RHETORIC AND REALITY IN AIR WARFARE

PRINCETON STUDIES IN

INTERNATIONAL HISTORY AND POLITICS

Series Editors
Jack L. Snyder
Marc Trachtenberg
Fareed Zakaria

RHETORIC AND REALITY
IN AIR WARFARE

THE EVOLUTION OF BRITISH AND
AMERICAN IDEAS ABOUT
STRATEGIC BOMBING, 1914–1945

Tami Davis Biddle

PRINCETON UNIVERSITY PRESS   PRINCETON AND OXFORD

Copyright © 2002 by Princeton University Press
Published by Princeton University Press, 41 William Street, Princeton, New Jersey 08540
In the United Kingdom: Princeton University Press, 3 Market Place,
Woodstock, Oxfordshire OX20 1SY
All Rights Reserved

Library of Congress Cataloging-in-Publication Data

Biddle, Tami Davis, 1959–
Rhetoric and reality in air warfare : the evolution of British and American ideas about
strategic bombing, 1914–1945 / Tami Davis Biddle.
p. cm. (Princeton studies in international history and politics)
Includes bibliographical references and index.
ISBN 0-691-08909-4
1. Bombing, Aerial—Great Britain. 2. Bombing, Aerial—United States. 3. Strategic
bombers—Great Britain. 4. Strategic bombers—United States. I. Title. II. Series.
UG705.G7 B54 2002
358.4'2—dc21   2001036865

British Library Cataloging-in-Publication Data is available

This book has been composed in Sabon

Printed on acid-free paper. ∞

www.pup.princeton.edu

Printed in the United States of America

1 3 5 7 9 10 8 6 4 2

Contents

Acknowledgments

WHEN I was a freshman in college, Carey Joynt convinced me that women could and should study national security policy—and then encouraged me to follow that path. Philip Towle furthered my interest in the topic. I have been blessed with unusually attentive and supportive mentors—scholars who take their teaching role very seriously—both during my graduate training and while a junior faculty member. Gaddis Smith made me want to become a historian, made sure I had a chance to become one, and then encouraged me all through graduate school. Paul Kennedy, who advised this project when it was a doctoral thesis, was an inspired role model for me in every sense. My Duke colleague Alex Roland has been no less an inspiring role model, and has helped to make working in the field of military history both a pleasure and a privilege. I thank him for his unfailing willingness to read drafts of my work and to offer—always—incisive advice.

Those who aided me and influenced my thinking in the early stages of this project include: Ashton Carter, Stephen Van Evera, Sir Michael Howard, Robert O'Neill, Noble Frankland, Ramsay D. Potts, David MacIsaac, and the late Lord Zuckerman. I am particularly indebted to Air Commodore Henry Probert, RAF (ret.), former head of the Air Historical Branch, RAF, who offered patient guidance to a novice researcher who first turned up in his office many years ago.

No project of this nature can be undertaken without substantial financial assistance. For their support of my work over the years I am greatly indebted to: Yale University, the Social Science Research Council, the John D. and Catherine T. MacArthur Foundation, the Belfer Center for Science and International Affairs at Harvard University, the U.S. Air Force Historical Research Center, The Brookings Institution, the National Air and Space Museum, and Duke University. Luke Arant, Lisa Kellmeyer, and D'Arcy Brissman provided able research assistance; Wayne Lee helped bring me into the computer age. Teresa Lawson and Kathy Goldgeier offered excellent editorial guidance on the final manuscript. I thank the U.S. Army's Military History Institute for support through the Harold K. Johnson Visiting Professorship, 2001–2002.

Over the years I have benefited enormously from the resources and assistance made available to me by the staffs of the Air Historical Branch, RAF (UK), the Office of Air Force History (USA), the Air Force Historical Research Center (USA), the RAF Museum (UK), the National Air and Space Museum (USA), the National Defence Headquarters (Canada), the Library of Congress (USA), the Public Record Office

(UK), the National Archives and Records Administration (USA), the National Library of Canada, the U.S. Army War College Library, and the Christ Church Library, Oxford. Special thanks go to Alec Douglas and Stephen J. Harris of the National Defence Headquarters, and Peter Elliott of the RAF Museum. I owe, as well, many thanks to the outstanding staff of Perkins Library at Duke University, especially Ken Berger and Margaret Brill. I thank Marc Trachtenberg and Chuck Myers for their interest in my work; I thank Linda Truilo, Bill Laznovsky, and Sylvia Coates for their help in transforming a manuscript into a book.

It is hard for me to imagine writing this book without the generous assistance and guidance of Sebastian Cox, the current head of the Air Historical Branch, RAF, who helped with the research process, made sure that I had ready access to key materials, and offered expert criticism all along the way. The voice in my ear these many years, he made this a better book than it otherwise would have been. Hays Parks very generously shared research materials with me, offered advice, support, and friendship—and cheered me on generally. John Ferris and Eliot Cohen provided invaluable commentary on the manuscript while it was still a dissertation; I am indebted to them for their many helpful insights and suggestions. Vincent Orange taught me to think in new ways, and became a good friend in the process. The late Edward Thomas was a source of lasting inspiration to me.

George K. Williams, whose knowledge of this topic is both broad and deep, very generously read every word of the manuscript and offered excellent commentary and superb editorial advice; indeed, some of the nicest turns of phrase in the book derive from his inspired suggestions. Robert Jervis twice read the manuscript carefully—offering thoughtful and perceptive assistance both times; his influence on my thinking about this topic was significant. My colleagues I. B. Holley and Richard Kohn helped me on many occasions. Lynn Eden had faith in me, and helped me have faith in myself.

I thank Mary Short, Chris Traugott, Ivan and Evelyn Oelrich, David Herrmann, and Sam Williamson for their loyal friendship, unwavering support, and unfailing ability to make me laugh and smile. Though Peter Schmeisser left this world far too soon, he gave those of us who knew him a gift beyond imagining. I thank my parents, Barton and Jacqueline Davis, and my aunt, Anna M. Morgan, for their dedicated love and support over the years. Finally, I thank my husband, Stephen Biddle, whose influence can be found throughout the pages that follow. He gave me the courage I needed to undertake and complete this project. Without his devoted support, advice, encouragement, and forbearance, it never would have been possible. With my deepest thanks and affection, I dedicate the book to him.

RHETORIC AND REALITY IN AIR WARFARE

Introduction

In late September 1941, Prime Minister Winston Churchill was frustrated with Bomber Command, his primary weapon against Hitler's offensive. The first rigorous evaluation of Bomber Command's performance in the war, the Butt Report, was discouraging: on any given night only about one in five crews put bombs within five miles of their targets.[1] This information came as a jolt—indeed, many in the Royal Air Force (RAF) could barely believe it. Sir Richard Peirse, head of Bomber Command, declared, "I don't think at this rate we could have hoped to produce the damage which is known to have been achieved."[2] What he "knew" came largely from pilot accounts, and these were now proved to be highly unreliable: Peirse and those under him had engaged in a great deal of wishful thinking.

For Churchill, however, the ramifications had sunk in. He directed his ire at Sir Charles Portal, former head of Bomber Command and, since late 1940, Chief of Air Staff (CAS). Portal had just sent Churchill a paper calling for 4,000 heavy bombers for use in a massive air offensive designed to break German civilian morale. The prime minister received the scheme with skepticism and despondency. Strongly implying that he had lost faith in Bomber Command, he responded to Portal with a note that pessimistically concluded, "The most we can say [about Bomber Command] is that it will be a heavy and I trust a seriously increasing annoyance [to Germany]."[3]

Portal, not one to shrink from the prime minister's tempests, pointed out that Churchill's own rhetoric and decisions to date had all relied on the strategic air arm—if not to win the war on its own, at least to help prepare the continent for an allied ground invasion. He defended the RAF scheme and then challenged Churchill directly: "We could, for example, return to the conception of defeating Germany with the army as the primary offensive weapon." Knowing that Churchill would find this distasteful, he continued, "I must point out with the utmost emphasis that in that event we should require an air force composed quite differently from that which we are now creating. If therefore it is your view that the strategic picture has changed since the issue of your original directives I would urge that revised instructions should be given to the Chiefs of Staff without a moment's delay." Portal thus called the prime minister to account with a response that one observer at the time called "masterly" and "audacious."[4]

Churchill, however, refused to be put on the defensive. Acknowledging the significance of Bomber Command's role, he nonetheless warned Portal against "placing unbounded confidence in this means of attack." He argued, "Even if all the towns of Germany were rendered largely uninhabitable, it does not follow that the military control would be weakened or even that war industry could not be carried on." He lashed out at the RAF's previous claims about strategic bombing, and the fears that they had aroused in Britain at the time of the Munich crisis: "Before the war we were greatly misled by the pictures [the Air Staff] painted of the destruction that would be wrought by Air raids. This is illustrated by the fact that 750,000 beds were actually provided for Air raid casualties, never more than 6,000 being required." He charged that "[t]his picture of Air destruction was so exaggerated that it depressed the statesmen responsible for the prewar policy, and played a definite part in the desertion of Czecho-Slovakia in August 1938."[5]

This was a tense moment. While bold interwar claims about the power of bombers and the vulnerability of enemy societies had helped preserve the RAF's institutional autonomy, they had also contributed to deep public anxiety about future wars. When he took office in 1940, Churchill had placed faith in Bomber Command's ability to make good on its claims and to turn them strongly to Britain's advantage. By 1941, though, those claims seemed empty. What had happened? And what would the future hold?

Just over two months later the United States, attacked at Pearl Harbor and drawn into the global conflagration, would also turn to strategic bombing. But the Americans, too, would encounter vast problems as they tried to fight the war from high altitude. Not only did American bombers fail to achieve a prompt decision, but, in 1942–43, they seemed to have little impact on the enemy. Indeed, by late 1943 the Anglo-American "Combined Bomber Offensive" (CBO) was all but grounded by the strength of German defenses. Allied air planners scrambled for a solution, eventually finding their way to tactical changes that salvaged the air offensive. By 1944 both the numbers and capabilities of Anglo-American bombers had increased dramatically, and a campaign of increasing fury and intensity would, by 1945, lay waste to German and Japanese cities and industry in an unprecedented campaign of death and destruction that has been hotly debated ever since.

The Churchill-Portal debate of September 1941—a short, sharp exchange between two men otherwise trying to cooperate in a larger, more consequential battle—evokes the dramatic history of strategic bombing in the Second World War. Controversy and emotional intensity have always surrounded the very concept of long-range or "strategic" bombing. The concept implies that aircraft carrying bombs to an enemy's "vital centers" can undermine its ability and will to fight. The idea is simple enough, yet few other claims about military power have provoked so many debates, or aroused so much intensity of feeling, both inside and outside the military. Time has neither stilled the controversy nor muted the arguments, which have recently focused on the 1991 Gulf War and the 1999 bombing of Kosovo. As a new century begins, the issue remains as contentious and consequential as it was at the beginning of the last one, when airplanes first took to the skies.

To make sense of these debates (and the emotions they stir), one must understand the assumptions that underpinned the concept itself, and the expectations bound up in those assumptions. This book's purpose is to trace and compare the development of ideas about long-range bombing in Britain and in the United States—the two nations that relied most heavily on this new form of warfare during the Second World War. I illuminate the factors shaping the evolution of those ideas from the turn of the century through the end of the Second World War. In this I seek not only to explain the development of a central mode of modern war, but also to shed light on the way military organizations think and behave. Obvious questions arise: Why were the British and Americans interested in strategic bombing in the first place? What did defense planners and policymakers expect of it, and why? How were these expectations influenced by experience and by broader debates? Why were many of their expectations ultimately at odds with reality? These in turn pose deeper questions: How do military ideas originate, and how do they establish themselves inside the staffs and organizations that plan for and undertake their implementation? How do expectations affect the way information is perceived and interpreted, and how do these perceptions and interpretations then shape plans, policies, and campaigns? How robust are ideas, once established, and why do they often seem resistant to new information that does not support them?

The development of aircraft in the early part of the twentieth century posed a problem of great significance to the military planners of all modern states. How were these new machines—as yet untested—to be integrated into existing military structures? In particular, how were planners to envision and implement aerial bombing of enemy lands? Examining the way the latter question was answered in two states offers insight into how their military organizations perceived and made sense of the world around them, interpreted experience, and coped with rapid change. It also enables us to examine the extent to which those organizations were influenced by the wider social and political contexts in which they operated.

Not all militaries, of course, responded to bombers the way the British and the Americans did.[6] In certain ways, then, this history is case-specific, explaining British and American uniqueness. Geopolitical issues were particularly important: neither the British nor the Americans found it essential to their survival to maintain large standing armies. Indeed, they had both eschewed such structures (and the political problems that often accompany them), and had instead relied on naval power to preserve their territorial integrity and to protect their interests. In relying on navies and exploiting the fruits of the industrial revolution, they reinforced national self-identities that celebrated mastery of science and technology. Over time they came to place the same reliance on new machines, aircraft—for deterrence, defense, and power projection—as they earlier had placed on ships. They came to see bomber aircraft as a means of fighting wars at relatively low cost to themselves, avoiding a repetition of the harrowing experience of the 1914–18 war. As I explain in chapters 2 and 3, this process moved more quickly in Britain than the United States, but both found themselves in essentially the same place by the Second World War.

Not all of the story is unique to Britain and the Unites States, however. Their thinking, planning, and decision making illuminates patterns generalizable to other military organizations in other places and times. Individuals and institutions have commonalities in the way they perceive new information, interpret experience, and respond to change. This exposes them to similar types of misperceptions, errors, and maladaptations, particularly in times of rapid change. My analysis relies on a few basic concepts borrowed from cognitive psychology.[7] These shed light on how and why air theorists in Britain and the United States perceived information and interpreted experience as they did.

All decision makers use cognitive processes to make sense of their complicated and stressful environments. Two forms of information-processing bias in particular seem pertinent here. The first derives from the problem of environmental complexity. To organize a vast array of incoming sensory information without being overwhelmed, we all use data-processing shortcuts. Most of the time, these shortcuts serve us well. Sometimes, however, they skew perceptions in ways that can have problematic consequences. For example, we tend to assimilate incoming information to fit existing beliefs and expectations. If all our basic understandings were subject to wholesale revision with every new datum, we would be in constant turmoil, changing direction so often as to become virtually aimless. Remaining impervious to new information would be just as useless. Thus, we are neither fully open nor fully closed to the implications of new information. While a preponderance of contrary information can eventually shift our beliefs, any given datum will tend to be interpreted consistent with our original predispositions. The result is that preexisting beliefs, once organized and established, have a staying power in the face of new information that one might not expect, looking only at the new data itself. In general, we also prioritize incoming information according to its emotional vividness. Emotionally remote information, such as written memoranda, statistics, or second- and third-hand reports, carries less impact than first-hand personal experience, especially when the latter is unusually painful, strikingly positive, or uniquely formative. The medium influences receptivity, independent of the analytical merit of the information per se. In particular, early personal experiences of decision makers often have an effect that later analytical input cannot easily match.

A second broad class of information-processing bias relates to the effects of stress on decision making. Few of us respond the same way to stressful and to banal situations. In particular, most people rely on a variety of mechanisms to enable continued functioning in very difficult conditions. For example, choosing between two mutually exclusive goods—or between two apparently unattractive alternatives—is difficult and unpleasant. Either something valued must be given up, or something repugnant must be accepted. Neither is easy to do. We therefore tend to deny that stressful choices really have to be made. Overlooking or discounting the real virtues of one good reduces the apparent scale of loss when both cannot be had; overlooking or discounting the real drawbacks of one bad option moderates apparent costs when one must be chosen anyway. Either strategy, however, leads to a mistaken assessment of at least one choice, and a tendency to overlook potentially important information. The higher the stakes—the more repugnant or the more attractive the options—the greater the stress and the greater the tendency to misperceive.

When a choice between unattractive alternatives cannot be postponed, avoided, or miscast, the result can be especially stressful. The process of such decision making is often so onerous as to create powerful barriers to reconsideration, even when new information casts doubt on the initial choice's validity. Thus, rather than revisit the original choice, decision makers discount, misinterpret, or ignore new information bearing on that choice. Finally, in addition to seeing what we expect to see, and not seeing what we find too stressful to absorb, we often see what it is in our interest to see. Decision makers with powerful organizational goals or self-interests may discount or minimize incoming information that conflicts with those interests, and highlight information that supports them. This may reflect cynicism or deliberate misrepresentation of the facts, but, more commonly, these strongly felt desires have a subtler effect, coloring our interpretation of data in ways we may not fully recognize.

All of these information-processing biases influenced thinking about strategic bombing in Britain and the United States, and in the narrative that follows I draw attention to the places where their influence and effect are most evident. In writing this book, I have relied on a combination of extensive primary source research, a comparative perspective, attention to the social and intellectual context in which planners and policymakers worked, and a sensitivity to the insights derived from the concepts outlined above. By examining British and American ideas through the whole sweep of time from the pre–World War I period through 1945, I am able to trace the way in which the "lessons" of World War I were interpreted and applied, highlight the differences and similarities in British and American thinking as well as the reasons for them, and offer a critique of the operations and effectiveness of the Combined Bomber Offensive (CBO) of World War II.[8]

In this study, institutional responses to bomber aircraft take center stage. The invention of aircraft prompted important organizational modifications in the military structures of Britain and the United States. In a dramatic wartime reorganization, the British in 1917–18 established a separate air force. Its autonomy was not guaranteed after the war, however, and its new leaders had to find ways to justify its continued existence. The American Air Service did not win organizational independence during the First World War, but its personnel nonetheless had high hopes for autonomy, and sought to hasten its achievement. Thus, the interwar experience of Anglo-American airmen was heavily conditioned by the quest for institutional autonomy, to preserve it or win it. To acquire legitimacy, any institution must make the argument for its existence in reason and in nature.[9] This is precisely what British and American airmen sought to do, but the process was inherently liable to error and bias.

No institution speaks with a single, wholly unified voice, but, among any group of individuals, particular preferences and views come to be privileged, and these form the basis of what may be called organizational thought. I trace organizational thought by examining the rhetoric used by British and American airmen, in intra- and inter-institutional conversations and in public statements. This rhetoric resides in a variety of places: the minutes of meetings, internal policy and planning documents, speeches, lectures, journal articles, letters, and teaching materials for the air staff schools. All these sources reveal the ways in which two nascent air organizations envisioned and articulated their function as well as their plans for carrying out that function. As new organizations dealing with brand-new, rapidly evolving technologies, they faced challenges, but their members brought energy, stubborn determination, and, sometimes, an almost religious fervor and commitment to their work. These qualities helped secure the place of air forces and elevate their status, but they also contributed to problems of conception and rigidity of thought.

My approach is premised on the assumption that articulations of function and policy reveal fundamental ideas within military organizations and that such ideas matter. They matter because they often serve as guides to action, in whole or in part. Thus, to understand actions we must understand the premises on which they rest. And once articulated in a formal way, the premises have consequences outside the institution itself. Of course, public or "declaratory" policy may not be wholly consistent with actual practice. Even if later modified, a declaratory policy promulgated for any length of time not only creates echoes and socializing effects inside an organization, but also produces independent consequences: it conveys information to other organizations, which may then modify their own behavior in response, and—particularly in the case of national institutions within democracies—it sets up public expectations about the future.

My approach is premised as well on the assumption that fundamental ideas are not formed in a vacuum, but rather in a specific temporal context. In order to understand how the British and American air forces became interested in strategic bombing and formed expectations about it, we must understand the context in which the organizations' members lived and worked, and the early experiences that helped mold their beliefs and predilections. This means beginning the story early in the century, when initial conceptions about aircraft in war were being articulated in response to the long-anticipated arrival of heavier-than-air flight. A body of ideas about long-range aerial bombing began to take shape, based on assumptions about and perceptions of the behavior of modern societies. I argue that these helped determine how World War I aerial experience of aerial bombing was interpreted and, in turn, affected subsequent thinking and planning. While much of the strategic bombing literature has tended to overlook or minimize the World War I experience, I argue that it played an important role in determining what came afterward.

A fundamental assertion that became central to Anglo-American thinking about long-range bombing was that modern, complex, urban-based societies are fragile, interdependent, and therefore peculiarly vulnerable to disruption through aerial bombing. This idea took slightly different but essentially overlapping forms in Britain and the United States. It involved not only political and military concerns about the steadfastness and political reliability of civilians (particularly urban dwellers) in modern, increasingly "total," war, but also concerns about the structure of modern economies and their susceptibility to disruption. This assumption derived from a particular historical context: the anxieties felt by Edwardian-era politicians and military planners who looked with increasing trepidation on the forces transforming their societies.

Arguments about enemy vulnerability gave validity to air force claims for existence and continued (or increased) autonomy; they gave weight to assertions about air power as a coercive tool in war.[10] If modern states were in fact highly vulnerable to long-range bombardment—which took war directly to industry, political leaders, and populations—then it made sense to maintain an organization that might either deter wars or win them in what promised to be a direct, expeditious way. Indeed, any state wishing to survive in the great contest of nations would be obliged to maintain an air force, not only to deter potential enemies, but to prevail against them should deterrence fail. Ultimately it was this argument that sustained the postwar RAF and gave credence to those voices calling for an independent U.S. air force. But ideas about vulnerability rested more on assumptions and assertions than established fact. The World War I experience seemed to confirm notions undergirding arguments about social and economic vulnerability, but the interpretation of that experience had been conditioned by preexisting expectations, individual and organizational interests, and a general lack of analytical rigor in methods of assessment.

During the interwar years, bold claims for the power of bombers were combined with a lack of focused attention to how, precisely, they would operate in war, and how, exactly, bombing an enemy might lead to its political capitulation. This inattention to what, in hindsight, seems like crucial and essential detail stemmed from several important causes—but most powerfully, perhaps, from the way in which airmen perceived their world and made assumptions about it. Even where effort and good intentions were apparent, problems often crept in.[11] For instance, both the British and the Americans carried out interwar exercises and field trials, but they ran them with rules and premises that skewed the results to match prevailing assumptions about the power of bombers and the frailty of those under the fall of bombs. Likewise, both the British and the Americans observed the air battles of the late 1930s, particularly those of the Spanish civil war, but they largely discounted results that did not accord with their preexisting beliefs. They did this principally by dismissing the wars (and whatever insights they may have offered) as largely irrelevant: they were not "first-class" wars between major states.

In Britain the consequences were particularly acute given the nation's proximity to Germany. The RAF's declaratory policy had long been far ahead of its capabilities with respect to long-range bombing. While this did not matter so much when there were few real enemies, it mattered a great deal when a resurgent Luftwaffe appeared to threaten everything in its range. Bomber Command was unready for war, but the British people had heard, for nearly two decades, about the vast power of bombers. The RAF's earlier bold claims now had a deterrent effect on Britain itself in a time of crisis. Adding to the problem was the tendency to assume that the German air force had been designed and built not as a predominantly army-oriented force (as it in fact was), but primarily for the purpose of independent long-range bombing. The uncertainty and fiscal stringency of the 1930s complicated Britain's existing problems, and Bomber Command would enter the war still in the opening phases of a hurried and onerous effort to close the distance between its claims and its capabilities. Ironically, British air defenses, which had received far less attention in RAF declaratory policy, were in much better shape.

Although the Americans had invested somewhat more effort than the British in working out the details of long-range bombing, they nonetheless fell victim to a range of similar problems. Like the British, they failed to analyze the World War I experience as rigorously as they might have; they underestimated the difficulties in finding and bombing targets from high altitude; and they overestimated the ability of bombers to penetrate enemy airspace. They also failed to heed the warnings inherent in Britain's traumatic experience of 1939–42. Thus, they too entered war unready. And they failed—even more than the British—to realize just how unready they were.

During World War II, British and American air forces sought to prove the soundness of the central claim of the interwar years: that modern societies and economies are vulnerable to aerial bombardment. The claim proved weaker than expected. From the start its proponents faced two major problems: the vulnerability of bombers themselves to enemy defenses, and the inaccuracy of bombers operating in wartime conditions. But the limited power of bombers in the early years of the war was not the only undermining factor. Modern economies and societies proved to be surprisingly robust, capable of coping, responding positively to stress, and, ultimately, withstanding tremendous punishment. In trying to produce the outcome they sought, British and American airmen made modifications that took them steadily toward heavier, less discriminate bombing. By 1944–1945 this trend was reinforced by another: Allied leaders' desire to end the long war as quickly as possible. The result was nothing less than a form of aerial Armageddon played out over the skies of Germany and Japan.

The first three chapters that follow treat the early development and evolution of Anglo-American ideas about aerial bombing; the fourth and fifth chapters discuss the way in which their adherents attempted to implement them in the Second World War. The first chapter begins by reviewing some of the earliest conceptions of strategic bombing and explaining how these ideas developed, within British and American military institutions, during the First World War. It traces the history of long-range bombing in the war, and concludes by summarizing the British and American post-armistice bombing surveys. The second chapter examines the RAF during the interwar years, revealing how arguments about long-range bombing were developed and presented in the 1920s, and how they were (or were not) modified in the tense and uncertain years leading up to 1939. The third chapter, on the American Air Service (later Air Corps) in the interwar years, shows how American thinking about strategic bombing evolved through the 1920s and 1930s, and contrasts this with British developments.

The fourth chapter covers the early World War II years, 1939–42. It focuses on the crises faced by British and American airmen, and the decisions that they made in response. It reveals the abrupt clash between interwar assumptions and wartime realities. The fifth chapter examines the the British and American "Combined Bomber Offensive" of 1943–45, detailing the sometimes desperate Anglo-American quest to make bombing into an effective tool of war against Germany, and how this quest ultimately led to the kind of aerial onslaught both predicted and deeply feared in the interwar years. This chapter also covers the American strategic bombing campaign in Japan—a campaign that, though an extension of the trajectory of strategic bombing begun in the early part of the century, also began a new chapter in the history of warfare through its climax at Hiroshima and Nagasaki. Chapter 5 ends by examining the many contested claims about Anglo-American strategic bombing in World War II. In the conclusion, I bring together the main themes of the narrative and suggest ways in which they influenced thinking about air warfare in the second half of the twentieth century.

CHAPTER ONE

The Beginning: Strategic Bombing
in the First World War

THE history of strategic bombing in the twentieth century is a history of the tension between imagined possibilities and technical realities. In seeking the roots of this tension, it is necessary to turn to World War I, where combat aircraft made their first serious appearance in both tactical and strategic roles—from short-range battlefield reconnaissance to long-distance bombing of enemy cities. In the end, tactical aviation received a fuller test than did strategic flying: the latter's demands on plane and pilot were more onerous, and armies, unsurprisingly, prioritized their tactical forces since they were of greater immediate use to the war effort. The result was that, by 1918, strategic bombing had received only a brief trial. Because its possibilities seemed far-reaching, however, this experience left a legacy with an important impact on postwar thinking; it formed a foundation for extrapolation, speculation, and zealous advocacy.[1] But the perception and interpretation of the experience itself had been shaped by expectation.

AERIAL BOMBING AND PUBLIC EXPECTATION

The First World War commenced only eleven years after the Wright Brothers made their first successful but brief ascent over the windy dunes of Kitty Hawk, North Carolina. The airplanes of 1914 were frail machines constructed mainly of wood, cloth, and wire; their capabilities were speculative at best. Military experts had varying expectations for these craft, but even the most conservative understood that an aerial perspective would facilitate observation and reconnaissance. Indeed, the aerial perspective quickly proved so valuable that it was aggressively sought and fought for, prompting the development of purpose-built fighter aircraft. Throughout the war, increasingly capable fighters sought control of the air to allow other aircraft to carry out reconnaissance work, including trench mapping and artillery spotting. Other tactical missions evolved, such as contact patrol (for tracking ground troops), close air support, and battlefield interdiction bombing.

The role aircraft might play beyond the battlefield had long been the subject of intense anticipation.[2] For centuries before flying machines were invented, they were envisioned as platforms for dropping explosives onto the vulnerable earth. From the beginning, this speculation imagined bombers not only as agents of physical destruction, but also of psychological shock and social disruption; the earliest conceptions of strategic bombing assumed it would impair both the enemy's capacity *and* will to fight. Much of this speculation came from futurist writers, inventors, and visionaries of various sorts.[3] In 1670, Jesuit monk Francesco Lana produced an important treatise with two chapters on the "Aerial Ship." While he believed his theoretical machine to be viable, he warned that God might not allow such a ship to be successful, "since it would create many disturbances in the civil and political governments of mankind."[4] The successful balloon ascents of the Montgolfier brothers and Jacques Charles in 1783 inspired an outpouring of imagination driven by a growing faith in the promise of science and technology; this manifested itself in prints and engravings depicting great flying ships dropping their deadly ordnance on those below. The emerging industrial revolution encouraged even more daring leaps. In Britain, where the people had been aroused to fear of invasion during Napoleon's continental successes, a rash of war speculation appeared in print and prose.[5]

Even after the invasion tide had ebbed, concerns over air warfare continued. In his poem "Locksley Hall" (1842), Lord Tennyson "dipp'd into the future, far as human eye could see," and postulated a "ghastly dew" raining from the heavens as "the nations' airy navies" grappled in "the central blue."[6] Just one year later, British inventor Samuel Alfred Warner sought to interest British officials in his balloon called the "long range," which, he argued, could ascend, travel to a point, and release its bombs on a target "with accuracy and mystery," thus enabling a commander to destroy forts and towns, and spread consternation among both troops and civilians. Twenty years later, Henry Tracy Coxwell contemplated a kind of "ghastly dew" when he sent a letter to the *Army and Navy Gazette* suggesting that balloons might drop chemical agents designed to cause "stupefication" of enemy populations. Jules Verne's widely read novel *Clipper of the Clouds* (1886) asserted that the future belonged to aerial warfare machines.[7]

As scientific progress continued, notions of air war were modernized, and infused with the hopes, concerns, and fears of the day. A recurring theme was that air warfare would be terrible. Like Francesco Lana, many concluded that future air battles might be so awful as to prompt men to mitigate their behavior, or even abolish war altogether—fostering a better, more peaceful world. In 1862, Victor Hugo speculated that aircraft would bring about the universal abolition of borders, leading to the end of wars and a great "peaceful revolution."[8] In 1893, Maj. J. D. Fullerton of the British Royal Engineers anticipated an aerial "revolution in the art of war," arguing that the arrival of an enemy air fleet over a capital city would have such an impact as to end hostilities. A year later, inventor Octave Chanute argued that because no territory would be immune from the horrors of air war, "the ultimate effect will be to diminish greatly the frequency of wars and to substitute more rational methods of settling international misunderstandings."[9]

In the hands of some Victorian novelists and purveyors of sensationalist fiction, however, speculation about air war was infiltrated by nationalism and xenophobia, and linked explicitly to imperialist fantasies of technical domination and subjugation of foreign peoples. These themes reflected the period's pervasive acceptance of Social Darwinism and highly competitive forms of colonial conquest. William Delisle Hay's 1881 novel, *Three Hundred Years Hence*, envisioned a war wherein a European air fleet destroys Asian armies and ravages their lands. American writers produced similar fantasies. In S. W. Odell's *The Last War; Or, Triumph of the English Tongue*, published in 1898, English-speaking peoples win their final battle against inferior races via an air force that rains incendiary bombs down upon the enemy. In the end, the English speakers impose the English language and the "customs of civilization" on the "ignorant and savage inhabitants" of Russia and Asia. Roy Norton's 1907 story *The Vanishing Fleets* imagined American scientists devising radioactive weapons to cope with a sneak attack by the Japanese, who were aided by communists operating within the United States.[10]

The fertile mind of H. G. Wells produced a more sophisticated scenario. In his famous 1908 novel, *The War in the Air*, bombers hold enormous power to inflict both physical and psychological damage on an enemy; indeed, they bring terror to a world in which technological developments have outstripped the political and moral means to contain them. Air war brings catastrophe as bombers destroy the very fabric of modern civilization, leaving chaos, famine, and political upheaval in their wake. Wells speculated that urban populations already weakened by the war's dislocations would, upon the appearance of an air fleet, fall victim to "civil conflict and passionate disorder."[11]

From its outset, aviation was "a very public technology" in England.[12] Some military writers of the early twentieth century denounced popular speculation on the topic, expressing concern over the deleterious impact on the public mind of unrestrained imaginings about aircraft. But their own writings echoed some of the same themes, especially air warfare's potential psychological effects.[13] In 1905 the British War Office's *Manual of Military Ballooning* argued that the balloons dropping gun cotton charges might have a "moral effect" on the enemy that "should not be lost sight of" in estimating their combat value. The moral effect (pronounced "morale" but spelled without the "e," as in the French) reflected a widespread fixation within contemporary European militaries. It revealed in part the influence of Carl von Clausewitz, whose writings had become particularly popular after the Franco-Prussian war when von Moltke claimed that they had influenced him. Clausewitz's *On War* (1832) had been translated into English by the end of the century, and was studied at the Army Staff College in Britain.[14] The work of Ardant du Picq, Foch, Langlois, and Grandmaison added to a trend emphasizing the role of "will" and moral factors in warfare. The French writers argued in particular that soldiers were sustained by powerful psychological elements such as élan, espirit de corps, and a willingness to seize and maintain the offensive. These ideas helped shape strategy, war planning, and conceptualizations of future conflict in Britain. Indeed, the 1913 Gold Medal Prize Essay topic for the Royal United Services Institution was, "How Can Moral Qualities Best Be Developed During the Preparation of the Officer and the Man for Duties Each Will Carry Out in War."[15] In a 1914 volume called *Principles of War Historically Illustrated*, Maj. Gen. E. A. Altham argued, "The moral effect of the bayonet is all out of proportion to its material effect, and not the least important of virtues claimed for it is that the desire to use it draws the attacking side on."[16] The emphasis on moral effects reflected and highlighted the qualities valued by upper-middle-class Victorian and Edwardian society—courage, initiative, resourcefulness, tenacity, and willpower—but it also resonated with prejudices and darker trends therein, including social Darwinism, anti-intellectualism, aggressiveness, and a strict class system.[17]

Psychological factors could be a double-edged sword—an army's greatest strength, but also its greatest weakness. If this were true for armies, might it not be true for nations as a whole? Would civilian populations, ever more directly vulnerable to the effects of modern war, be uniquely susceptible to social-psychological factors—especially in light of what one contemporary observer would later call "the nervous complexion of the modern mind"?[18] In particular, how might untrained, undisciplined civilians hold up under the pressures of a war fought directly over their heads? In its usage relating to long-range bombing, the moral effect came to represent qualities needed not only by fighting men and their leaders but also by entire societies. Wellsian fiction argued that modern war would require the highest organization of the national polity into "one organic, efficient whole."[19] But Wells's speculation on the behavior of urban populations was hardly reassuring. The "German School" of military thinkers had also made prominent the idea that modern war would depend on the total mobilized resources of a nation and its people. Colmar von der Goltz, in his influential bestseller *The Nation in Arms* (1883), argued, "War is now an exodus of nations and no longer a mere conflict between armies. All moral energies will be gathered for a life and death struggle." But this work had a prominently racist theme, reflecting German attitudes and expansionist ambitions. Influenced by a Hegelian conception of history, von der Goltz argued that Germany was destined to take the place of older, decaying empires. To achieve this, the German people would have to embrace those martial, antiliberal qualities that would insure success and provide for continued political dominance.[20]

This writing, emerging from an increasingly restive Germany, could not have been anything but unsettling to late Victorian and Edwardian Britons, who already felt a range of anxieties about their nation and its place in the world. Germany's imperial and naval ambitions were particularly worrisome. But other issues entered in, elevating to new heights a sense of national foreboding. Edwardian Britain was a vigorous, dynamic society, brimming with the products of modern science: electric power, automobiles, photography, telephones, cheap newspapers, and the cinema. But it was also a society adjusting to modernity—and full of the stresses of that adjustment. Along with the new came a yearning for and sentimentalization of the old and familiar. The societal changes that technology had wrought through the industrial revolution seemed to be a cause for particularly acute concern. Would the new urban classes erode the national characteristics that were believed (by the elite) to have made Britain great? The growth of industry had concentrated working populations in congested, polluted cities. For government officials, concerns over sanitation and public health took center stage along with concerns over the political stability of vast populations forced to endure hard labor and stressful living conditions. What would be the reliability of urban masses under the burdens of modern war? Would the dislocations produced by aerial bombardment trigger social and political upheaval in dense, vulnerable urban areas?[21] The worries of those in the military were conditioned, additionally, by longstanding organizational views on discipline: steadfastness in the face of danger, they believed, came either through breeding (as in the officer class) or through instilled training and drill (as in the enlisted ranks). The urban poor had neither.[22]

Generalized concerns about the urban poor had grown throughout the latter half of the nineteenth century. But the Edwardians rediscovered the problem at the turn of the century, and found it deeply troubling. Thirty-seven percent of the applicants examined for service in the Boer War were deemed unfit, and a similar percentage were turned away as too obviously unfit even for consideration. The root of the problem was not hard to find. Two important studies, Seebohm Rowntree's *Poverty: A Study of Town Life* (1901) and Charles Booth's *Life and Labour of the People of London* (1903), both reached the same conclusion: wages paid to workers condemned one-third of the British population to conditions that barely supported the lowest level of human existence. These poor were, as Samuel Hynes has explained, "a mysterious and frightening new force" inhabiting the nation's cities and towns.[23]

The blunt statistics were quickly absorbed into the extant cultural-intellectual preoccupation with social Darwinism, producing anxiety about decadence (which conservatives believed to be at the heart of the problem), degeneracy, and national decline. Speculation was widespread not only about how competing states would stack up against one another, but also about how different races and classes within a state affected its overall strength, virility, cohesion, and steadfastness under stress. So great were these concerns that a 1905 pamphlet, "The Decline and Fall of the British Empire" (a weakly written tract by an author of dubious historical qualifications), became a bestseller. In its list of the eight causes of British decline, it ranked first "the prevalence of Town over Country life, and its disastrous effect on the health and faith of English people."[24] Similarly, an amateurish 1909 play, "The Englishman's Home," became a box office hit when it struck a chord with audiences anxious about national weakness and unpreparedness. When enemy troops from "Nearland" (a thinly-veiled reference to Germany) invade and occupy a private residence, they are met by inept civilians and military volunteers with all manner of physical and moral deficiencies. Social reformer C.F.G. Masterman, in his *Heart of Empire* (1901), had lamented the handicaps faced by a new class of urban poor. "The physical change," he wrote, "is the result of the city upbringing in twice-breathed air in the crowded quarters of the labouring classes. This is a substitute for the spacious places of the old, silent life of England: close to the ground, vibrating to the lengthy, unhurried processes of Nature." The consequence, he gloomily explained, was "the production of a characteristic physical type of town dweller: stunted, narrow-chested, easily-wearied; yet voluble, excitable, with little ballast, stamina or endurance—seeking stimulus in drink, in betting, in any unaccustomed conflicts at home or abroad."[25]

Indeed, concern over England's perceived inability to defend itself was at the heart of a new round of invasion literature that peaked between 1906 and 1909. In William LeQueux's *The Invasion of 1910* (1906), England's problems were attributed to the fact that a strong aristocratic government had been replaced by a weak administration "swayed by every breath of popular impulse."[26] Lord Roberts, who had commanded troops in South Africa, and who on his retirement became an energetic campaigner for preparedness, endorsed LeQueux's book. A year earlier he had composed the preface to Maj. Stewart L. Murray's *Peace of the Anglo-Saxons*, which was written specifically to teach the working classes how to "maintain and defend the Anglo-Saxon heritage and pass it on undiminished to posterity."[27] In 1908 the flight tests of Count Ferdinand von Zeppelin's airships were watched closely and anxiously by the British. Lt. Gen. Baden-Powell (founder of the Boy Scout movement) made a vigorous call to arms in the *Daily Mail* on 13 July. Indeed, first-hand witnessing of Germany's airship mania helped prompt David Lloyd George to propose the formation of a coalition government in England—a government designed to bring unity and national purpose in the face to unprecedented external and domestic worries. "There were ominous clouds gathering over the Continent of Europe and perceptibly thickening" he later wrote in his memoirs. "The submarine and the Zeppelin indicated a possible challenge to the invincibility of our defence."[28] The mass-circulation press raised the profile of the preparedness issue, and stirred popular passions by serving as an outlet for invasion stories and scare literature.

The year 1909 saw increasing reports of strange airships as the British people tried to come to terms with their potential vulnerability to air attack. "The Phantom Airship Scare" of that year spoke to the deep anxieties provoked by unhappy speculation. The *Daily Mail's* powerful overseer, Lord Northcliffe, urged the British to eschew sightings of imaginary dirigibles and instead focus on real threats.[29] Earlier, Northcliffe had offered a prize for the first airplane flight across the English Channel; in June 1909, he reminded his readership of the award, designed to stimulate aeronautics in Britain. On 25 July, French aviator Louis Blériot made the flight in just over a half hour. The next day Northcliffe made good on his offer, presenting the Frenchman with a check for £1,000. His newspaper drew characteristically dramatic conclusions: "British insularity has vanished. We would not be understood to say that in a few weeks or months hordes of aeroplanes will follow where M. Bleriot has led, but his example has shown the way. . . . The British people have hitherto dwelt secure in their islands. . . . But locomotion is now being transferred to an element where Dreadnoughts are useless and sea power no shield against attack."[30] Winston Churchill, then a critic of what he felt were the often mindless enthusiasms of the "Dreadnought fear-all school," opined, "We live in a period of superficial alarms, when it is thought patriotic and statesmanlike, far-seeing, clever and Bismarckian to predict hideous and direful wars as imminent."[31]

In the United States, the late nineteenth and early twentieth centuries were marked by blatant xenophobia and deep-seated concerns over an influx of poor immigrants hailing mainly from southern and eastern Europe.[32] On both sides of the Atlantic, the urban underclass and foreigners were viewed warily; they were not held to possess the character strengths native to individuals of traditional Anglo-Saxon heritage. Indeed, a particularly clear window into these attitudes can be found in American press coverage of the *Titanic* disaster of April 1912. The majority of accounts portrayed the wealthy first-cabin passengers as behaving with dignity and calm, while describing those in steerage as cowardly and prone to panic. Rather than attributing any differences in behavior to the structural problems in steerage (the smaller proportion of crew to passengers, the lack of information and language barriers, and the disadvantageous position of the third cabin within the ship), reporters and commentators systematically portrayed steerage panic as the result of class, ethnic, and racial predispositions.[33]

In both the United States and Britain, civil strife and industrial crises became endemic as laborers struggled for more humane working conditions; the problem was particularly acute on the eve of the First World War. In Britain frequent, bitter strikes—especially by miners and railwaymen—were marked by unusual assertiveness.[34] Naturally, this atmosphere fueled speculation about how workers would behave under the strain of war. Discussion and debate took place in both civilian and military realms; indeed, there was no clear separation between the two since the military operated squarely within the context of the broader society. Commentators worried that the subhuman conditions present in the nation's congested industrial cities created weaknesses in the national population that might cause fatal vulnerabilities in wartime.

Such worries were particularly evident in numerous lectures delivered to the Royal United Services Institution. T. Miller Maguire, in two 1909 lectures, associated what he called "the flotsam and jetsam of decaying British humanity" with the perversions of the factory system.[35] In a lengthy lecture given in November 1913, Maj. Stewart L. Murray, who worried that "popular passion" might trigger a war in the first place, concerned himself with the potential for civil strife generated by the rise of working-class radicalism during wartime. He argued that a major war might see the "explosion of those volcanic forces which underlie every modern democracy," and urged that "unless steps are taken to prevent the hardships of war pressing intolerably upon the new working classes, the whole organized political power of labour may be used to demand the cessation of the war, even at the price of submission to our enemies."[36] Later that month, Col. W. G. Simpson discussed "The Duties of Local Authorities in Wartime." Commenting on his remarks, the chair of the session, Major-General Dickson, argued, "During any Great

War there is certain to be danger, in a densely populated country like Britain, arising from the miseries of the poorer classes, especially in the manufacturing districts."[37] And in an April 1914 lecture, Col. Louis Jackson speculated that an enemy might be willing to attempt an aerial "knock-out blow" if it "seemed probable that such panic and riot would be caused as to force the Home Government to accept an unfavourable peace."[38]

These fears were based on speculation rather than broad evidence, since the actual experience of aerial bombing prior to 1914 had been quite limited. In 1849, during an Italian revolt against the Austrian Hapsburgs, Venice became the first city to be bombarded from the air, by projectiles carried by small linen and paper balloons. These seemed to have little if any impact on the defenders, even though the Austrian press made exaggerated claims about the "frightful effects" of the new weapons.[39] Just over sixty years later, the Italians scored another famous first when they sent airplanes and dirigibles to Libya during the Italo-Turkish war of 1911–12. Since many nations scrutinized this war as a testing ground for new weapons, it drew the attention of the world press; indeed, a wide range of publications sought to glean "lessons" from the Italian experience for the benefit of their own military organizations.[40] Perhaps because of aviation's dramatic hold on the public imagination, some observers seemed predisposed to view its contribution as revolutionary. The *Times* (London) correspondent remarked effusively that "it is already clear that no nation can afford to go to war with a marked inferiority in aerial strength."[41]

Italian bombing efforts were unsystematic—mainly pilots dropping small bombs arbitrarily over the sides of their planes. Nonetheless, a headline in Italy's *Gazzetta del Popolo*, printed after the initial raid, exclaimed that the bombs had scattered the "terrorized Turks."[42] The Italians seemed convinced of the psychological impact of the bombing; less subjective observers also were prepared to argue that even though the bombs had virtually no physical impact, they had produced a discernible moral effect.[43] The editors of *Scientific American* followed up this line of thinking in their commentary on aviation in the Balkan wars of 1912–13. In an article called "Bomb Dropping in the Balkans," they argued that "the importance of aeroplane bombs lies in their moral effect—in the impression created that the machine in the sky is a real source of danger."[44] This rhetoric reflected the dramatic effect that airplanes could induce when they appeared over battlefields and caused ground troops to feel trapped and vulnerable—an effect that would be seen again later in the century. But the rhetoric also reflected expectations embedded deep in the history of speculation over air bombardment, and reinforced by prevailing notions of the supremacy of psychological factors in war and of the fate of civilians in future conflicts. With regard to aerial bombing, the moral effect would soon take on a life of its own.

THE OPENING ROUNDS: ZEPPELINS OVER BRITAIN, 1914–18

Because interested nations grasped the potential utility of striking directly at an enemy state, ideas about strategic bombing developed simultaneously with ideas about other forms of aerial combat. During the First World War, both German and French pilots quickly began air attacks on targets not directly related to the land battles. On 14 August 1914, for instance, a German pilot flew to the outskirts of Paris and dropped two small (four-pound) bombs on the urban dwellers below.[45] Count Ferdinand von Zeppelin's airships offered the Germans another means of striking at enemy populations.[46] Perhaps the most aggressive advocate of the use of "zeppelins" for strategic bombing was Rear Adm. Paul Behncke, Deputy Chief of the German Naval Staff. In the summer and fall of 1914, he argued that by bombing London, its docks, and the Admiralty Building in Whitehall, it might be possible to "cause panic in the population which may possibly render it doubtful that the war can be continued."[47]

In Britain, decisions had to be made about how to utilize the nation's air assets. While it has often been argued that British aviation developed more slowly than in France and Germany, historian David Edgerton has pointed out that between 1908 and 1914 a large number of British private firms began to manufacture aircraft, and that by 1914 Britain owned the largest air force—in proportion to its ground force—in the world.[48] Britain's status relative to other aerial powers was hotly debated at the time, however, as was the question of air force organization. These debates were marked by divisions among groups with differing agendas and institutional interests. In 1911 the Air Battalion of the Royal Engineers had been formed, and in 1912 the Royal Flying Corps (RFC), originally comprising both a military and a naval wing, had been established. An Air Committee of the CID (Committee of Imperial Defence) took shape to preside over the new interservice institution. But this arrangement had not settled the issue, particularly in light of ongoing tension between the army and navy. Despite concerns about the vulnerability of Britain to air attack, air defense remained a thorny, unresolved issue within the larger debate over organization; indeed, the British had not overcome these difficulties to make fully adequate air defense preparations prior to the outbreak of war.[49]

Because the navy did not wish to lose control over its aviation, it managed to acquire, by July 1914, recognition of a separate Royal Naval Air Service (RNAS).[50] On the presumption that the "short" war in Europe would call for a full continental engagement of the British army's air arm, the RFC, the Secretary of State for War, Lord Kitchener, handed responsibility for home defense to the RNAS. To prevent or at least curtail zeppelin attacks on Britain, First Lord of the Admiralty Winston Churchill opted for preemptive strikes against zeppelin sheds at such places as Cologne, Cuxhaven, Düsseldorf, and Friedrichshaven. Churchill, thereafter associated for many decades with British air power and long-range bombing, also authorized development of a heavy bomber in December 1914. The RNAS's anti-airship raids were flown from various British toe-holds on the continent; by November, all RNAS aircraft in Flanders were concentrated at Dunkirk. Though RNAS pilots reported six successes against zeppelins in or near their sheds, it was not enough to prevent airship raids against England, which commenced January 1915.[51] The raids put the British in an unaccustomed situation: suddenly, the nation was uncomfortably exposed. Some officials reacted quickly and with alarm, proffering dramatic schemes to redress the situation. First Sea Lord Baron Fisher of Kilverstone, for instance, proposed killing a captured German civilian for every British citizen killed by the German raids.[52]

While Churchill and the RNAS pondered the zeppelin campaign, the kaiser and his advisors debated how to use the weapon to best advantage. Though zeppelins were powerful symbols of national prestige, not all German leaders were comfortable employing them as long-range bombing platforms against Britain. Adm. Alfred von Tirpitz had doubts about their utility, and Chancellor Theobald von Bettmann-Hollweg fretted over possible international reaction to German bombing of civilians. But the temptation to use an available weapon—one that had captured the popular imagination and was backed strongly by advocates like Admiral Behncke—eventually eroded the hesitation of German decision makers. Additional impetus was provided by German frustration with the naval blockade against them, and by a French air attack on Freiburg in December 1914. In January 1915 the kaiser authorized attacks on docks and military targets along the English coast and on the lower Thames.[53] In trying to confine attacks to military targets, he sought not only to protect the Royal family (to whom he was directly related), but also to keep Germany within the parameters of international law on bombardment, such as it was. The belligerents in the Great War, however, had no means by which to strike targets from the air with precision. Indeed, witnesses on the ground rarely could determine the intended targets of invading air attackers.[54]

Over time, the kaiser loosened the constraints on air attacks, and zeppelin pilots ranged widely over London and Britain. Even Admiral Tirpitz became intrigued with the possibility of setting London ablaze. Flown primarily at night, and often inhibited by weather, bombload limits, and army-navy service rivalry in Germany, the raids caused limited physical damage. But they drew British soldiers and resources away from the western front, provoked disruption, and enjoyed some notable early successes in London, Greenwich, and Hull.[55] Indeed, a zeppelin attack set fire to the heart of London on 8 September 1915, and during that month thousands flocked to the Underground stations for shelter.[56] For the RNAS, attempting to defend Britain against air threats was a frustrating task, and the poor early record of the defenders tended to convey the impression that little could be done to keep hostile craft from flying overhead at will. In early 1916, zeppelin raids against a variety of targets in the North, Midlands, and the South only added to RNAS frustration; the Midlands raid of 31 January 1916 highlighted the need for more deliberate attention to all aspects of air defense. Under heated public scrutiny, the Admiralty had been seeking to unburden itself of the home defense task for some time. In February 1916, responsibility for the defense of British airspace was finally transferred to the RFC, although the navy still had some responsibility for intercepting aircraft over water.[57]

On 10 August 1916, Commander Peter Strasser, head of the German Naval Airship Division, notified the Commander-in-Chief of the High Seas Fleet (Reinhard Scheer) that "airships offer a certain means of victoriously ending the war."[58] By the time the message was sent, however, British defenses had improved substantially. Fighter aircraft with greatly improved climb speeds, anti-airship weapons such as incendiary bullets and flechettes, more and better anti-aircraft guns with high explosive shells, and an improved defense communications network were now taking a substantial toll on the attackers. In particular, the British used signals intelligence to good effect.[59] On the night of 23–24 September, Germany's Imperial Navy lost two of its newest airships; on 1–2 October, another of the great ships went down along with one of Germany's most expert commanders, Heinrich Mathy. Though the airship campaign would continue sporadically to the end of the war, it never again posed a serious threat to Britain: "the newest and most marvelous products of Friedrichshafen were reduced to tangled piles of junk smouldering in the fields around London."[60]

By the end of the war, zeppelins had dropped some 6,000 bombs (a total weight of under 500,000 pounds) on Britain, causing 556 deaths and 1,357 wounded. British citizens generally received little public warning that a zeppelin raid might be imminent; nor were they given much information about the results of the raids in their daily newspapers. The authorities were concerned that air raid warnings would cause panic and, in particular, a loss of production in the factories so vital to the prosecution of total war. And they did not wish to aid German intelligence by providing timely information about the course of zeppelin routes, or the locations of successful attacks.[61] Government authorities kept careful tabs on the zeppelins, and monitored the population in order to assess the effects of the raids on national morale. Beyond question, the raids were a rude shock to a population that had felt itself insulated by both the English Channel and a tradition of naval strength. Some of the early raids caused disruption on the streets and in the factories. Sometimes following the more severe raids, public anger manifested itself in civil disturbances that usually took the form of angry groups attacking shops owned (or thought to be owned) by German nationals.[62] But even though some residents of Hull sometimes took shelter in the countryside, and though some Londoners did the same (or headed to the Underground for safety), it would overstate the case to argue that the zeppelin raids had provoked panic. Here it is crucially important to separate out "panic" and "anger"; even though they are two distinct reactions, they have tended to be conflated in the interpretation of the British reaction to World War I bombing. Certainly the British were angry and indignant about the poor state of their defenses, and outraged that their government seemed so inept at the whole business. But there is no evidence of persistent, widespread, or deep-seated panic over the zeppelin raids. If members of the government began to feel pressure regarding the state of British defenses, it was not pressure to sue for terms.

Newspaper accounts, and wartime letters written by average citizens, indicated that though the zeppelin raids caused strain, the population was angered rather than paralyzed by them. But these sources surely expressed frustration over the slow development of British defenses.[63] In a book written just after the war, Col. A. Rawlinson of the Royal Naval Volunteer Reserve explained the public reaction thus: "There was, of course, no sign whatever of any kind of panic, but there undoubtedly *was* a certain feeling of dismay. This was immediately followed by a deep and universal anger that such attacks should be made upon our defenceless women and children."[64] Accounts by Members of Parliament were similar. In a debate held on 16 February 1916, M.P. Ronald McNeill, whose constituency had recently been bombed, argued emphatically, "I want to avoid the language of exaggeration because if I were to speak as if those people were nervous or panicky or frightened in consequence of what they have been subjected to I should be guilty of mostly grossly misrepresenting them." He insisted that the attacks had merely made them "set their teeth" in determination to prosecute the war harder. In the course of the same debate, Cecil Harmsworth argued, "There is only one chance of a panic arising in this country, and that would emerge from a mistrust of the authorities responsible for the air defences of the country. At present, as every member of this House knows, there is no panic in any part of the country." He went on to say, though, that among the many bombing victims he had visited, there was "uneasiness" and "disappointment with the measures that have been taken hitherto to meet this very great danger." Mr. Evelyn Cecil representing the Midlands, asserted, "I am quite convinced that, while there is no panic, there is a very strong feeling of want of confidence in the general management. What we want is vigour, guidance, courage and determination."[65]

Indeed, the strength of public feeling about the inadequacy of British defenses accounted for the election of an otherwise unlikely Member of Parliament, Noel Pemberton Billing. Leaving the RNAS to run for political office, the audacious Pemberton Billing won success on a single platform: changing the government's policy on home air defense. He energetically fulfilled his public mandate, making himself "almost a daily pest" in the House of Commons as he called insistently for improved home defense and reprisals.[66]

The first great breech of British air space had left its mark: while the zeppelins caused no general panic or social upheaval, they nonetheless brought the war home to the British populace in an unprecedented way. The homefront population had sought a voice in the prosecution of modern conflict, and the government had been forced to take notice. In the popular reaction to the zeppelins, some British authorities thought they saw a manifestation of some of the upheaval that prewar speculation had predicted. After the war, British successes against the later zeppelin raids would tend to be overshadowed in public memory by uneasy recollections of frustrating impotence in the earlier instances. Some military officials looked with concern on the implications arising from the public's new place in the line of fire and its new voice in matters of war.[67] The influential military writer Capt. B. H. Liddell Hart was dismayed by scenes in Hull, which he personally witnessed.[68] Liddell Hart's experience undoubtedly did much to shape his widely read 1925 book, *Paris, or the Future of War*, which argued that homefronts were particularly vulnerable to aerial bombardment. His emotional account of "women, children, babies in arms, spending night after night huddled in sodden fields, shivering under a bitter wintry sky" led him straight to melodramatic extrapolation: "Imagine for a moment London, Manchester, Birmingham, and a half a dozen other great centres simultaneously attacked, the business localities and Fleet Street wrecked, Whitehall a heap of ruins, the slum districts maddened into the impulse to break loose and maraud, the railways cut, factories destroyed. Would not the general will to resist vanish, and what use would be the still determined fractions of the nation, without organization and central direction?"[69] In this way, the experience of the zeppelin raids would help to sow seeds of dramatic speculation and extrapolation in the 1920s and 1930s. And, in this speculation, anger tended to be conflated with panic.

DEVELOPMENTS ON THE CONTINENT: 1914–18

While lighter-than-air craft were the focus of attention over British skies, on the continent heavier-than-air craft were directed more and more frequently beyond the battlefield. French bombing theory had assumed that a war effort was an integrated whole: air forces were to cooperate with ground forces, eroding the enemy's will and capability at all levels. French long-range bombing missions to industrial targets therefore were not thought of as "independent" operations. In general, continental military organizations had to think in terms of their armies first; victory in war—and, indeed, political survival—had, for them, always rested on ground warfare. Equipped with Voisin aircraft, the early French bomber squadrons strove to extend the reach of French offensive power; by mid-1915 there were over 120 aircraft able to prosecute long-distance attacks on German industrial assets in the Rhine and Saar valleys. Pilots departed for their destinations individually, picking their way across country and taking their chances against enemy defenses. Initial bombing methods were crude and inaccurate.[70]

The French sought to identify those industrial sites key to the German war effort, including the Bädische Anilin und Sodafabrik of Ludwigshafen, manufacturer of poison gas and explosives. By late summer of 1915, however, German fighters were taking an increasingly heavy toll on French bombers. The French responded by flying in formation and adding improved engines and armament to reduce losses. Night flying was employed also, but it further complicated the already difficult task of locating targets. Because Paris was easily reachable by air, the French had to consider the prospect of reprisal attacks. Aircraft production problems and the increasingly urgent calls from the front lines caused the French program to be scaled back by 1916. Since the French were compelled to divide their resources in many directions, their bombing force never attained the size required to engage in sustained, punishing raids against the enemy. Nonetheless, they would continue their efforts throughout the war, choosing their targets on the basis of feasibility and significance to the enemy war effort.[71]

The Royal Naval Air Service, by 1916 free of the main responsibility for home defense, continued to stretch in new directions. Though Churchill had departed after the Gallipoli fiasco, the RNAS still had bomber advocates whose zeal for long-range bombing had been strengthened by the Germans' zeppelin campaign and public sentiment for reprisals. Operations continued out of Dunkirk, and by May 1916 an advance party had been sent to review the French facilities at Luxeuil-les-Bains, later to be the home base for the Royal Navy's No. 3 Naval Wing. Though delayed by the Somme campaign, the Wing was ready by October to commence strategic strikes (sometimes in cooperation with the French) against selected targets, mainly Saar Valley iron works and blast furnaces. Like the French bombing units, the Luxeuil Wing was hindered by aircraft production problems and adverse weather.[72]

Decisions about the allocation of resources and the missions to be carried out by aircraft created an ongoing source of tension between the army and navy in Britain. Field Marshal Sir Douglas Haig, Commander-in-Chief of the British Expeditionary Force since December 1915, naturally wanted every available aircraft for use at the Somme. The government attempted, largely without success, to mediate these conflicts and rationalize the use of aviation.[73] Haig's objections to the naval bombing program finally terminated the work of the No. 3 Naval Wing; not only did Haig feel that it threatened his ability to run a centrally controlled offensive, but he also remained unconvinced that the bombing had any significant impact on the ground war. He cited an increase in German aviation units all along the front, and cast doubt on the idea that the Luxeuil bombing had reduced German steel output. The Admiralty countered that their strategic campaign could claim a significant moral effect upon the Germans.[74] The winding up of the Luxeuil operations in April 1917 meant that the army-navy debate over the impact of bombing would remain unresolved, at least for the time being.

While the RNAS had focused much of its attention on long-distance bombing, the Royal Flying Corps had kept its focus squarely on aiding the ground war. In 1914, the RFC had sent four squadrons to France with the British Expeditionary Force. Sir David Henderson, Director-General of Military Aeronautics (DGMA), was the first commander of the field force in France, with Col. Frederick Sykes as his chief of staff. The remnants of the RFC left behind in England were overseen by Lt. Col. W. S. Brancker and Maj. Hugh Trenchard. In mid-November 1914 the latter arrived on the continent, commanding a new wing attached to Haig's First Army. By the summer of 1915 Trenchard, by then a brigadier general, had assumed command of the RFC in France.[75]

That Trenchard would go on to have a great influence on British air power and its history seems unlikely in retrospect. He had had an un-promising start, entering the army as a militia candidate on his third try, and being placed nearly at the bottom of the infantry list in 1893. Serving in India and then in South Africa during the Boer War, his fortitude and determination helped him overcome a series of injuries. In 1912, at the age of 39, he applied for leave to attain his pilot's license, which he received after one hour and forty minutes' flying time. He then became an instructor at the Central Flying School at Upavon, and later its adjutant. Like those of his generation, Trenchard never doubted that courage, élan, and an aggressive spirit were the most important qualities a soldier might possess. Blunt in manner, and lacking lucidity of speech, Trenchard nonetheless managed to cultivate a number of important professional and social relationships prior to the war: he could list Kitchener, Churchill, Henderson, and members of the Royal Family among those who favored him.[76]

Trenchard got on well with Field Marshal Haig from the first.[77] Indeed, the two commanders prosecuted their campaigns in similar ways: both wholeheartedly taking and maintaining the offensive, and stoically accepting high casualties. As commander of the RFC, Trenchard maintained a steady and unwavering determination to wear down the enemy through relentless attacks. Haig's and Trenchard's commitment to these tactics reflected their commitment to Edwardian martial culture, including the idea of the decisive battle.[78] In 1916, Trenchard implemented a policy that pushed his own fighters deep over the lines to interdict enemy aircraft and keep them on the defensive. In support of the plan, he cited the French experience at Verdun, where aviators were able to penetrate the Germans' defensive Luftsperre (air blockade) designed to deny Allied aerial freedom of movement.[79] He felt that taking and maintaining the offensive in the air could achieve moral as well as material dominance over the enemy. Over the course of the Somme campaign, RFC pilots flew aggressive patrols designed to win freedom of maneuver for British reconnaissance, artillery, and other ground support aircraft—and to deny such freedom to the enemy. In a memorandum of September 1916, Trenchard officially asserted that at the Somme British air policy was one of "relentless and incessant offensive" that "had the effect so far on the enemy of compelling him to keep back or to detail portions of his forces in the air for defensive purposes." He argued, "It is the deliberate opinion of those most competent to judge that . . . an aeroplane is an offensive and not a defensive weapon. Owing to the unlimited space in the air, the difficulty one machine has in seeing another, the accidents of wind and cloud, it is impossible for aeroplanes, however skillful and vigilant their pilots, however numerous their formations, to prevent hostile aircraft from crossing the line if they have the initiative and determination to do so."[80] The memorandum, much-quoted during the war, also influenced a summary of RFC results (printed in October 1917), which similarly stressed Trenchard's "lessons" of the Somme offensive.[81]

Trenchardian tactics did in fact cause anxiety on the German side of the lines. Astonished by the British determination despite heavy losses, the Germans worried about interference with their artillery work, and wondered if they might be in danger of losing control over the battle-field. But it is not clear that Trenchard's approach was the unqualified success he made it out to be. The high cost of the patrols offset their value to some extent. The RFC lost 20 percent of its total force in the first weeks of fighting at the Somme, and losses remained very high throughout the battle. Despite their smaller numbers, the Germans often were able to seize the initiative and impose heavy costs on their opponent when there was a critical engagement. In any event, Trenchar-dian tactics were problematical by 1917 when the Germans adopted a tactical posture that emphasized local air superiority in vital areas.[82]

Trenchard's "relentless offensive" generally received the support of his colleagues, in part because they complacently assumed that German casualties had to be higher than British casualties.[83] After the war, how-ever, it became clear that the opposite was true. Contributing greatly to the problem for the British was Trenchard's insatiable appetite for new pilots, which stretched the already inadequate pilot training program to a point where it could not turn out competent aviators fast enough—leading to a vicious spiral in which novices were often quick victims of the more experienced enemy. Many lower-ranking officers had ex-pressed serious misgivings about Trenchard's tactics, and these doubts had been reflected in the press and in Parliamentary debates. Indeed, a government committee of Enquiry investigated the situation, but since testimony came almost exclusively from senior officers (few junior offi-cers were willing to risk airing their views), no charges of wrongdoing were leveled.[84] In a widely read account of the war written shortly after the armistice, the noted British journalist Sir Philip Gibbs was sharply critical of Trenchard's style, which he argued wasted life needlessly. Sir Frederick Sykes later claimed that Trenchard "had been an exponent of the battering-ram tactics beloved by G.H.Q."[85] But Sir Walter Raleigh and H. A. Jones, official historians commissioned by the Air Ministry, came to Trenchard's defense. Though Jones admitted, "It may be said perhaps with truth that the offensive patrols were too much a matter of routine, that their direction and co-ordination were not always suffi-ciently characterized by an alert imagination," he nonetheless supported Trenchard, largely by arguing that since the army had chosen to take an aggressively offensive stance, its air arm could do no less.[86]

Whatever the realities of the situation or the debates that ensued over it, the main point is simply that Trenchard firmly believed that his tactics were correct, and incorporated them into the foundational body of British air theory—with important consequences both during and after the war. Throughout 1917 and 1918, British wartime aviation would remain devoted to the primary task of maintaining a continual air offensive over the western front. Indeed, Trenchard's offensive tactical posture had so defined the nature of British wartime aviation that it would continue unaltered, even as its heavy demand for aircraft helped compromise British strategic bombing efforts commanded, ironically, by Trenchard himself in 1918.[87]

THE GOTHA / GIANT RAIDS AND THEIR IMPACT

In the end, the RFC was not afforded the luxury of keeping its entire focus on land battles. German aviation—specifically long-range, heavier-than-air bombers—would compel changes, leading to a reorganization of the British military. Besides their immediate impact on the British war effort, these developments ultimately would have long-lasting consequences for the island nation.

From the beginning of the war, the Germans had been engaged in an effort to develop and produce a long-range bomber. Their work came to fruition when specially designed Gotha, and later, Giant, bombers (Riesenflugzeuge or R-planes) were positioned in Flanders to wage aerial attacks on Britain. Both were technological marvels for their time, indeed, the Giant's 138-foot wing-span was scarcely shorter than that of a World War II B-29 bomber. As with the zeppelin raids, the Germans not only hoped that the bomber offensive would cause both material and psychological damage; they also gambled that these raids, along with unrestricted submarine warfare, might help break the war's deadlock. In July 1917, Field Marshal Paul von Hindenberg pointed out to the chancellor (Bethmann-Hollweg), "The military advantages are great. They keep a large amount of war material away from the French front and destroy important enemy establishments of various kinds."[88]

Though the aircraft could carry only a fraction of a zeppelin's bombload, they were faster, more maneuverable, and able to attack in daylight.[89] German bomber raids on Britain commenced on 25 May 1917 against Folkestone and Shorncliffe, followed by attacks on London on 13 June and 7 July. The people of Folkestone had images of air war seared into their memories in a particularly traumatic way. A handful of German bombers appeared overhead on a bright and otherwise calm spring day; the bombs they dropped killed 95 people and injured another 195. Only one German plane was shot down by the seventy-four British fighters attempting to engage the intruders. Shortly after the war, the Folkestone citizenry described 25 May as a day "never to be effaced from memory."[90] The first two London attacks were, likewise, carried out in broad daylight by a handful of bombers flying in formation and taking advantage of full surprise.[91] On 13 June, fourteen Gotha bombers dropped high explosive bombs on London in the late morning, killing 162 and injuring 432. Some of the bombs hit an infant's school in the East End, causing intense grief and indignation. Despite the ninety-two British aircraft attempting to intercept, all the Gothas returned safely to their hangars. Less than a month later a second raid, on 7 July, killed 65 and injured 245 British persons. Only one Gotha was destroyed by the intercepting force of ninety-five. The impotence of the defenders caused the public to recall the RNAS's failure against the early zeppelin raids.[92]

In the end the raids had an impact disproportionate to the bombload they carried (only seven and a half tons total). In a *Times* (London) editorial commenting on the 13 June raid, the authors warned that repetition of air attacks against England "will assuredly lead to a constantly increasing demand for better defensive measures, for a more efficient system of warning, and for prompter retaliation." The *Times'* description of the raid, subtitled "No Warning of Midday Attack," pointed out that the German attack had "made London quiver, not with fear, but with sorrow and anger."[93] This point was reemphasized by journalists and other commentators (including those in the midst of the rescue efforts) who pointed out that the public had not panicked during or after the raids.[94] But anger was thick in the air. On 15 June, the *Daily Mail* published photographs of the child victims of the first raid, along with a "Reprisal Map" of German towns within 150 miles of the front lines.[95] Well-attended public meetings at Tower Hill and the London Opera House debated air defense and air reprisals. The *Times* described the latter as "crowded and enthusiastic." A resolution was passed "amid great cheering," which called on the government to undertake air reprisals on German cities.[96] Letters to the editor demanded air defense and reprisals. Most contended that the government must warn citizens of impending air raids and carry out retaliatory efforts. Some writers were careful to argue, however, that any steps taken against the Germans ought not to diminish the critical air effort on the western front and thus "play into the German hands"; they believed that German strategic attacks had been deliberately designed to draw British resources away from the front lines.[97]

The raid of 7 July caused a more dramatic, sustained reaction in the press. In an outpouring of description, commentary, and debate that continued for days, the pages of the *Times* were full of the air raid. Writers describing the raid again pointed out (and took pride in) the cool, calm reaction of Londoners. One article in the *Times* argued, "An extraordinary indication of the futility of the raid as a demonstration of 'frightfulness' was the rapidity with which people everywhere settled down to their business again once the last of the raiders had disappeared."[98] Indeed, the language used to describe the attack, which included such terms as "thrilling" and "magnificent" revealed that many had perceived the raid as a spectacle second to none.[99] In the United States, the *Literary Digest* cited British sources claiming that, "in the majority of our fellows we believe the evidence before us shows demeanor to have been unimpeachable, and to augur well for whatever days of trial may yet be in store."[100] But if the British were not in the throes of panic, they were not complacent either. News coverage made it clear that in the aftermath of the second attack, Londoners were more indignant than ever about poor defenses, inadequate warning, and the dearth of retaliatory efforts. A key story in the *Times* (London) of 9 July stated that British anger was provoked "because the enemy squadron had got away unscathed." The author added, "The attack was carried out with such confidence—'impudence' was the popular word among the people—that one got the impression that the Germans despised our defenses."[101] Opinion leaders, even those generally inclined toward moderation in war, began to take a hard line. The Reverend Bernard Snell, Chairman of the Congregational Union of England and Wales, preached in Brixton that the British people should no longer practice "patience, self-control and good behaviour" while its citizens were slaughtered at home.[102]

Another gathering of Londoners at Tower Hill produced a telling message for delivery to the King: "Thousands of Londoners appeal to your Majesty to instruct your Ministers at once to make rigorous and continual air attacks on German towns and cities as reprisals for the murder of civilians—men, women, and children, even infants at their school desks—and if your Ministers do not take steps to protect us we implore your Majesty to dissolve Parliament and appoint Ministers who will do their duty. Failing any other solution we suggest the revival by Royal license of Letters of Mark granting the right to privateers of the air to carry havoc and destruction as reprisals into Germany."[103] Popular anger again found an outlet in daily newspapers. Letters to editors called for defense restructuring, including the creation of a separate air force. And again citizens vented their anger by attacking the shopfronts of Germans (or those thought to be Germans) in neighborhoods like Lambeth, Clerkenwell, Hackney, Holloway, and Bethnal Green.[104]

The Gotha raids provoked several important official responses. After the attacks on London of 13 June and 7 July, the government requested that Haig send fighter squadrons from the front line back home to help defend Britain. He complied, but warned Chief of the Imperial General Staff Sir William Robertson that losing two squadrons would complicate his job in France.[105] In addition, the War Cabinet mandated that aircraft production—plagued with widespread problems of management and organization—was to be given priority over all other forms of weapon production. Further, the number of RFC and RNAS squadrons would be roughly doubled, and engine production would be trebled. Forty of the new squadrons would be devoted to reprisals against Germany.[106]

Following the raid of 7 July in particular, the government's reluctance to organize air raid warnings was sharply challenged by a number of public figures. In rebuttal, some officials argued that air raid alarms would cause production losses due to work stoppage. They argued further that diverting fighters to home defense would increase the German advantage on the western front. Since casualties from air raids had been relatively modest (as compared to the battlefront), they urged the public to remain steadfast.[107] The editors of the conservative journal *The Spectator* supported this rationale, chiding other publishers for exaggerating the German menace and encouraging public outcries of vengeance.[108] But there is no question that the government was concerned. Lloyd George had his hands full with labor troubles in 1917. In his memoirs he would later write, "Of all the problems which Governments had to handle during the Great War, the most delicate and probably the most perilous were those arising on the home front . . . the contentment and co-operation of the wage earners was our vital concern, and industrial unrest spelt a graver menace to our endurance and ultimate victory than even the military strength of Germany."[109] The Russian Revolution, and the deployment of four cavalry divisions to the interior of France to break strikes and suppress agitation, hardly lightened the mind of uneasy officials in Britain already deeply worried about the pressures imposed on the people by Germany's unrestricted submarine warfare. Lloyd George recalled that the government's "constant anxiety" about how to handle labor was, in those difficult days, "more than ever acute."[110] Sir H. S. Rawlinson, British representative to the Supreme War Council through April 1918, worried that the strained and wearied masses—egged on by "Bolshevist propaganda"—wished to take control of the war from the government and the Parliament. In a speech to the House of Commons on 21 February 1918, Sir William Pearce asserted that in order to avert disaster, the London poor had to be given the impression that everything possible was being done on their behalf.[111]

In this context, the public anger displayed in the aftermath of the 7

July raid was interpreted as ominous and, perhaps, prerevolutionary; it spurred the government to action. On 11 July the War Cabinet appointed a committee of two, Prime Minister David Lloyd George and the well-respected General Jan Christian Smuts of South Africa, to review the situation and make recommendations. Lloyd George left the work to Smuts, who first turned his attention to air defense organization, and then, in a second report, addressed the issue of counterattack.[112] The latter, articulating a futurist vision of the yet unrealized power of aerial operations, argued for a radical change in British aviation organization: the creation of an independent air arm emphasizing a counteroffensive through long-range bombing. Smuts used language that reflected expectations and anticipations far more than existing realities:

> Unlike artillery, an air fleet can conduct extensive operations far from, and independently of, both army and navy. As far as can at present be foreseen there is absolutely no limit to the scale of its future independent war use. And the day may not be far off when aerial operations with their devastation of enemy lands and destruction of industrial and populous centers on a vast scale may become the principal operations of war, to which the older forms of military and naval operations may become secondary and subordinate.[113]

Smuts had been assured that sufficient surplus aircraft would be available in 1918 to constitute such a strategic bomber force.[114] The War Cabinet, on 24 August accepted all of Smuts's recommendations in principle. So long as the army and navy were promised enough air strength to meet their own requirements (and they were), they could not easily delay or circumvent the report.[115] This did not mean, however, that they favored restructuring British defenses in the middle of a war. Many in their ranks feared that the creation of an independent third service would waste resources or divert them to sideshows. Neither Trenchard nor Haig, for instance, was the least bit enthusiastic about the Smuts Report. Committed to the primacy of the western front, Trenchard believed that the RFC existed to further Haig's ground campaign. In a letter of 30 August 1917, he complained that the idea that the war could be won in the air alone was "bare assertion." And he argued that an independent Air Ministry, susceptible to "popular and factional clamour," could "lose its sense of proportion" and be drawn "toward the spectacular" at the expense of providing essential support to the older services.[116]

Haig commiserated with Trenchard and shared his deep misgivings.[117] In a mid-September letter to the Chief of the Imperial General Staff, he raised serious questions about the Smuts report, arguing, "Apart from the question of advisibility from the point of view of morality and public opinion, of seeking to end the war by 'devastation of enemy lands and destruction of industrial and populous centres on a vast scale,' I am unwilling to agree that there is practically no limit to such methods in this war, or that—at any rate in the near future—they are likely to 'become the principal operations of war, to which the older forms of military and naval operations may become secondary and subordinate.'" In a particularly prescient section of this letter, he argued that "the science of defence against aircraft attack may develop considerably in the future."[118]

German raids continued in the autumn, under cover of night. Rear Adm. Mark Kerr of the RNAS, a supporter of long-range bombing and a recent Admiralty addition to the Air Board, warned that the Germans had recently developed a newer, larger, more powerful bomber; any delay in British plans for an air offensive would give the initiative to the enemy. Arguing that parts of London were in danger of being bombed flat, he called for the construction of 2,000 big bombers. Lloyd George saw the memorandum, and it was quickly printed up and distributed to the full War Cabinet. The latter recommended that arrangements be made for the creation of an Air Ministry and for the commencement of long-range bombing operations.[119] The Air Force Constitution Bill passed in November 1917, and in January 1918 an Air Council was constituted and charged with overseeing the administration of the new "Royal Air Force" (RAF), which came into existence officially on 1 April 1918.[120]

In the meantime, the Germans prosecuted their plan to invoke panic and confusion through the use of newly developed ten-pound incendiary bombs. Large numbers of these could be dropped from small numbers of aircraft; the effect, the Germans hoped, might be a great conflagration in the heart of the city. This did not come to pass. In early December the Germans expressed their disappointment with the incendiaries. Even the large raid of 18 December 1917, which set several fires in the city, caused a limited damage and casualty toll—the latter including twelve dead and sixty-six wounded.[121] The British government, however, concerned itself with the prospect of war-weariness, especially since the conflict had been so unexpectedly long and costly. Debates were rekindled over the adequacy of British defenses, alerts, and public safety. These questions seemed even more urgent following the night of 28 January 1918, when twenty-eight casualties, including fourteen dead, resulted from the crush of shelter-seeking crowds, and when a direct hit on the Odhams Printing Works (doubling as an air raid shelter) claimed eighty-five severely injured and thirty-eight dead. The following night the Germans flew R-planes, without Gothas, against London. On the night of 16 February an R-plane dropped the single largest bomb of the war: thirteen feet in length, it weighed one metric ton. As all this tran-spired, the Germans also raided Paris, shocking the city's inhabitants who had not been hit hard since a zeppelin attack two years before.[122]

British government debates reflected worries about the course of the war and anxiety about the future. Concerned about German efforts to terrorize the British population, the War Cabinet discussed the possi-bility of large-scale air attacks on London (by as many as five hundred bombers) that might overwhelm the capacity of the fire brigades.[123] In-deed, so profound were concerns about the stability of the homefront that government planners would develop (in the spring of 1918) Emer-gency Scheme L. This highly secret plan aligned military districts with police districts, and replaced civil authority with military control. It re-quired government authorities to maintain in Britain the equivalent of about eight divisions—units otherwise capable of overseas service. Though its purpose was not stated explicitly and must be deduced from the structure and requirements of the scheme, it was almost certainly to maintain control in a domestic emergency, and to counteract the emer-gence of revolutionary dissent.[124]

BRITAIN AND THE BEGINNINGS OF STRATEGIC BOMBING

In the meantime the British authorities had, in October 1917, hastily established a detachment of mainly single-engine aircraft at Ochey, France—the 41st Wing under Brig. Gen. Cyril Newall—to fly reprisal raids against Germany. In a foreshadowing of 1939–40, the French urged the British not to launch strikes that would encourage German retaliation on French cities. The 41st Wing (renamed the Eighth Brigade in February 1918) was the forerunner of an "Independent Force" (IF), which would operate as an air reprisal force during the final year of the war. Its activities were constrained by a shortage of suitable aircraft, inadequately trained crews, lack of navigational instruments, and poor weather.[125]

An ad hoc effort, Newall's offensive achieved only limited results. Though he would have preferred more resources, he believed that bombing which was ineffective on a material level nonetheless had a moral effect on the enemy. At the conclusion of his efforts in May 1918, he submitted a paper to London with the optimistic title "The Scientific and Methodical Attack of Vital Industries" to help inform a strategy for a larger-scale long-range bombing effort. In it Newall asserted, "Up to the present, judging from reports and photographs, actual experience goes to show that the material effect has not been very great, except perhaps in isolated cases, but the moral effect has been considerable."

He argued as well that if his limited effort had caused "so much fear and discontent," then it was not difficult "to foresee what the effect of twenty or more squadrons, whether day or night, or both, will produce."[126] Newall's paper displayed a number of qualities that would reveal themselves over and over again in the writings of later airmen. The first was a hopefulness about orchestrating sustained attacks on carefully selected targets. The second was a firm faith that bombing had a significant moral effect even in the absence of significant material damage. And the third was a ready willingness to extrapolate from the perceived results of earlier bombing raids to overwhelming, decisive air offensives.

While Newall struggled along as best he could, the effort to get a larger reprisal effort up and running was plagued by ongoing organizational difficulties. These have been documented elsewhere and will not be discussed in detail here.[127] Still, some of these problems deserve brief mention since they affected the results of Britain's first major strategic bombing effort. Air organization had troubled the British throughout the war, and the rather dramatic discontinuities of the Smuts Report only increased the tumult. Haig had been strongly opposed to any notion of removing Trenchard from his field command so that he could serve as an administrator of the new service, and Trenchard himself was just as firmly opposed.[128] Nonetheless, Trenchard was recalled from France to serve as the first Chief of Air Staff (CAS), and Lord Rothermere was named the first Secretary of State for Air. While Rothermere rosily imagined great reprisal raids against German cities, Trenchard hewed to the operational reality: the British effort involved only a few squadrons equipped with bombers of limited range, and not fully capable of coping in poor weather.[129]

At continual loggerheads with his minister, Trenchard chose to tender his resignation in March 1918. It was accepted in April, once the crisis of the great German ground offensive had abated somewhat. Trenchard was replaced by his old rival Sir Frederick Sykes—now a major general—who had long held a more ambitious view of strategic bombing possibilities than Trenchard.[130] Rothermere himself resigned shortly thereafter, and was replaced by Sir William Weir, a Scottish businessman with a long-standing interest in strategic bombing. Once in his new post, Weir persuaded Trenchard to take charge of the soon-to-be-established "Independent Force," emphasizing that it would be a "really big active command."[131] Weir's choice, in many respects an unlikely one, nonetheless capitalized on Trenchard's energy and command experience. Trenchard, in London and out of a job, finally agreed to take the post in the late spring.

Trenchard's reasons for accepting command of the bomber force in

1918 have remained somewhat obscure; historians have had to make deductions based partly on circumstances and partly on Trenchard's ex post facto explanations. Trenchard knew that he had the confidence of the field commanders on the continent and that he could maintain good relations with the Allied armies. As a pragmatist, he probably felt he was the best man for the job: it would give him an opportunity, at least, to prevent too much harm from being done. In written negotiations with Weir, Trenchard insisted that the "fundamental principles" of air warfare could not be understood by men with no experience of it. He also insisted that a bombing offensive could not be directed from London, but must instead be run from the field since "weather, wind, engine trouble, hostile machines, and anti-aircraft all have their voice in the matter."[132] On 8 May Trenchard, having concluded that the IF was an inevitability, reluctantly told Weir that he would do his best to make the command a success as far as possible.[133] Later in his career, Trenchard explained that he was opposed to an Independent Force at the time because he did not want to jeopardize the fighting on the western front; he implied, not quite genuinely, that he disagreed only on the timing of independence, not with the idea itself. But Weir's influence was certainly crucial. He was able to chide Trenchard—petulant, embarrassed, and sitting idly in Green Park—and insist that he get back into the fight.[134] As a condition of employment, Trenchard scrupulously arranged a direct relationship with Weir, allowing a great deal of freedom from Sykes and the Air Staff in London. This unusual arrangement would have important consequences since it would give Trenchard wide discretion in the operation of the Independent Force.[135]

A window into Trenchard's early thinking on long-range bombing can be discovered in a memo he wrote in late 1917, just before he departed his post as head of the RFC. At that time, he viewed long-distance bombing as a component of air warfare to be organized and run within the context of the army, as surplus resources permitted. He argued that it had a dual purpose: (a) to weaken the power of the enemy directly "by interrupting his production, transport and organization through infliction of damage to his industrial, railway and military centres, and by compelling him to draw back his fighting machines to deal with the menace"; and (b) to weaken the enemy indirectly "by producing discontent and alarm amongst the industrial population." He pointed out that "experience goes to show that the moral effect of bombing industrial towns may be great, even though the material effect is, in fact, small."[136]

For Trenchard, long-distance bombing was part of the essential task of keeping the enemy on the defensive at all times. He pointed out that bombers needed to be specialized aircraft able to "beat off attack or be escorted by other fighting machines with a large range of action." But, he argued, "No machine at present serving in the Royal Flying Corps is suitable for long distance day bombing." Trenchard concluded by stressing that all air work had to be centrally coordinated. "It is essential," he wrote, "that one hand and one brain should have a firm grip of these difficult operations as a whole, and there ought to be no doubt in the mind of any pilot as to the source from which his orders spring."[137]

His insistence on virtually sole control over bombing operations would, inevitably, bring him into conflict with his colleagues. Sykes in particular had greater ambitions for strategic bombing than Trenchard did. In addition, Sykes's staff in London was made up of men with practical experience of aerial bombing; they believed that their professional advice and insights merited serious consideration. Two of the most important were Brig. Gen. P.R.C. Groves, appointed to head the Air Staff's Directorate of Flying Operations (DFO), and Maj. Lord Tiverton (later, second Earl of Halsbury), who served under Groves. The latter may legitimately be considered one of the first true analysts of air warfare.[138] Tiverton articulated a comprehensive concept of long-range bombing in a paper he wrote on 3 September 1917, two months ahead of Trenchard's memorandum. At the time, he was serving with the naval section of the British Aviation Commission in Paris, as technical liaison officer with the French. He identified key target sets, listed geographically: the Mannheim region because it produced chemicals, especially nitrates; Düsseldorf and Cologne because of their machine shops; and the Saar Valley because of its steel works. Tiverton also evaluated a number of crucial operational issues: the location of bases; constraints imposed by weather; navigation; the number of machines required and the number of sorties one could expect from each machine; and the transport and storing of bombs.[139] He insisted that for bombing to have its greatest possible effect (either moral or material), it had to be concentrated. Rear Adm. Mark Kerr echoed this emphasis on concentration: "Bombing to be effective must be done on a large scale and be continuous. Sporadic and small bombings only cause the enemy to prepare field defenses and dug-outs for personnel and material."[140]

For Tiverton and others considering the problem at this point, it seemed self-evident that attacking the foundations of the German war economy would mean keeping war matériel out of the hands of the enemy. Their target lists included the Benz motor works, the Bosch magneto factory and aeroplane works, munitions works, petroleum refining stations and stores, and power stations.[141] One observer argued, "A modern Army cannot fight without an adequate supply of munitions and therefore the strategy will be directed along the lines which will best destroy such supply. . . . In order to effect this, the root industries in Germany, or if another word be preferred, the bottleneck of production must be attacked."[142] In a second paper on bombing written in November, Tiverton refined his target list, and sought the most efficient way for Britain to attack it. He prioritized the Bädische Anilin und Soda Fabrik (BASF) at Ludwigshafen, the Meister Lucius works at Hoechst, and the Bayer works at Cologne—all of which produced synthetic nitrates for explosives.[143]

If the material effect of bombing was prioritized by World War I British staff planners, the moral effect was never very far behind. Its conceptualization and articulation varied somewhat, but general trends were discernable. Admiral Kerr argued that bombs missing factory targets would often hit workers' dwellings and thus reduce output indirectly: "If [workers] houses are hit it produces panic and lowers the production."[144] Though Tiverton was mainly interested in destroying German factories and works, he understood that bombing would have a concomitant "moral" effect. He advocated daylight bombing over night bombing because in daytime workers in factories would feel more exposed than at night in their own homes.[145] In considering the bombing of chemical factories, Tiverton recognized that fires started could spread beyond the control of local fire brigades, precipitating effects out of proportion to the damage actually done by the immediate effect of the bombs.

When the IF ultimately commenced operations with a much smaller complement of aircraft than had been anticipated for it, the Air Staff realized that inflicting material damage would be problematic, and a temporary change of priority would be warranted. Under the circumstances, it seemed expedient to hope for a maximum moral effect. This philosophy applied as well to the force, then in development, of large four-engine Handley Page V/1500s designed to range all over Germany from bases in Britain.[146] A planning paper addressing the V/1500s argued, "It appears certain that this machine cannot be produced in sufficiently large numbers this year to obtain decisive results against the root munitions industries. It is therefore apparent that the best value can be obtained by aiming at the maximum moral and political results."[147]

To quantify and incorporate moral effect as an operational goal, Tiverton defined it as anything "which hinders the German output of munitions, apart from actual material damage done to works." In a grim foreshadowing of World War II, he requested from air intelligence a "list of towns and works which specialize in workmen's dwellings, such dwellings therefore forming a reasonable target, and also a priority list of towns (not targets) in which munitions are being manufactured."[148] The Air Staff also assessed the potential of a new type of incendiary bomb. One memorandum cold-bloodedly stated, "In an incendiary system we are harnessing the element fire and applying it as a war weapon. In deciding on this element, we need no stronger warranty than the universal dread in which fire is held by humanity." Such bombs, if used systematically, might produce "terrific" results that "no ordinary populace" could endure over time.[149] At one point Tiverton even recommended a type of early biological warfare in which the British would drop planeloads of Colorado beetles on German farmland in order to devastate their potato crops.[150]

Debates regarding the moral effect invariably reflected the subjective, evanescent nature of the idea and the hopes and motives of its partisans. Perhaps Tiverton put it best when he admitted that the moral effect "is strongly reminiscent of that sweet and blessed word 'Mesopotamia.' It is used most loosely to embrace all manner of different enterprises."[151] But whether long-distance bombing was likely to effect any result at all depended on the resources dedicated to it. In Britain, the organizing and equipping of a suitable force lagged considerably behind the proliferation of planning documents outlining its employment. Disparities between ideas and capabilities would have an immediate and a long-lasting effect on British bombing efforts.

THE INDEPENDENT FORCE IN ACTION

Aircraft shortages and problems as well as conflicts over priorities would plague the IF just as they had plagued its predecessors. When the 41st Wing (later the Eighth Brigade) had begun operations in the fall of 1917, Newall frequently diverted it to tactical targets in support of the army; this tendency was reinforced when the German ground offensive in March 1918 placed high demands on the air force.[152] Trenchard, in command of the IF, would follow a similar pattern.

At its inception, the IF had only five squadrons of the forty originally envisioned: three-day bombing squadrons (of DeHavilland two-seater biplanes), and two night-bombing squadrons (of FE2bs and large Handley Page bombers). Though the force would later be expanded by four additional night squadrons and one additional day squadron, its total strength would never amount to more than 10 percent of the total British air strength in France.[153] Inter-Allied command relationships further complicated the issue. In March 1918 the command of Allied forces had been unified under Field Marshal Ferdinand Foch of France as Supreme Commander of the Allied Expeditionary Forces. It took time, however, to work out an agreement with him regarding the overall direction of the various national forces. He was opposed to the concept of an air force outside of his control; he wanted all available aircraft oriented toward the defeat of the German army. Months would pass before the issue would be formally settled.[154]

Trenchard became General-Officer-Commanding (GOC) of the IF in early June, stepping into a position for which he felt ambivalence and perhaps even disdain. His discomfort may have been reinforced by a comment from Gen. Maurice Duval of the French Air Service, who in mid-June 1918 pointed out that the IF was something Trenchard never would have approved of a year earlier.[155] Trenchard was clearly uneasy with the role that the press and the public were playing in the war; he felt they had forced an organizational change that made little military sense. But while he grumbled about it privately, he accepted the demands of the new reality. Indeed, Trenchard quickly proved himself highly attentive to press accounts of his work, and to national opinion generally. He understood that public expectation had made the IF the object of hopeful attention and critical scrutiny; he knew he would be expected to produce results and avenge the insults of the Gotha / Giant raids. Within two hours of taking up his new post—even before he had sent a telegram to the Air Ministry announcing he was officially in charge—Trenchard sent his first press release back home. He upgraded the communications links to England, and made a point of complaining whenever his press releases were not printed, or not followed verbatim in major English papers. The IF organized an extensive program of daily, weekly, and monthly news releases and dispatches for public consumption.[156]

This public relations campaign, however, belied the IF's meager results. Trenchard's first operational dispatch to Lord Weir (in July) explained his strategy: to attack a large number of objectives "so as to force the enemy to disperse his defensive forces," and then to bomb the same objective repeatedly. He complained thereafter that he was not able to undertake this program because of weather, engine troubles, and under-trained pilots. His small force had strictly limited capabilities, and his airfields (south of Nancy, France) were subpar.[157] In early August, Trenchard summarized (for Weir) his force's second month in the field. After complaining about such obstacles as "high wind and cloud over the Rhine Valley," he highlighted a few long-distance raids against Stuttgart, Mannheim, Zweibrucken, and Rottweil. Many of these raids involved only a handful of bombers, however. Though Trenchard emphasized the numbers of bombs dropped, claiming that "shooting has, as a rule, been good," actual achievements remained ambiguous.[158] The aircraft available to Trenchard suffered frequently from engine troubles, including broken valve springs (in the unreliable DH9 machines), and overheating (in the Handley Page 0/400s). He requested replacement engines for the DH9s, but the process was slow. In addition, training in map reading was not up to the needs of long-range bomber pilots. And in the field it was no small task, even for experienced airmen, to read large maps in cramped, windswept, frequently dark cockpits.[159]

Similarly, target-finding and bomb-sighting capabilities were very crude: pilots had only a random chance of hitting their intended targets, and those on the ground could rarely discern what pilots were aiming at when they released their bombs. The bombsights on DH9s, for instance, had to be calibrated before the aircraft left the ground. Frequently the prevailing winds over the target were not what had been predicted three hours earlier and one hundred miles away. And, often, oil from the engines would partly or wholly obscure the bombsight view by the time a pilot reached the destination. DH9s were slow and had a ceiling of only 14,000 feet with bombs; they were dangerously less capable than the DH4s they were intended to replace.[160] The carefully chosen and vague phrases employed by the official historian of the air campaign are revealing in this respect. Jones explained that between October 1917 and November 1918, 76 percent of the airplanes sent out bombed "some objective." (Fourteen percent returned due to engine trouble and 10 percent due to poor weather.) Of the 76 percent dropping bombs, 55.5 percent attacked their "allotted targets," and 20.5 percent attacked targets "of their own choosing."[161]

Under the circumstances, Trenchard, like Newall before him, turned to attacking what was readily in range. This expedient suited Trenchard's predilection for using air power to support ground operations whenever possible, and also allowed him to comply with the special requests of French General Headquarters. He reported that his forces had made frequent visits to railway stations in the vicinity of the ground war. He also reported increasing activities by hostile aircraft against his day bombers, and observed that "on many occasions there has been considerable fighting."[162] By high summer both enemy resistance and poor weather had become unhappy refrains in Trenchard's dispatches. Though a spell of fine weather in August allowed opportunities for long-distance raids, the force was nonetheless grounded on eighteen days and sixteen nights. In October "extremely unfavorable" weather again kept his force grounded more than half the time. From mid-September into October, Trenchard's force was diverted to help support the American ground offensive on the St. Mihiel salient.[163] Though he reported long distance raids on Kaiserslautern, Frankfurt, Bonn, Wiesbaden, and Mannheim, these generally involved small numbers of aircraft dropping ineffective 112-pound bombs.

In the end, strategic attacks on German war industry comprised only about 16 percent of total raids by the IF.[164] Trenchard instead dedicated much of his time to attacking railways: in the three summer months of

1918, Trenchard devoted to the railways, respectively, 55 percent, 46 percent, and 31 percent of the total bombs dropped by the IF. And he argued that he had no choice but to attack enemy airdromes to reduce the threat to his own forces. By September more than 83 percent of total IF attacks were directed at railways and airdromes.[165] His extensive use of the IF for tactical purposes greatly frustrated members of the London Air Staff who believed that, despite the difficulties, he had more targeting flexibility than he let on. In September the Air Staff's Director of Flying Operations, Brig. Gen. P.R.C. Groves, submitted a critical review of the work of the Independent Force during its first three months. He pointed out that Trenchard's attacks on priority targets had declined drastically: for instance, attacks on chemical factories had gone from constituting 14 percent of the total bombings in June to only 8 percent in August. Attacks on iron and steel works had shown a similar trend.[166] On the other hand, the percentage of attacks on enemy airdromes had risen dramatically from June to August. While he left the latter alone (granting that only the field commander could judge what kind of counteroffensive was required), Groves argued that the number of attacks on railway objectives was indefensible since "every effort should be made to concentrate upon root industries, since to carry out the destruction of these industries is the object for which the Independent Force was created."[167]

Like Groves, Sykes sharply criticized Trenchard at the time for remaining too tactically oriented, and later (in his memoirs) complained that Trenchard "allowed the independent air force to be diverted in attacking purely military objectives of minor importance in the army zone."[168] By midsummer, Sykes had revealed his own views and aspirations in an ambitious, forward-looking planning paper titled, "Review of Air Situation and Strategy for the Information of the Imperial War Cabinet."[169] In July, Tiverton vented his frustrations over Trenchard's direction of strategic bombing, and the irrelevance of the Air Staff to the effort. He felt that the Air Staff needed to take a much more aggressive line regarding targeting priorities.[170] Tiverton was most troubled by Trenchard's refusal to develop and execute any systematic plan. He had long been convinced that the Air Staff should identify German targets, and then consult with engineers, civilian industrialists, and technicians for insights into the German war industry and its vulnerabilities. In addition he wished to undertake tests of equipment and to conduct exercises to generate data and models for analysis. In pursuit of these objectives, he had produced, by the end of 1918, a total of sixty-five studies for Sykes and the Air Staff.[171] To these, however, Trenchard seemed largely oblivious: a soldier of the old tradition, he preferred to command more by instinct than by science and analysis.

In related matters, Tiverton and the Air Staff fretted over Trenchard's apparently haphazard attacks and his reckless disregard for the IF's very high loss rates. And after reviewing Trenchard's September dispatch on operations, Tiverton questioned the accuracy of the field commander's reporting, especially claims about losses and objectives.[172] Also in September, veteran pilot Capt. H. McClelland calculated that although the IF flying-hour total for July 1918 exceeded June's total by 33 percent, the wastage rate in the second month doubled. A similar analysis for July and August revealed that the wastage rate increased by 2.5 times the flying rate. Indeed, while Trenchard lost twenty-one aircraft over German lines in August, he lost another fifty-four—a staggering number by any account—on the British side of the lines.[173] In mid-October, Tiverton's Air Staff colleague Lt. Col. J. Gammell pointed out that in September, 44 percent of the IF's total machines had crashed on the *British* side of the lines. Adding this to the thirty-seven machines lost over enemy territory, he explained that in only eleven flying days and twelve flying nights, Trenchard had lost 81 percent of his total establishment. Both McClelland and Gammell strongly suspected problems of organization and management in Trenchard's force.[174] In the last eighteen months of the war, RFC/RAF wastage was so high (51 percent per month on average) that every airplane had to be replaced once every eight weeks.[175] For his part, Trenchard thought he was making the best use of his assets. He believed in the idea of victory through the "relentless offensive," and showed contempt for air units (in the RNAS for instance) that displayed what he termed a "lack of ginger."[176]

It is unlikely that the IF's preoccupation with railway targets gave results proportional to cost, and the effort expended on enemy airdromes—undertaken to reduce the enemy's toll on British aircraft—came to represent a circular activity that consumed substantial resources to little or no avail. Because the IF's scattered long-range attacks lacked impact, they did little real damage to German industrial output. A modern calculation by the Canadian official historian S. F. Wise concluded that damage inflicted on German industry by Allied bombing amounted to a total of only 15,380,000 reichsmarks, or less than one-tenth of 1 percent of German war expenditure.[177] More recently, a scholar of German aviation concluded, "The expense of the RAF's destroyed aircraft exceeded the cost of the damage it inflicted on Germany."[178] Allied bombing did cause the Germans to divert resources to defense, including, by 1918, 896 heavy Flak guns, 454 searchlights, 204 Flak machine guns, and 9 fighter squadrons.[179] The ever-increasing effectiveness of air defenses—German Flak guns shot down 129 Allied aircraft in October 1918—prompted the British to believe that the Germans had invested very heavily in this realm. While this investment was by no means insubstantial, it was consistently overestimated by RAF officers after the war.[180]

At one point Trenchard wondered, privately, if the effort repaid the cost. In August 1918 he admitted in his diary that the material damage done by bombing was likely very small. And, though he believed that the moral effect was very great, he added that its greatest impact was perhaps "to give the newspapers copy to say how wonderful we are, though it really does not affect the enemy so much as it affects our own people."[181] Yet any misgivings he had at the time had not prompted him to reevaluate his own approach, to rely more substantially on Air Staff analyses, or to tone down his public pronouncements. Indeed, he used the latter to cover up his doubts in a rhetorical offensive that may have helped him cope with the ambivalence he felt about his job. By focusing attention on the vague and amorphous moral effect of bombing, he could argue that he had met his obligations and justified his losses. And he could do so without much fear of contradiction.

In highlighting the moral effect, Trenchard was amplifying a claim first made by his predecessors in the RNAS and RFC.[182] Over time the RNAS had relied increasingly on the moral effect as a way of justifying the existence of No. 3 (Luxeuil) Wing, and this tendency reached its climax when the unit was under pressure to disband and transfer its assets to the army. An excerpt of a letter from a German factory manager claiming that he could no longer give his clients firm delivery dates because of wartime disruption and aerial bombing was translated by the Admiralty into an assertion that Allied raids "have caused panic among the workmen, and they refuse to carry on their work. Nearly all of them have cancelled their agreements, fearing for the safety of their lives on account of the Allies' machines."[183] Likewise Newall had stressed moral effect as a primary achievement of the Eighth Brigade's work.

The ubiquitous phrase made sense to an audience that accepted it unquestioningly. In 1916 a brief essay in *The Spectator* had explained that the term "moral" (pronounced with the accent on the second syllable) is "on the lips of everyone." The author traced the term to the French (and noted that the British often misspell it by placing an "e" on the end).[184] For Trenchard, asserting the primacy of the moral effect mollified public opinion and permitted him to deal effectively with the press. In general, vaguely articulated pilots' claims—"considerable damage appears to have been done"—formed the heart of many field dispatches, and, subsequently, many official statements on air activities.[185] And Trenchard relied on the phrase in interviews. An article in the *Daily Mail* of 21 September 1918, for instance, highlighted the work of the IF in support of the American advance at St. Mihiel, and ended with a description of a raid (of 16–17 September) against Frankfurt, in which it was claimed that the attack—carried out by only one bomber—had killed 120 persons and left the Opera House a "heap of ruins."[186] Interviewed for the story, Trenchard repeatedly argued that, "the damage to moral is out of all proportion to the number of bombs dropped." Keeping German towns under constant apprehension about being bombed, he asserted, made unremitting demands on the enemy's defenses. Even bombers on their way to other targets would trigger air raid alerts: "Every big German town hit at once screams for assistance. In this way hundreds of guns, searchlights, planes, and thousands of men have been drawn away from the front to meet the occasional attacks of a comparatively small number of assailants. It would be no exaggeration to say that every unit of the Independent Force immobilizes at least 50 times its fighting value from the ranks of the enemy."[187]

Trenchard's mathematics were not based upon any rational calculation or operational observation, but instead concocted to impress the *Daily Mail* readership. Even though he felt that the press had helped lead Britain to some unfortunate choices, Trenchard clearly felt obligated to feed its ongoing appetite. Indeed, he was so insistent upon media coverage that the Air Staff became concerned that his habit of announcing virtually every raid might jeopardize the campaign by giving away too much information to the Germans.[188] Cultivating public opinion also meant satisfying politicians and the civilian leaders of the young RAF, who were often strident and vengeful in their desire for reprisal raids.[189] According to Trenchard's biographer, Lord Weir once said to Trenchard, "I would like it very much if you would start up a really big fire in one of the German towns." He added, "If I were you I would not be too exacting as regards accuracy in bombing railway stations in the middle of towns. The German is susceptible to bloodiness, and I would not mind a few accidents due to inaccuracy." And Prime Minister Lloyd George looked ahead to 1919 when the RAF would be in a position to wage "devastating raids" on the German homeland.[190]

If the Air Staff accepted the idea of the moral effect of bombing, they nonetheless ultimately parted company with Trenchard regarding the way to achieve it, the emphasis to be placed upon it, and the degree to which it should be elevated rhetorically as the "primary effect" of the Independent Force.[191] Immediately after Trenchard's story appeared in the 21 September 1918 *Daily Mail*, Lt. Col. J. Gammell fired off an angry memorandum to Groves. While Gammell accepted the concept of moral effect, he questioned Trenchard's exaggerated claims and apparent dismissal of bombing's material effects. He argued: "G.O.C., I.F. is alleged to have said that the moral damage is of far greater importance than the material. This is at variance with the policy of the Air Force submitted to the War Cabinet and adopted by them." He complained that Trenchard had not stressed the "war against vital German industries which is the real work of the Independent Force," and he pointed out in frustration, "If statements of this kind appear in the press . . . it is difficult to see how the public can be educated up to appreciate the real policy of the Air Staff and so give the War Cabinet enough support to enable their policy to be carried through."[192] Tiverton, who had diligently explored schemes to make terror bombing work, nonetheless remained committed to the primary importance of the material effect of bombing. In early October 1918 he composed yet another memorandum on the future possibilities for long-distance bombing. Working from the premise that it would be possible, realistically, to wage only about eighty long-range attacks on Germany before September 1919, he made the case that targets like Berlin earlier considered the ultimate "moral" target ought to be left alone and that, instead, targeting should concentrate on the Westphalian industrial region. In a not-so-oblique reference to Trenchard, he argued that each raid ought to be "thought out, not by one man only, but by the joint brains of all those who know the question from the commercial, the political, the flying, and the technical points of view."[193]

The war ended before a force large enough to test the Air Staff's ideas could be brought to bear on Germany. By the time of the armistice, only three super Handley Page V/1500 aircraft had been delivered, and none had flown over German territory.[194] What might have happened if the war had continued another year is hard to say, although it seems likely that, in 1919, the political pressure to bomb Berlin would have been very great. What matters here, though, was the way Trenchard handled his duties and how he explained his behavior publicly, since this would become important to the future of the RAF.

In December 1918, as European affairs began to slow to a peacetime cadence, Trenchard composed his final dispatch on the Independent Force.[195] Naturally, he wanted to put the best face on policies and decisions, especially since the document was for public consumption as well as the military record. He began with a straightforward overview of the circumstances leading to his assignment to the IF. A later section titled "Scheme of Attack" was the crux of the dispatch, and the part most often quoted because it articulated Trenchard's overall approach. "The question I had to decide," Trenchard wrote, "was how to use this Force in order to achieve the object, i.e., the break-down of the German Army in Germany, its Government, and the crippling of its sources of supply." He asserted that he had but two choices: the first, to deliver "a sustained and continuous attack on one large centre after another until each centre was destroyed"; and the second, to attack "as many of the large industrial centres as it was possible to reach with the machines at [his] disposal." He chose the second, arguing that it was the only course open to him based on the resources available.[196]

Trenchard asserted that such widely dispersed attacks had not squandered resources since attacking "as many centres as could be reached" enhanced "the moral effect" and insured that "no town felt safe"; indeed, he argued, the enemy required "continued and thorough defensive measures" so as "to protect the many different localities over which my force was operating." And he added, "At present the moral effect of bombing stands undoubtedly to the material effect in a proportion of 20 to 1, and therefore it was necessary to create the greatest moral effect possible."[197] It was a curious statement. If he had faith in his own mathematics, then bombing for moral effect would have been the most efficient strategy no matter how many bombers were available. There is no evidence, however, that Trenchard had thought through the full implications of his asserted rationale. The ratio itself (20 to 1) had no scientific or mathematical basis. Trenchard used numbers liberally but never based them on anything except his own hunches.[198] Emphasizing the moral effect in this instance was wholly consistent with his use of the phrase in summaries and press releases sent out during the course of the fighting: he argued that his long-range raids (no matter how dispersed or inconsistent), at least had caused lost hours to German manufacturing, forcing enemy defensive preparations that otherwise would have been unnecessary.

Trenchard singled out only a few raids for detailed analysis. Much of the dispatch simply offered lists of locations bombed and tons dropped. He outlined the unfulfilled plans for the use of super Handley Page V / 1500s and described the work of his force in cooperation with the American First Army. Significantly, Trenchard argued that before he could attack Germany successfully, "it was necessary to attack the enemy's aerodromes heavily in order to prevent his [the enemy's] attacking our aerodromes by night, and by destroying his machines to render his attacks by day less efficacious." He also pointed out that in September and October 1918 in particular, day bombers often had to fight their way into Germany and back out again, a hardship that necessitated formation flying. Overall, the dispatch echoed themes that Trenchard had highlighted in his press releases, in particular the moral effect, which combined vaguely articulated notions of psychological impact with broad categories of "indirect effects." These statements might not have been quite so important had events followed a different course, and had Trenchard not become the head of the interwar RAF.

AMERICAN AERIAL PARTICIPATION IN WORLD WAR I

While the United States eventually would become a world leader in aircraft design and manufacture, and come to possess the most powerful air force in the world, this would not happen until well after the First World War. Entering that war late in the day, the Americans never had an opportunity to gain first-hand experience of long-range bombing. Like other belligerents, the Americans underestimated the production demands of complex weaponry in mass, industrialized warfare: the grand plans they made for a large-scale aerial offensive never came to fruition. Nonetheless, American military planners observed their allies' checkered progress in planning and implementing a long-range bombing policy, and drew lessons from it.

Despite the Wright Brothers' achievements, the Americans took a leisurely approach to developing and exploiting the military possibilities for aircraft. In 1907 the U.S. Army established an Aeronautical Division within the Signal Corps to deal with air machines, ballooning, and related topics. In the same year, the service set out specifications for a military airplane, and accepted a bid by the Wright Brothers. But real progress was slow, and in 1911—only three years before the outbreak of war—the Signal Corps still had but one plane and one pilot.[199] That year Congress finally appropriated funds for army aeronautics: five new planes were ordered, and new pilots were trained. By then, however, the United States had fallen well behind the Europeans.[200] The U.S. War Department's *Field Service Regulations of 1914* acknowledged aviation only for reconnaissance and observation of artillery fire; aircraft were not mentioned in the section dealing with combined arms operations. While these guidelines were modified several times in subsequent years, the sections on aviation remained essentially unchanged.[201] The 1st Aero Squadron, which was formally established in September 1914 with eight planes and ten pilots, saw its first service in northern Mexico in 1916, during operations against revolutionary leader Pancho Villa. The frail planes could not cope with the weather and the demands of active field service; within six weeks all had either crashed or become unusable.[202] This outcome exposed the sorry state of American military aviation and helped prompt the National Security Act of 1916, which provided for "aero squadrons" to be developed as needed, but which kept most aviation firmly bound to ground troops.[203]

Between 1914 and 1917, aviation underwent rapid evolution among the belligerent powers, but the United States did not benefit much from this progress; poor liaison left the United States isolated and lacking knowledge about air warfare. As historian I. B. Holley has pointed out, "Doctrine in the Signal Corps was the product of two factors: extremely limited operational experience with a handful of training aircraft and domestic interpretations of the scanty reports of military attachés."[204] When the United States went to war in 1917, its Aviation Section consisted of 130 officers, and just over 1,000 enlisted men. Of approximately 200 aircraft, none was suitable for combat service, even reconnaissance. There was no overall plan for utilizing aircraft in the war.[205] Nonetheless, the Americans quickly pledged themselves to an ambitious plan suggested in May 1917 by French Premier Alexandre Ribot. In a burst of unfounded optimism, the Joint Army and Navy Technical Aircraft Board translated the Ribot recommendations into a plan calling for the production of 12,000 aircraft for service in France (in 1918), as well as 5,000 training planes and 24,000 engines. Funding for the plan was included in the $640 million appropriated by Congress (and signed by President Woodrow Wilson in July 1917) for an expansion of the Aviation Section.[206] The naive scheme failed to anticipate the time and effort required to raise American industry to such unprecedented levels of output. But it touched a chord in the American imagination, and the public was quickly captivated by aerial images of "slaying the Hun."[207] The patriotic fanfare and grandiose rhetoric inflamed public expectations of American aviation.

Ribot had not specified aircraft types, so Secretary of War Newton Baker sent a commission to Europe to determine what kinds and numbers of aircraft the United States could produce to best aid the Allied air effort. The commission, which set sail in June, was headed by Maj. Raynal C. Bolling, a former chief counsel for the United States Steel Corporation, and a staunch supporter of aviation.[208] Its members spent time in London, France, and Italy before tendering their report on 15 August. Significantly, the Bolling Report went beyond a conception of aircraft as support mechanisms and envisioned them ultimately performing a role separate from armies in the field.[209] It argued that American production should proceed in three phases: the first would concentrate on building aircraft for training purposes in the United States; the second on building aircraft and engines for use "strictly in connection with the operation of American forces in the Field"; and the third on building fighters and bombers "in excess of the tactical requirements [of the army in France]."[210] Bolling and his colleagues recommended creating a mix of day and night bombers, although they viewed the latter as having greater possibilities. They took pains to point out that an effective aerial bombing campaign would have to be concentrated and sustained.[211]

A number of events and individuals influenced the perceptions and recommendations of the commission members. In London, the German Gotha raids of June–July 1917 had commenced; British air organization was in a state of flux; and the debate over strategic bombing was simmering. On 29 June, Bolling's preliminary report, based largely on the views of Sir David Henderson of Britain's Air Board, emphasized the potential significance of bombers.[212] In France, commission members spent a good deal of time trying to work out the details of licensing arrangements and royalties to be paid to French aircraft manufacturing firms. Perhaps the most immediate influence on the Bolling Commission, however, was exerted by the Italians. Successful in their efforts to build a large bomber, the Italians had, by the summer of 1917, used concentrations of up to 250 such planes in raids on the Austrian front. The vital force behind the Italian air effort was the industrialist and entrepreneur Count Gianni Caproni. He offered his views to the commission, and in the end they nominated his aircraft as one of the types slated for American production. Special licensing and development issues, however, significantly delayed Caproni bomber production in the United States.[213]

By prioritizing aircraft for army cooperation, the Bolling Report helped insure that bombers would not be given primacy of production in the United States. More importantly, the report's recommendations proved far in advance of American industrial organization at the time. An overnight shift from famine to feast in U.S. aircraft production could not be supported, and the problem was further complicated by constantly upgraded designs.[214] By itself, money could not compensate for years of prior neglect. Production goals were set and reset; ratios for aircraft types were changed over and over; plans were drawn up but never implemented. Ironically, the grandiose American aircraft production goals had as their primary effect an urgent stimulation of 1917 German aircraft production efforts, the *Amerikaprogramm*.[215] By the end of 1917 it was clear that American promises to the Allies would have to be scaled back dramatically. In their brief seven months on the front, American pilots flew foreign airplanes—mainly French—the vast majority of the time. The American contribution to the Allied aviation effort was felt primarily in the production of training planes (especially the Curtiss JN or "Jenny") and engines (the Liberty engine being the most successful and extensively used).[216] Public frustration and disillusion expressed itself in congressional investigations: the verdict was that poor organization and incompetence, rather than fraud and conspiracy, were at the root of the problem.[217]

The energetic and often flamboyant Col. William (Billy) Mitchell, who would become the most influential American aviator of the war, arrived in Europe in late April 1917, well ahead of the Bolling Commission.[218] Sent over as an aeronautical observer, Mitchell took himself directly to the front. In May he spent several days with Trenchard, who stressed the importance of taking and maintaining the offensive in air warfare—even reading aloud his 1916 memorandum on the subject.[219] Mitchell served as Air Officer, American Expeditionary Forces (AEF) until 3 September 1917 when he was made Air Service Commander, Zone of Advance, under Gen. William Kenly, Chief of Air Service, AEF. In November, Kenly was replaced by Brig. Gen. Benjamin Foulois, fresh from the United States with a staff contingent—mostly nonflyers—to organize the Air Service in Europe in support of Gen. John J. Pershing's AEF. Mitchell looked upon Foulois's staff as interlopers, labeling them "carpet-baggers" with neither the experience nor the credentials to run an air campaign in the field.[220] In May 1918, Gen. Mason Patrick, an engineer, replaced Foulois as Chief of Air Service, AEF. Foulois was to be made Chief of Air Service, First Army, but instead asked to serve as an assistant to Patrick, recommending Mitchell for the crucial combat position. Mitchell took up his new post on 27 July 1918, and in October was promoted to brigadier general and appointed Chief of Air Service, Army Group.[221]

Early on, Mitchell prepared two papers on air policy and organization for General Pershing's Chief of Staff, Lt. Col. James G. Harbord. He urged that aviation be considered a separate branch, like infantry and artillery, and that aerial operations be divided into "strategical" and "tactical" functions. With respect to the former, he wrote, "The strategical phase . . . applies to the air attack of enemy material of all kinds behind his lines." He added, "To be successful, large combatant groups of airplanes must be organized, separate from those directly attached to army units." Then he argued optimistically that "this class of aviation . . . will have a greater influence on the ultimate decision of the war than any other one arm."[222]

Mitchell corresponded with Count Caproni, asked AEF intelligence to draw up a list of potential targets in Germany, and later received a French list of German industrial targets in the Ruhr.[223] But if Mitchell's enthusiasm for what he termed "strategical" bombing was emergent, he had to oversee daily the aerial support of armies in the field. At the time, he believed that an army "is composed of various arms and services whose complete interdependence and working together is necessary for efficiency. No one arm alone can bring about complete victory."[224] Mitchell's main task was to control the air over the battlefield. This led him naturally to emphasize what Americans termed "pursuit" (fighter) aircraft.[225] The American command influence reached its peak in the late summer and early autumn of 1918 when, at St. Mihiel, Mitchell controlled a great conjunction of British, French, and American forces, which placed nearly 1,500 planes under his direction.

His bombers were best suited to tactical work, so he used them against those targets he felt would have the greatest impact on the ground battle, including depots, ammunition dumps, and railway heads in the enemy's rear. Mitchell soon learned that it was costly to send bombers over enemy territory in small formations. Indeed, during the St. Mihiel campaign, American attacks on German targets ten to twenty kilometers behind enemy lines resulted in such high casualties that Mitchell felt compelled to use escorts regularly during the [later] Meuse-Argonne offensive. He learned also that when escort aircraft were tied too closely to the bombers, losses ran at a prohibitive level (of nearly 60 percent). Results were far better (falling to only about 8 percent) when escorts freely engaged enemy fighters. Mitchell staged his largest bombing attack on 9 October 1918, sending 200 day bombers and 100 fighters against German troop concentrations.[226] Throughout the campaigns Mitchell felt the impact of production problems at home. These failures, combined with high loss rates, meant that aircraft were always in short supply. On 26 September 1918, 646 airplanes could be counted in the U.S. effort; on 15 October there were 579. At the armistice, U.S. aviators had available only 457 airplanes.[227] Nonetheless, Mitchell believed that his stress on concentration protected American troops by dispersing and thwarting enemy air. His views, reinforced by the apparent success of the autumn campaigns, would establish the principle of concentration as aerial dogma in the United States.

"Strategical" Bombardment

At war's end, the United States had only one night-bomber squadron in operation. It had been equipped with DH4 aircraft, and had been assigned to the front only on 9 November 1918.[228] American thinking about long-range bombing was not completely stymied, though, as observers on the scene gathered some practical insights. And while optimism about production still existed, plans and guidelines for the long-range bombing campaign continued apace. The First World War gave American airmen a basis—however partial and rudimentary—on which to build future ideas about the role and nature of long-range aerial bombardment.

After the Bolling Commission disbanded in late August 1917, Major Bolling was promoted to colonel and made an assistant chief of the Air Service. Maj. Edgar S. Gorrell, an aeronautical engineer, took over the Air Service Technical Section in Paris, managing purchases of air matériel in Europe.[229] Through this period Gorrell's enthusiasm for strategic bombing continued to grow. As a member of the Bolling Commission, Gorrell had been receptive to Caproni's ideas and, in the autumn of

1917, the two men continued to interact. In a memorandum to Colonel Bolling dated 15 October, Gorrell argued that the Air Service could inflict "immense destruction" on German morale and matériel by initiating a systematic campaign of night bombing.[230] During that same month, Caproni gave Gorrell a book on aerial bombing—essentially a compilation of Caproni's views—by Italian journalist Nino Salvaneschi. Written in English, the slim volume was clearly intended to enhance American enthusiasm for long-range bombardment, and to instill a sense of urgency about it. After receiving the book, Gorrell wrote back to Caproni asking for additional copies, stating that he would "spread the gospel in all directions."[231] The British, however, would most influence Gorrell's views on strategic bombing. Indeed, during his service in Europe, Gorrell would turn repeatedly to his British colleagues for ideas and guidance.

Soon after General Foulois arrived in the autumn of 1917 to take up his new post as head of Air Service, AEF, Gorrell submitted to him (28 November 1917) a scheme for bombing Germany. The document was drawn up as part of a program to provide General Pershing with plans for the utilization of American air power. Shortly after submitting his plan, Gorrell was promoted to lieutenant colonel, and detailed to head the Strategical Section, Zone of Advance, American Expeditionary Forces.[232] What came to be known as the "Gorrell Plan" was later considered paradigmatically American: the "earliest" and "clearest" statement of "the American conception of the employment of air power."[233] This was ironic because the plan was based heavily on Tiverton's 3 September 1917 plan for long-range bombing. Tiverton and Gorrell were then in Paris; it is clear that the two men consulted and that Tiverton provided ideas to his American colleague. Gorrell added opening and concluding sections of his own, but adopted the Tiverton paper, virtually verbatim, for the body of his own paper.[234]

Gorrell began by pointing out that trench stalemate had called for a new policy, and he argued that the Germans and the Allies had both come to understand the promise held out by aerial bombing. He felt though that the Germans were gaining the upper hand, and might successfully pursue, in 1918, a day and night bombing offensive designed to "wreck" Allied commercial centers. The only solution, he believed, was a counteroffensive of greater weight.[235] "The object of strategical bombing," he wrote, is "to drop aerial bombs upon the commercial centers and lines of communication in such quantities as will wreck the points aimed at and cut off the necessary supplies without which the armies in the field cannot exist."[236] Like Tiverton before him, he emphasized that the output of enemy war matériel depended on a relatively small number of factories producing key components.[237] By singling out those, he believed, one could quickly alter the entire course of the war. In the body of the plan, Gorrell adopted Tiverton's four geographical target groups—Düsseldorf, Cologne, Mannheim, and the Saar Valley— around which were clustered Germany's main manufacturing and industrial centers. He also echoed Tiverton's staunch advocacy of sustained (night and day) mass attacks against single targets with the aim of completely destroying them.[238]

In his introduction, Gorrell cautioned that any German air offensive would have not only direct physical effects, but also a moral effect on civilians.[239] Later in the paper he included Tiverton's prediction that prolonged Allied bombardment against a German target might cause a breakdown of order, and other consequences disproportionate to the immediate effects of its bombs. Gorrell owed his commitment to the moral effect of bombing to Trenchard as well as Tiverton, however. His essay called "The Future Role of American Bombardment Aviation," written some months after he had completed his November "Plan," incorporated significant segments of Trenchard's November 1917 paper on "Long Distance Bombing."[240] Gorrell adopted Trenchard's definition of long-distance bombing, explaining that its basic purpose was to weaken the power of the enemy directly ("through the infliction of damage on his industrial, railway, and military centers"), and indirectly ("by producing discontent and alarm among the industrial population").[241] Owing a debt to his British colleagues, Gorrell infused American air power thought with Tiverton's emphasis on analytical planning and systematic implementation, as well as Trenchard's emphasis on the moral effect of bombing. The latter acted as a multiplier. As George K. Williams has pointed out, "Moral effect diminished uncertainty by making every bomb dropped on enemy soil count, thus neatly complimenting the direct, destructive effects of bombs that in fact hit what one was aiming at."[242]

In the end, Gorrell's plan was never implemented. Had production measured up and the war continued into 1919, American momentum toward strategic bombing very likely would have increased. Indeed, Trenchard showed a particular interest in having the Americans join the work of his Independent Force.[243] But ambivalent attitudes about strategic bombing existed within the U.S. military hierarchy in 1918. Gorrell's tenure as head of the Strategical Section, Zone of Advance was brief; by February 1918 he had been transferred to the Operations Section (G-3) of the General Staff.[244] Though in his new position he continued to work on bombing, he was more firmly under the thumb of the army. Over the summer, the army balked at shifting Air Service priorities to favor independent operations. Like Foch, General Pershing was reluctant to divert resources away from the battlefield to underwrite a proposition so uncertain as long-range bombing. And Pershing's Chief of Staff, Maj. Gen. J. W. McAndrew, directed that, despite the philosophy behind Trenchard's IF, "It is of special importance that the higher officers among our bombing personnel . . . be warned against any idea of independence and that they be taught from the beginning that their efforts must be closely coordinated with those of the remainder of the Air Service and with those of the ground army."[245] Also that summer, the name "Strategical Aviation, Zone of Advance" was changed to "G.H.Q. Air Service Reserve" to quell any heresies suggesting that this Air Service function was in any way independent of the rest of the army.[246] In the end, the American aerial effort never engaged the German economy; its focus remained the battlefield. No section on "strategical" bombing appeared in the "Final Report" of the history of the Air Service in World War I, a compilation managed largely by Gorrell. As his plan for strategic bombing had not been implemented, Gorrell may have decided that it had no business in an operational history. Indeed, Gorrell did not even include his tenure as head of the "Strategical Section" in a biographical note he provided later (in 1927) to the U.S. Military Academy Association of Graduates.[247] Apparently he judged it wise not to emphasize too strongly his brief foray into the realm of independent air operations.

If the RAF had gained only a tenuous toehold on independence in World War I, the U.S. Army Air Service had not even made its first footsteps in such a direction. Production failures and an "early" armistice (from the perspective of the airmen) foreclosed Air Service hopes for postwar autonomy. General Pershing devoted few words and little praise to the role of the Air Service when he wrote up his final report on the war.[248] A general review of AEF participation in the war, undertaken in the spring of 1919 at the request of Pershing, was convened under Maj. Gen. Joseph T. Dickman. It predictably concluded that aerial operations to support troops showed more potential than independent initiatives. Gen. Mason Patrick, who had served as Chief of the Air Service, AEF, noted that observation remained the key job of an air force; bombing distant factories was, at best, a "luxury."[249] Thus was the American debate on long-range bombing muted—but only temporarily. Writing retrospectively—during a similarly acute period for the institutional future of the air arm—the official historians of the United States Army Air Forces in the Second World War hypothesized, "Had the [First World] War lasted long enough to provide the Air Service with some experience in a bombardment program conceived independently of the movements of ground armies, its postwar history might have been far different."[250] How different is hard to say, however. Lack of operational experience and interservice antipathy ultimately did not prevent the development of a detailed, indigenous concept of independent, long-range bombing. That concept would mature gradually and, though it would never gain acceptance by the army hierarchy prior to World War II, it would win staunch adherents and advocates.

THE POSTWAR ASSESSMENTS

Curious to see what impact aerial bombing had had on the enemy, the British sent a small team of investigators, under the direction of Major H.W.M. Paul, to examine and evaluate the "material damage done" and the "moral effect caused" by British bombing, and to examine the defensive measures employed by the Germans. They assessed not only the work of the IF, but also that of the RNAS's No. 3 Wing and Newall's 41st Wing (later Eighth Brigade). Their reports on various target sets were sent to the Air Ministry on 26 February 1919.[251] In addition, a smaller survey of bomb damage in Belgium was undertaken in November–December 1918.[252] Subsequently, in January 1920, the Air Ministry issued a publication, A.P. 1225 (Air Publication 1225), titled, "Results of Air Raids on Germany Carried out by the 8th Brigade and Independent Force." It was produced by a staff headed by Major A. R. Boyle, who had been responsible for producing two wartime assessments—also designated A.P. 1225—analyzing the progress of British bombing. The earlier editions were published in August and October 1918.[253] The Americans also arranged for a team to investigate bombing. Undertaken as part of Lieutenant Colonel Gorrell's effort to put together a history of the Air Service, AEF, the work had as its mandate to secure "as complete and reliable information as possible upon which the Air Service may base its future bombing plans."[254] The investigators were, like the British, to seek out evidence of material and moral effect. The work of the Americans, discussed below, was done independently of British efforts.

The British Survey

Two principal conclusions were articulated in the original British field survey. The first was that the material damage done to the German war economy generally had been small; the second was that the "moral effect" of bombing had been "considerable." The first inescapably followed from physical investigation, but the second, less amenable to empirical analysis, could be established only through less direct means—usually interviews and interrogations of factory owners. British survey team members reluctantly admitted that, overall, physical damage had been quite limited. The survey of "Chemical and Munitions Factories," which included the important Bädische Analin und Sodafabrik (BASF) and the Oppau Works (both at Ludwigshafen), and a munitions factory at Kaiserslautern, concluded that while bombing had measurable results at Kaiserslautern, its effect had been minimal in the crucial Ludwigshafen works. On the first page of the survey, the authors stated, "Considering the weight of the bombs dropped, the material damage both from a military and destructive point of view has been small. . . . No signs of any extensive damage or repairs were seen."[255] The authors concluded that bombing had not directly diminished military output. Similar results were reported with respect to blast furnaces.[256] In a section of the survey called "General Material Damage," the authors reported, "It is very noteworthy how surprisingly little serious damage has been done throughout four years of war, and on no occasion has a works been forced to close down for more than a week as the direct result of bombing." An exception to this trend appeared in the report on damage to "industrial centres" (a term used interchangeably with "town"), where investigators claimed optimistically that the material effect of air raids was "considerable." In the third edition of A.P. 1225, the wording of this statement was changed so that it read, "The material damage has been great."[257] The evidence advanced to support the claim (in the original survey) included damage to buildings and numbers of persons killed or injured.

In general, though, the survey team stressed the moral effect (a term encompassing the "indirect effects") of bombing far more than its material effect. In the report on blast furnaces, for instance, the authors pointed out that work stoppages of two to three hours on account of air raid alarms were not unusual, and that this had an impact on production at the plants. Using the Röchling plant at Völklingen as an example, they noted that the works had been subject to air raid alarms forty-four times during the month of September, but attacked on only one occasion.[258] Likewise for chemical and munitions factories: while the BASF and Oppau works were bombed fifteen times (thirteen times by the British and twice by the French), they endured 256 air raid alerts during the war.[259] Examining output figures at the Völklingen foundry, the survey team argued that the output deficit in a month with over forty alarms and no actual attacks was more than double the deficit in a month in which there were nine alarms and three actual attacks (that caused some limited physical damage).[260] Indirect effects of bombing, especially air raid alarms, also were stressed in connection with the bombing of railway stations. While admitting that damage to railways had been, on the whole, "moderate," A.P. 1225 (3rd ed.) nonetheless emphasized that the interruption of rail traffic caused by alarms had been considerable, since, at times, trains were delayed outside of stations for hours. The report concluded that "even if actual damage was not done, the raids on railways had a very marked effect on the normal and smooth working of traffic."[261]

The loss of production caused by air raids was considered both an important and consequential indirect effect of bombing. Indeed, the significance attached to this idea would increase during the interwar years as British aviators contemplated the air campaigns of the future. But the British survey members were prepared to go even further, giving a wide and dramatic interpretation to moral effect that took the idea beyond calculations of lost work-hours and stretched it, dubiously at times, into the realm of speculation. They argued that the stress caused by air raid alarms had important consequences. Of raids on the BASF, the survey team explained, "In contrast to the material damage caused by air raids, the moral effect on the workmen and others at the BASF and the Oppau Works, was considerable." They argued that the mood had intensified when bombs hit workmen's housing in March 1918, and that, over the summer, the effects of a "general state of nervousness," especially among the women and children, became apparent.[262] In the same report, the authors argued that while balloon barrages and the construction of dugouts raised the morale of the German workers somewhat, "even these did not prevent continual alarms which caused great confusion throughout the works and intense nervousness in the workmen's dwellings." In reference to the workers, the survey authors were prepared to make the extreme claim that "constant alarms and raids ruined their nerves, in some cases for life." With reference to the foundries at Burbach and Hagondange, the survey team explained that during the frequent alarms of 1918, "war-weariness and undernourishment" were felt and rendered men "less able and willing to work their best" under the trying conditions. They concluded with the bold but unverifiable prediction: "Had the war continued a few months longer, a more or less total breakdown of labour at several of the Works might have been confidently expected."[263]

Not infrequently the survey team had to confront evidence that undermined the case they sought to make. For instance, German workers (including women, who were not choosing between factory work and the front) usually could be persuaded to stay on the job simply by salary raises. In addition, a number of the interviewed factory directors claimed that strategic bombing had no moral effect; one even explained that when the time came to enter shelters, the workers entertained themselves by dancing and enjoying other amusements.[264] While the investigators did not fail to acknowledge these things, they attempted to downplay their significance where possible. They argued, for instance, that "[a]lthough the Directors of one or two of the works visited effected to make light of the moral effect produced by air raids, there can be no doubt whatever that it has been very considerable in many cases, and, if we regard the results as a whole, relatively greater than the material damage achieved."[265]

Some of the German posters, bulletins, and official notices reprinted in the report on industrial centres revealed that the psychological effect of bombing may have been less profound than the British wished to assert. For instance, a message posted in Bonn on 7 August 1918 complained, "On the occasion of the last air raid alarm, the prescribed rules of conduct were very inadequately observed by the public. During the alarm the streets were as full as ever of pedestrians and vehicles. *Such levity is incredible* [original emphasis]. . . . It is particularly regrettable that the adults should set the children such a bad example in neglecting the prescribed precautionary measures."[266] But the very existence of civil defense efforts also served as evidence for the British of the fact that their bombing had caused German authorities to attend to the protection of their population.

Word choices made by investigators injected ambiguity into their reports. For example, they repeatedly described the moral effect (and, in one instance, material effect) of bombing as "considerable," without further useful explanation. In addition, speculation and extrapolation were regular features of the reports: their wording frequently dwelt more on what might have happened (had the bombing continued) than on actual consequences. For example, the survey of bomb damage in Belgium, headed by Maj. Erskine Childers, initially conceded that the bombing in Belgium had been "at best a secondary and very imperfect method of attack." But the report nonetheless asserted that "with the progress in air science that seems likely to continue, it will be possible in a few years . . . for a powerful military nation . . . to obliterate cities in a night and produce the stunning moral effect necessary to victory."[267]

While investigators certainly saw indirect effects of bombing as real and important, there can be little question that they gave them so much play because evidence of the direct, material effect of bombing was thin. Investigators sent out specifically to assess bombing results would have had little desire to contradict official assertions that had been made publicly for some time. Further, they would have been keenly aware that scarce resources had been expended in strategic bombing, and that British lives had been lost in the prosecution of the campaign. Even if only subtle or subliminal, pressure to justify the effort certainly would have existed and would have been felt by those responsible for reporting the results of the surveys. Under these circumstances, their flights into extrapolation are, perhaps, unsurprising.

The two wartime versions of A.P. 1225, which relied heavily on captured letters and intelligence agents' reports, had insisted upon the moral effect of bombing: "Though information as to results is increasingly hard to obtain, it is certain that the *moral* of the German population becomes lower as the range and power of our bombing squadrons increases." As George K. Williams has argued, "the wartime editions of A.P. 1225 . . . had firmly established an analytical precedent for the widely cited third edition of January 1920." Boyle's staff, Williams argues, did not produce a comprehensive, analytical report based on "substantive analysis of captured materials or thorough cross-checking against R.A.F. wartime records." A.P. 1225 (3rd ed.) was dedicated more to "advocacy than accuracy."[268] An April 1919 Parliamentary paper, Command 100 (titled "Synopsis of British War Effort during the War"), trumpeted the official verdict on British bombing: "The effect, both morally and materially, of the raids on German territory carried out during the summer of 1918 can hardly be overestimated."[269]

But such glowing official British pronouncements contrasted with the more understated conclusions arrived at by the German General Staff. The Germans certainly had felt compelled to erect defenses to protect their population against long-range bombers, and they had seen their routines disrupted by Allied raids. But they determined that those raids had been neither a major threat to their population, nor a major hindrance to German war production. A detailed General Staff study of all the Allied raids (undertaken in August 1918) revealed a number of important insights. The German civilians who encountered bombers were initially fascinated by them, and most casualties occurred during initial attacks on cities when fascination overtook a willingness to heed precautions. Many casualties sustained might have been avoided if civilians had followed simple procedures like taking proper shelter. In subsequent raids, citizens generally followed the civil defense regimen established by local authorities, thus curtailing casualties dramatically. In ten of the largest raids undertaken in July 1918, the Germans suffered no casualties at all. Night raids, due to their inaccuracy, were little more than a nuisance.[270]

Greater attention to such conclusions might have tempered somewhat the tone of British pronouncements, or prompted more searching evaluations. But German conclusions received little notice in Britain. Because of its status as the officially sanctioned Air Ministry final report, A.P. 1225 (3rd ed.) not only bolstered RAF policy, but also provided the main database upon which historians would rely. The official historian of the air war, H. A. Jones, cited the bombing surveys to argue that British long-range raids on German industry and cities had three major effects: (1) a weakening of the national will, particularly in 1918 when the nerves of the people, through hunger and general war weariness, were acutely sensitive; (2) a falling off in the production of essential war materials, partly because the morale of the workers was lowered by the attacks, but chiefly through loss of time as a result of air-raid alarms; and (3) a diversion of fighting squadrons, anti-aircraft guns, and searchlights, and of a great amount of material and labour, to active and passive schemes of defense.[271] Jones, like the members of the RAF field survey, was impressed by the idea that air raid alarms had caused disruption and impaired production in Germany. Though he admitted that "the effect on the morale of the workers was uneven" (being much more significant where at least one prior raid had had some impact), he fully accepted that Trenchard's scattered raids had helped to undermine the will of the German people.[272]

Both the postwar assessments and the official history reflected a set of assumptions that their authors believed to be valid. These were conditioned by widely held prewar expectations about the likely effects of aerial bombing, and by mirror imaging that projected interpretations of the British experience of being bombed onto interpretations of the German experience. But institutional factors were at work here as well. Because Trenchard continued to have influence over the assessment process, there is no doubt that the documents pronouncing a verdict on the effectiveness of RAF bombing were strongly influenced by the field commander's desire to justify and defend his record, and to protect the autonomy of the RAF. His imprimatur was evident throughout: the phrasing and editing of both the wartime assessments and the postwar survey reflected his preferences and prerogatives. And the tone of these, subsequently, was adopted by supportive official historians. On this foundation Trenchard, as Chief of Air Staff in the 1920s, would develop the declaratory policy of his young service. And from this, further expectations would evolve.

The U.S. Survey

At war's end Lt. Col. Edgar S. Gorrell oversaw a history of the Air Service in wartime and a "Final Report" for General Pershing. Though it acknowledged that tactical bombing of troops had a "great effect," the absence of any reference to independent bombing operations reflected the American wartime experience and the American position after the armistice.[273] Nonetheless, the Americans, like the British, were intrigued by the potential of aviation, including strategic bombing. To preserve the history of the war, Gorrell coordinated and compiled a series of "lessons learned" reports from leading American aviators, and organized an investigative survey of Allied bombing efforts. For help, he turned to the Intelligence Section (G-2), General Headquarters, AEF. The American field work, which did not coincide with that of the British survey, was begun in early March 1919 and was concluded in late May. Twelve teams were formed, each consisting of one German-speaking officer and two enlisted men. They were directed to go to factories and towns looking for information on both the material and the moral effect of bombing. The region surveyed was west of the Rhine and south of a line from Düsseldorf on the Rhine to Meziéres on the border between Belgium and France. It contained all of the places bombed by the Americans (who never ventured more than about sixty miles from their base of operations), all of those bombed by the British except for a few cities east of the Rhine to which the Allies did not have access after the war, and some of the targets bombed by the French.[274]

While American bombing efforts had directly supported the St. Mihiel and Meuse-Argonne campaigns, discrete data on the effects of those efforts were hard to obtain after the war; it was especially difficult to distinguish the effects of aerial bombing from those of long-range artillery. Most of the American survey dealt with British and French operations against industrial and communications targets well behind the lines. In all, the teams visited 140 towns, 60 percent of which were able to provide pertinent data. In other places, data were either not available or had been destroyed or taken away by retreating Germans. The teams produced sixty-five separate reports, a few of which surveyed more than one location. In addition, the survey included a concluding overview and suggestions for the future.[275] Comparing the American survey to the British survey allows one to detect both the consistencies in and differences between the two assessments. The Americans, because they focused mainly on British and French bombing, could be reasonably objective: no wartime claims had to be defended for the U.S. Air Service. For the most part, they reported damage matter-of-factly: estimates and monetary totals were drawn from factory and town records, police reports, and insurance claims. But the analytical methods employed by the Americans were no more sophisticated than those used by the British, and American reports—like the British reports—were peppered with general and undefined phrases like "considerable damage."

As most long-distance attacks involved only a limited number of planes dropping a handful of small bombs, extensive damage rarely resulted from any one raid.[276] An exception that impressed itself on the Americans was the Thionville raid of 16 July 1918, where a bomb hit a munitions train and caused shells to explode, setting fire to the freight station and other buildings in the vicinity.[277] Besides such dramatic episodes, the Americans obtained information on railway traffic delays as well as the average time needed for repairs. They reported that while bombing held up railway traffic at smaller stations, at larger stations more extensive marshaling yards allowed trains to maneuver around damaged tracks and stay more or less on schedule.[278] The American survey concluded that the majority of damage done at the important BASF of Ludwigshafen was caused by falling shells and debris from German anti-aircraft guns. It also claimed that the moral effect of bombing had done the most to curtail output at the plant through lowered worker morale and losses in production due to air raids.[279] Reports on German towns frequently specified lost working hours due to raids or air raid alerts. Like the British, the Americans were impressed with the indirect effects that might be realized from bombing—specifically the loss of production (from both time in air raid shelters and lowered worker morale), the cost of establishing and maintaining defenses (including shelters, anti-aircraft batteries, and home defense flights), and, in general, the diversion of resources from offensive to defensive purposes.[280]

Estimations of the moral effect in the American survey suffered from the same limitations as the British survey, namely, the phrase did not lend itself to ready or reliable quantification. In reporting on it, American survey members conscientiously wrote up summaries of interviews with factory owners and municipal officials. In general, though, the task was difficult and elusive. And the simple fact that they had been sent out to search for evidence of bombing effects set up expectations in the minds of survey members that such evidence existed. On the other hand, in some instances the Germans revealed a tendency to downplay such effects for the sake of national or personal pride.[281] Even if all assessments of moral effect were inherently imprecise, however, the U.S. survey's repeated references to it indicate that it was accepted as a significant, integral element of aerial bombardment. The report on Coblenz stated for instance that, "everyone interviewed [was] of the opinion that the morale of the people was very much shaken by air raids, and the chief engineer at the railroad station stated that the efficiency of his employees was greatly impaired."[282] Such explicit attention highlighted the concept and extended its influence into future studies.

Like the British, the Americans portrayed civilian workers as subject to nervous strain under bombardment; indeed, the U.S. survey suggested that women were particularly vulnerable and prone to hysteria.[283] Perhaps the most dramatic statement regarding the moral effect was included in the report on Metz, where it was argued that bombing "had a tremendous effect upon the morale of the workers and civilians," and "a crew of 250 civilians as well as several hundred soldiers were kept on hand to repair the damage from bombs." Extrapolating in a manner similar to the British team, the authors concluded that if the bombing had continued "a month or so longer, it would have been impossible to keep employees at their duty."[284] But the American survey also made clear that when workers were exposed to consistently dangerous conditions, they frequently could be mollified by increased wages—and this step was necessary only on rare occasions. Most workers stayed on the job, and, when required, proceeded to shelters in an orderly fashion. Officials at Burbach claimed, for instance, that "[t]he workmen maintained a fairly good working standard in the factory and many were glad when an alert was signalled because it meant a loaf for a while." Similarly, officials at the Meister Lucius works claimed that their employees were "most loyal," and put "their best efforts into their work at all times."[285]

When civilians (other than factory workers) were considered as a separate category, the reported results were similarly inconclusive. At Düren, where one raid (on 1 August 1918) had caused thirty deaths, it was reported that "the German population consider the attack on the unfortified town of Düren an outrage and there is no doubt but that the morale of the people was greatly lowered and later alerts nearly caused panics." The Thionville report argued that while the morale of the people had generally held up well, it "rapidly dropped" toward the end of the war when the bombing became heavy, "and the mental strain under which the people labored seemed to have been enormous." The burgomaster of Ehrang said that the raids had a great effect on the people of the area, causing nervous breakdowns, calls for a cessation of hostilities, and agitation for a ban on the bombing of towns. The concluding section of the survey argued that during one raid against Ehrang, three people had died from fright.[286] On the other hand, the survey report on Cologne (which had been said to suffer a decline in factory worker morale) claimed generally that "[t]he moral effect on the people was rather insignificant," and added that "the people were in general quite stoical, the feeling being that Cologne was a fortified city and the Allies had a right to bomb it. After the first raid, the people became quite resigned."[287] Bonn was bombed for the first time on 31 October 1918. If its people were aware of raids in other towns they did not seem to be terribly worried about them: it was reported that the people "would not take shelter during alerts."[288]

As would be discovered again in the Second World War, the cause and effect relationship between bombing and civilian morale was complex and not conducive to ready generalization. The public reaction to bombing might vary a great deal according to local circumstances and, in particular, the degree to which the population felt the government was making efforts on its behalf. And popular anger and indignation could be mistaken for panic, even if there was no clear evidence of the latter.

The conclusions of the American investigators were compiled in a final "Narrative Summary," which included the main observations salient to the Allied effort. Some of these paralleled British observations, including an emphasis on German production losses due to both raids and alerts. In the subsection titled "Moral Effect," the authors ringingly declared, "It is certain that air raids had a tremendous effect on the morale of the entire people." With reference to the German air defense system, they asserted, "The enormous expense of maintaining balloon barrages, home defense flights, and anti-aircraft artillery must be an indication that the material was needed as well as that the popular clamor for protection was great."[289]

But the conclusions of the American survey did not completely coincide with those of the British survey. Indeed, in the subsection of the Summary called "Criticisms of Bombing in the Present War," the Americans took issue with the British—that is, Trenchard's—operational approach. Making a point in common with the Air Staff in London, the Americans claimed that the greatest failing of British bombing was that it was inefficient, suffering from "the lack of a predetermined program carefully calculated to destroy by successive raids those industries most vital in maintaining Germany's fighting forces." The U.S. survey further stated, "Evidence of this is seen in the wide area over which the bombing took place as well as the failure of crippling, beyond a limited extent, any one factory or industry."[290]

The Americans perspicaciously noted dissent among the British ranks regarding targeting policy, pointing out that "these [British] officers . . . did not believe they were getting the best results possible and that while the wish . . . to 'bomb something up there' might have appealed to one's sporting blood, it did not work with the greatest efficiency against the German fighting machine."[291] Their survey also explained that, upon visiting the British for three days, one American officer learned of the attitude of "disgust" held by one "British bombing expert" toward the Independent Force's policy of pursuing "unintelligent targets."[292] That the British displayed such internal dissension indicates that the divisions between Trenchard's staff and the Air Staff in London were deep and bitter. Interestingly, the Americans also criticized the British tendency to attack cities in general rather than specific military targets within cities; they referred to the latter alone as "legitimate targets." While the Americans were quite willing to concede that bombing had indirect effects on the state subjected to it, they were not convinced that it had translated into distinct military advantage with discernable effects on the enemy fighting forces. Addressing this, they wrote, "This investigation has decidedly shown that the enemy's morale was not sufficiently affected to handicap the enemy's fighting forces in the field." They concluded that bombing targets erratically was inefficient and unproductive.[293] Stressing the point, they argued, "Bombing for moral effect alone . . . which was probably the excuse for the wide spread of bombs over a town rather than their concentration on a factory, is not a productive means of bombing. The effect is legitimate and just as considerable when attained indirectly through the bombing of a factory."[294]

Finally, and significantly, the American survey concluded that to obtain useful results in future wars, one must first make a "careful study" of the different kinds of industries in an enemy nation, and ascertain "how one industry is dependent on another and what the most important factories of each are." The authors added, "A decision should be reached as to just what factories if destroyed would do the greatest damage to the enemy's military organization as a whole."[295] In this they clearly favored the Tivertonian rather than the Trenchardian approach to long-range bombardment. Of course it is impossible to determine whether the Americans, if they had had the chance, would have followed their own advice: their virgin status with respect to bombing surely gave them the freedom to be critical of their allies' efforts. In any event, the criticisms leveled at Trenchard by the London Air Staff clearly resonated with them. American air planners took these seriously, not only at the time of the survey, but in the years following the war. The American observers were convinced that a more systematic analysis of target sets, and a more deliberate, concentrated attempt to destroy one key target after another, would prove beneficial in the prosecution of a program of strategic bombing. Ironically, the ideas in which Tiverton and his colleagues had set such store were heeded by the Americans and incorporated into what eventually would become the American canon on strategic bombardment.[296]

* * * * *

While there had been no consensus on the role that aircraft might play in war prior to 1914, there had been a good deal of speculation—particularly on the potential role of aerial bombers. These were used in the war, and while they remained on the margins of overall national effort, they nonetheless captured public and governmental attention. The limited experience of bombing—and of being bombed—would provide the foundation on which speculation about future air wars would come to rest. In Britain, that experience was interpreted in a context that highlighted prewar concerns and anxieties about the robustness of national polities, particularly urban working classes, at war. And the interpretation was shaped in accordance with the predilections and views of a particular individual—Trenchard—and the institutional needs of the service he would head after the war. This would cast a long and important shadow over the RAF's interwar years.

The Americans were little more than observers in this early phase of air warfare, but their interpretations of World War I strategic bombing would come to matter as they assumed an increasing role in world affairs and ultimately prepared to fight the Axis powers. They borrowed heavily from the British, but they also applied their own analysis to what they observed, emerging with a set of ideas that was in certain respects hostile to the Trenchardian view. Significantly, however, both British and American airmen believed that long-range bombing could be used to important effect in war, and that modern industrial nations had exploitable weaknesses and vulnerabilities (in large part because of their complexity and interdependence). The next two chapters will examine how these ideas evolved in the context of the turbulent 1920s and 1930s, how they interacted with public expectation, and how they influenced national defense policies on both sides of the Atlantic.

CHAPTER TWO

Britain in the Interwar Years

IN the aftermath of the war, the young RAF faced an immediate fight for its institutional life. Though it survived, it had to articulate an ongoing raison d'être as a separate service. This requirement had the effect of elevating the role of strategic bombing above other tasks, and compelling the RAF's leadership to continue protecting its wartime bombing record in the exaggerated terms that Trenchard had employed in his own defense. Aggressive arguments for the continued existence of an independent air force helped establish a pattern of exaggeration that ultimately would help to create a gap between RAF declaratory policy and its actual capabilities. In addition, Trenchardian policy was vague; it lacked clear guidance, particularly on questions of targeting. Public articulations of RAF thought worried the other services, and fostered popular expectations about air warfare that would prove, ultimately, self-deterring for Britain. As a new war approached, RAF leaders would struggle to close the divide between rhetoric and reality by figuring out—in ways that Trenchard had not—how actually to plan and wage a major strategic air campaign.

The chapter necessarily begins with a further examination and elaboration of two important and related ideas from the World War I experience that would strongly influence British interwar thinking about strategic bombardment: the theory of the offensive and the "moral effect" of bombing. Indeed, they would prove central to RAF planning and decision making in the 1920s and 1930s.

THE OFFENSIVE THEORY OF AIR POWER

Trenchard attached great weight to offensive tactics, embracing the conviction that air war must be guided foremost by a commitment to the "relentless and incessant offensive." This emphasis fit into his preexisting conception of effective behavior in wartime, and it was, in addition, reinforced by his wartime experience and by his subsequent need to explain his actions in the two key posts he held during the most difficult and consequential war his nation had ever fought. In particular, Trenchard's emphasis on the offensive helped to justify the heavy casualties that otherwise might have been an embarrassment to him.[1]

Trenchard had spent the formative years of his career in a military environment wholly permeated by the idea that wars are fought and won through an unshakable commitment to the offensive. The forces shaping this environment have been explained in detail by others. What is important here is simply that the theory of the offensive, which suffused European military thought at the end of the nineteenth century and the beginning of the twentieth, stemmed from both the interpretation of past war experience and the inherent ability of an offensive posture to serve particular and important institutional needs of military organizations.[2] Certainly the Royal Flying Corp's commitment to offensive tactics was influenced by observed French experience at Verdun and cemented by the interpretation of experience at the Somme in 1916. Trenchard's September 1916 memorandum on offensive tactics was widely cited and reproduced, and it became part of the early canon on air tactics—a guide to action in a new war-fighting medium.[3] RAF papers written just after the war consistently stressed the offensive. For instance, an early postwar paper titled "Air Superiority" argued, "An enemy air offensive more intensive than our own must be met by renewed efforts on our part. Never must a defensive role be forced upon us."[4] Once Trenchard had drawn particular lessons from his Somme experience and had committed himself to these publicly, it was natural that he would remain largely consistent in his views even as he applied them to a new realm.[5] But the application of an offensive posture to tactical and strategic aviation would pose different problems. With regard to long-range bombing, the key question was how to fly deep into enemy airspace repeatedly, without suffering prohibitive losses in the face of enemy defenses.

During World War I, the underdeveloped state of communication between air and ground often worked to the advantage of enemy bombers. Fighter scouts had to fly sweeps over large areas in the hope of finding bombers—a practice that was difficult in the daytime, and doubly difficult at night. This made it possible, though risky, for bombers to operate without escorts to defend them. While at the helm of the Independent Force, Trenchard became well aware of the threats to his bomber force. His earliest conceptions for a long-range force, articulated in 1917, had envisioned a need for fighter escorts and for self-defending bombers.[6] In his negotiations with Lord Weir over command of the IF, Trenchard addressed the requirement for "fighter types of aircraft" to enable bombers "to carry out their work properly." In taking up his new job as General-Officer-Commanding (GOC), IF, however, Trenchard was reluctant to divert too many fighters to the IF from RFC units, and so requested only that he be given a future claim on aircraft allotted to the Expeditionary Force. By the time of the armistice, however, Trenchard had only one fighter squadron attached to the IF. Existing aircraft were tied up with the ongoing German offensive, and continued production problems slowed the pace of new construction.[7]

Trenchard sought, on repeated occasions, to persuade his colleagues to provide him with increased numbers of fighters to aid the work of the IF. In a letter to Sykes of 4 August 1918, for instance, he requested fighter squadrons "to drive the Hun fighter scouts still further back into their own country." He also discussed the possibility of using some bombers as fighting machines, and of increasing the armament on bombers so that they would be better able to protect themselves. But until such steps could be taken, he argued, his best recourse was "to try to educate everybody to think as I do, i.e., that if we bomb them harder than they do us this is the best and only defence." He concluded, "I want you to impress upon all your people at home and upon everybody else you can that we must not be allowed to become a defensive force."[8] The Air Staff in London, also concerned about the problem, suggested that the GOC, IF employ massed bomber formations for greater self-protection. This solution had its limitations since the IF was under-strength to begin with, but it at least implied that Trenchard might have rethought his tactics.[9] Short of this, he chose to make do, ultimately falling back on his predilection to "bomb them harder than they do us."

After the war, Trenchard downplayed the bomber escort issue; he instead argued that the key to a successful bombing campaign was to press it harder than the enemy by maintaining a constant offensive with the bombers available. Writing at the outset of the Second World War, aviation author J. M. Spaight recalled Trenchard once telling him that "ten bombers can be made to do the work of thirty, or of a hundred. All that is needed is to send them in again and again." Elaborating on Trenchard's views, Spaight wrote, "And it is not the destruction of life of property which the bombers cause that matters; it is the destruction of *morale*, the disturbance of life, the dislocation of routine. The moral effect is far more important than the material. Keep on raiding: that is the right strategy in the air, according to the Trenchard school."[10] Such a strategy presumes, of course, that sufficient bombers survive—or that adequate replacements will be forthcoming.

As the first postwar Chief of Air Staff, Trenchard could insure that his ideas received attention. The RAF's January 1921 paper "Air Power and National Security" argued that "in the offensive lies the surest defence, and it will be necessary to carry the war into the enemy's country, to attack his aerodromes, factories, military and naval establishments and generally force upon him a defensive role." By 1924, Air Staff documents were beginning to argue that it was more effective to launch an immediate bombing offensive against vital centers than to bother with initial counterforce attacks on the enemy air force.[11] A determination to seize the initiative and force upon the enemy "a defensive role" became the Air Staff's cardinal objective. While this had organizational benefits, it also reflected the interpretation of past experience.

Trenchard and his colleagues had been heartened by their perception (articulated in the bombing surveys) that IF efforts, even though largely without apparent material result, had caused German industrial facilities to issue repeated air raid alarms. In this they saw important indirect effects (a major component of the phrase "moral effects"): widespread inefficiencies and loss of production caused by the threat of imminent bombardment by small numbers of aircraft. This perception had been reinforced by German raids on Britain, when small contingents of zeppelins and bombers had imposed disruption and delay—in addition to physical damage—during the early raids in particular. This apparently large payoff for a relatively small investment seemed to argue strongly in favor of an offensive stance; indeed, fearing this payoff to Germany, the British government had resisted instituting air raid alarms to warn of potential attacks. Similarly, in the aftermath of the 1917 Gotha raids, members of the government had been highly exercised by the need to recall fighters from the western front to meet public demands for improved protection. Those demands had been unsettling to a government already concerned by labor unrest and the prospect of political upheaval stemming from the many dislocations of a long and unprecedentedly costly war. Policymakers were equally concerned by the large numbers of personnel and material ultimately devoted to coping with the German Gotha / Giant threat—a threat very modest in terms of the numbers involved. Indeed, policymakers understood that a driving motive for the German air offensive had been to force the British into a defensive stance that would drain resources from the fighting front.[12] Extrapolating, Trenchard argued that the side willing to prosecute a sustained and relentless offensive would eventually "throw" its enemy into a defensive stance characterized by a deeper and deeper commitment to homefront industrial and civil protection.

These themes began to appear with regularity in official writings. In a paper written for the newly opened RAF Staff College (and published by that body in 1923), Wing Commander J.E.A. Baldwin focused on the idea that air raids could cause long periods of delay and disruption at a factory, even when the raid itself did little or no physical damage. He pointed out that the British offensive effort had compelled the Germans to pull resources back from the front, to divert labor to defense, and to expend "vast sums" on shelters and warning systems.[13] Similar sentiments were articulated by Air Vice-Marshal Sir H.R.M. Brooke-Popham, who would become the first commandant of the Staff College.

In a lecture to the Royal United Services Institution, given shortly after the war, he drew pointed attention to "the amount of manpower and material that is absorbed in the endeavours to obtain protection from aircraft."[14] Following up on this theme in a 1924 lecture to the RAF Staff College, he offered an officially sanctioned RAF interpretation of the past and the future of air power in warfare. One of its key sections discussed the effects of German bombing of Britain—in particular the scale of the British defensive effort needed to cope with a handful of German bombers: in order to respond to a limited German offensive, the British had, from February 1918 onward, some 270 aircraft and over 13,000 men employed on searchlights and anti-aircraft guns. Brooke-Popham emphasized that "[t]he total number of German aeroplane flights over to England was 452; the total number of aeroplane flights made to beat off their attacks was 1,882, over four times as many."[15]

In Trenchard's eyes, these human and material resources devoted to defense represented a potentially significant loss to the critical offensive aspect of the war effort. In fact, the wartime experience had traced only the very steep, initial portion of a diminishing marginal returns curve. The relationship between defenders needed and attackers faced is sharply nonlinear: defenders require a certain number of aircraft simply to cover the relevant airspace, even if few bombers attack—the requirement is driven more by the area to be defended than the size of the attack. Hence a small attack still requires a relatively large defense to defeat it. But once defenders have deployed enough fighters to make it likely that any given raid will be intercepted, further increases in bomber fleets do not much increase the number of fighters needed to defeat them. All air forces discovered this in the Second World War, but by 1918 none had seen more than small raids, and thus all they had observed were the needs of defending against small attacks, which seemed disproportionate.

Trenchard adamantly insisted that an air force simply could not afford to surrender voluntarily the strategic initiative, and therein start down the slippery (and inevitable) slope to defeat. In language that echoed his Edwardian mindset and training, he emphasized national character, declaring that the aim was the destruction of the enemy's will power: "The one that stood it longest would win. . . . If we could keep going longer than the enemy, that was where we would score. It was not a matter of mathematical calculation."[16] Here Trenchard downplayed analysis—not to mention the often staggering losses endured by his own forces in wartime—in favor of exhortation. But his argument nonetheless would help to form a foundation on which a significant piece of the RAF's interwar declaratory policy would come to rest.

The lessons drawn from World War I experience were attempts to make sense of perceived reality. But they, too, were selective and problematical.[17] The need to put a positive face on British bombing results caused a greater emphasis to be placed on "indirect effects" than was warranted. Limited feedback, rudimentary methods of analysis, and organizational interests contributed to the problem. A more systematic and detailed look at the effects of bombing and its costs might have helped clarify the picture, setting up a better basis for future planning. Certainly the British raids had imposed a defensive cost on Germany and compelled nontrivial investments in air defense. In the end, though, the damage and disruption caused by air raids in Germany lowered output and production only marginally, and the temporary deficits often could be quickly recouped by those bombed.

Another factor complicating interpretations of wartime experience was the tendency (in some RAF circles, among certain popular writers, and among the public at large) to overemphasize the impact of early zeppelin and Gotha raids and, conversely, to deemphasize the outcomes of later raids. To be overly impressed by initial experience and to minimize subsequent information that diverges from it is a common cognitive error. Once a particular interpretation of an event has taken hold, new information bearing on it will not have the same impact it would have had earlier.[18] In this case, the early raids were an indelible trauma that could not be wholly erased by subsequent events. The early zeppelin and Gotha raids, when the British were caught unprepared, managed to inflict damage disproportionate to the size of German resources committed. And the lucky shot later on, such as the direct hit on the Odhams Printing Works in 1918, helped perpetuate the perception that British defenses were somewhere between inadequate and futile.[19]

But with respect to both zeppelin and Gotha/Giant raids, British defenses improved over time, and the cost to the Germans increased correspondingly. Indeed, from the German perspective, the air war looked very different. While it did manage to tie up resources in Britain, it was disappointing in other respects. Improved British defenses forced night flying, which in turn complicated the nemeses of long-range bombing—mechanical difficulties and weather. These took an inevitable toll: of the sixty-two German planes lost during the Gotha/Giant raids, forty-three were lost to operational accidents. British defenses accounted outright for the downing of another nineteen planes—nearly one-third of total German losses. Indeed, during its year of operation, the German bomber force "England Wing" was, in effect, wiped out nearly twice over. The German bomber raid flown on the night of 19 May 1918 had been so costly to its perpetrators—over 20 percent of the attacking force was lost—that it helped persuade them to reorient their bombers to tactical roles on the continent. The Germans came away from the war unconvinced that the investment in the Giant bomber—in construction costs, maintenance, and servicing—had been worth the effort.[20]

After the war, Trenchard took the stance that defense-oriented expenditure should be minimized so as to free as many resources as possible for the prosecution of an all-out bomber offensive against the enemy. As we shall see, Air Staff opinions were not uniform on the issue of the offense-defense balance for indigenous forces, and Trenchard would not have his way entirely in this particular realm. Many in the RAF felt it was essential to do the kind of mathematical calculation that Trenchard eschewed: to find the ideal proportion of fighters and bombers that would both facilitate an aerial offensive and enable the homefront to hold out in the meantime. This meant that home air defense was never neglected in the interwar RAF; in fact, it would develop successfully—albeit out of the limelight—through the interwar years.[21] If he had to compromise on this issue, however, Trenchard did what he could to insure that RAF *public* proclamations strongly emphasized an offensive posture. This was a way of maximizing both the organizational strength of the RAF and the deterrent value of aircraft, but it had some problematical ramifications. First, it implied that victory corollated mainly with an immediate, all-out air offensive. And second, it helped to encourage an environment in which the fallacy that the bomber "will always get through" could thrive.

These ideas were particularly consequential when combined with fears of future air war, and official interwar civil defense planning assessments. (As early as 1922 Lord Balfour was issuing dire predictions that a continental enemy could drop on London "a continuous torrent of high explosives at the rate of seventy-five tons a day for an indefinite period.") In the early 1920s, the Air Staff claimed that in a future war involving attacks on Britain, one could assume fifty casualties per ton of bombs dropped. But this multiplier was highly problematical because of the error-laden way in which it was derived from the World War I experience. Richard Titmuss, official historian of Britain's World War II social policy, explained, "This simple and easily remembered multiplier soon acquired a validity to which, in statistical theory and for other reasons, it was hardly entitled."[22] The Air Staff's math went largely unquestioned even though there were plenty of grounds for questioning it, and was maintained through the interwar years. As a result, the question of how to fill the requirement for enormous numbers of doctors, ambulances, and hospital beds became an unhappy and constant refrain for domestic planners. And, as the estimated tonnage of bombs deliverable by the Luftwaffe grew throughout the thirties, the multiplier of fifty produced continually higher estimated casualties. Trenchard's solution, to bomb the other side harder, was of limited comfort at best to those approaching the issues from a civil defense perspective.

THE "MORAL" AND THE "MATERIAL"

The Trenchardian notion that an enemy state could be thrown on to the defensive through bombing presumed that its government would be required to devote more and more resources to civil protection in response to popular demands for it. Since it would be impossible wholly to control one's own domestic population, the only way to cope would be to steal a march on the enemy and remain more aggressively committed to a continuous aerial offensive. When pared back to its essential premises, the "relentless and incessant offensive" theory rested on the assumption that one's own state, if possessed of an adequate air force and the right notions about how to use it, could be tougher and ultimately more determined than one's enemy (who, presumably, would be attempting the same thing). Aiding in the effort to predominate would be any qualities of steadfastness and strength of character possessed by one's population. These were, of course, relative rather than absolute: even if one's own population possessed weaknesses and vulnerabilities, they needed only to be less than the enemy's. Trenchard had to be able to argue that the British, despite inherent weaknesses, would not succumb first. Here he relied on the *relative* qualities of the British compared to other European states, and an insistence that British leaders be prepared to dedicate themselves with incomparable determination to an early, large-scale air assault.

For the enemy state's civilian population, being "thrown" onto the defensive would come about mainly through the cumulative "moral effect" of being bombed: popular fear, disillusion, and demoralization leading to lost work hours, lowered production, and, ultimately, perhaps, political upheaval. These were the national-level parallels to the battlefield moral effect felt by soldiers and groups of soldiers in war. Expectations about the moral effect had been, as we have seen, imbedded in the prewar literature on air power, and were repeatedly articulated during the war itself. But perhaps the reason the idea was deeply rooted and broadly accepted was because it seemed intuitive. The prospect of aerial bombardment aroused in many a primal fear of total vulnerability: there would be no shelter, no refuge from the worst ravages of technology. When combined with the apparently commonsense extrapolation that air forces would grow in size and that chemical weapons (gas) would form part of the future arsenal of long-range bombers, the fear became particularly potent.

By emphasizing moral effect during the war and in his final dispatch, Trenchard exploited a phrase already well understood in his social and cultural milieu, and firmly established in the professional context in which he worked and fought.[23] In his 1916 memorandum on the primacy of an offensive posture in the air, he wrote, "[T]he moral effect produced by a hostile aeroplane . . . is all out of proportion to the damage which it can inflict." He added, "The sound policy which should guide all warfare in the air would seem to be this: to exploit the moral effect of the aeroplane on the enemy, but not to let him exploit it on ourselves."[24] The March 1917 edition of the RFC's manual "Fighting in the Air" had asserted that the psychological impact of aircraft is similar to the psychological impact of a successful cavalry action, and that the "moral effect produced by an aeroplane is also out of all proportion to the material damage which it can inflict, which in itself is considerable."[25]

In moving from the tactical realm to the strategical realm, Trenchard took the idea with him. Now, however, it applied not just to fighting men and their leaders, but to entire societies. The transfer seemed natural enough: the idea that modern war was nothing less than an all-out struggle between states (requiring all their resources) had been a fundamental tenet of the German school, and the argument had resonated in England. In 1905, for instance, Maj. Stewart Murray referred to "these days of scientific warfare when wars are waged by great empires with the whole united force of their peoples." The "total" nature of the Great War had been lost on no one who lived through it. Sir Frederick Sykes, in his June 1918 paper, "Review of Air Situation and Strategy for the Information of the Imperial War Cabinet," described what he called "national attrition": "The entire population and the whole weight of the resources and industries of the opposing nations are thrown into the balance. The success of the armies or fleets entirely depends upon the energy and 'moral' of the nation supporting them."[26]

The personnel of the new Royal Air Force well understood that their service had been brought into existence largely as a result of popular demands for protection and reprisal raids against Germany in the face of the 1917 air attacks on Britain. Indeed, soon after the war, Trenchard characterized the birth of the RAF as "owing to the great popular outcry." While he certainly resented this fact at first, he nonetheless had felt compelled to answer to public expectations for air power.[27] After the war, Trenchard appropriated "the great popular outcry," promising to provoke and exploit it, through aerial bombing, amid Britain's enemies.

If one believed that urban industrial workers already were burdened by their crowded, demeaning environment and alienated from their labor, then it was certainly reasonable to think that the overwhelming stresses of modern warfare might lead to popular rebellion. During

World War I, British policymakers had been pleased to discover that the war was genuinely popular initially, but they were nonetheless deeply concerned by homefront trends they perceived in 1917–18. As noted above, Lloyd George's government could not escape ongoing worries about labor troubles and nagging fears about the robustness of the homefront in general: the munitions strikes in London, industrial unrest in Tyneside, and the rail strike of 1918 resonated with officials' gravest fears since, as historian Brock Millman has pointed out, "a rail, ship-building, or munitions shutdown in total war is tantamount to defeat."[28] The potentially volatile situation inherent in these circumstances kept many authorities on edge and wondering if domestic events might undermine the morale of soldiers on the front, and generally imperil the prosecution of the war.[29] Fears of possible domestic collapse in wartime Britain almost certainly facilitated the interwar tendency of the British to accept the idea that Germany had succumbed, in the autumn of 1918, to an unraveling homefront.

The interpretation of First World War experience and the ramifications it seemed to hold had been conditioned by expectation, which, in turn, had rested on nagging fears about social stability, degeneracy, and the potential for political upheaval; initial experiences and "might have beens" strongly influenced official memory of events. In the absence of such expectation, a somewhat different interpretation might have been possible. The behavior of the British public in the First World War had been generally admirable. Overall, the public had revealed (and taken pride in) a propensity for steadfastness, orderliness, and determination. Though there was certainly disruption, exhaustion, and popular resentment of perceived government incompetencies, the likelihood of homefront collapse was less than officials had feared. Despite the very large numbers of people using the Underground and public buildings for shelter, for instance, stampedes of panicked crowds were very rare.[30] While the zeppelin and Gotha / Giant raids had caused some outbreaks of public discontent and disorder, these had rarely become grave, uncontrolled problems for civil authorities. For many, the raids had the effect of exciting British desire to prevail in the war; it was not infrequently the case, for instance, that the numbers of prospective soldiers turning up at recruiting stations increased in the aftermath of the zeppelin raids.[31] Lost work hours were inefficient, and labor problems were certainly unsettling to authorities—but neither had been paralyzing to the war effort. Finally, as noted above, air defenses had, in fact, improved markedly following the early zeppelin raids, and again following the early bomber raids. The public mood always strengthened when citizens felt that government and military officials were making genuine and energetic efforts on their behalf.

Some officials perceived this. Chief of the Imperial General Staff Sir William Robertson was convinced that, instead of panic, the raids had caused greater determination among the British people. And Winston Churchill made a similar argument while serving as Minister of Munitions. Though an advocate of air power, Churchill nonetheless had a sense of its limitations. In a memo he wrote in late October 1917, "Munitions Possibilities of 1918," he argued, "It is improbable that any terrorization of the civil population which could be achieved by air attack would compel the Government of a great nation to surrender. . . . In our own case we have seen the combative spirit of the people roused, not quelled, by the German air raids." He added, "Nothing that we have learned of the capacity of the German population to endure suffering justifies us in assuming that they could be cowed into submission by such methods, or, indeed, that they would not be rendered more desperately resolved by them."[32] Competing hypotheses on the steadfastness of civil populations under bombs were never reconciled, however. In the absence of detailed analyses, a debate remained. The interwar years saw ongoing labor-management strife, constant and frequently intense fears of Bolshevism, and deep concerns about technological determinism. All these helped maintain an atmosphere of anxiety that nurtured alarmist prognostications and ultimately stirred support for the RAF in political circles. This atmosphere proved to be a growth medium for air force institutional interests, allowing Trenchard to stress the centrality of an aerial deterrent to British defense, and to rely on claims about the moral effect in relation to past and future air wars.

Trenchard was able to use his "twenty to one" calculation to good effect: after the war, echoing proclamations of the moral effect appeared consistently in official RAF memoranda, policy statements, essays, lectures, and examinations. In his December 1919 lecture to the Royal United Services Institution, Brooke-Popham would tell his audience that "[t]he material effect of bombs is . . . small compared to its moral effect, and I think most people will agree that bombing from aircraft has considerably greater moral effect than ordinary shelling. This of course applies with still greater force to towns and places far behind the line which, at any rate previous to the war, considered themselves immune from attack."[33] Likewise, the January 1921 Air Staff paper, "Air Power and National Security," warned that in a future air war, the material damage would be great, but "the moral effect will be more far-reaching still." Significantly, the authors argued, "The dislocation of national life and of the work of factories, the damage to centres of food supply . . . and the widespread fear of personal injury . . . may force us to comply with the demands of the enemy without a single surface action being fought." The remedy, they explained, would lie in the prosecution of an aerial offensive designed to carry the war into the enemy state and force upon it a defensive role.[34] Countless examples of such arguments are available to any researcher willing to delve even briefly into Air Staff documents of the early postwar years.[35]

Hewing to Trenchard's line, the Committee of Imperial Defence's first committee on Air Raid Precautions concluded in 1924 that the moral effect of bombing in a future war will be "out of all proportion greater" than the physical consequences.[36] Writing later about such committee conclusions, official historian Richard Titmuss argued, "[I]t seems sometimes to have been accepted almost as a matter of course that widespead neuroses and panic would ensue." Yet he found that this conclusion rested on assumption rather than analysis: "In sifting the many thousands of papers, which passed through Governmental agencies during the nineteen-twenties and nineteen-thirties, it is difficult to find even a hint that this fear of a collapse in morale was based on much else than instinctive opinion." And he added that the evidence, such as it was, had been passed through "a dense and reduplicated veil of human interpretation." Among the details sometimes cited were the number of people sheltering in the tubes during 1917–18, the work stoppages among the railways, and the number of industrial work hours lost due to air raids. But there was little systematic evaluation of what had actually taken place during the war. The consistently dire prognostications of the interwar years, he argued perceptively, could not be understood "if divorced from the public temper and the time when they were written."[37]

Like its emphasis on the "offensive," the RAF's focus on the moral effect would have important long-term consequences. Trenchard believed that material effect would be necessary (at least initially) to provoke a moral effect, but he elevated the latter, arguing specifically that it was the more important of the two consequences of long-range bombing. This was problematic because it downplayed the fact that bombing designed to maximize the material effect would not necessarily require the same operational approach as bombing designed to maximize moral effects. Also, the emphasis on the moral effect tended to make bombing seem a simpler enterprise than it really was, since it implied that it might be enough for bombers merely to get in the vicinity of their targets. If air raid alarms were virtually as important as raids themselves, then the operational details of bombing accurately probably did not matter all that much: it might be enough for bombers simply to trigger lots of alarms. This helped remove incentives for close, sustained attention to targeting and navigation.[38] Finally, the RAF's rhetorical reliance on the prospect of causing enemy collapse helped contribute to *domestic* popular anxiety about air power and long-range bombardment.

With the Trenchardian theory of aerial offensive, the RAF had to walk a fine line between deterring the enemy and frightening the domestic polity into a state of self-deterrence. If this could be done in the 1920s when there was no terribly serious air threat on the horizon, it was far more difficult to do in the 1930s when such a threat appeared in abrupt and ominous form.

THE RAF's EARLY POSTWAR YEARS

The early years after the war held challenges for all three services in Britain as they coped with demobilization, the return to a peacetime footing, and the requirement for a new conceptualization of British grand strategy. In 1919, Winston Churchill took over the dual post of Minister for War and Air. Though he chose to keep Air as a separate service, he found Sykes's plans for the postwar RAF too grandiose and expensive; instead, he prevailed upon Trenchard to oversee a smaller force. It was indeed ironic, in view of Trenchard's earlier antipathy toward RAF independence, that he came to play the central role in defending the postwar RAF. After some deliberation, the former GOC, IF chose to accept the position; on 15 February 1919, he became the Chief of Air Staff (CAS) once again. This time, however, he would stay, holding the post for nearly a decade, during which he would have a dominating voice in the public articulation of RAF thought.[39] Once established in his new job, he fiercely defended his organizational turf, coping as the older services jealously eyed the RAF and jockeyed to regain control over their air components. He proved himself shrewd when the situation called for it, and he found ways to fend off challenges, often by arguing that the RAF could accomplish tasks that the other services could not—and could accomplish them efficiently and inexpensively. Indeed, Trenchard's bureaucratic talents, intransigence, and force of will were to make him a crucial asset to the survival of the still-fragile RAF.[40]

Trenchard initially resisted Churchill's fiscal constraints, but compromised—insisting that, in return, the RAF be treated as an independent service. He realized he would have to move carefully and, initially at least, avoid a fight to the death with the older services. He soon realized, too, that he could use fiscal issues to his advantage. He played his hand skillfully—at one point even implying that he might be willing to release air cooperation units to the army and the navy.[41] While he probably never intended to allow this, it bought him some time and temporarily kept his rivals from combining forces against him. He was quite prepared to make promises that served his short-term interests.

And he felt he had time: the armistice had removed any serious threat to Britain for the foreseeable future. In July, Trenchard stated that he did not think a British strategic bombing force would have to operate in Europe for twenty or thirty years.[42]

In August 1919, Lloyd George's cabinet adopted what John Ferris has called "strategic axioms" to guide service planning and expenditure: (1) that there would be no war for the next five to ten years, and the chief concern would be policing colonial areas; (2) that service strengths similar to those of 1914 (now including the RAF) would meet those needs; and (3) that scientific weapons should, to the greatest extent possible, replace manpower. Though these were never entirely accepted by the services—and though the Treasury failed to gain any real control over the military planning in the first few years after the war—they nonetheless established parameters within which service debates and struggles were conducted.[43] Outmaneuvering the army, Trenchard argued that the RAF could offer substantial economies in colonial policing by substituting aircraft for soldiers and horses (and all their required supplies). Relying on the concept of "air control," he sought to secure the RAF's independent status by making the service useful in the near term. Air control was, very simply, using aircraft to threaten, intimidate, and thereby "control" native populations in British colonial territories. Trenchard used RAF assets, too, in the ongoing struggle against Britain's tenacious enemy, the so-called "Mad Mullah" of Somaliland, and took the opportunity to fulfill Churchill's desire for cost-effective policing in Iraq and Palestine.[44] The army resented the encroachment, and both the army and navy condemned as immoral the aerial bombing of tribal peoples. The RAF countered that bombing was no more indiscriminate than long-range shelling by the army or the navy.[45] Although air control exacerbated interservice problems and has remained controversial to this day, it helped insure the RAF's continued survival since it served Churchill's interests and offered apparent economies in the regions where it was applied.[46] Air control did not entirely replace troops on the ground, though. Indeed, despite the fact that it raised bureaucratic tensions between the army and the RAF, in practice it produced a rare interwar phenomenon: examples of sound army-RAF cooperation in the field.[47]

Air control also reinforced the RAF's attachment to the rhetoric of the moral effect of bombing. One Air Staff Memorandum (1920) argued, "Aircraft depend to a great extent on the moral effect they create: this is at present considerable owing to ignorance in the native mind." Another claimed, "In the later stages of operations when the enemy has learnt to conceal himself . . . air action must rely for its effect less on material damage inflicted than on the effect on the tribal morale of constant liability to attack and the consequent continuing dislocation of daily life."[48] And certain aspects of air control were retained as a mental model for action, even as the Air Staff contemplated air warfare against an industrialized enemy: an Air Staff paper of September 1941 explicitly linked the attack on German morale and interwar air control. It argued that the former was "an adaptation, though on a greatly magnified scale, of the policy of air control which has proved so outstandingly successful in recent years in the small wars in which the air force has been continuously engaged."[49]

By the end of 1920 all the services were under pressure from the government's Finance Committee. With support from Lloyd George, who saw his political fortunes increasingly tied to the imposition of drastic economies, the nation's economic planners sought to gain greater control over strategic planning. At this point, Trenchard felt he had to attack the other services in order to keep the RAF alive and autonomous, and his tactics became bolder. By early 1921 he was prepared to argue that the RAF could solve all of Britain's defense problems. In May he told the Committee of Imperial Defence (CID) that only the RAF could attack civilian morale, the decisive target in a future war.[50] Though the other services resented his audacity, he found a willing ear among those concerned about the future of air power and its relationship to Great Britain. The cabinet accepted his case and gave the RAF primary responsibility for aerial home defense. Trenchard managed another coup in dealing with the independent committee of businessmen, under Sir Eric Geddes, assigned by the cabinet to propose cuts in government spending. Though both the War and Admiralty offices had by then joined forces to argue that disbanding the RAF would provide economies, the CAS fought off the threat, once again preserving RAF independence and funding.[51]

Trenchard was able to tap into what David Edgerton has termed "liberal militarism": a means of maintaining national security and protecting national interests without having to build and sustain a large standing army. This sentiment, already strong in Britain, was redoubled in the aftermath of a costly, disillusioning war fought with mass armies. The hopeful side of bomber aviation's Janus face was that, in the event it failed as a deterrent, it might be able to bring about a swift and decisive victory that would preclude the horrors of the 1914–18 western front. The Treasury, liberal and powerful as it was, saw air power and mechanization as a substitute for manpower.[52] But many conservative voices pushed in the same direction; indeed, aviation held strong connections to the right-wing in England. A largely conservative air lobby in Parliament had supported the development of British aviation, and the right wing press gave prominence and support (financial and otherwise) to aeronautical causes. By 1914 the *Daily Mail* had dispensed some £24,050 in prize money for aeronautical contests. The aviation trade press (including *Flight*, 1909, and *The Aeroplane*, 1911) was likewise conservative, as were the various leagues and clubs (paralleling army and navy lobbies) agitating for British world leadership in aviation. William Joynson-Hicks, Home Secretary from 1924 to 1929—and a man "capable of seeing Red under every bed"—was also a key supporter of aviation.[53]

Trenchard was quick to exploit another opportunity in the early 1920s: the French "air threat." Unresolved problems with France—especially French policy in the Ruhr—contributed to a strained atmosphere between Britain and its World War I ally. These tensions fostered among some a gnawing fear of the French air force as a potential threat. Looking back, it may seem hard to account for this sudden francophobia: France's air assets (which the Air Ministry overestimated) were organized to support its army against Germany and posed no true strategic threat to Britain. But the case illustrates the reflexive fears of many politicians regarding British vulnerability to an air threat. In 1922, Lloyd George stated that "if we quarreled with France," its air force "would be across the Channel in a few hours."[54] Trenchard, who later admitted that he was never very concerned about the French, nonetheless exploited the situation. One Air Staff memorandum warned of ruthless attacks on London, comprised of "high explosive or incendiary bombs" and "chemical warfare in the most horrible form" including "lethal or toxic gas containers" and even "infection by bacilli."[55] Parliament debated the issue, and the cabinet responded with calls for greater air strength. By June 1923 it approved an expanded home defense air force (to include both fighters and bombers) allowing for the formation of fifty-two squadrons by the end of 1928.[56] In discussions about the nature, content, and structure of the newly authorized force, held in the summer of 1923, the CAS insisted that the goal of the RAF was to drop the heaviest possible bomb load on the enemy, in order to "trust their people cracking before ours." He added that "though there would be an outcry, the French in a bombing duel would probably squeal before we did. That was the really final thing. The nation that would stand being bombed the longest would win in the end."[57]

Left to his own devices, Trenchard might have kept to a minimum the number of fighter squadrons included in the new force. The majority of his RAF colleagues, however, were not prepared to take so unorthodox a stand. Christopher Bullock, the dominant civilian in the Air Ministry, claimed rightly that Trenchard's views on air defense were colored by his experiences on the western front.[58] After lengthy and important discussions in which several individuals—including senior staff officer

T.C.R. Higgins, an expert on home defense in 1918—argued on behalf of air defense, a compromise was reached that authorized the inclusion of seventeen fighter squadrons for the fifty-two-squadron force. This was twice as many as Trenchard preferred.[59] It represented a political compromise within the organization, but it also pointed to a difference of opinion in the RAF over the allocation of resources in strategic planning, and—though not fully countenanced at the time—a potential disconnect in the logic of emerging RAF declaratory policy. The stridency and consistency of Trenchard's position in this debate implied that it was undergirded by more than a cynical view of institutional interests or an attempt to maximize deterrence through assertive rhetoric and posturing. He argued that "it is easy to lose sight of the effect one is making on the enemy if one is too anxious to safeguard oneself from attack. . . . Our people would undoubtedly squeal if they were bombed, but we should find, if we bombed the enemy enough, that he would collapse before we did."[60] Full and unhesitating commitment to the offensive would be paramount. But the air defense advocates were not prepared to accept all the ramifications of Trenchard's orthodoxy on offensive planning, and their arguments provided for the continued and crucial evolution of a system of air defense for Britain. Pushing in this same direction was the fact that the army not only insisted that the RAF maintain effective air defense, but threatened to seize the role for itself.[61] Though its public rhetoric and declaratory policy would remain fixed on the "relentless offensive," the RAF would not ignore the air defense mission.

In an address given to the War Office Exercise at Buxton (April 1923), Trenchard had claimed that a battle for air superiority would form an initial and separate phase of a continental air war; he also argued that winning air superiority would depend in large part on such factors as a "combined organisation composed of night fighting squadrons, searchlight companies, anti-aircraft guns and other devices to fight the enemy's bombing aircraft by night." In the same talk, the CAS developed familiar themes, warning that a future war in Europe would resolve itself "into a contest of morale between respective civilian populations." He asserted that the population which suffered most from air attacks, or which lacked "moral tenacity" would likely "bring such pressure to bear on their government as to result in military capitulation." "It follows," he concluded, "that if we could bomb the enemy more intensively and more continuously than he could bomb us, the result might be an early offer of peace."[62]

Just a year later, though, the Air Staff was moving away from the idea of a separate battle for air superiority. A March 1924 memorandum argued that even though the "lessons of military history" seemed to call for a preliminary attack on the enemy force, the Air Staff did not share this view. More efficient would be a direct attack on "military objectives in populated areas" with "the object of obtaining a decision by the moral effect which such attacks will produce, and by the serious dislocation of the normal life of the country." Since long-range, self-defending bombers were essential to this overriding task, the Trenchardian document argued (in purposefully vague terms): "it may be stated as a principle that the bombing squadrons should be as numerous as possible and the fighters as few as popular opinion and the necessity for defending vital objectives will permit."[63]

In the course of events, production of the fifty-two-squadron force fell behind schedule; and when the "French threat" had abated in light of the 1925 Locarno Treaties, the leverage of the economizers in the Treasury grew. With easing international tensions, Prime Minister Stanley Baldwin's government (November 1924–June 1929) chose to concentrate its efforts on domestic programs, and on strengthening the war-battered British economy.[64] With the backing of the cabinet, Chancellor of the Exchequer Winston Churchill was able to impose economies on the services in 1925. Trenchard helped Churchill attack the navy in order to further his own agenda for the RAF, but the ultimate result was not as he had hoped or planned. In arguing that the RAF should be the keystone of British defense, he alienated the older services even more, and, in provoking a new round of interservice struggles, Trenchard "helped the exchequer create a change in strategic principles," which ultimately worked to his disadvantage. The Treasury argued that it should rationalize the competing claims of the services in their bid for budgets; it argued, as well, that finance was a more important component of power than military strength. The date for the completion of the fifty-two-squadron program was moved again, to 1935.[65] Since fighters were cheaper and easier to build, they were produced at a faster rate than bombers. Indeed, only by 1928 did the RAF have more bombers than fighters; even in 1934 the figure was twelve fighter squadrons to fifteen bomber squadrons.[66]

In the late 1920s the lack of an enemy on the horizon seemed to obviate any governmental sense of urgency for defense expenditure. The RAF turned its attention back to the immediate tasks at hand, including air control of colonial territories and the need to serve as a general imperial air reserve behind Britain's extra-European air forces. Central to the latter role was the Defense of India Plan, which from 1929 onward called for the dispatch of bomber and fighter squadrons to aid the army in operations against the Soviet Union in Afghanistan and the northern frontiers of India. These roles put a premium on the existence of versatile, easily serviced aircraft able to operate in primitive conditions—a requirement also amenable to Treasury wishes since it offered the maximum number of aircraft for the least money. The result was a concentration of light bombers of short range and little striking power, mainly Harts and Wapitis.[67] If these were rational for the purpose at hand, they certainly could not close the gap between the RAF's dramatic public proclamations and its actual capabilities.

A bleak economic picture dominated the scene, and, in 1928 the completion date of the fifty-two-squadron home defense force was postponed again, until 1938. Also in 1928, Churchill took the first of the 1919 strategic axioms—that the services should plan on the assumption that there would be no war for a period of up to ten years—and placed it on a rolling basis, insuring that the "ten years" would continuously start anew. When Air Minister Sir Samuel Hoare protested the decision, Churchill replied that his action "would not in any way hamper the development of ideas, but would check mass production until the situation demanded it."[68] This statement deserves particular notice since explanations of Britain's unpreparedness in the air at the start of World War II often have rested on assumptions about the cumulative effect of economic stringency. Slimmer budgets certainly slowed aircraft construction, curtailed pilot training, and eroded operational readiness. And the repeated delays of the fifty-two-squadron program certainly helped widen the cleavage between RAF declaratory policy and RAF capabilities. But the story here is less simple than it has been made out to be. The literature on interwar air power has typically overstated fiscal constraints as a cause of the RAF's unpreparedness at the outbreak of World War II.

The defense preparations of any given state need to be assessed against other states at the time, not against an artificial standard removed from context. The RAF had not been starved of funding from the end of World War I onward; moreover, British defense budgets were not unreasonable in the political context of the late 1920s.[69] If the Treasury by 1926 gained an increased voice in strategic matters relative to the services, it was because policymakers deemed it appropriate. Equally, between 1924 and 1932, RAF procurement expenditure increased rather than declined, and in the mid-1920s, the Air Ministry spent a higher proportion of its total budget on research and development than did the Admiralty or the War Office.[70] Nor was the British aviation industry in dire shape. Clearly (and naturally) its size was much reduced after the war, but, as David Edgerton has pointed out, the situation had stabilized fairly quickly and, into the early 1930s the British aircraft industry was as large as any other in the world. (In the mid-1930s Britain, the United States, Germany, Italy, and France were the only net exporters of aircraft.) In 1940, the United Kingdom was the largest aircraft producer in the world.[71]

Churchill was right to argue that an era of restraint ought not to impede ideas and analytical thinking. The problems that the RAF faced in 1939 and 1940 were due less to reduced funding per se than to the failure to analyze thoroughly the requirements of its own declaratory policy, which had as its centerpiece a strategic bombing offensive at the outset of a major air war between industrialized states. Interestingly, the RAF in this period made more progress in thinking through the demands of air defense than those of a strategic air offensive, even though its public rhetoric stressed the latter. In the 1920s and early 1930s, the most important operational aspects of waging a strategic air campaign received inadequate attention, including those—like navigation—that could have been treated seriously and adequately even by a financially strapped air force. Beginning with rearmament in the mid-1930s, the RAF had either to develop or reframe its thinking with respect to everything from navigation to targeting to matching aircraft types to missions. And even when this got underway, the RAF moved slowly. Funding was less the reason than a tendency to rely overmuch on prevailing assumptions and assertions, and to promote simplistic interpretations that eschewed real analysis and begged many important questions about strategic bombing. While these types of problems were unique neither to the RAF (the army and the navy had similar troubles) nor Britain, they must be considered if we are to comprehend the fortunes of the RAF through the early years of World War II.

THE SEEDS OF LATER TROUBLES

So long as the central tenets of Trenchardian thought remained unchallenged externally there was no incentive to question them, particularly since they served institutional interests very effectively. The war had highlighted any number of crucial but only partly resolved issues, including the problems of night and bad weather flying, the vulnerability of bombers, and the nature of civilian will. But little work had been done since 1918 to help shed light on these problems. Since Trenchard felt that he understood the World War I experience (and since analyzing it more carefully might have meant calling some of his decisions into question or placing the RAF in a less favorable light), he had little incentive to undertake such an evaluation, even though it would have been inexpensive and instructive.

Even though the Independent Force had little choice but to fly most of its missions at night in 1918, scant interwar attention was given to the difficulties of night flying and night bombing. This oversight was especially problematical since, during the war, distances covered had been short, flying had been done at low level, and operations had been attempted only in relatively good weather. During the interwar years, the standard navigational technique taught and trained in the RAF was map reading. And yet the obvious practical difficulties of relying on maps when flying in darkness over large stretches of blacked-out territory were never taken nearly so seriously as they should have been. Night flying training took place at the squadron level, and rather sporadically at that. And the lessons provided by these few trials were rarely heeded at higher command levels.[72] In general, navigation training was left to languish during the interwar years. No Air Ministry department had responsibility for navigation, nor was there a perceived need to train a special class of aviators for the task; pilots simply were expected to fly and navigate simultaneously. With no incentive or reward for proficiency in navigation, few airmen invested their time in it. The navigational knowledge of the wartime observers—many from the RNAS—was simply lost after the war. Celestial navigation, a common and important practice among civil airlines, was largely ignored in the RAF until the late 1930s. And though it was assumed that direction-finding wireless would play a large role in future operations, it was rarely practiced, and few studies were undertaken to assess its operational shortcomings.[73]

Other important issues also received inadequate attention. These included bomber tactics, in particular: how bombers might defend themselves, the types and calibre of guns they might use, and the armor they might require. In addition, bombing trials held in the interwar years generally allowed bombers to fly without opposition, at altitudes too low (14,000 feet and below) to determine bombing accuracy under operational conditions. Further undermining any semblance of a wartime environment was the illumination of targets during night trials. Not enough was done to determine what effects different types of bombs might produce, and what improvements might be made in them. Finally, until 1929, no adequate air intelligence organization was set up to accumulate information about the industry and infrastructure of potential enemies, and to identify and evaluate targets. And even after such an organization was established on a permanent basis, its staff was too small for the task at hand.[74]

Though trials pitting bombers against fighters were held beginning in 1927, they never truly challenged Trenchardian assumptions. This was true even though a reading of the results, at least in hindsight, strongly suggests that they should have. Aided by a range of technical developments, air defense against both daylight and nighttime raids was greatly improved over the World War I standard. In 1933, for instance, squadrons intercepted 55 percent of enemy day-formations as they flew toward the target, and another 26 percent as they left it; 67 percent of individual night raiders were intercepted.[75] But what might have seemed clear defensive victories were not perceived as such: proponents of the strategic air offensive did not seem to grasp the problems raised for them by these exercises. When assessing results, bomber advocates applied both formal rules and cognitive filters that insured they would see what they expected to see: the primacy of the aerial offensive waged by determined bombers. The rules under which the exercises were run gave advantages to bombers, and umpire rulings explained away unexpected results.

As there was no means of determining how many bombers intercepted in a given exercise would likely have been shot down under combat conditions, the Air Staff determined its own rule of thumb. Defensive fighters were accorded only half the "killing power" of twin-engined bombers. The Air Staff argued that "the fighting value of a good formation of bombers is higher than that of the same number of single-seat fighters; as an arbitary figure, the fighting value of the bombers is assessed as 2 and that of the fighters as 1."[76] This guidance, unfortunately, was not based on a careful assessment of historical experience; had it been, fighters would have garnered more respect. Other assumptions were curious at best. For instance, exercise umpires seemed to have had as much professed faith in the relentless offensive and the "moral effect" of bombing as Trenchard himself. A 1930 exercise, for instance, applied the "Blueland" tactic of direct attack against enemy "Redland" resources, while Redland put up an air defensive battle and also attacked Blue aerodromes. While the Red Force was given credit for destroying large numbers of Blue aircraft, this did not determine the outcome: Blueland was instead adjudged the victor by dint of its initial offensive. Writing up the exercise for publication, Flight Lt. M. W. Yool observed, "Blue's policy of commencing the operations by practically ignoring the existence of the enemy air force, and of concentrating on the attack of those objectives, the destruction of which would best achieve his aim, was fully justified by the results."[77] In his analysis of the 1931 exercises, Maj. C. C. Turner tried to grapple with some of the problems of assessment and interpretation of a staged operation. He explained, "Of the 112 bombers detailed for the exercises, it was judged that 84 were destroyed in the three days' operations. This may or may not be a sound estimate; but, after all, the crux of the matter is the amount of damage they would have inflicted on London and London's nerves." In the opening section of his essay, he pointed out that the exercises were important not only for the RAF, but also for the British people: "Air exercises of the kind now under discussion imply attacks on cities, and if disastrous panic—possibly from small cause—is to be averted, measures must be taken in peace time to instruct civilians, to organize protective measures, and to ensure discipline."[78]

Although air officers understood that the exercises were artificial and that their result—to some degree—could be open to interpretation, their perception was guided by some general assumptions: that Britain would outdo its enemy in terms of commitment to a swift and relentless offensive; that enemy morale could be made to break under such pressure; and that bombers flying at night, at high altitude, or on instruments through cloud would more than hold their own against fighters. Developments in bomber speeds and altitudes in the early 1930s legitimately bolstered their views: some exercises testing new techniques and models bore this out, and, in the 1934 exercises there was a 10 percent dip in interception rates across the board. But the slide was reversed a year later when (despite exercise rules tilted against fighters, and bombers flying at twice the altitude of earlier exercises) 79 percent of the 110 raids flown were intercepted, and 56 percent of them by superior numbers.[79] While these exercises gave crucial practice to air defense personnel who later put it to good effect, they did not—as one might have expected—force a reevaluation of the bomber advocates' position. Bomber advocates found a range of ways to see what they wanted to see, and to avoid seeing what contradicted their views. As John Ferris has pointed out, "They adopted the future conditional tense about material developments, assuming that marginal increases in the speed of altitude of bombers would cripple air defence, while ignoring the possibility that other developments could bolster it. The errors were multiplied by the erroneous assumption that just a few raids would wreck an enemy's morale and production."[80]

Of the dominant RAF view in the interwar years, Sir John Slessor later wrote, "Our belief in the bomber, in fact, was intuitive—a matter of faith."[81] This faith came partly from prevailing assumptions about societal and economic vulnerability, partly from the need to preserve a lever—in the form of the strategic air offensive—in interservice wars, and partly from cultural norms inside the service. Though formally professionalized, the military services in interwar Britain continued to be pervaded by a spirit of traditional amateurism.[82] While by no means unique to the RAF at the time, this attitude told heavily on a service that was born of technology, and whose future rested on developments in that realm.[83] Slessor summed it up well when he confessed in his memoir the main difference between soldiering in the 1950s and soldiering in the interwar years: "[T]he amateur status has disappeared, and today it is no longer an agreeable part-time occupation for a gentleman, but a serious and very wholetime profession."[84]

Though it would have been the logical place for forward, analytical thinking about air warfare and strategic bombing, the RAF Staff College often served more as a disseminating station for the accepted organizational viewpoint than it did as a center for critical thinking. The Staff College, which Trenchard had helped establish at Andover in 1921, sought "to draw lessons from World War I to form doctrine." Among the first courses taught were: "The Nature of War," "The Employment of Aircraft in War," "The War of 1914–1918," and "Air Force Organization."[85] But the curriculum did not encourage analysis or innovative thinking. Prospective students were accepted for admission if they passed an entrance exam administered under the direction of the Air Ministry and the Staff College. Answers were expected to conform with RAF established views. Examiners' comments were published, and these "left no doubt in prospective candidates' minds that if one wished to do well on the qualifying examination, it was safest to adopt the prevailing Air Force view in matters of doctrine." Thus, indoctrination began even before students matriculated. Even when candidates lacked knowledge or had difficulty expressing themselves, they were nonetheless commended for their "offensive spirit."[86]

Beginning with the college's third cycle, a starting point for class discussions was the "Notes"—copies of or extracts from original documents related to RFC and RAF policy in World War I. Much of the material served to reinforce for students the dominance of the offensive and the importance of the moral effect of bombing. Because of the small size of the Staff College, both the Commandant and the Chief of Air Staff could be personally acquainted with the instructors, and it was common for exceptional students to be posted on as instructors at the College. Thus, internal ideologies perpetuated themselves.[87]

In the mid 1920s and early 1930s it was not unusual to find articles in *The Hawk* (the RAF Staff College Yearbook and Journal) and the *Royal Air Force Quarterly* about the virtues of horseback riding, or bazaars in Baghdad. The pull of the old cavalry mentality—in a service that until recently had been part of the army—was evident. Riding, with all the romantic, nostalgic images it evoked, remained part of RAF culture. For several years *The Hawk* devoted most of its essays on the annual combined exercise at Camberly (including the Army, RAF, and Navy Staff Colleges) to the "outstanding event of the week": the annual "Drag Hunt," designed to test the students' strength of character by placing them on horseback (even those who could not ride well) and sending them over a course of difficult obstacles at breakneck speed. Sir John

Slessor would later write laconically, "There was a slight tendency for the Drag to assume undue importance in the curriculum at Camberly."[88]

Though a key part of the RAF Staff College mission was to articulate the assumptions on which wartime air strategy would rest, its leadership often seemed resistant to grappling with details in advance of events. They preferred to stress general principles and leave plenty of room for improvisation in the event. This was part of a broad tendency in British military thought, and, while it had certain advantages, was increasingly risky in the age of mechanization and ever more complex methods of warfare—all of which demanded analysis and calculation. Brooke-Popham, the first commandant of the Staff College, cautioned that regarding air warfare, "it is impossible to be so definite on the correct method of procedure as it is in the case of operations at sea or on land." Arguing that air tactics and air strategy necessitate "extreme flexibility," he advised his listeners to focus on the future, and warned them against limiting their thinking "to the range of material at our disposal today."[89] A later commandant of the Staff College, Edgar Ludlow-Hewitt, admonished students in 1928 against becoming "dogmatic." After explaining that in war there are "no universal remedies—no panaceas," he went on to warn against "being impressed too much by the actual letter and figure of our calculations" and developing "a habit of mind which calculates results purely in mathematical terms."[90]

Though writing about the First World War, H. A. Jones captured something fundamental about the interwar tendencies of British military organizations when he wrote that "the British character inclines to the taking of a sporting chance in preference to making fussy and apparently endless preparations for something which may never happen."[91] While it is clearly the case that not all operational details of wartime practice can be worked out in advance, it is clearly the case, too, that a modern military organization is best served by trying to work out as many as possible.

If Ludlow-Hewitt was wary of peacetime calculation, he nonetheless embraced certain general principles. Continuing in the tradition of Trenchard, he argued, "The demoralising effect of air bombardment is exceptionally high compared to its destructive effect." While he ruled out "terrorizing the enemy civilian population," he nonetheless accepted that the "demoralising force should be applied where it will have the quickest and most decisive results": the enemy nation's production, distribution, transportation, and communication centers. He suggested that industrial organizers and factory workmen would be particularly susceptible to the disruptive "indirect effects" of bombing.[92] RAF leaders stressed many of the same ideas when, later in 1928, they sought to convey the essence of air force strategic thinking to the other services.

SPREADING THE WORD:
PUBLIC PRONOUNCEMENTS OF RAF THOUGHT

By the end of a decade as Chief of Air Staff, Trenchard had left an indelible mark on the organization that he initially had not wanted but later worked fiercely to protect. By 1928 Trenchard's independent RAF was ready to articulate its mission and identify its place in British defense policy. Selected key documents from that year explain the way that the RAF presented itself and its organizational views to the other services and to the public. These included Trenchard's memorandum for the Chiefs of Staff Subcommittee on "The War Object of an Air Force" (May 1928); the RAF War Manual of 1928 (July 1928); and Trenchard's address to the Imperial Defence College (October 1928).

Immediately after the war, Trenchard had been cautious in his wording regarding the main objective of an air force. He did not argue that an air force could win a war on its own, or could operate on different terms than the other services. Over time, however, this began to change. Though Trenchard knew he could not afford to alienate totally the other services, he became more assertive in his public claims. While he did not dismiss the idea of a contest for air superiority, he argued that it would be won in the course of operations against enemy vital centers. In his May 1928 memorandum to the Chiefs of Staff Sub-Committee, he explained that, unlike the other services, an air force was not bound in war to destroy first the opposing force. Instead, "the object to be sought by air action will be to paralyse from the very outset the enemy's productive centres and munitions of war of every sort and to stop all communications and transportation."[93] Harking back to the Great War, the CAS argued that "the stronger side, by developing the more powerful offensive, will provoke in his weaker enemy increasingly insistent calls for the protective employment of aircraft. In this way he will throw the enemy on to the defensive . . . and air superiority will be obtained, and not by direct destruction of air forces."[94] He argued further, "The great centres of manufacture, transport and communications cannot be wholly protected. The personnel . . . who man them are not armed and cannot shoot back. They are not disciplined and it cannot be expected of them that they will stick stolidly to their lathes and benches under the recurring threat of air bombardment. . . . Each raid spreads far outside the actual zone of the attack. Once a raid has been experienced, false alarms are incessant and a state of panic remains in which work comes to a standstill."[95] This refrain persisted. Two years into the Second World War, Air Vice-Marshal Sir John Slessor, commanding a bomber group, wrote the following to his crews: "[B]y . . . attacking in widely different parts of Germany on successive nights you spread the moral effect not only of the actual attacks but of the air-raid warnings in all districts over which you pass. You know Lord Trenchard's slogan 'keep the Germans out of bed, keep the syrens blowing,' and there is the devil of a lot in it."[96]

The idea that one could "throw" the enemy on the defensive also depended crucially upon the enemy population being vulnerable, or—at least—more vulnerable than one's own population in a head-on offensive contest.[97] But this Trenchardian conception only made sense in a world in which bombers could penetrate successfully enough to bring about the desired effect. The RAF War Manual, published in July 1928, argued that "the wide space of the air and the condition of cloud and wind confers unique powers of evasion on the attacking aircraft and renders their timely interception uncertain." It argued further that "the defenders cannot be said to possess absolute stopping powers, and cannot altogether prevent the attackers reaching their objective if the attack is made with *sufficient determination* [emphasis added]."[98]

Downplaying escort fighters, Trenchard believed that if enemy defenses became a problem, they should be handled by offensive techniques. The War Manual read, "When, owing to the strength of the hostile defence, the casualties caused by enemy fighters become excessive, the remedy should first be sought in the improvement of the fighting efficiency and fire effect of the bomber formations themselves, rather than in the provision of escorts." Evasive techniques were emphasized, including flying at high altitude, use of cloud cover, avoidance of routine, cooperation between operating squadrons, and the use of feints.[99] In his May 1928 memorandum to the Chiefs of Staff, Trenchard stressed that the effects seen in the Great War would only be redoubled in a future war "with greater numbers of aircraft, the larger carrying capacity and range, and the heavier bombs available."[100]

After reading Trenchard's memorandum, both the Chief of the Imperial General Staff (Milne) and the Chief of the Naval Staff (Madden) expressed serious reservations on several key points. Neither was convinced that an air force could simply pass over the enemy army and navy and achieve its aim through a direct attack on the enemy's vital centers. Madden bluntly observed that in Trenchard's paper it "is taken for granted that direct air attack on the centres of production, transportation and communication must succeed in paralysing the life and effort of the community and therefore of winning the war." But, the Naval Chief argued, "No evidence has so far been produced that such bombing in the face of counter attack will have such a result." Milne likewise argued that in World War I "no military concentration either by the Germans or by the Allies was ever brought to a standstill by air action." Both Milne and Madden suggested that instead of undermining enemy morale, air attacks might have the effect of stiffening it. Milne also pointed out that developments in "counter air action" might undermine Britain's all-out aerial offensive, and he argued that the RAF's air strategy, in any event, had the effect of placing Britain in a disadvantageous position due to the geographical vulnerability of London.[101]

Milne and Madden raised further objections to Trenchard's memorandum on ethical grounds; to them, Trenchard's articulated policy sounded like advocacy of indiscriminate attacks on civilians. In fact, the issue of targeting would pose a chronic dilemma for the RAF. The problem—as the army and navy critics of RAF policy understood—was that most industry was located in or very near cities, and it was not clear where "dislocation" would slide into terrorization. The issue was obscured by international legal difficulties over what constituted a "military target" and who constituted "civilians" in the brave new world of total warfare. But the Trenchardian concept of moral effect depended on weaknesses and points of vulnerability in the enemy population— and these in turn rested on assumptions about civilian reliability and worker steadfastness. Attempting to clarify his service's position, Trenchard argued that his means of undermining enemy morale would be within the bounds of the existing law of war, which permitted attacks on "military objectives" wherever located. Certainly, he conceded, civilian casualties would occur, but they would result from attacks on legitimate military targets. He argued that he was not interested in indiscriminate bombing for "the sole purpose of terrorising the civilian population." Rather his intention was to "terrorise munitions workers (men and women) into absenting themselves from work, or stevedores into abandoning the loading of a ship."[102]

But Trenchard's attempted distinction was largely lost on the other chiefs. Clearly, terms like "vital centres" and "centres of manufacture, communications, and transportation" meant cities would take the brunt of the attacks, whether civilians were an explicit target or not. And terms like "enemy morale" and "national will" implied that the RAF was seeking to apply leverage against something quite human. Trenchard did nothing to banish this impression when he said, "It will be harder to affect the will of an army in the field by air attack than to affect the morale of a Nation by attacks on its centres of supply and communications as a whole."[103] Madden pointed out that RAF strategy as articulated would mean that the civilian life of the enemy would be "endangered to a far greater degree than has ever hitherto been contemplated under International Law." And Milne stated simply that "it is for His Majesty's Government to accept or to refuse a doctrine which, put into plain English, amounts to one which advocates unrestricted warfare against the civil population of one's enemy."[104]

Debate continued among the chiefs, and Trenchard made another effort, in a speech to the Imperial Defence College in October 1928, to convey publicly his perception of the RAF mission. In a nod to the other services, he conceded that the new declared "war aim of the RAF" would be to break down the enemy's resistance "by attacks on objectives calculated to achieve this end and in addition to direct cooperation with the navy and army and in furtherance of the policy of His Majesty's Government at the time."[105] The CAS still insisted, however, that instead of engaging in counterforce work ("a waste of air power in a first class war"), the RAF would concentrate on "other objectives more vulnerable and which cannot be so readily defended." Regarding targets, he equivocated, noting only that "[a]t one time one kind of objective might be the best one for the air forces to attack, while at another the fullest effect might be gained . . . by attacking another kind of objective altogether."[106] His October speech reiterated the importance of "throwing" the enemy on to the defensive. "The issue to be fought out," Trenchard said, "is which side by maintaining its bombing attacks in the face of losses can continue to lead and keep the other on the defensive."[107] As in May, the CAS argued that the Air Staff was not "desirous of carrying out indiscriminate bombing attacks on the civil population as such." Air attacks, he said, "will be directed against military objectives using that term in the broad sense."[108]

CONFUSED LEGACY

At the 1930 RAF Staff College annual reunion dinner, Trenchard, recently retired as Chief of Air Staff, was the honored guest. To heartfelt applause, Commandant of the College, P. B. Joubert de la Ferte toasted him: "We owe our existence as a service to Lord Trenchard; we could not owe more."[109] In the view of those gathered, Trenchard had been responsible for preserving RAF autonomy, and thus deserved the service's gratitude and praise. From a bureaucratic point of view, Trenchard had been a great success: his positions and rhetoric had encompassed and promoted a vision of air war that had advanced the RAF's organizational needs. But his long-term legacy would be decidedly more mixed.

The ideas laid out by Trenchard in 1928 were left largely intact through the early 1930s. Joubert de la Ferté's 1932–33 lectures did not differ greatly from those of Brooke-Popham nearly a decade earlier. In a lecture titled "The Employment of Air Forces in War," he argued that air power allowed for "the direct application of pressure to the enemy people without any defeat of their armed forces," and that successful attack on the "weaker components" of a nation's fighting strength, including its "moral qualities" could "bring the whole edifice crumbling down."[110]

Even though Trenchardian rhetoric persisted, it remained less than limpid. Trenchard once admitted, "I am not good at writing. I cannot set my ideas out in nice order."[111] Whether a problem of articulation or conception, the consequence was confusion—both outside and inside the organization—over the real mission of the RAF and the practical means by which to achieve it. An avoidance of analytical rigor, combined with rhetorical flexibility designed to serve organizational needs, had left behind problems. Fundamental points of contention remained over interservice cooperation, counterforce operations, and targeting. RAF members debated the aim of their organization among themselves, while remaining on the defensive with respect to the other services.

The RAF's focus on its strategic mission in these years tended to edge out thorough consideration of missions shared by the other services, including tactical cooperation with the army. Indeed, Sir Maurice Dean has written that "[b]etween 1918 and 1939 the RAF forgot how to support the army."[112] So far apart did the army and RAF drift in the interwar years that they began to lose the ability to communicate with one another effectively. In one exercise in 1939, considerable confusion prevailed until personnel from each side got together to work out the meaning, in practice, of such terms as "close support" and "direct support."[113] If the significance of close support of troops had been recognized and understood during the First World War, it was not clear quite how it might play out in a future war—and this situation was hardly helped by the fact that the British had set themselves firmly against the possibility of another 1914-style continental commitment. In addition, postwar analyses of close air support often focused on its high cost in pilots and aircraft.[114] If high cost had been a feature of long-range bombing as well, its proponents were inclined to overlook it; with close air support—a use of aircraft which tied air forces to armies and did little to further a rationale for independence—airmen tended to highlight rather than overlook disadvantages. In general, the Air Staff frowned on those few cooperative initiatives that did develop with the army, and Army Air Forces maneuvers lacked the most basic features of practical cooperation.[115]

The problem of cooperation with armies was not wholly ignored in the 1930s, however. In 1936 Sir John Slessor published a book called

Air Power and Armies, which sought to address some of the army's concerns. It was a thoughtful effort and it revealed that not everyone in the RAF had forgotten about cooperation. But it did not change the central thrust of RAF thought, and Slessor did not abandon any of the things he had come to believe as a bomber advocate. Indeed, he worked hard to maintain the flexibility and maneuvering room of the RAF even as he sought to calm the fears of his sister service.[116] Little changed in practice, and, despite some proposals late in the day, the British aircraft industry produced no specialized types for close support. In 1940, Capt. B. H. Liddell Hart confided in his diary that the British had "no suitable machines for low-flying attack, and the Air Staff object to the idea of air counter-attack against troops moving up."[117]

Other problems remained. After Trenchard's retirement, RAF officers continued to be at pains to explain that their means of prosecuting a future war were not immoral or outside international law. Much of their writing uneasily addressed charges that long-range bombing would be less ethical than traditional forms of warfare, including naval shelling or blockading.[118] One frustrated writer lampooned the debate, pointing out that while an aerial bomb will, unfailingly, select as its target "the female sex and children under sixteen," a shell from an eighteen-pounder on land or a ship "proceeds with unerring aim directly to the target at which it is fired and . . . kills only the male population of fighting age."[119]

Part of the confusion left in the wake of Trenchard's departure manifested itself in a staff exercise for the Wessex Bombing Area Headquarters of the Air Defence of Great Britain (CADGB), held on 13–15 March 1933 and written up by Air Officer Commanding-in-Chief (AOC) Air Vice-Marshal T. Webb-Bowen. Based on the premise that the "Western European Confederation" was about to commence intensive air attacks on London, Webb-Bowen drew up a plan of response. While it met with general approval, it raised questions among some reviewers, who asked, rhetorically, if the targeting guidance laid out in the 1928 Manual had been clear enough. In brief, the AOC's objective was to attempt to "break the enemy's national resistance in the shortest possible time." Concerned that he would not be able to crush the enemy's will by material damage alone, Webb-Bowen argued, "Our effort must therefore be directed against the morale of the civil population with the object of so disorganizing the normal daily life of the individual that a continuance of such conditions becomes intolerable. This postulates striking primarily at targets located in *thickly populated* areas."[120] He settled on a plan that sent the bulk of his force against centers of government, and the rest against the aircraft industry and other industrial areas. He identified material damage as a "secondary consideration" behind "moral pressure," and defended his position with language that sounded remarkably similar to that found in Trenchard's final war dispatch of 1919.[121]

Over the summer of 1933, however, the exercise was drawn into an intraservice debate on the "war aim" of the RAF. Staff College Commandant Joubert de la Ferté opened the debate by bringing to the attention of the Air Ministry his concerns that the real "aim" of the RAF was being misinterpreted both inside and outside of the service. He listed five "common misconceptions" about the RAF aim:

1. that the air force will not fight the enemy air forces at all;
2. that the RAF will make ruthless air attack (baby-killing) its aim;
3. that military targets will be attacked in densely populated areas, where it does not matter if the bomb misses the target (the "near-miss theory");
4. that the RAF will not direct its efforts to what the other services argue should be the common aim: the attack on the enemy armed forces (a claim, he observed, that is "usually followed by an accusation of gambling on the effect of air attack on that imponderable factor—the moral fibre of the enemy people");
5. that the RAF is advocating a form of military action that no British government will allow to be put into effect on the declaration of war.[122]

Joubert was especially worried about the second misconception, which, he argued, was an incorrect interpretation of the 1928 War Manual's emphasis on the attack on enemy morale. Joubert explained that Trenchard had tried to "counteract" the same misconceptions through his lectures and the publication of the manual, but had not been entirely successful.[123] The Commandant admitted that "as a service, [we] may be to blame for this state of affairs," and added, "Not only is there a lack of knowledge as to the official Air Staff view, but there is much loose talk amongst junior officers, whose military education has not kept pace with their enthusiasm for pet theories, and few of them have had sufficient mental training to enable them to clear away the misconceptions that exist in their own minds as to the Air Force Aim."[124] That this confusion and lack of consistency occurred inside the service as well as outside indicates that it was not just a problem of the other services caricaturing the RAF aim, but rather that the aim itself was unclear, as were the means of achieving it. In the interwar years, mantras about air power were advocated and repeated, but without much practical detail, especially in regard to counter–air operations and targeting. This odd combination of dogma and ambiguity left plenty of room for confusion.

The ADGB March exercise, with its attack of "thickly populated areas," merely highlighted this problem. Joubert suggested that "[a] common doctrine on the interpretation of the Aim as laid down in the manual should be stated by the Air Staff at the Air Ministry, and accepted and worked to by all commands in all forms of training."[125] In his effort to help, he sent the Air Ministry examples of his own teachings, stressing those issues he thought most misunderstood. Though he attempted to tighten some definitions and to appease the other services, his language did not differ fundamentally from Trenchard's. In one (rather remarkable) passage, he made an argument that almost certainly was influenced by an "air control" model: "What we desire to do is to make an area in which exists some organisation of a military nature so uncomfortable that nobody can work in it effectively. Actual killing is not in any way essential to our purpose. It is sufficient to indicate that if a certain course of action is pursued, death or maiming is likely to ensue. . . . It should not be necessary to use large numbers of aircraft, since the weight of bombs does not matter."[126] Finally, Joubert insisted that the RAF must avoid the fatal flaw of devoting too many resources to a defensive force. In a statement worthy of his pre–World War I predecessors, he wrote, "The nation with the better fighting men, the stouter hearts, the better leaders and equipment will, in the end, out-fight the weaker, who will be forced more and more on the defensive, until finally the successful offensive of the stronger side will have given it the security it requires."[127]

From his position in the Directorate of Plans, Group Capt. Charles Portal also weighed in. He argued that the Wessex Bombing Area appreciation was "about as unfortunate as it could be," since the aim, as articulated by the AOC "leads directly to the idea that we can 'make war on our own' by 'indiscriminate attacks on the civil population,' which is exactly what . . . we have told the Government that it would not pay us to do." Portal concluded, however, that the misinterpretation was not due to a lack of clarity in the manual, which, he believed, emphasized the moral effect. He tactfully suggested that the AOC probably had insufficient data on the military situation, and this led him to put forward an aim that was "far too high and vague to form the basis of an A.O.C.'s appreciation."[128]

The war aim issue was never fully resolved before it was taken up again in early 1935 by Group Capt. Arthur T. Harris, Deputy Director of Plans, who concluded it might be worthwhile to revise and reissue an official statement of the war aim.[129] A draft, produced late in the year, stated simply that victory in war "goes to that nation which can the sooner break down the other's power of resistance." The author (very probably Harris) argued that a nation's power of resistance, which is comprised of the interdependent qualities of military strength, financial and economic power, manpower, industrial power and the strength of character and moral attributes of the enemy people, is susceptible to pressure at its weakest points. He recommended that bombers use evasion tactics and "sheer determination" to prosecute the offensive. He maintained, though, that it would be necessary to retain a home fighter force to prevent as many enemy bombers as possible from reaching their targets, and to reduce the accuracy of those that do get through.[130] The draft noted that the dependence of a "civilised community" on its urban centers (with their food, water, and sanitary organization) created an exploitable weakness. Its author recognized, however, that in a war for limited objectives, air bombardment or air blockade against "urban localities" might not be legitimate, and some "less devastating method of exerting pressure might have to be accepted in the early stages, or until such time as the enemy has himself shown such a lack of restraint as to attempt to apply urban blockade pressure himself."[131]

In *Air Power and Armies*, Slessor pointed out that the debate over strategic bombing in a future war had been much inflamed by "passions and prejudices" surrounding the issue of targeting. Realizing that he had to tread carefully, he asserted that he by no means underrated the "possibly terrible effects of air bombardment on the morale of a civil population," explaining that if the "moral effect" of air attack was serious in the Great War, it would be "immensely more so under modern conditions." But his conception of the RAF aim, he explained, focused on industrial dislocation and disorganization, and its impact on enemy functioning and war-related manufacture. He argued that industrial workers, who would bear the heavy brunt of attack, could not be expected to have "morale and sticking power . . . to equal that of the disciplined soldier."[132] Despite his earnest attempts to specify and delineate, Slessor did not clarify the issue very much—indeed, the debate over targeting, and the definition of "combatant" would continue right into the late 1930s when Slessor himself would be one of the ones most responsible for sorting out operational guidance and the practical meaning of terms.

VISIONARIES, ENTHUSIASTS, DISARMERS, CIVIL DEFENSE, AND PULP FICTION

The RAF's debate over its "war aim" took place against the backdrop of a bleak financial situation and increasingly ominous developments on the international scene. Antimilitarist sentiment ran strong in Britain, which in the late 1920s had been exposed to a flood of literature condemning the war of 1914–18. And frightening descriptions of air war, published in popular books and journals all through the 1920s and

1930s, undermined faith that Britain's existing bomber force might serve as an adequate deterrent to war, helping to create an outspoken public campaign supporting disarmament. Ironically, if the fear of strategic bombing had earlier helped to secure the independence of the RAF, it later lent energy and urgency to international disarmament efforts getting underway in Geneva through the auspices of the League of Nations.[133] The bomber, the most frightening weapon of the day, naturally was a main target of the disarmers. Increasing international tension, first manifested by the Japanese seizure of Manchuria in 1931, seemed to foreshadow an uncontrollable armaments race that would threaten Britain's vulnerable finances. Prime Minister Ramsay MacDonald's National Government backed the Geneva initiative, hoping that the international atmosphere might be right for real progress in placing curbs on war. Disarmament was of considerable and indeed passionate personal interest to both MacDonald and his Foreign Secretary, Sir John Simon.[134]

The Foreign Office, the War Office, and the Admiralty all favored banning the bomber. The latter was particularly adamant, noting (with a good deal of interservice animosity), "Only the Air Ministry wants to retain these weapons for use against towns, a method of warfare which is revolting and un-English."[135] But Air Ministry members argued vigorously against British initiatives regarding bombers, pointing out that no agreement could prevent civil aircraft from being transformed into bombers in wartime, and that banning the bomber would deprive the government of an inexpensive method of controlling colonial territories. Indeed, Arthur Harris, then a wing commander, took an almost conspiratorial view of the Geneva discussions, referring to them as "disarmament plots and counterplots."[136] Air Ministry resistance, however, did not prevent British participation in an armaments "truce," which lasted from 1 November 1931 to 31 March 1933. This precluded work on heavy bombers, and thus had a serious impact on the RAF's fifty-two-squadron program which was significantly behind its original schedule.[137]

Writing while the Geneva negotiations were ongoing, P.R.C. Groves, the World War I Director of Flying Operations, opined dryly, "To judge from the nature of the speeches of public men of all denominations, there is no clearer method of gaining popular applause than to anathematize war and eulogize peace. Unfortunately . . . reference is seldom made to the prodigious difficulties which must be overcome before any approximation to the ideal of 'Law—not War' is possible."[138] But if the public in Britain was inclined to endorse those who called for peace, their stance was not unrelated to their imaginative foreboding about the consequences of future air wars. Groves himself had helped establish this environment through articles he wrote for the *Times* (London) in the spring of 1922.[139] Widely cited afterward as a reliable account of future air warfare, the articles developed themes that would be repeated steadily through the interwar years in Britain. Echoing H. G. Wells, Groves pointed out that aviation had made war an affair of "areas" rather than "fronts": at the outset of conflict, each side would strike immediately at the "heart and nerve centers" of its opponent with high explosive, incendiary, and poison gas bombs. Certain that civilians would suffer these onslaughts, and pessimistic about the chances for successful air defense, Groves explained that the only course was therefore a "policy of aerial offensive-defensive" which would unleash a long-distance striking force against the enemy.[140]

Ministers, politicians, and other opinion leaders promulgated similar ideas in articles, public speeches, and House of Commons debates. Indeed, the annual Commons debate on the defense budget served as a regular catalyst for dire proclamations about the menace of air warfare.[141] Capt. Frederick E. Guest, who had a short tenure as Air Minister after Churchill, gave an ominous speech on air power to lead off the 1922 debates on air estimates in the House of Commons. And Sir Samuel Hoare, an admirer of Trenchard who served as civilian Air Minister from 1922 to 1929, argued that an aerial counteroffensive would be vital both for deterrence and for defense if deterrence failed. Sir Frederick Sykes, who was responsible for civil aviation after the war, wrote of great aerial armadas that would aim at the heartland of their enemy in future wars. And by 1925 Churchill himself wrote of aerial attacks on civilians by bombers carrying gas and other chemicals. Other noted figures, including Lord Balfour, Gen. Sir Frederick Maurice, Sir Sefton Brancker, Lord Salisbury, Sir Maurice Hankey, and Anthony Eden advocated for air power—and warned of the consequences of being left behind in that realm—during the 1920s.[142]

In his *Reformation of War* (1923), J.F.C. Fuller postulated that aerial bombing of cities, especially with gas, would be a notable feature of future wars. In 1925, Capt. B. H. Liddell Hart published what would become a deeply influential book, *Paris, or the Future of War*. It explored means by which an enemy nation could be subdued, not by deadly frontal assaults on armies, but by locating and exploiting national weak points. Taking his cue from Paris of the Trojan War, who shot an arrow into Achilles' heel, Liddell Hart sought a strategy of modern warfare that would exploit "moral factors." He argued that an enemy people can be subdued by "dislocating their normal life" to such a degree that they will have no choice but to surrender.[143] He explained that aircraft provided "boundless possibilities" for striking immediately "at the seat of the opposing will and policy." Using a metaphor from biology, he explained that "a nation's nerve-system, no longer covered by the flesh of its troops, is now laid bare to attack, and, like the human nerves, the progress of civilization has rendered it far more sensitive than in earlier and more primitive times."[144] Liddell Hart prophesied that, with its 990 airplanes, France could drop a greater weight of bombs on London in one day than the Germans dropped during the entire course of World War I—and could repeat the dose at "frequent and brief intervals."[145] He hypothesized that future weapons and delivery systems would be vastly more accurate and powerful than the "primitive instruments" of 1915–18. Indeed, he postulated that a state with superior air power could deliver to its enemy a blow so powerful as to paralyze its "nerve system" within a few hours or, at most, days.[146]

Paris, placed on the RAF list of recommended reading and highly touted by Trenchard, was written when the Red Scare—an aftershock of the Russian Revolution—still had much of Europe in its grip. Liddell Hart's argument assumed the intolerance of the civilian population for disruption of their normal routines. Disruption would lead to chaos, particularly among the lower classes, and such chaos would lead to the loss of government control—perhaps revolution.[147] Much early post–World War I popular fiction focused on the threat posed by Bolshevism and the laboring masses. A wave of postwar strikes contributed to fears already spawned by events in Russia in 1917. Underlying these works—which had titles like *London Under the Bolshevists*, *The Red Fury*, *The Red Tomorrow*, *Against the Red Sky*, and *Revolution*—was the assumption that postwar disillusionment would set in among peoples who had been falsely promised a "War to End All Wars" and a "Home Fit for Heroes." Embittered ex-serviceman figured prominently in most of these stories.[148]

The earliest deliberations of the Air Raid Precautions (ARP) Committee (1924–25), reflected this pervasive level of concern.[149] Even though the head of the committee (Sir John Anderson) was well known for his unflappability and objectivity, the report he oversaw incorporated (from Air Ministry estimates) an assessment that a future war might bring some 350 tons of bombs down on London in the first forty-eight hours, and 100 tons per day thereafter for a month. The Committee—again following the lead of the Air Ministry—put only limited faith in defense; it recommended partial evacuation of the city so as to minimize panic, chaos, and confusion. Conversations with Trenchard led committee members to conclude, pessimistically, that the only course open to them was to continue their investigations "with a view to mitigating, so far as possible, the evils attendant upon aerial bombardment." Regarding public morale, they wrote, "It has been borne upon us that in the next war it may well be that the nation whose people can endure aerial bombardment the longer and with greater stoicism will ultimately prove victorious."[150]

In 1926, the futurist novel *1944* envisioned a massive air attack against London with lethal gas. Its author, the second Earl of Halsbury—formerly Viscount Tiverton of the World War I Air Staff—had maintained an interest in air warfare despite returning to his civilian work as a lawyer. After the war he grew convinced that the new gas weapons becoming available would not require the specialized equipment and training needed for high explosive and incendiary bombs. His motive in writing the book was to bring the danger to the attention of the public, and to set up the conditions that might lead to international abolition of chemical weapons.[151] Such dire predictions—official and literary—had the effect of encouraging liberals and pacifists to lobby hard for air disarmament. For instance, A. S. (Susan) Lawrence, an undersecretary in the Labour government of 1929, argued in 1927 that the government was obliged to make a serious and genuine commitment to aerial disarmament. Citing the 1922 Groves articles, she asserted that there could be no defense against an attack that would produce such terror, disorder, and disorganization as to "break up" London as a civil community in two to three hours. She estimated that millions would die, especially from gas attacks.[152]

Lawrence's arguments anticipated a wave of popular fiction on air and gas warfare that continued until the outbreak of actual war in 1939. The perfection of instruments of destruction was at the heart of S. Southwold's 1931 book *The Gas War of 1940*, a tale set in the late summer of 1940: Germany attacks Poland and destroys France's defensive fortifications; London is smashed by a succession of air raids, and all of the world's great cities experience bombardment with high explosives and poison gas. Following closely in this genre were such interwar works as *The Poison War, The Black Death, Menace, Empty Victory, Invasion from the Air, War Upon Women, Chaos, Air Reprisal,* and *What Happened to the Corbetts.*[153] The impact of these was augmented not only by the futurist scenarios being played in the (increasingly popular) cinema, but also by the ominous and troubling events of the 1930s, including the Japanese attack on Manchuria, the Italian attack on Abyssinia, and the Spanish civil war.

By this time as well, the ideas of the Italian air enthusiast, Gen. Giulio Douhet, were becoming more widely known in English-speaking countries. Douhet's 1921 book, *The Command of the Air*, had painted a graphic vision of societal collapse in the face of air attack. Indeed, it was the futurist drama he conveyed rather than the analytical rigor of his ideas that gave Douhet a lasting place in the canon of air warfare.[154]

A poet, painter, playwright, and amateur novelist, Douhet brought to bear on his work "the intense modernist fascination with the latest advances in science and technology—with the automobile, with electricity, with gas and finally with the aeroplane—prevalent in prewar Italian protofascist *avant-garde* culture."[155] Though both British and American airmen developed indigenous theories of air warfare that did not depend on Douhet—and though there is no evidence that Douhet was widely read in Britain before the 1930s—his ideas were cited thereafter and used to support apocalyptic visions of air warfare.[156]

Douhet's vision stressed the offensive, indeed he referred to aircraft as the offensive weapon "par excellence." Postulating that vast destruction could be wrought by fifty squadrons of bombers, he asked his readers, "How could a country go on living and working under this constant threat, oppressed by the nightmare of imminent destruction and death?" Douhet was impressed by the possibilities of attack against those of "least moral resistance," such as factory workers.[157] His vision was one of technological determinism. He wrote, "The brutal but inescapable conclusion we must draw is this: in the face of the technical developments of aviation today, in case of war the strongest army we can deploy . . . and the the strongest navy we can dispose . . . will provide no effective defense against determined efforts . . . to bomb our cities."[158] But Douhet's perspective was narrow, and he saw only the evidence that supported his view. His idea of the future rested on crude extrapolation, and like many other interwar "prophets" of air power, he failed to see how, in the words of historian Michael Sherry, it "might evolve unpredictably, strengthening the defense as well as the offense, creating its own futile charges and bloody stalemates."[159]

In 1932 the Air Staff decided to move the annual ADGB exercises away from London. This was in part because the Geneva negotiations were ongoing, and in part because bombers over London seemed to have the effect of underscoring the concerns given voice in the popular fiction of the day. Maj. F. A. de V. Robertson, who wrote on the 1932 exercises for the *Journal of the Royal United Services Institution*, took the press to task for sensationalized coverage of previous RAF exercises, which had as its consequence "a considerable scare and a general belief that any enemy could bomb London at will."[160] But journalists were not the only ones helping to promulgate such views. The RAF's own official statements and predictions had fostered an environment for sensationalized stories. And members of the government, too, speculated about air war and the potency of the bomber. In November 1932, once and future Prime Minister Stanley Baldwin (then serving as Lord President of the Council) offered up one of the most repeated and remembered statements of the era when he declared in the House of Commons that "the bomber will always get through."[161] As time went on, his grim convictions remained unshaken. In 1936 he stated that the next war would be the end of civilization in Europe: "[T]he raging peoples of every country, torn with passion, suffering and horror, would wipe out every government in Europe" and would leave anarchy in their wake.[162]

When, in the spring of 1932, the government gave serious consideration to a Foreign Office plan to prohibit aerial bombing of the territory and shipping of another sovereign state, the Air Ministry redoubled its efforts to stave off a bomber ban. They argued that, so long as aircraft existed, no agreement could prevent Britain from being attacked by air in a future war; and they strongly implied that such attack—which would be all but inevitable—would involve heavy casualties. The only answer to it, they argued (unsurprisingly), was counterattack; fighters alone could not secure London. The Coast Defence Subcommittee of the Committee of Imperial Defence (CID)—which did not include the First Sea Lord or the Chief of the Imperial General Staff—was impressed by Air Ministry arguments and endorsed the RAF view.[163] Shortly afterward an even more radical plan for air disarmament, drawn up by Stanley Baldwin, was presented to a specially appointed cabinet committee. Sympathetic toward, but concerned about, Air Ministry arguments, the full cabinet recommended that Baldwin's plan become the basis of informal negotiations with the French. In the meantime, the Americans interjected a dramatic but problematic proposal that mainly had the effect of disrupting the Anglo-French discussions. By midsummer Britain's efforts were stymied. Despite the government's sincere commitment to air disarmament, it never managed to devise a workable policy. The dilemmas raised by the potential wartime conversion of civil aviation proved particularly resistant to solution, and there was no consensus on how to constrain bomber operations in war. The deliberations finally succumbed to the German demand for an air force equal to that of the other European powers; the negotiations were effectively over when the Germans withdrew from the talks in October 1933. Still, the British continued doggedly to seek, right up to1939, a way to head off the "knock-out blow" through international deliberations.[164]

Throughout those years there was no shortage of dire predictions regarding air warfare—not just in fiction but in scholarly accounts as well. Former RAF officer L.E.O. Charlton's 1935 book, *War from the Air* (developed from a series of lectures he gave at Cambridge), argued that since air defense was essentially futile, a future air war would be "like a team competition in a shooting gallery."[165] Charlton, who had been Britain's Air attaché to the United States, foresaw a war in which railway yards, docks, and market centers would be "drenched with gas," and power stations would be attacked with high explosive bombs, creating, in the dark shelter of the London Underground, "an interlude of blind panic" that "will beggar description."[166] He was particularly exercised over the likely behavior of Britain's working classes, explaining that it would be the "labouring masses, herded in the discomfort of overcrowded, antiquated dwellings in congested districts, themselves the most difficult people to control (factory employees in particular), who will be more susceptible than most to dismay and stampede when the air-raid warning goes."[167]

Two years later, Frank Morison took a less dramatic tone in his book *War on Great Cities*. He argued that gas was not something that governments would employ lightly. Writing in what may have been direct response to Charlton, he explained that the "drenching" of great cities with gas would be "profoundly obnoxious to the moral sense of mankind," with far-reaching political considerations. He argued, as well, that restraint might be brought about by the fact that "the real arbiters in a momentous decision of this kind must, by the irony of circumstances, become in their own persons among its first victims." Morison was greatly concerned, however, with efforts by a potential enemy to set fire to London from the air, using large concentrations of high thermal capacity incendiary bombs.[168]

For its part, the government was not prepared to take any chances with the prospect of gas warfare. Because gas had been the subject of much research in Britain, more was known about its effects than was known about the effects of high explosive or incendiary bombs.[169] The first ARP circular on civil defense (July 1935), provided information on gas masks, other antigas equipment, and the setting up of a gas school to train instructors. These measures were meant to instill within the population the sense that they could protect themselves through self-help measures. In regard to war preparations in general, though, the trend in Britain until the late 1930s was generally away from full public discussion. For political reasons the government kept under wraps the details of most of its home defense plans. A ban on the full disclosure of information regarding wartime measures, including naming the enemy, was not lifted until after the Munich crisis of 1938.[170]

The 1930s saw no diminution in the grim casualty estimates put forward for air war. The preparation of the 1935 circular prompted the Air Staff to produce a more ominous picture than ever before: it envisioned the German air force, operating out of the Low Countries, able to drop 150 tons of bombs daily for an unspecified period. After reports of air attacks on Barcelona in 1938, the government raised its multiplier of fifty casualties per ton of bombs to a higher ratio of seventy-two per ton.[171] A July 1938 report by the Advisory Committee on London Casualty Organization (under the Home Secretary and the Minister of Health) expected a rate of 30,000 casualties per day requiring hospital treatment; a rate that would continue over several weeks.[172] And the government continued to be as concerned as the popular writers about the prospect of civilian panic and hysteria in the wake of air attacks. Between December 1937 and September 1938, discussions among the War Office, Home Office, and Commissioner of Police recommended the provision of some 17,000 regular troops (with 20,000 reserve constables) to control crowds and panic in London and other cities.[173]

In October 1938 the Ministry of Health received, from eminent psychiatrists in London, a report indicating that psychiatric casualties might outnumber physical casualties by three to one. The previous month the director of one highly regarded London clinic predicted widespread outbreaks of neurosis upon a declaration of war, and especially after the first air raids. In April 1939 the Ministry of Health received another report indicating that war would trigger increases in mental and nervous disorders to "an extent never before experienced." In that same month, the Ministry issued one million burial forms to local authorities.[174] Unsurprisingly, medical journal articles speculated on the public health implications of a future war. In a typical assessment, Dr. John Rickman pointed out that "[t]he civilian population is not organized into regiments which, by special training and tradition, claim and inspire the self-forgetful devotion of individuals." As if to remedy the situation, Dr. Maurice Wright suggested that "[t]he civilian population must be treated as if they were combatant troops; they must be under authority and know what to do and what to avoid doing in case of emergency."[175]

REARMAMENT: THE EARLY YEARS

Even though the British government continued to seek a path to disarmament, it was forced, after the failure of the Geneva Conference, to face the prospect of rearmament. When the Geneva armaments "truce" expired in March 1933, Britain's first line possessed only six day- and five night-bomber squadrons. The Auxiliary Air Force and the Special Reserve contained eight day- and two night-bomber squadrons.[176] Building a new air force would be complicated and lengthy, and made all the more difficult by ongoing concerns about Britain's financial situation, the tense environment that seemed to preclude clear and sober thinking, and strained relations between the Air Ministry and the Foreign Office.[177] Though the process was underway by 1934, it got off to a slow and halting start. Air rearmament was marked by eight different stages, labeled expansion schemes A to M (the extra letters being those that did not achieve official approval). On the whole, the British aircraft industry would respond well under the circumstances, ultimately producing invaluable types.[178] But difficulties were inevitable in a telescoped and unavoidably stressful process, and these troubles had their reflection in the early years of the war. There were several underlying causes for the problems that arose.

First, the Air Ministry was hesitant to commit too rapidly to aircraft designs that might well become obsolete on the production line. Their concerns were not unjustified since aircraft technology was in a period of particular flux and development. The switch from wood to metal construction, for instance, demanded increased commitments to development and testing. Second, initial rearmament schemes were designed to insure that Britain maintained "parity" with Germany's expanding air force. The government saw parity as a means of deterrence, and as a way of maintaining diplomatic credibility without engaging in undue provocation. But parity was a problematical concept because defining and calculating force levels was difficult, and because it gave Germany the initiative.[179] Third, and perhaps most importantly, rearmament took place without adequate assessment of the purpose and development of the German air force.[180] This reflected not only a tendency to rely overmuch on preconceptions, but also a failure to appreciate and prioritize intelligence information that would form a basis for informed decision making. The underappreciation of intelligence also meant chronic staff shortages and underfunding in that realm. All this resulted in unhelpful fluctuations in Air Ministry attitudes and actions in the years leading up to war: after putting forward conservative estimates of the German Luftwaffe growth early on, Air Ministry officials became alarmed and remained so through the end of the Munich crisis in 1938. Lacking adequate information on the purpose of the Luftwaffe—information that would have included technical intelligence like aircraft performance characteristics and data on bombs and bombsights—British air planners assumed that its role would not be very much different from the role they envisioned for the RAF. Thus, as the Luftwaffe expanded, the Air Ministry ultimately relied on worst case scenarios that envisioned a massive German air strike aimed at producing a quick surrender, mainly by breaking civilian morale. As historian Wesley Wark has pointed out, "the public's apocalyptic vision was matched by a professional air staff nightmare about a future war."[181]

In late 1933 the government set up the Defence Requirements Committee (DRC) to sort out priorities and to remedy the "worst deficiencies" in Britain's defenses.[182] It suggested modernizing Britain's aging battle fleet; preparing an expeditionary force equal to that of 1914; and completing an updated version of the RAF's 1923 expansion scheme.

The decision to upgrade all three services reflected concern over the Japanese threat to British interests in the Far East, apparent since 1931.[183] The report was referred to the Ministerial Committee on Disarmament—dominated by Chancellor of the Exchequer Neville Chamberlain—which upended some of its premises. Concerned about the cost of rearmament, and not convinced that the public would support a large buildup in the Far East or an expansion of the army, Chamberlain opted for an aerial deterrent. He believed that Germany was the foremost threat, persuading himself that Japan would not attack Britain unless Britain were involved in hostilities with Germany, so a deterrent to Germany would deter Japan as well. Accordingly, he proposed cutting the DRC allocations to the army and navy, while increasing the allocation to the RAF to allow for eighty squadrons rather than the original fifty-two.[184]

In the early deliberations on the German threat and the British reaction, the Air Ministry had moved carefully and produced conservative estimates, believing that Hitler would develop strength rationally, and in depth (rather than in the "shop window"). This assessment reflected the Air Ministry's own concern for efficiency, as well as assumptions about the German national character. In a failure to understand the political dynamics inside Germany at the time, Air Staff members assumed that the Germans would follow a deliberate, measured rearmament pattern designed to create an effective military force with adequate spares and reserves. The Foreign Office, which was more alarmed by the situation, did not concur with the Air Staff's approach. Having failed to bring about disarmament, they sought to create a strong but nonprovocative deterrent. Foreign Office leaders—particularly Sir Robert Vansittart—criticized what they perceived to be the inwardly focused attitude of CAS Sir Edward Ellington and his deputy Sir Edgar Ludlow-Hewitt. But Ellington and Ludlow-Hewitt wanted to avoid being pressured into creating an air force of readily available but probably inadequate types, backed by insufficient reserves.[185] Reflecting back on this tension many years later, Sir John Slessor would admit that the Air Staff should have used Vansittart and others as allies to push the government toward a swifter, more energetic rearmament policy. The RAF, he opined, "lagged behind the political pressure that was only too anxious to back us."[186]

In House of Commons debates in late 1934, Winston Churchill thrust himself into the forefront of the issue: he challenged the government by demanding that it confirm or deny his own estimate that the Germans were already approaching parity and by 1937 would have three times the strength of the RAF.[187] The debate reached a head in March 1935 when Hitler announced—to senior diplomats who had gone to Germany to try to reopen the possibility of disarmament—that the Luftwaffe already had achieved parity with the RAF and would seek parity with the Red Air Force. Confusion dominated the scene; as Wesley Wark has pointed out, "There were inconsistencies in the record of what Hitler had said, doubts about the standard of British strength . . . and little clarity about what was actually meant when Hitler boasted of air parity."[188] Further exacerbating the situation was volatile British public opinion, which vacillated between alarm and pacifism. Nonetheless, when the tempest was over both the government and the Air Ministry chose not to take Hitler's parity claim literally.

But the episode had heightened tensions and exacerbated the concern of the Foreign Office. Mussolini's invasion of Abyssinia hardly created a hopeful mood; in general, militarism was casting an increasingly ominous shadow over global affairs—European affairs in particular. Though the Air Ministry did not wish to create a hollow force, the external criticism could not fail to have some impact. In addition, the Air Staff began to concern itself increasingly with overall German industrial potential, and its ramifications for German air power. When expansion Scheme F was accepted in early 1936, its goal was to see the completion of a 1,500 aircraft frontline force by April 1937, and the completion of a 1,736 aircraft frontline force by 1939. It represented a compromise between RAF priorities, growing alarm, and the continued desire to deter without undue provocation; but this collection of aims insured that none of them could be achieved particularly well.[189] The RAF won its case on two points, making full provision for reserves and creating new bomber types: light bombers were to be replaced by medium bombers and heavy mediums. This trend favoring heavier, longer-range aircraft—a first step in closing the gap between RAF declaratory policy and capabilities—would lead eventually to the Short Stirling, the Handley Page Halifax, and ultimately the Avro Lancaster, Britain's most effective World War II bomber.

By this time the dynamic and energetic Sir Philip Cunliffe-Lister (later Viscount Swinton) had become Secretary of State for Air, lobbying hard for reserves and industrial mobilization.[190] Organizational changes were underway as well. What had been the Directorate of Supply and Research (of the Air Ministry) was divided into separate research and development and supply organizations. During the spring and summer of 1936 the RAF command structure was also reorganized around four distinct divisions: Bomber Command, Fighter Command, Coastal Command, and Training Command—all responsible to the Air Council through the Chief of the Air Staff.[191] While this reorganization was viewed as an improvement, it had some inherent problems as well. Separating fighter and bomber functions reduced the incentive for the two divisions to work together, engage in joint tactical planning, or share advances and breakthroughs. The latter was particularly troublesome, as research done for Fighter Command progressively revealed defensive techniques that would increase the vulnerability of bombers.[192]

Throughout 1936 the Air Ministry was made well aware of the continuing anxiety felt by the various agencies and individuals trying to assess the Luftwaffe. In a meeting between the prime minister and representatives from both Houses of Parliament, Sir Austen Chamberlain and Lord Salisbury confessed to being "profoundly disquieted . . . at the contrast between the high degree of preparation which appears to have taken place abroad among those who might be our adversaries and the want of promptness with which we originally responded to that challenge." Churchill, also present at the meeting, took the opportunity to raise a multitude of pointed questions about Air Ministry assumptions and procedures.[193] More importantly, new and apparently reliable sources of intelligence painted an increasingly worrisome picture of Luftwaffe strength. By the autumn, the Air Ministry had changed its tune and was now adopting a very pessimistic view of the situation. While preserving the assumption that the main purpose of the German air force would be to wage long-range bombing attacks against an enemy, air planners abandoned the idea that German rearmament would be constrained by the pace and the demands of efficiency. The Air Intelligence Directorate was now inclined to accept information from every available source, including some of dubious reliability. This alarmist phase in air policy circles persisted through the Munich crisis, and would abate only in 1939 when more sober appreciations—of German weaknesses and limitations as well as strengths—would be put forward.[194]

In October 1936 the Joint Planning Committee (JPC), which performed detailed planning for the Chiefs of Staff Committee, assessed Britain's options in a war with Germany in 1939. A worst case scenario, their paper incorporated the pessimistic tone that had begun to characterize British military rhetoric. Indeed, its authors meant it to be a polemic designed to light a fire under government spending and formal war preparations.[195] A preface to the JPC paper was heavily influenced by the Air Ministry representative, Group Captain Arthur Harris. This took the view that the most immediate menace to Britain would arise if Germany were to use the Luftwaffe for unrestricted air attacks on the nation. Appendix II of the report, which tried to provide some idea of what such an attack might look like, pointed out that the Germans might wage intensive air strikes against Britain to persuade the population that "surrender was preferable to the continuation of the attacks."[196]

The planners—influenced by Harris—believed that this might be mitigated by air defensive measures, but nonetheless admitted that they had been "unable . . . to discover any method of direct defence sufficiently effective to guarantee the security of objectives in this country," and thus believed that "the only real answer lies in a counter-offensive of at least similar effectiveness."[197] But they could not identify any German target so valuable as London, nor any highly vulnerable economic target; they selected the "bases, communications, and maintenance organisation of the German bomber force" as the initial targeting priority. Though this course was seen to have serious disadvantages, they could envision no other short-term answer. They postulated however that in a later phase of the war the RAF would prosecute a broad bomber offensive designed to strike at the "sources of Germany's belligerent power as a whole" (which Harris would later interpret as Germany's great industrial cities). If a counteroffensive on land remained necessary, the RAF would be called upon to help prepare for it. These tasks would require a large, heavy bomber force able to deliver a great weight of attack on to the enemy.[198]

The plan failed to call for the initial, overwhelming offensive that Trenchard had envisioned, and it gave initial priority instead to counterforce targeting of aircraft on the ground—a strategy that Trenchard had largely eschewed. But Trenchard, who had never faced a serious aerial enemy after World War I, had been content to make vast claims that did not have to be backed up by deeds. Operating in a very different environment, Harris and the air planners of 1936 were forced to start closing the gap between rhetoric and reality; they had to think concretely about scenarios based on resources available in the near term.[199] The plan—which envisioned the ultimate use of a heavy bomber force with which to prosecute a vital counteroffensive—proved a prescient guide to RAF strategy in World War II. It also, however, revealed the extent to which RAF planners "mirror imaged" assumptions about Luftwaffe behavior in wartime. And, as Wesley Wark has explained, "Nothing distilled from the sources that became available during 1937 challenged the Air Ministry's preconceptions about the Luftwaffe's strategic air mission. The picture indicated instead that the German air force would have both an army-support and a strategic bombing role. On this basis, a German knock-out blow could not be dismissed."[200] In the midst of all this, the Air Ministry had to decide how to assess and utilize information arriving from real air wars overseas.

THE AIR WARS OF THE 1930s

Though the progress in air warfare during the Abyssinian crisis, the Sino-Japanese war, and the Spanish civil war was attended to by Air Staff members, it did not substantially change their attitudes. The war in Spain, which in particular might have been seen as a testing ground for air warfare ideas, did not appear to British planners to offer many clues to a future war between Germany and Britain. The relatively low level of resources involved and the paucity of industrial targets, they argued, made its utility for comparison limited at best. Prevailing images and assumptions were preserved since, at the end of the day, one could claim that air power had been mishandled, or that the war entailed unique circumstances that would not pertain to a future war involving large industrial nations, or to Britain in particular. Through selective interpretation of the available data, British air planners were able to avoid a reinterpretation of their existing hypotheses. In a similar vein, professional military journals in Britain did not give the Spanish war the kind of attention it might have merited.[201]

Some of the most dramatic information from Spain had to do with low-flying attacks on infantry. But even as they reported on this information, Air Ministry officials insured that it would not greatly alter their views. On 21 September 1937, Wing Commander R. V. Goddard, the Chairman of the Joint Intelligence Sub-Committee on Spain, reported that aerial attack had a great effect on ground troops. In a passage that foreshadowed later events in France, Goddard stressed the "terrifying roar of diving and zooming aircraft close overhead." Nonetheless, he insisted that such attacks cause high aircraft losses, and he reminded his readers that "these attacks have been carried out against troops whose standard of training and morale is lower than that of regular trained troops against whom the effect of such attacks would probably be less great."[202] In the same month, the Deputy Director of Operations (DDOps) sent a minute to the Deputy Chief of Air Staff (DCAS) arguing against drawing the RAF into close support duties, which he viewed as "uneconomical." He insisted that, in accordance with the War Manual, the RAF had not contemplated (in a war in the European theater) "any organized close support by aircraft at all" as "no units are really trained in such work." He said that the RAF should contemplate close support work only "to turn defeat into a rout, or to prevent defeat of our own Forces becoming a rout."[203]

Writing in December 1937, the Deputy Director of Plans (DD Plans) argued, "I think we may be getting exaggerated ideas from the results of low-flying attack in Spain and China; we must remember that in those campaigns it has mainly been directed against semi-organised and semi-disciplined troops who have neither the cohesion nor the morale to stand up to it, nor the firepower nor fire-discipline necessary to reply to it effectively." He pointed out that in the last war, the British had found such attacks useful, "in an emergency," but that they had been expensive in casualties. While suggesting that such conclusions ought to be subject to modification based on new information and experience, he argued that nonetheless he was "very doubtful" whether there was sufficient evidence from Spain and China to justify such modification.[204]

In February of 1938 Goddard had an opportunity to go on a fact-finding mission to Spain (as a result of a personal invitation from the War Minister of the Republican forces). Though he admitted that it was not always possible to get all the information he wanted, he reported back in some detail on aerial bombardment.[205] First, he explained that even though many Spaniards believed that bombardment by insurgent forces had been directed toward demoralizing the population (an idea that was taken up by the international press as well), he had concluded that nearly all of Franco's bombing "had been directed towards military and important material objectives."[206] He believed that the indigenous perception resulted from the frequent inaccuracy of the air raids, and he felt that the Italians had been more responsible than the Germans for inaccurate bombing.[207] He reported as well that attacks against power stations had been neither "sustained" nor "daringly executed." And he asserted generally that "Franco's Air Forces have had no sustained bombing policy."[208]

In reporting on attacks against "the habitations of industrial and dock workers," Goddard pointed out that in many cases such attacks had resulted in evacuations, and surmised that this must have led to a very great moral effect. At the same time, though, he explained that in the factories themselves output had not declined. He pointed out that repeated attacks on the vital Sagunto works "have apparently not appreciably reduced the output of steel"; and that despite being put out of their homes and suffering 150 deaths (among 3,000 workers), the workers had displayed "amazingly high spirit," and only two had deserted. But, he wrote (in what can only be seen as a strained attempt to explain this outcome), "[I]t must be hard for people of a gay temperament to take a morbid view of things in the halcyon sunshine which seems to prevail nine days out of ten in Spain. The shattered steel works at Sagunto would have seemed very depressing in the wet and gloom of Sheffield, but in Spain it was not so."[209] (Later that year the British Consul at Valencia would write up a report for the Foreign Office specifically on the moral effect of bombing. After explaining the difficulties in getting reliable information, the Consul reported that the indirect results of the bombing had been negligible. But he implied—in a way that downplayed the impact of his news—that this was due to the fact that the bombing was inaccurate and sporadic, and that, on the whole, the war revealed an "excellent example of how not to utilise a complete mastery of the air." He argued that half a dozen planes could, if employed intelligently, keep the port cities in an almost constant state of alarm.)[210]

Goddard argued that in zones outside the battle area "aircraft have not fully exploited their advantages," and that the air effort had been "dissipated over a wide range of objectives instead of concentrated time and time again on certain important objectives to ensure their destruction or the demoralization of local personnel."[211] This enabled him to draw two general conclusions. First, "The well-known principles governing the employment of men and machines in war both on a large scale and in minor tactics, appear to require no modification in the light of experience gained in Spain." And second, "The nature of this civil war and the limitations in material and command cannot, it seems, be expected to produce military information which is wholly capable of direct application to our own problems."[212] A Joint Intelligence Sub-Committee Report of 10 June 1939 likewise accepted that, with respect to the attack on industry, there was very little analogy between the wars in Spain and China and any future war between Great Powers in Europe.[213]

This tendency to eschew parallels was evident as well in British thinking about fighter escorts. Many British observers of air operations in Spain contended that escorts had to fly only short distances, and that therefore the "lessons" of Spain did not apply.[214] From his own observations, Goddard reported, "The escort of bomber formations proceeding to and from their objective by double, or more than double, their number of fighters, has been found by both sides to be a necessity notwithstanding the ability of the bomber to shoot down fighters."[215] (Interestingly, his observations on escort fighters were reprinted and distributed within the Air Ministry when the question resurfaced in the spring and summer of 1939.)[216] But even though he had sounded a tocsin, Goddard soothed his readers by pointing out that bombers could defend themselves with speed, and forward and rear gun defenses; he added that "bomber crews were confident in their ability to bring down fighters, and many successes by bombers were claimed."[217]

Prior to Goddard's visit to Spain, the DDOps (Richard Peirse) had sent a memorandum to the DCAS indicating that escort operations in Spain ought to be observed, as the war provided "the only examples of modern air forces in actual conflict with each other since 1918." He was interested in German tactics for using fighters as escorts or "as a sort of advanced guard for the bombers." Nonetheless, he remained skeptical, stating, "While . . . I still feel it would be a confession of weakness and a waste of effort on our part even to contemplate the use of fighters in this way, I cannot help feeling that we ought to be prepared for such an eventuality."[218] He asked that the Bombing and Fighting Committees look into the question, and that a specification be drawn up for an escort fighter. But he admitted, "I confess I am not at all clear in my own mind as to the type of fighter that should be provided."[219] Commenting on the minute sheet a week later (30 November 1936), the Director of Staff Duties (Sholto Douglas) wrote, "My own feeling in the matter is that the bombers should be able to look after themselves without the addition of an escort of fighters; although certain of the bombers might be more heavily armed than the remainder at the expense of their bomb load."[220] In his response, the DCAS listed a set of concerns about escorts that was fairly representative of RAF thinking: specialized escorts would demand resources that might otherwise be put into bombers; they would have to be tied to their formation; and they could not necessarily be better armed than the aircraft they were escorting. He concluded that though he did not wish to constrain free discussion of the question, he felt that "the whole conception of fighter escorts is essentially defective."[221]

In June 1937 the Air Fighting Committee of the Air Ministry found itself stymied over the question of escorts. After listening to detailed arguments first in favor of and then against the development of escort fighters, they decided it was not the right time for special requirements to be drawn up.[222] Instead, they recommended exploring the possibility of fitting certain bombers with more (and larger) guns, more ammunition, and better protective armament.[223] In the late summer of 1938, Ludlow-Hewitt, then Chief of Bomber Command, suggested very serious reconsideration of the Air Staff's policy on escorts. Confessing to his own past pessimism over escorts, and confusion over what an adequate type might look like, he was nonetheless concerned enough to advocate some action. He envisioned, ultimately, a bomber force working out of France, aided by heavily armed escorts.[224] At an April 1939 meeting on Bomber Command readiness, the Director of Operational Requirements reported that further discussion on the issue had yielded the opinion that the defense of bombers could be better undertaken "by bomber aircraft carrying fewer bombs, but more ammunition and guns."[225]

As war approached, Air Staff members realized that they had not made sufficient progress on this "hardy annual"—the question of escort fighters, and the protection of bombers in general. Though increased urgency characterized their discussions, they were unable to determine how an escort could be made fast enough, maneuverable enough, and sufficiently long-ranged to be feasible for deep penetrations into enemy air space. What they envisioned, in the end, was more an escort bomber than an escort fighter.[226] In general, in the years leading to war many unresolved questions remained about how the RAF ought to proceed, and how it ought to think about the Luftwaffe. Air planners were handicapped by their late start on many of these issues, and simply by their inability to come to a consensus on how to predict the increasingly complex and uncertain future of aerial warfare. They also did not help themselves with their selective reading of the evidence available to them, which tended to interpret new information in such a way as to preserve and indeed reinforce prevailing conceptions.

REARMAMENT: THE EVE OF WAR

As the RAF cast about for ways to conceptualize and prepare for the future, a number of important changes took place that would influence the early stages of the coming war. In May of 1937, Neville Chamberlain replaced Stanley Baldwin as Prime Minister; Sir John Simon became Chancellor of the Exchequer, and Anthony Eden took over at the Foreign Office. Largely due to the experience of World War I, Chamberlain was distrustful of the military; he understood the horrors of the Great War and the profound desire of the British people to avoid a repetition of the disaster.[227] He had gone through his political development at a time of austerity in Britain and was convinced, as were many of his contemporaries, that sound finances were absolutely essential to security. While Chamberlain had earlier (as Chancellor of the Exchequer) increased the RAF's portion of the budget relative to the other services, he was gravely concerned with the overall economics of British defenses; he feared handing Hitler a bloodless victory by undertaking a large-scale armaments construction program that the nation could not afford.[228]

In June 1937 all three services were asked to articulate their needs in order to ascertain the cost of the necessary programs. The army and navy took the opportunity to argue for large increases in their estimates. The air force proposed that the bomber force be rearmed with heavy bombers that could operate entirely from British bases, and continued to demand full accommodation for reserves (for bombers and fighters). RAF requests called for increases of 40 percent in bomber strength and 25 percent in fighter strength over the existing program (Scheme F). However, it would be no small task to produce the airplanes, the engines to power them, and the crews to fly and maintain them. In addition, runways and airdromes would have to be reworked in order to accommodate the heavier planes, and no one was certain that some sort of catapult system might not be necessary to get the planes off the ground.[229] In putting forward the new program, Lord Swinton found himself telling the cabinet that it was very unlikely the goals of the plan could be met before the summer of 1941 at the earliest.[230]

As it turned out, the new plan (Scheme J) was met by a challenge from Sir Thomas Inskip, a civilian appointed Minister for the Coordination of Defence in March 1936 and who was charged with the thankless task of trying to coordinate and prioritize the views of the different services—a role performed unofficially by the Treasury in the late 1920s and early 1930s. In an aide-mémoire of 9 December 1937, Inskip argued that German aircraft could be better destroyed over Britain by fighters than by an attack on German factories and airdromes.[231] At the most basic level, fighters would be cheaper and easier to construct. The fighter force, he argued, should be made as strong as possible and given full reserves. Inskip's own view of future strategy was in line with the methods Britain had traditionally used over the centuries: relying on sea power and superior economic resources to repulse any initial assaults, and then engaging the enemy in a war of economic attrition.[232] While his actions were motivated mainly by a concern for economy, their immediate consequences confronted some of the premises of Air Staff planning.

Despite hostility from the Air Ministry and protest from the Foreign Office, Inskip managed to win his case in the cabinet, which on 22 December 1937 accepted his program. He declined to put the Air Staff program forward, and placed a spending limit of £110 million over Scheme F.[233] The new Scheme K retained fighter numbers with full reserves, but cut bomber squadrons and reserves. The Inskip program was, in actuality, less radical than some authors have argued. While Inskip did change the ratio between bombers and fighters, he did not change the number of fighters ordered for Britain—this number had already been agreed to by the Air Ministry. And his program retained nearly the same *front line* strength in bombers, as well as a plan for rearming the air force at some future point with new heavy bombers. After further deliberation, in which the Air Ministry warned against cutting reserves for heavy bombers, monies were shifted out of the training establishment and the construction of permanent buildings, and into reserves.[234]

Still, the near-term deemphasis of bombers worried the Air Ministry; its members did not take kindly to being second-guessed on issues of such fundamental importance. Thus, part of their reaction to Inskip was dismissive and defensive in nature—indeed, one officer complained that Inskip's plan was the equivalent of putting all of one's players in goal.[235] Sir Cyril Newall, who had become CAS in September 1937, believed that Inskip was driven only by economics, and not by the necessities of strategy. And he believed that, in any event, it was not Inskip's place to tell the services how to spend their money. The Air Staff suspected, as well, that the navy might be influencing him.[236] But the Inskip report had found the RAF in a moment of pessimism and low confidence. The JPC report of 1936 had acted as a catalyst for more detailed planning within the services, and the RAF duly followed through on its part. The results that followed were wholly discouraging. As the official historians of the World War II bombing campaign acknowledged, "It was soon revealed that there was no clear idea as to what was operationally possible, what targets could be reached, how far they could be hit, what would happen to them if they were hit, or what were likely to be the casualties incurred."[237]

Air planners believed, of course, that a determined air offensive had to be part and parcel of any victory plan for a future war: this idea had been the centerpiece of their identity, so its disruption, even temporarily, was disturbing and disorienting. But, with their counteroffensive capabilities so uncertain, they were hardly in a strong position to parry successfully Inskip's thrust—at least at the moment. The Air Ministry's layered reaction to Inskip was later summed up best, perhaps, by Sir John Slessor's internally inconsistent reflection: "To multiply fighters is the usual refuge of the ignorant about air power, but in this case it was undoubtedly justified."[238] Air Staff members, however, could take solace in reminding themselves that the situation was only temporary, and that they still would be able, eventually, to wage a war more or less as they had envisioned. Relying on the sound work that had been done on air defense through the interwar years, they focused their near-term energies on resisting a German attack. But all along they intended to preserve their commitment to the offensive, and reemphasize it at the earliest possible moment.

Still, building the basis of an offensive force would be no mean feat: the problems facing Bomber Command were manifold—and daunting. When Sir Edgar Ludlow-Hewitt had assumed leadership of Bomber Command in the autumn of 1937, he had taken an inspection tour to assess the state of the organization. In reporting the results to the Air Staff on 10 November, he was frank. He told them he had expected some confusion due to the rate of expansion, but found the current situation with respect to war preparedness "most disquieting." He announced to his colleagues that Bomber Command was "entirely unprepared for war, unable to operate except in fair weather, and extremely vulnerable both in the air and on the ground."[239] His unvarnished revelations made him an uncomfortable figure among his colleagues, many of whom preferred to try to convince themselves that things were not so bad.[240] Ironically, the man who had once warned against "calculations" was now having to make very many of them. To his credit, he set about the task with great energy and determination.

Problems of reconnaissance, target acquisition, intelligence, tactics, and navigation had received inadequate attention through the early and mid-1930s. There were no specialized reconnaissance units, and there was no organization for the interpretation of photographs; indeed, the need for damage assessment was hardly considered at all.[241] Navigation was done largely by dead reckoning with occasional visual checks, but the lack of career opportunities for navigators meant that few men were attracted to it. In the two years before the outbreak of war, there were no less than 478 forced landings due to pilots losing their way.[242] A similar state of affairs existed with respect to the operational details of bombing. There had been, for instance, no consensus on how bombers ought to proceed to their targets while minimizing the risk of fighter interception.[243] In 1938 a Bombing Policy Sub-Committee (of the Bombing Committee) was formed to consider the tactical details of different methods of bombing, and to determine the most suitable types of aircraft and apparatus for these.[244] At its first meeting, on 22 March 1938, the Sub-Committee recommended the investigation of methods for improving high-level bombing accuracy. The members argued that inadequate attention had been given to bombing problems, and that there was a "crying need for a *Bombing Development Establishment* [original emphasis], which could concentrate on the necessary experiments." It was pointed out that a similar proposal had been made at the 2nd, 3rd, and 10th meetings of the Bombing Committee, "but nothing had eventuated."[245] Such an establishment was brought into being only after the Munich crisis. Until then, many of the most urgent questions surrounding bombing policy remained unsolved.[246] Regarding bombs themselves, there had been actual retrogression. The need for heavier bombs, which was seen in World War I and was reemphasized by Trenchard in 1923, was apparently forgotten; in 1935, the Air Staff rejected a proposal (from the Commander-in-Chief, ADGB) that the standard 500-pound bomb be replaced by those of 1,000 and 2,000 pounds.[247]

The RAF was, in the late 1930s, an organization facing the fact that it could not carry out its own declaratory policy. But the situation was brighter with respect to defense. Despite its overwhelming declaratory commitment to the aerial offensive, the RAF had never ceased thinking about fighters and methods of home defense generally. This hedging of bets would pay off in crucial ways. By the late 1920s, the funds available to the Air Ministry for research were devoted largely to scientific and technical experiments examining possibilities for defense.[248] General E. B. Ashmore, who had directed British air defense in World War I, argued after the war for the development of an information network to enable the communication of data to facilitate interception of incoming aircraft. The resulting system made use of ground observers and dedicated phone lines to support fighters and anti-aircraft artillery. Progress was made in radio telephony that would allow for a greatly improved communications system for defenders. Other important developments took place in intelligence, and in fighter defense organization. During his tenure as Chief of Air Staff (May 1933–August 1937), Sir Edward Ellington oversaw the drawing up of specifications that led to the Hawker Hurricane and the Supermarine Spitfire. When experiments in methods of aircraft detection began to reveal the first glimpses of what would later become radar, these could be readily and successfully positioned into a preexisting framework.[249]

If the Germans can lay claim to key innovations (in terms of technical change) regarding radar, the British employed their systems more effectively and efficiently.[250] In Britain, concern about the improving capabilities of bombers, especially following the 1934 exercises, prompted investigations into improved aircraft detection techniques.[251] H. E. Wimperis, Director of Scientific Research in the Air Ministry, proposed that a scientific committee to survey air defense be formed under Henry Tizard, Chairman of the Aeronautical Research Committee; it met for the first time in January 1935.[252] Tizard consulted with R. A. Watson-Watt, Superintendent of the Radio Department of the National Physics Laboratory, who, in February, wrote a paper proving the feasibility of radar; in March members of the committee saw a demonstration of the principle.[253] Between 1936 and 1940 the existing defensive net was enhanced by the Chain Home and Chain Home Low (for low-flying aircraft) radar systems. The centralization of the Command enabled information to be disseminated quickly.[254]

In March 1938 the Deputy Director of Plans (Slessor) requested from the Air Staff an overview of the effectiveness of fighter defenses; he needed the information for meetings of the Joint Planning Committee. He sought answers to questions about such things as the likelihood of bomber interception, the value of defensive armament for bombers, and the margin of speed between fighters and bombers. In his covering note to the Assistant Chief of the Air Staff, he admitted that, on many issues involving the tactical performance of new fighters and bombers, there was a dearth of useful information. And he pointed out that while he believed the value of the fighter was declining due to increased bomber speeds and blind flying methods, his general view of their value was, he thought, more generous than that of the Air Staff.[255] In answering the query, Air Staff respondents conjectured that some 60 percent of day raids and 40 percent of night raids could be intercepted (though the figure might fall to 20 percent and 10 percent respectively in heavy cloud). Actual shoot-down rates would depend on such things as the tactical formations utilized by the bombers, but the chances of a fighter taking a bomber out of action were thought to have increased in general. These good rates were attributed to such things as increased fighter climb speeds, better communications and observer corps organization, balloon barrages, and more accurate anti-aircraft fire. Counteracting this trend, however, were cloud flying techniques and the greater speed and operating heights of modern bombers.[256]

Significantly, an attached document called "The Composition and Strength of the Royal Air Force—Air Staff Policy" sought to address the perception that recent increases in the strength of the RAF had "lead to some erroneous deductions that a change of policy is thereby implied in the direction of a defensive strategy at the expense of our capacity for counter-offensive action." The authors asserted that "no such change is implied by the measures recently announced or is in any way contemplated." They pointed out that increases in the numbers of fighters were tied to the development of the German bomber force, but insisted that British strategy had not changed, arguing that "[i]t is not enough to avoid losing a war . . . A boxer cannot win a fight if he does no more than parry his opponent's blows—he must have an equivalent punch, he must be able to deliver it at the right time and place; and he must be able to keep on punching until his opponent is out." Though willing to admit that there "had been a tendency in the past to over-state the case that 'the bomber will always get through,'" the authors nonetheless staunchly upheld the importance of the counteroffensive.[257] In November 1938 the Air Staff circulated a memorandum stating that the counteroffensive had not been abandoned or replaced by a defensive orientation.[258]

But there was a fundamental tension at work that the RAF never fully countenanced. If air defense methods were improving, then very likely they were improving in Germany as well. And if this were so, might it not call into question the entire basis of a strategy that ultimately rested on an aerial offensive? In analyzing this problem long after the fact, R. J. Overy succinctly summed up the dilemma facing the Air Staff: "To admit that there was a defence against the bomber was to question the whole basis upon which an independent air force had been built."[259] To have posed such a question would have been profoundly stressful for the organization, already in crisis. Though planning was put on a much more solid and serious footing than ever before, planners tried nonetheless to hold on to as many of their foundational ideas as they could. The tendency of the organization was to preserve its fundamental assumptions whenever possible, and to modify them only when there was little other option but to do so. This precluded a full examination of the tension inherent in simultaneously believing that one could fend off a Luftwaffe attack and also prosecute a successful offensive against Germany.

While a determined faith enabled air planners to find hope on the horizon, it did not help them to solve their near-term problems. Chamberlain did not set before the House of Commons all the implications of the Inskip program, but that body already was exercised about RAF inadequacies and a possible German "bolt from the blue." Churchill, still playing a leading role in the drama, called for an inquiry into the workings of the Air Ministry. Though the issue was debated, the potential crisis never came to a head because the resignation of Lord Swinton in May 1938 was enough to placate the critics, at least for the time being.[260] By then, however, the perception of British vulnerability played a part in the conclusion drawn by the Chiefs of Staff that very little could be done to help Czechoslovakia, the object of Hitler's latest territorial demands.[261]

Wesley Wark has argued that three factors dominated the air intelligence picture at the time of the Munich crisis: lack of technical insight into the Luftwaffe's real capabilities; an assumption that the Luftwaffe was developed for a strategic air offensive; and a two-year history of increasingly pessimistic readings of the air power balance. All of this added up to a reliance on worst case scenarios. And these could not fail to contribute to the deep sense of alarm and pessimism felt by policymakers responsible for coping with Hitler. Although the Air Staff did not assume that the Germans were in fact looking to launch a bolt from the blue at that moment, air-intelligence estimates of that worst case were dire: fifty thousand casualties in a twenty-four hour period. Because senior military advisors to the government did not analyze the bolt from the blue scenario, the issue was left "to the imagination of the ministers."[262] With images of a "knock-out blow" casting a shadow over his thinking, Chamberlain opted to settle with Hitler at Munich rather than risk war at that point. Britain was "outdeterred by Germany."[263]

In many ways, the RAF's aggressive declaratory policy had come home to roost. If it had helped preserve RAF autonomy, it had also troubled and confused the other services, and frightened the public, the politicians, and the diplomats. As a deterrent in a time of peace, it probably had much to recommend it. But, because the words had not been backed up by actual capabilities, or even very much systematic thought about how to achieve them, it proved terribly stressful in a time of sudden, serious threat. The 15 September 1938 issue of the *Times* (London) referred to the "intolerable sense of impotence and tension" felt throughout the nation. Reflecting back on the period before and during the Munich crisis, Sir John Slessor described the "gnawing dread of national shame and disaster that curdles the tummy and wakes one up at three in the morning to lie tossing and wondering what can be done and what will happen if nothing is."[264]

In London, workmen toiled through the nights to dig sheltering trenches in the city's many parks, to distribute sandbags, and to dim the city's traffic lights. Air Raid Precautions (ARP) personnel tested sirens, distributed posters, made public announcements at sporting events, and prepared instructional films for the cinemas. Gas mask distribution centers stayed open twelve hours a day, and "laggards" who had not yet picked up their masks were implored to do so via loudspeakers mounted on roving trucks. Airplanes circled overhead, trailing streamers asking volunteers to join the auxiliary fire service. Hospitals prepared to discharge stable patients to make room for emergency cases; their staffs inventoried equipment and stocked up on surgical supplies. The Church of St. Martin-in-the-Fields held day and night prayers for peace. Factories and shops made emergency accommodation for their employees and patrons: one shop readied "brandy for the nervous, chocolate for the hungry, and games for the restless." The London Zoo made plans to destroy its poisonous snakes and spiders, and to shoot any large animals that might escape their cages due to bombing.[265]

The crisis over Czechoslovakia removed whatever patience or tolerance remained in Britain for Hitler's revision of the World War I settlement. Up to that point, more than a few Britons had felt, as Slessor later explained, "that this fellow Hitler had a case," that the Germans could not "permanently be held in a position of inferiority vis à vis the French."[266] Indeed, Churchill was in a unique position: opposed to *both* the appeasers and the pro-German right wing.[267] But Munich had finally begun to reveal the Führer's true face, and this brought with it the dawning realization that war, even if averted for the time being, was unlikely to be averted for long. The gap between claims and capabilities would now have to be closed for good. In the breathless months leading up to war, the Air Staff would concern itself with a great many questions pertaining to British and German capabilities regarding strategic bombardment. In addition, Air Staff members would concentrate on drawing up plans for war based on the resources available to Britain in the near term. This crucial process will be examined in the early pages of chapter 4.

CHAPTER THREE

The United States in the Interwar Years

THIS chapter traces the intellectual progress of American airmen during the interwar years. It examines how theories about long-range bombing developed, gained influence, and established themselves in the organizational mind of what ultimately became the United States Army Air Corps (and later Army Air Forces). It points out parallels and contrasts between the American experience and the British experience. Though there are clear and important similarities in the way ideas evolved in the two nations, there are also some notable differences. The Americans, like the British, would rest their ideas about long-range bombing on assumptions about the complexity and vulnerability of modern industrial societies, but they would take a particular interest in what they believed to be the inherent weaknesses of interdependent, interlocking national economic systems.

In comparing the British and American interwar experiences, several issues must be acknowledged from the start. First, American interwar air doctrine was not formulated by an independent service. While the Royal Air Force came into existence as a separate organization in 1918, American airmen required nearly thirty more years to achieve such standing. The U.S. Army was not willing to condone any statement that implied a revolutionary role for long-range bombers based on their ability to impose, independently, a shattering blow on the enemy. In an attempt to make itself very clear on the subject in 1934, the War Plans Division of the War Department argued, "The effectiveness of aviation to break the will of a well-organized nation is claimed by some; but this has never been demonstrated and is not accepted by members of the armed services of our nation."[1] The latter clause was untrue: members of the U.S. Air Corps were among the "some" making strong claims for aviation. Indeed, a 1928 document from the Office of the Chief of the Air Corps had argued, "It is not hard to visualize a situation in which the destructive power of the air force will be adequate to subdue the enemy's will and in which both the Army and Navy would operate in support."[2] Throughout the interwar years a debate raged inside the U.S. military—sometimes quietly and sometimes openly—about the degree to which an air force could and should act independently in war. A desire for greater autonomy naturally inclined the airmen to focus their attention on strategic bombing—a role that promised them greater independence, responsibility, and prestige. Their subordinate status caused them to behave differently from the British, but the differences were, ultimately, more in the realm of official action than in the realm of ideas. RAF leaders defended themselves and Air Corps leaders sought to assert themselves by using similar claims about the possibilities for independent air operations. In both cases, the circumstances caused them to become heavily invested in those claims.

Second, the United States and Britain faced distinctly different geopolitical situations; these, necessarily, produced different interwar perspectives on aerial bombing among their leadership and within their general populations. If the First World War had been a grievous and disillusioning experience for the Americans, it had not scarred them with the shock and trauma that had defined the British experience of war. With the English Channel no longer serving as the useful moat it had been for centuries, the British felt their new vulnerability acutely. Though the postwar dismantling of the German air force had provided an important measure of security for them, the British had to pay close attention to all aerial developments on the continent, and had to assume that if another general war came, it would involve air attacks on London and other British cities. The Americans, isolated from potential enemies by two oceans—and, after the war, more determined than ever to stay that way—felt they could afford to be more complacent about developments in aviation. Their perspective on bomber aircraft and the future of air warfare was more distanced—and far less visceral—than the British perspective.[3] Like their British colleagues, American airmen believed that bombers were inherently "offensive" tools of war. But the official American national security posture circumscribed the way in which this could be interpreted and articulated. This posture was defensive in orientation, and bomber aircraft were given a defensive mission: to find and attack naval threats to the U.S. coastline. Until the eve of war, American airmen had to use conditional language and hypothetical scenarios whenever they discussed theories of air warfare involving strategic bombing.

Differences in geography and politics produced a corollary for theories of aerial bombing. The greater immediacy of the air threat to Britain—and the heightened sensitivity to class issues prevailing there—inclined the British to focus somewhat more than the Americans on the specifically social ramifications of aerial bombing. This was a difference in degree, but it nonetheless mattered since it shaped fundamental conceptions. If Trenchard concerned himself mainly with the upheaval, disruption, and dislocation caused by bombers getting into the general vicinity of a target, the Americans tended to keep their focus more on the nature of the damage that might be directly imposed on a given target. The destruction of the target itself—and the resulting impact on the enemy's economic structure—mattered primarily.

Third, because the Americans had no direct experience of strategic bombing in World War I, they had no record to explain or protect in the interwar years. As we saw in chapter one, much of what the Americans learned about "strategical" bombing in World War I came from observing the experience of their allies, and from the bombing survey that they undertook independently at the end of the war. While they were strongly influenced by the British experience, American airmen developed an approach to air warfare and strategic bombing that reflected their own circumstances and predispositions. For example, the Americans never distanced themselves so much as the British did from the assumption that the first objective in war would have to be the enemy air force. When they imagined air warfare, Americans generally envisioned large-scale counterforce operations through bomber attacks against the enemy air force on the ground (airfields, hangars), and through air-to-air combat waged by armed bombers flying in defensive formation.

Like the British, the Americans felt that victory in war came to the side able to undermine most effectively its enemy's will to war. The Americans did not privilege the elusive "moral effect" of bombing in the same way that Trenchard did, and therefore it did not come to have the high-profile rhetorical role that it had in the RAF. The Americans believed, however, that bombing did produce a "moral effect." But though they discussed it throughout the interwar years, they never fully specified what it meant or how it might be quantified. How did it interact with and overlap the material effect of bombing? How, exactly, might it bear on war? These questions never were adequately answered, and the Americans would never come to a consensus on the meaning, significance, and operational definition of the moral effect. In addition, uncertainty and vagueness surrounded the American conceptualization of what constituted enemy morale, and what might be the most effective and efficient means of undermining it. Failure to specify and reach consensus in this regard also complicated American debates over the legal and ethical aspects of long-range bombing. These problems, and the confusion and uncertainty that they engendered, were reflected in inconsistent and even contradictory writing on the subject.

The Americans, however, felt they had a clearer idea of how to achieve "material effect," even though they never closed with how, exactly, this might translate into victory in war. From the moment that Edgar S. Gorrell first borrowed the ideas articulated in Tiverton's September 1917 paper, American airmen embraced the assumptions underlying the selective targeting of key elements in an enemy's industrial economy. The American critique of British World War I bombing, influenced by the London Air Staff, chided Trenchard for not following through on a systematic program based on analysis. The Americans, impressed by the potential frailties and weaknesses in the interlocking structure of a modern industrial economy, postulated that careful analysis could guide planning in crucial ways and produce effective results. They came to believe that their own long-range bombers would be able to undermine efficiently the integrity of an enemy's war economy by attacking specific targets crucial to the functioning of that economy. This conviction gained momentum through the years as Air Corps planners dedicated themselves increasingly to understanding and preparing for air operations independent of the army and its ground combat function, and as they invested themselves in the concept of "precision bombing." Indeed, this line of thought eventually would take on a life of its own as the "industrial fabric" (or "industrial web") theory of bombing, articulated and promoted most aggressively by the Air Corps Tactical School of the 1930s. But though the Americans would embrace the "industrial fabric" theory, they would fail to back it up with the intelligence apparatus necessary to turn it into a coherent and sophisticated foundation for an operational plan. And they would fail to understand fully the conditions and requirements necessary to enable it to succeed.

Thus, even if American airmen were free of the burdens of defending a wartime record, they were not immune from problematical assumptions, faulty analyses, oversights, and a tendency to make bold, unsubstantiated claims. The latter in particular stemmed from a desire to win greater freedom from the institutional confines of the army. But many of the problems they faced stemmed from the way in which they perceived their world and, in turn, how they interpreted new information based on those perceptions. These inevitably influenced their decisions and their behavior, with important ramifications during the Second World War.

IDEAS AND INSTITUTIONAL CONSTRAINTS:
THE EARLY INTERWAR YEARS

The early postwar writing of American airmen reflected the organizational constraints they operated under; but it revealed, as well, the lure of wider horizons. While commanding the Air Service First Army, Gen. Billy Mitchell had drawn up a set of guidelines for his observation, day bombardment, and pursuit (fighter) units. Initially published in a series of operations bulletins, these were later incorporated, with some revisions, into the "Provisional Manual of Operations," which appeared officially in December 1918. Even though Mitchell's units had not undertaken long-range bombing, many of his ideas were relevant to the formation of American thought on independent air operations. He emphasized for instance that bombers must fly in defensive formation, with up to eighteen aircraft per group.[4]

Maj. William C. Sherman, who had been Chief of Staff of the First Army Air Service, added to the Air Service's early body of thought by preparing an extensive "Tentative Manual for the Employment of Air Service" in early 1919. Hewing to army orthodoxy, Sherman reminded his readers that "the final decision in war must be made by man on the ground, willing to come hand to hand with the enemy. . . . It is, therefore, the role of the Air Service, as well as that of the other arms, to aid the chief combatant: the infantry.[5] But Sherman also revealed enthusiasm for what he perceived to be the vast possibilities of air operations, arguing that the commanding position of an airplane, which renders concealment useless, "induces the instinctive belief in the heart of every man on the ground that he himself is being watched by hostile eyes and being made the target for bomb or bullet; and that this hostile man can pursue him intelligently and ultimately destroy him." He explained, "To this is added a feeling of utter helplessness, not justified by facts but none the less instinctive and not to be overcome wholly by reason or training."[6] In a passage that reflected the early appeal of "bottleneck" theories and also foreshadowed a theme Sherman would develop more fully later, he compared the morale of an army to the human body, arguing that in order to destroy it, it is necessary only "to destroy one of several of its component parts."[7] In June 1920, portions of Sherman's Tentative Manual were published in the *Air Service Information Circular*; the opening section on day bombardment repeated Trenchard's "twenty to one" rule, albeit without attribution.[8]

Like Sherman, the majority of officers accepted the organizational situation and identified army aviation as a supporting arm for infantry operations. In the early 1920s, official army publications on the role of the Air Service emphasized its position as an auxiliary service, and focused on support missions including observation and defensive pursuit. Without experience in independent operations, the Americans had little leverage in arguing for a separate identity and organization. The Army Reorganization Act of June 1920 made the Air Service a part of the combat line of the army; no changes were made in its relations with the General Staff.[9] And another constraint operated: Secretary of War Newton Baker had objected fundamentally to strategic bombing. In a section of his 1919 annual report, Baker made his thoughts clear. Addressing himself to the question of whether the United States required a separate service for the air, his answer was a resounding "no." To him, air forces were utilized best when supporting troops in the field, particularly through observation. He argued that by far the most effective use of air power in the war had been for observation.[10]

With respect to long-range bombing, Baker first noted the wartime proliferation of anti-aircraft defenses, and he observed that "the actual loss of life caused by these bombardments was relatively small and the destruction of property, while large, had no appreciable effect upon the war-making power of either nation." More importantly, he felt that bombing enemy industry and cities had violated the Hague principle that bombardment be restricted to "fortified places." Aside from the ongoing legal debate over that phrase, he had no doubt that strategic bombing fell outside of the bounds within which civilized states should conduct warfare. Though cognizant of the appeal of air power and its compelling hold on the public imagination, Baker nonetheless refused to sanction the "inevitability" of long-range air campaigns for the future; indeed, he suggested ruling out strategic bombing on the most "elemental ethical and humanitarian grounds." And he argued that advocates of strategic bombing created their own paradox: "[I]t is most likely that history will record these manifestations of inhumanity as the most powerful aids to [military] recruitment in the nations against which they were made."[11]

Partly because of Baker's strong views, the Air Service was compelled to develop a dual personality: externally (and in official documents) it followed the army line, while internally it developed and nurtured a more congenial, independent ideology. As time went on, the latter philosophy became increasingly dominant among the restless American airmen. This trend toward independent thinking was greatly facilitated by the establishment of a school system. In October 1919 the Director of Air Service sought permission to establish an "Army Air Service School of Application" at Langley Field, Virginia, to "develop and standardize the instruction and training of officers in the tactics and techniques of the Air Service."[12] In July 1920 Maj. Thomas DeWitt Milling (assisted by Sherman) oversaw the organization of the Air Service Field Officers' School (renamed the Air Service Tactical School in 1922 and then the Air Corps Tactical School [ACTS] in 1926). The curriculum included pursuit, observation, bombardment, and attack aviation; combined air tactics; aeronautical engineering; navigation and meteorology; and armament.[13] Course texts consisted of an ad hoc and occasionally inconsistent collection of items. In its fledgling years the school did not in general stray too far from the prescribed line of policy handed down from the General Staff, but faculty sometimes dwelt at length on theories of independent air operations.

The 1922 "Air Tactics" text, written by Milling, paid lip service to the official constraints while it offered insights into broader thinking among airmen. It revealed both the influence of the British as well as American points of divergence from British theory. Moving beyond army conceptualizations, Milling divided the work of the Air Service into the "Air Service," which consisted of observation in cooperation with the infantry, and the "Air Force," made up of the offensive elements of pursuit, attack, and bombardment aviation. He argued unequivocally that pursuit was the "backbone of the Air Forces": the means by which it undertakes its "first duty" to gain and hold control of the air.[14] Indeed, in the years right after the war, the Americans devoted considerable attention to the development of pursuit (fighter) tactics and aircraft for specialized missions.[15] Milling pointed out that day bombardment had increasingly fallen victim to hostile pursuit, and that even night pursuit was beginning to make strong progress by the end of the war. The response, he explained, had been the tactic of formation flying for mutual defense. In addition, the Americans utilized escort fighters that were not tied to the formation but instead sought out enemy fighters and attacked them as they came up to engage.[16]

Milling's conceptualization of aerial bombing revealed some British influences, but also the building momentum of indigenous views. His text's "Bombardment Aviation" section stated that the twenty to one rule (which he attributed to Trenchard) "is undoubtedly a fair approximation"—although he did not explain it. He argued that bombing, once it had attained "efficiency," would then produce an effect "so marked that violent enemy reactions were naturally called forth." Inevitably, populated areas of strategic or political importance would demand elaborate anti-aircraft defenses. He further asserted "the concussion of masses of high explosive is a thing under which human nerves simply cannot stand up."[17] Likewise, in 1923 the commander of the U.S. 1st Pursuit Group, Maj. Carl A. Spaatz, observed, "The first bomb dropped by an enemy on one of our cities will cause such a clamor for protection that no executive would be strong enough to withstand it."[18]

But Milling's work contained ambivalence (and perhaps confusion) about Trenchardian dictums. On the one hand, he acknowledged the Trenchardian notion of pushing the enemy population on to the defensive, and the indirect effects of bombs (on industrial workers); on the other, hand he cautioned, "A strong government will recognize that the enemy's armed forces are the true objective, and will not permit popular clamor to weaken materially the forces at the front." Milling identified headquarters, munitions depots, and railways as key bombardment objectives. He also reasoned that, though the threat of the hostile air force would be countered chiefly in the air, enemy airdromes must also be placed on any target list. Echoing the American bombing survey, he insisted that aerial bombing should not be haphazard, but must instead "have a definite objective in some war industry."[19] Similarly, the 1924 Air Service Tactical School's "Bombardment" text noted that during World War I, bombing squadrons had "operated in a more or less haphazard fashion, their efficiency varying with the initiative of the commanders and the resistance they happened to encounter."[20] Nonetheless, its authors went on to say that "[d]espite the fact that it was hampered in its early development by a confused idea of its mission and an utter lack of comprehension of its potentiality, bombardment . . . proved itself to be a powerful combatant arm."[21] The text strongly recommended that targets be selected carefully.

By 1925 American airmen were beginning to move steadily toward a more independent line than the one authorized by the army, and they were doing so self-consciously. This was reflected in a 1925 memo from the Office of the Chief of the Air Service to Maj. Carl Spaatz (later the commanding general of the U.S. Strategic Air Forces in Europe in World War II). Sent shortly after Spaatz graduated from the Air Service Tactical School (and titled "Suggestions for improvement of The Air Service Tactical School"), it posed the question: "Is the independent mission of the air force sufficiently stressed or is the entire course based on the thought that the sole mission of the Air Service is to assist the advance of the Ground Force?"[22]

The status of the Air Service was one of the most continuously debated topics in Washington in the 1920s. It was addressed repeatedly by an array of boards and commissions, most of them populated by distinguished individuals opposed to change.[23] The Air Service's weak institutional standing caused airmen to look outward, to Congress and to the public, for support. Congress was not without its self-proclaimed aerial visionaries: between 1913 and 1920 it had put forward eight bills proposing an independent air force. In 1919 both Sen. Harry New of Indiana and Rep. Charles Curry of California called for a separate Department of Aeronautics. Neither these nor a subsequent bill by New made any real progress: the War Department was unsympathetic and the Naval lobby used its considerable power to preserve the status quo. Those in the highest leadership positions in the Air Service, including Chief of Air Service Gen. Charles Menoher, had achieved their status in part by accepting army constraints; they were not inclined to make a play for early independence. Naturally, this circumscribed the activities of more junior officers who took a different view of things.[24]

Most Air Service officers perceived that the forces arrayed against them were too great to be overcome immediately. Alternatively, they worked to bring about change incrementally.[25] But one prominent officer was entirely unprepared to move at a slow pace: Gen. William ("Billy") Mitchell single-handedly campaigned for Air Service independence. Disdainfully referring to the Army General Staff as the "long-bowmen," he challenged the auxiliary status of the Air Service, running a "bone-crushing interference" for the rest of the organization. Ultimately his tactics left a mixed legacy, but his flamboyant performances brought the debate over air power to the center of the national stage.[26]

Outspoken, impetuous, and stubborn, Mitchell rejected gradual change and compromise. Trenchard had noted, presciently, that Mitchell would go far "if he [could] only break his habit of trying to convert opponents by killing them."[27] Believing that military changes come only after disaster in war or through public pressure, he assaulted the public with speeches, articles, books, and endless appearances before congressional committees. To challenge the dominance and self-perceived omnipotence of the navy, he staged a much-publicized series of air attacks on unmanned, stationary battleships in the summer of 1921. Mitchell believed that the navy's role as national "first line of defense" was soon to be wholly eroded by bomber aircraft. Only by possessing its own independently directed bomber fleet would the United States be able to remain safe at home and project its interests abroad.

Mitchell advocated positions well beyond what the army was prepared to sanction. He insisted on a new paradigm for warfare based on the independent operations of aircraft. The forward to his 1921 book, *Our Air Force*, was a sustained plea for a Department of Aeronautics. His 1925 volume, *Winged Defense*, was in fact a manifesto for winged offense. His last book, *Skyways*, argued that defeating an industrialized enemy would mean controlling its vital centers, which consist of "cities where the people live, areas where their food and supplies are produced and the transport lines that carry these supplies from place to place."[28] An unabashed advocate, he asserted that any future war would commence with air battles: "[T]he nation winning them is practically certain to win the whole war, because the victorious air service will be able to operate and increase without hindrance."[29] Like the Italian general Giulio Douhet, Mitchell emphasized the importance of winning and maintaining control of the air. Defying Newton Baker, he argued that in total war an enemy nation's entire population—women and children included—would be subject to bombardment as contributors to the enemy war economy.[30] But—again like Douhet and many other interwar air "prophets"—he argued that air power, by making wars shorter, would offer a way around the stalemate and slaughter seen in the Great War. Further, he believed that the very prospect of large-scale bombardment would serve as a deterrent to war.

Echoing Trenchard, Mitchell stressed the indirect impact of bombs upon the morale of a nation during World War I: "When industrial districts were attacked," he wrote, "the workers were made so nervous that whenever the buzz of an airplane was heard it made them stop work . . . while at night the constant fear of the bombardment attacks prevented sleep."[31] He also was attuned to the possible use of chemical weapons over urban areas.[32] But while he was confident in the psychological effect of aircraft on fragile civilian will, he did not make clear precisely how to break that will, or how doing so would translate into peace.[33] Indeed, Mitchell never articulated a coherent body of doctrine that devolved from consistent theories or logical postulates. Rather, he was an energetic publicist who elevated his conception of omnipotent air power above the heads of his colleagues, and directly to the masses. He had such faith in his convictions and found them so instinctively correct that he was confident the public, once roused to awareness, would rally to his cause.

But this did not happen. Though intrigued by Mitchell's antics and exploits, the American public did not feel any corresponding urgency to demand a Department of Aeronautics over Army and Navy resistance. Indeed, following World War I many Americans felt a general revulsion to war (and preparation for war); this was accompanied by support for isolationism, later manifested in the Neutrality Acts of the 1930s, and vigorous investigation, under North Dakota Republican Sen. Gerald Nye, of "Merchants of Death" (an alleged collusion of bankers and munitions manufacturers). Nonetheless, Mitchell persisted. He was perceived as a gadfly by army leaders, and as "General of the Hot Air Force" by navy leaders.[34]

Another round of congressional interest in aviation matters (1923–25) elicited further aggressive testimony from Mitchell, capped by a series of articles for the *Saturday Evening Post*. In the latter he argued that a powerful air force could make war a briefer, more humane, and cheaper affair by obliterating an enemy's industrial centers.[35] His examples presumed that all industrial states were essentially alike. As one scholar later explained, "he bestowed on the governments under attack a degree of rationality that ignored the war aims of the enemy and the possibility that the population would willingly suffer to avoid capitulation."[36]

In 1925 the army, finally fed up with Mitchell's maverick behavior, demoted him to colonel and assigned him to an obscure post in Texas. But this only pushed him to a more radical stand. He used the loss in a storm of the navy dirigible *Shenandoah* as a pretext for issuing a highly inflammatory statement to the press, indicting the War and Navy Departments on charges of "incompetency, criminal negligence, and almost treasonable administration of the national defense."[37] The army promptly ordered Mitchell to Washington to stand before a court martial. On 28 October he was charged with conduct prejudicial to military discipline and of a nature to bring discredit upon the military service; in December he was found guilty and suspended from duty for five years. He resigned from the Army in early 1926, but continued to be a champion of air power and something of a celebrity in public circles.

Despite Mitchell's strident campaign, the eventual fate of the Air Service was largely determined within various governmental bureaucracies. The House Committee on Military Affairs formulated its own "Air Corps Bill," which the Senate then amended heavily. Their compromise became law on 2 July 1926.[38] The Air Service was redesignated the Air Corps: an air section for each division of the General Staff was established, and a new Assistant Secretary of War was named for aeronautics. The bill also authorized a program for expanding and equipping the Air Corps over five years. But representation on the General Staff lacked real influence, meaningful reforms were not carried out (to the satisfaction of the airmen), and funds for a five-year expansion program were not always authorized in full amounts.[39] The Air Corps remained very much a part of the army.

PROGRESS AND PROBLEMS FOR THE AIR CORPS

When the Air Service became the Air Corps in 1926, the renamed Air Corps Tactical School (ACTS) continued to train officers in the mission of the new service. Neither Congress nor Mitchell had settled any of the major debates on the future of air power. But most airmen were content simply to look to the future, a sentiment reflected in the ACTS motto adopted in 1929: "*Proficimus More Irretenti*" (We progress unhindered by tradition).[40] They forged identity and unity through their shared sense of mission, their readiness to accept the dangers of early flying, and their defiance of army ways. Youthful and daring, they took pride in the fact that they stood largely outside the West Point fraternity.[41]

Army Training Regulation 440–15, "Fundamental Principles of Employment of the Air Service" (26 January 1926), was conservative in tone, assigning airmen a supporting role in a future war: "to aid the ground forces to gain decisive success."[42] The 1926 version of the "Bombardment" text used at the Air Corps Tactical School revealed many of the tensions and unresolved disputes of the day. In it, a conservative conception of air power competed, sometimes uneasily, with a more independent, "air-minded" line of thought.[43] Its authors pointed out that bombardment "will have an important bearing on the outcome of the war, but it must not take precedence over the support of ground operations by proper tactical employment."[44] They argued that, at war's onset, "strategical" bombardment might be used to retard the enemy's concentration of troops, hamper the manufacturing of war matériel, and weaken the morale of enemy civilians by attacks on population centers. But they lacked clarity regarding the latter. Concerned that attacks on "political centers" might be prohibited by the laws of warfare, they rationalized that since these were the "nerve centers of the nation," they would be "important targets for bombardment in reprisal for attacks made by the enemy on such centers in our own country." Nonetheless, the authors questioned the potency of such reprisal raids (including those waged against London and Paris in World War I): "Whether such bombing actually accomplishes its avowed purpose—to weaken the morale of the hostile nation and thus hasten the end of hostilities—is doubtful in some cases. The reactions may be in exactly the opposite direction."[45]

In the same year that this text appeared, however, the Air Corps produced a less conservative one for a course called "Employment of Combined Air Force." It signalled the increasingly confident posture of the Air Corps; it especially emphasized the concept of enemy will, arguing that the aim in war is to destroy the enemy's will to fight—a goal not necessarily accomplished by a direct attack on his armed forces. Instead, this objective might be achieved by attacking, via air power, vital points in the enemy interior.[46] This language, now common among air theorists, was reinforced by trends in Britain, in particular by the 1925 publication of B. H. Liddell Hart's *Paris, or the Future of War*. Endorsing the book during a speech to the Army War College, Gen. Mason Patrick (the new, less conservative Chief of the Air Service) asserted that in the future the objective in war should be to crush the enemy's will to fight rather than to concentrate on his armed forces.[47] In calling attention to the text, Patrick was bound to give it a wide audience among American airmen. Maj. Gen. James E. Fechet, who became Chief of the Air Corps in November 1927, likewise promoted a more independent line of thinking. Proposing revisions in the existing ACTS texts, he wrote, "The objective of war is to overcome the enemy's will to resist, and the defeat of his army, his fleet, or the occupation of his territory is merely a means to this end and none of them is the true objective." He added, "At present the Air Force provides the only means for such an accomplishment."[48]

Clearly the Americans were in the throes of working out just how to think about the future of bombing, and how to articulate it. Though organizational policies and authorities had sought to limit the debates, a growing iconoclasm inclined instead toward the forward-looking visions of those who had perceived an aerial shortcut to the accomplishment of a Clausewitzian dictum: to end a war one must destroy the enemy's will to fight. Americans drew on their limited World War I experience and British rhetoric to underpin their evolving concepts. But while they embraced the idea that the real objective in war is to overcome the enemy's will, they wrestled unsuccessfully with it. Phrases like "national will" and "moral effect" (and their connection to victory) remained elusive and underspecified. Americans did somewhat better when they focused on particulars. They found instinctive appeal in the idea that strategic bombardment must be governed by a well-thought-out program based on a thorough evaluation of the enemy's war economy.

These evolving themes were evident in the mature work of William C. Sherman, who had gone from the Air Service Tactical School to instructor in air tactics at the army's Command and General Staff School at Fort Leavenworth, Kansas. His 1926 book, *Air Warfare*, revealed much about the corpus of thought extant among the Air Corps's most active theorists. His opening section, "Some principles of Air Warfare," reflected Clausewitz specifically: "War is essentially a conflict of moral forces. A decision is reached not by the actual physical destruction of an armed force, but by the destruction of its belief in ultimate victory and its will to win."[49] On World War I bombing, Sherman argued, "The Germans believed that the clamor of civilians for protection would find a ready echo among the governing politicians who would force the military authorities to protect their city. The event seems fully to have justified their belief."[50]

From these premises he moved toward an explanation of the future of the bomber, pronouncing enthusiastically, "The bomber now stands forth as the supreme air arm of destruction. . . . When nations of today look with apprehension on the air policy of a neighbor, it is the bomber they dread."[51] While Sherman recognized the bomber's potential against civilian populations, he guardedly cautioned that any decision to bomb cities had to be political and not strictly military. In addition, he believed that the trend toward bombing civilian populations might be mitigated by the practical fear of reprisals. Influenced perhaps by his experience as a member of the U.S. team sent to participate in the drafting of the 1922–23 Hague Air Rules, Sherman believed that the direction in international law was toward proscribing deliberate air attacks on civilian populations. Though he understood all the difficulties (including the persistent problem of defining "military targets"), he nonetheless argued, "Among peoples in whom the spirit of sport has been strongly inculcated, it is peculiarly abhorrent to contemplate the waging of war on unarmed civilians of all ages and sexes."[52]

Building on a traditional interpretation of the importance of interdiction in war, Sherman asserted that "the military objective of bombardment aviation, par excellence, is the hostile system of supply." Therefore, "The long-range of the bomber should be utilized to the full, and every sensitive point and nerve center of the [supply] system put under pressure, in an effort to paralyze the whole." Rejecting haphazard or dispersed attacks, he added, "Not a mission should be executed which does not fit in with a well defined strategic plan."[53] In language similar to that used by Tiverton and the London Air Staff during World War I, Sherman cogently articulated a set of ideas that would shortly thereafter take on a central doctrinal role at ACTS as the "industrial fabric" or "key-node" theory of targeting:

> Industry consists . . . of a complex system of interlocking factories, each of which makes only its allotted part of the whole. . . . Accordingly, in the majority of industries, it is necessary to destroy certain elements of the industry only, in order to cripple the whole. These elements may be called the key plants. These will be carefully determined, usually before the outbreak of war. . . . On the declaration of war, these key plants should be made the objective of a systematic bombardment, both by day and by night, until their destruction has been assured, or at least until they have been sufficiently crippled.[54]

Sherman took the lead in outlining what would come to be embraced by Americans as the "American" view of air warfare. It was not uniquely American, since its provenance could be traced back to Gorrell's 1917 appropriation of Tiverton's ideas. But it had become an important refrain for Americans, and one that they seemed to adopt instinctively. Sherman had now articulated it clearly and fully in a book-length treatise on aircraft in war. His low-key style and his untimely death prevented him from receiving full recognition for his ideas, and from becoming a leading name in the history of U.S. Air Force thought.

By the end of the decade, American airmen were increasingly lured by the promise of the bomber and its cardinal role in the offensive theory of air warfare, and they were increasingly willing to run the risk of chafing their parent service. In 1928 the Air Corps Tactical School committed to paper a statement on "The Doctrine of the Air Force." It went beyond what the War Department would have been prepared to endorse. Even so, the Office of the Chief of the Air Corps argued that it was too guarded and subordinate in tone.[55]

As advocates of independent air power found their stride, they increasingly began to brush aside the candid observations about bomber vulnerability that had appeared in American writing just after World War I. And this tendency was furthered by a growing consensus that increasingly shut out dissenting voices. Subsequent trends in annual maneuvers, which had begun in 1925, portended a decline in the prominence once accorded the pursuit plane in the United States.

Air exercises annually brought units of the Corps areas together to train and test equipment, tactics, and logistics. The maneuvers of May 1929, held in Ohio, were more sophisticated than in previous years. Results were determined by rules established by the umpires. As in Britain, these gave the advantage to attackers: for instance, bombers would be declared to have succeeded in their mission unless they were intercepted by pursuit aircraft (fighters) possessing two to one superiority.[56] As chief umpire for the 1929 maneuvers, Maj. Walter H. Frank (the serving commandant of ACTS) reported that pursuit aircraft found it difficult to locate and intercept bombers. He argued, "There is considerable doubt among the umpires as to the ability of any air organization to stop a well-organized, well-flown air force attack."[57] Back at ACTS, Lt. Kenneth Walker, a Billy Mitchell protégé and instructor of bombardment aviation from 1929–34, sanctified this idea in a pithy dictum: "A well-organized, well-planned and well-flown air force attack will constitute an offensive that cannot be stopped."[58] Walker's statement, much cited in subsequent years, succinctly captured an idea that would reach full flower at ACTS in the 1930s.

In the meantime, aviation had been advancing, paced by technology and human fascination with flight. Interwar air races and flying competitions captured the public's attention and imagination, and helped spur developments in airframe construction and engine design. Long-distance flying established the airplane as a vehicle for transport and travel. As early as 1919, a crew led by noted Australian aviator Capt. Ross Smith had flown a Vickers Vimy to victory in the first England to Australia race. In 1927, Charles Lindbergh flew his small plane, alone and nonstop, from New York to Paris. The following year, Capt. Charles Kingsford Smith crossed the Pacific. In 1931, Wiley Post and Harold Gatty circumnavigated the world in the *Winnie May*, and the following year Amelia Earhart became the first woman to fly the Atlantic alone. New records were also set by those seeking to take both balloons and aircraft higher than they had ever been taken before.[59] While these breakthroughs did not revolutionize attitudes toward military aviation, they did help to maintain an increasing background pressure for service autonomy by affirming the abilities and versatility of aircraft.

Slow progress toward autonomy in the 1920s had conditioned most American airmen to accept that a General Headquarters Air Force (GHQ), a centrally controlled aerial strike force, would be the best organizational arrangement that they could achieve in the short run. Mobilization plans of the 1920s had assigned attack, pursuit, and observation aircraft to armies, and observation units to army corps, for the support of ground troops. The plans also called for a GHQ Air Force of 2,300 aircraft under an air officer who would report directly to the commander in chief in the field. As one historian explained, this GHQ existed only as "a vague 'something' that would come into being when the army took the field for defense of the United States."[60]

High-ranking officers in other branches of the army had also been growing gradually more aware of the combat potential of aircraft. They understood that the Air Corps desired greater freedom, but they were also concerned about their own service priorities and budgets. They were inclined to believe that the Air Corps might be appeased by a GHQ Air Force arrangement. Thus, the early 1930s saw progress toward the centralization of combat aircraft in an increasingly formalized GHQ. By 1932 the War Plans Division of the General Staff viewed the GHQ Air Force (Provisional) as incorporating all bombardment, attack, and pursuit aviation, as well as some observation. Soon after, the War Department approved and formed the GHQ Air Force (Provisional) for maneuvers in May 1933, establishing a GHQ office in Washington in October. Finally, a permanent GHQ Air Force was approved in March 1935.[61]

A number of developments contributed to this outcome. The first centered on a January 1931 agreement between Army Chief of Staff Douglas MacArthur and Chief of Naval Operations William V. Pratt, which sought to settle the hotly contested question of how to define and delineate the functional responsibilities of the army and navy regarding coastal defense and seaborne operations. The MacArthur-Pratt agreement established that naval aircraft would be based on the fleet and would accompany it, while the army's aircraft would be "land-based and employed as an element of the army in carrying out its missions of defending the coasts, both in the homeland and in overseas possessions." It allowed that the air force of each service would be "free to develop within well-defined limits and each with a separate and distinct mission."[62] The agreement, which was vague and which the army and navy tended to interpret in different ways, came after years of haggling between the services over respective responsibilities for defending the nation's coastlines. Many members of the navy were unhappy with the agreement and continued to protest the Air Corps' right to operate distant, over-water patrols. (Indeed, the navy ultimately rescinded the agreement unilaterally.) Still, the agreement became the thin edge of a wedge for the Air Corps in its quest for expanded responsibility and matériel. In his January 1933 policy letter, "Employment of Army Aviation in Coast Defense," MacArthur divided the nation into four coastal frontiers, in each a field army was commanded by the senior corps area commander. He directed the Air Corps to "conduct the land-based air operations in defense of the United States and its overseas possessions."[63]

The plan gave the GHQ Air Force wartime control over bombardment, pursuit, and attack aircraft, as well as observation for long-range reconnaissance. The latter function required special equipment suited to long-range reconnaissance over land and water. The Air Corps could also agitate for a GHQ Air Force to exist in peacetime and for a GHQ Headquarters to be established in Washington. The General Staff demurred, anxious that a permanent GHQ Air Force would cause airmen to slight their support duties. Nonetheless, the Air Corps won War Department approval to form a GHQ Air Force (Provisional) for maneuvers in May 1933.[64]

The coastal defense and long-range reconnaissance mission provided the Air Corps with a doctrinal rationale—accepted by the army's ground combat arms—to develop long-range reconnaissance aircraft. This new responsibility ultimately resulted in the production of larger planes, including bomber prototypes. The Air Corps's preoccupation with long-range aircraft had more to do with strategic bombing than reconnaissance, but that sentiment could not be fully articulated as long as U.S. military policy remained defensive in nature. Coastal defense operations were integrated into Air Corps training. Australian navigator Harold Gatty, who had flown the world in Wiley Post's airplane *Winnie Mae*, was hired to instruct. In October 1933 the Air Corps formed units at Langley Field, Virginia, and Rockwell, California, for navigation and instrument flying. In addition, Chief of the Air Corps Gen. Benjamin Foulois set up a school at Bolling Field to develop coast defense navigation and plotting equipment. But the Depression years put a strain on Air Corps resources for coastal defense missions.[65] National belt-tightening meant fewer flying hours as well as frequent furloughs, pay cuts for both officers and enlisted men (in 1933 a $21-a-month private saw his salary cut to $17.85), and limits and delays for new aircraft. Even the *Air Corps Newsletter* suspended publication from October 1933 to January 1935.[66]

Over the summer of 1933, General Foulois was asked to recommend the employment of GHQ air power in the national war plans ("Rainbow" plans).[67] Trouble in Cuba and the prospect of U.S. military action there highlighted the need for efficient air planning and mobilization. In August the Secretary of War appointed a committee, headed by Deputy Chief of Staff Maj. Gen. Hugh Drum, to review the Air Corps plan. The final report of the committee, approved in October, recommended the establishment of a permanent GHQ Air Force.[68] Between the time that the Drum recommendations were issued and the permanent force finally was established in 1935, however, the air mail "fiasco" of 1934 focused attention on the need for increased funding and improved organization for military aviation.

Concerned about fraud and collusion among those airlines holding government contracts to fly the mail, the Roosevelt administration asked the Air Corps to step in. General Foulois agreed to make the necessary preparations in only ten days for a job that was to begin in mid-February.[69] The episode highlighted the disparities between commercial and military aviation. The former possessed better and more sophisticated equipment and better-trained pilots who were more familiar with instruments and radios.[70] Indeed, fatal Air Corps crashes halted the operation shortly after it began. When additional safety measures fell short, the Roosevelt administration reevaluated its options. Newspaper outrage over the situation heightened animosities. The government began to reassign contracts to commercial airlines, and by June 1934 the Air Corps was out of the mail business.[71]

The Air Corps mail debacle was dissected by a committee headed by former Secretary of War Newton Baker. The Baker Board recommended a more comprehensive and sophisticated training program for pilots, better instruments and communications, and strengthening of the national meteorological infrastructure. Air Corps leadership blamed its woes on insufficient funding and support. General Foulois, arguing that the Baker Board recommendations comprised the first "comprehensive outline of War Department policy" relative to the Air Corps, asserted that the loss of life had finally "forced" the president and congress to free up funds for the Air Corps.[72] Without doubt the Air Corps, like the RAF, had been stressed by the constraints of financial stringency. But again like the RAF, it had fallen victim to a certain amount of internal complacency about the operational details of its mission, allowing itself to be outpaced by the achievements of nonmilitary aviation.

Once the airmail fiasco had ended, however, the Air Corps quickly sought to regain its equilibrium. Speaking at the Indiana Department of the American Legion in early May 1935, Chief of the GHQ Air Force Gen. Frank M. Andrews described the probable wartime mission of his force, emphasizing that the "most important operation for the United States Army Air Forces is to defeat the enemy aviation." Noting that the initial phases would be characterized by a struggle between opposing air forces, Andrews explained that the GHQ would then undertake "independent air operations," attacking enemy aviation and aviation bases, naval forces, choke points (including railway lines, highway bridges, canal locks), troop concentrations, and war industry.[73] Andrews' words reflected the expanding ambitions and aspirations of his service. With burgeoning responsibility for American national security policy, airmen knew that they also would have increased opportunity. By 1935, Congress expanded Air Corps appropriations—and the trend continued, spurred on by the growing threat of Hitler's Germany and of wars in China, Ethiopia, and Spain. Air Corps expenditures nearly tripled in five years, ballooning from $30 million in 1935 to over $83 million in 1939.[74]

In addition, the Air Corps won a powerful ally in President Roosevelt, who, despite his naval background, viewed military aviation as increasingly central to the national defense.

The ominous tones emanating from Europe had been heard across the Atlantic, not only by politicians but by military planners who would be responsible for protecting American interests and, indeed, waging war if it became unavoidable. The 15 May 1935 issue of the *Air Corps Newletter* reprinted an editorial from the 12 April issue of the *Manchester Guardian*, under the title, "Widespread Air Bombardment Contemplated by European Powers," which asserted that "[a]ir power will strike at the very outset of a future campaign," and explained that "since in a war of 'areas' and not of 'fronts' the advantage is throughout with the attacking air force, no large success by the defense can be expected."[75] Increasing awareness of the probable role of bombardment in a future war, concern about events abroad, and the growing technological sophistication of bombers all spurred ACTS to focus even greater attention on strategic bombardment.

The difference between the MB-2 bomber of the 1920s and the Martin B-10 of the early 1930s was striking: the service ceiling was raised from 7,700 to 24,400 feet, the normal bomb load from 1,040 to 2,260 pounds, and the top speed from 98 mph to 213 mph. Indeed, the B-10 marked a new generation of machines: it proved that greater size did not necessarily mean slower speeds (instead, aerodynamic efficiency could be increased with size). But the B-10's range did not extend beyond that required for support missions. With the long-range reconnaissance mission in its pocket, however, the Air Corps had the opportunity to change its future, and to move closer to becoming the radically new tool of war that so many of its members hoped it might be. The real breakthrough in this realm—pregnant with policy implications—was the development of a plane with much greater range than the B-10.[76]

In response to a 1933 design proposal circulated by the Air Corps, the Boeing Company put forward a four-engine bomber of radical design. In 1935 tests, the prototype YB-17, which had a top speed of 250 mph, made a record-breaking flight from Seattle to Dayton. It could carry a load of 2,500 pounds for 2,260 miles at cruising speed. The Air Corps was, unsurprisingly, very enthusiastic about the new plane; it recommended the purchase of sixty-five of them for delivery in 1936. Formal testing and acquisition was held up when the prototype crashed in October 1935 (due to human error rather than mechanical failure).[77] In August 1937 the Air Corps finally was in possession of its first thirteen B-17 bombers. Training and maneuvers soon confirmed its advantages for sea-search and bombing operations. Using the newly developed Norden bombsight, B-17 pilots were able to score hits (with water-filled bombs) against battleships. Col. Hugh Knerr, Chief of Staff of the GHQ, exclaimed that his headquarters believed that the B-17 was the "best bombardment aircraft in existence."[78] The American official historians of the World War II bombing campaign summed up this momentum perceptively: "The Air Corps after 1935 was characterized not so much by its concern to change the basic organization of national defense as by a purpose to find in the mission assigned to the GHQ Air Force the basis for an ambitious program of bomber development. The Army airman thereafter was, above all else, an advocate of the big bomber, and around the potentialities of that type of plane he built his most cherished hopes."[79]

ENTHUSIASTS, ADVOCATES, ARMS CONTROLLERS, AND DEBUNKERS: THE PUBLIC DEBATE IN THE UNITED STATES

As in Britain, American interwar conceptions of future aerial conflict were influenced by general assumptions and concerns about the impact of modernity and urbanization, and the intricate, interlocking nature of modern economies and societies. These issues remained less immediate for Americans than for Britons, but common assumptions, ideas, and fears helped to establish a shared foundation. And, as in Britain, the military debate over the future of air warfare could hardly occur in isolation from the public debate.

Belief in the exploitable vulnerabilities of urban areas was not restricted to Europe. By the last decades of the nineteenth century, Americans had largely lost confidence in the notion that their individual communities could continue to be autonomous and self-sufficient. The old order was increasingly being supplanted by governmental bureaucracies, centralized authority, and the regulative hierarchies of urban-industrial life. Cities were, for many, "monolithic in their strangeness, centers of alien ways and murky power," displacing old notions of self-sufficiency by a new dependence on centralized bureaucracies. This change was exacerbated by the inflow of immigrants (nearly nine million between 1900 and 1910), and by labor unrest that was frequently interpreted as a harbinger of mass sedition or political revolution.[80]

During the interwar years Washington, D.C., was witness to hunger marches and protests. Unemployed veterans demanded payment of Adjusted Service Certificates; demonstrations supported by the Communist party, the Trade Union Unity League, and the Unemployment Councils drew over 100,000 participants in New York City and Detroit in March of 1930.[81] The "Red Scare" and the labor unrest of the Great Depression also heightened political uneasiness, and social stability seemed unrealizable. But the linkages between these trends and speculation about air warfare, so prevalent in Europe, were far less clear in the United States. They existed, but as background to what still seemed a remote and theoretical problem. Reflecting on the contrast in European and American attitudes, Michael Sherry has argued, "Europeans seemed to grasp almost desperately at the airplane, knowing its terrible role in war but hoping it might prevent war. Americans either seized on it eagerly or ignored it complacently, inspired by a confidence about man's ability to control his creations."[82]

Americans, however, understood that their "free security" would not last forever in a world of ever-developing technology and increasing international tension. The advances and potentialities of air warfare were thus of interest, even if that interest could remain—for the time being—less immediate than in Europe. Like the Europeans, Americans worried about the prospect of gas warfare. Their fears were heightened by, among others, Thomas Edison, who proclaimed in 1921 that aerial bombing with poison gas could destroy a great city in five minutes and leave every creature either burned to death or suffocated.[83] Edison's stature and dramatic rhetoric insured that his doomsday argument garnered attention. The combination of the bomber and the poison gas bomb was a potent one, and it flourished in the hands of sensationalist writers. By the 1930s, Americans had been introduced, too, to the dramatic arguments of Italy's Gen. Giulio Douhet, whose name quickly became associated with the bombing of cities and the use of gas weapons.

Publicity surrounding the annual Air Corps maneuvers captured public attention and produced newspaper coverage accompanied by photographs, maps, and drawings (the latter usually having more to do with an imagined future than existing realities). A special "bombing mission" to New York, part of the 1929 maneuvers, prompted one reporter to write, "The Army post on Governor's Island was reduced . . . to a 'smoldering heap of ashes.' The city's defenses were hopelessly 'crippled' and the 'enemy' might have taken New York without trouble."[84] A *Popular Science* article from 1931 asked (above a depiction of bomber darkened skies and a burning city), "Can Enemy Planes Wipe Out America?" Speculation about Europe lent drama and immediacy to these kinds of tales. In a 1929 article for *The New Republic*, Stuart Chase postulated that fifty tons of gas dropped by two hundred planes would have the effect of destroying "every living thing in the London area." Arguing that legal conventions and arms control agreements would be useless in holding back the tide of future war, he asserted that "it hardly pays to discuss any mechanism of warfare except the aeroplane" and added that offense was the only true defense against air attack. At the end of his essay, he consoled his readers by pointing out that even if bombing destroyed one or more nations in a future war, it would probably not destroy all of Western civilization.[85]

Those affiliated with the Air Service / Air Corps, and those with ties to the aviation industry also attempted self-consciously to create an "airminded" culture in the United States by producing a steady stream of speculative literature and air war fiction. As we have seen, Billy Mitchell worked tirelessly to convince Americans that their powerful navy could no longer be relied on to protect them from hostile outside forces. By 1921 he was arguing that those "who have had experience in aviation thoroughly believe that the great battleship on the water is as vulnerable to air attack today as was the 'knight in armor' to the footman armed with a musket."[86] Handsome and articulate, he made himself into a kind of American icon: the brash, committed individualist who bucks the establishment for the sake of a deeply held conviction. News footage of his exploits kept him in front of a nation that had become captivated by the cinema. Equally suited to the newsreels were the great distance flying exploits of the 1920s and 1930s, and the air races of the same era. And even those without ready access to the cinema might still witness the derring-do of Depression-era barnstormers and acrobatic flyers.

Other members of the Air Service also set out to build public support for military aviation. Henry Arnold and Ira Eaker, officers on active duty, coauthored three books on aviation for popular audiences. Arnold also wrote a six-volume adventure series for boys—based on the exploits of a young flyer named Bill Bruce—designed to raise "airmindedness" and to create a favorable image of the "airman" for America's youth. In the 1930s, boys' aeronautic organizations flourished: the Junior Birdmen of America had no less than 500,000 members by 1936.[87] Alexander de Seversky, a World War I Russian fighter pilot who subsequently emigrated to the United States and worked as an aircraft designer and entrepreneur, also worked as a tireless advocate of air power, proselytizing about its revolutionary impact on war. Though he did not evoke original ideas, he brought enormous energy and enthusiasm to his task.[88]

Throughout the interwar years, though, the American debate over military aviation and strategic bombing was never so highly charged as it was in England—nor was it so high-profile a political issue. Mitchell's fate serves as a paradigm: though clearly captivated by him, Americans remained detached from his prognostications and uncommitted to his demands. The navy remained a powerful and assertive force, able to work against any erosion of its power and influence. And dramatic speculation about air war was frequently offset by writers who took rather more sober views. Sometimes (but not always) associated with navy opinions, these critics sought to burst what they perceived as an overinflated air-power balloon set aloft by "enthusiasts," "propagand-ists," "devotees," "advocates," "fact-dodging contributors," and "Jer-emiahs of the press."

In his 1932 essay, "Death from the Sky" (for *The American Mer-cury*), Arlington B. Conway complained, "The flyers . . . have taken to playing the politician's game, i.e. conjuring up a terrible bogey and then representing themselves as the only sorcerers capable of exorcising it." He was concerned that the "air terror myth" was "rapidly penetrating the mass consciousness." Similarly, John Edwin Hogg thundered in "The Bogey of War" that aviation had produced "a grotesque coterie of writers and editors who have subscribed to the unproven theory that the airplane is a substitute for every other weapon of war." A naval reserve officer particularly incensed by Mitchell, Hogg argued that the "only warships ever seriously damaged or destroyed by aerial bombing were some obsolete old hulks . . . motionless, undefended vessels—naval relics with none of the structural strength and armored decks of modern fighting ships." In 1935, W. F. Kernan, warning that the bomber held an "insidious appeal to the imagination," cautioned that "sweeping generalizations about the opportunities for conquest which modern science has placed in the hands of the aviator are easy to make and difficult to refute." He added, "When such eminent authorities as Captain B. H. Liddell Hart and Mr. H. G. Wells predict misery, ruin, and desolation from the air . . . the average citizen is inclined to believe in the reality of the menace."[89]

Conway's essay presented a sober, informed account of the history of strategic bombing and its limitations in wartime. Beginning with an overview of British and German bombing in World War I, he explained that since little material damage was done, emphasis had been placed upon the indirect effects and the moral effect of bombing, particularly in the British postwar bombing survey. He also summarized British mis-givings over public demands for reprisals and over the diversion of large numbers of aircraft to home defense missions. But he held, nonetheless, that bombers had operated with real limitations (including weather and navigation problems), and that improving air defenses had made suc-cessful raids increasingly rare as the war continued.

Conway then postulated a scenario in which a hostile northern neigh-bor waged air attacks upon the United States with a force roughly equal to that of France (the largest air power at the time). Basing his estimates on the number of bombs that could be carried by planes getting through fighter and anti-aircraft defenses (and their possibility of bombing accu-rately), he calculated that .23 percent of Manhattan and the Bronx might suffer damage on the first day, and that their populations would suffer 1,240 killed and 3,560 injured. He suggested that while this would produce "moral" effects including fear and an exodus from the city, it was unlikely to cause collapse. He added that, over time, the efficiency of the offensive force would deteriorate as weather and fatigue took their toll, and as defenses—including anti-aircraft techniques and better communications—improved.[90] To include the possibility of gas weapons, he recalculated his numbers, again using his best estimate of what could feasibly be delivered by a 1932 air force. Rather than death to every living thing, he predicted about 12,000 casualties, pointing out that a population equipped with respirators would be more resilient and resistant to terror than many doomsday speculators assumed.[91]

As Conway's article appeared, European disarmament negotiations were underway in Switzerland. As noted in the previous chapter, the British government took the conference very seriously, considering that failure with respect to bombardment aviation would have disastrous political consequences. The Americans could afford a far more disinterested approach; indeed, the Disarmament Conference itself highlights the wide gulf then separating British and American attitudes toward defense issues. If Ramsay MacDonald and Sir John Simon felt themselves engaged in a struggle for their national security and the maintenance of their way of life, American participants saw themselves acting mainly as friendly facilitators in an effort to solve a European problem. While it is impossible to know—in light of political developments in Germany, whether any useful outcome at Geneva was possible—it is clear that American "help" ultimately served more as a hindrance to progress than an aid to it.

Concerned that the participating governments were not making satisfactory headway, President Hoover in May 1932 prepared a sweeping proposal that included dramatic reductions in ground armies, navies, and military aviation. He hoped that the initiative would build on the momentum that he believed the United States had generated through the Washington Naval Treaty and the Kellogg-Briand Pact of the 1920s, and also bring him favorable attention prior to the upcoming presidential election. Initially, U.S. Secretary of State Henry Stimson warned the president that "the best method of promoting . . . progress was by helpful private discussion and not by dramatization or publicity."[92] But Stimson was in sympathy with the president's intent and was prepared eventually to endorse the proposal with significant modifications. The revised plan suggested cutting battleships and aircraft carriers by one third, greatly reducing the size of national armies, and abolishing all military aviation except that used for observation and intelligence. It contained no security arrangement designed to allay French concerns about a resurgent Germany. Even though the proposal had the official endorsement of the Secretary of War and the Chief of Staff of the Army, there was little desire within the Air Corps to see a severe curtailment of military aviation. And the Department of Commerce, concerned for the future of American civil aviation, did not wish to see any restriction in that realm.[93]

The Hoover Administration hoped that the British would be prepared to endorse the plan (indeed, Norman Davis of the American delegation at Geneva had indicated that MacDonald "was very anxious that something big and definite" be done at the conference), and they sought to work openly with MacDonald and Simon.[94] Even though he admired the aim of the Hoover plan and was thus prepared to give it general support, MacDonald wanted time prior to its announcement to discuss it with the cabinet in London; he was particularly concerned about the naval provisions.[95] Sir John Simon also asked that the Americans not push ahead before the ground could be properly laid. But Hoover was unwilling to give them the time they desired.[96] Sir John Simon viewed the American timing as little short of disastrous. He conveyed his feelings in no uncertain terms to the Americans; indeed, Norman Davis reported to President Hoover that Simon was "terribly upset and almost takes it as an insult." In the days preceeding Hoover's 22 June announcement, the British and French had made some headway on the question of bombers, and Simon did not want the American intervention—which was well intended but full of practical problems—to interrupt the progress of those discussions. In addition, Simon felt it would embarrass MacDonald to have to pronounce on the American proposal prior to consulting his cabinet.[97]

As it turned out, the American announcement did disrupt the flow of negotiations, which were focused on restricting air bombardment to battlefields alone. In July Simon was able to work up a formula (which tried at least to echo the Hoover Plan), designed to rekindle the bomber discussions, but his efforts were not entirely successful. When German demands for *Gleichberichtigung* (equal treatment) prompted British policymakers to explore more radical solutions by late 1932, including the international control of civil aviation, the solutions were hung up in part by American unwillingness to accept any restraint in this realm.[98]

By the mid-1930s worldwide tension over the possibilities of air warfare had increased, and Americans, like others around the globe, were increasingly confronted with highly disturbing news emanating from Ethiopia, China, and Spain. Descriptions of "cold-blooded, wanton, purposeless" attacks on noncombatants at Guernica helped to raise public concern and to encourage further Congressional funding for the

Air Corps.[99] Public analyses of the impact of bombing in foreign wars did not yield a consensus: "Prophets found the evidence necessary to sustain their arguments or merely ruled the record before 1939 too inconclusive to merit much attention, while skeptics usually had their doubts reinforced."[100] Articles addressing the bombing raids did not shy away from detail or graphic imagery, and they professed outrage at the perpetrators of such cruel and inhuman acts. But their conclusions varied. Many commentators described the raids as self-defeating in that they roused the affected populations to higher levels of indignation and determination.

New York Times reporter Herbert L. Matthews, on assignment with the Leftist forces in Spain, argued that terror by air is a real phenomenon. He cabled the following: "Human beings are not built to withstand such horror . . . makes one either hysterical or on the verge of hysteria . . . hard to remain sane."[101] American political leaders reacted with anger and outrage at the aerial attacks that gripped the attention of the world in the 1930s, often responding in rhetoric that echoed the stigma Newton Baker had attached to strategic bombing. But it was not clear whether declarations of outrage and efforts to stigmatize the air attacks would have any chance of reducing their future occurrence in war. And international law seemed a thin reed on which to rest much hope. Informed American readers would have been aware of the difficulties of successfully applying international rules of warfare—such as they were—to aerial bombing. In a 1937 essay for The New Republic, Jonathan Mitchell offered a clear overview of the problems in this regard, explaining that the Hague Rules, drafted in 1922–23, foundered on definitions of what constituted a legitimate military target in an age of total war. The rules, he pointed out, "still remain unratified, and many American experts believe them too vague to be of practical importance."[102] If Americans were not quite sure of what kind of threat foreign air forces posed to their shores, they realized that modern warfighting forces would now include aircraft engaged in a daunting range of activities.

THE AIR CORPS TACTICAL SCHOOL:
THE EVOLUTION OF THOUGHT IN THE 1930s

In July 1931 the Air Corps Tactical School moved from Langley, Virginia, to Maxwell Field, Alabama. The relocation proved a fortuitous one as the school prospered through the remainder of the decade. The Works Progress Administration built base housing, garages, and a variety of other needed structures.[103] While the physical plant of the school expanded, so too did the body of thought applied to the potential role of bomber aircraft in war. ACTS personnel deliberately sought to create at Maxwell a center where air force ideas would be amassed, evaluated, and disseminated. Explaining this initiative, ACTS Commandant Lt. Col. John F. Curry told the Chief of the Air Staff in 1932 that ACTS needed to become a "clearing house into which tactical ideas can flow, where they can be tried, and where the doctrine can go out to the service to be put into practice and evaluated."[104] In large part this worked. So long as the airmen remained formally committed to army conceptualizations, they found themselves with some leeway since the army did not look *continually* over the shoulder of ACTS. Its personnel thus had some opportunity to envision the future as they wished.[105]

But anticipating and preparing for the future was by no means a simple or straightforward task for these self-appointed visionaries: the technological and political ground was shifting rapidly beneath their feet, and the organizational context of their efforts remained complicated. Throughout the 1930s the Air Corps continued to have a dual personality, aspiring to evolve in a radical direction while proclaiming its official commitment to a more conservative one. By the end of the decade, though, it was speaking in ever bolder terms about strategic bombing, and straying increasingly from army-oriented conceptualizations of aviation. The text for the "Air Warfare" section of the 1938 "Air Force" course asserted confidently, "The possibility for the application of military force against the vital structure of a nation directly and immediately upon the outbreak of hostilities, is the most important and far reaching military development of modern times."[106] But this was an internal dialogue that remained unsanctioned by the army and largely ignored by the navy. As such it was risky, and held room for potential conflict and confusion among the services.

Even if the Air Corps had carved out some space for itself, official doctrine continued to be contested ground between the army and the air insurgency movement within its ranks. Much of the army effort manifested itself in the official "Training Regulations" for the Air Corps and the wartime role it authorized. Those seeking greater freedom for aviation in war could hardly have been excited by wording, put forward in a 1935 proposed revision of the Training Regulations, which specified that "Air Corps troops further the mission of the territorial or tactical commands to which they are assigned or attached."[107] The first volume of an Air Corps field manual, drawn up in 1937–38 and forwarded for comment to the War Department, did not by any means receive the whole-hearted endorsement of that body. After six months of review, the War Department sent it back demanding changes: the manual was not to make mention of "independent" operations, nor was it to discuss air attacks designed to destroy civilian morale.[108]

And even as it contended with externally imposed constraints, the Air Corps also had to face up to its own internal attachments to army legacies: despite professing a future-oriented perspective, Air Corps members (like their RAF colleagues) had to overcome their own cultural connections to social anachronisms and to outdated elements of training harkening back to once-favored but now obsolete methods of war. While, for instance, the requirement for twenty-five hours of equine stable management was eliminated early on, horseback riding was required from 7:15 to 8:15 every other morning. Indeed, students spent many more hours on horseback than they did addressing themselves to more useful topics such as air logistics.[109] The riding requirement was increasingly resented as the years passed. Hoping to be exempted, Lt. Col. E. L. Hoffmann wrote to the school's commandant in 1935: "I have never liked a horse, nor admired one, except at a safe distance. . . . I fail to see that horses have any place in the science of aviation." His request was denied.[110] In a 1936 article for the *Air Corps Newsletter*, Maj. Ira Eaker explained that "the present class has suffered five major casualties from riding to date, including broken bones—an arm, a leg, and miscellaneous ribs. There is considerable agitation on the part of the present class to make riding optional. The student council has recommended that the Tactical School Cavalry be placed high on the army's priority list for early mechanization."[111]

Other training methods were more obviously relevant. The Department of Air Strategy and Tactics covered attack, bombardment, pursuit, and observation aviation, as well as "Air Force," which included a mixed bag of general topics such as "air warfare, anti-aircraft defense, and air operations."[112] If the texts for ACTS courses, updated frequently, were not always consistent with one another, this body of writing nonetheless revealed trends and patterns representative of Air Corps thinking—patterns that continued to reflect both Trenchardian and Tivertonian ideas, and the problems and unresolved questions inherent in them. At Maxwell the Air Corps allowed itself the freedom to articulate ideas, to wrestle with them, and finally to endorse them in print. But this process did not always resolve debates or lay the foundation for successful wartime operations. Just as in Britain, assertion and conjecture retained loose ends that were not satisfactorily tied off by the airmen themselves. Even if the Air Corps had been allowed or required to present its case more completely to the public, it is not certain that the process would have produced greater clarity. It had not done so for the RAF.

By the late 1920s and early 1930s, the rhetoric of ACTS was evolving ever more rapidly toward a full and unconstrained articulation of a theory of independent strategic bombing. The 1930 text for the "Bombardment Aviation" course took its readers through the history of long-range bombing, seeking to draw lessons from the World War I experience. It continued to acknowledge the difficulties posed to bombers by pursuit planes, pointing out that in World War I both fighters and ground-based defenses had taken their tolls and had forced attackers to bomb by night. The authors observed that by 1918, "certain of the principles governing the employment of bombardment aviation were definitely recognized," including disruption of lines of communication and destruction of important factories and airplanes on the ground.[113] The authors printed portions of Trenchard's 1916 memorandum on the "relentless and incessant offensive," claiming simply, "It is evident that this policy was adhered to."[114] Echoing the British, the authors were impressed by the difficulties of defending against an aerial offensive. They argued that German bombing of London and Paris had forced the British and French to tie up a "large number of personnel and a vast amount of material to defend against the German airplanes." Extrapolating, they asserted "it is apparent that the damage suffered by London throughout the war did not equal that which could be caused by one heavy bombardment group with modern equipment."[115] The text supported the case for strategic bombing in war, arguing that it had caused losses of production in factories, inconvenience to the enemy (which could not always be directly measured in monetary terms), and a lowering of morale among both the fighting forces and the civilian population.[116]

But while the authors of the text were willing to cite certain aspects of British experience, they were not afraid to criticize Trenchard. In describing the policy of the Independent Force, the authors quoted Trenchard's decision, articulated in his final war dispatch, to bomb many targets scattered throughout Germany as opposed to concentrating on a few major ones. They then presented the criticisms of this approach offered in the post–World War I U.S. Bombing Survey: the British lacked a systematic program for destroying those industries most vital to the German war economy. They added that with the small bombs then available, "concentration rather than dispersion would have gained the greater results."[117] The "Air Force" text of that year included the same criticisms of British bombing, along with Trenchard's rationalization, which the authors rejected: "His defense of the plan he adopted is not convincing, except in that he seemed to believe that the bomb was a weapon of moral effect rather than that of destruction."[118]

Earlier in the same "Air Force" text, however, the authors had nonetheless underscored some assumptions Trenchard would have found congenial. In a section titled the "Human Element," they accepted that modern commerce, industry, and communication had "intensified the effect of war upon a nation's population as a whole" and they asserted that the ability of an air force "to strike directly the rear of the enemy's army, or the heart of his country, may have a profound effect upon his will to wage war."[119] Because entire societies now went to war, rather than just armies or navies, nations themselves became vulnerable. The route to victory was no longer through the enemy forces alone: the nation itself was subject to defeat, either along with or independent of the defeat of its armed forces. The goal in war was to break the enemy's national will, and to do it directly through the application of the air arm.

The "Air Force Objectives" section of the 1934–35 "Air Force" text asserted, "The ability of a nation to wage war fundamentally rests in a collective national courage or morale . . . that must be sustained if war is to be prosecuted to a successful conclusion." The authors argued that morale is the "pivotal factor," since the collapse of the civilian will would be "decisive."[120] The 1938 "Air Force" text emphasized many of the same tenets: "Whether or not the means to fight and the will of the armed forces remain intact," the authors argued, "the necessary capacity for war cannot be maintained when the *civil will* is broken."[121] Speaking to the National Aeronautic Association in January 1939, GHQ Air Force Commander Maj. Gen. Frank M. Andrews explained that air power could be used to apply direct pressure against a nation's "moral fiber."[122]

Critical and expedient assumptions of civilian vulnerability underpinned all this. The 1930 "Air Force" text had explained that "[t]he decision of the commander of the Confederate forces in the Civil War, as well as that of the Central Powers in the World War to accept defeat, was largely based upon the condition and sufferings of the non-combatants at home."[123] The "Air Force Objectives" section of the 1934–35 "Air Force" text bluntly concurred, arguing that in World War I, "Germany, in spite of the intensity and duration of the fighting, did not lose through the military defeat of her armed forces but through the moral collapse of her civilian population."[124] This sentiment was echoed in speeches delivered throughout the 1930s by ACTS instructors. Maj. Harold L. George, Director of the Department of Air Tactics and Strategy, lectured for instance that the defeat of Germany had followed inevitably from "the breakdown of the German people through the continuous denial of those things which are essential, not only for the prosecution of war but to sustain life itself."[125]

George's comment is instructive in that it brings together a number of ideas that, explored more deeply, led to dilemmas for the Air Corps. It rested fundamentally on an assumption that Allied victory in World War I had been won mainly by the erosion of the "will to resist" of the German homefront, and it implied that a similar process of erosion could be facilitated in future wars through the application of air power, not only against those things essential to the prosecution of war, but also to the sustenance of life itself. This interpretation of the history was at least problematic, and spoke to the widespread acceptance of the *Dolchstoss* ("Stab in the Back") myth stressed emphatically by interested parties in Germany. Beyond this, the interpretation raised thorny issues for the Air Corps: when and how might an air force pressure an enemy population—deny it those elements necessary to sustain life itself? The RAF had faced similar dilemmas, and had faced them more publicly. Trenchard's solution was to remain vague and to avoid being pinned down on issues of targeting. In part this was because it gave him bureaucratic flexibility, and in part because he was disinclined to work out details in advance of events. But the elusive way in which he handled the question, combined with his emphasis on the inherently vague moral effect, had led to a good deal of confusion (and consternation) both inside and outside the RAF.

American air theorists could not predict the latitude the Air Corps might be given to prosecute a future air war, especially since American security policy remained defensive, isolationist, and officially hostile to any proposal for bombing noncombatants. Under the circumstances, they attempted to think through possible futures even as they sought to avoid raising the eyebrows of their colleagues in the other services. The "Air Force" course text of 1931 (rev. ed.) pondered the possibility of direct attacks against "political objectives," specified as attacks on cities (with high explosive or chemical bombs) or on civilian water and food supplies and utilities. The authors recognized that these would entail terrific suffering among noncombatants, and suggested that a decision to undertake such raids could be made only after careful political consideration by the "highest authority."[126] They then quoted several European sources to show that the possibility of air warfare directed at civilians could not be dismissed.

The ACTS text for the 1933–34 "International Aerial Regulations" course noted that since the Hague Rules of Air Warfare had not been ratified by any nation, there were "no conventional rules in actual force which directly effect aerial bombardment."[127] Within the arena revealed by this legal ambiguity, the ACTS staff argued that the first object in war, in any case, would be the destruction of the enemy air force. But they promptly added "When control of the air has been gained, then military objectives other than the hostile air force will receive increasing attention, including perhaps political capitals and centers of population." They added that "political considerations will govern, and warfare of terrorization will probably be conducted only as a matter of reprisal."[128] But these equivocal statements left plenty of room for speculation, and opinions varied. Some commentators handled the issue very delicately. Maj. B. Q. Jones, lecturing on the role of the GHQ Air Force, argued, "In opposition to Europe, we have no belligerent neighbors. And, if we ever did have trouble with them, we would most assuredly hang back on the employment of any weapon that might jeopardize the lives and beings of their defenseless women and children. America doesn't wage war that way."[129]

Grappling over how to wage a future war manifested itself in the "Air Force Objectives" section of the 1934–35 "Air Force" text. The authors argued that the "interlaced social, economic, political and military divisions of a nation acquire a state of absolute interdependence during war. Offensive action in one of these spheres will produce sympathetic disturbances of varying intensity in all the others."[130] Under the heading "the social sphere," the authors examined both direct attack on population centers and direct attack on those targets "upon which the social life of the nation depends for its existence." They postulated, "Civilization has rendered the economic and social life of a nation increasingly vulnerable to attack. Sound strategy requires that the main blow be struck where the enemy is weakest." In rhetoric reminiscent of contemporary RAF proclamations, the authors wrote, "The object here is the dislocation of normal life to the extent that the people are willing to surrender in the hope that they can at least regain a normal mode of living. Large urban populations . . . add length to the lever that an air force can apply against morale."[131] Fully aware of the moral and legal problems raised by bombing social centers, the authors justified addressing the possibility of such action nonetheless: while it was "an undeniable fact that the consensus of world opinion is opposed to such employment of air power, it is common knowledge that nearly all of the leading powers are facing the actualities of war by recognizing the probability of this employment in the preparation of plans and the training of civilians to the end of minimizing the effects of such an attack."[132]

All of this indicated clearly that the Americans continued to think about the impact of bombing on enemy morale and civilian will to fight. At no point during the interwar years did the Americans cease to contemplate either the psychological or indirect effects of bombing. They wrestled with it, tried to make sense of it, and sought out the connections between the material and the moral effects of strategic air raids. But they usually found themselves conflicted and confused about it, and they avoided raising the moral or psychological effects of bombing to a privileged rhetorical position.

Indeed, the authors of the "Air Force" text were clearly more comfortable with and confident in their subsection titled "The Economic Sphere," which received nearly twice as much attention as any other category in the text. In this realm they believed they could escape uncertainties and deal instead in practical analysis. Unsurprisingly, they endorsed a campaign of selective targeting based on a careful analysis of the enemy's economic structure. In language reminiscent of the American World War I bombing survey (to ascertain "how one industry is dependent on another and what the most important factories of each are"), they wrote, "The specific objective for the offensive will be selected only as the result of a careful and complete scientific analysis that would evaluate the effects upon the economic system and estimate the force necessary for suppression or destruction."[133] Targets analyzed under "the economic sphere" included petroleum, coal, electric power, and transportation facilities. Direct pressure on these might undermine the enemy's national morale without raising the kinds of ethical questions that might be posed by attacks on targets considered to be "social" or "political" in nature. Resting on assumptions about the complex and fragile nature of modern industrial economies, the "industrial fabric" approach postulated that by carefully choosing the right card at the base of an intricate structure, an air force could bring the whole house of cards crashing down. It depended on the same logic that had led British air planners in 1917–18 to talk about "root industries" and "bottleneck targets." And it was the same argument that William Sherman had explicated in his 1926 book, *Air Warfare*. Its appeal in the United States had continued unbroken since the First World War.

The ideology of selective targeting was fully articulated at ACTS by several young officers who happened to be posted together as instructors there in the early 1930s: Donald Wilson, Harold George, Kenneth Walker, and Robert Olds. Walker, in particular, had helped orient thinking toward high-altitude bombing. Herbert Dargue, who became the new assistant commandant at ACTS in 1934, brought with him an appreciation of technological advances in precision bombing and targeting, including the new Norden bombsight.[134] All bomber advocates, they reinforced one another's intuitions and logic, and helped to create loyal and tenacious support at ACTS for their mature ideas.[135] These ideas were expressed in the "Air Warfare" section of the 1938 "Air Force" text:

> [T]he economic structure of a modern highly industrialized nation is characterized by the great degree of interdependence of its various elements. Certain of these elements are vital to the continued functioning of the modern nation. If one of these elements is destroyed the whole of the economic

machine ceases to function. . . . Against a highly industrialized nation, air force action has the possibility for such far-reaching effectiveness that such action may produce immediate and decisive results."[136]

The requirements placed on American bombers for coastal defense and sea search put a premium on their ability to find and hit specific targets, and this in turn encouraged the existing orientation toward "precision bombing" of selected targets in an enemy war economy. This was further reinforced by the development of American bombsights, in particular the Norden Mark XV bombsight of 1933, produced by inventor Carl Norden, the navy's in-house designer of cutting-edge technologies.[137] Precision bombing of selected targets would require, necessarily, a process of identifying vulnerable points in the enemy war economy—a process that had already been understood as necessary and vital. Thus, the new capabilities inherent in the B-17 and the Norden sight both facilitated and reinforced the prevailing U.S. conception of air force doctrine: scientific and technological developments dovetailed not only with the existing emphasis on careful selection of targets, but also with the requirements of prevailing moral and ethical strictures. Technology (in a self-proclaimed "high-tech" nation) seemed to make all things possible and, equally, seemed to solve all potential problems.

Along with some ACTS colleagues, Donald Wilson in 1933 engaged in a grapeshot-style letter-writing campaign to solicit information for use in lectures and problem sets. He began by searching for "key node targets" in the American industrial infrastructure; this would serve as a model for similar analyses of other states. His civilian experience with railroads led him to think in terms of critical junctions and potential bottlenecks.[138] In a note of thanks to a colleague who had sent him a list of the components in B-10 and B-12 aircraft, he wrote, "This sort of information puts a new angle on air force operations. . . . It seems to hold the promise of solving all problems of destruction in the most efficient way."[139] From the Office of the Assistant Secretary of War, he requested information on the industry in the northeastern United States, including "principal electric power plants" and "key items and their source in each of the major industries such as: steel, automobiles, clothing, printing, chemicals, rubber, etc."[140]

In August 1935 the Commandant of ACTS asked the Chief of the Air Corps for vital information on the makeup of German cities; the Office of the Chief of the Air Corps in turn requested that the military attaché in Berlin obtain the information.[141] A power outage in New York City triggered intense interest in urban power grids. This culminated in an ACTS lecture called "Air Power and the City," which determined that the New York metropolitan area relied upon twenty-six generating plants within a radius of twenty-two and a half miles. The author assumed, optimistically, that one direct hit with a large bomb might take a power plant out of action for up to six months.[142]

Attempts by ACTS faculty to compile a data base for comprehensive analysis fell short however. An instructor in the "Air Force" course in 1937, Maj. Muir S. Fairchild, wrote to the Army War College to discuss ways to determine the amount of destruction a particular target might require to have a "decisive" effect.[143] Fairchild raised the possibility of ACTS personnel working with the Industrial War College or the Brookings Institution to answer such questions. He expressed concern that ACTS instructors alone could not authoritatively answer such "fundamental national questions." Putting all the pieces together would require excellent intelligence information, augmented and assessed by economists and statisticians.[144] He was correct in this. Unfortunately, however, the esoteric arts of intelligence and target analysis did not mature before the war: they would develop, instead, in the crucible of wartime events. Only in 1939 would a tiny economic analysis section be established inside the Office of the Chief of the Air Staff. This meant, however, that the fundamental and foundational data on which the theory necessarily rested remained underdeveloped. In addition, the connections between air force action and enemy responses remained vague and speculative.

In both the RAF and the Air Corps, the general objective of the bomber advocates was the same: to undermine the enemy's will to fight—directly and efficiently—by aerial attacks on an enemy's points of vulnerability. Their enthusiasm for this new approach to warfare stemmed from the assumption that it would prove more powerful, more effective, and more expeditious than any mode of warfare ever previously tried. Thinkers and planners in both air forces concentrated on the social and economic sinews that held together modern societies, and tried to envision means of eroding them. Precisely how the goal might be achieved was less clear, however, than the goal itself. The phrase "to undermine the enemy's will to fight" contained much room for interpretation. Trenchard's emphasis on the moral effect, which prioritized the psychological and the indirect effects of bombing, only intensified the vagueness of an inherently imprecise idea. The Trenchardian vision of two air forces largely ignoring each other to strike directly at one another's "vital centres" implied that cities might be early—perhaps immediate—objectives for long-range bombers. Even though this powerful implication (useful for purposes of deterrence) was widely internalized by politicians and government agencies, and constantly reinforced by a steady stream of popular writing, the RAF was not at liberty to elaborate upon its grim ramifications. Those were highly controversial and, in themselves, politically unacceptable. For a variety of reasons Trenchard was disinclined either to specify targeting carefully or to erect any preemptive boundaries around it. The flexibility served many purposes, suited his nature, and had few disadvantages in the relatively benign security environment of the 1920s. As his successors grappled with questions of targeting they realized that the course of a given war would determine what might be open to them; contingencies and political factors would bear heavily on actions. No planner on either side of the Atlantic could predict the exact course of a future air war or the amount of political leeway that air forces might be given with respect to targeting.

The Americans understood this just as well as the British did, but the lure of the "industrial fabric" theory—and their growing rhetorical attachment to it—inclined them in a particular direction with respect to targeting. They focused on teasing out the main threads in the complex fabric of industrial economies, which they believed could be identified and assessed well in advance of hostilities, providing an almost foolproof strategy for rapid victory through the precise application of offensive air power utilizing the best and most ingenious American technologies. In addition, the moral constraints articulated by Newton Baker (and maintained by policymakers after him), and the long-standing trend in American political thought toward moral "exceptionalism" had put boundaries around Air Corps thinking, reinforcing its inclination toward the relatively tangible "economic sphere." The luxury of geography and the absence of any worry about sudden "bolts from the blue" unquestionably played a role as well: the Americans were not at this point trying to deter attacks on their own cities, nor were they so worried as the British about the unpredictable and potentially uncontrollable behavior of their working classes. Also, the absence of any World War I long-range bombing experience meant that the Americans felt no obligation to be consistent with past history. Finally, the Americans *were* inclined to dither over the details of air warfare well in advance of actual operations. Unlike Britain's Ludlow-Hewitt, who in 1927 had eschewed overreliance on "peacetime calculations," Laurence Kuter of ACTS insisted (if overoptimistically) that "[i]t is highly desirable to base our computations upon sound mathematical considerations. We would avoid chance, luck, or hazard and deal only in concrete facts."[145]

To a greater extent than their RAF counterparts, American airmen labored to derive scenarios and target sets, and to identify and assess the most vulnerable points of attack for an air force. This analytical outlook probably owed much to the progressivist tradition and the strong appeal of Taylor's "scientific management" in the United States.

It was reinforced by bitter lessons from the economic crash of 1929 and the subsequent Great Depression that hit the United States particularly hard: specifically, complex, fragile modern economies are subject to major dislocation.[146] Writing in *Colliers* magazine in 1939, Republican Congressman Bruce Barton gave voice to a widely held impression: "Industry is a living body, highly integrated, with nerves extending to every part. Cripple a limb, and the whole body limps, prick even a finger, and the pain is felt throughout."[147]

The American preoccupation with science and technology could not resolve all the many unforeseen problems inherent in the planning process, however. This process was undermined by flawed assumptions and by a failure to comprehend fully the heavy—indeed central—demand for high-quality strategic intelligence. Also, overarching enthusiasm for "precision bombing" and faith in American technology seemed to crowd out any concern that such a course of action might prove difficult—even impossible in some circumstances. In the 1930s, test results "showed that bombing was accurate only in excellent weather against a clearly outlined, undefended target in the middle of wide-open terrain." Committed to an idea, the airmen chose not to countenance completely those things that undermined it. Even as war loomed on the horizon, bomber crews rarely dropped bombs from heights above 12,000 feet.[148] But this was not the only potential problem facing American bomber advocates. Being able to attack selected targets and bomb them precisely rested on the assumption that one would be able to reach them without sustaining prohibitive losses in the process.

THE BOMBER WILL ALWAYS GET THROUGH

Through the 1930s, ACTS emphasized bombers at the expense of observation, attack, and pursuit.[149] So obvious was this favoritism that the Air Corps sometimes referred to its observation units as "orphans." The ground army, though it tried continually to rein in the Air Corps, was preoccupied with its own affairs and did little to force a change. Additionally, army and Air Corps units were scattered among isolated locations, and funding for joint training exercises was limited. Indeed, not until 1941 were there maneuvers with two army-sized teams.[150] Favoritism toward bombers was especially reflected in aircraft procurement. As Lee Kennett has pointed out, the U.S. Army Air Forces deployed two generations of strategic bombers in World War II (and would have fielded a third if the war had continued), but neither developed a satisfactory plane for light observation and liaison, nor identified the proper aircraft for ground attack.[151] Pursuit (or fighter) aviation's demotion to a distinct second on the American priority list occurred gradually but inexorably as the bomber ascended.

As the bomber advocates envisioned longer-range missions, they had to come to terms with the problems of bomber penetration and survivability. They pinned their hopes on the self-defending bomber flying to distant targets unescorted: their vision required that sleek, fast, high-altitude bombers would use formation flying techniques, their own armament, and natural possibilities for evasion to reach their targets without prohibitive losses. As Trenchard and the RAF had done, the Americans sought to convince themselves that bombers would "get through."

Claiming bomber survivability in a future war meant downplaying bomber vulnerability in the last war. While this was a bit awkward, it could be done by asserting that improved tactics and greater bomber speeds would change the equation. The technology of the early 1930s eased the process initially: the development of the B-9, B-10, B-12, and B-17 bombers—all modern combat aircraft with greatly improved speed and range—furthered the idea that fast, well-armed bombers could operate on their own. (Indeed, bomber advocates believed that the the speed differential between bombers and fighters would only increase.) Before radar, the assumption that fast bombers would use speed, altitude, and cloud cover to achieve their objectives seemed rather straightforward. Drawing these apparently sound conclusions, American planners deemphasized the requirement for a suitable escort. At the same time, though, one finds in U.S. discussions of bomber vulnerability an underlying current of subtle but nagging doubt that kept the question of escorts alive. Despite the faith of many in the self-defending capabilities of bombers, some Americans never entirely abandoned the quest for a suitable escort. This search was ensnared by design and engineering challenges, oversights, and conceptual blind spots—all helping to insure that the doctrine of the self-defending bomber would remain largely intact until wartime experience would rudely challenge its assumptions.[152]

Examples from past military experience (aside from the World War I aviation experience) were invoked to reinforce subtly the idea that armed forces of an enemy state, when utilizing the initiatives of space and time, were difficult to find and intercept quickly. Armies had been able to maneuver around one another throughout decades of European history, and navies—even as recently as World War I—had successfully evaded one another much of the time. Both the British and the Americans would point to the "vast expanse of the air above the earth" as a factor in the promised dominance of bombers. But if conclusions rested in part on perceived reality, they rested as well on selective memory and filtering. Like the RAF, the Air Corps generally downplayed information—available by the late 1930s and based on techological developments—suggesting that bombers would become increasingly vulnerable in light of new breakthroughs enhancing the capabilities of defensive fighters. And (as we shall see next) they largely interpreted the wars of the 1930s in ways that did not disrupt their assumptions about bombers.

The evolution of American thinking about bomber vulnerability is not hard to trace in documents, speeches, and texts. Early post–World War I aviation studies by Americans had revealed a healthy respect for the ability of fighters to intercept bombers. Fighter escorts were recommended for bomber formations, even though it was recognized that this would not always be feasible in all situations. In 1922 the commander of the 1st Pursuit Group, Maj. Carl Spaatz, had called for maneuverable, heavily armed escort fighters with speeds superior to the bombers they were to protect, and ranges equal to them.[153] In *Air Warfare*, William Sherman made the case for fighter escorts. He argued that while pursuit might not remain continually with bombers, they should arrange to be with bombers during crucial phases of missions.[154] But limited fighter range vexed the problem of providing escorts for bombers of ever-increasing range and speed. The authors of the 1926 Manual proposed that bombers be made as fast as possible to increase their chances of avoiding hostile interception.[155] In addition, they devoted considerable space to particular types of self-defensive formations for bombers.

In 1925 and 1926 the Air Service had undertaken tests of airplane performance with auxiliary, droppable tanks. These revealed that the extra weight did not seriously affect the general flying characteristics of the aircraft.[156] Unfortunately, despite the feasibility of external tanks to increase range, they were not immediately embraced by the Air Corps for military use. Concern focused on the fire hazard posed by the tanks, and the possible reduction in performance caused by their weight and increased drag. Droppable tanks were discussed at ACTS beginning in 1929, but the "Pursuit" manual concluded that cruising speeds of bombers and fighters differed so much that an escort group would not be able to support bombers all the way to and from their targets. It recommended using two escort groups: one for the outbound phase and one for the return trip. A conference of Air Corps leaders, held at Langley Field in April 1929, discussed the topic of escorts but reached no consensus.[157]

Texts used at ACTS in the 1930s reflected both the tensions surrounding the question of bomber survivability, and the increasing lean toward the idea that they could defend themselves. The 1930 "Bombardment" text readily acknowledged that pursuit had taken a toll on daytime bombing in World War I, forcing all the belligerents toward night operations. But it also made clear the distance limitations faced by pursuit aircraft trying to escort bombers on longer strategic missions.[158] The authors accepted Trenchard's policy of "relentless and incessant offensive." Concomitantly, they cast doubt upon French concerns, expressed during the war, that the losses from bombing sometimes outweighed its benefits.[159] The 1930 "Air Force" text incorporated in bulk arguments that Trenchard had used: "It is not possible to secure control of the air over a wide front. The hostile attack and bombardment with their great range may be expected to avoid the area over which the other belligerent has control of the air, and to enter elsewhere."[160] Later in the text the authors drew an analogy with the oceans: "Even the surface of the sea, which represents a much smaller field than the air above the sea and earth, was large enough to permit units of the German Navy . . . to elude the unquestionably superior British and Allied Navies for a long period of time during the World War."[161] Conceding that high altitude bombardment could be detected, the authors nonetheless asserted that "hostile pursuit will not be able to make contact with it in effective force, until after the bombardment has reached its objective and is on the journey home. . . . As the speeds of attack and bombardment increase, the time available to the hostile pursuit to gain contact, and to attack them as they fly home, diminishes."[162]

Though they had earlier relied on World War I examples for guidance, ACTS instructors at this point sought to distance themselves from the inconvenient fact that bombers had often been vulnerable to the enemy. They implied that better tactics and increased speeds would solve the problem, arguing (tautologically) in the 1930 "Air Force" text that lessons derived from the World War experience of bombers versus pursuit could not be conclusive because the war had offered few examples of "*well flown* [emphasis added] bombardment formations". They pointed out that both "bombardment and attack have very great powers of self-defense against pursuit": high altitudes and speeds would allow bombers to reach their targets before defensive pursuit could reach them. If attacked, a bomber could "defend itself with its flexible machine guns . . . while flying directly home."[163] Bombers could defend one another through interlocking fields of fire from their own rapid fire weapons. Again stressing tactics, they wrote, "Formations of attack, bombardment and observation airplanes, *properly flown and tightly maintained* [emphasis added], provide adequate protection except against an attack by hostile pursuit overwhelmingly superior in numbers and firepower."[164]

In Trenchardian-sounding tones, they claimed, "Victory will accrue to him who is best able to withstand the blows of the enemy and at the same time strike first, hardest, and strike most often."[165] But while Trenchard had failed to emphasize counterforce operations, the Americans maintained that they were important, and very likely essential. The 1930 Air Force text argued, "The contest for air superiority will start immediately upon the declaration of war, and will result in every means being employed to destroy hostile aircraft." The use of modern bombardment and attack aviation directed against airdromes, depots, and aircraft construction facilities would result in "losses of aircraft on the ground greatly in excess of those suffered during the World War."[166]

Exercises held in 1931 seemed to reinforce the idea that fast bombers could fare well on their own. Lt. Col. Henry ("Hap") Arnold reached this conclusion, as did the umpires, one of whom proclaimed: "[I]t is impossible for fighters to intercept bombers and therefore it is inconsistent with the employment of air force to develop fighters."[167] Commenting on 1933 exercises designed to test the GHQ Air Force (Provisional), Asst. Chief of the Air Corps Brig. Gen. Oscar Westover observed what he termed the "woefully obsolete" speed characteristics of pursuit aviation. From this he was moved to postulate that "no known agency can frustrate the accomplishment of a bombardment mission." Specifically, he argued, "Bombardment aviation has defensive fire power of such quantity and effectiveness as to warrant the belief that with its modern speeds it may be capable of effectively accomplishing its assigned mission without support."[168]

Of the 1934 exercises in California pitting B-12 bombers (a modified version of the B-10) against the less capable P-26 fighter, Arnold wrote, "Pursuit or fighter airplanes operating from frontline airdromes will rarely intercept modern bombers except accidentally."[169] In a speech to the Army War College in the same year, Major General Foulois argued, "Observation, bombardment and attack have advanced in speed development much faster than has pursuit."[170] The progress of American pursuit aircraft in the latter half of the decade was not promising. The awkward two-seater P-30 served mainly, as one historian observed, "to demonstrate the superiority of the single-seat pursuit." While they represented improvements over the P-26, neither the Seversky P-35 nor the Curtiss P-36 was a match for the B-17.[171]

Not everyone, however, accepted the intellectual orthodoxy of bomber invincibility. Lt. Col. Millard Harmon, while a fan of bomber development, nonetheless lamented the short shrift given to pursuit at ACTS. On a board that reviewed the 1935 "Air Force" text, he argued that it was fully conceivable to imagine an enemy air force defeated by hostile pursuit. Likewise, Lt. Col. A. H. Gilkeson, in charge of the 8th Pursuit Group, argued that dismissiveness toward pursuit had led to "the teaching of doctrines which have not been established as being true and might even be fatally dangerous to our aims in the event of armed conflict." And Major O. S. Ferson pointed to improved radio communication as a factor bearing on the future of defensive pursuit and bomber penetration.[172]

Capt. Claire Chennault, in charge of pursuit aviation at ACTS from 1931 to 1936, acerbically observed that the bomber ought not to be made "the first exception to the ancient principle that for every weapon there is a new and effective counter weapon."[173] At ACTS, Chennault's frequent verbal battles with bomber advocate Kenneth Walker became legendary. He believed that a responsive ground agency—a defense warning system using improved radio technologies—could solve the intercept problem. Outraged that fighter design had been neglected relative to bomber design, he believed that interpretations of the 1930s exercises were flawed and selective. This position, pregnant with implications for an attacking force, brought him into direct conflict with Lt. Col. Hap Arnold. Indeed, in response to Arnold's interpretation of the 1934 exercises, Chennault wrote an eight-page critique, arguing that the P-26 was outmoded compared to foreign fighters of far superior quality. He argued further that, instead of proving the invulnerability of bombers, the maneuvers only proved the need for improved interceptors, better tactics, and effective ground control.[174] In 1936 the Air Corps's Chief of the War Plans and Training Division felt compelled to dispute and disown a critical article Chennault published in the May–June 1936 *Infantry Journal*.[175]

So convinced was Chennault of the soundness of his own ideas that he successfully tested an experimental air defense system that included ground observers, a centralized communications agency, and alert fighters. But while he was able to influence a group of young fighter pilots—one of whom suggested that if the bomber boys could be lured into a fair test, real bullets should be used—Chennault did not make much of a dent in the bomber orthodoxy then ascendent. His retirement in 1937 due to physical disability meant that the bomber advocates were freed from the naysayings of their most persistent and vocal critic.[176]

As in Britain, this issue was hindered by rivalry and compartmentalization. No disinterested central authority successfully mediated the debate. Once the theory of the long-range self-defending bomber had taken hold, it proved surprisingly robust. The 1935 "Bombardment" text prescribed that escorts for bombers would not be provided unless bombers could not in fact penetrate enemy resistance.[177] This contingent statement implied that escorts would be on call if experience ever contradicted theory. But, though a fitful quest for an escort continued, it never enjoyed high priority before the war. In 1935 the Air Corps Board chose to handle the escort issue by recommending that bomber aviation seek out every means for self-defense; only if all other means failed should additional aircraft be provided to support long-range missions. It suggested that if the need for an escort was fully demonstrated, then a search for a suitable machine should be made among existing aircraft types. The board did not want to see time, resources, or attention taken away from other projects of higher status. Several two-seater designs received preliminary consideration, but the greater promise was seen to reside in a larger platform—perhaps a modified bomber.[178] Larger planes, however, would not match the maneuverability and fighting characteristics of the defensive fighters they would have to face.

The heightened tensions of the late thirties, and greater investment in aviation generally, drew some attention back to fighters and to the question of escorts particularly. But a 1938 conference on escorts reflected ongoing confusion regarding design possibilities, and a 1939 study concluded pessimistically that there was "little, if any, possibility" of building an escort fighter with the necessary range and performance to cope with the enemy's short-range interceptors.[179] Continuing concern over fire hazards led the Chief of the Air Corps in May 1939 to order that no tactical plane be equipped with a droppable tank.[180]

At the same time, the bomber units themselves tended to consider escorts largely superfluous in light of increased bomber speeds and tactics using altitude, cloud, and movement to evade enemy defenses. In June 1939, Lt. Col. Donald Wilson, Director of Air Tactics and Strategy at ACTS, cautioned the Air Corps against diverting too many resources to the escort issue. He argued that bombers modified with additional firepower could serve the purpose. Opinion was divided, however. Indeed, the Air Corps Board took another look at the issue in early 1940 and concluded that bombers would need protection on daylight missions where heavy opposition was likely: "The pertinent technical problems incident to the provision of such protection merit thorough investigation." But several studies that year led to inconclusive results on whether, and to what degree, the United States should continue the search for a viable escort.[181]

This atmosphere of conflicting opinions—and doubts as to the technical feasibility of a long-range escort—hardly was conducive to the development of a satisfactory plane. Unfortunately, American designers continued to focus on large, twin-engined types like the Bell YFM-1A Airacuda, the Lockheed XP-58, and the Northrop XP-61 (which belatedly went into production as a night fighter). Equipping heavy bombers to serve as escorts to the others was considered, yielding the wartime YB-40 (a modified B-17), which proved eventually to be a complete failure.[182]

"LESSONS" FROM FOREIGN WARS

Air theorists and planners in the United States hesitated to draw firm conclusions or lessons from the "little" wars of the late 1930s. Indeed, American interpretations did not differ substantially from those in Britain, and they were remarkably similar in rhetorical style. Observations were heavily weighted with qualifiers that circumscribed the significance of the information reported or the value of the information itself.[183] Air Corps officers insisted that these scattered foreign conflicts differed fundamentally from any potential war between "first class powers" in Europe. Despite this attitude, evidence from Spain heightened concerns in the United States about the ability of the bomber always to "get through," subtly undermining the certainty with which the self-defending bomber theory was asserted.

Several branches of the U.S. Army took an attentive interest in the Spanish civil war, and many of the articles produced in their professional journals cast doubt on the notion that strategic bombing would be decisive in the next war: bombed civilian populations had quickly learned to adapt, and various types of defenses had thwarted the notion that the bomber would "always get through." The Air Corps Tactical School, however, seemed strangely indifferent to the event: in 1937–38, only one lecture was offered at ACTS on the Spanish civil war.[184] The official historians of the American air war in World War II would later point out that: "The U.S. Army Air Corps . . . saw nothing in the aerial warfare in Spain or in China to suggest the advisability of change in its own doctrines. In both conflicts, the combatants employed relatively small numbers of aircraft, and the bomber appeared to be regarded chiefly as a means of intensifying artillery fire and of increasing its range."[185]

In a chapter for a book titled *This Flying Game*, written with Col. Ira Eaker during the war in Spain, Gen. Hap Arnold explained that aircraft in the Spanish war had been used principally to attack troops and to assist infantry assaults and offensives. Drawing a distinction between these "air cooperation missions" and "air force missions" (which he held to include attacks on manufacturing establishments, rail centers, and populated areas), he argued that the latter had been little practiced in Spain. Consequently, parallels between the war in Spain and any European war in which the United States might become involved were limited at best.[186] Arnold summed up his initial views on Spain: "A few first class planes and heterogeneous legionnaire pilots operating under loose control can never be called an air force and no true lessons can be drawn therefrom. We cannot assume that air experiences in Spain are equally applicable to ourselves or to any first class air power. That is a civil war of loosely integrated and poorly armed opponents."[187] He was equally dismissive of the war in China, stating, "The air picture any observer sees in China will be out of focus unless it be remembered that a nation with an air force is opposing one without any worthy of that name."[188]

Readers of the *Air Corps Newsletter* may have been reassured by their April 1938 issue containing a translated article by Lt. Col. Emilio Canevari, an Italian, titled "Forecasts from the War in Spain." Colonel Canevari noted, "Great care is necessary in drawing conclusions from the use of aircraft in this civil war and applying them unhesitatingly to a possible European war." He pointed out that the air forces involved had "constituted themselves hesitatingly and gradually" and only in small scale. Therefore, "it is . . . reasonable to assume that the situation of aerial warfare in a European struggle would differ greatly from what it is today in Spain. In the case of a large war, aerial warfare would start with great masses of modern aircraft in full readiness on both sides, well armed and supplied with munitions, directed by perfectly trained pilots accustomed to act in concert."[189]

The 1941 book *Winged Warfare*, again coauthored by General Arnold and Colonel Eaker, expressed retrospective views that were not substantially different from those they had articulated in the late 1930s. They still qualified the "lessons" from Ethiopia, China, and Spain, claiming that they were derived from wars that differed significantly from any future war between "first class powers." The only targets in Ethiopia, they explained, were troop concentrations and primitive supply columns; it possessed none of the manufacturing establishments, lines of communication, or great centers of population and industry that were of interest to planners in advanced industrial states.[190] Arnold and Eaker claimed that the war in Spain had produced only "the first crude air warnings, the first faint evidence about what could be expected later in some other and more important localities."[191] They argued that the "uncertain and indiscriminate undertakings" of these wars did not foreshadow "what the power and effect of a great air force might be and how best it might be combated."[192]

Nonetheless, those responsible for planning and policy at the time did not feel they could completely ignore events overseas. Incoming information prevented them from doing so, and kept them alive to the complexities and difficulties of air warfare. They had to admit, for instance, that anti-aircraft guns and machine guns had made great strides, and that certain "passive" defenses, such as the dispersal of factories and matériel, could be effective in combating the effects of air strikes. In addition, they could not entirely overlook the threat to bomber invincibility posed by fighter interceptors. In December 1936, U.S. Army intelligence requested information from military attachés in Rome, Berlin, Paris, London, and Moscow on the types of aircraft being used in the war in Spain, their performance, and their tactical employment.[193] The attaché reports were supplemented by articles written by both foreign and American observers of the war. Conclusions varied with each observer, but a few key themes were articulated repeatedly: airplanes could effectively disrupt and demoralize troops on the ground; and unescorted day bombers would be repeatedly harassed and attacked by defending fighters. Indeed, Condor Legion bombers were driven to nighttime attacks just as the bomber forces of World War I had been. Nationalist Air Chief Alfredo Kindelan argued that bombers had to have friendly fighter escort whenever enemy fighters were expected in their area.[194]

In August 1937 the *Air Corps Newsletter* had reprinted an article from *Revue de l'Armée de l'Air*, whose author noted, "It proves to be very difficult for a bombing multi-seater to get away by day from the attacks of a single-seater pursuit plane; the only effective protection is then in the escorting single-seater.[195] Maj. Harrison G. Crocker, who had given the sole lecture on the Spanish civil war at ACTS, argued that to prevail against enemy interceptors, bombers required armament, tight formations, and escort protection. And in the summer of 1938 the U.S. attaché for Air in Spain reported that Spanish military leaders unanimously agreed that pursuit must come first.[196] In addition, American intelligence reports made clear that bombers' defensive armament had not deterred their attackers.[197] Other independent reports from Spain and China, brought to the attention of the Office of the Chief of the Air Corps, also cast doubt on the invincibility of bombers.[198] All of this helped to keep discussions of escorts alive, even if they were not accorded first place on the Air Corps priority list.

The pangs of concern felt at this point by some bomber advocates were intensified when war broke out in Europe in the late summer of 1939. Despite his desire to downplay the impact of the air wars of the late 1930s, General Arnold found himself having to rethink his earlier views on the ability of bombers to penetrate to their targets without assistance. Indeed, Arnold's discomfort over this issue was such that in November 1939 he wrote a memorandum complaining about the neglect of pursuit tactics and technological development. He attributed much of the blame to the way doctrine had been taught in Air Corps schools. Distancing himself from any responsibility, he wrote, "A doctrine which has been widely propounded in certain Air Corps circles for many years, to the effect that fighter craft cannot shoot down large bombardment planes in formations, has now been proven wholly untenable."[199] In *Winged Warfare*, published after radar had shown its impact on air war, Arnold (and Eaker) commented revealingly that, "[d]uring daylight and in good weather, when pursuit aviation is present in strength in an area, it can pretty nearly bar the air to the bomber."[200] Despite this, enough difficulty, muddle, and self-delusion surrounded the problem of long-range escorts to insure that little progress was made toward a really workable solution. The Americans continued to hang their hats on the self-defending, high altitude bomber. Indeed, only in 1943—after disastrous losses—would the Americans decide finally that unescorted bombers could not successfully shoot their way in and out of foreign territory.

With repetition, both the British and the Americans bomber advocates became so committed to what they believed to be the fundamental concepts of long-range aerial assault that they downplayed or dismissed plausible alternative scenarios. A passage from the ACTS 1935 "Bombardment" text read, "During the time devoted to the sighting operation and release of bombs, the bombing teams must disregard the hostile pursuit and concentrate entirely upon the task at hand." The authors added, "A well-trained and well-disciplined unit having full confidence in its ability to defend itself . . . may be depended upon to perform effective and accurate bombing even under the most unfavorable circumstances."[201] The sentiment was worthy of any pre–World War I army text pronouncing on the soundness of the *offensive à outrance*.

When the events of the late thirties began to erode the certainty of bomber invincibility, the selective reading and interpretation of information insured that reaction would be delayed and disjointed. Faith in bombers, and the long-standing pessimism about building an adequate escort type, helped to obscure avenues—such as the droppable auxiliary fuel tank—that might otherwise have been more readily recognized and explored. Though it is of course far easier to identify such things in hindsight than it is to see them at the time, there is no question that the airmen's attachment to particular ideas inhibited their openness to new information bearing on those ideas. Their expectations, as well as their response to a competitive organizational environment, shaped their view of reality.

But bomber advocates on both sides of the Atlantic would have a chance to see their ideas tested extensively in the crucible of war. This would not have been possible if British and American politicians and publics had not found bombers a potentially attractive form of warfare (or, at least, relatively more attractive than other means). This attraction rested in large part on geography and a resulting strong tradition: resistance to the use and maintenance of large standing armies. In both nations, but perhaps even more so in the United States, this combined with optimistic faith in technology. As Michael Sherry has perceptively asserted, "Air power appealed . . . to a deeper strain of antistatism and antimilitarism in American culture because its reliance on a small, technically sophisticated elite apparently avoided the burdens of conscription, taxation, and death. It was the perfect weapon for a nation that wanted the fruits of centralized state power without challenge to traditions of decentralized authority and individual autonomy."[202]

CHAPTER FOUR

Rhetoric and Reality, 1939–1942

On Sunday, 3 September 1939, just moments after Prime Minister Chamberlain had announced "this country is at war with Germany," an air raid warning began to wail over London and other places in Britain. It proved, however, to be a false alarm and the "all clear" was signaled a half hour later.[1] The air war did not commence with an all-out strategic bomber offensive pitting the aerial strength of each contestant against the vital centers of its enemy. No revolution in warfare had yet taken place; the older forms of warfare were not yet obsolete. Indeed, the contrast could hardly have been sharper between what happened and what many had expected to happen.[2] By the end of the Second World War, however, the combined Anglo-American air forces were waging strategic bombing attacks on a scale that approached the most dramatic and assertive interwar predictions. In the intervening years, Anglo-American air planners, supported by their governments, struggled to find means and methods of using aerial bombardment to achieve national war aims. Their efforts, which came at a high cost to their own bomber crews and to enemy civilians, were sustained by a stubborn faith in the potential of bombers. The combined bomber offensive was characterized by constant adaptation and adjustment; its history is one of ongoing, real-time reconciliation of plans and capabilities, sustained by an optimism often at odds with the realities of the situation.

Unable at the outset of war to follow through on Trenchard's strident policy of relentless offensive, RAF decision makers put a premium on air strategies designed to shield Britain and avoid pushing Germany into a "gloves off" all-out aerial assault against cities. Weakness circumscribed the range of possible action: defending Britain and conserving the bombing force for a later day became the new priorities.[3] The RAF fitfully adjusted its plans and tactics to cope with losses, limited capabilities, small force size, and the lingering array of problems that had never been solved during the interwar years. But British reliance on the bomber as a tool of war was hardly abandoned. In June 1940, those who stood with Prime Minister Winston Churchill and rejected accommodation with Hitler did so in part because of their faith in the prospects for aerial bombing. Later, German defeat in the battle of Britain did not dampen British enthusiasm for waging a strategic air campaign against Germany: British planners were able to persuade themselves that their conception of air power was more sophisticated than Germany's, and that they would not make the same mistakes that their enemy had made. But the early years of the British air offensive saw one disappointment after another. Bomber Command's weak performance raised a chorus of critical voices demanding that the RAF justify its sizable portion of the national defense effort. Churchill endured his own crisis of doubt about Bomber Command, but he was not prepared to reallocate radically British defense resources in the midst of the war.

Under pressure to bring greater results despite persistent operational shortcomings, air planners turned their attention to the "area bombing" of German cities; by late 1941 Bomber Command was shifting the bulk of its effort in this direction. When Air Chief Marshal Sir Arthur Harris took up the reigns of the force in late February 1942, he was under instructions to use his force to attack the housing of urban workers in order to undermine their productivity and morale. Harris, convinced that city bombing was unquestionably the best and most efficient course for Bomber Command to pursue, assumed his new job with single-minded determination to prove his point. Indeed, he would remain tenaciously committed to city bombing throughout the remainder of the war, well after most of his colleagues had lost faith in it and shifted their attention to other targets. As was true in the First World War, the British bomber offensive was shaped in part by ongoing tensions between the field commander and the Air Ministry. Harris's views on bombing, and the conflicts they triggered with his colleagues, formed an important part of the history of Britain's strategic air war.

Across the Atlantic the Americans watched, waited, and finally began a military expansion program of their own. But the freeing up of funds did not solve problems of scale or banish persistent cognitive hurdles. Despite their vast resource base, the Americans would be plagued with the inevitable organizational and production problems of rapid rearmament in a highly demanding and dynamic environment. The Air Corps, soon to become the United States Army Air Forces (USAAF), would enter into war with limited numbers of aircraft and an untested faith that high altitude, "precision" daylight bombers would be able to reach their targets unescorted. This point of view would bring them into conflict with their British allies who understood, through direct experience, the risks and hazards of trying to fly over Germany in daylight. No small issue, this conflict not only dominated early discussions about an Anglo-American Combined Bomber Offensive (CBO), but also shaped the nature of the wartime interaction between the two national air forces. The early years of the war saw the British and the Americans seek out ways to work together during a hazardous and often bleak period of mutual dependence, and to develop the means of waging a sustained air offensive over Europe in the face of effective German defenses.

PLANS, TARGETS, AND LIMITATIONS

As we saw in chapter 2, preparation for war in the late 1930s finally had forced the RAF to harmonize the strategic goals of the Air Staff with the actual capabilities of Bomber Command; overarching guidance and plans had to be informed by operational realities. The planning process in general had been a sobering exercise for the RAF, and the process of drawing up operational guidance was especially so. The development of the "Western Air Plans" (WA Plans) for the first time "caused the strategy and tactics of the bombing offensive to be considered with due regard to the actual conditions under which warfare would be carried on."[4] The plans and their updates rested in part on intelligence provided by a number of specialized committees that would evolve over time in capability and sophistication.[5] By the end of 1940 the Ministry of Economic Warfare (MEW) Intelligence Department would have a permanent representative on the Joint Intelligence Committee (JIC) of the Committee of Imperial Defence, and some influence over policy. But the system that emerged was not perfect, and tension would exist throughout the war between the Air Staff and the various agencies offering it advice and counsel.[6]

Though serious war planning had begun earlier, Bomber Command's role in the process had greatly increased in late 1937 when the Air Staff sent it a list of plans, including instructions to concentrate on three of them: W.A.1, the attack on the German air striking force; W.A.4, the attack on German military rail, canal, and road communications; and W.A.5, the attack on German war industry, particularly oil.[7] These three target sets headed a more extensive list that was reevaluated constantly throughout the early years of the war. Some of the more unusual targeting possibilities (recalling some of the odder schemes of WWI), included attacks on German forests and crops using air-delivered incendiary bombs, weed seeds, and entomological and biological vectors. Despite their technical difficulties, some believed that such attacks might have a great "moral effect" on the German civil population.[8] Implementation of any of the plans would depend on developing contingencies and on the behavior of the Germans in war.

W.A.1 assigned Bomber Command a role in defending the nation and thwarting a "knock-out blow" by attacking the infrastructure and supply of the Luftwaffe. But neither the Air Staff nor Bomber Command was very happy with the plan, since they saw it as a defensive interim step prior to the counteroffensive needed for victory.[9] The plan came to center on the dislocation of the German aircraft industry itself—a set of targets known to Air Intelligence, and believed to be reasonably identifiable. The Commander-in-Chief of Bomber Command, Sir Edgar Ludlow-Hewitt, thought it might be possible to mitigate the German offensive somewhat by striking directly at the Luftwaffe, but he worried deeply about the costs of such an offensive if undertaken while his force remained very weak.[10] It would be necessary, as well, for the RAF to assist the army in repulsing a German offensive through the Low Countries and France, an outcome also anticipated by the Joint Planners and Chiefs of Staff. This scenario generated W.A.4, the attack on German military rail, canal, and road communications. Again, though, the Air Staff and Bomber Command lacked enthusiasm: neither was much interested in seeing the bulk of the bombing force used to support armies in the field. Moreover, Air Staff views differed from General Staff views regarding optimum aerial tactics for slowing a land advance.[11]

Of the prioritized alternatives, the Air Ministry clearly favored W.A.5: direct attacks on German industry, to be commenced once a full-scale air war had begun. The Air Targets Sub-Committee offered up a number of targets considered both feasible and vulnerable to air bombardment, including the German electric power grid; the canal locks and aqueducts connecting the Ruhr to northern Germany; coking stations; and repair depots and workshops of the main railway lines. By 1 September 1939, W.A.5 had evolved into three sub-plans: W.A.5(a) the attack on German war industry; W.A.5(b) the attack on the Ruhr (and its military lines of communication in Western Germany); and W.A.5(c) the attack on Germany's oil resources.[12] Planners favored quick, focused strikes against Germany's "weakest link": oil, plus concentrated attacks in the Ruhr to inflict both material and moral damage. They warned, "The longer we postpone the attack of oil after the 'gloves are off' and serious operations begin, the weaker our Air Striking Force will become and the stronger the enemy defenses will grow." While the strategists recognized that they could not account for all contingencies, they felt that their plans were sufficiently flexible to "attain the degree of dislocation aimed at in the particular industry."[13]

Bomber Command was more optimistic in its assessment of W.A.5 than the other plans, and Ludlow-Hewitt showed a particular interest in night attacks as a means of causing the maximum disruption and inconvenience for Germany. He cited World War I, referring specifically to "bombing for purposes of disturbance," which, he argued (in a way that reflected the tone of the post–World War I assessments) had caused 70–75 percent of the effect of bomb raids on Britain in World War I.[14]

The Air Ministry hoped that W.A.5, through the general dislocation it would cause, might also help indirectly to stem the German ground advance. When joint staff talks opened between the British and French, however, the French were unconvinced that British air plans would appreciably assist the ground war: they would not commit to the British view that a "serious attack on the Ruhr" would interfere with the movement of the [German] army, and also "break the morale of the German people and their will to fight."[15]

But while Ludlow-Hewitt felt that W.A.5 was the best of the available alternatives, he remained pessimistic about Bomber Command's capabilities. His proximity to the problem meant that he could not avoid what he knew to be a crisis. His views were reflected in a series of bleak letters to the Air Ministry that sought to instill a sense of urgency, and to drive home the need to achieve a high technical standard in all aspects of long-range bombing. In a letter of 30 August 1938, he even challenged the Air Ministry's conventional wisdom on long-range escorts, arguing that, while he too saw no ready answer to the problem, evidence from China and Spain suggested that the question be revisited. Subsequently he pointed out that the assumed range of the Blenheim bomber (792 miles) had proved in practice to be only 700 miles.[16] In a November 1938 meeting to discuss the assumptions for war planning, he argued that any early attempt to send bombers deep into enemy territory might "end in a major disaster." He therefore recommended that Bomber Command "start with targets fairly close in and gradually to penetrate further and further."[17]

In March 1939, Ludlow-Hewitt submitted a detailed, thirty-one-page report on the requirements and deficiencies in Bomber Command. In late May 1939, he continued his Jeremiad, complaining that Bomber Command's crews were insufficiently trained (especially in navigation and air gunnery) and that inadequate provision had been made for such necessities as a permanent bombing range and practice in low-flying attacks.[18] While conceding some of Ludlow-Hewitt's points, the CAS (Air Chief Marshal Sir Cyril Newall) was not prepared to face the full implications of them. The Air Staff had kept itself from comprehending the full scope of Bomber Command's problems in the 1930s, and when these were finally and unambiguously laid out by Ludlow-Hewitt, the Air Staff found his candor rather too jarring. Though recognizing the soundness of force conservation, Newall nonetheless insisted in early 1939 that Bomber Command must be prepared in an emergency to carry out attacks on essential enemy targets. Later, in May 1939, he argued that Ludlow-Hewitt's outlook was overly pessimistic.[19] This tension not only recalled the general problem of opposing views that had arisen during the First World War, but foreshadowed future wartime conflicts within the bureaucratic machinery of the British air offensive.

Whether and how Bomber Command might carry out Air Staff war plans was not the only issue bedeviling strategy however. Another concern was how British planning might be squared with the new imperative of doing everything possible to encourage Germany to keep the "gloves on" until the British bomber force could be enlarged and made more capable. This required a reexamination of the frustrating, unresolved issue of what was to be considered a "military target," and who in Germany ought to be considered "noncombatants." Attitudes and interpretations varied from person to person, even within the RAF. As the Hague Draft Rules of 1923 had not been ratified, international law provided no definitive guidance on the issue. And yet the question could not be avoided. The government, which had only recently abandoned the fruitless quest for an international agreement on aerial bombing, was in favor of doing anything it could to reduce the chances of Germany's attempting a "knock-out blow" against cities in the early stages of war. Prime Minister Chamberlain choose to adhere to the Hague Draft Rules, such as they were. On 21 June 1938 he had declared in the House of Commons that it was against international law to make deliberate attacks on civilian populations, and he specified that targets of air bombardment should be "legitimate military objectives" capable of identification. Reasonable care should be taken in attacks on such targets so as to reduce the chances of collateral civilian casualties. The devil, as ever, lurked in the details of the phrase "legitimate military objectives." Nonetheless, these guidelines had provided the basis for a directive issued to the Chief of Bomber Command in September during the Munich crisis.[20]

The following month the Chiefs of Staff's Joint Planning Sub-Committee weighed the relative advantages and disadvantages of a restricted bombing policy. Its disadvantages included the loss of deterrent value, reduced ability to apply economic pressure on Germany from the air, and lessened means to reduce Germany's air strength (although it had already been admitted that the prospects of doing this were limited). The advantages included reducing the danger of an initial German air offensive and winning over world public opinion (especially American opinion) if Germany chose to start an air offensive against Britain. In the end, the advantages of restriction looked more compelling. If the immediate weaknesses of Bomber Command meant that the force would have to be conserved to the greatest extent possible, it made no sense to risk provoking an all-out German attack.[21]

Planners working on targeting policy assumed that it would be legitimate to attack military targets in populated areas.[22] The prospect of imminent war forced discussion of the thorny legal issues that had remained unsettled for so long. But even determined and focused efforts did not wholly solve the intrinsic difficulties embedded in the problem. Sir John Slessor later recalled these debates as "difficult and depressing." The seriousness with which air planners considered the issues, he wrote, was motivated by a desire to avoid bringing down "upon our then virtually defenceless heads a terrible weight of attack, without any counterveiling advantages to ourselves or our allies." He added, "We never had the least doubt that sooner or later the gloves would come off; but our policy was to gain time—to improve our own defences and to build up the great force of bombers of the Scheme M programme."[23]

In August 1939 an interservice committee under Sir William Malkin, the legal advisor to the Foreign Office, examined the whole question of legal targets for all the services in the event of war. The resulting report noted specifically that large numbers of civilians must not be bombed lest the good opinion of neutral countries, notably the United States, be forfeited. On 22 August, instructions were issued to commanders to guide operations in the initial stages of war. (They would not be cancelled until 4 June 1940.) The covering letter explained that while the limitations were more strict than the Hague Draft Rules, they were subject to modification if the enemy commenced indiscriminate bombing. Commanders were warned that heavy civilian casualties "might well be the cause of great embarrassment to His Majesty's Government in the critical opening stages of a war, and might produce serious reactions in neutral countries."[24] The instructions sent to all—down to the squadron level—listed acceptable targets ("purely military objectives in the narrowest sense of the word") as including naval forces, naval ships, dockyards, barracks, army units, fortifications, barracks, billets, military airdromes, depots, bomb stores, troop transports at sea and in harbor, military railways and roads, and military stores. Factories and bulk stocks of fuel were proscribed.

On 1 September 1939, President Roosevelt issued an appeal for every government engaged in war to affirm publicly that it would not be the first to bomb civilians or "unfortified cities."[25] In response the British and French declared jointly that they intended to spare civilian populations and cultural property. The Germans said that they welcomed the president's appeal and that they had issued orders that only military targets were to be bombed. The British Government heralded the cooperation of its French partner. Indeed, the French, even more anxious than the British, thoroughly endorsed their ally's intention of bombing only "military objectives in the narrowest sense of the word" in the initial stages of war.[26] New guidance issued during the battle of France would allow for attacks on military forces; fortifications; military facilities and depots; shipyards; factories "and other establishments engaged in the manufacture, assembly or repair of military material, equipment or supplies, and power stations ancillary thereto"; fuel and oil-producing plants; refineries and storage installations; and lines of communication and transportation serving military purposes. Commanders would be reminded that the "intentional bombardment of civil populations as such is illegal," and that bomber crews must take reasonable care to avoid "undue loss of civil life in the vicinity of the target."[27] In almost every sense the reality of these plans—as conservative and nonprovocative as possible—were strikingly different from the bold "relentless offensive" rhetoric of the Trenchard era.

THE OPENING PHASES

In September 1939 Britain could call upon only 1,460 first-line aircraft, including 536 bombers of limited capability, 608 fighters, 96 aircraft for army cooperation, and 216 for coastal reconnaissance.[28] The first eighteen months of the war saw the bomber force used mainly for maritime operations and for tactical support of armies in France and Belgium, including attacks on German air bases in France and the Low Countries. But Bomber Command had only very limited effectiveness in any of the roles it attempted to undertake. It is surely understatement to argue that this period represented a crisis for the RAF: the gap between rhetoric and reality proved to be nothing less than an abyss. But the grim present had the effect of focusing attention on the future, and the Air Staff looked toward it with a hopefulness that, in hindsight, appears overly optimistic and even naive. They persuaded themselves that heavy bombers, when strengthened in numbers and put on a true war footing, would make good on all the promises issued for them over the years.

Rather than waging an all-out air offensive designed to throw the enemy on to the defensive, Bomber Command was reduced to limited attacks on shipping and to dropping propaganda leaflets in the hope of convincing the German population that Hitler's war was a grave error. Hours after Britain's declaration of war, twenty-seven Vickers Wellingtons and Handley Page Hampdens were sent to search for German shipping off the coast of Denmark, but none found targets. The following day twenty-nine bombers were sent to attack warships around Wilhelmshaven. Seven crews failed to return, and ten failed to find the target; those that did caused only minimal damage.[29] In actions on 14 and 18 December 1939, small groups of Wellington bombers flying over the North Sea in daylight were mauled by German defenders, losing half the attacking force in each encounter. These demoralizing outcomes quickly began to cast doubt upon the theory that the bomber would "get through" in daylight, although the pessimism was not widely acknowledged right away. As historian Anthony Verrier later argued, "Few aspects of this phase of the strategic air offensive are more striking in retrospect . . . than the disparity between the claims made for and the hopes entertained about mass bombing before 1939 and the virtual absence of all reference to it at the• highest policy-making levels for many months thereafter."[30]

The poor early results of the initial daytime raids caused Ludlow-Hewitt to begin to pull back from the prospective plan then favored by the Air Ministry: an attack on the Ruhr power plants. On 28 January 1940 he expressed his doubts about it to the Air Ministry. Losses of 50 percent or more of the attacking forces would not only demoralize British bomber crews, but would also kill those men who might later fly more capable bombers. These conclusions caused the Air Ministry to shift its planning efforts from the Ruhr plants to the German oil industry. The latter was encouraged by a variety of intelligence sources, and was further stimulated by the expectation that oil facilities would have the useful property of being relatively self-destructive when attacked. The Ruhr plan would be adopted only if a German attack on the Low Countries produced an emergency.[31]

The nighttime leaflet-dropping missions, which had commenced on 4 September 1939, gave the Air Staff an early opportunity to test Bomber Command as an arm of psychological warfare. The Air Staff had earlier expressed the hope that warning notices of impending attacks by British bombers might cause panic and disrupt the industrial life of the Ruhr. In the last months before the war, the Foreign Office had cooperated in the task of creating suitable leaflets.[32] Hopes that this effort would have some discernible impact on Germany proved to be greatly mistaken, however. Instead, the missions told of the difficulties of finding distant cities, the constant battles with weather, and the physical discomforts crews would encounter in such operations. Crews were sent out with maps, astro-sextants, and directional radio. With these means, which required a high degree of skill to use effectively, they were expected to find their way about; in essence, crews were expected to navigate at night by observation—an all but impossible task under the weather conditions so frequently prevailing. The interwar lack of attention to navigation told heavily. RAF crews mistakenly overflying and crashing on neutral Belgian, Dutch, and Danish territory led to a temporary ban on nighttime leaflet drops.[33] But the missions made clear something else: the relative absence, at night, of enemy fighters, and the comparative ineffectiveness of anti-aircraft fire, even at middle heights. This, along with the shift away from the Ruhr plan, provoked the first steps in the conversion of Bomber Command to a night attack force.

At the same time, some elements of Trenchardian thinking were already working themselves back into planning. A variant of W.A.5, prepared in January 1940 without any pretense of overriding earlier versions, pointed out that Bomber Command might be best served in the near term by a night offensive designed for maximum moral effect. Its authors looked to dispersed harassing attacks at night to disrupt industrial production and disturb the population generally. Like Trenchard, they presumed that continuous air raid warnings would have an important cumulative impact on the nerves of the German people. Though they recognized that they were placing their faith in an "imponderable factor"—the will and morale of the German population—they felt that it was a "practicable course to adopt."[34]

By early March 1940, Ludlow-Hewitt already was beginning to turn the focus of his force to night bombing. It had many drawbacks, but these seemed, at least, less formidable than the ones posed by daylight attack. On the night of 19 March 1940, in response to a German air attack near Scapa Flow, Bomber Command struck its first land target, the isolated seaplane base at Hornum on the isle of Sylt, chosen in part because of the low likelihood of collateral casualties. Although the crews claimed to have identified and bombed the target, photoreconnaissance revealed no evidence of damage done. (In one bit of good news, only one of the dispatched bombers failed to return.) Bomber Command would soon admit that only about half of its average crews could be expected to identify and attack targets at night except in the very best conditions of visibility. This was an inauspicious start to what would become a five-year campaign of increasing tempo and fury.[35]

In early April, Air Marshal Charles Portal took over from Ludlow-Hewitt the leadership of Bomber Command. Shortly thereafter Germany invaded Norway and Denmark. A month later Hitler commenced his ground offensive against the Low Countries and France. German air attacks against Rotterdam made it clear that Germany intended no special treatment for Western Europe. Bomber Command was unavoidably drawn into the ground war. But, as the Wehrmacht rolled westward, the RAF could not substantially aid the French or the British Expeditionary Force, and the French were understandably nervous about any RAF bombing that might provoke retaliation against them. On 4 June, DCAS Air Vice-Marshal Sholto Douglas summed things up when he told Portal laconically: "the strenuous and gallant efforts of your squadrons against objectives in collaboration with the land battle since the 10th May have not always had results commensurate with the effort exerted."[36]

At the end of May, the Chiefs of Staff had undertaken a plan for coping with "a certain eventuality": the fall of France.[37] Their review of the situation called for defeating Germany through a combination of economic pressure, bombing, and the fostering of revolt in the occupied territories. Following a shift that had commenced earlier, the Air Staff chose to concentrate Bomber Command on attacks against the German oil supply. This Tivertonian approach, designed to eliminate (or at least reduce) a crucial commodity, was coupled with its Trenchardian alternative: a continuous interruption of German industry to be sought on nights when weather would not permit the location of oil targets. The decision to target oil rested on optimistic intelligence reports combined with a hope—however faint it may have been at that point—that Bomber Command could actually find and hit such targets. Back in April, Portal had revealed hopefulness regarding Bomber Command's prospects against oil.[38] Indeed, RAF optimism at this point rested far more on hopefulness than direct experience: it was largely a case of good news being generated by those who wanted very badly to believe it.

A little unfounded optimism can be a good thing, however: the hope that Bomber Command might play a role in fighting Germany helped Winston Churchill win the day against those who felt that Britain had no choice but to seek terms with Hitler. The new prime minister felt that, before any negotiations with the enemy, the British had to prove they would not be beaten. Proving this would depend on maintaining effective defenses and carrying out offensive operations designed to erode German industry and the German homefront. The latter would rely on methods Britain had traditionally used in continental warfare: economic pressure rather than a direct clash of ground forces. In this, Bomber Command would have a key role, especially since the effectiveness of naval blockade had been undermined by Hitler's conquests. Bombers would "pulverise the entire industry and scientific structure on which the war effort and economic life of the enemy depend." Bomber Command, Churchill insisted, must be rapidly expanded "since no other way of winning the war has yet been proposed."[39]

Churchill's views came to dominate debates on grand strategy: in late July the Chiefs of Staff relegated the army's role largely to an occupation force in the final stages of Germany's defeat. "Massive bombing" would be relied upon to destroy the Germany economy and morale.[40] Churchill's faith in this view rested not only on implicit assumptions about the effect of bombing, but also on assumptions about weaknesses in the German economy. Several of these proved to be misguided, ill-founded, or simply overly optimistic, including the assumption that the German economy was already nearing capacity; that it had readily exploitable Achilles' heels, like oil; and that the German people already were greatly worn down by privation and the effort involved in war preparation. The British assumed that Hitler fully intended war in 1939, and that he would have undertaken it only if his economy were in full gear. The führer, they presumed, had organized his industrial war machine in an efficient, regimented way. But they presumed, too, that it was not up to the demands of a long war—it would collapse under sustained pressure. In September 1940 deliberations, the Chiefs of Staff concluded that if Britain maintained economic pressure on Germany, its deficiencies in oil, food, and textiles "may prove disastrous" by 1941. In the same month the MEW speculated that since the German economy was more brittle than in the First World War, "an acute shortage of oil or a tie-up of the transport system might cause a breakdown of the closely-knit Nazi system." Earlier, in a public speech of 18 June, Churchill had reminded his countrymen that in 1918 their terrible German foe had "quite suddenly, quite unexpectedly . . . collapsed before us."[41]

If these views had sustained the hopes of nervous policymakers in their darkest days, they also set up exaggerated expectations for Bomber Command. Pressuring the German war economy would prove far harder than planners expected. In the meantime, urgent issues dictated immediate priorities: Bomber Command was called upon to aid in the battle of Britain by attacking German airframe assembly factories, aluminum plants, air fields, and stores. In addition, Bomber Command was told it must help forestall a military attack from the sea; accordingly, German ports and shipping were to receive renewed attention. The net result was that the force divided its attention in multiple directions, and the effect was minimal. For instance, in return for 1,097 sorties against airfields (and a loss of sixty-one aircraft), Bomber Command destroyed five German planes on the ground and damaged twelve. Damage to airfields was hard to assess, but, as the official historian of the battle of Britain explained dryly, it "seems to have caused the enemy no serious embarrassment."[42]

Though engaged in a close-run thing, RAF fighters managed to prevail in the air battle over British skies. Victory was due to prewar attention to air defense, scientific and technological advances, the dogged determination of Fighter Command, and some crucial German errors. The Luftwaffe, headed by the rash, self-indulgent Hermann Göring, discovered that waging a successful air offensive was no simple matter. Paradoxically, however, the Luftwaffe failure did not seem to blunt the Air Staff's enthusiasm for its own planned air offensive: the latter managed to convince themselves that the Germans had misused their resources. The German bombers of 1940–41, they argued, could not match the ordnance payloads of the heavy British bombers then in the works. And the Germans would not hold up very well under air attack: taking the war to Germany would undermine the "gloss of national unity" that the Nazis had labored to create.[43] Perhaps under the circumstances, this attitude was not surprising. Britain was in a desperate situation: the bombers provided the only means of offensive action against Germany. Looking stoically ahead, the British kept themselves from despair by cultivating a selective blind spot. As one historian has argued, "[T]he Air Staff, and indeed the government, were sustained by a faith wholly at variance with the known facts of the situation."[44] Through the summer, however, reality often intruded on grasping optimism. Oil targets proved very difficult to find and hit with any reliability. Sir Charles Portal complained to the Air Staff that his force was incapable of performing all of its tasks. In particular, he believed neither that his force could consistently hit oil targets, nor that its light scale of attack against such targets could generate worthwhile results. He argued that for tactical reasons scattered bombing was unavoidable. Using an old argument of Trenchard's, he rationalized that dispersal "largely increases the moral effect of our operations by the alarm and disturbance created over the wider area."[45]

German air attacks on Britain peaked in August. Following the fall of some German bombs on London the night of 24 August 1940, Bomber Command retaliated with attacks on industrial targets in Berlin (25 August). Portal believed that German behavior in the war to date had freed Britain to "take the gloves off" and give as good as she got. Churchill's thinking ran along the same lines. In July he had written to Lord Beaverbrook, Minister for Aircraft Production, about the need for an "absolutely devastating exterminating attack by very heavy bombers from this country upon the Nazi homeland."[46] Churchill suggested that Portal might spread his attacks as widely as possible over cities in Germany. But most Air Staff members still preferred to prioritize selective attack, despite Portal's reservations.[47] Indeed, one memorandum from the Air Ministry's Plans Division—suggesting curious gaps in organizational coordination, and revealing the extent of misplaced optimism in some circles—argued that, since Bomber Command had been adequately trained for precise bombing of important selected targets, anything less would have little appeal.[48] A new bombing directive, issued 21 September, continued to stress the disruption of Germany's oil supply as the basis for long-term offensive policy. In the meantime the Germans had begun to supplement the daylight battle with nighttime bombing. Initially this concentrated on London but was soon extended to other British cities.[49]

Portal, acutely aware of the limitations of his force, wanted to follow

Churchill's advice. The prime minister's encouragement and the expectation of poor winter weather allowed Portal to make some headway against Air Ministry arguments. His views, however, complicated the careful consideration given to civilian casualties and collateral damage in the August 1939 and June 1940 guidance. Though he had no authority in political matters, Portal believed that events had justified a direct attack on the "will of the German people to continue the war." He argued that if heavy material destruction could be "periodically meted out to different towns," it would produce a generalized fear of bombing that would then facilitate "panic and exaggerated reports," even following scattered raids.[50] The debate took on a new complexion as a result of a reshuffling within the RAF hierarchy: Vice Chief of Air Staff (VCAS) Sir Richard Peirse took over the helm of Bomber Command, while Sir Charles Portal went to London to take over as Chief of Air Staff. As CAS-designate and later as CAS (beginning 25 October 1940), Portal could directly shape Air Staff policies. At a meeting to discuss bombing policy, held on 23 October, he advocated a program of heavy incendiary attacks on large, populous areas. He argued that if the air war resolved itself into a contest of wills, the British "will prove themselves to be tougher than the Germans." In the end, the meeting produced a compromise: attacks on oil would continue to be the focus of long-term strategy, but Bomber Command would turn more of its attention to assaults on German morale.[51] On the night of 16 December 1940, Bomber Command attacked the city of Mannheim in its first deliberate "area raid" of the war.[52]

Ideas about what comprised enemy morale, or how to undermine it, however, remained muddled at best. Britain's domestic experience reflected this. The government, recognizing the crucial role of public support and steadfastness in war, had created a Ministry of Information to handle government propaganda and sustain homefront morale. But more than two years passed before its officials "made any attempt to define what it was they were charged with sustaining."[53] Lacking a clear sense of its objective, the Ministry floundered about, becoming the object of considerable criticism and ridicule in the early years of the war.[54] Even as they worked out the requirements for implementing air raid policies and emergency medical procedures, they struggled with the more ethereal aspects of preserving the public will to fight. Despite the government's grave fears that breakdown on the homefront would mean defeat in war, its efforts to think through and shape the social and psychological aspects of the problem were flailing and largely irrelevant. If the elusiveness of the term "morale" had been an asset to Trenchard, it was a problem for those recruited to serve in the Ministry of Information.

Much to the relief of officials, the British homefront proved robust during the battle of Britain and the "blitz" against British cities (particularly London) that followed for six months afterward. As we saw in chapter 2, there had been no clear consensus on how the British public might fare in air war, but many official prognostications (often reflecting a problematical analysis of the World War I experience) had been alarmist and bleak. In the 1930s predictions offered up by many professionals (including doctors, psychologists, and social scientists) were grim: panic, social upheaval, radical increases in mental illness and emotional breakdown.[55] The stresses imposed by the immediacy of the German threat in the summer of 1940 intensified the concerns of some officials in positions of high authority; some of the most anxious scenarios came from those concerned with Britain's class cleavages, or the potential appeal of pacifist or communist propaganda. Harold Nicholson, then working in the Ministry of Information, worried about the resilience of Londoners and the potential appeal of peace petitions being circulated in air raid shelters by the communist party.[56] The reliability of the working classes came up once again as a topic of urgency in government circles, but concerns were based on assumptions rather than empirical evidence. In fact, surveys undertaken by Home Intelligence indicated little sign of class resentment, and every sign that the nation had achieved an unprecedented degree of national unity spanning class boundaries. Still, even when working-class robustness was acknowledged, it was sometimes attributed to unflattering causes like ignorance of the military and political situation.[57]

Unsurprisingly, assessments of the impact of specific enemy air attacks often reflected the prevailing assumptions of those doing the assessing. And it took time to understand what indicators were meaningful. With no available precedents to follow, the Ministry of Information had to make things up as it went along. On occasion, Ministry officials perceived worrisome trends: occasional looting; depression and some signs of hysteria following the serious Coventry raid of 14 November 1940; despondency in Bristol; frayed nerves in Portsmouth. But these problems, it was discovered, were very often symptomatic of inadequacies in local aid and relief efforts. And certain behaviors that were viewed as worrisome, like trekking (leaving a town for the safety of the countryside), were actually quite rational, sensible responses to danger. Contrary to prewar prognostications, hospital admissions for neurosis declined, suicide rates fell, and drunkenness declined by half.[58] The experts had been proved wrong. To their credit, however, they were quite prepared to admit it. Writing in *The Lancet* in 1941, Dr. Felix Brown explained, "The incidence of genuine psychiatric air-raid casualties has been much lower than might have been expected; the average previously healthy civilian has proved remarkably adjustable." He added that women had not been "a weakening element in the general population"; indeed, his data indicated that women fared better than men.[59]

The stress of the raids had not exacerbated class or ethnic differences; instead it created a sense of shared purpose and national identity. Many commentators pointed out that citizens took overt pride in traditional British calm in the face of adversity; indeed community spirit developed around the idea that "The British can take it." As psychologist P. E. Vernon pointed out, "Each newly raided city has wished to emulate the example of London."[60] In addition, the analogies drawn between soldiers and civilians under air attack (which had almost always been drawn to the disadvantage of civilians) were subjected to more rigorous analysis—with surprising results. Civilians subjected to air attack were now seen to possess a number of advantages over soldiers in the same circumstance. Civilians had the enormous psychological advantage of being able, simply, to move out of the way. They had far greater physical (and thus psychological) freedom than soldiers who had no choice but to stay put. And civilians were not forcibly separated from their homes and from familiar social conditions. This sense of connectedness to the familiar was an important element of mental stability.[61]

In response to a Gallup poll asking what had made them most depressed that winter, Londoners in early 1941 ranked the weather over aerial bombing.[62] Overall, the British endured their ordeal with calm, determination, and public-spiritedness. But if this news was felicitous for those charged with keeping homefront morale high, it was rather more problematical for those who argued in favor of air attacks aimed at German morale. As noted above, though, the contradiction was not grasped: the British were "tougher" than the Germans, and the British would pursue a more determined, overwhelming air offensive than their enemy had done.[63]

Optimism about the potential of British bombing was revealed in an interesting correspondence between Bomber Command chief Sir Richard Peirse and Polish authorities. In January 1941, Peirse received a letter directly from Count Stefan Zamoyski, writing on the authority of the Commander-in-Chief of the Polish Army, asking if it might be possible for Bomber Command to attack a German concentration camp in southwest Poland called Oswiecim (Auschwitz). Peirse put the question to Portal, stating, "If you judge it to be a desirable diversion . . . then I could undertake it with a small Wellington force under suitable moonlight conditions." Portal did not judge it to be a desirable diversion since he could see no way to carry it out with any hope of success. He told Peirse to prepare a letter to Zamoyski explaining the difficulties. Peirse thus regretfully informed Zamoyski that limitations on accuracy and the weight of bombs that could be carried to such a distance would inhibit chances for a successful mission. And, significantly, he added that it was important for him to concentrate every one of his bombers against industrial targets in Germany since "we are likely to precipitate a crisis in Germany's war economy this year."[64] Peirse's optimism, re- markable in retrospect, nonetheless reflected a truly held belief about the likelihood of causing hardship in Germany in the near term. And it held up despite the fact that he was able to complete only three opera- tions against oil targets in January and February 1941.[65] In general it was not uncommon for intelligence assessments undertaken in late 1940 and early 1941 to be wildly optimistic—and Air Staff assessments often were not far behind. One of these claimed that industrial output in the Ruhr-Rhine and Frankfurt-Main districts had fallen by more than 30 percent (due to the lack of sleep among workers), and that bombing had affected 25 percent of the total productive capacity of Germany.[66]

In February, Portal informed Peirse that the mood in London was swinging from oil and toward the "general dislocation of industry by mass attacks on industrial centres." He also told him that the RAF was "on the defensive with a vengeance owing to the situation in the Atlan- tic" and added that "a very high proportion of bomber effort will inev- itably be required to pull the Admiralty out of the mess they have got into."[67] Portal at this point forcefully argued that in the poor weather prevailing over northern Europe much of the time, it was "virtually impossible for a pilot to select and bomb a particular object"; but it was at least possible to attack areas successfully. He noticed, as well, that secret reports were indicating no German anxiety about oil production due to the availability of Rumanian oil fields.[68] Peirse resisted Portal's drift, pointing out that there was no reason voluntarily to abandon the oil directive "unless we are convinced . . . that whatever we might do to oil within the next two moon phases will not be worthwhile; and can offer some very attractive alternative which, at the same time, is likely to have more effect."[69]

The debate became less urgent in early March, when, at the behest of the Prime Minister, Bomber Command received a directive stating that in the near term, attention would be devoted to "defeating the attempt of the enemy to strangle our food supplies and our connection with the United States" by attacking U-boats at sea, in docks, and in building yards, and by attacking the Focke-Wulf and other bombers used against shipping. In the event, some room narrowly remained for continued attacks on oil. The British official historians have argued, though, that the rather dramatic refocusing compelled by the battle of the Atlantic was actually a saving grace for Bomber Command since any attempt to drive home an all-out offensive at that point would have been doomed to failure.[70] In the meantime, a Trenchardian trend continued to emerge. Deputy Chief of the Air Staff (DCAS) Air Vice-Marshal Arthur Harris argued that—even within the bounds of the existing directive—some targets ought to be selected to impose ARP (Air Raid Precautions) measures over wide areas in Germany. Thus, as the official historians pointed out laconically, in this period "some ostensibly naval targets were whole German towns."[71]

Later in the year Portal held out against resurrecting the oil plan. In May, DCAS Air Vice-Marshal Sir Norman Bottomley argued that in the five months since the oil directive had been issued, it had been shown that the plan was not feasible due to the difficulty of reaching and recognizing the targets. Bottomley recommended a campaign aimed at the "destruction of the morale of the population of certain vital industrial centers."[72] As their hopes for selective targeting faded, the members of the Air Staff increasingly accepted Portal's view. Unsurprisingly, events had led them to become more receptive to arguments and "evidence" that area attacks designed to undermine German morale might prove efficacious. The wish became father to the thought.

Despite their lack of clarity about the meaning of the term, officials engaged in a good deal of speculation about enemy morale. By late 1940 it was widely held in policymaking circles that German morale was weaker than British morale: the German people, already wearied by rearmament and fearful of further wartime burdens, would not withstand widespread bombardment.[73] This view was endorsed by the Chiefs of Staff at the beginning of 1941, in a report arguing that the Germans had been undernourished and subject to strain throughout the whole period of Hitler's regime, and were thus more subject to collapse than a nation of greater stamina. The report suggested that harassing action and incendiary attacks on the centers of German population might produce internal disruption. One of the several factors it ignored, however, was that the German standard of living under Hitler was higher than it had been in the years of economic depression.[74]

In May 1941 the retired Lord Trenchard weighed into the debate through a memorandum to Churchill, which was then forwarded to the Chiefs of Staff. Using his peculiar mathematics to support the notion that no bomb is wasted on a city, he proclaimed that "ninety-nine percent of the bombs dropped on cities would contribute directly to the destruction of German morale." Resurrecting his own views about the relentless and incessant offensive, he argued further that the attacks should be made every night, even if only one bomber could be sent over. Since British aircrew casualties would be heavy (he postulated 70 percent of the front line in a month), 400 to 500 percent of the reserves would be necessary, and aircraft production would have to receive top priority.[75] In early June, Trenchard offered his views at a meeting held by Portal to discuss bombing policy. He argued exactly what he had argued in 1918 and 1928, pointing out that everything turned on "the difference between the German and British mentality." He said that reports from a wide variety of sources indicated that, in contrast to the British populace, the German civil population stood up "very badly" to the strain of repeated bombing attacks. Undermining German morale, he argued, ought to be Bomber Command's primary aim; he recommended repeated attacks designed to force the population into air raid shelters, into a state of demoralization, and ultimately into a defensive stance from which they would not recover.[76] The former CAS argued that the weakening of morale could have an important effect on industrial ouput: "damage to essential services caused by indiscriminate bombing in a town was far greater than that caused by the aimed bombing of factories." Trenchard asserted that the destructive synergy of these two effects should be exploited since the Germans were more susceptible than the British. He insisted that "no town of any size should consider itself safe," and specified that morale raids should be held at frequent intervals to prevent the people from recovering. Finally, he argued that while the "primary plan" for attacking morale could be combined with a "secondary military plan" for attacking particular types of targets, priority ought to be given to the former when a choice presented itself.[77]

Having presented his case, Trenchard departed to allow the other participants to dissect his ideas. Some wished to postpone an all-out campaign against morale until the following year when Bomber Command's attacks could be more intense and frequent.[78] Peirse still advocated selective targeting, arguing that maximum moral effect followed from material damage. At the end of the meeting, Portal asked the Director of Plans to draft a paper for the Chiefs of Staff and the Defence Committee arguing that while the battle of the Atlantic would continue to have priority, the principal objective of the bomber force should be "the morale of the German people linked with suitable transportation targets." He cautioned that the paper would have to be carefully worded to secure political support in the Defence Committee, and pointed out that, were the plan adopted, the presentation of news concerning the results of the attacks would have to be "carefully handled."[79]

Trenchard had his critics. The First Sea Lord, Sir Dudley Pound, thought Trenchard's views overstated; both Pound and Sir John Dill (Chief of the Imperial General Staff) were concerned that Trenchard did not allow for cooperation with the other services. And Portal acknowledged that Trenchard's vision assumed an unfettered air force free of all other demands imposed by the war. Nonetheless, the Chiefs of Staff endorsed Trenchard in principle when they concluded that "the most vulnerable point in the German nation" is "the morale of her civilian population under air attack." Since there was no chance that a force as large as Trenchard wanted could be built in the near term, the spirit of his dictum had to be reconciled with a small Bomber Command subject to frequent diversions from its preferred primary role.[80] The new directive, which called on Bomber Command to attack transportation and communications targets (in particular marshalling yards), was a compromise: it satisfied those who wished to produce direct economic results from bombing, and also those who wished to see indirect effects accrue, partly due to bombs missing their targets and falling in the built-up areas around railway stations. Issued on 9 July 1941, the directive argued that the weak points in the German armor were the inland transport system and the morale of the civilian population. In addition, the Air Ministry resurrected (from the W.A. plans) a plan for burning German forests, instructing Peirse to carry out fire-raising attacks when the weather did not permit the attack of specific targets outlined in the new directive. Forest attacks, it was argued, would have both a material effect and a psychological effect "on the rural population who are not normally subjected to attack."[81]

New information arriving late in the summer of 1941 had the effect of pushing Bomber Command further in the direction that Portal had been trying to guide it. In August a photo-reconnaissance survey (the Butt Report) revealed that, despite aircrew claims, only about one in five crews were bombing within five miles of their intended targets.[82] The report forced even the staunchest optimists to rethink the situation. Peirse was dismayed and discomfited.[83] The prime minister, who had begun harboring doubts about the bomber offensive, told Portal that the report required "most urgent attention." Days later he reflected, "It is an awful thought that perhaps three-quarters of our bombs go astray. If we could make it half and half we should virtually have doubled our bombing power."[84] At the same time, the Chiefs of Staff discussed the very high losses then being sustained by Bomber Command: no less than 107 aircraft had been lost between mid-July and mid-August. The prime minister suggested that attacks be scaled back in the face of bad weather.[85]

Portal at this juncture undertook to improve navigation, develop marker bombs, and to train "expert fire raising crews." In addition he urged that it had become necessary, under the circumstances, to undertake a careful reconsideration of bombing policy. He explained that there was a growing body of opinion to the effect that "by keeping as many Germans out of bed as possible for as long as possible every night we shall achieve far greater moral effect and not much less material effect than by attempting concentrated attacks with the primary object of material destruction."[86] Vice Chief of the Air Staff Sir Wilfrid Freeman entered a strong objection to the momentum of events, however, arguing that material damage could be achieved only by concentration and not by the dispersal of effort that Portal was recommending. He rejected the notion that British policy should rest on the assumption that German civilian behavior was fundamentally different from British civilian behavior. Freeman emphasized that "Lord Trenchard's theory . . . depends on a basis which is fundamentally unsound. Material damage would be negligible and the enemy's morale, if not stimulated, will certainly be strengthened in a very short time." But Portal held his ground, arguing for "dispersal so as to set the sirens blowing in as many areas as possible."[87]

Churchill's intense disappointment with the record of Bomber Command spurred him to lash out at Portal, triggering the autumn confrontation detailed in the introductory chapter of this volume. Though Churchill vented his many pent-up frustrations over the disparity between prewar RAF claims and its actual performance to date, he did not take up Portal's challenge to reengineer British grand strategy to shift resources away from Bomber Command and toward other fighting arms. Despite its failure to contribute much of anything to the early war effort, Bomber Command still looked to Churchill like a much-needed tool in the British arsenal; after all, no other service could take the offensive, however limited, against Germany and thereby help sustain British homefront morale. Churchill remained anxious, however, about whether Bomber Command would "justify the large proportion of the national effort devoted to it."[88]

Though the existence of Bomber Command helped buoy the homefront, it is just as well that its early operations were not disclosed in much detail. In the autumn of 1940, Bomber Command lost through crashes six times the number of aircraft shot down or lost over enemy territory through other causes.[89] And a year later when, on 1 October 1941, Bomber Command's assigned targets were in Stuttgart and Karlsrühe, its planes were reported wandering over twenty-seven other cities.[90] Without sophisticated scientific aids for navigation and target finding, the job of finding anything smaller than a city became a matter of chance—and, often, locating cities themselves was beyond the ability of British crews. Also, Bomber Command crews in 1940–41 occasionally dropped remarkably high percentages of their total load on dummy installations, erected carefully and elaborately by the Germans to draw British fire away from real targets. During one raid on Berlin in 1941, for instance, RAF crews dropped forty-three times more high explosives and forty-seven times more incendiaries on a dummy installation than on the city itself.[91]

During this period Bomber Command's offensive remained viable only because of the commitment, determination, and stoicism of its crews. Throughout the six years of its campaign, about half the total aircrews who served were killed. Out of every hundred men who joined operational training units, only twenty-four would avoid death, injury, and/or German prisoner of war camps. As Mark Wells has pointed out, "No other Western Allied combatants, except for their American daylight bombing counterparts, suffered the same huge casualties, nor faced the mathematical certainty of their own deaths so routinely and so unflinchingly."[92]

Whether fair or not, the performance of a military organization inevitably is associated with its commander. In light of Bomber Command's 1941 record, Sir Richard Peirse's reputation was hardly on the rise. Portal's patience with Peirse had already run thin when, on the night of 7 November 1941, Bomber Command lost thirty-seven aircraft in bad weather. Peirse claimed that the weather had deteriorated unexpectedly and that the inexperience of his crews had contributed to the debacle. But Portal concluded that Peirse had ignored his own meteorologists.[93] The stage was set for a change in leadership. Before that change was effected, however, a new bombing directive came to dominate Bomber Command's operations. It represented the culmination of momentum that had been building since 1940—momentum guided by Portal all along the way. On 14 February 1942, Bomber Command was directed to attack area targets with the aim of undermining "the morale of the enemy civil population and in particular, of the industrial workers." The directive suggested that, "This is the time of year to get the best effect from concentrated incendiary attacks."[94] Only in late October did the Air Ministry finally get around to revising formally its policy regarding the rules of bombardment to be adhered to by field commanders. Restrictions that had applied at the outset of the war—and still pertained to bombing in occupied territory—no longer applied to Germany itself: "Consequent upon the enemy's adoption of a campaign of unrestricted air warfare, the Cabinet have authorised a bombing policy which includes the attack of enemy morale."[95]

A week after the 14 February directive was issued, Air Chief Marshal Sir Arthur Harris took the helm of Bomber Command. Harris had acquired a reputation as a man of action able to work toward a goal with great energy and determination. During the interwar years he had amassed an impressive record as a commander who paid attention to the technical and operational details often overlooked by others. In the opening days of World War II, he gained crucial combat experience as the head of Bomber Command's No. 5 Group. Then, from late 1940 to mid-1941, he served as Deputy Chief of Air Staff, where he developed further insight into the problems facing Bomber Command and took a special interest in the technical issues involved. Before being brought in to lead Bomber Command, Harris served as the head of an RAF delegation to the United States.[96]

Though very much a product of Trenchard's RAF, Harris bristled at Britain's overall military unpreparedness during the interwar years. He had coauthored the important 1936 Joint Planning Committee report assessing Britain's options in a war with Germany in 1939. A worst-case scenario, the paper was intended by its authors to light a fire under governmental decision makers. But it had proven a stronger tonic than the Chiefs of Staff were willing to put before the cabinet, and it was circulated in a toned-down form that had the unhelpful effect of heading off serious ministerial discussion.[97] The episode did not prompt Harris to be more circumspect in the future; indeed it had just the opposite effect.

Harris was brusque, opinionated, outspoken, and searingly perceptive. He was also somber in spirit, single-minded, dogged, determined, and, in certain respects at least, thick-skinned. Taking the helm of Bomber Command when he did, he needed these qualities. Throughout 1941 arguments had raged about whether Bomber Command ought to receive the budget and material its advocates claimed would be necessary for a successful offensive in the future. Harris set out to convince the nonbelievers. He moved quickly to try to restore the morale of Bomber Command crews, and to win the respect and confidence of the prime minister. With Harris's headquarters at High Wycombe only a short drive from Chequers the Commander-in-Chief could, and did, frequently impress his views on Churchill in person. Though a strong relationship between the two men did not last through the end of the war, it nonetheless helped to secure and bolster the position of Bomber Command at a crucial moment.

When Harris was brought in to take command, his colleagues at the Air Staff knew exactly what they were getting. Harris had never been one to hide his personality, his predilections, or his prepossessions. In his autobiographical account of the war, written in 1947, Harris would explain that for nearly twenty years he had "watched the army and navy, both singly and in concert, engineer one deliberate attempt after another to destroy the Royal Air Force."[98] Among airmen, Harris seemed particularly to have internalized this threat to RAF independence; it had made him defensive and bitter throughout his RAF career, and it would bear heavily on his behavior during World War II. Aside from Trenchard himself, no other RAF officer of the period was so consistently antagonistic toward the other services as Harris.

A committed bomber advocate, Harris had a perspective on strategic bombing that did not fit neatly into either the Trenchardian or Tivertonian camp. Like Trenchard, Harris fully expected that bombing would have a psychological effect, but he did not separate this out or elevate it above the impact of actual physical destruction. To Harris it was all of a piece: the moral and the material—the direct and the indirect—were inextricably linked. As he would later explain to Lord Trenchard, his own view of efficient bombing was simply to do the maximum amount of damage possible to Germany's most important industrial-politico-morale objectives."[99] In the same vein, he viewed attempts to seek out Tivertonian "bottlenecks" or "key nodes" (to use a later American term) as too clever by half. Indeed, he would scornfully refer to quests for such targets as "panacea mongering," making derisive reference, for instance, to the "Schweinfurt fans" who wanted to strike German ball bearings, and the "oily boys" who sought to prioritize petroleum targets. Harris believed, instead, that cities concentrated everything important to a modern state, and therefore the most efficient way to use bombers in war was to direct them against the main cities of an industrialized enemy. He was certain that if he could destroy vast stretches of Germany's largest cities—the edifices sustaining and supporting modern industrial life—he would surely bring the war to a close on his own terms. This approach was not about short cuts particularly (although Harris did believe and expect that an all-out bombing campaign would preclude having to land Anglo-American troops on the continent). It was a form of aerial warfare that was more akin to a Clausewitzian frontal assault on the enemy than a clever Sun-tzu-like attack on a point of particular vulnerability. The destruction of a high enough percentage of the enemy's infrastructure and urban factory floorspace would eventually and inevitably stop the enemy in its tracks. For Harris, it was as simple and straightforward as that.

The early war years seem to have cemented Harris's commitment to city bombing. Not only was he well aware of the operational limitations of the RAF, but he was increasingly convinced of the soundness of his instincts about targeting. He would later write, "The Germans again and again missed their chance, as they did in the London blitz that I watched from the roof of the Air Ministry, of setting our cities ablaze by a concentrated attack." Harris explained that the blitz caused British air planners to appreciate the principle of concentration: "the principle of starting so many fires at the same time that no fire fighting services, however efficiently and quickly they were reinforced . . . could get them under control."[100] But Harris did not feel that the German attacks on Britain had offered much of a window into what a larger and more determined British air offensive might accomplish. He was convinced, in particular, that the effects of accretion would be decisive: "There was every reason to expect not only that one thousand acres of devastation in a town would cause more than ten times the loss of output resulting from the destruction of one hundred acres, but also that when a large number of towns was similarly devastated the total loss of output could not be estimated merely by adding together the various acreages of devastation in all the towns."[101] Along with this, Harris believed that non-industrial damage caused from air raids—damage to public utilities, gas lines, sewers, and so on—had an important impact on the enemy. All this left him well suited to implement the directive of 14 February 1942. Some air staff members, however, viewed the area bombing directive as a temporary expedient to be implemented only while Bomber Command was expanding its strength and improving its target-finding abilities. This difference of views would lead to great difficulties later on.[102]

Harris's efforts to bolster the fortunes of Bomber Command and to focus it on city bombing received some assistance early on from Churchill's scientific advisor, Lord Cherwell. On 30 March 1942, Cherwell addressed a memorandum to the prime minister asserting that bombing Germany's fifty-eight principal towns would be decisive. The claim drew on data from a Ministry of Home Security report, still being written up, on air raids in the British cities of Birmingham and Hull. But, according to one of the two authors of that report, Cherwell's use of the data was problematical, and his interpretation of its main finding on morale was "misguided." Cherwell argued that the "de-housing" of people in those towns had produced signs of strain, and that if such effects could be multiplied by a factor of ten, "there seems little doubt that this would break the spirit of the [German] people." Cherwell also expected that worker productivity would be greatly depressed. But the Birmingham-Hull report had concluded, in fact, that there was no evidence of panic in either town, and, aside from some alarm and anxiety always associated with air raids, there was no mass antisocial behavior. Loss of production was caused almost entirely by direct damage to factories, and that loss had been only about 5 percent.[103]

Though the report on Birmingham and Hull could not have spoken directly to the likely effects of much larger raids, it provided no basis for the assumptions that Cherwell drew from it; his conclusions rested on equal parts selective reading and wishful thinking. Similarly, the Air Ministry's own summary of the report drew policy conclusions, in a section titled "Practical Application," that did not flow naturally from the evidence. Many years later the official historians would point out, "[T]hese policy decisions could not be justified by the probability calculations themselves because the calculations seemed probable only to those who, in any case, believed in the policy."[104]

Nonetheless, Cherwell's intervention had an important impact at a crucial moment. Both Portal and Sir Archibald Sinclair, Secretary of

State for Air, supported the conclusions of his memorandum, and Churchill, eager to hear some promising news, lent an ear. He could find little solace elsewhere. On Christmas Day 1941 the British had surrendered Hong Kong to the Japanese; on 1 February 1942 British forces evacuated Derna; two weeks later Singapore capitulated. Rommel advanced while German U-boats shredded Allied shipping. Pressing questions of Allied grand strategy soon would have to be settled, and Churchill needed options to pose against those preferred by the Americans and, especially, the Soviets.[105] The members of the RAF delegation in Washington also needed official commentary on the bomber campaign to resonate, positive and unqualified. They were determined to encourage all-out American production and avoid giving American navalists any opening for concentrating on Japan instead of Germany.[106] Timing did, indeed, make the difference. Harris now had an apparent green light from the highest policy levels to proceed full speed ahead.

On the night of 30 May 1942, Bomber Command launched the first of its "thousand bomber raids" on Cologne. In a dramatic but risky effort to create support for Bomber Command by showing what it might achieve if expanded, Harris scraped together his assets by calling upon reserves, including crews in training. The raid produced dramatic results, damaging about one-third of the total area of the city. It greatly strained the capacity of the force, however, and could not be regularly repeated without a serious increase in resources. But it provided impressive copy for the newspapers and raised the spirits of those on the homefront. With Harris in charge, new aircraft types coming into production, and improved target-finding techniques in development, there seemed reason to hope that the bomber offensive might offer some check on Hitler's plans. When Churchill met Stalin in mid-August, news about the progress and prospects for Bomber Command was the only thing that pleased and brightened the Soviet leader who felt, otherwise, that the British were not making a significant enough contribution to the war effort.[107]

Like Churchill, Harris dreaded the thought of sending men back to the continent to fight a ground war against the Germans; unlike Churchill, Harris believed that Bomber Command—given the right support and resources—could win the war entirely on its own. But this would require that Bomber Command be free of the influence of those Harris derisively called the "diversionists": those who, he believed, were frittering away Bomber Command's potential on operations other than city bombing. Many of these "diversionists" were from the other services, but Harris had even more disdain for those lurking inside Air Staff offices. Hoping for a sympathetic ear from the old air marshal who had been through it all, Harris would tell Trenchard, "I sometimes wish you could do something to help us to get the Air Ministry *as a whole* more bomber offensive minded. Our greatest difficulties and our greatest opposition . . . arise surprisingly enough in the Air Ministry."[108]

Harris's dislike and distrust of the other services was so strong that he had great difficulty accepting their claim on RAF assets, even for urgent causes. Those air commanders who, early in the war, had gained diverse experience had an easier time than Harris seeing the war effort as a joint utilization of resources, rather than a competition for them. Air Chief Marshal Sir Arthur Tedder, for instance, had had no alternative but to learn to get along with the other services while he served in the Middle East and the Mediterranean. Maj. Gen. Carl A. Spaatz, who would later head the U.S. Strategic Air Forces in Europe (USSTAF), had his early war experience forged in a similar way.[109]

In mid-June 1942, Harris sent the prime minister a personal minute in which he argued vigorously for giving Bomber Command the support it would need to defeat Germany without resort to a large-scale ground campaign that might, Harris speculated, see Britain's youth slaughtered once again in the mud of Flanders.[110] Harris felt so strongly about the issue that later in the summer he reiterated his argument to Churchill and, in an even more passionate form, to Portal. In planning for an eventual invasion, Harris argued, "United Nations' soldier strategists" were driven by a "blind and even pathetic urge to do that only thing which they know how." He insisted that the war would have to be won in the air, and that Bomber Command could not be diverted repeatedly from its main purpose. He stressed, in underlined text: "*When it becomes possible to defeat the German army on land by United Nations' forces transported overseas, there will no longer be any need to defeat them. They will already have broken.*"[111]

Harris's vision was a radical one, and in the end Churchill was not prepared to commit himself to it. If Harris was disappointed by Churchill's refusal to bet solely on the air power horse, he was nonetheless the beneficiary of the prime minister's great desire to wear Germany down prior to a direct confrontation between Allied ground forces and the Wehrmacht. Throughout the war Churchill had complex and ambivalent attitudes toward strategic bombing, and these attitudes made him frequently anxious, impatient, and unpredictable. Back in March he had summed up his views on bombing to Secretary of State for Air Sir Archibald Sinclair: "[I]t is not decisive but better that doing nothing, and indeed is a formidable method of injuring the enemy."[112] The conflicted phrasing betrayed much. Churchill had been, at various points in his extensive political life, one of the most potent supporters of bombing as a means of war. During World War I he had encouraged the Royal Naval Air Service to wage preemptive strategic air attacks against

German zeppelin sheds. In the 1930s he had actively warned of the Luftwaffe threat, and had encouraged a build-up of the RAF. And his World War II strategic plans all relied heavily on air power. But at the same time he had doubts—first expressed in 1917 while he served as Minister of Munitions—about the ability of bombers to break civil will. He reiterated these in a January 1939 article he wrote for the American magazine, *Colliers*.[113] If he had embraced the Cherwell report (thereby ignoring arguments he himself had made in September 1941), he had almost certainly done so because other options were lacking at a crucial moment in the course of the war.[114] And, if he relied on Bomber Command, he nonetheless was deeply concerned not only about its many weaknesses, but also about possible criticism of its operations on moral grounds. Thus, when the Americans began planning and preparing their own strategic bombing offensive, the prime minister took careful notice. He was acutely desirous of guiding American policy. Churchill's faith in Britain's ability to hold Germany off had depended to an important extent on his expectation that the United States would enter the war in a timely fashion. This hope had proven too optimistic early on, but the consequences of Pearl Harbor filled him with a sense of renewed energy: now that the Americans were in, he believed, the fate of the Axis was sealed.[115] All the details of cooperation remained to be worked out, however.

THE UNITED STATES AND THE PREPARATION FOR WAR

In late January 1938, President Roosevelt, declaring American defenses inadequate in light of the troubling world situation, had asked for appropriations for naval construction and air defense. By year's end he recommended an augmented Army Air Forces of 20,000 planes and an annual capacity of 24,000 aircraft. Army Chief of Staff Gen. George C. Marshall likewise supported the Air Corps request for the newest B-17B bombers. In January 1939, Roosevelt asked congress for $300 million for the Air Corps, which, at the time consisted of 1,700 tactical and training craft, 1,600 officers, and some 18,000 enlisted men. Within three months Congress had approved a program to procure 3,251 aircraft, and to increase the strength of the enlisted force by 150 percent. A press release of 3 April 1939 explained that the War Department was prepared to acquire "the best types of aircraft now in existence," beginning an expansion that would continue through 1944.[116]

During the interwar years, Roosevelt had hoped for an international agreement that would limit the effects of aerial bombing. When this hope faded and war came to Europe, he came full circle and advocated the creation of a serious American air force. Fearful of the Germans, particularly of their scientific and technological abilities, Roosevelt felt he had to support a bomber force to deter German attacks on the American east coast, and, if necessary, to help fight and win a war in Europe. Roosevelt's concerns about Germany were reinforced by the highly inflated German production figures given him by U.S. Army intelligence sources. One estimate postulated that Germany would produce 42,500 aircraft in 1941; in fact, the true figure was 11,776—with no true strategic bomber of long range.[117] Nonetheless, the perception mattered more than the reality. Roosevelt hoped that a vast air program would deter Hitler, bolster American confidence, and arm the British and French against German aggression.[118]

When war broke out in Europe in September 1939, the United States declared its neutrality and concentrated on developing the strength to keep the Axis powers out of the western hemisphere; Roosevelt's first concern was hemispheric defense. But American planners soon realized that the survival of the Allies in Europe, especially Britain, would help forestall an attack on the United States. Thus, long before it was drawn into the conflict, the United States undertook to provide material aid to those states fighting the Axis. This task, on top of an ever-expanding domestic military build-up aimed at hemisphere defense, war preparation, and deterrence of Japan in the Far East, put an enormous initial strain on American production. By late 1939 the U.S. aircraft industry had a backlog of orders totaling $630 million; of this, $400 million was attributable to foreign orders.[119]

By 1940, when aid to the Allies had become avowed American policy, a radical expansion of facilities enabled the United States to begin to become the "arsenal of democracy." On 16 May 1940, for instance, the president called for an annual output of 50,000 aircraft: the American aircraft industry was asked to expand twentyfold.[120] Just as they had in 1917, the Americans turned to the prospect of an aerial fighting force. Preferable to a large land army, a high technology alternative like air power promised a way to prosecute war in a cleaner, briefer, and more effective way than had been the case during the disillusioning and distasteful 1917–18 ground war in Europe. Even though U.S. military spending expanded across the board, it was easiest to get congressional approval for aircraft. Newspapers and journals made the case for airplanes instead of ground troops, and the public readily accepted it.[121]

But with expansion (and despite good intentions), military and industrial efforts sometimes went in circles. British air officers in the United States frequently had their patience tried as they waited for aircraft that did not materialize. Naturally the British wanted priority; just as naturally, the Americans sought to avoid gutting their own programs.[122] Sir

John Slessor, sent to the United States in the autumn of 1940 to explain British Air Staff plans for expansion, committed his impressions to paper some months later: when the United States woke up to the danger of war, "all three services . . . immediately aimed for the moon and set about building up the most immense forces that they could think of, without any proper coordination or examination of what their military policy should be and what forces they required to implement it." Service rivalries in America concerned Slessor, as did the absence of a workable chiefs of staff system: "It is one of the most unfortunate aspects of Service policy in the United States that the Army and Navy really seem to hate each other more than they do the Germans."[123]

In September 1941, Sir Arthur Harris, then with the RAF Delegation to the United States, had sent an acerbic letter back to London (to VCAS Air Chief Marshal Sir Wilfrid Freeman) complaining about army and air force leadership in the United States: "[Hap] Arnold and [George] Marshall are in the position of having expended, or rather accepted, vast sums of money for the production of Forces which exist only on paper or in their own rather muddled minds. They have literally nothing to show for it, and are covering up in self-defence lest their bluff be called. In that situation to demand from them any substantial part of the little that is being produced is in effect like asking them for blood in a bucket."[124] In the same skeptical vein he bet Freeman that if the Americans came into the war short of being "kicked in," then he would eat "a pink elephant, trunk, tail, and toenails—and raw at that." Harris did suggest, however, that if the war were to go on long enough, unlimited American resources and manpower would make up in "smothering effect" what they lacked in careful implementation.[125]

In addition to expanding their infrastructure for wartime aircraft production, the Americans began to formulate a detailed strategy for employing their own air power. Unsurprisingly, the ideas that had been developed by those at the Air Corps Tactical School now came into prominence. As the airmen saw it, their long battle for recognition, validation, and greater autonomy was finally yielding fruit. Like the British, American bomber advocates held fast to their ideas: nothing in the European air war to date had shaken ACTS faith in the potential of independent strategic air operations. Carl A. Spaatz, then a colonel, was sent to Britain in 1940 to observe the RAF at close hand. He came back with all of his existing views intact. Despite British and German experience, he remained convinced that groups of self-defending bombers could operate without the aid of escorts, and that "precision" attacks of selected targets would be necessary for maximum results. His time in Britain did convince Spaatz, however, that civilian populations were robust and therefore it would be harder to shatter enemy morale than some proponents of bombing had expected.[126] Spaatz held fast to those ideas that defined the thinking and self-identity of his organization. Thus, he failed to realize, for instance, that acquiring a long-range escort fighter ought to be an immediate priority for the Americans. He reacted more flexibly to those things less dear to the heart of his service, such as the impact of bombing on morale. Like his RAF colleagues, he observed the battle of Britain through cognitive filters that carefully preserved his preexisting views. "The English have developed real air power," he argued, "whereas the Germans so far appear to have developed a mass of air geared toward the army and [are] lost when confronted with properly applied air effort."[127]

At this point, American air planning went forward as part of a broader effort to determine national strategic priorities in the event of American entry into the European war. Ironically, just as the British were beginning seriously to contemplate a shift to area attacks, the Americans were confirming their commitment to the selective attack of industrial targets. This commitment was codified in AWPD/1 (Air War Plans Division), written in August 1941. Triggered by President Roosevelt's request for aircraft production information from the newly designated U.S. Army Air Forces (USAAF), the plan assumed that a "sustained air offensive" would prove crucial in a war against Hitler. Ranging well beyond the original request, it was developed in just over a week by a handful of officers who had been heavily indoctrinated into the "industrial fabric" mentality of the Air Corps Tactical School: Lt. Col. Harold George, Maj. Lawrence Kuter, Maj. Haywood Hansell, and Lt. Col. Kenneth Walker. They designated "key node" targets in the German war economy for destruction by American bombers flying in self-defending formations in daylight.[128]

AWPD / 1 called for attacks against the industrial and economic structure of Germany to "break down the capacity of the German nation to wage war." While it assumed that the air force would support a final invasion of the continent, it held out the possibility that if the strategic air offensive itself were successful, it might preclude the need for such an invasion. Overall it called for 2,164,916 men and 63,467 aircraft. Target selection was at the heart of the plan, and this was supported by analyses of bomb tonnage, aircraft attrition estimates, and airfield and crew requirements. In the end, the planners selected 154 targets, including the German electric power system, transportation, petroleum, aircraft assembly plants, and aluminum and magnesium factories. Planners assumed that "precision" attacks on approximately fifty electric generating stations would, along with attacks on transportation and petroleum targets, collapse the German military and civilian establishments.[129] Even though AWPD/1 was based on selective targeting of key points in the German war economy, it also incorporated ideas about the psychological effect of bombing. Specifically, it included the possibility that at the right moment—when the enemy was already worn down and weary—air attacks for psychological effect against German cities might hasten enemy surrender. A carefully timed attack on Berlin was envisioned as the most likely scenario for such an operation.[130]

In line with the thinking developed at the Air Corps Tactical School, the authors of AWPD/1 believed that bombers could rely on speed, high-altitude, massed formations, armament, and defensive firepower to penetrate to their targets in daylight. Regarding the latter, they called for increased gun power in larger calibre machine guns and in cannon; power-operated turrets; and adequate armor plate protection for the combat crew and vital parts of the airplane.[131] Still, the planners thought it wise to hedge their bets by paying at least some attention to the question of long-range escorts. Following a pattern established in the interwar years, they misjudged the type of aircraft required when they called for a large, heavily gunned, two-seater type that would have a range equal to the bombers they would escort, and would have armor to protect each of the crew members. They requested that prototypes be built and that production be expanded if such planes proved necessary in numbers.[132]

The long-range escort fighter still proved a vexing problem, even though the means of solution—the auxiliary, droppable fuel tank—was within reach if only the right people had been able and willing to grasp it. The need to keep aircraft design simple in order to facilitate high volume production was apparently the reason why Col. Spaatz, who had some sway in these matters by virtue of his work in the AAF's Plans and Matériel divisions, passed up an opportunity to have auxiliary fuel tanks placed on 623 P-39D aircraft.[133] Later, in October 1941, a board convened especially to discuss the future development of pursuit aircraft and failed, again, to perceive the issue with insight and clarity. One of its members, Col. Ira Eaker, would be influenced by the attitudes of the RAF, which still had not found any solution to the escort problem. While the board saw a need for auxiliary tanks for fighters, and also for increasing the safety of bombers on deep penetration raids, it "never connected the single engine pursuit aircraft and drop tanks with the bomber protection problem."[134] If this oversight seems remarkable in hindsight, it speaks to the power of cognitive filters and the enduring blind spots they can produce. Undaunted by either the German or British conversion to night operations in the face of unacceptable daylight losses, the Americans convinced themselves that the superior speed and armament of the B-17, along with the maintenance of tighter formations, would avoid the troubles faced by European bombers.

Another key assumption of the plan was that American bombers would exploit the accuracy and precision of the gyro-stabilized Norden bombsight to destroy targets at the rate calculated. The faith placed in high-altitude "precision" bombing had yet to be challenged. It rested on data derived from artificial training conditions and bombing competitions that bore little resemblance to the operational demands of war in Europe.[135] Although the AWPD/1 planners tried to account for the differences, they still made some mistaken assumptions, such as the number of sorties required to destroy a target, and the number of sorties that could be flown per month given the weather in northern Europe. These problems insured that the plan would have to be altered later, sometimes dramatically, based on operational experience.

In December 1941 the shock of Pearl Harbor focused Allied attention on the American plan for air warfare. Despite the direct attack by Japan, President Roosevelt saw Hitler's Germany as the more immediate threat to American security. This perception, which had been formalized in Anglo-American staff conversations earlier in the year, underscored the priority of American planning for a European war. For Churchill, the attack on Hawaii was, ironically, a bright spot in an otherwise bleak year. He immediately journeyed to the United States in order to observe and guide American war planning.[136]

THE FIRST STEPS TOWARD A COMBINED BOMBER OFFENSIVE

A reorganization of the American defense establishment, which had become effective on 20 June 1941, had created the U.S. Army Air Forces and had placed Gen. Hap Arnold at its helm. Arnold was directly responsible to the Army Chief of Staff, and was responsible for establishing all policies and plans for army aviation. After Anglo-American consultations in January 1942, a Combined Chiefs of Staff Committee was formed to meet regularly in Washington.[137] U.S. strategy, which, like Britain's would rely heavily on aerial bombardment, would be implemented by using Britain as a base of operations. This required not only that the Americans work out plans for bringing the Army Air Forces across the Atlantic to join the offensive against Hitler, but also that the British make organizational changes in order to have the personnel in place to help facilitate those plans. Finally, the two allies had to hammer out a mutually acceptable command hierarchy and a coordinated plan for the air offensive. In early February 1942, Gen. Arnold designated Carl Spaatz (now a two-star general) to serve as the head of the Army Air Forces in Britain.

The Americans made clear from the start that their interest was in selective attacks on German industry based on high altitude "precision" daylight bombing. On 19 February 1942, just days after Bomber Command's new directive had focused it on the morale of German workers, the British Air Staff in Washington conveyed to the Air Ministry in London the essentials of U.S. air plans. The Americans were "very firmly convinced of the inadequacy of the night bombing and consequently of the need to intensify the day bombing effort."[138] Heavy bombers would be sent to Britain, and the Americans hoped that with improved armament and crew training these bombers could operate without fighter escort.[139] The British knew that this commitment to daylight "precision" bombing would cause a number of difficulties, and they made clear to the Americans their doubts about deep penetrations into Germany during daylight. They urged the Americans to join them, with the RAF as senior partner, in a bomber offensive waged by night.[140]

Clearly, the Americans and the British were heading in two very different directions, and these had to be reconciled somehow. In the event, the process would prove to be tumultuous. The British, due to their own grim experience, had no faith in the Americans' ability successfully to conduct a daylight precision campaign over Germany. The Americans, for their part, had no interest in changing their plans. Historian Noble Frankland, in a paper he delivered at the United States Air Force Academy long after the end of World War II, argued that there were three reasons why the Americans had clung so tenaciously to daylight bombing of selected military targets even though there was plenty of evidence to indicate that it was a problematic strategy: (1) they believed that the B-17 was better suited to daytime operations than to nighttime ones; (2) they were unimpressed with the British effort; and (3) they were simply determined to operate their own air forces independently.[141] He was quite right on all counts, though his third point deserves elaboration. USAAF commanders, focused as they had been on the fight for organizational independence, were determined not to relinquish their air assets to British control, or to jump to British tactics before trying out their own. But more was at work than national assertiveness. American airmen had a genuine, unshaken conviction in their theory of air war. They found it elegant, straightforward, and promising. It helped them around the ethical concerns raised about bombing, and it promised leverage in the ongoing struggle for service autonomy. By emphasizing these things, and simultaneously downplaying British doubts, they held fast to their convictions. Still, as the American official historians have pointed out, the Americans were committed to daylight precision bombing "more as a matter of faith than of knowledge empirically arrived at."[142]

On 8 June 1942 the United States' European Theater of Operations opened officially with Spaatz at the helm of the Eighth Air Force, comprised of VIII Bomber Command, VIII Fighter Command, VIII Air Support Command, and VIII Service Command. Brig. Gen. Ira Eaker was in charge of Eighth Bomber Command operations. Only in September was a joint U.S.-British directive on day bomber operations finalized. It stated that the aim of day bombardment by Allied air forces based in Britain was to achieve continuity in the bombing offensive against the Axis. It further stated that night bombardment policies, which fell under the purview of Bomber Command, would remain as defined in existing Air Ministry directives. The day bombing offensive, to be directed toward the "destruction and damage of precise targets vital to the Axis war effort," would develop in three phases. First, U.S. bombers, aided by U.S. and RAF fighter protection, would attack targets within the radius of action of RAF fighter forces. Second, U.S. bombers would attack objectives within the radius of action of both U.S. and RAF fighters, relying principally on U.S. fighter cover, and extending the range of attacks. Finally the United States would "develop its full day bomber offensive," drawing upon RAF cooperation and support as needed.[143]

As had been the case for the RAF, target selection for the Eighth Air Force initially was governed by the limitations of the force. Targets prioritized early on included aircraft factories and repair depots, marshalling yards, and submarine installations. The early efforts were designed as well to determine U.S. capacity to destroy point targets by "daylight accuracy bombing" and to "beat off fighter opposition and to evade anti-aircraft opposition."[144] AWPD/42, an update of the original U.S. air war plan, and the most comprehensive plan produced by USAAF Headquarters, was completed in September 1942. However, AWPD/42 appeared before a satisfactory body of intelligence had been developed to serve as its foundation. A program for selective targeting necessarily had to rest on very detailed and accurate analyses of the enemy war economy. In order to provide this analytical infrastructure, General Arnold authorized in December the creation of what would become the Committee of Operations Analysts (COA), a group of service and civilian personnel tasked with assimilating and analyzing industrial intelligence from all available sources. Subcommittees were established to study crucial elements of the German economy, including petroleum, aircraft production, transportation, and food.[145] For the remainder of the war, the COA strove to put American target planning on as sound a foundation as possible. Nonetheless, hunches and best guesses sometimes had to substitute for facts. Target planning remained a very imperfect science. And planners erred when they assumed that the industrial systems of highly developed states would be essentially similar; information, plans, and blueprints from U.S. plants were not always the useful mirror-images that analysts assumed them to be. And, though the COA was comprised of knowledgeable personnel, it lacked industrial engineers and managers among its ranks.[146]

The early U.S. raids, which had begun with an attack on marshalling yards at Rouen, France, on 17 August, probed only the fringes of European airspace. Wishing to get the force off to a good start, American commanders insured that the raids were flown in good weather conditions and with heavy fighter escort. Even so, bombers were often subjected to intense German fighter attacks. For instance, the USAAF mission flown on 2 October, which included 156 aircraft, saw 3 B-17s lost and 36 damaged, and 1 B-24 lost and 10 damaged. U.S. crews claimed high numbers of kills against German fighters, but these were questioned by the British and subsequently shown to be greatly exaggerated.[147]

Although subsequent reconnaissance often belied claims of accuracy and extent of damage, the American bomber crews appeared at first to be hitting their objectives. Indeed, General Eaker was so encouraged that he predicted that 40 percent of bombs might fall regularly within 500 yards of the aiming point, so that adequate numbers of American bombers might shut down German aircraft factories and submarine activities in a matter of months.[148] The British, more guarded in their assessments, pointed out the orchestrated quality of these early raids. A further source of Anglo-American frustration was the slow build-up of American aircraft and infrastructure, as well as the diversion of air assets to support the North African invasion. Both the British and General Arnold were disturbed, as well, by the drain of air assets into the Southwest Pacific Theater.[149]

Churchill became increasingly concerned about the limited size and capabilities of the American force, and the Americans' tenacious commitment to daylight bombing. On 16 September he wrote directly to Roosevelt urging him to prioritize the production of aircraft.[150] One month later Churchill diplomatically informed Roosevelt's special assistant, Harry Hopkins, that the British were not as optimistic as the Americans about the initial efforts of the USAAF over France. He warned against the danger of committing too fully to producing bombers suited only to daylight work.[151] In London, a debate over "what to do about the Americans" raged between Churchill and his air advisors.[152]

Both Churchill and Portal feared that the Americans would commit resources to a campaign they could not ultimately carry out, at which time it would be too late for a tactical volte-face. Decisions made in 1942 would determine the operational possibilities for 1944. In a memo of 26 September, Portal asked rhetorically if it were not "essential" to persuade the Americans at least to lay the foundations for night bombing.[153] Assistant CAS Sir John Slessor, who had spent the winter of 1940–41 in the United States, was by far the most optimistic about the Americans' prospect for success on their own terms. He argued that the Americans are "a bit unwarrantably cockahoop as a result of their limited experience to date." But, he added, "[T]hey are setting about it in a realistic and business-like way, paying special attention to gunnery training, distribution of ammunition in the aircraft, cutting the bomb-load and increasing the ammunition of wing aircraft, and so on. And making all allowances for their natural optimism, I have a feeling they will do it." He warned, "They have hung their hats on the day bomber policy and are convinced they can do it . . . to cast doubts on it just at present would only cause irritation and make them very obstinate."[154] In a memorandum to Sir Archibald Sinclair, he expressed confidence in the American plan and argued that massed formations might make daylight bombing feasible.[155]

Neither Churchill nor Portal was convinced, however, and their letters and minutes accurately foresaw many of the problems that the US-AAF would face in the coming year. But Sinclair stepped into the fray as a voice of diplomacy. He urged Churchill not to force the issue before the Americans had made a real try at their "cherished policy of daylight penetration." He was certain they would not be convinced of anything except through their own experience. And he further warned that to be fractious over bombing policy would play right into the hands of navalists like Adm. Ernest King, and might tempt the Americans to focus on the Pacific.[156] At this point Portal followed suit and argued to Churchill that the Americans at least be given a fair trial. He suggested, though, that the Americans should look into radar navigation and bomb-aiming aids, and "press on with night adaptation as an insurance." Though still harboring deep concerns, Churchill chose to keep quiet.[157]

Discord between the British and the Americans over the other's approach to strategic bombing sometimes emerged in staff memoranda and in public discourse. For instance, a May 1941 letter from the Director of the Air Corps Board to the Chief of the Air Corps complained that the British "lack appreciation of the value of accuracy in bombing," and that they had made no "material effort . . . to determine and use effective methods of bombing."[158] The American press, which had made American bombsights a symbol of American technical prowess, and had helped to convince the public that American bombers could drop their ordnance into a "pickle barrel," was often critical of highly inaccurate early British efforts. Equally, the British press decried the meager results, in the summer and autumn of 1942, of the highly touted American "precision" bombing force. Peter Masefield, writing in the *Sunday Times* (London) even before the first raid was flown, argued that the B-17 and B-24 were not suited to daylight operations in Europe.[159] The U.S. Air Staff reacted promptly and aggressively. As the American official historians explained, "a good deal of special pleading was done in behalf of precision techniques, and comparisons were sometimes drawn to the disadvantage of the British doctrine."[160] Indeed, an American study of British bombing at Rostock, Cologne, and Osnabruck, dated 19 October 1942, went so far that General Eaker had to distance himself from its conclusions in an effort at alliance damage control. The study asserted that British area bombing was unreliable and inefficient, and that "precision" bombing of selected targets would provide greater results through concentration of effort.[161]

Despite the disappointments, setbacks, and bickering, however, both the British and American air forces maintained a gritty optimism. Largely undaunted by the gap between prewar promises and wartime results to date, the leaders of both forces figured that success would be a matter of time and resources. If Churchill had had deep concerns about Bomber Command—and even deeper concerns about the USAAF—he nonetheless continued to feel that they had to carry a significant part of the war effort. American military and political leaders felt, too, that bombers had an important role to play in the prosecution of the war. Their determination that bombers would be able to carry out the tasks envisioned in prewar theory caused them to downplay or discount the indications that it might not be possible, at least in the way they had thought. Neither the British nor the Americans realized the extent of the struggle that lay ahead, still, for the Allied air forces. Though they would continue to gain in size, strength, and operational efficiency, they would continue to face vast problems. Indeed, by the end of 1943 the entire Allied strategic bombing effort was in danger of collapse. The next chapter will examine how that crisis in Allied strategy was met and overcome. It will examine, as well, the many problems and dilemmas faced by the Combined Bomber Offensive in the later years of the war, and the many ethical questions posed by those problems.

CHAPTER FIVE

The Combined Bomber Offensive: 1943–1945

By the end of 1942 no theory of strategic bombing had been proven or disproven. The Americans were just out of the starting blocks with their nascent air campaign. Sir Arthur Harris had helped bring Bomber Command through the many crises it faced in 1942, and he was gearing up for the vast campaign he planned to implement. But losses in Bomber Command remained high enough for Chief of Air Staff Sir Charles Portal to insist that the statistics be confined to "the smallest number of people." In the early months of 1943, only 17 percent of Bomber Command crews could be expected to complete the required thirty-mission tour of duty, and the life expectancy of new bombers was only forty hours flying time. Bomber Command was held together by the courage and determination of its crews.[1]

Competing claims and rivalry between the British and the Americans had characterized the closing months of 1942, as various interested parties in the bombing debate sought to assert the soundness of their own ideas and to lobby for influence. Clashes over how best to utilize bombers would become a central feature of the Anglo-American air campaign, and these would become particularly intense during the latter stages of the war. Harris would continue his steadfast commitment to city bombing and would lose no opportunity to convince those around him that his path was the correct one. Other Allied air commanders would survey a wider range of options, looking for whatever clues to German vulnerability they could find in available intelligence information. In the Far East, the Americans would first try to pursue the selective targeting of key industries, but poor results and the attractions of applying fire techniques to vulnerable Japanese cities would move the American Twentieth Air Force toward the prosecution of a campaign that, in practice, had little to distinguish it from Bomber Command's nighttime city raids over Germany.

IDEAS AND REALITIES:
THE COMBINED BOMBER OFFENSIVE IN 1943

British doubts about daylight "precision" bombing made the Americans all the more determined to press the case for it. The issue was taken to the January 1943 Casablanca conference on Allied grand strategy. In a presentation to Churchill, Gen. Ira Eaker lobbied hard for the American position. His briefing text was designed to help the Americans hold their ground against the prime minister's persuasive powers. What Eaker and his colleagues did not know, however, was that Churchill's own advisors had worked to persuade him to allow the Americans to go their own way.

Eaker argued that the entire orientation of American strategic aviation was toward daylight bombing, and that the Americans simply were not trained and equipped to join the nighttime offensive. He also highlighted the potential of the American bombsights for accuracy against small targets. He pointed out that American "precision" bombing would allow Germany no rest, and would benefit the Allies by reducing the strain on Britain's airdromes, airspace, and communications. Significantly, he argued that daylight bombing would aid in the destruction of the German day fighter force: the enemy "has to fight our bombers when we hit his vital targets." Eaker's discussion of German day fighters revealed his continued faith that the firepower of the B-17s would enable them to cope adequately with the enemy; he made the case that the Americans would knock down "at least 2 or 3 fighters for every bomber lost."[2] But his estimate was built on greatly exaggerated pilot claims; if the Americans did not comprehend this point, the British surely did.

In the end, despite some optimistic and high-sounding rhetoric about "round the clock" bombing, each side gave the other one the freedom to go its own way, and the resulting bombing directive was an agreement to disagree. The Casablanca directive stated that the "primary object will be the progressive destruction and dislocation of the German military, industrial, and economic system, and the undermining of the morale of the German people to a point where their capacity for armed resistance is fatally weakened."[3] Such general language contained something for everyone, and gave a good deal of latitude for interpretation to the field commanders. Harris found in it a continuing endorsement of his approach. Though Portal was theoretically in control of what was now called the "Combined Bomber Offensive" (CBO), the real power was in the hands of Harris and Eaker, since the tactical decisions of field commanders often were as consequential as higher-level strategic plans.

In March, the American Committee of Operations Analysts (COA) submitted targeting recommendations to Gen. Hap Arnold, endorsing selective targeting designed to "cause a high degree of destruction in a few really essential industries or services."[4] American operational plans, drawn up by Eaker and finalized in April (as the "Eaker plan"), rested on the assumption that "precision pattern bombing" was tactically feasible from high altitude (20,000 and 30,000 feet) in the face of enemy defense—a proposition the Americans felt had been "proven" by their bomber raids waged in the first three months of 1943. But Eaker understood that the success of his plan would hinge on winning air superiority; he would attack the Luftwaffe in the factories where its aircraft were made, and, to the greatest extent possible, in the air as well.[5]

The primacy of counterforce operations and the general thrust of the Eaker plan, which drew on long-standing themes in American bombing theory, were reflected in the draft of the Pointblank bombing directive. Drawn up with the assistance of American and British economists and operations analysts, revised, and then submitted to the Combined Chiefs of Staff in May, Pointblank identified six target systems comprising seventy-six precision targets, the destruction of which, it was claimed, would gravely impair the Axis war effort.[6] It warned that the Germans were rapidly building their fighter defenses so as better to protect their vital industries. The authors stressed that "if the growth of the German fighter strength is not arrested quickly, it may become literally impossible to carry out the destruction planned and thus to create the conditions necessary for ultimate decisive action by our combined forces on the Continent."[7] Thus, the German fighter force was designated the "intermediate objective" that would take initial priority as a means of establishing the conditions for an extension of the bomber offensive, and also as a means of establishing air superiority over Germany prior to the opening of an Allied second front.

In endorsing Pointblank, Portal and his staff accepted many of the assumptions that underlay American air theory. Significantly, Pointblank acknowledged that German fighters threatened both the American daylight and the British nighttime campaign, and endorsed a counterforce campaign against the Luftwaffe over an aerial *guerre de course*. The plan directed that Eighth Air Force day raids should be complemented by RAF bombing attacks against the surrounding industrial area at night; the authors pointed out that, "Fortunately the industrial areas to be attacked are in most cases identical with the industrial areas which the British Bomber Command has selected for mass destruction anyway."[8] Harris, however, was guarded in his attitude to Pointblank. While he had posed no major objections to the Eaker plan, he would allow himself to be pulled only so far toward selective targeting, even to denude Luftwaffe strength. He was much less interested in "intermediate objectives" than in what he believed to be a more direct and effective utilization of bombers: the attack on cities. Accordingly, he managed to revise the language of the Pointblank draft to give him the latitude necessary to continue the general area offensive.[9] In the event, he only infrequently coordinated Bomber Command's raids with those undertaken by the Americans. In order to maintain support for his command, though, he knew he had to produce results. Under such circumstances, 1943 became—in the words of the British official historians—a "bombing competition" rather than a combined offensive.[10]

The years 1942 and 1943 had brought ever-increasing operational strength to Bomber Command; indeed, the British official historians have argued that 1942 was "the turning point" in the operational development of the force. The incendiary technique was demonstrated against Luebeck in March of that year and many more such attacks followed, aided by new target-finding devices.[11] The Pathfinder Force, in which skilled crews marked targets at night, was created in August. And special units proved themselves capable of remarkable accuracy on occasion. But the whole of the force, which continued to focus on area bombing, became increasingly deadly in light of special developments in pyrotechnic bombs and incendiary clusters. In July 1943, Bomber Command raised a firestorm in Hamburg that leveled five square miles of the city center.[12]

On 7 June 1943, just days before Pointblank officially took effect, the cover of *Time* magazine featured Harris's profile superimposed over a drawing of repeated hammer blows against a gradually shattering Nazi swastika. The opening paragraph of the story read, "The air offensive against Germany and Axis Europe is suffering from understatement. The objective is not merely to destroy cities, industries, human beings, and the human spirit on a scale never before attempted by air action. The objective is to defeat Hitler with bombs, and to do it in 1943." But the author (anonymous) took a generally skeptical tone, pointing out the slower than expected build-up of American forces, the generally rapid recovery of German cities from bombing raids, and the lack of evidence of any imminent collapse of the German people. Harris's faith, however, did not waver.[13]

Evidence of Harris's commitment to city bombing could be found in the "Blue Books" he maintained at his High Wycombe headquarters. These oversized volumes were intended to make his case—in diagrammatic form—to all who would listen. In them, each of the major towns in Germany was assigned a "key point rating," which was an index of its overall industrial importance. Each town was portrayed as a circle, the area of which varied with its key point rating, and each circle was divided into colored segments showing the proportion of various main groups of industry making up the whole. The diagrams, constantly updated, also indicated the proportion of a town's inhabitants directly engaged in or dependent on its industries ("key point factor"), as well as the area of the town that Bomber Command had destroyed. Harris, very proud of this inventory of destruction, showed the leather-bound volumes to all important visitors who came through his headquarters.[14]

Harris's successes had afforded him a certain amount of autonomy, but not as much as he would have liked. Moreover, Harris continued to believe that Bomber Command was under siege from the "diversionists" and "panacea mongers." In a pointed letter to Deputy Chief of Air Staff Sir Norman Bottomley at the end of the year, he noted sarcastically that the "panacea mongers" must have been planted by the enemy in a deliberate attempt to insure that only the minimum amount of damage be caused to Germany through aerial bombardment.[15] Determined that the way to victory was through relentless attacks on cities, Harris resisted any efforts to divert his bombers from this mission. And he agitated constantly for better resources and increased respect for Bomber Command's achievements.[16] He felt that those who criticized the bomber offensive for not doing enough had no idea of how thin bomber assets had been spread, in large part due to the demands of the battle of the Atlantic. The naval use of air power, he complained, consisted of "picking at the fringes of enemy power, of waiting for opportunities that may never occur . . . and of looking for needles in haystacks."[17]

Not all of his bitterness was without foundation. In early 1943, Bomber Command was enjoined to attack submarine pens in a campaign that ultimately aided the navy very little, due to the great difficulty of damaging the structures. But many of Harris's complaints about the navy were parochial, since naval-oriented aviation had made crucial contributions to Allied survival.[18] Virtually the whole of the Western war effort—including Bomber Command's own fuel supply—depended on sea lines of communication. Certainly Harris was obligated to prioritize and fight for the interests of the strategic air offensive, but his vigorous protests against "diversions" were often narrow in outlook and caused no end of headaches for his colleagues and superiors. He was too quick to assume that those who prioritized naval targets were short-sighted or insufficiently "air-minded." In August 1943 the Secretary of State for Air, Sir Archibald Sinclair, wrote to Harris in exasperation: "I know that nothing I can say will undermine your conviction that we in the Air Ministry are all in a nefarious conspiracy to ham-string Bomber Command! I only wish that you could hear what the other commands say to me about the favouritism with which your command is deliberately . . . treated by us here."[19] Harris's views stood in stark contrast to those with a wider perspective. Tedder, in particular, had developed a vision of war "as a single problem in which the strategy, the tactics, and the technique of sea, land and air warfare respectively are inevitably and closely interlocked."[20]

Harris felt, also, that he had to battle for adequate press coverage for Bomber Command, and to combat enemy propaganda, which, as he saw it, was designed to prevent Allied leaders from understanding the effectiveness of their own air offensive.[21] Throughout the war Harris was aggrieved over two main issues pertaining to the media: that Bomber Command's contributions were badly slighted relative to the other services, and that the press coverage Bomber Command did receive focused all too delicately on damage to German industrial sites instead of the devastation visited upon German cities and the German population. For the former, he blamed "interested parties in the other services," "certain members of Parliament with axes to grind," and "other influential people" who "ought to know better."[22]

Regarding the latter, Harris believed that all the resources—material and human—fueling a state's capacity to wage war were legitimate targets of attack. He did not feel compelled to shroud his work in a guise designed to make it more palatable for the public, and he felt disdain for those who felt it necessary to do so, including the personnel of the Ministry of Information, the government's official propaganda arm.[23] His position was not only a matter of principle to him, but also a matter of protecting the morale of his crews. He understood the tension inherent in their performing a given mission on a certain night, and then later seeing a censored or manipulated version of it in the newspapers. Unsurprisingly, Harris's determination to pull no punches troubled his colleagues who either convinced themselves that much of the destruction wrought by Bomber Command was incidental or collateral, or that it had to be portrayed as such. They found it difficult to understand the stubbornness of his position, perhaps in part because they realized that the British public might raise questions about bombing later on, even if they were disinclined to do so in the midst of intense warfighting. Though he had been prepared to argue the case vigorously for city bombing, Portal had recognized that it had to be handled carefully in order to avoid stirring public discomfort. Churchill, too, was concerned about the potential for postwar backlash against Bomber Command's methods.

Harris's differences with his colleagues led him into an extended correspondence with the Under Secretary of State, Air Ministry, Sir Arthur Street. Writing to Street on 25 October 1943, he argued that too little attention had been paid to his force relative to the Allied ground forces, and that too much attention had been focused on "the bombing of specific factory premises" rather than "the obliteration of German cities and their inhabitants as such." He complained that, instead of stressing that the recently attacked city of Kassel "contained over 200,000 Germans, many of whom are now dead and most of the remainder homeless and destitute," official handouts emphasized that the Henschel locomotive works and various other important factory premises were in or near the city. "The result of this presentation," Harris wrote, "especially since the highly effective raids recently carried out by the VIII Bomber Command which *were* aimed at specific factories, is inevitably to give the impression that Bomber Command is trying to do the same thing as the Americans, and is doing it comparatively ineffectively."[24] This, he argued, compelled his crews to think that "the authorities are ashamed of area bombing." Concluding his letter, he asserted that the aim of Bomber Command should be unambiguously stated as "the destruction of German cities, the killing of German workers, and the disruption of civilised community life throughout Germany." He added, "It should be emphasised that the destruction of houses, public utilities, transport and lives; the creation of a refugee problem on an unprecedented scale; and the breakdown of morale both at home and at the battle fronts by fear of extended and intensified bombing are accepted and intended aims of our bombing policy. They are not by-products of attempts to hit factories."[25]

In mid-December, Street answered Harris, telling him that the Air Staff did not intend to change the orientation of publicity regarding Bomber Command operations. He explained, "No attempt has been made to conceal from the public the immense devastation that is being brought to German industrial cities." But he added, "In all official communiqués and pronouncements, however, the emphasis is such as to bring out what . . . is an obvious truth, i.e., that the widespread devastation is not an end in itself but the inevitable accompaniment of an all-out attack on the enemy's means and capacity to wage war."[26]

This answer, which Harris saw as disingenuous semantic hair-splitting, only outraged him. He responded in the blunt, unflinching manner that so often characterized his discourse: "It is surely obvious that children, invalids and old people who are economically unproductive but must nevertheless consume food and other necessaries are a handicap to the German war effort and it would therefore be sheer waste of effort to attack them." He went on, "This however does not imply . . . that *no* German civilians are proper objects for bombing. The German economic system, which I am instructed by my objective to destroy, *includes* workers, houses, and public utilities, and it is therefore meaningless to claim that the wiping out of German cities is 'not an end in itself but the inevitable accompaniment of an all out attack on the enemy's means and capacity to wage war.'" Harris understood that the Air Ministry sought, in Street's words, to "provoke the minimum of public controversy" and "avoid conflict with religious and humanitarian opinion." But he felt the issue went deeper than publicity policy. Unless his interpretation of the situation was accepted "without ambiguity or evasion of the issue," then Bomber Command crews were being sacrificed "in a deliberate attempt to do something which the Air Council do not regard as necessary or even legitimate, namely eliminate entire German cities."[27] Harris's concern that the British public did not comprehend the nature of Bomber Command's effort was, in fact, misplaced. Reports of Home Intelligence indicated not only that the public understood the nature of Bomber Command's war, but that they wished to see Germany punished.[28]

Harris's belief in the efficacy of city bombing was intuitive, but it also was supported by the selective reading of data, and by a number of problematical assumptions about the German war economy and German morale. The Bomber Command staff continued to assume that Germany had little slack in its economy and only limited ability to recuperate from bombing raids. In a 1942 report the staff claimed that the enemy was already "strained to the limit." (Conversely, the failure of German bombers to cause serious disruption in Britain from 1940–41 was explained away as a result of the island's economic "fat and tremendous recuperative power.") Though there was no systematic, analytical evaluation of enemy morale, the British continued to assume that Germany was worse off than Britain had been during the blitz.[29] If reports on the state of German morale were not always consistent with one another, they usually contained enough positive information to sustain the hopes of those who wanted to believe that bombing could seriously erode Germany's will to fight. A British Air Intelligence report of September 1942, for instance, had indicated that Germany was facing significant housing shortages for its population as a result of Bomber Command raids. A Directorate of Intelligence paper covering 15 February to 15 March 1943 argued that the period under review saw a "sudden, and in some cases a severe, decline in morale in the areas attacked, and increase in the areas over which the indirect results of raids have been apparent." And a March 1943 letter from the U.S. Embassy, which conveyed information from its Legation in Helsinki, claimed that an eyewitness to Bomber Command attacks on Berlin reported terrific devastation and panic among the city's citizens.[30] But these assessments, like all assessments of moral effect, were inherently subjective and liable to be interpreted according to the predispositions of the interpreter.

In addition, Harris believed that bomb damage assessments resting on photographic interpretation were inaccurate and failed to tell the whole truth. He expressed his views to Portal on this matter several times, pointing out that damage to German housing was more extensive, according to some German sources, than British sources indicated. He asserted that, particularly when built-up areas were at issue, damage was generally much more widespread than official reports implied. By questioning the work of British intelligence, Harris could retain his views about city bombing even as evidence mounted against its efficacy; and he could remain optimistic that the continued growth and improvement of Bomber Command would soon push Germany to collapse.[31] Such collapse, he hoped, might be provoked by an air assault on Berlin, planned for the long winter nights of 1943–44.

American airmen, too, were finding sources of optimism, and were reassuring themselves with wishful thinking. A report done under the auspices of the Chief of the Air Staff and the Commanding General of the U.S. Eighth Air Force, covering the period February to October 1943, argued that "all evidence points to the fact that conditions in Germany are resolving themselves into an ever more acute conflict of priorities, and a marked deterioration in morale." The report argued, as well, that concentrated daylight attacks on single vital systems (like fighter factories) "are likely to have produced within that industry far in excess of the sum of the visible damage." Like Harris, General Arnold was convinced that photos of bomb damage did not reveal the whole story. In an October 1943 talk to a conference of editors, writers, and news broadcasters in Washington, he argued, "You can't always measure damage done by what you see in the photograph."[32]

If the Americans and the British were taking heart from similar hopes and were working toward the same ends, they nonetheless utilized different means. In contrast to Harris, General Eaker was interested in the quest for efficiency through the careful selection of targets. In an October 1942 letter to General Spaatz, he had written optimistically, "I believe it is clearly demonstrated that the efficiency of day bombardment over night bombardment is in the order of ten to one." He told Spaatz that he anticipated losses, but he saw no evidence to indicate that "losses will be of such a high order as to make day bombing uneconomical."[33] Eaker fully endorsed the work of the operations analysts whose efforts had been utilized in the preparation of the Pointblank directive; indeed, he called their efforts "eminently sound" and their report "a magnificent piece of work."[34] He welcomed attempts to rationalize the targeting process, and he sought the kind of analytical advice and input that Harris consistently shunned.

Of course, the bomber offensive Eaker sought to undertake was in many respects the same one the British had hoped to wage in 1940–41. The failure of the British to fly successfully in daylight did not deter the Americans who were convinced that they would succeed where the British had failed.[35] As we have seen, initial USAAF raids were limited in both range and scope, and they rarely challenged targets the Germans felt compelled to defend. The concentration of German fighters on the eastern and Mediterranean fronts also helped insure that the early American efforts would be relatively unmolested. Indeed, nothing in the American's experience of bombing had yet forced a reexamination of their faith.

During the spring of 1943 the USAAF turned its primary attention from U-boat pens and construction sites to the German air force. But the campaign against the Luftwaffe, prioritized by Pointblank, proved harder than anticipated: American sorties against German airframe, engine, and component factories—limited in number at first because of ongoing production holdups back home—fell victim to the German fighters and anti-aircraft artillery increasingly assigned to the Western Front. In mid-April, 16 of the 115 U.S. bombers dispatched were destroyed in a raid on the Focke-Wulf plant at Bremen; a further 44 were damaged. Realizing that the Americans were looking to wrest air supremacy from them, the Germans set up a defense that, by the summer of 1943, contained a fighter command system covering a geographical zone up to 480 miles deep.[36]

General Eaker retained his faith, however, that daylight bombers operating in "well-flown formations" could penetrate enemy air space successfully—with a loss rate of 5 percent or less—in their pursuit of the German aircraft industry.[37] A September 1943 essay for the *Royal Air Force Quarterly*, written to defend and promote the American bombing effort, argued triumphantly that the Americans had "given the proof" that they could "hit the target from the sub-stratopshere" and "defend themselves against enemy fighters well enough to keep losses within reasonable bounds." It credited success to the .50 caliber machine gun arming U.S. bombers and to the tight formations used by bomber groups.[38] But events would prove that the Americans had not yet earned such bragging rights. Indeed, the basis for their optimism was fast evaporating. Continuing production problems meant that by the end of the summer, the Eighth Air Force was short of strength by some 240 bombers. In the meantime, German fighter strength on the western front had increased at a staggering rate: single-engine fighters had doubled in number, and the repertoire of deadly fighter tactics was expanding just as rapidly.[39] Also, American attempts at "precision bombing" were consistently hindered by pervasive cloud cover over northern Europe, and by the extreme altitudes forced upon the bomber pilots by German flak, fired by increasing numbers of anti-aircraft guns. The highly touted and publicized Norden bombsight, which had shown such promise in controlled test environments, had distinct operational limitations in Europe. Under the circumstances, Eighth Air Force bombers began to divert with disturbing frequency to area targets or to fringe targets less likely to exact a high price in bombers and crews.[40] Despite these setbacks, however, USAAF leaders were determined to maintain the daylight campaign.

Both the U.S. Committee of Operations Analysts (COA) and British intelligence sources had concluded that antifriction bearings represented a potential bottleneck in the German war economy, and that the Germans had not stockpiled them. The factories around Schweinfurt, Germany—sixty-five miles east of Frankfurt—were known to manufacture approximately one-half of the total Axis supply; they looked to be a concentrated and potentially lucrative target.[41] Harris had sought to resist pressure on him—maintained by those he dismissively called the "Schweinfurt fans"—to attack the target. But the Americans were interested. On 17 August 1943, to celebrate the first anniversary of USAAF operations in Europe, American bombers attacked the Schweinfurt antifriction bearing plants and the Regensberg Messerschmitt factory. It would be the largest and costliest mission U.S. bomber crews had flown to date, with 16 percent of the force shot down. This, however, did not deter a second attack on Schweinfurt in the autumn. The raid of 14 October, which can only be considered a disaster for the Americans, finally brought an end to the theory of the self-defending bomber. Of the 291 bombers dispatched, 198 of them were shot down or damaged. Indeed, in four raids carried out over six days in October 1943, 148 American bombers had failed to return to their bases.[42]

In a press conference where he explained that 593 Americans had been lost in the second Schweinfurt raid, General Arnold nonetheless sought to put a positive face on things. He argued that the losses were worth the goal, since Schweinfurt's production was essential to the German war effort. He pointed out, in what would prove to be a mistaken assumption, "We know the ball-bearing industry represents a potential bottleneck, for it is impracticable to assemble any considerable stockpile of ball-bearings." Arnold also sought to reiterate the American commitment to "precision" bombing, pointing out that the bombing was undertaken "with the care and accuracy of a marksman firing a rifle at a bullseye." The *New York Times* article conveying Arnold's commentary also gave optimistic assessments by Sen. Sheridan Downey (D) of California, who insisted that full-scale bombing would "bring the Nazis to their knees in four months," and by the USAAF's Brig. Gen. Curtis LeMay, who asserted that Germany would be neutralized "by Allied air power's systematic destruction of Nazi industry during the winter months."[43]

But the terrible losses had been a blow, and despite efforts at 1940s-style "spin control," there was no getting around the implications. Answering a question about bombing that came up in a press conference at that time, President Roosevelt pointed out laconically that the Americans could not afford to have sixty bombers shot down on a regular basis.[44] Whether Arnold was prepared to admit it publicly or not, the Americans had finally found inescapable a conclusion they had earlier refused to confront despite British warnings: unescorted raids deep into Germany were prohibitively costly.[45] The Allies' intermediate objective of the German fighter force was now, obviously, in serious jeopardy. Those planners, both American and British, who believed that Pointblank was key not only to a wider bomber offensive but also to an Allied second front, understood that it could not be allowed to fail. Heightened tensions led to recriminations. General Arnold wrote to Portal asking why Fighter Command could not be of greater help to American bombers. Explaining that Fighter Command aircraft had inescapable range limitations, Portal went on to argue that, in his view, the difficulties faced by the Eighth Air Force were due to the Americans' failure to make good on their production and reinforcement schedule.[46]

Realizing that the year's setbacks may have put his command in jeopardy, Eaker wrote to Arnold on 16 November 1943. Following the Trenchardian pattern of falling back on moral effects, he argued, "I am concerned that you will not appreciate the tremendous damage that is being done to the German morale by these attacks through the overcast, since we cannot show you appreciable damage by photographs. . . . The German people cannot take that kind of terror much longer."[47] At the Cairo and Teheran conferences of November and December 1943, Allied air leaders struggled to put a good face on things by offering up a quantification of square miles destroyed and asserting that German morale was "at an extremely low ebb."[48] But the reality was grimmer than they let on. Both the Americans and the British were struggling: Bomber Command's Berlin offensive, highly touted by Harris as a potential war winner, had yet to show results. In the meantime, more and more bombers were falling to Luftwaffe night fighters. Indeed, it is hardly overstatement to argue that, in the winter of 1943–44, the entire Combined Bomber Offensive (and therefore the operations that depended upon it) hung in the balance. Official Allied policy continued to call for attacks on the Luftwaffe, but the means by which to do it successfully were not entirely clear. The Americans were facing a crucial choice: either they would have to change targets, as the British had earlier in the war, or change tactics.

Eaker's rhetorical emphasis on German morale was not enough to save his position. At the end of the year General Arnold sent him to take command of air operations in the Mediterranean. Maj. Gen. James

Doolittle was installed as the field commander of the Eighth Air Force, and Maj. Gen. Nathan Twining took command of the Fifteenth Air Force, established in northern Italy in November. Carl Spaatz (now a three-star general) assumed overall leadership of the two air forces as commander of the United States Strategic Air Forces (USSTAF) in Europe.[49] When Spaatz took up his new post in late December 1943, he arrived at a critical moment. The pressures on him were very great, but he was able to take advantage of some things Eaker had been denied: American production finally was hitting its stride, and victory in the battle of the Atlantic meant that it was now much easier to transport the fruits of that production to Britain. And, despite heavy attrition from September 1943 to May 1944, the number of fully operational heavy bombers in the Eighth Air Force increased from 461 to 1,655, and fighter aircraft rose from 274 to 882. By mid-February, the Fifteenth Air Force was able to add twelve heavy bomber groups and four fighter groups to the total Allied effort in Europe.[50] Just as critically, the supply pipeline from the United States was beginning to include new aircraft—long-range fighter escorts—which would ultimately turn the tables for the Allied air war in Europe.

As we have seen, the problem of building a long-range escort capable of holding its own against enemy short-range defensive fighters had looked largely intractable to both the British and Americans. And their motivation to push onward toward a solution was surely undermined by their readiness to believe that escorts might not be needed anyway if bomber crews were adequately motivated to wage an aggressive offensive. During the early years of the war, the British remained pessimistic about the possibilities for escorts, while the Americans maintained the same conflicted attitudes that had characterized their interwar machinations on the subject.[51] On the one hand, they recognized the problem and, on occasion, expressed a desire to address it; on the other, they tried to reassure themselves that there might be no need for such a plane. If the 1941 American plan AWPD/1 had called for the development of escorts as a kind of insurance policy, it nonetheless sent planners down an unproductive path toward heavy two-seaters. AWPD/42 did not reemphasize the problem of fighters; instead, it argued that "our current type bombers can penetrate existing German defenses to the limit of their radius of operation without excessive losses."[52]

The failure to prioritize escorts and their supporting technology earlier meant that possible solutions to the bomber penetration problem were slow to be conceived. The demands of the war intervened too. In 1942 the invasion of North Africa diverted aircraft from Europe and stripped the Eighth Air Force of its P-38 fighters, replacing them with shorter-range Republic P-47 fighters suffering engine and radio troubles.

Over the summer of 1943 hopes pinned on the YB-40, a B-17 modified to serve as a bomber escort cruiser, proved unfounded.[53] Earlier, however, in the autumn of 1942, the USAAF had made preliminary inquiries into a technology that ought, by rights, to have received more attention sooner: the jettisonable auxiliary fuel tank. Work on suitable tanks proceeded in the spring of 1943, and, in July, the USAAF used them on a combat mission for the first time. Production difficulties in both Britain and the United States held up more extensive use of improved tanks, even as mounting bomber losses in the late summer and autumn gave greater urgency to their manufacture and employment. Not until December 1943 were they arriving in numbers that would allow them to make a difference.[54]

Adequate numbers of capable fighters were also slow in coming. Following a tour of operational units in England in the spring of 1943, Asst. Secretary of War Robert Lovett realized the importance of escorts; he informed General Arnold that there was an "immediate need" in Europe for long-range fighters and "proper tanks"—not only for P-47s, but for P-38s and P-51s as well. The P-51 had been produced originally for the British in lieu of the Curtiss fighters they had requested from North American Aviation, Inc. But the initial model, in which the Americans took little interest, had disappointing performance capabilities. Not until the British replaced its Allison V-1710 engine with a much more capable Rolls Royce Merlin 61 did the plane begin to show real promise. American interest in the plane picked up, and, equipped with the American-built Packard-Merlin engine, the P-51 quickly outclassed other aircraft of its type.

Even in the summer of 1943, however, the Americans had not totally recognized the potential of a solution so near at hand—in large part because they had not yet completely acknowledged that there was a problem to be solved. Of the first 145 P-51B machines produced between June and August 1943, none was sent to Britain as a long-range fighter. Only after the second Schweinfurt raid was the production schedule for the P-51s (and P-38s) reconfigured to give priority production to long-range escorts over reconnaissance types. Once they had been forced to recognize the problem, however, the Americans took advantage of the available solution.[55] Relying on a fully-functioning industrial production base, they built escorts and brought them into the European theater in large numbers.[56] Soon, escorted USSTAF bombers were flying regularly to strategic targets that the Germans felt compelled to defend, provoking furious battles of attrition between German and U.S. fighters. These contests ultimately proved to be a first step in the destruction of the Luftwaffe.

In this same period, the Americans took other steps to intensify the results of their bombing campaign. Quietly they had moved away from their emphasis on "precision" bombing and toward an acceptance (though certainly not an embrace) of instrument bombing aids. In his book on H2S radar, scientist Bernard Lovell argued it was no coincidence that the dramatic change in the negative American attitudes toward H2S coincided with Eighth Air Force operations in Europe, so often hindered by cloudy weather.[57] In late 1942, General Arnold had expressed interest in nonvisual bombing methods by ordering a study of navigational aids used in homing and target location by radio means, and Eaker urged and prioritized the acquisition of such equipment.[58] Early in 1943 individual bomb sighting (by bombardiers in each airplane) was abandoned and replaced by a procedure in which all aircraft dropped their bombs simultaneously on a signal from the leader of a combat "box" of 18 to 21 aircraft. Because each box covered a sizable stretch of territory below, the result was, inevitably, pattern bombing. Under combat conditions—when bombers had to contend with fighters, anti-aircraft fire, and smoke—it became very difficult to bomb in tight patterns. "Precision bombing" was simply not an applicable term for this practice.[59] In early November 1943, following on the heels of the second Schweinfurt raid, Arnold gave American bombers permission to operate "blind"—to attack area targets through cloud.[60] This enabled them greatly to increase the tempo of their bombing operations; indeed, "blind" raids quickly came to comprise a significant portion of the American effort in Europe. But Arnold, mindful of American public opinion and comparisons with the British, warned against the use of the term "blind bombing," as he believed it gave "both the military and the public the wrong impression." He preferred phrases like "overcast bombing technique," or "bombing through overcast."[61]

The urgent need the Americans felt to bomb through cloud meant that they would rely heavily on their few B-17s equipped with the H2X (derived from Britain's H2S) radar bombing aid. The H2X planes, equipped earlier in the autumn, served as pathfinders for American bomber groups. But there were problems with the H2X program, especially at its outset. American crews and commanders thought of themselves as part of a visual bombing force, and they resisted the imposition of new methods. Commanders, when called on to furnish crews for H2X training, often sent their poorest personnel. Pathfinder crews tended to be overworked and, initially at least, overburdened with extra duties and debriefings. Inadequate maintenance of the highly technical equipment (exacerbated by a lack of parts and maintenance personnel) was common, leading to equipment failures. And the aircraft in which H2X was installed were sometimes substandard. While some of these problems were solved, others lingered.[62] In February 1944, General

Doolittle remarked that hitting a precision target with H2X "has been largely luck." He added, "Ordinarily bombs are scattered over at least ten times as much area as with visual bombing. It is analogous to shooting into a flock of ducks rather than selecting your duck." Overall, American crews never became as skilled as their British counterparts when bombing on instrument.[63]

Early in 1943 the Americans already had begun to raise the percentage of incendiary bombs used in the bomb "mix" dropped on enemy targets. In a memorandum of 26 April 1943, Arnold pointed out that the Eighth Air Force would use incendiaries for (1)"burning down suitable precise industrial objectives" (when a more lasting degree of destruction could be obtained than with a similar tonnage of high explosive bombs); (2)"starting fires by day in the densely built-up portions of cities and towns to serve as beacons for the RAF to exploit at night"; and (3)"burning down the densely built-up portions of cities and towns by day attack alone when the occasion warrants."[64]

Arnold's concerns about phrasing aside, the simple fact was that the USAAF was resorting to area bombing. Though the fundamental intent of the campaign remained different from that of the RAF, its practical effects were now identical on many occasions. In periods of sustained bad weather, overall American accuracy was no better than—and often worse than—that of Bomber Command. In nonvisual bombing undertaken between October and December of 1943, for instance, the USAAF achieved accuracy rates no better than those documented by the RAF's 1941 Butt Report.[65]

While the American crisis over escorts was at its peak, Sir Arthur Harris was meanwhile engaged in the aerial attack on Berlin. As ever, he remained uninterested in searching for key nodes ("panaceas") in the German industrial structure. Encouraged by the weight of the raids his force had been able to inflict in previous months, Harris continued to hold out hope of a German collapse due to the sheer devastation of unrelenting city bombing. His successes in the summer of 1943 seemed to mitigate in favor of his case: heavy strikes like the one that engulfed Hamburg in fire made conceivable the idea that he might indeed be closing in on his objective.[66]

No one believed this more than Harris himself. By early November 1943 he believed he was rounding a corner. He sent Churchill a report that included a list of forty-seven German towns, nineteen of which were "virtually destroyed," nineteen of which were "seriously damaged," and nine of which were "damaged." Pointing out that most of the damage had been done since March 1943 "when the heavies came into full production and Oboe, H2S and the Pathfinders served to concentrate the effort," he went on to propose Berlin and eight other target complexes as the remaining priority targets for his force. Harris asserted confidently, "We have not far to go. But we must get the USAAF to wade in in greater force. . . . We can wreck Berlin from end to end if the USAAF will come in on it. It will cost between us 400–500 aircraft. It will cost Germany the war."[67] He believed, of course, that the Americans had to eschew their "disastrous diversions" (a clear reference to the Schweinfurt raids). Tellingly, he made no reference to an Allied second front.

Even though the Casablanca and Pointblank directives had sought to accommodate both Bomber Command and the USAAF, the guidance under which the two organizations were operating was fundamentally incompatible: if Harris was right, then all Allied bombers ought to have been thrown into the attack on German cities. Increasingly, however, members of the British Air Staff were coming to support the American approach. Sir Norman Bottomley, the Deputy Chief of Air Staff, took this view, arguing for a more committed and vigorous attack on the Luftwaffe by both Bomber Command and the USAAF. Sir Charles Portal was also supportive of the logic of Pointblank, but he, like Churchill, was intrigued nonetheless by the promise of a major campaign against Berlin.[68]

Still flush with expectation, Harris wrote to the Air Ministry on 7 December 1943, claiming that it would be possible for his Lancasters singlehandedly to bring about a German surrender. Portraying his progress in acres destroyed, Harris argued that surrender could be compelled "by the destruction of between 40% and 50% of the principal German towns." This, he believed, could be accomplished by 1 April 1944 provided that Lancaster production was maintained, that navigational aids were delivered on schedule, and that the bomber offensive be given unchallenged priority.[69] The goals of the Berlin campaign would be to undermine worker morale (by killing the workers, to the greatest extent possible) and to wreak havoc with industry and communications in the Nazi capital.

Berlin accounted for 8 percent of Germany's total industrial output, and no less than 40 percent of the German electronics industry. But much of this industry was hard to find—located in small, undistinguished buildings. And because the city had many broad avenues and generally nontimber construction, it was less susceptible to fire than many other German cities. Finally, Harris and others underestimated the degree to which the Germans would find technological countermeasures to British initiatives in the radar and radio wars. The Germans, having sensed that Berlin would be Bomber Command's next focus, had made the capital the most well-defended place in the Reich.[70]

As the long winter campaign was to prove, Harris had set his hopes too high with respect to Berlin: over time, rates of damage diminished while bomber losses continued to rise. Some 9,000 sorties were flown, but they brought Britain no closer to victory. There was no obvious decline in the war economy, and no crack in morale. In the meantime, German night fighters took an ever-increasing toll, and Bomber Command had no answer to them. Portal and his staff, like the Americans, were disheartened by intelligence reports indicating that total Luftwaffe fighter strength on the western front had continued to swell; indeed, one report estimated that at the planned date for Operation Overlord, the total front line strength of the Luftwaffe fighter force would be 2,865.[71]

Evidence about the state of affairs inside Germany continued to vary from source to source and from week to week. Harris, heavily invested in his own statements and predictions, held firm in his convictions; indeed, he dug in his heels, continuing to insist that German morale was near to a breaking point. In late February 1944 he wrote to the Under Secretary of State at the Air Ministry to protest the language used in press statements about "the state of mind of the German populace." He insisted that "incontestable evidence derived from Most secret sources" predicted a "German defeat comparatively quickly" through a "collapse of morale as well as of production on the homefront." Harris protested use of the word "apathy" to describe the popular mood in Germany; he found the term weak and misleading, and argued that the situation was better described as one of "the utmost despair, of terror and of panic not always held in control by the authorities." He insisted that the Joint Intelligence Committee (JIC) investigate the evidence on the state of German morale, and that descriptions more in line with his views be offered to the public.[72]

In fact, both the JIC and the Assistant Chief of Air Staff (ACAS) for Intelligence were then undertaking evaluations of German morale, and the results did not support Harris's assumptions. The latter argued that since the Berlin campaign had been spread out over time, the effect of concentration was lacking: "while therefore the sequence of attacks has had a great and progressive effect, it has not caused the break in morale which the German Authorities themselves seem to have feared might result from attacks on the capital." The report pointed out further that repression and fear would make organized revolt against the government unlikely, and concluded that, despite the difficulties of assessing the situation with certainty, "most responsible observers are inclined to discount the possibility that the factor of morale will alone exercise a decisive influence on the outcome of the war."[73] In early April the Air Ministry Weekly Intelligence Summary argued that bombing had not been sufficient to rouse the Germans "from their apathetic resignation" or "to overcome their fear of the repressive measures of the Gestapo."[74]

The answer to the problems then faced by the CBO would not lie in continued attacks on Berlin. The disastrous Nuremberg raid of 30–31 March 1944, in which Bomber Command lost 11.9 percent of the bomber force dispatched, made it clear to most authorities that the RAF was losing the battle against the Luftwaffe.[75] Instead, the Combined Bomber Offensive would be rescued largely by ongoing aerial combat pitting German fighters against American long-range escorts. This battle for control of the skies not only salvaged the efforts of the USAAF, but gave essential help to the RAF: the attrition campaign had a direct impact on the German night fighter forces through the dislocation of pilot training, practice flying, and fuel supplies.[76] Harris never fully appreciated the extent to which this pulled British chestnuts out of the fire—or, if he did, he never acknowledged it during the war.[77]

THE COMBINED BOMBER OFFENSIVE: 1944

In a forward he wrote for a December 1943 report on the progress of the Combined Bomber Offensive, General Arnold stated, "To hasten the end of the war we must achieve the maximum flexibility in our bombing operations, by altering our technique, employing new gadgets, and by any other means found practicable . . . to secure an uninterrupted bombing offensive of the greatest possible effectiveness."[78] As noted above he had already employed "new gadgets" allowing the Americans to rely much more frequently on blind bombing, and he moved to implement other forms of flexibility. He was, for instance, in agreement with a decision already taken by Spaatz and Doolittle to use escort aircraft in a more aggressive air-to-air combat role instead of tying them to the bombers.[79]

A break in the weather in mid-February allowed USSTAF to commence a mission that had been in the works since the previous November: Operation Argument (or "Big Week" as it came to be called) concentrated the full available weight of American resources against the Luftwaffe, on the ground and in the air. The campaign, prosecuted not only by the strategic bomber forces but also by the tactically oriented Ninth Air Force, caused a temporary decline in German fighter production—for a cost of 266 heavy bombers and 2,600 aircrew. Although German production levels were thereafter restored, the pause gave American bomber crews some room to commence attacks on other targets considered crucial to the longer-term goals of the strategic campaign, including German synthetic oil.[80] Though dramatic in terms of effort expended, Big Week in itself was not a fatal blow; German munitions output would continue to rise through July, and in the autumn a new and formidable threat would emerge in the form of German fighter jets. Nonetheless, Big Week was encouraging at the time since it indicated that the Allies could make some headway through concentrated effort.

In early February the senior air force commanders in Europe had been formally notified that the Allied strategic and tactical air forces would be directed toward the completion of tasks designed to facilitate and support the Allied landing on the continent (Operation Overlord) and "to deal with the subsequent activities of the enemy." A proposed key mission, along with securing air superiority, would be to "paralyse the railways from western Germany to the assault area to such an extent that major reinforcement by rail would be virtually impossible."[81] The Anglo-American strategic air forces would be placed at the disposal of Supreme Headquarters Allied Expeditionary Force (SHAEF) under the guidance of the Supreme Allied Commander in Europe, Gen. Dwight D. Eisenhower, and his deputy, Air Chief Marshal Sir Arthur Tedder. The latter, an architect of the railway plan, was influenced by investigations into the effects of air attack on the railway network in Sicily and southern Italy, led by civilian advisor Solly Zuckerman, and completed at the end of 1943.[82]

Both Spaatz and Harris had earlier hoped that strategic bombing might obviate the need for a major Allied amphibious landing but, in light of the difficulties faced by the Combined Bomber Offensive (CBO) in 1943, they had recognized that such a landing would go ahead, and that their forces would be called upon to play a direct role. Thus, they both sought to shape the nature of that role. On 13 January 1944, Harris had written a memorandum explaining that the heavy bomber had evolved as an independent strategic weapon designed to operate at night and, as such, had significant limitations as a "tactical weapon." He concluded that "the best and indeed the only efficient support which Bomber Command can give to Overlord is the intensification of attacks on suitable industrial centres in Germany as and when the opportunity offers."[83]

The Air Ministry countered his memorandum point by point, and came to two significant conclusions: that the failure of Overlord would result in far graver repercussions than a temporary cessation in the bombing of German centers, and that Bomber Command's role in Overlord would be "determined by the C.C.O.S. after they have had General Eisenhower's recommendations."[84] Harris, undeterred, told Portal that it was harmful for Bomber Command to be tied to the same target list as Eighth Air Force, since it committed him in advance to targets in regions where the weather was questionable, resulting in frequent cancellations or ineffective raids. Angling for the flexibility he had won under Pointblank, he asked for "full discretion" regarding the targets he would attack on any given night.[85]

For some time Portal had worried that Harris was relying on an increasingly outdated concept of Bomber Command's capabilities, and was using this as an excuse to focus on city raids. In a challenge to his field commander, Portal ordered Bomber Command to undertake trial raids, on moonlit nights, against airfields, transport targets (including six French marshaling yards), and ammunition dumps. These would determine the real operational capabilities of the force. As the British official historians pointed out, the results, "though not universally successful, were outstanding."[86] They foreshadowed Bomber Command's important contribution to the preinvasion bombing campaign.

Spaatz made his own bid for influence over planning. He had his staff draw up an overall assessment of the CBO's progress and put forward targeting recommendations pertaining to Overlord. They rejected morale as an object of attack, arguing that "neither fear, war weariness, nor the prospect of impoverishment is likely to be sufficient to enable important political and social groups to overthrow the efficient, terroristic Nazi social controls." They likewise rejected Axis railway and motor transport arguing that the former involved too many targets with "too great a cushion of long-term civilian and industrial use." (Spaatz was concerned, as well, that attacking railway targets would not compel German fighters into the air, thus jeopardizing the crucial battle for air superiority.) Instead, they proposed attacking the sources of German oil, along with ball bearings and fighter aircraft production. Oil had been given attention and priority by the Enemy Objectives Unit (EOU) of the Economic Warfare Division of the U.S. Embassy in London, charged with analyzing German military and industrial assets to determine the enemy's most vulnerable points.[87]

Neither Harris nor Spaatz saw his preferences prevail however. On 25 March, Eisenhower and Tedder met with Harris, Portal, Spaatz, and others representing the Air Ministry, the United States Strategic Air Forces (USSTAF), the War Office, and the wartime intelligence organizations. After discussing at length the various targeting plans that might be employed to support Overlord, Eisenhower chose the plan calling for attacks on the French and Belgian railway system as a means of inhibiting the movement of German supplies and soldiers in the Normandy region, thereby constraining the enemy's ability to reinforce the front and wage a war of maneuver.[88]

The decision, however, was not taken without considerable debate among all parties about whether strikes against railways would have major and direct military effects. Spaatz made his case for oil, which was considered seriously by the parties present.[89] In the end Eisenhower and Tedder concluded that neither area bombing nor oil strikes promised an immediate impact on the ground battle. They reasoned that even if the railway plan offered only a limited hope in this regard, it would be worth the effort.[90] Once a conclusion was arrived at, though, Eisenhower and Tedder still had to cope with concerns expressed by both Spaatz and Churchill regarding French civilian casualties likely to be caused by the transportation plan. The prospect of French deaths alarmed Churchill and caused him to refrain from supporting the plan, which he feared might "smear the good name of the Royal Air Force across the world." Since the Combined Chiefs of Staff backed Eisenhower, the prime minister felt he had but one route of appeal: Roosevelt. But FDR's argument ultimately ended the matter. He said simply, "I am not prepared to impose from this distance any restriction on military action by the responsible commanders that in their opinion might militate against the success of 'Overlord' or cause additional loss of life to our Allied forces of invasion."[91] Sensitive to the prospect of killing friendly civilians, Spaatz would try to insure that his forces used visual sighting and small bomb groups as often as possible. Even with such precautions, however, about one hundred French civilians died in each of the American attacks waged on rail yards in the preinvasion campaign.[92]

Harris, too, put up some verbal resistance and continued to agitate for greater freedom. Indeed, he never truly accepted an Allied grand strategy oriented ultimately to a ground battle in northwest Europe. He complained that day bombing as practiced by the Americans was not, except under clear weather conditions, a very serious menace to Germany, and argued (tellingly) that its effect on morale, as compared to that of "night bombing on a large scale" was slight. He argued, "In any case the Germans know that any factory can be replaced relatively easily in the post-war period provided that the city on which it depends is not too badly damaged to be repairable in a reasonable time. But factories without cities are valueless."[93]

In an April letter to U.S. Assistant Secretary of War Robert Lovett, Harris lambasted Zuckerman: "Our worst headache has been a panacea plan devised by a civilian professor whose peacetime forté is the study of the sexual aberrations of the higher apes."[94] The relationship between Portal and Harris, never an easy one, was growing increasingly testy. A debate over night fighter equipment dissolved into an acrimonious struggle over loyalty and the lines of authority between Bomber Command and the Air Ministry. Much of Harris's venom on this point was directed at several members of the Air Ministry Staff who were critical of his commitment to city bombing, in particular Air Commodore S. O. Bufton, the Air Ministry's Director of Bomber Operations.[95]

To Harris's surprise, Eisenhower's first bombing directive, dated 17 April, gave him more leeway to bomb cities than he had expected. In a second surprise, Bomber Command proved perfectly capable of hitting the tactical targets Eisenhower and Tedder had prioritized. After trying hard to excuse himself from the transportation plan, Harris made a significant contribution to it: between 17 April and 6 June Bomber Command waged nearly one hundred attacks on railroads, coast defense installations, and airfields in France and the Low Countries. These raids, flown with the latest navigational aids and using well-developed Pathfinder marking techniques, helped dramatically to reduce rail traffic on lines in France.[96] With a big bomb bay, a crew of only seven, and less weight of armament for self-defense than their American counterparts, Lancaster bombers could carry a more sizable bombload (with bigger, more destructive bombs) than B-17s. With their increased accuracy, and with less to fear from the Luftwaffe, they were a potent force capable of fulfilling tasks that were sometimes beyond the capabilities of American day bombers.

Spaatz also found himself able, in a limited way, to follow his own instincts. Though respecting the 25 March decision he continued to press his case, and to find—and make—opportunities as he could. Each of the important oil refineries in Ploesti, Rumania, had a marshaling yard located nearby. On 5 April, Spaatz used the Fifteenth Air Force to attack the refineries, under the guise of attacking the marshaling yards. And Spaatz found another "back door" method to legitimize oil targets in central Germany. The 17 April directive had called on USSTAF to maintain pressure on the German air force. Spaatz knew, of course, that the Luftwaffe relied on oil, and that they would defend their sources heavily. Thus, he viewed it as wholly within the terms of his directive to attack oil installations—indeed, he felt such attacks were essential to bring German fighters into the skies in large numbers. Eisenhower concurred, and on 19 April gave Spaatz permission to attack oil during the next two visual bombing opportunities. The results were promising enough to sustain Eisenhower's interest and thereby open the door for increased activity against the target set.[97]

In a further modification of the 25 March decision, Allied strategic bombers attacked bridges over the Seine and Meuse Rivers prior to D-day (and the Loire bridges thereafter). This came about as a result of renewed debate over the utility of bridge attacks in the Mediterranean, and, in particular, of new information from General Eaker's office indicating that bridge attacks in Italy's Po Valley had added to the effectiveness of interdiction efforts there. The advocates of bridge bombing would later stress its significance for the success of Overlord and the Normandy campaign.[98]

By the time the D-day landing took place, strategic bombers had helped insure its success. The winter-spring battle for command of the skies meant that the Luftwaffe had a compromised ability to interfere with the landing and inhibit the progress of Allied ground troops thereafter. Indeed, the Luftwaffe mounted only 100 sorties on the first day of the invasion, and only 175 ineffectual sorties on the night of 6–7 June. A "decisive battle" over the beachhead, which some planners had anticipated, was unnecessary.[99] The attacks on French transportation did much to undermine the Germans' ability to take advantage of interior lines of communication on the continent. After the landing, strategic bombers continued to provide tactical support to the Anglo-American armies, and they performed a range of other duties as well. In addition to supporting the ground battle, they assisted on the Italian front, aided preparations for an Allied landing in southern France, and prosecuted attacks on Hitler's V-weapons sites (Operation Crossbow). Because of the incessant V-1 strikes against England (over 300 V-1s were launched on 15–16 June alone), Crossbow was given high priority over the summer. Indeed, in July and August the Allied air forces sent 16,566 total sorties against V-weapon targets—one quarter of their total tonnage for those months. General Spaatz was frustrated by this since he thought the raids were of doubtful efficacy, but he could do little about it without appearing callous to the plight of British civilians.[100]

Spaatz was interested in doing all he could to promote attacks on the German oil supply. In his eyes, German synthetic oil looked to be the long-sought key node—a genuine bottleneck in the German war machine. There was no ready substitute for it, and the pressure on the Germans increased as Soviet armies moved east, denying the Reich the fuel sources of southeastern Europe. In May, the Fifteenth Air Force followed up on its initial attacks on Ploesti, and the Eighth attacked synthetic oil at a number of sites including Zwickau, Merseburg-Leuna, and Politz.[101] In a June memorandum to Tedder, Eisenhower drew up a bombing directive, which, though it ranked Crossbow first, added, "[W]hen we have favorable conditions over Germany and when the entire Strategic Air Force cannot be used against Crossbow, we should attack—*a*. Aircraft industry; *b*. Oil; *c*. Ball bearings; *d*. Vehicular production."[102]

Portal, too, was sympathetic to Spaatz's thinking, which was increasingly supported by Ultra-based intelligence (derived from breaking enemy codes) indicating that the Germans were facing critical shortages.[103] On 9 July, for instance, a deciphered message from Luftwaffe chief Reichsmarschall Hermann Göring argued that "[t]he deep inroads made into the supply of aircraft fuel demand the most stringent reduction in flying. Drastic economy is absolutely essential." Indeed, the Germans were so concerned about their oil situation that they transferred large numbers of anti-aircraft guns from their cities to the synthetic oil plants (SOPS).[104] Spaatz thus tried to balance his obligations so as to direct as much effort as possible toward oil. In June and July, despite suffering heavy losses to flak, USSTAF bombers took a serious toll on Germany's diminishing oil supply.[105] In August and early September the Eighth and Fifteenth Air Forces continued to divide their resources between supporting the ground campaign, attacking V-weapons sites, and attacking strategic targets, mainly oil. The Eighth flew seven missions against German oil, and the Fifteenth flew thirteen missions against German and Balkan oil.[106]

For the American bomber forces, good results against oil facilities demanded visual conditions. But not all clear days could be dedicated to this end, since bomber crews were called on repeatedly to aid in ground operations, including close support for troops in the field. Though these tactical operations could be effective, they did not always live up to expectations. In addition, they entailed serious risks due to the challenges of controlling a large and inherently inaccurate force. The heavy bomber missions flown in support of Lt. Gen. Omar Bradley's Operation Cobra in late July 1944, for instance, were a mixed blessing. Though they aided the Allied advance, they killed over one hundred American troops and wounded hundreds more.[107] The inability of Allied supply lines to keep pace with the advance of ground troops caused the diversion of an entire bomber combat wing (approximately 200 B-24s) to the ferrying of supplies to forward troops. And the preparation for and execution of Operation Market Garden in September placed serious demands on Allied strategic bombers: under dangerous and ultimately costly conditions, they shuttled supplies forward for the paratroops and engaged in close support operations. General Doolittle estimated that Market Garden cost the Allies four major and two minor heavy bomber missions in September.[108]

In the meantime, the attempt on Hitler's life in July had prompted the USSTAF director of intelligence to note that "there has been widespread unrest within the German armed services." Though it was hard to assess what this meant, it at least suggested that the Reich might be edging toward some sort of crisis. This development, along with the success of the attack on oil and the rapid progress of troops immediately following the Normandy breakout, inspired the hope—among some at least—that victory in Europe might be near at hand and that a collapse of German morale might be effected and put to use in the war's endgame. Indeed, optimism about the course of the war already had helped spur a joint venture between the Air Staff, USSTAF, the Ministry of Economic Warfare, and the Foreign Office, resulting in a plan called Thunderclap, which envisioned a massive attack (by both American and British strategic bombers) on German morale at a crucial moment.[109]

Portal stressed that timing was critical: the raid would be undertaken when the Allies sensed Germany might be particularly vulnerable psychologically. This sense of vulnerability would be influenced by the state of the German political, economic, and military situation. Thunderclap was not so much a triumph of Trenchardism as it was an acceptance of the idea that the conditions for victory in war are evoked not just by air warfare, but by ground and naval warfare as well. The plan, which would focus on Berlin, would be carried out when this interplay of forces had brought Germany to the point of collapse. Much of the motivation for Thunderclap was to help hasten, consolidate, and control the German surrender."[110]

In August, Eisenhower was invited to prepare plans for an attack on Berlin along the lines suggested by Portal. Spaatz was wary of it; he told Eisenhower that he thought Thunderclap would compromise American claims regarding "precision" targeting of military objectives. Eisenhower imposed his own view, however, stating that while he, too, had "always insisted that U.S. Strategic Air Forces be directed against precision targets," he was nonetheless "always prepared to take part in anything that gives real promise to ending the war quickly."[111] Spaatz instructed Doolittle to be ready to bomb Berlin "indiscriminately" on Eisenhower's order. In the midst of his debate with Eisenhower, though, Spaatz protested to Arnold: "There is no doubt in my mind that the RAF want very much to have the U.S. tarred with the morale bombing aftermath which we feel will be terrific."[112]

Spaatz's protest calls for some elaboration. There was no single, coherent attitude among American airmen about bombing for psychological effect: some were lured by its promise; some perceived it as inefficient; and others, including Doolittle, perceived it as both inefficient and ethically troubling. The desire to see the war over in 1944 was strong— so strong, in fact, that it caused American air planners to hope that by creating enough disillusionment and chaos in Germany they might force an internal crisis. In certain respects, Thunderclap might be thought of as a manifestation of the idea, set out in 1941 in AWPD/1, that at a moment of particular weakness toward the end of war the enemy might be vulnerable to a major air attack for psychological effect.[113] As the governmental and administrative center of the Third Reich, Berlin held an enormous attraction: between early March and late June 1944 the Americans bombed it nine times. Spaatz's concern may well have been aroused by the idea of a massive attack on Berlin *in conjunction with* Bomber Command. Though the Americans had relied increasingly on inaccurate nonvisual bombing, and though they had attacked targets defined simply as "cities and towns" throughout 1944, they still continued to think of themselves as "precision bombers" with a mission distinct from the British. Maintaining that distinction meant keeping a careful distance from Bomber Command. Historian Richard G. Davis put it succinctly when he pointed out that the American airmen "judged themselves by their motives rather than their results."[114] They wanted others to do the same.

But even as they sought to protect their image and to keep their distance from Bomber Command, the Americans looked at ways in which the moral effect of bombing might be employed to Allied advantage. In response to the V-weapon attacks on England, USSTAF had worked up a plan (Operation Shatter) to bomb over one hundred German cities in a single day, thus demonstrating the demise of the Luftwaffe and the vulnerability of the German people. Its planners paid close attention to terminology: aim points would be transportation links, government buildings, and minor industries. In the autumn, the prospect of widely scattered air raids over Germany—employing both strategic and tactical aircraft—was raised again in plans called Hurricane I and II. Spaatz supported the plans for a "full-out beating up of Germany" in attacks on industry, oil, ordnance and motor transport depots, and transportation. He was not blind to its potential psychological impact, arguing that a multiple-day attack "was bound to have considerable effect on morale" and might be the only way to end the war in 1944 with air forces.[115] Ultimately though, neither Thunderclap nor the Hurricane plans materialized in 1944. The right strategic moment did not arrive, in part because the Anglo-American armies ran into setbacks. Had Operation Market Garden gone well, Thunderclap might have been launched on its heels.[116]

At this same time another unusual prospect was in the works; it, too, revealed conflicted American attitudes about the need to pursue "precision bombing" and the degree to which the moral effect of bombing might be used as a lever to compel victory. In June, Spaatz had suggested that the AAF Proving Grounds in Florida investigate the prospects of using new methods (special bombs or radio-controlled aircraft) to attack V-1 sites. At the same time, he had his own units look into using remotely controlled "war-weary" B-17s to carry heavy explosive loads to targets. When early testing went poorly, Spaatz began to lose interest. He discontinued testing when the Germans switched to mobile V-weapon launchers. But planes had already been collected for the purpose, and Arnold's interest in the project kept it alive. A handful of aircraft were sent against a variety of targets, with mixed results. Doolittle, who was in charge of the tests, was critical of the project, dubbing it a failure as a strategic weapon.[117] Later in the year the project was examined for tactical purposes, with aircraft to be launched from forward bases. This, too, generated little enthusiasm from field commanders. In the meantime the Joint Chiefs of Staff in Washington, no doubt urged on by Arnold, began to shape their own ideas for the project—specifically, a plan to launch over 500 war-weary bombers against industrial targets in Germany, with the aim of producing dislocation and disruption. Arnold felt that the raids might be "a means of breaking down the morale of the people of interior Germany."[118]

In November the Americans requested authority from the British to proceed with the development and implementation of the plan.[119] British representatives in Washington pointed out that the Americans "feel that anything that can be done to increase the enemy's difficulties and lower their general morale is worthwhile." Nonetheless, some Air Ministry personnel balked at the plan on grounds of operational effectiveness and political factors: "This proposal has on the face of it little to recommend it. . . . The idea appears to be a rather labourious copy of the flying bomb."[120] Portal's reaction was more sympathetic, although he argued that the feasibility of the project would have to be proven to justify the expenditure of resources. Presuming that Churchill would agree, the British Chiefs authorized the continuation of the project. But Churchill, concerned about possible German retaliation in kind against London, would not give his assent and the Chiefs had to rescind their original answer in January 1945.[121]

The negotiations continued, and Arnold's commitment to the project insured that the negotiations took place at high levels. Roosevelt, who generally did not interject himself into debates about strategic bombing, wrote directly to Churchill: "My Chiefs of Staff inform me that they consider this weapon to be most valuable in our all-out offensive against Germany . . . many lucrative targets in the industrial areas in Germany can be levelled and the German war effort correspondingly weakened." Roosevelt had been told, as well, that tests of the weapon would be of great value to the postwar development of guided missiles. Portal, now more conservative in his assessment, warned the British Chiefs that use of the war-weary bomber might constitute a "useless provocation" and a "direct invitation to the enemy to retaliate." But he argued that the final decision was a political one for Churchill to make. Months passed without a resolution. Ultimately the prime minister handed the decision back to the newly sworn-in U.S. president, Harry S Truman, in a telegram that nonetheless argued against the plan. The matter would be closed finally on 17 April 1945, when Truman laid the idea to rest.[122] But the episode spoke to continuing American interest in the psychological effects of bombing, and also to fissures between Washington and some field commanders.

The rapidly changing fortunes of war had provoked the discussion of all manner of schemes for employing bomber aircraft. But the negotiations over such plans as Hurricane and Thunderbolt were not the most important discussions undertaken by Allied air planners in the late summer and autumn of 1944. When, in September, the formal obligations of Overlord had been completed and SHAEF ceased to have primary authority for the guidance of the bomber forces, a new targeting debate commenced; it would be just as charged and consequential as the pre-Overlord debate. Tedder favored extending (into Germany) attacks on transport and communications lines, so as to cripple Reich military efforts and industry; Spaatz pinned his hopes on reducing the German oil supply; and Harris sought to maintain his focus on city raids.

Spaatz, whose progress in the spring and summer had made him more committed than ever to oil, knew that he was working against time: his crews, dependent on visual bombing methods for significant results, would be handicapped once the autumn weather closed in. Other Allied leaders shared his concerns.[123] Harris, whose crews had also begun to attack oil, remained true to the assumptions he had held since taking charge of Bomber Command: cities were the best, most efficient targets of Allied bombers. The debate resulted, again, in a compromise. On 25 September executive responsibility for control of the Allied strategic bombing campaign reverted to Portal who, under a new arrangement, would share his authority with Arnold. The bombing directive issued at the same time identified priority targets: the petroleum industry, with special emphasis on petrol (gasoline), the German rail and waterborne transportation systems, tank production and plants, ordnance depots, and motor transport production and plants. But Harris was able to find plenty of room to continue his offensive as well, since priority targets were listed "subject to the exigencies of weather and tactical feasibility," and the directive specified that when "weather or tactical conditions are unsuitable for operations against specific primary objectives, attacks should be delivered on important industrial areas, using blind bombing technique as necessary."[124]

In a conception of air strategy he would make explicit in October, Tedder essentially integrated the oil plan into his overall transportation plan. He pointed out that strategic air operations could take advantage of the fact that German road, water, and rail transport were interdependent and complementary, and that the oil plan would affect movement by road and air. He perceived his strategy as coherent and comprehensive: it could not fail but to have a direct impact on the German capacity to continue the war since any loss of transport traffic would produce a shortage or a delay that unavoidably would affect the Reich war effort. In Germany—in contrast to France during the pre-Overlord campaign—bombed-out transport lines could be replaced only at the cost of other key programs. Also, the campaign in Germany—unlike the the one in France—would be unhindered by the need to avoid collateral casualties to the greatest extent possible.[125]

In October, U.S. bombers were able to launch only three completely visual attacks on oil targets, allowing German production of aviation gasoline to triple. Even in the best conditions, oil plants were demanding targets. A postwar study by the United States Strategic Bombing Survey, which covered the effects of fifty-seven American "precision" strikes on three separate synthetic oil plants, revealed that only 2.2 percent of the bombs dropped hit "damageable" buildings and equipment; no less than 87.1 percent "were spread over the surrounding countryside"—outside the perimeter of the plants.[126] Weather affected Bomber Command's campaign as well: in October Harris dedicated only 6 percent of his force's bombs to oil.

A review of strategic priorities resulted in a new directive, put forward in late October, which listed simply the petroleum industry and transportation/communications. Again, though, it authorized attacks on "Important Industrial Areas" whenever weather or tactical conditions made other operations infeasible. In November the Eighth Air Force was able to put 39 percent of its bombs on oil targets—although continuing bad weather insured that none of it was purely visual; the Fifteenth was able to achieve 28.4 percent on oil. The overall effect was not enough, however, to maintain the crisis situation imposed on the Reich over the summer.[127]

Even as USSTAF formally committed itself to "precision targets" in its public rhetoric, it continued the practice of area bombing through overcast. Back in July 1944 variable weather had caused USSTAF to place a high percentage of its total tonnage on the target category "cities and towns."[128] The worsening weather in the autumn meant a continuation—and intensification—of this trend. Between 1 September 1944 and 31 December 1944, weather forced the Eighth Air Force to rely heavily on H2X bombing. Of 140,807 tons dropped on the primary targets, 81,654 tons of it was H2X-guided. And of that total, only 674 tons got within 1,000 feet of the aiming point.[129] Poor weather continued to plague bomber operations in early 1945, and Spaatz pressed Arnold to hasten the ongoing implementation of H2X equipment. A March 1945 joint British-American conference on bombing accuracy revealed the situation faced by American bombers: in conditions of heavy cloud cover, which included the majority of missions for the Eighth Air Force over the winter of 1944–45, 42 percent of bombs fell more than five miles from the target. Of those inside the five-mile radius, the average circular error was 2.48 miles. Gross errors (bombs falling more than 3,000 feet from the aim point) and mission failures (when less than 5 percent of total bombs dispatched fall within the 1,000 feet around the target) became common. Gross errors ran at 66 percent for the Eighth Air Force in poor weather, and 29 percent in good weather.[130]

A special study of American H2X attacks on Ludwigshafen and Mannheim, flown in September 1944, had indicated that "a disturbingly high proportion of our attacks failed to reach the general area of the target, . . . of 186 formations dispatched . . . the bombfalls of only 80 have been identified within the area of photographic coverage. Presumably the balance, somewhat over 50 percent, either represent errors of very large magnitude or mistaken attacks on other targets."[131] Various analyses of American H2X bombing explained that inaccuracy was due to a range of factors, including the unfamiliarity of H2X Pathfinder techniques and "the lack of understanding by the combat wing commander of the requirements for good radar bombing"; insufficient training of radar navigator-bombardiers; overworked crews; inadequate maintenance; equipment failures; combat fatigue and enemy opposition (especially flak); navigational errors; unfamiliarity with the target; lack of maneuverability with a large formation; interference from other formations in the target area; inability to observe results and profit from them; and (to a lesser degree) the inherent inaccuracy of the bombsight.[132]

Because they were so often blocked by weather from attacks on oil facilities, U.S. strategic bombers dedicated ever-increasing tonnages to marshaling yards in German cities. And escort fighters accompanying bombers increasingly undertook low-level attacks and strafing raids against enemy matériel. This had an important consequence: attacks on marshaling yards (large, identifiable targets in urban areas) had the effect of greatly inhibiting the German transport of coal, which was the backbone of the German industrial economy. Tedder had indeed identified a crucial artery in the German war machine. But such attacks were done by blind bombing techniques, and they utilized high percentages of incendiary bombs. Though they were designated and recorded as attacks on transport targets, these were, in essence, area raids on German cities. As Richard Davis has argued, "a well-hit marshaling yard meant a well-hit city, with block upon block of residential areas gutted, families left homeless, small businesses smashed, and workers and others— including women and children—blown to bits or, more likely, burned or crushed by the hundreds if not thousands."[133] Standard U.S. incendiary bombs, with their poor ballistic properties and lack of blast or fragmentation effects, were not well suited to rail yard bombing. They were utilized in the role, "to take advantage of the known inaccuracy of H2X bombing in order to maximize the destruction of warehouses, commercial buildings, and residences in the general vicinity of the target."[134]

A memorandum of 29 October 1944 specified the procedure for operations when weather precluded higher priority targets, explaining that to meet the criteria for "secondary" and "last resort" targets, a town or city in Germany had to contain within it (or immediately adjacent to it) one or more military objectives, defined to include railway lines, junctions, marshaling yards, road bridges, industrial plants, military camps, oil storage tanks, airfields, and ammunition depots. It pointed out that towns and cities large enough to produce an identifiable return on the H2X scope "generally contain a large proportion of the military objectives listed above," opening them to attack. This criteria applied to just about any German city with a population of 50,000 or more.[135] If marshaling yards were considered legitimate military targets under the laws of war, air force leaders were nonetheless aware of the full impact of their rail yard program: they described it euphemistically as "pressure" on the enemy.

The American wartime and postwar emphasis on "precision bombing" and "pickle barrel accuracy" was for public consumption: the Americans wanted very much to distinguish themselves from the British and distance themselves from the RAF's area campaign. But these oversold phrases ought not to obscure the reality of American bombing in Europe. While there is no doubt that the Americans generally believed in and identified themselves with the selective targeting called for by the industrial web theory—their initial unwillingness to join the British in area bombing was only one indication of this commitment—belief and practice were by no means one and the same.

The fact that the Americans reflexively returned to "precision" targets whenever weather permitted meant that they were motivated by a theory of air war distinct from that which animated Harris. And the USAAF never sought to develop or employ in Europe the specialized fire-raising methods used by the RAF. Certainly, intent and motivation matter for ex post facto judgments. But the problems posed by operational circumstances and the lure of finding a quick end to the war caused the Americans to stray very far indeed from their "precision" ideal. The toll this took on German civilians—formally considered "collateral casualties"—was enormous.

HARRIS'S BATTLE FOR CITY BOMBING

Battles over targeting priorities took place at practically every level of the Anglo-American wartime hierarchy. One of the most hard-fought battles developed between the British Air Staff and the chief of Bomber Command. Portal—who had led the RAF's transition to area targets early in the war—at this point found himself in the position of arguing exactly the opposite case he had made four years previously. Though he had hoped that the general area offensive would significantly aid the war effort, he remained attentive to other approaches. Looking closely at *Ultra* intelligence, he had become increasingly convinced that Spaatz was on a fruitful path: oil was now a key German weakness—and city bombing had brought no similarly apparent result. In July the Air Ministry had announced the formation of an Anglo-American oil targets committee, which diligently monitored the Axis oil supply. The American raids under Spaatz, and the advance of the Red Army (neutralizing first Polish oil sources and later Romanian ones), had created a situation that could not fail to arouse the Air Staff's interest. By late summer of 1944, Allied oil attacks—even in the face of bad weather—had reduced by two-thirds the level of oil production achieved by the Germans in January of that year.[136] Bomber Command's contribution had the potential to be very great. The liberation of France and the overrunning of the German early-warning net had allowed Bomber Command to conduct some daylight raids on oil targets. These were more accurate than night raids, and, because they were undertaken with powerful Lancaster bombers (with a bombload capacity higher than that of American bombers), they were capable of doing very serious damage: every single raid made a difference.

Portal worried (with cause) that Harris continued to see oil and transport targets as the latest in a long list of "panaceas," and that he had found—and would continue to find—a variety of reasons to avoid them and pursue his own priorities. In the same way that the Air Staff had failed to control Trenchard during World War I, they now faced the prospect of failing to control Harris.[137] Thus Portal felt compelled to persuade Harris of the significance of oil. The vigorous written debate that ensued between the two men was about the close calls—the times when weather might or might not permit something more accurate than area bombing. Portal did not want Harris to opt for a city when there was any reasonable chance of successfully hitting an oil target. Though targeting was the main topic of discussion, the letters spanned the range of issues shaping the relationship between the CAS and his principal field commander; they were, in many ways, an eruption of built-up tension and exasperation that had accumulated over the years of the war. Portal and Harris wrestled over power, authority, loyalty, and mutual respect. Indeed, the debate was even about personal style, and—to some extent at least—class, as the refined, restrained, Oxford-trained Portal squared off against the blunt, outspoken Harris. Both men felt strongly about their views, and both were highly articulate.[138]

In his effort to persuade Harris about the merits of oil, Portal faced an uphill struggle. All through 1944 Harris had campaigned hard to retain his freedom. Back in January he had warned that the defensive burden imposed on Germany by city bombing had been enormous, and, if the campaign were to cease, all those men and resources tied up in defensive operations would be suddenly free to join and support the ground war in the west. "There could be no greater relief afforded Germany than the cessation of any ponderable reduction of the bombing of Germany proper," he wrote. "The entire country would go wild with a sense of relief and reborn hope, and get down to the prosecution of a purely land war with renewed determination and every hope of success." He added that a break in the area offensive would also give tremendous relief to the German army on the eastern front. He was convinced that the German homefront was incapable of withstanding many more heavy night attacks. And, significantly, he was also convinced that the German people would not tolerate the prospect of a postwar situation in which all their cities were obliterated—leaving them to face long years of difficult economic recovery.[139]

Harris had pitted his own views and assumptions against those held by other individuals both inside and outside the Air Ministry. Wary of intelligence and the input of "experts," he systematically discounted information that did not accord with his expectations. Instead he relied on his own hunches and assumptions, and on any incoming information that seemed to support his case. At first, Harris was largely in step with his colleagues in this: as we have seen, following the February 1942 directive, Portal and others in the Air Ministry had seized upon data that seemed to support the area offensive. But after the battle of Berlin, many had begun to have doubts: German morale did not appear to be at a breaking point, and German production had not been so thwarted as to slow the Wehrmacht down very much. Lingering hopes still existed in one form or another, but by the autumn of 1944, Portal and his staff were increasingly inclined to focus their efforts in a new direction. Now that reliable intelligence sources seemed able to identify targets with the potential to cripple Germany—and now that Bomber Command was capable of significantly aiding in the attack of those targets— did it not make sense to embrace a new approach? In the absence of perfect information, all the parties in the debate were guessing. But Portal and his associates at the Air Ministry felt, increasingly, that their guesses were better informed than Harris's. And by this time they may very likely have felt, as well, that they had an obligation to protect Bomber Command's reputation for the postwar world, when wartime passions would die down and the area bombing policy would be scrutinized on grounds of both efficiency *and* morality.[140]

For some time Portal had suspected that Harris was using an outmoded conception of Bomber Command's capabilities as an excuse to continue city bombing. The CAS, as we have seen, had already challenged Harris on this earlier in the year, with results foreshadowing the strong record Bomber Command would amass prior to D-day. But Portal was not convinced that Harris had taken these lessons to heart. His poor showing against oil in October aroused Air Staff concern that he was not committed enough to the letter and spirit of the new directives. The weather had indeed been bad, but Portal feared that Harris's strategic preferences were coloring his tactical decisions.

Bottomley reminded Harris of his obligation, under the existing directive, to attack oil and transport. And Portal sent Harris a memorandum by Tedder critiquing Bomber Command. If by this Portal had been looking to provoke a debate, his tactic worked. On 1 November, Harris sent back a lengthy response that argued, in no uncertain terms, for maintaining the area offensive. Throughout their detailed exchange, which continued well into the new year, Harris argued two things in particular: (1) the weather and other variables strictly limited his ability to attack selected targets, and that under the circumstances it made more sense to attack targets that had a guaranteed payoff—cities—than to gamble on single-target theories that might well prove meritless; and (2) the Germans were likely to disperse their oil production or to find substitutes for it, as they had with so many other "panacea" targets.[141] If the implication of the first was, "I can't do it," then the implication of the second was, "It's a bad idea anyway." This aroused Portal's suspicion: if the first part of the argument was really true, then there was no need to add the second part.

Portal responded by questioning Harris's decisions to eschew oil attacks on two specific nights when weather appeared, to Portal at least, to support such attacks. He had hoped to provoke a clear and convincing response from Harris, but he mainly provoked a mini-debate on how to interpret weather data. In addition, he worked vigorously to convince Harris that the quality of intelligence work supporting the targeting directives was very high and very reliable. Portal figured that he might make his case through sheer force of logic. But Harris put up resistance. He had always resented what he felt was the Air Ministry's micro-management of Bomber Command, and he reacted defensively to Portal's specific queries on targeting. He insisted to the CAS that he took oil seriously, and that he sought to attack it on every suitable occasion.[142]

With respect to intelligence, Harris was jaded by the early war years when the search for selective targets deemed crucial to the German war effort had been fruitless, or when a declared "bottleneck" was later discovered not to be one. "You will recall," Harris wrote, "that in the past MEW [Ministry of Economic Warfare] experts have never failed to overstate their case on 'panaceas,' e.g. ball bearings, molybdenum, locomotives, etc. in so far as, after the battle has been joined and the original targets attacked, more and more sources of supply or other factors unpredicted by MEW have become revealed." Asserting that "the oil plan has already displayed similar symptoms," he insisted, "I am quite certain that there are dozens more benzol plants of which we are unaware, and when and if we knock them out I am equally certain we shall eventually be told by MEW that German M.T. [motor transport] is continuing to run sufficiently for their purposes on producer gas, steam, industrial alcohol, etc., etc." Later he told Portal that while he was doing his best to attend to oil, he felt compelled nonetheless to inform the CAS that the plan, "like all previous panaceas so enthusiastically put forward by MEW" was "chimerical." Indeed, Harris's enmity for the MEW was so deep—and his desire to discredit it so strong—that he accused it of "amateurish ignorance, irresponsibility, and mendacity."[143] The alternative, Harris pointed out, made far more sense. He argued, "If the Germans were asked today 'oil plants or cities,' they would reply 'bomb anything you fancy except the cities'—that is the whole tenor of everything we hear from Germany today."[144]

The more Harris dug in his heels the more Portal harnessed the energies of his entire staff in an effort to push him—or drag him—in the preferred direction. Oil facilities, Portal patiently explained in his letter of 8 January 1945, were too large and too complex to have easily escaped the notice of determined and competent intelligence efforts.[145] Attaching to the letter several intelligence files on oil—including the latest Ultra information—Portal sought one more time to deploy the facts in his favor. He particularly pointed out that the "prodigious efforts" the enemy was making to protect its remaining oil was incontrovertible proof of the soundness of the oil plan. But he suspected all along that his efforts were falling on deaf ears. He believed, and there was plenty of evidence in Harris's letters to fuel the belief, that Harris was simply too invested in city attacks to be able to develop enthusiasm for another approach. Portal wondered whether the "magnetism of the remaining German cities" had not been the principal driver in Harris's targeting decisions. Later on, both the official historians of the British strategic bombing campaign, and the official historians of British intelligence in the Second World War, would suspect the same thing. Some of the new writing on the subject, however, has been more open to Harris's arguments at the time.[146]

Portal tried to wear down Harris's commitment to cities, challenging his stubborn belief that Germany was being brought to the brink of collapse through urban area attacks. He argued that while the Hamburg and early Berlin raids had surely shocked the Germans, they had not been brought to a point of collapse. And he added that the Germans had successfully weathered the subsequent Berlin attacks.[147] In late July and August the Joint Intelligence Committee (JIC) again had argued that the majority of the German population accepted the bombing with hopeless resignation. In the view of the committee, Allied bombing was "most unlikely to foment such opposition or produce such chaos as might lead to a collapse of the home front."[148] Harris, preferring to trust his instincts, put little store in such information.

Portal feared that Harris's conception of what was "possible" on any given night had been overly influenced by his strong investment in the city campaign. Not only had Harris staked his own prestige on it, but he had convinced himself that the built-up momentum of the attack— intensified almost daily by the increase in Allied strength and the deterioration of the German position—virtually guaranteed success in the near term. This conviction, along with the inability to believe that oil could be anything but another "panacea," kept him from seeing the world as Portal did—and prevented him from understanding the history of the war, up to that point, as Portal had understood it.[149] Harris might have avoided a long and painful debate with Portal by simply reassuring him that Bomber Command was doing all it could for the oil campaign, given the weather. But Harris refused this course: he felt compelled to fight for the cause he believed in, even if it alienated others and compromised his position in the eyes of his colleagues. He would not accommodate, conciliate, or play along in a collegial consensus. His actions were determined not only by the way he had come to perceive the war and his investment in a particular course of action, but also by his stubborn personality.

Harris's sensitivities about the position of the RAF among the services played a role as well, inhibiting his willingness to prioritize targets in Germany that offered potent, synergistic effects with the ground war. Very much a central element of Harris's debate with Portal was the former's contention that to use bombers "to deprive the enemy fighter aircraft in order to stop the enemy opposing us in the air, or to deprive him of oil to the same end in the air and on the ground" was to use them "defensively." This, in Harris's mind, was a fundamental mistake that denied air power the benefits of its greatest strength: the relentless offensive designed to force the enemy into a hopelessly defensive position.[150] Here were strong echoes of Trenchard. Harris, far more than Portal, Spaatz, Eaker, or Tedder, held a radical view of the role of strategic bombardment in war. "A point of major difference between us," Portal wrote, "seems to be that you would apparently regard the oil plan as a failure so long as the enemy continued to be able to fight at all, whereas we would regard it as successful as soon as the shortage of oil began to have a really substantial effect on the enemy's power to resist."[151]

After receiving Harris's letter of 18 January 1945, Portal had to acknowledge that his great efforts at persuasion had failed.[152] Harris simply could not overcome his earlier prejudices against intelligence agencies to see their work in a new light; indeed, he even suggested that the Germans were likely locating oil plants underground or "inside ordinary farm, village, town, and city housing." Nor could he persuade himself that attacks on oil facilities would do more damage to the German war effort than city attacks had done—and would continue to do if the Air Ministry would simply let him finish the job. Even in the face of all Portal's efforts to persuade him otherwise, Harris remained as committed as ever to city bombing, which he felt certain was responsible for Germany's distress and for the ongoing advance of Allied ground forces on both the eastern and western fronts.[153] When Harris closed with a threat to resign (it was not the first time he had done so), Portal backed off, writing, "I willingly accept your assurance that you will continue to do your utmost to ensure the successful execution of the policy laid down. I am very sorry that you do not believe in it but it is no use my craving for what is evidently unattainable."[154] Portal was not at that point prepared to remove Harris from command. Because of the inherent difficulties in interpreting weather data, there was no way to be absolutely sure that Harris was operating in contravention of Allied bombing directives.[155] Perhaps seeking a different approach to his problem, Portal (in February) raised the possibility of sending Harris to Russia so that he could point out to Stalin, in person, the contribution of strategic bombing to the Allied war effort. Harris, however, revealed no enthusiasm for the mission.[156]

Despite all the attention that has been given to it in the literature, no clear victor can be declared in the Portal-Harris debate. Even if one were to gather all the existing weather records for the period, there could be no final resolution to the question of whether Harris took every opportunity to attack oil: weather data itself was subject to interpretation that varied from individual to individual.[157] It may be the case that Harris did take every opportunity—as he perceived it—to attack oil. And it may be the case that he did not. After the war, the Chiefs of Staff's Committee's Technical Sub-committee on Axis Oil concluded that oil "might possibly" have been bombed, but was not, on seven nights and three days in the last three months of 1944.[158] Despite the difficulty of resolving the issue finally, several observations are worth raising. First, despite his grudging rhetoric, Harris responded to pressure from the Air Ministry: knowing he was under Portal's scrutinizing eye seems to have made him inclined to devote more overall effort to oil. For instance, Harris raised his total tonnage on oil from 6 percent of Bomber Command's total in October, to more than 24 percent in November. None of the November total, however, relied on visual methods.[159] While this shift does not prove anything in itself, it seems at least to imply that what was "possible" depended in part on what the commander-in-chief was motivated to do. Second, a major part of Harris's argument had nothing to do with weather or operational limitations: the assertion that the Germans would continue to find ways to work around their oil shortage had everything do to with Harris's own assumptions, which were unrelated to data then available from reliable intelligence sources. This in itself could not fail to raise Portal's doubts about the degree to which Harris had committed himself to attacking oil on every possible occasion. And third, if Harris had been willing earlier to change tactics only on the margin—an additional one or two raids against oil per month by the enormously potent Lancasters—it might have made a discernable difference to the German war effort. Whether it might have precluded or greatly inhibited the Ardennes offensive of December 1944 is very difficult to know, but it is certainly one of the more intriguing "what ifs" of the war.

From January through April 1945, Bomber Command carried out 74 operations against 49 oil targets (38 at night and 36 in daylight). On eleven occasions more than one oil target was attacked in a single night. "Thus," the official historians concluded, "if by no means a maximum effort, the Bomber Command part in the oil campaign of 1945 was intensive and concentrated. It was also exceedingly destructive and, in combination with the even more frequent but somewhat lighter attacks of the United States Strategic Air Forces, it proved to be a great deal more than the already badly mauled oil industry could withstand."[160] In a letter (on another matter) to Portal of 22 February 1945, Harris described the oil plan as "a faith to which I am not only not a convert, but against which I have waged unceasing and unrelenting opposition within the widest limit of my duty and my subordination." But, at the end of the letter, he added, "I have tried my best in the Oil Plan, and in everything else which I have been ordered to undertake."[161] Harris and Portal remained in a truce of sorts until the end of the war, and Harris never lost what was a genuine respect for Portal. Responding to a congratulatory note sent by the CAS on 9 May 1945, Harris wrote (in an unusually open and expansive way), "If we had differences of opinion they were not personal—and in the outcome you were always right on the things that mattered."[162]

In the winter of 1944–45 the dispute over targeting was all the more sensitive because the Air Staff was becoming increasingly concerned about its public image in the postwar period, in particular because of the degree to which it had strayed from its initial intent to bomb only military targets narrowly defined. Certainly they believed that their own actions had been justified by German attacks on such places as Warsaw, Rotterdam, and Coventry—as well as the V-weapon attacks on British soil. But over time, and in particular as opportunities for more selective targeting opened up, the issue had became more complicated. Still, concerns of this nature were certainly tempered by the prevailing crisis atmosphere surrounding the Ardennes offensive, and the realization that Germany was not yet defeated. New technologies including V-2 rockets and jet-fighters (specifically the Messerschmitt 262) had revealed that the führer still held an arsenal of daunting lethality. The first test of an Allied atomic weapon was still months away. On 21 January 1945, USSTAF's Office of the Director of Intelligence circulated a grim memorandum pointing out that Anglo-American armies had lost the initiative in the West, and that the Luftwaffe had been able to rebound to a degree "not considered possible by Allied intelligence some eight months ago." Though it recognized the many ways in which Germany had been seriously weakened, it drew attention to the enemy's Houdini-like feats of recovery and, specifically, to jet aircraft, U-boats (which then included Schnorkel-equipped submarines), and "secret weapons" that the Reich might employ at any time. It recommended that the Allies make every effort possible to deal Germany a "knock-out blow."[163] Finally, the Soviets were becoming increasingly difficult, and the upcoming conference at Yalta promised to be tumultuous.

THE COMBINED BOMBER OFFENSIVE: 1945

This uneasy environment dominated the mood in early 1945. On 3 February, USSTAF waged a large-scale attack against the city of Berlin, implementing the remnants of the Thunderclap idea.[164] The raid was prosecuted in a less grandiose way than had been envisioned in the original proposal, but the fact that it took place at all indicated the lingering intuitive appeal of targeting for psychological effect, and the overwhelming desire to see the war brought to a prompt end. Indeed, USSTAF's wide-ranging targeting choices for the month of February revealed an almost desperate quest for a decisive use of strategic air power. One of the targeting priorities, in accordance with Tedder's transportation plan, was railways. During the Normandy campaign, American bombers had dropped about nine tons of incendiaries per month on French rail yards. In contrast, they dropped roughly 600 tons per month on German rail yards between September 1944 and April

1945. Of 38 marshaling yard raids (each containing more than 200 tons of incendiaries) flown between 1 January and 30 April 1945, fully 75 percent were blind.[165]

The centerpiece of the war in Europe in early 1945, however, was the Red Army's move on Berlin. The Joint Intelligence Committee in Britain postulated that a heavy flow of refugees from Berlin coinciding with the westward trek of civilians fleeing the advance of the Soviet armies would create great confusion and would interfere with the movement of German armies to the battlefront. When DCAS Sir Norman Bottomley discussed it with Harris, the latter argued that Chemnitz, Leipzig, and Dresden might be added to Berlin as places where Bomber Command could apply pressure to the Germans on behalf of the Soviets. The issue developed urgency when Churchill became involved. The prime minister was then interested in the role that air would play in the endgame in Europe. He asked Sir Archibald Sinclair what plans the RAF had for "basting the Germans in their retreat from Breslau." After some debate the Air Staff decided that, while oil should continue to be the priority target, poor weather intervals would create opportunities for attacks on eastern German cities such as Berlin, Leipzig, Chemnitz, and Dresden for the purpose of causing confusion and hampering the eastward movement of German troops. Sinclair sent Churchill a minute to that effect.

The prime minister, anticipating something more dramatic, sent back a sharp reply, which said in part, "I asked whether Berlin, and no doubt other large cities in East Germany, should not now be considered especially attractive targets." His response implied that he was not only interested in making life rough for the Germans, but also impressing the Soviets (on the eve of the Yalta conference) with the power of the Allied strategic air forces. Churchill's reaction prompted the Air Staff to instruct Harris to attack the previously identified cities in eastern Germany in an effort to cause confusion behind the German lines.[166] Portal and Bottomley discussed the plan with Spaatz and Tedder, and, at a meeting of the Allied air commanders on 1 February 1945, Spaatz read his colleagues a copy of the new directive placing Berlin, Leipzig, and Dresden on the target priority list just below oil.[167]

On the night of 13–14 February, the city of Dresden, swollen with refugees fleeing the Eastern Front battles, was attacked by a force of over 800 RAF bombers. On 14 February American bombers, using visually assisted H2X, bombed the Dresden marshaling yards with an ordnance mix of 60 percent high explosives and 40 percent incendiaries. The city was already an inferno.[168] The attack on Dresden was at once routine and exceptional. There had been nothing unusual in the planning or execution of the raid—nothing in particular to distinguish it from the other operations carried out by the Allied air forces at the same time. The Eighth Air Force had already bombed the city's "industrial area" on 7 October 1944 and would do so again on 17 April 1945. In addition, the Eighth would bomb Dresden's marshaling yards again on the nights of 15 February and 2 March. On the night of 14 February, Bomber Command carried out a raid against Chemnitz, and on 26 February the Eighth Air Force carried out another massive attack on Berlin with over 1,000 bombers.[169] At the end of the month, the United States took the lead in Operation Clarion, which dispersed thousands of bombers and fighters all across Germany to bomb and strafe transport targets and targets of opportunity in Germany's smaller cities and towns.[170] The Eighth's bombers extended their Clarion operations over two days (22–23 February) in part because of the perceived good results of the first day's attacks. At the Allied air commanders' meeting held the day after the Dresden raids, the results were announced matter-of-factly along with the results of other raids for the previous fortnight. The minutes of the meeting did record, however, that Gen. Doolittle pointed out "with the 'greatest reticence'" that the smoke over Dresden rose to 15,000 feet.[171]

New York Times coverage emphasized Dresden's role as a transport center, and stressed that its attack was part of a "great aerial offensive in support of the Russian front." Readers of the *Times* (London) were told on 15 February that "Dresden is a place of vital importance to the enemy" as "the centre of a railway network and a great industrial town," and as "a meeting place of the main lines to eastern and southern Germany."[172] But a *Times* (London) editorial of 16 February pointed to the air campaign's "unprecedented fury." The observation was embedded in a largely congratulatory argument about strategic bombing's heavy impact on German oil and communications, and the difficulties this posed for Reich Gen. Heinz Guderian. But perceptive readers would have picked up on the implications of what was called "a new and terrifying prodigy of air power." In key respects, the Combined Bomber Offensive had become different from previous years. Both British and American raids were, at this point in the war, unprecedented in their size and sustained fury. With less to fear from the Luftwaffe and with the results of an immense Anglo-American aircraft production effort fueling their efforts, the allies could lay waste to locations of their choosing.[173]

Conditions in Dresden proved conducive to a firestorm. The 1,181 tons of incendiary bombs (of 2,646 tons total) falling from Lancaster bombers kindled fires that merged into a vast, self-sustaining conflagration. There are no agreed-upon casualty figures from the Dresden raid; they vary from 35,000 to over 100,000. It was impossible to count the dead, but the vast majority were women, children, and elderly—noncombatants trying to escape war's crossfire.[174] In 1968 one historian wrote perceptively, "In every sense, Dresden exemplifies the dangers of carrying an idea to its logical conclusion."[175]

The nature of the *Times* reporting on the allied strategic bombing campaign (along with the almost daily accounting of British citizens killed by German bomber and V-weapons attacks) had given British citizens little reason to question that campaign, and—aside from some notable exceptions like the Bishop of Chichester—they had not.[176] Reading about Dresden, *Times* readers learned that the raid had caused "fires everywhere, with a terrific concentration in the center of the city."[177] As the results became known in Britain, questions were raised about the means and ends of the strategic bombing campaign. Dresden contained important railway lines and some industry, but it was certainly not one of Germany's foremost industrial cities. Educated Britons knew it mainly for its cultural life and its fine examples of Baroque architecture. Was the raid, which took such a heavy toll on noncombatants, really warranted, especially at what was clearly a late stage in the war?

Churchill, who always had one eye toward posterity, was now becoming uneasy with the "fury" of the strategic air campaign. In a pointed minute to the Chiefs of Staff, on 28 March, he argued that there was no longer very much to be gained by continued heavy bombing, and that the time had come for a review of the "question of bombing of German cities simply for the sake of increasing the terror." After stating that "the destruction of Dresden remains a serious query against the conduct of Allied bombing," he insisted there was a need for "more precise concentration on military objectives . . . rather than on mere acts of terror and wonton destruction, however impressive."[178]

Portal, unwilling to accept the prime minister's sanctimonious turn-about, took the bold step of demanding that the statement (which the British official historians described as "among the least felicitous of the prime minister's long series of wartime minutes") be withdrawn and replaced by a version the Air Staff could more readily stomach. The CAS was not prepared to allow Churchill to stand in harsh after-the-fact judgment of a raid he had urged and was fully informed of ahead of time. The prime minister's revised minute of 1 April 1945 concluded, "We must see to it that our attacks do not do more harm to ourselves in the long run than they do to the enemy's immediate war effort."[179] In a telegram to Truman of 14 April, Churchill argued that "the war situation has now turned so much in our favour that the making of these great explosions in German cities is no longer of its former importance."[180]

Harris, unsurprisingly, was offended by allegations that Bomber Command had attacked German cities "simply for the sake of increasing the terror." In a 29 March letter to Bottomley, he insisted that he had followed and implemented government policy all along, and that that policy had sanctioned attacks on German cities. Harris did not believe that city raids constituted "terror bombing," which to him meant bombing solely for psychological effect. City attacks, he pointed out, were not wanton, but strategically justified; they had "produced the strategic consequences for which they were designed and from which the armies now profit." He argued further that city attacks ought to be continued so long as they helped to save the lives of Allied soldiers, which, he felt, had been their justification all long. "To my mind," he wrote, "we have absolutely no right to give them up unless it is certain that they will not have this effect."[181]

Harris's continuing obstinacy on this issue was derived in part from his utter unwillingness to engage in pretense about the nature of Bomber Command's wartime work, and from his strong and wholly undiminished view that such work had been worthwhile in its effects and that it was fully justified as an act of war designed to shorten the conflict and spare the lives of Allied soldiers. He was convinced and defiant, and his natural stubbornness caused him to dig in his heels ever harder as those around him raised the frequency and stridency of their questions about Bomber Command. Harris felt that the Allied reaction to Dresden was based on the same kind of misplaced sentimentality that had caused the Air Staff to try to prettify the language used to describe strategic bombing to the public. At the Allied air commanders' conference of 1 March 1945, Harris had reiterated his unflinching commitment to area bombing. Rather than the Dresden raid, he singled out a Bomber Command attack on Pforzheim, explaining with satisfaction that the whole town had been burned out, and that Bomber Command "had now destroyed 63 German cities in this fashion." He noted with more than a hint of sarcasm that this kind of raid, "popularly known as a deliberate terror attack" had "disputed value in certain quarters."[182]

At this juncture Harris also was deeply concerned that the strategic air offensive was not receiving appropriate credit for the work it had done in clearing a path for advancing Allied armies, and that artillery and tactical air forces were instead reaping an unearned reward in the press. He was so troubled by this that he wrote directly to Eisenhower, asking him to "see to it that as the armies advance, credit is given to us for our efforts, and that what we have achieved is neither ignored by army correspondents nor still less credited solely to the magnificent efforts of the ground forces."[183] All throughout the war Harris felt that Bomber Command was shortchanged in recognition compared to the army and navy. This was a matter of perspective, of course: there was no dearth of press coverage of Bomber Command's activities in wartime British newspapers. But Harris's perception that his crews were denied press attention and that the Air Ministry did nothing to change the situation helped fuel the sense of alienation and indeed persecution he felt by the end of the war.[184]

In the meantime, the Americans were in the midst of their own tempest. On 17 February an Associated Press war correspondent had issued a dispatch (which had inexplicably cleared the censors) stating that the Allied air chiefs "had made the long-awaited decision to adopt deliberate terror bombing of German population centres as a ruthless expedient to hastening Hitler's doom." The story was widely circulated in the United States and to say the least it produced an awkward situation.[185] The USAAF, with one eye fixed firmly on a postwar struggle for service independence, had worked hard to maintain its image as a "precision" or "pin point" force—an image frequently sought through comparisons to the RAF. For instance, the USAAF's glossy public relations magazine, *Impact*, consistently attempted to stress the distinction between American and British bombing.[186]

Members of the American press, who generally took a pro-air power stance and seemed to be enamored of the "precision bombing" image, rarely challenged the official USAAF interpretation of events, even as their stories described American bomb damage in terms of acres or square miles destroyed. Convinced, perhaps, that strategic bombing was the best possible substitute for costly ground battles of attrition, Americans were disinclined to demand more rigorous and searching analysis from reporters. During the war even liberal and religious journals of opinion were, generally, either supportive of or silent on American strategic bombing. *The New Republic* for instance, largely dodged the issue of bombing from 1943 to 1945, publishing one article the purpose of which was simply to celebrate the capabilities of the B-29 bomber. In April 1943 the journal did, however, run a short news brief pointing out that two respected British papers (*The New Statesman* and *The Tribune*) had printed stories indicating that American bombing was killing innocent civilians. Disinclined to give credence to the British view, which conflicted with their own interpretation of events, the editors suggested that the newspapers had been "misled." Arguing that more information was needed, the editors added, "The impression among Americans has been that high level bombings from our planes is not wildly inaccurate, as these papers claim."[187]

Unsurprisingly, the AP story generated a great flurry of uncomfortable activity inside the USAAF.[188] Arnold requested an immediate clarification of USSTAF targeting policy—perhaps ironic in light of his ongoing interest in the war-weary bomber project. Maj. Gen. Frederick Anderson responded for Spaatz, who was then in the Mediterranean. He argued that nothing in American policy or practice had changed. USAAF representatives in Washington—attempting hurriedly to rectify the situation—held a press conference on 21 February, which pointed out that while the story was sent to newspapers in good faith, it was based on a grave misunderstanding and did not reflect the policy of either Supreme Allied Headquarters in Europe, nor the Headquarters of the Army Air Forces.[189] The spokesman explained that American airmen had concluded that indiscriminate attacks were "wasteful and ineffective" and thus such attacks were passed over in favor of the policy of "precision bombing of selected military targets." He concluded by emphatically assuring the gathered press that *"we have never done deliberate terror bombing . . . we are not doing it now . . . we will not do it."*[190]

General Marshall and Secretary of War Henry Stimson explained that the Dresden raid had been undertaken at Russian request. This was not technically correct because while the Soviets had suggested that Anglo-American bombing might aid the advance of Soviet armies by attacks on Berlin and Leipzig, they had never specified Dresden.[191] As it turned out, the story did not generate profound public interest in the United States. Headlines in those weeks tended to concentrate on the great battles being waged in the Pacific, the Yalta Conference, and the advance of ground armies in Germany and the Philippines.[192]

The flap following the Dresden raid caused USSTAF to implement a new press policy that called on public relations officers to emphasize the military nature of targets attacked and always to describe raids (even if they were aimed at city centers) in terms of specific targets contained within them. Concerns about acknowledging "city areas" as targets found expression in some statistical compilations. One USSTAF working paper, "Review of Bombing Results," ceased to acknowledge any city area targets after January 1945—whereas from January 1944 to January 1945 it acknowledged 45,036 tons on "cities and towns."[193] The two most frequently cited Eighth Air Force statistical summaries for the entire war period do not list the target categories "city areas" or "towns and cities" at all, whereas monthly statistical surveys always listed a "city areas" category. The postwar United States Strategic Bombing Survey ultimately edged around the problem by using the term "industrial areas," a category defined to include cities, towns and urban areas, public utilities (including gas, electricity, water), and government buildings.[194]

As the long winter of 1944–45 faded into spring, it became ever clearer that the Third Reich finally was in the throes of collapse. Despite admitting that the "operational considerations which have in the past necessitated area attacks still exist," the British Joint Chiefs of Staff argued in early April that "at this advanced stage of the war no great or immediate additional advantage can be expected from the attack of the remaining industrial centres of Germany." (At a practical level, the Allies were now beginning to concern themselves, too, with reconstruction.) While recognizing that area bombing might still be required to overcome remaining pockets of German resistance—and thus no directive should exclude it—they argued that "area bombing designed solely with the object of destroying or disorganizing industrial areas should be discontinued."[195]

Harris felt this was one more denial of his opportunity to deliver Germany a coup de grace. Since he had become so deeply invested in the area campaign—dedicating all his efforts for nearly three years to prosecuting it ever more efficiently—it was very difficult for him to change course. In the waning months of the war he felt that the Air Staff had denied him not only the opportunity to bring his efforts to a crescendo, but also the credit that would have accompanied such an achievement. In January 1945, long after his battle of Berlin had failed, Harris still insisted that attacking the remaining major cities in Germany, and "bringing a great weight to bear on Berlin" would be "the end" of the Third Reich. "It is for this reason," he told Portal, "that I am personally so upset at this sudden change of horses in mid-stream after the three years of tremendous effort we have put into the alternative policy."[196]

On 19 April the Combined Chiefs of Staff recommended a new bombing directive, which came into effect formally on 5 May. It specified that the main mission of the strategic air forces would be to provide direct assistance to the land campaign.[197] On 25 April the American Eighth Air Force flew its last raid of the war; the following day the Fifteenth Air Force flew its last raid. Bomber Command Lancasters, which recently had been dispatching twenty-two-thousand-pound "Grand Slam" earthquake bombs, could now take up the rather more pleasant duty of bringing Allied prisoners of war out of formerly Nazi-occupied lands. But the war, for Bomber Command crews and for Sir Arthur Harris in particular, would end on a bitter note. Churchill, in a further effort to downplay strategic bombing in the public mind, declined to offer Bomber Command its own campaign medal. The prime minister had not mentioned Bomber Command in his victory speech, and he scarcely mentioned strategic bombing in the six-volume epic he would later write on the war. For Harris, the denial of recognition to his personnel, in light of the sacrifices they had made throughout the war, was an inexcusable affront—further evidence of the preference continually given throughout the war to the older services. In early June, he vented his bitterness to the Secretary of State for Air: "[W]henever the armies succeed in doing anything more useful and spectacular than a retreat, a medal is immediately announced for them. When Bomber Command carries on the offensive alone for two years no medal is struck for them—and a share in one is only awarded as an afterthought for crews only."[198]

THE USAAF AND THE FIREBOMBING OF CITIES: JAPAN, 1945

As the war in Europe reached its end stages, British and American bombers in that theater began preparing for redeployment to the Far East, where their combined power, added to existing might of the Pacific bombing fleet, would be loosed on the Japanese home islands.[199] In a letter to Bottomley at the end of March, Harris concluded with the following rhetorical question: "Japan remains. Are we going to bomb their cities flat—as in Germany—and give the armies a walk over—as in France and Germany—or are we going to bomb only their outlying factories and subsequently invade at the cost of 3 to 6 million casualties?"[200] At the time of his writing, the Americans already were in the midst of a campaign to bomb Japanese cities flat.

Beginning in 1944, American bomber forces operated in the Japanese theater under the direction of the U.S. Joint Chiefs of Staff, with Gen. Arnold in direct command of the newly formed Twentieth Air Force.[201] Just less than a year later, on the night of 9–10 March 1945, American B-29 bombers launched what proved to be the single most deadly raid of the war: sixteen square miles of Tokyo were burned out, and no less than 80,000 residents were killed. The Tokyo raid had marked a turn in the American air campaign in the Far East; it came after months of frustration and stagnation. But it was not an abrupt turn. Plans to attack Japanese cities with incendiary bombs had been in the works for years.

The Americans had long been aware that the structure and nature of Japanese cities made them especially vulnerable to fire. In the 1920s, while the U.S.-Japanese antagonism was yet in its early stages, Billy Mitchell had noted that Japanese cities were built from inflammable materials like wood and paper. This idea influenced thinking at the Air Corps Tactical School and, in 1939, instructors there taught their students that large sections of Japanese cities "are built of flimsy and highly inflammable materials." They argued that the earthquake disaster of 1924 "bears witness to the fearful destruction that may be inflicted by incendiary bombs."[202] In 1940, Gen. Claire Chennault, who had been hired in 1937 as an advisor to the Chinese Air Force, suggested a China-based air campaign against Japan that would include the use of incendiary bombs against Japanese cities. Washington policymakers, including the president himself, enthusiastically embraced the plan as a way to check Japanese advances without arousing domestic opposition to war. But plans to put bombers in the hands of the Chinese aroused concerns in the War Department—in particular, such an effort would delay getting more bombers to the British, who were then making immediate and desperate demands for them. As anxieties about Japan continued and intensified, a number of highly placed Washington officials maintained an interest in the prospects for air war against Japan—and for fire raids against Japanese cities.[203]

In 1941 theory and speculation were increasingly replaced by concrete plans as the Intelligence Division of the Air Corps began to collect data on Japanese economic targets. By July, the Air Corps was ferrying B-17s to the Philippines, hoping to deter Japanese expansion, and to interdict it if it flowed southward. This decision, as Michael Sherry has pointed out, "measured the desperation about the Far East and the optimism about the bomber's potential that arose despite the formidable practical obstacles to deployment of the big bombers." This optimism was nowhere so strong as in civilian circles: Secretary of War Henry Stimson proclaimed that the bomber had "completely changed the strategy of the Pacific."[204] Such optimistic assessments rested in part on the idea that the Japanese were intensely afraid of aerial bombing, and that they would be prone to panic or collapse in the face of it. In an ultimately vain effort to deter the Japanese, Gen. George Marshall in mid-November threatened to "set the paper cities of Japan on fire." But the comment was more than simply a deterrent threat: Marshall knew that incendiary weapons, which had limited use against military targets, were being shipped to the Philippines, and that U.S. airmen were preparing plans for an aerial offensive against Japan. The Americans hoped to overcome the long distances in the Pacific by having Luzon-based bombers land in the Soviet Union once they had bombed their Japanese objectives. General Marshall made vigorous though ultimately futile efforts to win Soviet permission for the plan.[205] In the meantime, popular American journals speculated about U.S. incendiary attacks on Tokyo. By February 1942 the U.S. Air Staff had identified areas of Tokyo particularly vulnerable to fire attack.[206]

Once the war was underway, planning for the air campaign against Japan went on in several different circles, including the Air Staff and the Committee of Operations Analysts (COA). President Roosevelt, fearing that the Pacific war might be an intolerably protracted affair, urged a shortcut, again suggesting the possibility of using Siberian airfields in a bid to attack "the heart of Japan."[207] Earlier he had endorsed another route to the same end. On 18 April 1942, sixteen B-25 bombers had departed the carrier Hornet to wage an aerial assault on Tokyo. Led by Gen. James Doolittle, the raid was intended to deliver a blow to Japanese morale, to give the Chinese a shot in the arm, and, more concretely, to persuade the Japanese to pull fighter squadrons out of combat theaters and back to the home islands. Though the targets of the "Doolittle raid" were industrial and military facilities, the bombs scattered into residential areas. Though the brazen attack was heralded in the American press, and though it caused the Japanese to rethink some parts of their grand strategy and reallocate resources in ways that were ultimately advantageous to the Americans, it made clear the operational difficulties of operating in the Far East: the planes were lost in their attempts to make it back to Chinese (and in one case Siberian) territory. The Japanese government used the raid as an excuse to tighten controls over its population.[208]

As government officials prioritized aircraft manufacture, planners sought ways to employ bombers in the Far East. New B-29 bombers offered greater range if suitable bases could be found for them. Looking for a solution (and under continued pressure from Roosevelt), the Air Staff fastened on the idea of staging bombers out of India, using advance bases in China for refueling and loading bombs. This plan went forward even though it was understood that, in time, the Marianas Islands would offer even better staging opportunities for bomber operations. And new weapons entered the scene as well. In 1943 a cloth streamer attached to the recently developed M-69 incendiary bomb (filled with jellied gasoline, or "napalm") stabilized it in flight. It proved the most successful incendiary bomb employed in trials (May–September 1943) against the mock "Japanese village" at the Dugway Proving Ground, Utah, which consisted of two dozen houses made with construction materials like those used in Japan.[209]

By 1943 targeting for the Japanese theater reflected the ongoing prioritization of selective bombing of key industries, along with the increasing lure of urban incendiary bombing. A March report prepared by AAF Headquarters selected eight target systems consisting of fifty-seven key targets. At the same time, a COA plan and a joint U.S.-British targeting effort were underway. The latter indicated that bombing would likely be a prelude to invasion, and thus would need to deal a significant blow to Japanese war industry. Bomber bases would be spread over a wide area, but basing in China—despite logistical difficulties—would offer the best operational possibilities. A Combined Chiefs of Staff plan released shortly thereafter listed the Japanese aircraft industry as the most important immediate target. This plan, too, envisioned operations out of China. But it postulated that the planned offensive could not be completed until October 1945.[210]

At the same time, investigations into the potential of urban incendiary attacks were ongoing. A study appearing in early 1943 indicated that Japanese industry and population were concentrated in a small number of large cities, and that these were vulnerable to the effects of fire. The Americans, however, had not lost their concern about moral and legal questions; indeed, a May 1943 request for a study of the prospects for urban incendiary raids admonished, "It is desired that the areas selected include, or be in the immediate vicinity of, legitimate military targets."[211] Such a request not only helped to ease the consciences of those requesting the report, but allowed for urban and selective targeting to be conflated in the minds of those doing the targeting. A patina of legitimacy was thereby applied to raids that were, in both conception and in operational technique, urban-incendiary attacks. This would mean, inevitably, that the "indirect effects" of bombing would be elevated to a position of increased prominence, thereby upending the theory revered at ACTS. But planners worked around this problem by looking for the advantages of indirect effects. Applying logic similar to that used by the British when they switched to area bombing, they specified the disruption and dislocation of the work force as an explicit motive for their targeting decisions. At the Quebec Conference of September 1943 General Arnold presented "An Air Plan for the Defeat of Japan" in carefully chosen but rather tortured language, including "the dislocation of labor by casualty."[212]

Inherent in any plan for incendiary attacks on cities is the acceptance of large numbers of casualties among those not in military uniform. Some of those, surely, would be engaged in war work—but many more would not be. This was well understood by planners, although it was eased in many instances by self-justifying rhetoric. And, while it raised the concerns of some of them, it did not prevent them from going ahead with both the conceptualization and prosecution of urban incendiary raids. Another targeting report, released in October, highlighted the congested, flammable nature of Japanese cities. Twenty cities, noted the authors, contained 22 percent of the Japanese population, 53 percent of all the targets, and 74 percent of all the targets listed on the March 1943 target priority list. Some 1,600 tons of M-69 incendiary bombs might destroy all twenty cities. A COA report released two weeks later came to similar conclusions.[213] This line of thinking was similar to that elaborated in the detailed and careful graphics contained in Harris's "Blue Books."

While two different approaches to targeting were now clearly on the table, nothing had as yet been settled. The groundwork for urban incendiary attacks had been established, but the AAF's instinct for selective targeting continued to coexist with it. In November 1943 a COA targeting list prioritized shipping, aircraft, steel, and urban areas. And targeting lists produced by other agencies in 1944 continued this pattern. An updated COA list (of June) listed in order: aircraft, coke, oil, electronics, bearings, urban areas, and shipping. It noted that urban areas could be attacked using blind bombing methods. In the same month, the COA established the Joint Incendiary Committee, to focus on the possibilities of destroying six important urban areas on the island of Honshu. In September its subcommittee recommended undertaking such a campaign with massive force in a concentrated time frame. Planners estimated 560,000 casualties. In October 1944 the National Defense Research Committee suggested that just over nine thousand tons of incendiary bombs could burn out twenty-two Japanese cities. This approach, the authors maintained, held the prospect of shortening the war and saving lives. They edged around the ethical questions by asserting simply that they would have to be settled at higher levels.[214]

When bombing operations began in the Pacific theater, they slammed immediately into the daunting logistical and operational difficulties of functioning over enormous distances and in difficult conditions.[215] In the summer of 1944 the Twentieth Bomber Command began operations in the China-Burma-India theater. Its B-29s had reached Karachi via Gander, Newfoundland, Marrakech, and Cairo. But the Twentieth, commanded by Gen. Kenneth Wolfe, faced a painfully slow build-up of fuel, ordnance, and supplies, due to the formidable problems of bringing it in by air "over the hump" of the Himalayas. (To deliver eight tons of fuel and cargo, a converted bomber required twenty-eight tons of gas for the round trip.) Other problems proved overwhelming as well. Not only did crews have trouble reaching and finding targets, they had trouble getting home again. Fully 70 percent of the Twentieth's bombers lost were lost to causes *other than* enemy action. General Arnold fired General Wolfe less than a month after the Twentieth's first combat mission.[216] Wolfe was replaced by Gen. Curtis LeMay, who, in Europe, had proven himself a determined and technically proficient combat commander— much like Harris.

LeMay did what he could to improve the combat performance of his organization, but, in light of the problems posed by the theater, he had only modest expectations. He insisted that an alternative staging area be sought. In the meantime he used the opportunity to train his crews and to learn from experience. In December, LeMay was persuaded by his immediate superiors to fly an incendiary attack on Hankow, a Chinese city being used as a base for Japanese operations. The raid was considered a great success by the Americans.[217] By that time the Twenty-First Bomber Command, under Gen. Haywood Hansell, had commenced its own bombing operations out of the Marianas Islands. On 24 November the Twenty-first carried out its first large-scale attack on the Japanese homeland. General Hansell, a former staff officer, was a product of ACTS and one of the authors of AWPD/1. Unsurprisingly, he was a proponent of selective targeting. But Hansell's early attempts against Japanese industry, with priority placed on the aircraft industry, were disappointing—indeed they produced little consequential damage. This made Arnold particularly uneasy, for he feared that if American bombers did not make headway in an air force controlled operation, they would be parceled out to army and navy theater commanders.[218]

The B-29 bomber was the backbone of the Twenty-first Bomber Command. The large plane—the air force's "three billion dollar gamble"— was to be a war-winning airplane, and thus it had much to prove. The AAF and General Arnold in particular had staked a great deal on the plane. After the second experimental B-29 flew successfully on 27 June 1943, manufacturing sites were set up in Wichita, Kansas; Marietta, Georgia; Omaha, Nebraska; and Seattle, Washington. B-29s were hurried off assembly lines to meet President Roosevelt's pledge that 200 of the aircraft would be ready for combat in Asia by March 1944. But the rush—off the drawing board and off the assembly line both—had costs: the aircraft suffered engine failures, fires, dead power plants, and jammed gear boxes. Thousands of modifications were required to make the plane operationally reliable and effective.[219]

The manifold teething problems of the B-29 were a major factor in Hansell's (and Wolfe's) difficulties, but the weather over Japan was even more of an obstacle. Constant cloud cover, and the prevailing winds of the jet stream (which were imperfectly understood at the time), made it nearly impossible for bombers to keep and hold formation and to bomb their targets accurately. These problems were exacerbated by the unsatisfactory nature of weather forecasting in the theater and the fact that, due to the long distances being flown, navigational errors could not be corrected: aircraft that went astray either had to return early or bomb a target of opportunity.[220]

As the failures mounted, General Arnold grew impatient with Hansell. Like other American commanders and politicians, Arnold was anxious to see the war end as quickly as possible; he hoped that aerial bombing would play a conspicuous role in final victory, vindicating expenditure on the B-29, and enhancing the USAAF's chances for full independence after the war. The setbacks in the European theater in the autumn of 1944 only increased his determination to push hard in the Far East. In mid-December, Arnold's deputy, Gen. Lauris Norstad, conveyed to Hansell an "urgent requirement" for a full-scale fire raid on Nagoya. Hansell undertook it reluctantly, arguing that he did not want to diverge from the priority mission of "precision bombing" just at the moment when, he believed, results were within his grasp.[221]

Hansell fully understood that the COA had emphasized the vulnerability of Japanese cities to incendiary attack, and his own daylight tactics had included incendiaries, in particular for use against "home shop" production in Japanese cities. He knew, too, that nighttime incendiary raids were in the original plans for the air war in the Far East. But he had an instinctive attraction to selective targeting and he believed—in accordance with the plans he had seen before leaving Washington—that nighttime area raids were to be undertaken as a "last resort, and only if precision bombing proved infeasible or failed to do the job."[222] He did not feel that events yet compelled such drastic measures. His read of the situation, however, was too complacent. Arnold was impatient, and, while Hansell had been dedicating himself to tactical and operational considerations in the theater, Washington-based plans for the air war in Japan had been changed to raise the priority of area incendiary missions. As Michael Sherry has pointed out, Hansell's failure to comprehend fully the situation was understandable: "[T]he vague circumlocutions employed and the incremental way by which new assumptions crept into planning obscured the shift." It was obscured as well, by the unwillingness of Arnold and his staff to admit that they were contemplating a marked change in tactics.[223]

In January, Arnold opted for a reshuffling of command in the Far East. He was anxious to consolidate operations in the hands of his more experienced field commander, but he was anxious as well to move Hansell out of the way. When LeMay took over the consolidated B-29 operations he did so with the understanding that he was to produce results as rapidly as possible. In his memoir, Hansell would argue that Arnold had become more impressed by tonnages dropped than by (less-knowable) estimates of damage done: "[S]tatistics of tons of bombs dropped and of sorties flown," he complained, "are easily compiled, seem factual and specific, and are impressive. Photographs of burned out cities also speak for themselves." While recognizing the many pressures that had made Arnold impatient, Hansell nonetheless pointed out that "time had become an obsessive compulsion" in the Washington headquarters of the USAAF. He was right: Washington was in a hurry. Convinced that he had been diverted from the right course, Hansell lamented that "General Arnold did not understand what the Twenty-first Bomber Command had gone through or had achieved."[224]

LeMay's assumption of a new position, consolidating the operations of the Twentieth Air Force, coincided with a strengthening of the B-29 force in the Pacific. But LeMay acted on his own initiative to enhance the prospects for planned incendiary attacks. Knowing that his decisions would not be censured, he made tactical changes that would intensify the nighttime raids. He stripped his B-29s of their defensive armament, filled their bomb bays with incendiaries, and flew them over Japanese cities at low-level. Against the bloody backdrop of the battle of Iwo Jima, General LeMay said of the 9 March raid, "If the war is shortened by a single day the attack will have served its purpose."[225] Over the course of the following months, LeMay and his bomber force waged an area bombing campaign of terrible fury, attacking sixty-six Japanese cities with incendiary weapons.[226]

On 2 August, just days before the attack on Hiroshima, American bombers flew the largest single aerial strike in history, dropping 6,632 tons of bombs and burning out the cities of Hachioji, Toyama, Nagaoka, and Mito.[227] Once the incendiary campaign was underway, it generated few questions among the American press or public, even though the details of the tactics being used were readily discernable to newspaper readers. The Disney-produced film *Victory Through Air Power*, based on Alexander de Seversky's 1943 book of the same title, had helped prepare the ground. Using the destruction of Tokyo for its climactic final scene, the film "cultivated popular expectations for a virtuous campaign of annihilation against Japan."[228] *The Nation* was one of the few journals to question the bombing. Addressing raids flown against Tokyo, Nagoya, Osaka, and Kobe, the anonymous author of one article observed, "At least twenty-nine square miles of the four cities were burned out in the first four attacks, which makes the A.A.F.'s insistence that these were 'precision' raids a little puzzling."[229]

In its internal history written at the time, the USAAF did not cite "undermining enemy morale" as a reason for the shift to the nighttime incendiary attacks. While recognizing that their tactics represented a "radical departure from the traditional doctrine," they attempted to maintain consistency by arguing that they "were not conceived as terror raids against the civilian population." The authors explained, "The Japanese economy depends heavily on home industries carried on in cities or settlements close to major factory areas. By destroying these feeder industries the flow of vital parts could be curtailed and production disorganized." And they added, "A general conflagration in a city like Tokyo or Nagoya might have the further advantage of spreading to some of the priority targets located in those areas, making it unnecessary to knock them out by separate pinpoint attacks."[230]

In the European theater the Americans focused on intentions rather than outcomes. In doing so, they had persuaded themselves that they were being true to the concept of "precision bombing" even when such bombing was desperately inaccurate. In the Far Eastern theater, the Americans worked hard to link their actions to the general philosophy behind the industrial fabric theory. But in many respects the Americans followed a path similar to the one the British had followed in Europe: rationalizing their choices by reference to the particular psychology of the Japanese, and to the indirect effects of area bombing. To this the Americans added arguments about the peculiar structure of Japanese industry. Looking for a way to end the war quickly, and faced with operational problems even more daunting than those in Europe, Arnold further loosened whatever constraints remained on American bombing; he was unwilling to wait around for those slow to embrace the new methods.

If the inflammability of Japanese cities was folded into an argument about efficiency, it was also recognized as a way of capitalizing on an exploitable weakness and on Japanese fears of air attack. And the tone of the public relations information on the air war in Japan belied the notion of a campaign based *solely* on economic considerations. As the noose tightened around Japan, the air force was anxious to claim its share of the credit. Once victory was achieved, this desire intensified. The exuberant language of the New York-based Office of Information Services, Headquarters Army Air Forces, revealed that if killing Japanese and lowering popular morale was not the principal focus of the incendiary raids, it was certainly seen as a beneficial side effect. One release, called "Highlights of the Twentieth Air Force," displayed an unrepentant tone of vengeance and celebration, exclaiming that the "Twentieth Air Force Blitz" against Japan culminated in a "fiery perfection" of "jellied fire attacks" that "literally burned Japan out of the war." The "vaunted Twentieth" had "killed outright 310,000 Japanese, injured 412,000 more, and rendered 9,200,000 homeless." For "five flaming months . . . a thousand All-American planes and 20,000 American men brought homelessness, terror, and death to an arrogant foe, and left him practically a nomad in an almost cityless land."[231]

In his final war dispatch (published after the conclusion of hostilities), General Arnold included a map of Japan, showing each of the sixty-six cities that had been firebombed. To help policymakers and the American public appreciate the nature of the achievement, each Japanese city had listed next to it the name of an American city of roughly the same size. In the text accompanying the graphic, Arnold admitted that casualties had caused "significant effects in the dislocation of industrial manpower and on enemy morale." "The Japanese," he noted with satisfaction, "have stated that air attacks killed 260,000, injured 412,000, left 9,200,000 homeless, and demolished or burned down 2,210,000 houses."[232] Just as Harris had celebrated Bomber Command's destruction of over sixty German cities, so too did Arnold celebrate his destruction of over sixty Japanese cities.

If race alone did not determine the nature of the air war in the Far East, it certainly intensified a campaign already characterized by strong emotions and forces: temptation, frustration, momentum and zeal. And race did account entirely for the rhetoric associated with the Far Eastern air campaign. Hatred of the Japanese, and the course of the war in the Pacific made American planners confident that the American people were unlikely to object to or to raise many questions—at the time or later—about fire raids against Japanese cities.

In Japan the Americans did not wholly abandon their preferred theories of air warfare. As in Europe, American bombers typically returned to selective targeting whenever weather permitted. But the willingness of American planners and policymakers to cross the line and prosecute mass fire raids on a repeated and systematic basis represented a descent to a new and terrifying level in the hell of total warfare. And it surely helped to smooth the way—intellectually and emotionally—for the atomic attacks that would follow. On 6 August, over Hiroshima, no moral threshold was crossed that had not been crossed much earlier in the year.[233] Those military planners who knew about the atomic bomb before it was dropped viewed it as another tool in the Allied arsenal. If they hoped it might have an impact, they did not assume it would end the war. Planning for a ground invasion went on as usual, conventional air raids on a variety of Japanese targets took place in between and after the two atomic attacks, and the navy continued its stranglehold on enemy shipping and supply. The Japanese military, government, and population were to be afforded no relief and no quarter until surrender was achieved under terms then being contested at the highest political levels.

ASSESSMENT AND RESULTS

On 30 April 1945 the Air Ministry and USSTAF issued a joint statement on the strategic bombing offensive. Naturally, both organizations were interested in highlighting the contributions of bombing to victory in Europe. They stressed the following: (1) the achievement of air superiority before the invasion of Normandy; (2) the reduction of the German oil supply; (3) the use of bombers to isolate battlefields, to interdict supplies, and to encircle ground troops; (4) the delivery of unprecedented levels of explosives; and (5) the reduction of the numbers and potency of enemy special weapons, including V-bombs and jet aircraft.[234] This assessment of the contribution of the bomber forces to victory in

Europe would not be the last word on the subject, however. Other, more elaborate evaluations were already underway and would come to fruition in the aftermath of the war. But the significance of the air campaign—the political and moral arguments that grew up around it during and after the war, and the high stakes involved for the different organizations affected by the results—would insure that evaluations of it would be contentious and contested. Lives had been lost, large sums had been invested, and national and individual reputations had been put on the line. Neither the American bombing survey nor the more limited British evaluation would fully answer critics' questions or establish unchallenged guidance for future air campaigns. Indeed, the British survey would remain a rather obscure document, narrowly circulated and, until recently, available only in a few archives.[235]

The British were interested from the outset in a joint survey to assess the Combined Bomber Offensive. But the Americans, particularly General Spaatz, resisted this vigorously. In the spring of 1944, when the first suggestions for a survey were circulated in USAAF circles, Spaatz insisted on a wholly American effort. He put forward some official and bureaucratic reasons for avoiding a joint assessment, and these had their own validity. But they were largely cover for Spaatz's primary concern: that the USAAF and RAF efforts would end up merged in the public mind, with deleterious consequences for the USAAF. The question was not settled until late in the summer, when American delays finally convinced the British that a joint survey was not a live option.[236]

The American survey got underway formally in the autumn of 1944 when General Arnold inquired if Franklin D'Olier, the president of the Prudential Insurance Company of America, would be willing to serve as the chairman of a comprehensive survey of the effects of strategic bombing by the USAAF. D'Olier accepted, ultimately heading up an organization of some 350 officers, 500 enlisted men, and 300 civilians—many of them highly trained economists, managers, and businessmen. Those in key posts, besides D'Olier, included Henry Alexander (vice-chairman), George Ball, Paul Nitze, Theodore Wright, Fred Searls, and John Kenneth Galbraith. Their job was to produce an independent, objective report (not issued under the auspices of the United States Army Air Forces) on wartime bombing.[237] Though USAAF leaders initially supported a wholly independent report, they grew anxious that it might evaluate only the results of the war, without adequately considering the course of the war, and the challenges it posed. Their concern was acute enough that General Spaatz authorized a separate study, under his director of intelligence, titled "The Contribution of Air Power to the Defeat of Germany." It stressed the long struggle for air supremacy and the large air effort devoted to ground support operations.[238] Fully cognizant of their upcoming battle for service independence, USAAF leaders wanted to insure that their own perspective on the war was known and available to others.

The personnel of the United States Strategic Bombing Survey (USSBS) followed the advance of front line troops in the end stages of the war, examining bomb damage and interviewing factory managers and local German officials.[239] This work, undertaken so closely on the heels of advancing armies, was often dangerous. USSBS personnel produced reports on key targets systems, as well as more than 200 special reports on a variety of topics, such as the influence of weather upon bombing operations. In all, over 330 reports and annexes were released for printing in 1946. Two special reports on the war in Europe—the Over-all Report (European War), and the Summary Report (European War)— were the focus of attention when the survey conclusions were released publicly and became the most widely cited portions of the survey for Europe.[240] The Summary Report for the Pacific war, written mainly by Paul Nitze, was the most widely read portion of the survey assessing the Far Eastern campaign. These three reports were the only ones that bore the unqualified approval of the USSBS chairman's office.[241]

The statistical analyses supporting the USSBS European reports were based on questionnaires submitted to industrial firms in Germany, examination of the internal records of those firms, and interrogation of their managers. While these methods were more rigorous than those employed for the First World War bombing surveys, they had inherent disadvantages based on the unreliability of the answers. Frequently the firms questioned did not have all the data required, and in some cases it was impossible to know if the figures utilized by analysts were actual or instead merely estimated production levels. Survey officials sought to do the best they could under the circumstances, and attempted to correct for errors as often as possible.[242] The nature of the USSBS, with so many different reports under the control of so many different individuals, meant that it would be large, unwieldy, and comprised of a variety of opinions—some radically at odds with one another—regarding the contribution of strategic bombing to the war effort. Because the survey was so broad in scope and contained so much data, it subsequently has been used to support a range of differing arguments about bombing.

Though disappointed by their failure to persuade the Americans to undertake a joint survey, British officials continued making plans for an independent investigation. The British Joint Chiefs approved a plan in principle by the Chiefs of Staff on 10 August 1944, and in the autumn various parties having some stake in the outcome of a British survey began jockeying for position. Professor Solly Zuckerman, who had been Tedder's principal advisor and who was now a guiding force in the newly established Bombing Analysis Unit of the Supreme Headquarters, Allied Expeditionary Forces (SHAEF), urged a scientific study to compare the results of area and precision bombing. Harris suggested a limited survey done mainly by Bomber Command personnel who had an intricate knowledge of the workings of the force, but who, soon after Germany's defeat, would depart for their civilian occupations. These individuals, Harris suggested, would spend six to eight weeks investigating a small sample of German cities "with a view to confirming or refuting theories which have already been built up on the evidence available."[243]

But the Air Ministry set out its own course, planning the establishment of a British Bombing Survey Unit (BBSU), which was ultimately to be absorbed by a larger British Bombing Research Mission (BBRM). In November 1944 this plan went to Churchill, who did not respond until January, when—to the surprise of those involved—he refused it. The prime minister, who was anxious about what such investigations might reveal, was prepared to support only a small-scale survey that would be in a position to have results "soon enough to be of material assistance in the war against Japan." In light of this news, Portal made preparations for a more modest program, but Churchill erected more roadblocks in March and April 1945 against what he termed a "sterile task." He was insufficiently moved by Portal's strong warning—issued in late March 1945—against allowing the USSBS to be the sole record for posterity.[244]

The Air Ministry scrambled to do the best it could within the narrow bounds set by the prime minister, ultimately turning to SHAEF where Professor Zuckerman had been attempting to make investigations with the few people available to him. With Tedder's endorsement as a boost, Zuckerman became scientific advisor to the BBSU. Nine panels were constituted, and they relied heavily on the statistical data provided by the U.S. Survey teams. The study of area bombing was based on statistical inquiry and was not checked by direct observation. Once the report was completed it might have been possible to submit it to an impartial body for review, but this was not done as the Air Ministry by then showed little interest in such a course, and other departments had lost interest—and much of their wartime personnel as well.[245] Bomber Command's Operational Research Section (ORS) also undertook some limited investigations; these were independent of the BBSU effort.

In the meantime, the USSBS studies came together, and results of the European assessments were ready to be made public in the autumn of 1945. The USSBS Over-all and Summary reports on the European war gave a positive endorsement to the role of aviation. The vice-chairman, Henry Alexander, read sections of these to the press on 24 October

1945. In particular he emphasized that "Allied air power was decisive in the war in Western Europe." He went on, "Hindsight inevitably suggests that it might have been employed differently or better in some respects. Nevertheless it was decisive." The phrasing had been carefully selected by the editors working for the chairman's office. Newspaper writers generally took their cue from these statements when they devised headlines for the next day's copy. In fact, the argument was more qualified than it seemed: "air power" was used instead of "strategic bombing," and "Western Europe" instead of "Europe." The term "decisive," in the context of the overlapping influences affecting the war's endgame, is so hard to specify as to be almost meaningless. Still, most Americans heard Alexander's statements as endorsements of bombing—a fact that no doubt came as a relief to the personnel of the USAAF.[246]

The authors of the Over-all and Summary Reports could not resist highlighting the bombing campaign's final crescendo. Alexander told the press, "It [bombing] brought the economy which sustained the enemy's armed forces to virtual collapse, although the full effects of this collapse had not reached the enemy's front lines when they were overrun by Allied forces. It brought home to the German people the full impact of modern war with all its horror and suffering. Its imprint on the German nation will be lasting."[247] Even here, though, the argument was not as strong as it appeared: admitting that Allied air forces had not stymied the Wehrmacht independently of Allied ground forces, Alexander stressed the psychological impact of bombing on the German people.

The summary reports and quotes to the press were obliged, to some degree at least, to stay within the boundaries established by economist John Kenneth Galbraith, who had directed the USSBS study of the impact of bombing on the German war economy. He had concluded, in a report titled "The Effects of Strategic Bombing on the German War Economy," that its impact was limited until the latter part of 1944 when the air campaign worked in combination with other factors to contribute to Germany's collapse. (Galbraith's report made clear that, despite bombing, Germany's total munitions output reached its peak in July 1944.) Indeed, Galbraith argued that strategic bombing may have helped streamline the German war economy by allowing German economic czar Albert Speer to impose more stringent measures and restructuring than he would have been able to otherwise. In his memoir, written in 1981, Galbraith referred to the "disastrous failure of strategic bombing"—a rather more dramatic description than the one conveyed in his survey report, which could more appropriately be characterized as damnation by feint praise. In any event, the memoir made Galbraith even more disliked by air force supporters than he had been immediately following the war.[248] Galbraith felt that he had fulfilled his brief and had come to the only possible conclusion: bombing had been important in collapsing the German war effort, but only late in the day and in combination with other effects.

Critics of the report believed that he had been too narrow in his assessment, and that his conclusions failed to convey the possibilities of air power for the future.[249] General Orvil Anderson, who had been Deputy for Operations in the Eighth Air Force, felt that any assessment of the USAAF's role in the war had to consider the many difficulties under which the service operated, and the uphill battle to establish air superiority in Europe. Anderson wanted a fuller accounting of these issues in the Over-all and Summary reports than eventually appeared there. Those reports, however, did not fail to acknowledge the problems faced by the USAAF, nor did they fail to acknowledge that some target sets had been far more effective than others. But even if Galbraith's report had not been everything that air advocates hoped, it still acknowledged that "the attack on transportation beginning in September 1944 was the most important single cause of Germany's ultimate economic collapse." The author explained, "The operation of Germany's raw material industries, her manufacturing industries, and her power supply were all dependent on coal. By January [1945] their stocks were becoming exhausted and collapse was inevitable. . . . From December 1944 onwards, all sectors of the German economy were in rapid decline. This collapse was due to the results of air raids working in combination with other causes."[250]

A separate USSBS report titled "The Impact of the Allied Air Effort on German Logistics," which examined the effect of aerial attacks on German army supply lines, argued that attacks on transport targets prevented the enemy from effectively concentrating men and matériel at critical times and places. Transport, the authors argued, was the weakest link in the German logistics chain, and thus "its failure was the immediate cause of the breakdown of the supply system, and consequently was a decisive factor in the breakdown of the German army." Both the strategic and tactical air forces were credited for their contribution to this outcome.[251] The Over-all and Summary reports accordingly stressed the importance of transport attacks in undermining Germany's ability to fight the war.

The USSBS also highlighted the utility of General Spaatz's pet project, the oil campaign; unsurprisingly, perhaps, the USSBS gave a good deal of attention to the oil plan, which came closest to fulfilling the aspirations of the "industrial fabric" theory. The American official historians of the bombing campaign reflected and reinforced this finding, writing, "The air offensive against German oil production was the pride of the

U.S. Strategic Air Forces. Initiated through the insistence of its officers, effective immediately, and decisive within less than a year, this campaign proved to be a clear-cut illustration of strategic air-war doctrine."[252] Galbraith's report on the German economy explained, "Heavy Allied attacks on German oil production began in May 1944; two months later oil had replaced aircraft as the first priority strategic bombing target. From the German point of view, this was disastrous."[253]

The USSBS Oil Division Final Report suggested that attacks on oil, if carried out earlier in the campaign, almost certainly would have had more of a deleterious effect on the Luftwaffe than the campaign against the German aircraft industry did. The Galbraith Report concurred, arguing, "From the point of view of grounding enemy aircraft, the attacks on synthetic oil works were the most effective of all strategic bombing." The Oil Division Final Report suggested as well that the oil campaign would have been enhanced if the Americans had earlier recognized the important links between the German oil, chemical, and rubber industries, and if they had used larger bombs, more incendiaries, and fewer defective bombs on oil targets.[254]

After the war it was recognized, often with the help of German officials, that certain relatively untouched target sets might have been useful in helping to bring about the collapse of the German war economy. The German Quartermaster General Department ranked powder and explosive plants second behind oil targets. USSBS analysts argued that concentrated attacks on German rubber manufacture would have served Allied ends. Finally, Albert Speer, German Minister for War Production, argued that the German electrical power net was highly vulnerable to attacks. Even though this target had been prioritized by AWPD/1, it did not receive dedicated attention because American authorities in England believed the system to be more highly developed and robust than it actually was.[255]

The USSBS and British Survey both affirmed the importance of air supremacy. The USSBS Over-all Report on the European war had recognized it implicitly in its statement, "Allied air power was decisive in the war in western Europe."[256] The American official historians were more direct on the point, claiming, "Of all the accomplishments of the air forces, the attainment of air supremacy was the most significant, for it made possible the invasions of the continent and gave the heavy bombers their opportunity to wreck the industries of the Reich."[257] The impact and import of air superiority was recognized particularly in a report by Gen. Omar N. Bradley titled "Effect of Air Power on Military Operations." After V-E day, Eisenhower suggested that Bradley serve as a military advisor to the USSBS, to offer the views of a ground commander to the overall evaluation of wartime strategic air power. Bradley's report stressed that, though some air commanders may have wished it otherwise, air forces did not function outside an operational context that used air power as "a prelude to and preparation for ground operations." He gave pride of place to the destruction of German air power and its key role in the Normandy landing, and hailed the contribution of the oil campaign in eroding the power of the Wehrmacht. But while he heralded these two accomplishments, he concluded that they were not in themselves decisive without exploitation by tactical air, and Allied ground and sea forces. With regard to rail transport, Bradley drew a distinction between tactical attacks (designed to destroy military traffic), and strategic attacks (aimed at railway facilities well behind the lines of battle); he concluded that the former was of more significant help to Allied armies, and praised the efforts of the fighter bombers attached to the tactical air forces in Europe. Bradley was critical of Operation Clarion, however, which he claimed "had no immediate or apparent results on the ground battle" since it did not concentrate on transportation facilities immediately available to the opposing forces or their reserves.[258]

USSBS assessments of bombing's impact on German morale were not uniform, but they contained some overlapping general conclusions. USSBS reports stressed that though bombing demoralized civilian populations, this did not have a direct reflection in either production or pressure for surrender. The "Area Studies Division Report" (which evaluated area attacks for the European theater) echoed the World War I American survey, arguing that lowered German morale had not contributed directly to a decline in German war production. While pointing out that factory managers reported declines in worker efficiency due to air raids, specifically area attacks, the authors claimed that they could find "no concrete evidence of such a decline." They did, however, argue that city attacks had "a permanent effect on morale and political thought," and "made life in Germany . . . progressively more difficult."[259]

The USSBS report titled "The Effects of Strategic Bombing on German Morale" argued that heavy bombing was not proportionally more effective than moderate bombing, and that sustained heavy bombing led to diminishing returns in morale effects (not stiffened morale as has been sometimes argued based on a misreading of the reports). It also maintained that though "bombing was less important than other military developments in producing defeatism," it nonetheless "aided greatly in convincing civilians of Allied superiority" and discrediting Nazi propaganda. While bombing "seriously depressed the morale of German civilians" the effect was not necessarily transferable into active opposition, since "German controls . . . helped to prevent depressed morale from being translated into subversive activity seriously detrimental to the war effort." And though lowered morale "expressed itself in somewhat diminished productivity," this only became a serious problem at the end of the war when German controls failed to overcome the "increasing apathy induced by bombing." The Over-all Report on the European War, explaining that German armaments production continued to mount through 1944, claimed that depressed and discouraged workers were not necessarily unproductive workers: the German people "continued to work efficiently as long as the physical means of production remained."[260] In a 1958 volume entitled *The Social Impact of Bomb Destruction*, Fred Charles Iklé would argue that "[f]indings from Hiroshima, Nagasaki, Hamburg and other areas of large bombings in World War II do not indicate that serious mass panic occurred at any time."[261]

The authors of the report on German morale highlighted the vagaries and assumptions that pervaded both Allied and Axis thinking on the subject. Basing their work on interviews with 3,711 German civilians and on official German documents, the authors explained that the enemy had collected "no accurate, quantitative data on the effect of bombing on the morale of their civilian population or on the relative effectiveness of the various control steps which they took." They pointed out that the Allied Command had not made systematic attempts to gain such data either, and suggested that if either side had in fact sought such information, it would have been useful to them.[262]

Several USSBS Pacific theater reports reinforced and emphasized the general arguments about morale made in the European survey. While two key reports—"The Effects of Air Attack on Japanese Urban Economy" and "The Effects of Strategic Bombing in Japanese Morale"— went to great lengths to point out that USAAF raids had caused profound social disruption, absenteeism, and deprivation, neither one argued that lowered morale and apathy produced by the raids were decisive factors in the outcome of the war. The authors of the first report argued that the economy had been so badly battered by the naval war prior to the area attacks that the raids could have had little direct economic impact in most cases anyway. The authors of the second report maintained that, regardless of low morale, loyalty to the Emperor meant that the Japanese would go on working and fighting so long as they were physically able.[263] Taken together, these assessments revealed not only that civilians could and did endure very high pain levels inflicted by bombing, but also that the relationship between high pain levels and surrender is anything but straightforward.

Despite these findings, the Pacific War "Summary Report" asserted that conventional strategic bombing had been crucial in pushing Japan toward unconditional surrender, and would have culminated in that result even if the atomic bombs had not been dropped. The difference of views could be traced back to Paul Nitze, principal author of the Pacific Summary Report. In the summer of 1945, before heading to Japan to participate in the Pacific survey, Nitze helped draft an air plan for ending the war in the Far East, based on information gained in the European war. By July he apparently had concluded that conventional bombing would be enough to force Japan's surrender. His pre-Hiroshima conclusion was incorporated into the Summary Report, even though it did not flow naturally from arguments presented elsewhere in the Pacific Survey. In a much-quoted section of the report, Nitze argued, "It seems clear that, even without the atomic bombing attacks, air supremacy over Japan could have exerted sufficient pressure to bring about unconditional surrender and obviate the need for invasion."[264]

Supporters of the navy had felt vindicated by the conclusion that the Japanese economy had, in effect, been destroyed by strangulation prior to the onset of the great air raids in March 1945. Thus they were pleased with neither the Summary Report's assumptions about bombing nor its failure to credit the antishipping campaign with being "decisive." Air force-navy antagonism over the Pacific war survey reached its peak, however, in the conflict between the Military Analysis Division and the Naval Analysis Division. The rift was personalized by the Navy's Adm. Ralph Ofstie and the USAAF's Gen. Orvil Anderson, and intensified by the USAAF's postwar bid for independence. Ofstie's Naval Analysis Report, "The Campaigns of the Pacific War" (USSBS Pacific Report #73), had come to conclusions quite different from Anderson's report, "The Over-all Air Effort against Japan." The latter was an unabashed propaganda tract claiming that air power dominated both naval forces and ground forces. The report also recommended a preventive war against the Soviet Union—an argument which, when he made it more explicitly in 1950, would usher Anderson out of command.[265]

Ofstie, appalled by what he read, fired off his critique to Nitze:

> The volume presents a completely inaccurate and entirely biased account of our war against Japan which is of absolutely no historical value, consistently misrepresents the facts, and indeed often ignores facts and employs falsehoods. . . . Underlying the main theme that air power alone won the war is a vicious and deliberate attempt to discredit the naval service. No opportunity is lost to belittle the efforts of the navy, to charge the navy with incompetence and to ridicule the navy concept of warfare."[266]

This was an early round in what ultimately would develop into an all-out war between the navy and the postwar air force.

General Arnold produced his own opinion of the World War II air campaign, issuing three public reports on wartime bombing operations (on 4 January 1944, 27 February 1945, and 12 November 1945). Arnold's reports were, unsurprisingly, celebratory in tone. The first highlighted the "growing pains" that the USAAF had suffered in the early years of the war and the lessons it had learned from experience. The second emphasized the attack on the German aircraft industry during Big Week, the defeat of the Luftwaffe, and the contribution made by strategic bombers to the success of the Normandy landing. His third report stressed the fact that as Allied bombing grew increasingly intense, the Germans failed to keep pace with it in terms of repair and dispersal. He called attention to attacks on oil and transportation and took a special pride in Operation Clarion. He also put a great deal of emphasis on the strategic bombing campaign in the Far East, writing, "Fully recognizing the indispensible contributions of other arms, I feel that air power's part may fairly be called decisive."[267]

The third volume of the American official history of the air campaign, which offered a summary assessment, acknowledged that the "magnitude, resilience, and reserve strength of the German economic system" enabled it to hold out against all but the greatest efforts of the Allies. As noted above, its authors particularly celebrated the attainment of air superiority by the Allies, recognizing and appreciating all the ramifications of that achievement. The U.S. official history also drew attention to the contribution of U.S. tactical air forces in aiding the progress of Allied ground forces. They pointed to intelligence errors as a cause of certain mistakes in the air war, but acknowledged the contributions of the oil and transportation campaigns.[268] Again crediting tactical air forces for helping with the latter, they argued that its impact was profound: "It was clear toward the end of the war that the transportation campaign had paralyzed Germany."[269]

The report of the British Bombing Survey Unit also heralded the contribution of the transportation plan. This is unsurprising since the principal author of the report, Solly Zuckerman, had been the plan's guiding force and most determined advocate. As we have seen, though, both Galbraith and the American official historians agreed with his assessment. And subsequent studies, too, have not only reinforced but strengthened the argument.[270] Like Galbraith, Zuckerman invested the attack on transportation with primary responsibility for collapsing the German economy by the end of the war. BBSU authors argued that perhaps the most telling evidence of the effectiveness of the transport campaign was in the number of trains that were assembled but not moved as a result of loading difficulties and other problems caused by air attacks: in June 1944 the average daily figure was 275; by October 1944 it was 1,000; by March 1945 it was 2,000.[271]

The BBSU report argued against the efficacy of city bombing, particularly for moral effect but also as a means of reducing industrial production. The BBSU final report concluded, "In so far as the offensive against German towns was designed to break the morale of the German civilian population, it clearly failed. Far from lowering essential war production, it also failed to stem a remarkable increase in the output of armaments." Later in the report the authors argued that "area attacks against German cities could not have been responsible for more than a very small part of the fall which actually had occurred in German production by the spring of 1945." The British official historians were unimpressed with area bombing, which, they argued, had by the end of the war shown itself to be an "uneconomic" and "largely self-defeating policy."[272]

The report of the BBSU was initially classified, and—until very recently—was only available in special repositories such as London's Public Record Office. Likewise, Sir Arthur Harris's official dispatch on his three and a half years at the helm of Bomber Command was not made public; it became widely available only in 1995.[273] Since the USSBS focused on American efforts, it downplayed the role of Bomber Command in the war generally. And the conclusions of the USSBS were often harsh in their attitude to the British contribution, reflecting the Americans' ongoing desire to distance themselves from the taint of area bombing in Europe, and to use British bombing as a foil against which to argue the effectiveness and "precision" of their own campaign. Indeed, the bias was so evident that the American official historians felt compelled to apologize for it in 1951, writing, "the deprecating tone with regard to the contribution of the RAF which ran through much of the survey's work, especially the specialized reports, did not reflect a judicious appraisal of the RAF effort."[274] If RAF leaders had feared a scenario in which an American survey would provide the only public, authoritative analysis of wartime strategic air operations, their fears proved justified.[275]

Harris, whose views had been essentially silenced by the noncirculation of his final dispatch, attempted to correct the situation and get his perspective across through his war memoir, *Bomber Offensive*, published in 1947. In it, he offered a straightforward if not overly reflective account of his years at the helm of Bomber Command. It defended area bombing and stressed that its contribution to the Allied war effort was enormous.[276] Emphasizing the many handicaps under which Bomber Command labored, and the endless "diversions" to which it was subjected, Harris maintained his long-held argument that bombing might have won the war essentially on its own: "I am certain that if we had an adequate bomber force to attack Germany a year earlier, that is, in 1943, or if we had not had the pre-invasion bombing and the bombing of the V-weapons sites to divert us in 1944, we should never have had to mount an invasion on anything like the scale that proved necessary."[277]

Harris took issue with some of the conclusions reached by the USSBS "Area Studies Division Report." In particular he pointed out the discrepancies between the results of the USSBS and the investigations of Bomber Command's Operations Research Section (ORS). He argued, for instance, that a difference in the definition of "destruction" caused the USSBS to list much lower percentages of German housing destroyed by Bomber Command than ORS did. Harris also found much to criticize in the USSBS's attempt to assess the loss of production as a whole resulting from Bomber Command's attacks on cities. He felt that American measures did not adequately account for the vast expenditure of labor and material necessitated by German efforts to cope with city raids.[278]

Not until 1948 did the Air Staff send Harris's final dispatch into limited circulation—and did so with an accompanying written statement that took issue with both the tone and substance of the document. Unsurprisingly, the dispatch was wholly consistent with Harris's strong views throughout the war, and, equally unsurprisingly, the postwar Air Staff was ill at ease with it. The Air Staff statement pointed out that the dispatch did not take into consideration the subsequent conclusions of the bombing surveys; it argued as well that Harris tended to inflate the impact of area bombing. Additionally, it explained that while area bombing had been seen by the Air Staff as a temporary expedient, Harris had not perceived it that way and had delayed switching to selective targeting later in the war when his Command had the means to do so.[279]

The dispatch itself stressed the destruction of German cities, which, Harris argued, not only disorganized and dislocated the whole of the German economy but also demoralized the German people. He stressed also that city bombing forced the enemy on to the defensive ("a veritable army of at least 2,000,000 men") and caused a shortage of war materials on all fronts. He admitted that the results of Bomber Command's attacks on oil "exceeded my expectations and frustrated the German hopes."[280] Harris argued that though the demands of the Normandy campaign gave German cities a "virtual respite from bombing" for "nearly half a year," he resumed the all-important campaign against cities in September 1944, achieving record tonnages in October. To support his case and his wartime decisions, Harris highlighted assessments made by Bomber Command's own analysts and commentary derived from postwar interrogations of Albert Speer. In his conclusions he maintained that the "enemy's sinews of War were to be found in his industrial cities." Harris added, "German propaganda tried very hard to convince us that German war industry was wholly dispersed, or was underground, or concealed in forests, or indeed was anywhere except where one would expect to find it—in the great industrial cities."[281]

The years after the war saw ongoing debates about the history and record of strategic bombing. In his 1947 book, *Bombing and Strategy: The Fallacy of Total War*, Adm. Sir Gerald Dickens called on his naval instincts to caste doubt upon the entire concept of strategic bombing. Maj.-Gen. J.F.C. Fuller implicated strategic bombing in an overall decline in the civility of war, which he linked to the demise of aristocracy and the effect of general conscription. Marshall Andrews' 1949 *Disaster Through Air Power* and David Divine's *The Broken Wing* also rebuked arguments supporting strategic bombing. In 1948 noted British scientist P.M.S. (Patrick) Blackett, writing about the broader consequences of nuclear war, launched his own critique of strategic bombing on grounds of both efficacy and morality.[282]

A different perspective on the issue was offered by Lord Tedder when he delivered the Lees Knowles Lectures at Cambridge University in 1947 on the topic: "Air Power in War." Arguing that air power—though "interlocked with sea and land power"—was essential in World War II, he insisted that its usefulness rested on the achievement of air superiority.[283] He added that the value of air power had to be assessed in terms of the way it was used in the war: the Allies, he pointed out, had not attempted "to win [the war] by means of air power alone—or even by air power as the primary factor." Tedder's conception of targeting, articulated during the war, rested on the idea of air power as part of a larger joint effort by all the services. He identified what he termed "common denominator" targets, the destruction of which could "collectively affect the whole war effort." These included railways, canals, power plants, iron and steel plants, and oil. Bomber attacks on these affected enemy efforts, and the German economy in general, in myriad and interrelated ways, allowing all of the Allied fighting services to benefit.[284]

Only in 1961 did the British produce an official history of their World War II strategic bombing campaign. Its authors noted that, in the intervening years, "myth and misconception have grown and been unassailed."[285] But if the delay had allowed misconceptions to emerge, it had also given the official historians, Sir Charles Webster and Noble Frankland, the time and distance required to produce an exceptionally thorough and informed account. Their volumes, which allowed that Bomber Command had made a crucial contribution to the defeat of Germany, were nonetheless critical of the area bombing to which Harris had remained so steadfastly loyal. In their concluding remarks they argued that Bomber Command's operations gave essential aid to the campaign against oil and transport, and that even area bombing ultimately contributed "important by-products to the achievement of the main plans for oil and transport"[286] Tedder, who read the draft of the manuscript twice through, commended the authors on their "masterly" and "courageous" work; he admitted that he "had not thought that anything so near the truth would ever be likely to go on record." But Harris, who would not read the draft, was determined to discredit it and its authors, whom he, for false and contrived reasons, deemed unfit to the task.[287]

The great contribution of the British official history was the application of balance, judgment, and in-depth knowledge (of a highly technical and complex subject) to the assessment of the strategic air war. While Bomber Command was their main focus, Webster and Frankland provided a sophisticated analysis of the work of the USAAF—and the interaction of the two air forces comprising the Combined Bomber Offensive. Their writing offered up consistently perceptive comparisons of the ideas, behavior, and relative strengths and weaknesses of the British and American air forces during World War II. The authors highlighted, for instance, "the most important strategic problem of the bomber offensive": that Anglo-American strategic air forces could not in the end avoid a battle for supremacy in their own medium. The future of the bomber campaign—and the Allied ground campaign too—depended on the neutralization of German fighters. Success in the battle for air supremacy was largely due, they argued, to the eventual American decision to force the Luftwaffe into air-to-air battle against long-range escort fighters.[288] A wartime improvisation, this decision nonetheless reflected a firm determination on the part of Americans to pursue their own course: "A less resolute force than the Eighth Bomber Command," they wrote, "would have broken down and a more versatile one would almost inevitably have followed the German and British example of changing to night attack."[289] But they argued, as well, that the achievement of the Americans could not have been exploited nearly so well had it not been for two British aircraft, the Lancaster and the Mosquito, which were responsible for a great amount of the damage wrought by the air campaign.

Some thirty years after the British official history appeared, the Canadians produced an official history of their World War II air war—set squarely in the context of the Allied offensive as a whole. Stephen J. Harris, author of the strategic bombing sections of that history (titled *The Crucible of War, 1939–1945*), reached conclusions not dissimilar to—if somewhat more critical than—the Webster and Frankland volumes. While fully appreciating the bravery and sacrifice of Allied bomber crews, he took issue with some of the decisions imposed upon them by their commanders. Taking a lead from the British and American surveys, he questioned the efficacy of area bombing, pointing out the remarkable recovery capacity of both German industry and the German people. He also critiqued the mass incendiary attack on Dresden, and the stubborn insistence of Sir Arthur Harris that cities were the only targets that mattered.[290] He argued, however, that bombing had in fact served as a kind of "second front," forcing a significant diversion of German resources into a defensive effort. He pointed out, for instance, that of 19,713 88-mm and 128-mm dual purpose flak/antitank artillery pieces produced between 1942 and 1944, all but 3,172 were allocated to air defense—denying the Wehrmacht a critical tool for the ground battle.[291]

Recent analyses of the German war economy and of World War II in general have drawn on expanded bodies of evidence, further economic analysis, and prior scholarship to add to the ongoing debate about bombing in World War II. Though critical of Harris and fully cognizant of the many problems inherent in the bombing campaigns, Gerhard Weinberg made clear both the direct and indirect effects of bombing on the Nazi economy.[292] In his recent book *Why the Allies Won*, Richard Overy argued that, in general, the bombing offensive caused German military leaders to drain much-needed air strength away from the main fighting fronts to protect the Reich, giving relief to the Russians and helping ease the situation in the Mediterranean. Less directly, money and resources that went into making anti-aircraft guns could not simultaneously be used to build tanks—and soldiers operating those guns could not simultaneously drive tanks. In addition, he argued that bombing set a "strict ceiling" on German economic output: "By the middle of the war, with the whole of continental Europe at her disposal, Germany was fast becoming an economic superpower. The harvest of destruction and disruption reaped by bomb attack, random and poorly planned as it often was, was sufficient to blunt German economic ambitions."[293] Overy argued that strategic bombing achieved all that was realistically asked of it. And bombing, he added, allowed the Allies to rely on their preference for bringing economic and scientific power (as opposed to large armies) to bear on their enemies, resulting in lower Allied casualties.[294]

Overy's conclusions, written for a wide-ranging account of World War II intended for a general readership, relied to a great degree on his scholarly investigations of the German war economy. In that realm he has argued that the rationalization of the German war economy, achieved under Speer, was the chief factor in transforming Germany's wartime economic output. Rationalization, based on methods of industrial efficiency, necessarily concentrated production in the largest and most efficient enterprises, and reduced the stocks of raw materials held at the factories. But, Overy argues, strategic bombing undermined key features of the rationalized system, thereby placing a ceiling on the additional gains in output afforded by the increased scale and speed of production. Bombing interrupted "in arbitrary and unpredictable ways the web of supplies of materials and parts on which the whole industrial structure depended." And bombing forced dispersal just at the time when concentration was paying off. Paradoxically, the only way for Speer to cope was to insist on "even more rigorous rationalization—concentrating production on a handful of weapons, reducing all unnecessary and sophisticated equipment, and cutting back on all military production not directly concerned with priority weapons."[295]

Using Overy's work on the German economy, Sebastian Cox has recently critiqued the BBSU study for its conclusions on area bombing, pointing out that dispersal of industry—which he argues was provoked mainly by the area offensive—made the German economy more vulnerable in the long run because of the increased importance of the transportation system. He contends that the BBSU report "credits the transportation attacks of 1944–45 with enormous success in destroying the German economy, but it perhaps fails to give due credit to the area attacks in helping both to cap the German economy, and to handicap rationalisation and force dispersal, thus making transport a more lucrative target."[296] What Harris might have made of this analysis is hard to say; he never envisioned city attacks as a way of making other targets more lucrative. He did, however, believe that his campaign had had a tremendous impact on every element of the German war infrastructure.

As scholarship reveals more and more about the wartime German economy, it may become possible to piece together ever more sophisticated analyses of what bombing contributed to the Allied war effort. But, because it is a difficult and complex question, there is unlikely ever to be a final answer to it. And arguments about effect will not, in the end, put to rest the many moral and ethical debates that still weigh heavily on discussions of bombing in World War II.

* * * * *

The record of strategic bombing in the Second World War has deserved the attention historians have given it to date. Though its contribution to Allied victory was hard to specify and to separate out from other effects—and though there can be no final answer regarding its "decisiveness"—several points can be made about it nonetheless. It placed a heavy defensive burden on the Germans and prevented them from creating and sustaining an even more powerful war machine than they did create. It undermined the German war economy in general by forcing dispersion of industry and then limiting the means to sustain that dispersion, and it helped strangle the German fuel supply. By the end of the war it had crippled the Wehrmacht's ability either to supply itself or to maneuver on the battlefield. Those air commanders who, like Tedder, searched for ways to use aerial bombing to exploit opportunities created in part or wholly by the other services, discovered in this role its greatest strength. In addition, bombing kept a check on the development of new weapons in Germany, and aided—crucially at times—in the war at sea. It made possible a successful Allied landing on the coast of France and contributed to the collapse of Japan in August 1945.

The Second World War made it obvious that a military force able to win and hold dominance in the air would have a profound advantage over its enemies. The lesson was clear enough: any state with international interests and powerful enemies would have to be prepared to wage, and to defend against, air war. Strategic bombing did not, however, fulfill the bold and dramatic claims of the 1917 Smuts prophesy: "[T]he day may not be far off when aerial operations with their devastation of enemy lands and destruction of industrial and populous centers on a vast scale may become the principal operations of war, to which the older forms of military and naval operations may become secondary and subordinate." The other services had not, in fact, become "secondary and subordinate." If airplanes had made themselves, in every imaginable way, fixtures of modern warfare, they had not yet evoked a revolutionary change in its conduct. This insured that interservice rivalries—which after the war would be complicated by the issue of nuclear weapons—would continue to affect and condition all arguments about strategic bombing in war.

The Smuts claims had not been fulfilled because modern societies and economies had proven far more resilient than the advocates of strategic bombing had predicted they would be. In March 1945, the peak month of the Combined Bomber Offensive, the USAAF and Bomber Command together dropped more than 130,000 tons of bombs—well over their combined total effort for the *year* in 1942, and just under the total tonnage Bomber Command had dropped for the year in 1943.[297] Still, the Red Army had to batter its way into Berlin. Both the Tivertonian and Trenchardian theories had presumed that bombing would offer a shortcut to victory: a prompt and direct means of exploiting newly exposed enemy vulnerabilities. But both theories had underestimated the robustness of urban societies and economies, and the potential effectiveness of enemy defenses. And they had, similarly, overestimated the likely efficiency of strategic bombing itself.

The difference between expectations and realities caused both the RAF and USAAF to make constant wartime adjustments to their plans, tactics, and machinery. The kinds of shifts they made were consistent with (and articulated in terms of) their individual circumstances and predilections, but in some cases the practical effects were nearly identical. Most notably, both air forces moved toward much less discriminate forms of bombing than they had used in the opening phases of the war. The British translated the shift into a formal directive and brought in a field commander who believed in the new approach. The Americans avoided any explicit change in announced policy in Europe, and, to the greatest extent possible, clung to their self-identity as "precision" bombers. But they nonetheless grasped an expedient that frequently caused their efforts to be virtually indistinguishable from those of the British, and they experimented late in the day with aerial attacks designed to evoke a primarily psychological effect on the enemy. In the Far East, they adopted an operational policy that depended on area incendiary attacks against cities, thereby laying the groundwork for the later use of atomic bombs. The consequences of all these adaptations were profound; in addition to their immediate effects, they raised urgent moral questions—and established legal and ethical dilemmas—that would linger long after all the guns of war had been silenced.

Conclusion

How aircraft might be employed in war—and what they might accomplish—were among the most pressing military questions of the early twentieth century. Those who envisioned radical answers followed in a long tradition of speculation about the power of both flight and aerial bombardment, and the vulnerability of civilian societies to aerial onslaught. Two ideas, in particular, drove this kind of imagining. The first was that the overwhelming power of bombers—especially their ability to inflict wanton destruction anywhere their pilots chose to fly—would prove overwhelming to human nerves. The second was that since modern societies were complex and interdependent, they were vulnerable to the kinds of pressures bombers could impose. These notions have retained a remarkable tenacity into the twenty-first century, even in the face of evidence that has called them into question.

* * * * *

The advent of aircraft forced governments and militaries to respond to them. During the First World War, sustained German air attacks on Britain—London in particular—aroused anger among the British people and convinced a nervous government to act. The Smuts Report of 1917 set in train a far-reaching and consequential reorganization of British military resources, and furthered the development of ideas about long-rang bombing. Remarkably, most of the key ideas shaping strategic bombing in twentieth century were developed rapidly—and articulated by 1917–18. In Britain, Tiverton perceived a natural opportunity to attack "bottlenecks" in the enemy's war-fighting infrastructure. Direct attack on key industries and resources would offer an efficient means of undermining and ultimately collapsing the enemy war effort. To him—and the Americans who appreciated and indeed appropriated his thinking—the idea was obvious and logical.

If the gap was great between the heady promises of the Smuts report and the reality of Britain's Independent Force, Trenchard sought to close it through rhetoric of his own, emphasizing the "moral"—including indirect—effects of aerial bombing and the disruption it caused. If his claims were expeditious, they were nonetheless readily grasped from the prevailing military culture, and resonant in the public and political realms. They derived from an overly optimistic assessment of the IF's impact and from a particular interpretation of British public behavior under the fall of bombs—an interpretation that was neither objective nor disinterested, but instead influenced by prevailing concerns about the likely behavior of urban workers under stress. Trenchard's instinct to protect his own record and his own version of the war effort was a natural enough response to finding himself in charge of RAF postwar interests. But it also closed off deeper and more searching analyses of what bombing had or had not accomplished in the war.

After the First World War, American airmen combined certain elements of Trenchardian thinking about the moral effects of bombing with an instinctive interest in Tivertonian ideas. For a time, though, these preferences were largely academic since the Air Service's parent service, the army, had little interest in long-range bombing. But in the United States—just as in Britain—the airplane's appeal as a tool of war would come to be strong. Among both British and American airmen, arguments for power and autonomy came to rest heavily on claims about bomber's role in war: if they were to determine the outcomes of future wars, then air forces should have institutional independence and a major claim on national resources. But any argument about the centrality of bombers in war had to rest on claims about enemy vulnerability to disruption and dislocation. Trenchard worked to insure that his service would be committed to the prosecution of a prompt and determined offensive against enemy "vital centers." In the 1920s this assertive rhetoric promised an inexpensive deterrent to such remote threats as appeared on the horizon. The details of *how* to prosecute an air war were less pressing. Trenchard was not inclined to dwell on these, and, in any event, it did not serve his bureaucratic interests to do so.

Useful for its immediate purpose, Trenchard's rhetoric nonetheless remained vague and underspecified—an Edwardian artifact in a world that had moved on. This created problems both inside and outside the RAF, particularly as a gap developed between the RAF's official declarations and its actual capabilities. In emphasizing the moral effect of strategic bombing, Trenchard overestimated its impact on a future war and downplayed the operational challenges it posed. He left his service confused as to its mission's scope and nature—especially in light of implicit prohibitions against the bombing of civilians—and his far-reaching claims intensified the other services' animosity toward the RAF. Upon his retirement, the RAF had institutional security, but no clarity regarding how it might perform its self-proclaimed mission. In the 1930s, Trenchard's successors had to sort out these problems under the pressures of an increasingly ominous political situation. As they did this, they reevaluated and pulled away from many of the central elements of Trenchardism—at least temporarily.

During the interwar years American airmen were increasingly attracted to claims centering on the economic vulnerability of modern societies—and the bomber's ability to exploit it. They postulated that an air force, having determined the key elements in an enemy's industrial infrastructure, could destroy that economy efficiently through aerial attacks against those "key nodes" or "bottlenecks." If the credit due Tiverton and his colleagues was largely lost along the way, the ideas survived and helped form a body of thought that the Americans embraced and developed further, adding an emphasis on "precision" bombing by groups of high-altitude, self-defending bombers. This "industrial fabric theory" assumed that modern economies were made up of an intricate weave of highly integrated threads, and that pulling on a key thread could unravel the entire fabric. It assumed, too, that one could identify these vulnerable points and attack them with sufficient precision and weight to create the desired effect. Both would prove problematic in the event.

None of the assumptions on which British and American ideas rested was pulled from thin air. The airmen's expectations—and hence their arguments—revealed the way in which they interpreted the world around them and in which they sought to promote their own interests. The claims they made and the policies they advanced reflected specific cultural, political, social, and institutional contexts. Likewise, their failure to see the potential problems and flaws in these ideas—and the ramifications that might flow from them—reflected the cognitive shortcuts of seeing what we expect to see and what is in our interest to see. But, these particular ideas—and their flaws—would prove tremendously consequential during the Second World War.

Both the British and the Americans had overestimated bomber's ability to penetrate enemy defenses and reach targets unaccompanied by long-range escorts. Similarly they had both been far too optimistic about bombardiers' ability to find and hit specific targets in cloud-shrouded northern Europe. And they had overestimated their enemy's frangibility: civilians, industrial workers, and war economies all proved much more robust and resilient than interwar theories had presumed. These problems might have been anticipated to a greater degree if airmen had scrutinized more objectively their experience in World War I. But that experience had been seen through particular lenses and was interpreted selectively. There was, in addition, too great a readiness to focus on the future without rigorously considering the past. This is an endemic problem in air forces, which develop their institutional identity around claims to see and understand the future more clearly than other services do.

During the Second World War, Anglo-American air planners had to make constant adjustments and real-time modifications to cope with the many problems they faced, not only as a result of the gaps they discovered between expectations and realities, but also from the shifting demands imposed by the course of the war itself. Their responses reflected the cognitive patterns one might expect in such circumstances. In shifting to a general area offensive, British planners embraced (or more accurately reembraced) arguments about the power of the moral effect of bombing. As elements of the German war economy came to appear more robust than expected, German morale increasingly seemed like the most promising target. Hopes and expectations converged and, for a time at least, influenced interpretations of progress.

Sir Arthur Harris brought his own ideas about strategic bombing to the table: neither purely Trenchardian nor purely Tivertonian, his perspective combined elements of both. He assumed that by hitting hard at German cities—the nation's nerve and production centers—he could do enough damage and cause enough disruption and demoralization to bring his enemy to its knees. But as the war continued, British planners struggled increasingly to find sufficient evidence that Harris's approach was sound. Portal, who had done the most to move the British toward city bombing, now became the most outspoken advocate for a revised strategy that would refocus British efforts on key elements of the German war economy. In particular he wanted to follow Spaatz's lead and prioritize oil strikes whenever weather permitted. Harris, however, was too firmly entrenched in his beliefs and too personally invested in Bomber Command's efforts to be able to make the shift readily or gracefully.

The Americans for their part held to their search for the most important bottlenecks, hoping that their destruction might unravel the German war economy. Their resistance to joining the British nighttime offensive and Spaatz's determination to strike at German oil supplies reflected this commitment to the American concept of a military-industrial holy grail. But mounting frustration with weather and the length of the war provoked the Americans to try other approaches as well. By the winter of 1944–45 they targeted just about everything they could think of, hoping to hit upon some means of affecting enemy behavior, directly or indirectly. While claiming adherence to "precision" bombing of industrial targets, they often engaged in area attacks on cities.

In Europe, strategic bombing did not prove the case of its most outspoken advocates. Harris would claim that it might have, had he been left alone to prosecute the air war as he saw fit. Others, albeit in more moderate tones, would sometimes appropriate his argument. The ensuing struggle over what bombing had or had not achieved in Europe was political, partisan, and subjective. The problem was exacerbated by the hushed and stifled debate in Britain and by the unwieldy and often internally inconsistent nature of the United States Strategic Bombing Survey. In the Far East the debate was just as acrimonious, and was obscured by the use of atomic bombs; indeed, the new weapon looked so different and so revolutionary as to make discussions about mere "conventional" bombing seem outdated and obsolete. Under the circumstances, both advocates and critics of bombing would continue to argue their positions vigorously.

At the end of the war, American airmen found themselves in a position similar to the one the British had faced in 1919: battling for autonomy. Clearly the Americans could make their argument on the basis of much fuller experience than could the British at the end of World War I, but the often acrimonious post–World War II debate had parallels with the earlier British experience—and similar effects. In particular, it encouraged an assertive tone in USAAF (later USAF) rhetoric that encouraged overclaiming. Once again, airmen emphasized the strategic bombing mission, stressing it as the justification for service autonomy and downplaying other more modest and cooperative roles for aircraft, however important they might be. This rhetoric was only intensified by a major debate over the structure of the American military and by tight postwar budgets. The result was, as in interwar Britain, an overselling of "air power" and, in consequence, inflated expectations among policymakers and the public about strategic bombing.

The USAAF's position as the nation's only nuclear-capable arm reinforced this propensity to focus almost exclusively on strategic bombing and to pronounce on the unlimited power of bombers. In his final war dispatch in 1945, General Arnold stated simply, "It [atomic energy] has made Air Power all-important."[1] And, with the 1946 establishment of their postwar long-range bomber arm, Strategic Air Command (SAC), American airmen proclaimed triumphantly that, with nuclear weapons, the airplane was "the greatest offensive weapon of all times."[2] But atomic bombs were, in some sense, a parallel to the RAF's moral effect: they aided claims to autonomy and placed a heavy focus on deterrence—but they made it easier to avoid thinking through the still poorly understood relationship between bombing and enemy capitulation. Like Trenchard's immediate and incessant offensive, they postulated a scenario that was attractive for purposes of deterrence (and cost cutting), but unrealistic in terms of the way states actually enter into and fight wars.

These problems made themselves felt in the 1950s and 1960s when American airmen found themselves fighting limited wars in Asia, where the theories underpinning Anglo-American strategic bombing had little relevance to the circumstances at hand. At the outset of the Korean War in 1950, SAC bombers were moved overseas to reinforce the Far Eastern Air Force (FEAF), under the overall control of Gen. Douglas MacArthur, commander-in-chief in the Far East. The commander of SAC's Fifteenth Air Force, Maj. Gen. Emmett O'Donnell, became commander in chief of FEAF Bomber Command (Provisional). In consultation with SAC chief, Gen. Curtis LeMay, he quickly requested MacArthur's permission "to do a fire job on the five industrial centers of northern Korea." He thought MacArthur should announce that the communists had forced him, against his wishes, to use "the means which brought Japan to its knees."[3] This approach reflected traditional air force warfighting concepts as well as recent experience: fire raids would undermine the enemy's will and capacity to fight; waging them immediately would intensify their psychological effect.

Initially, though, MacArthur was unwilling to escalate so dramatically. O'Donnell chafed under orders that saw his bombers "diverted" to tactical support of ground troops. In late summer, bomber missions were expanded to include interdiction strikes and attacks on North Korean industry. Following Chinese entry into the war in November, MacArthur permitted attacks on a wide range of targets—including fire raids on North Korean cities—in order to do everything possible to stem the tide of Chinese advance. He held back on striking North Korean hydro-electric plants, though, hoping they might prove useful bargaining chips for negotiations. Incendiary attacks on Pyongyang in early January 1951 burned out 35 percent of the city. Training for atomic missions went forward, but authority for actual use of A-bombs was withheld.[4] The wider use of bombers, however, did not translate into discernable progress toward victory, and, as time passed, American B-29s became increasingly vulnerable to North Korean air defenses: by the end of 1951 they were forced to fly almost exclusively at night.[5]

Airmen were frustrated by the politics of the limited war, which kept enemy supply sources outside North Korea permanently off the target lists, ensuring that the industrial fabric theory would remain a poor fit with the reality of the situation. After the war General LeMay would argue, "We never did hit a strategic target."[6] When MacArthur was fired in April 1951, General Matthew B. Ridgway assumed command of UN Forces. Though he generally restrained the use of bombers, he continued to use them to maintain pressure on Chinese troops. Such pressure included interdiction-oriented attacks on Pyongyang (on 30 July and 14 August). But negotiations made little headway, and, in the meantime, overworked air crews began to suffer morale problems and high abort rates.[7]

In May 1952 Ridgway was replaced by Gen. Mark Clark, who was interested in using aircraft to compel movement in the negotiations. Clark authorized a FEAF-designed "air pressure" campaign designed to destroy military targets so situated as to have a "deleterious effect upon the morale of the civilian population actively engaged in the logistic support of enemy forces."[8] The rhetoric attempted to frame it carefully and identify it as a logistics campaign, but the emergence of the "air pressure" campaign signaled a familiar pattern of an air force, in frustration, turning to an increased emphasis on civilian morale.

The first targets were the previously off-limits North Korean hydroelectric power plants. The attacks saw FEAF destroy 90 percent of North Korea's hydroelectric potential in less than a week. The campaign also renewed full-scale attacks on North Korean cities, beginning in July. The 29 August attack on Pyongyang was designed to "punish the enemy with air power," yielding a psychological payoff during the Moscow Conference between the Chinese and the Russians.[9] Following a course similar to the one the USAAF had followed in World War II, FEAF's Bomber Command was, by early 1953, attacking small cities and towns deemed important to the communist supply system. Still, however, negotiations dragged on, with little apparent change in the enemy's determination to hold out.

The campaign's last phase was particularly dramatic. In March 1953 FEAF targeteers began to study North Korea's irrigation system. His patience exhausted, General Clark told the Joint Chiefs that he was prepared to breach twenty dams, which would flood areas producing approximately 250,000 tons of rice. At the same time FEAF Bomber Command made plans to destroy what remained of Pyongyang. In the course of events, the campaign went forward more modestly, with mid-May attacks on three dams situated near railway lines. (Officially, these could have been designated "interdiction" attacks against those railway lines—although neither FEAF planners nor the communists perceived them that way.) The raids flooded nearby villages and rice fields. The North Koreans worked vigorously to repair the Toksan dam site in particular: thirteen days later they had repaired the dam and the railway lines around it, and had placed anti-aircraft artillery around the dam itself. Two more dams were struck in June, and planners anticipated further strikes. These, however, were delayed pending the outcome of armistice negotiations. Those talks resulted, shortly thereafter, in a truce.[10]

There has been no consensus on the dam raids' impact. Historians recently have tended to argue that they probably had some effect on the negotiations, even though that impact is difficult to specify and separate out from other factors, including, in particular, the death of Stalin. Conrad Crane's recent conclusions are representative: "The resort by the UN to such extreme measures as the dam attacks might have alarmed the enemy enough to influence their negotiating position to some degree, though there were many other factors involved in their decision to sign the armistice."[11] If the exact impact of the raids was hard to specify, however, its effect on Korean civilians was not. In 1954 Brig. Gen. Don Z. Zimmerman, FEAF Deputy for Intelligence, argued, "The degree of destruction suffered by North Korea, in relation to its resources, was greater than that which the Japanese islands suffered in World War II." He believed that "these pressures brought the enemy to terms."[12] Many others agreed, and this interpretation cast the debate over means and ends in a positive light, problematical evidence not withstanding.

USAF planners wished to declare the war a success and move on. Most of all, they wished to put the experience—which they viewed as an aberration—behind them. FEAF's 1954 final Report on the Korean War repeated a conclusion that Lt. Gen. George E. Stratemeyer had already drawn in 1950: the Korean conflict contained so many unusual factors as to make it a poor model for planning. In particular, the USAF wished to distance itself from the close air-support operations that had been a main a feature of the war. The report stated, "Because FEAF provided UN ground forces lavish close air support in Korea is no reason to assume this condition will exist in future wars."[13]

Air Force leaders were instead anxious to reassert their priority: preparing for strategic air war against the USSR. The funding allotted to the services as a result of the Korean War had greatly increased Strategic Air Command's size and strength; now, more than ever, SAC's mission reigned supreme in the USAF. General LeMay was appointed Vice Chief of Staff in 1957 and Chief of Staff in 1961; in 1964 three quarters of the Air Staff's upper echelon came from SAC. Between 1954 and 1962 the United States' total nuclear arsenal grew from 1,750 to 26,500 weapons. SAC, which controlled the majority of them, planned to deliver them in a "massive pre-emptive bomber assault." Other contingencies received little attention. Despite the political upheaval in Southeast Asia in the 1950s, the *Air University Quarterly Review* published (in the whole of the decade) only two articles relating air power to insurgency movements there.[14]

USAF Manual 1–8, "Strategic Air Operations" (May 1954), drew upon teachings of the Air Corps Tactical School and the interpretation of World War II experience to make claims much like those highlighted in the Air Service's post–World War I assessment, Sherman's 1926 *Air Warfare*, or the ACTS doctrine manuals of the 1930s. Long-range bombers would strike the enemy nation itself so as to collapse the enemy's capacity and will to fight. Though nuclear weapons would make any claim to "precision" bombing absurd, the industrial fabric theory still took pride of place:

> The fabric of modern nations is such a complete interweaving of major single elements that the elimination of one element can create widespread influence on the whole. Some of the elements are of such importance that [their] complete elimination . . . would cause collapse of the national structure. . . . Others exert influence which, while not immediately evident, is cumulative and transferable, and when brought under the effects of air weapons, results in a general widespread weakening and eventual collapse."[15]

The manual was not revised until 1965.

In the meantime, the USAF found itself in yet another limited war in Asia. Unlike the Korean War, it had no clear starting point. When President Lyndon Johnson and his advisors dramatically increased the U.S. commitment to South Vietnam, they hoped that air power might facilitate a quick, painless campaign that would not divert too much time or too many resources from their domestic agenda. They hoped that air strikes would demonstrate U.S. resolve, bolster morale in the South, erode the Viet Cong's morale, and generally intimidate the insurgency's leadership.[16]

In April 1964, the Joint Chiefs of Staff had compiled a list of ninety-four bombing targets in North Vietnam. The air force wanted these attacked immediately and heavily, to impose psychological shock as well as physical damage. But the Johnson administration chose a more graduated approach that would punish, by reprisal, acts of terror by the Viet Cong. After guerillas struck a U.S. Special Forces camp at Pleiku in February 1965, American policymakers implemented Operation Rolling Thunder, an aerial interdiction campaign characterized by increasing pressure on the enemy. In August 1965, Secretary of Defense Robert McNamara rejected a JCS recommendation for attacks on North Vietnam's strategic oil facilities and electric power plants. Hanoi began to disperse the nation's limited industry and build up its air defenses, aided by supplies and workers from the USSR and China. Given this, the JCS called for expanded bombing late in 1965. Johnson did in fact expand the air campaign in 1966 and 1967: in June 1966, North Vietnamese oil storage was bombed for the first time; in May 1967, Hanoi's main power station was attacked.[17]

Unsurprisingly, the air force chafed at the early restrictions: both during and after the war the air force claimed that Rolling Thunder had been undermined by civilian meddling in timing and targeting. Gradualism, they argued, flew in the face of well-established war-fighting principles. While it is true that all major targets were not destroyed until 1967 (whereas the air force would have preferred an all-out assault in 1965), the civilian intervention may not have been so consequential as the USAF has maintained. The JCS list grew from 94 to 242 targets shortly after Rolling Thunder began, and the latter number changed little through the rest of the campaign. In 1965, 158 of these targets were destroyed (nearly all of them military targets below the 20th parallel); in 1966, 22 more were destroyed. Johnson released nearly all the remaining targets for attack in 1967, and by December almost all of North Vietnam's industrial war capacity had been destroyed. There was, by the end of the war, virtually no target left unbombed that might have been bombed. Indeed, during the course of the war the USAF dropped some 6,162,000 tons of bombs—vastly more than had been dropped by the Allied powers in all of World War II.[18] Yet this had not brought capitulation.

Robert Pape has argued that there is "no evidence that executing the sharp knock in 1965, instead of 1967, would have produced better results."[19] Structural factors (including Vietnam's economy and geography) and the nature of the war itself helped insulate the North Vietnamese and Viet Cong against interdiction and coercive air power. This insulation was furthered by evacuation programs in all major towns and villages. Finally, even if an earlier all-out air assault had convinced the North to stop supporting the Viet Cong, this was no guarantee that they would not have continued the war on their own, and at their own pace.[20]

The Nixon administration instituted a program of "Vietnamization"—a means of reducing American involvement by returning the main responsibility for the ground war to the South Vietnamese. In addition, the president allowed the JCS to give more freedom to U.S. air commanders. Operation Linebacker, an aerial interdiction campaign to halt Hanoi's 1972 spring offensive, largely succeeded and appeared to put a settlement within reach. But North Vietnamese negotiators stalled, prompting Linebacker II, an eleven-day campaign (18–29 December) to bring enemy negotiators back to the table to sign a final accord. Linebacker II concentrated on military assets in and around Hanoi. On 29 December, communist leaders indicated their willingness to resume serious negotiations. This reflected the success of both Linebacker campaigns, which were oriented toward fundamentally different circumstances and goals than Rolling Thunder had been.[21]

Many observers, civilian and military, argued that if a Linebacker-style campaign had gone forward from the outset, the war would have ended much sooner. Frustrated over the political constraints placed upon them, airmen argued—in the tradition of Harris—that they might have won had they been free to fight as they saw fit. Writing in the June 1975 *Air Force Magazine*, General T. R. Milton, USAF (Ret.) argued that Linebacker II was "an object lesson in how the war might have been won, and won long ago, if only there had not been such political inhibition."[22] But this perspective overlooked the crucial differences between 1965 and 1972. Linebacker I's success was facilitated by the fact that, when it took place, Hanoi had shifted to a conventional strategy that was far more vulnerable to air power's effects than the earlier guerilla war had been. And when Linebacker II commenced, Hanoi had already achieved most of its political goals and was prepared to sign an accord that would put it, ultimately, within easy grasp of its final aims. These important distinctions often were overlooked, however, leaving a false impression of bombing's utility and reinforcing proclamations about its future application in war.[23]

The air force's response to criticism implying that it had not lived up to public expectations was not to try to modify those expectations but rather to insist that bombing could be decisive—if only it could be freed from political restraints. Those air leaders who had held important positions during World War II particularly resented the constraints placed on them later. But two observations are worth noting here. First, there were few important targets in Korea and Vietnam that were not hit hard by bombers (often multiple times). Even when heavy pressure can be brought to bear on enemy economies and societies, they can prove resilient and robust. In the economic realm, industry can be dispersed, repairs can be made, and resources can be obtained externally. In the social realm, civilians can move out of the way of bombs, they can become acclimated to their effects over time, or they can choose to accept high levels of discomfort and sacrifice. Motivated and mobilized civilians backed by determined governments can sustain very high pain thresholds.[24] In addition, discontented civilians may simply lack the mechanisms to convey their discontent into political leverage against the national leadership.

Second, World War II was the exception rather than the rule: most wars have been fought within distinct political parameters—not to mention legal and ethical ones. For political reasons it will rarely, if ever, be possible to implement what air forces have traditionally believed to be the most effective campaign: an immediate, all-out strike on the enemy's most valuable assets. Even in World War II (the most "total" of modern wars), limits on Anglo-American bombers were lifted only slowly, over a period of years. And, even though the war was later considered a "good war" fought for the right reasons, the Anglo-American public has proven uneasy with its legacy of unconstrained bombing.

After Vietnam, defensiveness inhibited USAF dialogues and, for a while, proscribed a thorough and searching analysis of doctrine (and the applicability of that doctrine to differing circumstances). There was still no satisfactory understanding of the crucial relationship between bomber raids and desired political outcomes. In the conclusion to his 1989 book, *The Limits of Air Power*, Mark Clodfelter, a junior officer in the air force, wrote, "The tremendous rush of technology—which has produced gargantuan B-52s and sleek B-1s capable of carrying 30 tons of ordnance, and supersonic fighters capable of directing laser-guided bombs into a single warehouse in the heart of a densely-populated city—has not guaranteed military success. What it has done, however, is to create a modern vision of air power that focuses on the lethality of its weaponry rather than on that weaponry's effectiveness as a political instrument."[25] His critique was notable not only because it was perceptive, but because it was delivered by a serving USAF officer.

In the thirty years since Vietnam, strategic bombing has, if anything, become even more prominent as a mode of warfare. For America alone, wars in the Persian Gulf in 1991, Bosnia in 1995, and Kosovo in 1999 have seen air attacks against opponents' vital centers in an effort to coerce concessions from hostile regimes. In many of these conflicts, air power theorists have claimed to have developed a new mode of strategic bombing. Pinpoint precision attack of leadership, political control, and civilian economic targets is now said to offer coercive leverage unattainable by older methods; some even see a "revolution in military affairs" in this apparent combination of new technology and new ideas.[26]

It is probably too early to judge the efficacy of precision air attack as a political tool; certainly its effectiveness remains hotly contested as this book is written.[27] Yet much of this new debate has a familiar ring. Since 1918 airmen have sought to find and destroy a critical Achilles' heel in an opposing society, polity, or economy so as to win wars without fighting one's way through the mass land armies of previous eras. Through more than eighty years and the experience of World War II, Korea, and Vietnam, the underlying philosophy and central implementing ideas of strategic bombing have changed remarkably little. The *tools* of air warfare have changed dramatically since the canvas and plywood planes of the First World War, but it is striking just how little the basic ideas behind the *use* of those tools have changed. Profoundly influential for nearly a century, these foundational ideas continue today to animate a debate over bombing in an era otherwise almost unrecognizably different from the world of Tiverton and Trenchard.[28]

Yet these ideas are neither self-evident nor the inevitable consequences of aircraft or the technology of flight. Rather, they are the product of a complex social, political and cognitive context in which airmen have tried to understand their world and their missions. This context has been formed from overlapping and interactive influences, including the perceived social consequences of industrialization, urbanization, and increasing economic interdependence; popular concerns and expectations about the development of new technologies for war-fighting; the intellectual demands of envisioning uses for a new tool of war, and the inevitable cognitive hurdles and obstacles to which that process inevitably is subject—including the tendency to be overly impressed by initial experience, and the resistance to new information that does not conform to previously formed ideas; and the pressures imposed by the requirement for organizational survival in hostile bureaucratic environments.

To suppose that strategic bombing doctrines have been mere reflections of the demands of good practice is to overlook the experience of the world's most energetic attempt so far to wage war from the air—the Anglo-American strategic bombing campaign in the Second World War. The near-catastrophic failure of the RAF, and later the USAAF, to make good the prewar claims for their new methods cannot be explained by looking at the methods and the equipment alone. This failure lay fundamentally in a process of learning and perception in which the larger environment conditioned thought in powerful and ultimately very problematic ways. To understand the history of strategic bombing thus requires an understanding of the process by which those ideas took form and the influences that molded them.

But this is more than an issue of historical understanding alone. The continuing influence of these ideas highlights the importance of their sources and the influences that made them what they are. A major dimension of the waging of war and the use of force in a new century rests on these foundations, and a crucial ongoing debate turns on them. The better we understand how these ideas came to be, the better positioned we will be to make wise decisions on their use in the world of today and tomorrow.

Notes

Introduction

1. This figure is based on total sorties, rather than on the number of aircraft that were recorded as actually attacking the target. For the latter, one in three got within five miles. The Butt Report is discussed in the British official history of strategic bombing in World War II: Sir Charles Webster and Noble Frankland, *The Strategic Air Offensive Against Germany, 1939–1945*, vol. 1 (London: HMSO, 1961), 178–80 (hereafter referred to as WF, with volume number). The full text of the report is reprinted in vol. 4 (Annexes and Appendices), 205–13.

2. Peirse quoted in WF, 1:179.

3. "The Development and Employment of the Heavy Bomber Force," forwarded to Churchill with a covering note from Portal, 25 September 1941, in the Papers of Lord Portal, folder 2 (Prime Minister's Minutes, October–December 1941), Christ Church Library, Oxford; and Personal Minute, Churchill to Portal, 27 September 1941, in Papers of Lord Portal, folder 2c (hereafter PP, with folder number).

4. Portal to Churchill, 2 October 1941, in PP, folder 2c. Sinclair quoted in WF, 1:183.

5. Minute, Churchill to Portal, 7 October 1941, 1–3, in PP, folder 2c.

6. For an elaboration of the very different path taken by the French Air Force, see Pascal Venneson, "Institution and Air Power: The Making of the French Air Force," *The Journal of Strategic Studies* 18, no. 1 (March 1995). Also on the French Air Force, see R. J. Young, "The Strategic Dream: French Air Doctrine and the Interwar Period, 1919–1939," *Journal of Contemporary History* 9 (1974). On the German Air Force, see James Corum, *The Luftwaffe: Creating the Operational Air War 1918–1940* (Lawrence: University Press of Kansas, 1997); Richard Muller, *The German Air War in Russia* (Baltimore: Nautical and Aviation Publishing, 1992); Williamson Murray, *Luftwaffe* (Baltimore: Nautical and Aviation Publishing, 1985); R. J. Overy, *Goering: The Iron Man* (London: Routledge and Kegan Paul, 1984); Hoorst Boog, *Die Deutsche Luftwaffenfuehrung, 1935–1945* (Stuttgart, 1982); R. J. Overy, "From *Uralbomber* to *Amerikabomber*: The Luftwaffe and Strategic Bombing," *Journal of Strategic Studies*, 1 (1979). On the Russian Air Force, see Von Hardesty, *Red Phoenix: The Rise of Soviet Air Power, 1941–1945* (Washington, D.C.: Smithsonian Institution Press, 1982); Robert Kilmarx, *A History of Soviet Air Power* (New York: Praeger, 1962). For comparative perspectives, see R. J. Overy, "Strategic Bombardment before 1939," in *Case Studies in Strategic Bombardment*, ed. R. Cargill Hall (Washington, D.C.: Office of Air Force History, 1998); James Corum, "Airpower Thought in Continental Europe between the Wars" in *The Paths of Heaven: The Evolution of Airpower Theory*, ed. Phillip Meilinger

(Maxwell AFB, Ala.: Air University Press, 1997), 151–82; and, generally, Hoorst Boog, ed., *The Conduct of the Air War in the Second World War: An International Comparison* (Providence, R.I.: Berg, 1992).

7. Political scientists have applied cognitive psychology to explain decision makers' behavior in governmental and international affairs. Since that literature bears the most relevance to the issues I seek to understand here, I rely principally on their work. See Robert Jervis, Richard Ned Lebow, and Janice Gross Stein, *Psychology and Deterrence* (Baltimore: Johns Hopkins University Press, 1985), esp. 18–33; Richard Ned Lebow, *Between Peace and War: The Nature of International Crises* (Baltimore: Johns Hopkins University Press, 1981); Robert Jervis, *Perception and Misperception in International Politics* (Princeton: Princeton University Press, 1976); Chaim Kaufman, "A Method for Testing Psychological Explanations of Political Decision Making," *International Studies Quarterly* 38, no. 4 (December 1994): 557–86; Robert Axelrod, *Framework for a General Theory of Cognition and Choice* (Berkeley: Institute of International Studies, 1972); Robert Axelrod, ed., *Structure of Decision: The Cognitive Maps of Political Elites* (Princeton: Princeton University Press, 1976); John Steinbruner, *The Cybernetic Theory of Decision* (Princeton: Princeton University Press, 1974); Irving L. Janis and Leon Mann, *Decision Making: A Psychological Analysis of Conflict, Choice and Commitment* (New York: Free Press, 1977). On the use of psychology in historical research, see Richard Immerman, "Psychology," in *Explaining the History of American Foreign Relations*, ed. Michael J. Hogan and Thomas G. Paterson (Cambridge: Cambridge University Press, 1991), 151–64.

8. There is a large literature on strategic bombing. With some exceptions, most of it focuses on only one nation in a discrete time period, such as World War II or the interwar years, and tends to treat the evolution of bombing plans and policy as responses to specific political, military, economic, or organizational circumstances. On the First World War, some of the most important recent works include John H. Morrow, Jr., *The Great War in the Air* (Washington, D.C.: Smithsonian Institution Press, 1993); George K. Williams, "Statistics and Strategic Bombardment: Operations and Records of the British Long-Range Bombing Force During World War I and Their Implications for the Development of the Post-War Royal Air Force, 1917–1923" (D.Phil. thesis, Oxford University, 1987; recently published as *Biplanes and Bombsights: British Bombing in World War I* [Maxwell AFB, Ala.: Air University Press, 1999]); Neville Jones, *The Beginnings of Strategic Air Power, 1923–1939* (London: Frank Cass, 1987) and *The Origins of Strategic Bombing* (London: William Kimber, 1973); Malcolm Cooper, *The Birth of Independent Air Power* (London: Allen and Unwin, 1986); and S. F. Wise, *Canadian Airmen and the First World War*, vol. 1 of *The Official History of the Royal Canadian Air Force* (Toronto: University of Toronto Press, 1980). On the interwar years, see Scot Robertson, *The Development of RAF Strategic Bombing Doctrine, 1919–1939* (Westport, Conn.: Praeger, 1995); John Robert Ferris, *The Evolution of British Strategic Policy, 1919–1926* (London: Macmillan, 1989); (Ferris's book has been published by Cornell University Press under the title *Men, Money, and Diplomacy* [1989]; references are to the Macmillan edition); Maurer Maurer, *Aviation in the U.S. Army, 1919–*

1939 (Washington, D.C.: Office of Air Force History, 1987); and Malcolm Smith, *British Air Strategy Between the Wars* (Oxford: Clarendon, 1984). On World War II, see Christina J. M. Goulter, *A Forgotten Offensive: Royal Air Force Coastal Command's Anti-Shipping Campaign, 1940–1945* (London: Frank Cass, 1995); Brereton Greenhous et al., *The Crucible of War, 1939–1945* (Toronto: University of Toronto Press, 1994); Richard G. Davis, *Carl A. Spaatz and the Air War in Europe* (Washington, D.C.: Smithsonian Institution Press, 1993); Conrad C. Crane, *Bombs, Cities and Civilians* (Lawrence, Kans.: University Press of Kansas, 1993); Michael S. Sherry, *The Rise of American Air Power* (New Haven: Yale University Press, 1987); Ronald Schaffer, *Wings of Judgment: American Bombing in World War II* (Oxford: Oxford University Press, 1985); and R. J. Overy, *The Air War, 1939–1945* (London: Stein and Day, 1980). Overviews include John Buckley, *Air Power in the Age of Total War* (London: UCL Press, 1999); and John Gooch, ed., *Air Power: Theory and Practice* (London: Frank Cass, 1995).

9. Mary Douglas, *How Institutions Think* (Syracuse: Syracuse University Press, 1986), 45.

10. For an important critique of air power as a coercive tool, see Robert A. Pape, *Bombing to Win: Air Power and Coercion in War* (Ithaca: Cornell University Press, 1996).

11. For a similar problem in a different context, see the discussion of the Roberts plots experiments in Ashley L. Schiff, *Fire and Water: Scientific Heresy in the Forest Service* (Cambridge: Harvard University Press, 1962), 25–33. Also, Lynn R. Eden, *Deconstructing Destruction: Organizations, Knowledge, and the Effects of Nuclear Weapons*, forthcoming from Cornell University Press.

Chapter 1
The Beginning: Strategic Bombing in the First World War

1. Michael Sherry has written that, in the aftermath of World War I, "both extravagant hopes and unreasoning fears were still possible" with respect to bomber aircraft. See Sherry, *The Rise of American Air Power* (New Haven: Yale University Press, 1987), 21.

2. See Robert Wohl, *A Passion for Wings* (New Haven: Yale University Press, 1994), 2; Michael Paris, *Winged Warfare* (New York: Manchester University Press, 1992). On predictions of future warfare generally, see I. F. Clarke's pioneering study, *Voices Prophesying War, 1763–1984* (New York: Oxford University Press, 1966); John Gooch, "Attitudes to War in Late Victorian and Edwardian England," in *The Prospect of War* (London: Frank Cass, 1981), 35–51.

3. Among his many prophetic designs later made manifest as weapons of modern warfare, fifteenth-century artist and inventor Leonardo da Vinci included a "flying machine." The technological hurdles were immense, however, and would require centuries of work. See Laurence Goldstein, *The Flying Machine and Modern Literature* (Bloomington: Indiana University Press, 1986), 26.

4. Francesco Lana, quoted in Sir Walter Raleigh, *The War in the Air*, vol. 1 (Oxford: Oxford University Press, 1922), 29–30.

5. Clarke, *Voices Prophesying War*, 6–7.

6. Alfred, Lord Tennyson, *Works: With Notes by the Author*, ed. Hallam, Lord Tennyson (New York: Macmillan, 1935), 98.

7. On Warner and Coxwell, see C. F. Snowden Gamble, *The Air Weapon*, vol. 1 (Oxford: Oxford University Press, 1931), 39, 45; on Verne, see Paris, *Winged Warfare*, 22–23.

8. Hugo quoted in Clarke, *Voices, Prophesying War*, 3.

9. On Fullerton and Chanute, see David MacIsaac, "Voices from the Central Blue: The Air Power Theorists," in *Makers of Modern Strategy from Machiavelli to the Nuclear Age*, ed. Peter Paret (Princeton: Princeton University Press, 1986), 625–27. Chanute is quoted on 626.

10. On Hay, see Paris, *Winged Warfare*, 23–24; Clarke, *Voices Prophesying War*, 62–63. On Odell and Norton, see H. Bruce Franklin, *War Stars: The Superbomb and the American Imagination* (New York: Oxford University Press, 1988), 30, 41–44.

11. See T.H.E. Travers, "Future Warfare: H. G. Wells and British Military Theory, 1865–1916," in *War and Society: A Yearbook of Military History*, ed. Brian Bond and Ian Roy (New York: Holmes and Meier, 1975), 74–75, also 70–71; David Edgerton, *England and the Aeroplane* (London: Macmillan, 1991), 44–45; Franklin, *War Stars*, 84–85; and Sherry, *The Rise of American Air Power*, 8–9.

12. Edgerton, *England and the Aeroplane*, 13.

13. For examples of the debate in military circles in the years prior to World War I, see, for instance: Bvt. Maj. Sir A. Bannerman, "The Difficulty of Aerial Attack," *Journal of the Royal United Services Institution* 53, no. 375 (May 1909); Maj. B. Baden-Powell, "How Airships are Likely to Affect War," *Journal of the Royal United Services Institution* 54, no. 387 (May 1910); W. F. Reid, "Explosives in Aerial Warfare with Some Remarks on Methods of Defence," *Journal of the Royal United Services Institution* 55, no. 400 (June 1911); Col. Louis Jackson, "The Defence of Localities Against Aerial Attack," *Journal of the Royal United Services Institution* 58, no. 436 (June 1914). Since all of these were first delivered as lectures, the printed commentary from the audiences is also helpful.

14. Moltke's statement is noted in an essay by Bernard Brodie titled, "The Continuing Relevance of *On War*," in M. Howard and P. Paret's translation of Clausewitz's *On War* (Princeton: Princeton University Press, 1984), 53. On Clausewitz, see also M. Howard's essay, "The Influence of Clausewitz" in Howard and Paret, trans., *On War*, 39; Howard, *Clausewitz* (Oxford: Oxford University Press, 1983); Azar Gat, *The Development of Military Thought: The Nineteenth Century* (Oxford: Clarendon Press, 1992); Christopher Bassford, *Clausewitz in English* (Oxford: Oxford University Press, 1994), esp. 104–12.

15. Maj. A. Lawson's prize essay is printed in the *Journal of the Royal United Services Institution* 58, no. 434 (April 1914). See also Tim Travers, *The Killing Ground: The British Army, the Western Front and the Emergence of Modern Warfare, 1900–1918* (London: Unwin Hyman, 1987), 37–97. On similar ideas in Germany at the time, see Antulio J. Echevarria II, "On the Brink of the Abyss: The Warrior Identity and German Military Thought before the Great War," *War and Society* 13, no. 2 (October 1995): 23–40.

16. Altham cited in M. Howard, "Men Against Fire: Expectations of War in 1914," in *Military Strategy and the Origins of the First World War*, ed. S. Miller (Princeton: Princeton University Press, 1991), 11; first printed in *International Security* 9, no. 1.

17. See Travers, *The Killing Ground*, 37–38, chap. 2 generally.

18. Caroline E. Playne, *The Pre-War Mind in Britain* (London: Allen and Unwin, 1928), 104.

19. Travers, "Future Warfare," 80.

20. See Gat, *The Development of Military Thought*, 79, also 78–88.

21. On turn of the century changes wrought by the industrial revolution, see, generally, Geoffrey Barraclough, *An Introduction to Contemporary History* (London: Watts, 1964); and Gareth Stedman Jones, *Outcast London* (New York: Pantheon, 1984; London, 1971). Also, Edgerton, *England and the Aeroplane*, p. 12. On ideas about urban populations and strategic bombing generally, see Joseph Konvitz, "Cities as Targets: Conceptions of Strategic Bombing, 1914–1945," Woodrow Wilson International Center for Scholars, paper no. 85 (Washington, D.C., 1987); "Why Cities Don't Die," *Invention and Technology* (Winter 1990): 59–63; Sherry, *The Rise of American Air Power*, 26.

22. Travers, *The Killing Ground*, 40. For an example of the military emphasis on discipline, see Lt. Stewart L. Murray, *Discipline: Its Reason and Battle-Value* (London: Gale and Polden, 1894).

23. Samuel Hynes, *The Edwardian Turn of Mind* (Princeton: Princeton University Press, 1968), 21–22, 54–55, 63.

24. See ibid., 24.

25. Masterman quoted in Hynes, *The Edwardian Turn of Mind*, 61–62. In his "frontline diary," published under the title *Gallipoli Correspondent*, First World War journalist C.E.W. Bean would write, "The truth is that after 100 years of breeding in slums, the British race is not the same, and can't be expected to be the same, as in the days of Waterloo" (*Gallipoli Correspondent* reprint, Sydney: Allen and Unwin, 1983), 154.

26. See Hynes, *The Edwardian Turn of Mind*, 42–46; Playne, *The Pre-War Mind in Britain*, 100.

27. Maj. Stewart L. Murray, *The Peace of the Anglo-Saxons* (London: Watts, 1905), 2.

28. Lloyd George quoted in Alfred Gollin, *No Longer an Island: Britain and the Wright Brothers, 1902–1909* (Stanford: Stanford University Press, 1984), 351; see also p. 345. On Baden-Powell, see Travers, *The Killing Ground*, 39.

29. See Alfred Gollin, *The Impact of Air Power on the British People and Their Government, 1909–1914* (London: Macmillan, 1989), 49–63.

30. The *Daily Mail* cited in Gollin, *The Impact of Air Power*, 72; see also pp. 64–76.

31. Churchill quoted in Playne, *The Pre-War Mind in Britain*, 101. Playne's own critique of the popular press, and its frequent resort to sensationalism, can be found on 104–24.

32. See G. S. Jones, *Outcast London*; Judith R. Walkowitz, *City of Dreadful Delight* (Chicago: University of Chicago Press, 1992), esp. 26–27; Richard Hofstadter, *Social Darwinism in American Thought*, 4th ed. (Boston: Beacon

Press, 1992); John Higham, *Strangers in the Land*, 3rd ed. (New York: Atheneum, 1963); and Thomas F. Gossett, *Race: The History of an Idea in America* (Dallas: Southern Methodist University Press, 1961).

33. See Steven Biel, *Down With the Old Canoe: A Cultural History of the Titanic Disaster* (New York: Norton, 1996), 38, 46–47. Biel points out (38) that overall, 60 percent of the first-cabin passengers were saved, compared to 44 percent of second-cabin passengers and 25 percent in steerage.

34. There were 399 industrial disputes in Britain in 1908; by 1911 there were 903. In the months before the outbreak of World War I, there were approximately 150 strikes per month. See Allen Hutt, *The Postwar History of the British Working Class* (New York: Coward-McCann, 1938), 3. See also, Paul Addison, "Winston Churchill and the Working Class, 1900–1914," in *The Working Class in Modern British History*, ed. Jay Winter (Cambridge: Cambridge University Press, 1983), 43–64; David Lloyd George, *War Memoirs*, vol. 4 (London: Ivor Nicholson and Watson, 1934), 1926–27.

35. See two lectures by T. Miller Maguire to the Royal United Services Institution, published in the *Journal of the Royal United Services Institution* as "Readiness or Ruin" (53, no. 382 [Dec. 1909]), and "National Recuperation" (54, no. 385 [March 1910]).

36. Maj. Stewart L. Murray, "Internal Condition of Great Britain During a Great War," *Journal of the United Royal Services Institution* 57, no. 430 (December 1913), 1564, 1566, 1587–1588. I am grateful to David Silbey for bringing this article to my attention.

37. Col. W. G. Simpson, "The Duties of Local Authorities in Wartime," *Journal of the Royal United Services Institution* 58, no. 431 (January 1914). For Dickson's comment, see 20.

38. Col. Louis Jackson, "The Defence of Localities Against Aerial Attack," *Journal of the Royal United Services Institution* 58, no. 436 (June 1914), esp. 713.

39. See Lee Kennett, *A History of Strategic Bombing* (New York: Scribners, 1982), 5–6.

40. On aviation (and reaction to its use) in the Italo-Turkish war generally, see Paris, *Winged Warfare*, 106–115. A 1914 commentary on aviation in the Italo-Turkish war can be found in Eric Stuart Bruce, *Aircraft in War* (London: Hodder and Stoughton, 1914), 137–43.

41. "The Italian Army and Aviation," *Times* (London), 12 August 1912, p. 5.

42. Kennett, *A History of Strategic Bombing*, 13.

43. For an official overview of the war, compiled from reports of the Italian General Staff, see *The Italo-Turkish War* trans. Lt. Renato Tittoni, USMC (Kansas City, Mo.: Franklin Hudson, 1913); see esp. 100. See also "Lessons of the War in Tripoli," *Aeronautics* (February 1913): 65.

44. See "Bomb Dropping in the Balkans," *Scientific American*, 11 October 1913. See also "The Aeroplane in War," *Scientific American*, 28 June 1913, which pointed out, again, that the effects of bombing in the Turko-Balkan campaign were "decidedly moral rather than material."

45. Barry Powers, *Strategy Without Slide Rule* (London: Croom Helm, 1976), 11.

46. On the German zeppelin program, see generally Douglas Robinson, *The Zeppelin in Combat, 1912 to 1918* (London: G. T. Foulis, 1962); Peter Fritzsche, *A Nation of Flyers* (Cambridge: Harvard University Press, 1992); Marian C. McKenna, "The Development of Air Raid Precautions in World War I," in *Men at War*, ed. Timothy Travers and Christon Archer (Chicago: Precedent, 1982); and Powers, *Strategy Without Slide Rule*, 11–51.

47. Behncke quoted in Robinson, *The Zeppelin in Combat*, 50; see also p. 52.

48. Edgerton, *England and the Aeroplane*, 8–14.

49. For a detailed examination of these issues prior to the outbreak of war, see Gollin, *The Impact of Air Power*, 159–290. Also, see generally, Malcolm Cooper, *The Birth of Independent Air Power* (London, Allen and Unwin, 1986); and Eric Ash, *Sir Frederick Sykes and the Air Revolution, 1912–1918* (London: Frank Cass, 1999).

50. "Memorandum on the Organization of the Air Services," by Lt.-Gen. Sir David Henderson, July 1917, reprinted in H. A. Jones, *The War in the Air*, Appendices (Oxford: Clarendon Press, 1937), 1–8. For excellent coverage of the development of British naval aviation, see Christina J. M. Goulter, *A Forgotten Offensive: Royal Air Force Coastal Command's Anti-Shipping Campaign, 1940–1945* (London: Frank Cass, 1995).

51. Powers, *Strategy Without Slide Rule*, 15–17; Raleigh, *The War in the Air*, 1:357–409; and S. F. Wise, *Canadian Airmen and the First World War*, vol. 1 of *The Official History of the Royal Canadian Air Force* (Toronto: University of Toronto Press, 1980), 126–33, 260–61.

52. On Fisher, see Lloyd George, *War Memoirs*, 3:1846; Powers, *Strategy Without Slide Rule*, 21.

53. See Powers, *Strategy Without Slide Rule*, 12–13; Fritzsche, *A Nation of Flyers*, 44; Wise, *Canadian Airmen*, 234–35.

54. See Tami Davis Biddle, "Air Power," in *The Laws of War*, ed. Michael Howard, George Andreopoulos, and Mark Shulman (New Haven: Yale University Press, 1994), 142–46.

55. The most damaging raids included the June 6th (1915) raid against Hull, which caused rioting and the sacking of German (or supposedly German) shops; the 15 June raid against Tyneside shipbuilding works; the 9 August raid, against Hull again, which killed sixteen people; the 7 September raid against the Millwall, Deptford, Greenwich, and Woolwich docks; the 8 September raid against London; and the 13 October raid against London. The latter saw the greatest number (seventeen people) killed by a single bomb in the raids up to that time. See Robinson, *The Zeppelin in Combat*, 76–113.

56. Ibid., 107–8; Powers, *Strategy Without Slide Rule*, 40; Wise, *Canadian Airmen*, 130–31.

57. Wise *Canadian Airmen*, 130–31; Powers, *Strategy Without Slide Rule*, 14–51; H. A. Jones, *The War in the Air*, 3:116–49; T. H. O'Brien, *Civil Defence* (London: HMSO, 1955), 7.

58. Strasser's memorandum is reprinted in Robinson, *The Zeppelin in Combat*, xv.

59. On improvements in British defenses, see A. Rawlinson, *The Defence of London, 1915–1918* (London: Andrew Melrose, 1923), 121–28; Powers, *Strat-*

egy Without Slide Rule, 30–37. Particularly useful is John Ferris: "Airbandit: C3I and Strategic Air Defence during the First Battle of Britain, 1915–18," in *Strategy and Intelligence: British Policy During the First World War*, ed. Michael Dockrill and David French (London: Hambledon Press, 1996), 23–66; and John Robert Ferris, "Fighter Defence Before Fighter Command: The Rise of Strategic Air Defence in Great Britain," *The Journal of Military History* 63, no. 4 (October 1999): 845–84, esp. 853.

60. Robinson, *The Zeppelin in Combat*, 165.

61. The casualty figures are from Powers, *Strategy Without Slide Rule*, 51. On warnings and information, see "Precautions for Dwellers in London," *Times* (London), 10 June 1915; "Hushing Up 'Zeppelin' Raid Results," *Literary Digest*, 2 October 1915, pp. 701–2; Charles Stienon, "The Zeppelin Raids and Their Effect on England," *The New York Times Current History*, 6 (April–June 1917): 333–38; O'Brien, *Civil Defence*, 8–10.

62. See AIR 1/569/15/16/140, Public Records Office, London; O'Brien, *Civil Defence*, 7; Powers, *Strategy Without Slide Rule*, 21–22; Wise, *Canadian Airmen*, 236–38.

63. See, for example, "The Zeppelin Raids: An Official Report," *Times* (London) 18 September 1915, p. 1, which claimed that among those who witnessed the raid, "the feelings everywhere aroused were of interest and curiousity rather than of fear." Also, Stienon, "The Zeppelin Raids and Their Effect on England," 333–38. On wartime letters, see, for instance, the letters of Mrs. Dayrell Browning, the diaries of Viola Bawtree, the recollections of Mr. W. M. Hughes, and the letters of J. B. Evans, all filed under "Zeppelin Raids," Imperial War Museum Archive, London.

64. Rawlinson, *The Defence of London*, 4–5.

65. Parliamentary Debates (Official Report), fifth series, vol. 80, 6th Session of the 13th Parliament: House of Commons, 16 February 1916. For the McNeill quote, see col. 95; Harmsworth, cols. 130–31; Cecil, col. 141.

66. See Powers, *Strategy Without Slide Rule*, 22–27; Lloyd George, *War Memoirs*, 3:1848–49; Edgerton, *England and the Aeroplane*, 15–16.

67. Sir John Slessor, *The Central Blue* (London: Cassell, 1956), 14–15; Air Vice-Marshal E. J. Kingston-McCloughry, *Defence Policy and Strategy* (New York: Praeger, 1960), 207.

68. Capt. B. H. Liddell Hart, *The Memoirs of Captain Liddell Hart*, vol. 1 (London: Cassell, 1965), 17–18. In his memoir, Slessor reflected, "Perhaps in those early days it was the novelty of the unknown—the shock of finding for the first time in nearly nine hundred years that we were no longer secure behind our sea frontiers—that temporarily unnerved some of us" (*The Central Blue* 15).

69. B. H. Liddell Hart, *Paris, or the Future of War* (New York: E. P. Dutton, 1925; reprint, New York: Garland, 1972), 39–42.

70. On early French bombing efforts, see John H. Morrow, Jr. *The Great War in the Air* (Washington, D.C.: Smithsonian Institution Press, 1993), 93–94; Wise, *Canadian Airmen*, 261–62; "The French Air Bombing Units in the Great War," *Journal of the Royal United Services Institution* 67, no. 508 (November 1932): 825–27 (an essay adapted from the *Militaer Wochenblatt* [11 October 1932]).

71. On the French bombing program in the latter part of the war, see George K. Williams, "Statistics and Strategic Bombardment: Operations and Records of the British Long-Range Bombing Force During World War I and Their Implications for the Development of the Post-War Royal Air Force, 1917–1923" (D.Phil. thesis, Oxford University, 1987), 94–111. This work has recently been published, in slightly abridged form, as *Biplanes and Bombsights: British Bombing in World War I* (Maxwell AFB, Ala.: Air University Press, 1999). See also Morrow, *The Great War in the Air*, 94–103.

72. On the operations of the Luxeuil (No. 3) Wing, see Williams, "Statistics," 15–64; also Wise, *Canadian Airmen*, 263–77; Cooper, *The Birth of Independent Air Power*, 63–66; Neville Jones, *The Origins of Strategic Bombing* (London: William Kimber, 1973), 103–29. The Wing undertook only eighteen raids, dropping an average weight of just over a ton of bombs per raid. Many of the bombs used were the nearly useless 65-pound type.

73. Continuing naval interest in long-distance bombing prompted the government to create the Joint War Air Committee, headed by Lord Derby, to look into the rationalization of the air services. But the navy remained determined to pursue strategic bombing, and Derby found himself unable to close the distance between the two organizations. The failure of the Joint War Air Committee in April 1916 triggered the creation of another body, the Air Board, headed by Lord Curzon. But this, too, turned out to be a weak organization, unable fully to resolve the ongoing disputes over aerial resources.

74. George Williams, "Statistics," 32–37.

75. For a detailed (and critical) overview of the early organization of the RFC, see Cooper, *The Birth of Independent Air Power*, 9–10, 13–24, 31–32; also, Robin Higham, *The Military Intellectuals in Great Britain, 1918–1939* (New Brunswick, N.J.: Rutgers University Press, 1966), 132–39; and Gollin, *The Impact of Air Power*, 309–13.

76. Higham, *Military Intellectuals*, 132–39.

77. Andrew Boyle, *Trenchard* (New York: W. W. Norton, 1962), esp. 128, 163; Higham, *Military Intellectuals*, 136; Malcolm Cooper, "A House Divided: Policy, Rivalry and Administration in Britain's Military Air Command, 1914–1918," *The Journal of Strategic Studies* 3, no. 2 (September 1980): 183–84.

78. See Trenchard's memoranda on air tactics and strategy in AIR 1/522/16/12/5. Also, Cooper, *The Birth of Independent Air Power*, 71–83, and "A House Divided," 187–89; Paris, *Winged Warfare*, 220–22; Higham, *Military Intellectuals*, 141; Wise, *Canadian Airmen*, 326, 381.

79. On aviation at Verdun, see Alistair Horne, *The Price of Glory: Verdun 1916* (London: Macmillan, 1962), 203–9. Also Morrow, *The Great War in the Air*, 132–35; Richard P. Hallion, *The Rise of the Fighter Aircraft* (Baltimore: Nautical and Aviation, 1984), 27–29; Lee Kennett, *The First Air War* (New York: Free Press, 1991), 70–73; James Corum, *The Luftwaffe: Creating the Operational Air War 1918–1940* (Lawrence: University Press of Kansas, 1997), 24–25.

80. The memo is reprinted in Maurice Baring, *R.F.C. H.Q., 1914–1918* (London: G. Bell, 1920), 180–84. See also AIR 1/522/16/12/5. On the Somme, see Higham, *Military Intellectuals*, 132–59, appendix B; Wise, *Canadian Airmen*, 358–92, esp. 362–76.

81. "Memorandum of the Results Obtained by the Royal Flying Corps During September with Some Notes on the Work of the German Flying Corps," 5 October 1917, in AIR 1/522/16/12/5. Trenchard's sympathetic biographer labeled the September 1916 memorandum "prophetic." See Boyle, *Trenchard*, 188.

82. See Morrow, *The Great War in the Air*, 168–75; Neville Jones, *The Beginnings of Strategic Air Power, 1923–1939* (London: Frank Cass, 1987), xvi–xvii; Paris, *Winged Warfare*, 237–39; Cooper, *The Birth of Independent Air Power*, 78–79; Wise, *Canadian Airmen*, 575.

83. See, for instance, Cooper, "A House Divided," 188.

84. See N. Jones, *The Beginnings of Strategic Air Power*, xvii–xviii; Denis Winter, *The First of the Few* (Athens: University of Georgia Press, 1982), 76–77.

85. Sir Philip Gibbs, *Now It Can Be Told* (Garden City, N.Y.: Garden City Publishing, 1920), 387 (in Britain the book was published under the title, *The Realities of War*); Sir Frederick Sykes, *From Many Angles* (London: Harrap, 1942), 220. See also Lt. Col. J. Gammell to Director of Flying Operations, 15 October 1918, in AIR 1/461/15/312/107. For Boyle's comments on criticism of Trenchard, see his *Trenchard*, 184–85.

86. H. A. Jones, *The War in the Air*, 6:555, also 552–58. In the first volume of the official history of the air war, Sir Walter Raleigh was laudatory of Trenchard's style. See, for instance, Raleigh, *The War in the Air*, 1:417.

87. See Cooper, *The Birth of Independent Air Power*, 81.

88. Quoted in S. Wise, "The Royal Air Force and the Origins of Strategic Bombing" in *Men at War*, ed. Timothy Travers and Christon Archer (Chicago: Precedent, 1982), 158.

89. On the German bomber program, see Morrow, *The Great War in the Air*, 220–21.

90. J. C. Carlile, D.D., ed., *Folkestone During the War, 1914–1919* (Folkestone: F. J. Parsons, n.d. [1920?]), 87 and generally, chapter 6, "The Air Raids." The casualty figures are from WF, 1:34.

91. Signals intelligence had not, in this case, helped the British to predict the arrival of the aircraft. See Ferris, "Airbandit," 41–42.

92. On the London raids, see WF, 1:35; and, generally, Raymond Fredette, *The Sky on Fire: The First Battle of Britain, 1917–1918* (New York: Holt, Rinehart & Winston, 1966). For the War Cabinet responses to the raids of June and July, see CAB 23/3/163 (163rd meeting, War Cabinet), and CAB 23/3/178 (178th meeting, War Cabinet), Public Record Office, London.

93. "The Air Attack on London," *Times* (London), 14 June 1917, p. 7; "Story of the Raid," *Times* (London), 14 June 1917, p. 7.

94. See for instance, "The Air Attack on London," *Times* (London), 14 June 1917, p. 7; letter from Maj. Gen. Desmond O'Callaghan, *Times* (London), 16 June 1917, p. 7. Writing after the war, C. S. Peel stated, "In spite of the danger of these raids the generality of those who endured them remained very calm" (*How We Lived Then* [London: Bodley Head, 1929], 161).

95. See Powers, *Strategy Without Slide Rule*, 55.

96. "Air Raid Warnings for the City," *Times* (London), 18 June 1917, p. 8.

97. See in particular the letters printed under the heading "Air Raids: Strong Demand for Retribution" *Times* (London), 16 June 1917, p. 7.

98. See "No Panic" and "Clear Streets," *Times* (London), 9 July 1917, p. 9, cols. 4 and 5.

99. See "The Spectacle," *Times* (London), 9 July 1917, p. 9; "Germans' Biggest Air Exploit," *Times* (London), 9 July 1917, p. 10.

100. Unsigned article, "The Psychology of the Air Raid," *Literary Digest*, 8 September 1917, p. 23.

101. See "The Enemy's Escape Unscathed" and "Trust in British Coolness," *Times* (London), 9 July 1917, p. 9.

102. "The Reverend Bernard Snell on Reprisals," *Times* (London), 9 July 1917, p. 10.

103. Reprint of telegram sent to the King, in "Appeal to the King," *Times* (London), 10 July 1917, p. 8.

104. See, for instance, the letters printed under the heading "The Air Raid: Lessons of Saturday's Attack," *Times* (London), 10 July 1917, p. 5; "Air Raid Disorders," *Times* (London), 10 July 1917, p. 3; "Anti-German Disturbances," *Times* (London), 11 July 1917, p. 3.

105. See H. A. Jones, *The War in the Air*, 4:152–53. Because the second raid had taken place immediately after the fighter squadrons (sent home after the first raid) had returned to France, the War Cabinet suspected "effective German espionage." See CAB 23/3/178.

106. On these events, see Sykes, *From Many Angles*, 215–24; Wise, *Canadian Airmen*, 278–80; N. Jones, *The Origins of Strategic Bombing*, 130–39; J. M. Spaight, *The Beginnings of Organized Air Power* (London: Longmans, Green, 1927), 126–30; WF, 1:37.

107. These debates are articulated in various articles appearing in the *Times* (London), 9, 10, and 11 July 1917. Steps finally were taken toward the creation of an air raid warning system for London on 12 July. See Powers, *Strategy Without Slide Rule*, 58: also O'Brien, *Civil Defence*, 10. Air defense and warning for London are discussed in several documents in AIR 9/69.

108. In an October 1917 editorial, they reiterated that policy had to be based on sound military grounds, not on public demands for protection and revenge. See "Topics of the Day," *The Spectator*, 14 July 1917 and 6 October 1917.

109. Lloyd George, *War Memoirs*, 4:1925, see also 4:1960–61.

110. Lloyd George, *War Memoirs*, 4:1932. Of the Russian Revolution, he wrote, "The coming of the Russian Revolution lit up the skies with a lurid flash of hope for all who were dissatisfied with the existing order of society" (1933). Regarding domestic labor difficulties in particular, he pointed out that during the year, there were 688 disputes, affecting 860,727 people. "The total," he wrote, "though still well below those of the years 1912–1914, showed how serious was the problem, when every day lost diminished the means of effective prosecution of the War on land and sea and in the air" (1938).

111. Rawlinson quoted in Brock Millman, "British Home Defence Planning and Civil Dissent, 1917–1918," *War in History 5*, no. 2 (April 1998): 224; Pearce quoted in Powers, *Strategy Without Slide Rule*, 62. See also generally: R. J. Overy, "Air Power and the Origins of Deterrence Theory," *The Journal of*

Strategic Studies 15, no. 1 (March 1992): 73–101; Malcolm Smith, "The Air Threat and British Foreign and Domestic Policy: The Background to the Strategic Air Offensive," in *The Conduct of the Air War in the Second World War*, ed. Horst Boog (Providence, R.I.: Berg, 1992), esp. 621–24; Joseph Konvitz, "Cities as Targets," 6–7; Arthur Marwick, *The Deluge: British Society and the First World War* (Boston: Little Brown, 1965), 189–210.

112. See W. K. Hancock, *Smuts: The Sanguine Years, 1870–1919* (Cambridge: Cambridge University Press, 1962), 438–42; Lloyd George, *War Memoirs*, 4:1844–70; Cooper, *The Birth of Independent Air Power*, 97–107.

113. From "The Second Report of the Prime Minister's Committee on Air Organisation and Home Defence Against Air Raids," 17 August 1917, in AIR 1/515/16/3/83 ("Precis for the Army Council, Air Organization"). The report is also reprinted in H. A. Jones, *The War in the Air*, "Appendices," 8–14.

114. See Hancock, *Smuts*, 441; N. Jones, *The Origins of Strategic Bombing*, 138–39; Matthew Cooper, *The Birth of Independent Air Power*, 101–2.

115. Cooper, *The Birth of Independent Air Power*, 104–5.

116. See letter from Trenchard to Adv. Headquarters, RFC, 30 August 1917, in AIR 1/521/16/12/3.

117. Regarding Trenchard's initial view of the prospect of an independent air force, Haig wrote, "The War Department has evidently decided on creating a new Department to deal with Air operations, on the lines of the War Office and the Admiralty. Trenchard is much perturbed as to the result of this new departure just at a time when the Flying Corps was beginning to feel that it had become an important part of the Army." Haig's diary entry of 28 August 1917, cited in *The Private Papers of Douglas Haig 1914–1919*, ed. Robert Blake (London: Eyre and Spottiswoode, 1952), 252.

118. Letter from Field Marshal Commanding-in-Chief, British Armies in France to Chief of the Imperial General Staff, 15 September 1917, in AIR 1/521/16/12/3.

119. N. Jones, *The Origins of Strategic Bombing*, 151–53; Cooper, *The Birth of Independent Air Power*, 105 and 109–17; Williams, "Statistics," 77–79; Fredette, *The Sky on Fire*, 197–98.

120. See Lloyd George, *War Memoirs*, 4:1875.

121. Fredette, *The Sky on Fire*, 171–72, 176–77.

122. Ibid., 181–83 and 186–88.

123. Powers, *Strategy Without Slide Rule*, 60–61; O'Brien, *Civil Defence*, 11; Fredette, *The Sky on Fire*, 180.

124. See Millman, "British Home Defence Planning and Civil Dissent," 204–9, 212, 216–25, 231–32.

125. The best overview of the operations of Newall's force is found in Williams, "Statistics," 113–92.

126. The Scientific and Methodical Attack of Vital Industries," 27 May 1918, p. 5, in AIR 1/460/15/312/101.

127. See in general Cooper, *The Birth of Independent Air Power*, and "A House Divided"; N. Jones, *The Origins of Strategic Bombing*.

128. For Haig's views, see Haig to Chief of the Imperial General Staff (CIGS), 2 October 1917, in AIR 1/522/16/12/5. See also Boyle, *Trenchard*, 249–55;

Cooper *The Birth of Independent Air Power*, 120, and "A House Divided," 194; Fredette, *The Sky on Fire*, 201.

129. "The Bombing of Germany," 13 January 1918, in AIR 1/522/16/12/5; Williams, "Statistics," 203–5.

130. Cooper, *The Birth of Independent Air Power*, 119–27; Higham, *Military Intellectuals*, 155; Malcolm Smith, *British Air Strategy Between the Wars* (Oxford: Clarendon, 1984), 20–21. For the personal opinions of Sykes, see his *From Many Angles*, 216–17.

131. Lord Weir to Trenchard, 30 April 1918, Papers of Sir Hugh Trenchard (hereafter TP), MFC 76/1/20, c I 17, RAF Museum, Hendon. See generally W. J. Reader, *Architect of Air Power: The Life of the First Viscount Weir of Eastwood* (London: 1968), 68–74; Williams, "Statistics," 211–13.

132. Trenchard to Weir, 1 May 1918, in TP, MFC 76/1/20, c I 17.

133. Trenchard to Weir, 8 May 1918, in TP, MFC 76/1/20, c I 17.

134. See Boyle, *Trenchard*, 284–88. Also, Smith, *British Air Strategy*, 21; Cooper, *The Birth of Independent Air Power*; 129; Fredette, *The Sky on Fire*, 223.

135. Williams points out that aside from ad hoc initiatives taken by staff officers, no organizational provision existed for the coordination of operations and intelligence below the level of Sykes himself. See "Statistics," 218, 222.

136. Trenchard's memo "Long Distance Bombing," 26 November 1917, in TP, MFC 76/1/67.

137. Ibid.

138. For background on Tiverton and an analysis of his impact, see George K. Williams, "The Shank of the Drill: Americans and Strategical Aviation in the Great War," *Journal of Strategic Studies* 19, no. 3 (Sept. 1996): 386; N. Jones, *The Origins of Strategic Bombing*, 142–47.

139. Lord Tiverton, "Original Paper on Objectives," 3 September 1917, in AIR 1/462/15/312/121 (also in the Halsbury Papers, AC 73/2, Box 3, RAF Museum, Hendon).

140. Rear Adm. Mark Kerr, memo on bombing, 27 November 1917, in AIR 1/461/15/312/107.

141. One planner, C.R.J. Randall, argued, "For instance, if the whole of his production of high explosive can be stopped, the need to attack those factories in which he is making guns, shells, etc., at once disappears." See untitled notes on bombing by Wing Commander C.R.J. Randall, 12 November 1917, in AIR 1/460/15/312/97. See also Kerr memo, 27 November 1917, in AIR 1/461/15/312/107.

142. Unsigned paper (possibly written by Tiverton), "Notes for the D.F.O. on Paper for War Cabinet," n.d., in AIR 1/461/15/312/107. This same idea is expressed in similar but slightly varying forms in strategy papers scattered throughout AIR 1/460 and AIR 1/461.

143. Tiverton's 2 November 1917 paper is detailed extensively in N. Jones, *The Origins of Strategic Bombing*, 154–57.

144. Kerr memo, 27 November 1917, in AIR 1/461/15/312/107.

145. Tiverton, "Original Paper on Objectives," 3.

146. This unit, Group 27, under the command of Lt. Col. R. H. Mulock,

began to organize early in September 1918 in Norfolk. See H. A. Jones, *The War in the Air*, 6:173.

147. [Tiverton?], "Notes on Potentialities of Norfolk as a Base for the 'V' Type Handley Page Aeroplanes," [June ?] 1918, in AIR 1/461/312/107. An earlier paper on this subject had proposed the use of these bombers primarily against German munitions works, and secondarily against other cities for moral effect.

148. Tiverton to Air Intellegence, 26 August 1918, in AIR 1/460/15/312/97. The list was provided and an attached note by J. Gammell (dated 8 September 1918) read, "Your list above gives us which factories (in the priority list already supplied) have got the workmen's dwellings belonging to them concentrated in such a way as to make it possible to attack them successfully if required." See also, Tiverton, "The Possibilities of Long Distance Bombing from the Present Date Until September 1919," 1 October 1918, in AIR 1/460/15/312/101.

149. See "Incendiary Operations as a Means of Aerial Warfare," 30 September 1918, in AIR 1/461/15/312/111. The War Cabinet had ruled on 18 September that incendiary raids would be undertaken only as a "defensive act of retaliation." See memo from FO3 to DFO, 18 September 1918, in AIR 1/461/15/312/107. See also Wise, *Canadian Airmen*, note at the bottom of p. 316.

150. See memo from Tiverton to Groves, 12 June 1918, in AIR 1/461/15/312/107. In the end, the plan, though "well worth considering," was not implemented because it was not clear how to prevent the beetles from invading French territory. See Groves to Tiverton, 14 June 1918, in AIR 1/461.

151. Tiverton, "The Possibilities of Long Distance Bombing from the Present Date Until September 1919," 1 October 1918, in AIR 1/460/15/312/101.

152. On this point, see Cooper, *The Birth of Independent Air Power*, 131–32. Newall also revealed a tendency to discount or ignore Air Staff thinking and intelligence work available to him. See the Air Staff critique (titled "Notes for the D.F.O." and probably written by Tiverton) attached to his paper, "The Scientific and Methodical Attack of Vital Industries," in AIR 1/460/15/312/101.

153. On the number of planes originally envisioned for the force, see H. A. Jones, *The War in the Air*, 6:173. On the actual strength of the IF, see H. A. Jones, *The War in the Air: Appendices* (Oxford: Oxford University Press, 1937), Appendix XII, "Statistics of Work of Squadrons of the Independent Force, Including Wastage, June–November 1918."

154. Not until 24 September would an agreement be worked out for the establishment of an Inter-Allied Independent Air Force. Trenchard finally would be confirmed as its head just two weeks before the armistice. See H. A. Jones, *The War in the Air*, 6:104–6. Some of Foch's views, including his insistence on the primacy of the army, are documented in his "Memorandum on the Subject of an Independent Air Force," 14 September 1918, reprinted in Jones, *Appendices*, 29–30.

155. Williams, "Statistics," 230–31.

156. See George K. Williams, "Measure by Micrometer, Cut with an Axe: The Air Staff and General Hugh M. Trenchard, June–November 1918" (paper delivered to the Society for Military History, Montgomery, Ala., 11 April 1997).

157. Trenchard to Weir, 2 July 1918, in AIR 1/458/15/312/69 (also in AIR 1/2000/204/273/275).

158. At times Trenchard claimed that results were hard to determine because the towns were enveloped in mist. See "Operations of the Independent Force, R.A.F. During July, 1918" (including covering note to Weir), in AIR 1/458/15/312/69 (also in AIR 1/2000/204/273/275).

159. See Trenchard's report on operations in June and July in AIR 1/2000/204/273/275; Wise, *Canadian Airmen*, 295.

160. On these problems, see Trenchard's report on July operations in AIR 1/2000/204/273/275. See also Squadron Leader J. C. Quinnell, "Experiences with a Day Bombing Squadron in the Independent Force, 1918," in *A Selection of Lectures and Essays from the Work of Officers Attending the Second Course at the Royal Air Force Staff College* (Andover), 1923–1924" (London: Air Ministry, 1924); in the former Library of the RAF Staff College, Bracknell, Berkshire; now part of the Joint Services Command and Staff College, Swindon, Wiltshire, United Kingdom.

161. H. A. Jones, *The War in the Air*, 6:163.

162. He attributed the loss of fifteen of his own aircraft to such fighting.

163. "Operations in August," "Operations in September," "Operations in October," all in AIR 1/2000/204/273/275.

164. A record of all industrial targets bombed by the 41st Wing, and the Independent Force (between October 1917 and November 1918) is reprinted in H. A. Jones, *Appendices*, 42–84. See also Wise, *Canadian Airmen*, 301–27; Williams, "Statistics," 327–32.

165. See Groves (DFO) to Sykes (CAS), "I.F., R.A.F. 'Policy,'" (11 September 1918), in AIR 1/460/15/312/97; Cooper, *The Birth of Independent Air Power*, 134–35; and Williams, "Statistics," 330–33.

166. Groves to Sykes, "I.F., R.A.F. 'Policy.'"

167. He put the percentage of attacks on airdromes as 55 percent of total in June, 46 percent in July, and 31 percent in August. Groves allowed that the attacks on railways "have some connection with intended operations by the Allies," but added that "this contention cannot be advanced in defence of a policy carried out over a period of three months" (ibid.).

168. Sykes, *From Many Angles*, 231.

169. "Review of the Air Situation," in ibid., appendix 5.

170. Tiverton to DFO, 4 July 1918, in AIR 1/461/15/312/107.

171. On Tiverton's efforts, see Williams, "Measure by Micrometer," 4–5.

172. Tiverton to Lt. Col. R. H. Mulock, 17 August 1918, in AIR 1/460/15/312/97; Tiverton to SO1, 10 October 1918, in AIR 1/458/15/312/69.

173. McClelland quoted in Williams, "Measure by Micrometer," 11. See also H. A. Jones, *The War in the Air*, 6:146, where the official historian noted laconically that fifty-four aircraft were wrecked "from various causes" on the British side of the lines.

174. Lt. Col. J. Gammell to DFO, 15 October 1918, in AIR 1/461/15/312/107. To make his point, Gammell cited the loss figures for 5th Group, RAF, which had only three aircraft lost on the British side of the lines during August and September. While Gammell allowed that pilots flying longer distances might be more prone to accidents, he still found the numbers telling.

175. Williams, "Statistics," 298. He has calculated that "[b]attle casualties alone [for] the day component of the I.F. amounted to 257 aircrew between

June and November 1918, or 178 percent of total assigned strength at the Armistice. Total losses to these squadrons amounted to 407 flyers, equal to nearly twelve full squadrons." See also Air Commodore H. R. Brooke-Popham, "The Air Force" (lecture delivered to the Royal United Services Institution on 3 December 1919) printed in the *Journal of the Royal United Services Institution* 65, no. 457 (February 1920): 49.

176. Wise, *Canadian Airmen*, 326.

177. Ibid., 321, 324–25. Wise points out that "[t]he success of the German interceptors . . . led to a natural exaggeration of their magnitude by Trenchard and by later commentators." It might be pointed out, as well, that British losses behind *British* lines surely reduced the numbers of aircraft the Germans had to commit to defensive operations.

178. Corum, *The Luftwaffe*, 40.

179. Ibid., 43; Edward B.Westermann, "Sword in the Heavens: German Ground-Based Air Defenses, 1914–1945" (Ph.D. diss., University of North Carolina, Chapel Hill, 2000), 34–50.

180. Wise, *Canadian Airmen*, 325.

181. Trenchard's private diary entry (18 August 1918) quoted in Williams, "Statistics," 350.

182. Williams, "Statistics," 58.

183. Quoted in ibid., 59, also 58.

184. "Moral," *The Spectator*, 11 March 1916, pp. 344–45.

185. Official statements that made their way into the American Expeditionary Force's air intelligence bulletin (titled "Summary of Air Information") habitually emphasized the "moral effect" of bombing. See, for instance,"Summary of Air Information," Air Intelligence Bulletin, GHQAEF Second Section, General Staff, 4 April 1918.

186. "Huns Raid Panic," *Daily Mail* (London), 21 September 1918, copy in AIR 462/15/312/116. The claims about Frankfurt came from a letter taken from a German prisoner of war.

187. "Huns Raid Panic," in AIR 462/15/312/116.

188. Unsigned document, "Remarks for D.F.O.," 18 June 1918, in AIR 1/461/15/312/107. See also Williams, "Statistics," 236–37.

189. In response to a toast in his honor in December 1917, Secretary of State for Air Lord Rothermere said, "It is our duty to avenge the murder of innocent women and children. As the enemy elects, so it will be the case of 'eye for an eye, and a tooth for a tooth,' and in this respect we shall slave for complete and satisfying retaliation" (quoted in Williams, "Statistics," 203). On 25 March 1918, M.P. Sir Henry Norman drew up an elaborate bombing scheme. He envisioned a force that would deliver twenty tons of bombs hourly for ten consecutive hours, so as to bring victory 'in sight' in a month. He was, however, a bit out of step with reality as it had taken the 41st Wing five months to drop forty-eight tons of bombs on German targets. See Williams, "Statistics," 199–203.

190. See Boyle, *Trenchard*, 312; Powers, *Strategy Without Slide Rule*, 158.

191. See, for instance, Groves to Sykes, 12 September 1918, in AIR 1/461/15/312/107.

192. Minute, Gammell to Groves (DFO), 21 September 1918, in AIR 1/462/15/312/116.

193. See Tiverton, "The Possibilities of Long Distance Bombing From the Present Date Until September 1919," 1 October 1918, in AIR 1/460/15/312/101. See also Gammell to Groves, 5 October 1918, in AIR 1/461/15/312/107.

194. In July 1917, orders had been placed with both Handley Page and Vickers for the development of long-range bombers; the following April the Handley Page prototype was close to the testing stage. The first plane crashed in June and set back production. In October, Trenchard was still waiting for his new weapons. See H. A. Jones, *The War in the Air*, 6:174.

195. Trenchard's final dispatch was sent to the Air Board on 12 December 1918, and made public in January 1919 when it was printed in the *London Gazette*. The complete text can be found also in AIR 6/19; portions of it were reprinted in H. A. Jones, *The War in the Air*, 6:136. It is also available in the April 1919 edition of *The New York Times Current History*.

196. Trenchard asserted that a sustained, systematic campaign of material destruction would not have been possible "unless the war had lasted for at least another four or five years" (AIR 6/19).

197. Trenchard's dispatch, 12 December 1918, in AIR 6/19. The passage also appears in H. A. Jones, *The War in the Air*, 6:136.

198. Historian Malcolm Smith has called him "a master of the wholly unfounded statistic" (*British Air Strategy Between the Wars*, 61); also, Cooper, *The Birth of Independent Air Power*, 72.

199. "Signal Corps Specification, No. 486," Air Force Historical Research Center (hereafter referred to as AFHRC), Maxwell Air Force Base, Ala., file 167.6-1 (1907–1940). See also, generally, Alfred Goldberg, *A History of the United States Air Force, 1907–1957* (Princeton: D. Van Nostrand, 1957), 3–5; Gollin, *No Longer an Island*.

200. Between 1908 and 1913, Germany and France spent some $22 million on aviation, while the United States spent about $430,000. In 1911, France had fourteen times as many pilots as did the United States. Not until 1912 were U.S. pilots recognized officially (and given badges) as military aviators, and not until 1914 did statutory legislation put army aviation on a firm footing by formally creating the Aviation Section of the Signal Corps. See John F. Shiner, *Foulois and the U.S. Army Air Corps, 1931–1935* (Washington, D.C.: Office of Air Force History, 1983), 6; Goldberg, *A History of the United States Air Force*, 8.

201. Maurer Maurer, ed., *The U.S. Air Service in World War I*, vol. 2 (Washington, D.C.: Office of Air Force History, 1978), 23. This four-volume set reprints many of the documents produced by the Air Service during and after the war.

202. On the exploits of the First Aero Squadron in Mexico, see "Report of Operations of the First Aero Squadron, Signal Corps, with Punitive Expedition, U.S.A. for Period March 15 to August 14, 1916," reprinted in Maurer, *The U.S. Air Service*, 2:75–87. See also Shiner, *Foulois*, 8, and Goldberg, *A History of the United States Air Force*, 10.

203. Portions of the National Security Act of 1916 are reprinted in Maurer, *The U.S. Air Service*, 2:65.

204. I. B. Holley, *Ideas and Weapons* (New Haven: Yale University Press, 1953; Washington, D.C.: Office of Air Force History, 1983), 133 (page citation is to the more recent edition).

205. The Air Service was comprised of the First Aero Squadron, the Second Aero Squadron (formed December 1915), the Sixth Aero Squadron (formed in March 1917), the Seventh Aero Squadron (formed February 1917), and three other squadrons in various stages of development. See Maurer, *The U.S. Air Service*, 2:101.

206. Memo, Joint Army and Navy Technical Aircraft Board to the Secretary of the War and the Secretary of the Navy, 29 May 1917, reprinted in Maurer, *The U.S. Air Service*, 2:105. See also Robert Frank Futrell, *Ideas, Concepts, Doctrine: A History of Basic Thinking in the United States Air Force 1907–1964* (Maxwell AFB, Ala.: Air University Press, 1971), 10. On the Ribot cable specifically, see Holley, *Ideas and Weapons*, 41–46.

207. Historian John Morrow, Jr., has pointed out that Chief of the Aviation Section of the Signal Corps, Gen. George O. Squier, talked about "winged cavalry sweeping across the German lines and smothering their trenches with a storm of lead, which would put the 'Yankee Punch' into the war." See Morrow, *The Great War in the Air*, 266–68.

208. See Maurer, *The U.S. Air Service*, 2:131; Morrow, *The Great War in the Air*, 268–70; Futrell, *Ideas, Concepts, Doctrine*, 10–11.

209. Portions of the Bolling Report of 15 August are reproduced in Maurer, *The U.S. Air Service*, 2:131–33. See also Holley, *Ideas and Weapons*, 53–62.

210. See the Bolling Report in Maurer, *The U.S. Air Service*, 2:131.

211. "Day bombing," they argued, "presents much greater difficulties than night bombing because it cannot be conducted successfully by slow machines with great bomb carrying capacity, if the enemy have in the air any number of fast fighting machines or have great numbers of anti-aircraft guns effective at great altitudes" (ibid., 2:131–33).

212. Holley, *Ideas and Weapons*, 58–59.

213. See J.L.B. Atkinson, "Italian Influence on the Origins of the American Concept of Strategic Bombardment," *The Air Power Historian* 6, no. 3 (July 1957): 141–49.

214. In March 1917, only twelve firms were capable of producing aircraft for the government, and their total production the year before had been fewer than four hundred planes; see Goldberg, *A History of the United States Air Force*, 15. Also, Holley, *Ideas and Weapons*, esp. chaps. 7 and 8.

215. Futrell, *Ideas, Concepts, Doctrine*, 11; John H. Morrow, Jr., *German Air Power in World War I* (Lincoln: University of Nebraska, 1982), 95–120.

216. Eugene Emme, "The American Dimension," in *Air Power and Warfare: Proceedings of the Eighth Military History Symposium, USAF Academy 1978*, ed. Alfred F. Hurley and Robert C. Ehrhart (Washington, D.C.: Office of Air Force History, 1979), 62; Goldberg, *A History of the United States Air Force*, 18.

217. Futrell, *Ideas, Concepts, Doctrine*, 11; Goldberg, *A History of the United States Air Force*, 15.

218. On Mitchell's early history, see Alfred F. Hurley, *Billy Mitchell: Crusader for Air Power* (Bloomington: Indiana University Press, 1975).

219. Billy Mitchell, *Memoirs of World War I* (New York: Random House, 1960), 104–5. For other descriptions of the Mitchell-Trenchard interaction, see

Boyle, *Trenchard*, 298–301; Wesley Frank Craven and James Lea Cate, *The Army Air Forces in World War II*, vol. 1 (Chicago: University of Chicago, 1948), 12–13 (hereafter cited as CC).

220. "General Orders, No. 46, Headquarters, A.E.F., 10 October 1917," reprinted in Maurer, *The U.S. Air Service*, 2:139. See also Futrell, *Ideas, Concepts, Doctrine*, 12; Morrow, *The Great War in the Air*, 336; Hurley, *Billy Mitchell*, 33–34.

221. Futrell, *Ideas, Concepts, Doctrine*, 12. See also Shiner, *Foulois and the U.S. Army Air Corps*, 9.

222. See "Memorandum for the Chief of Staff, U.S. Expeditionary Forces," from William Mitchell, Aviation Section, Signal Corps, reprinted in Maurer, *The U.S. Air Service*, 2:108.

223. Hurley, *Billy Mitchell*, 32.

224. Mitchell, preface to "General Principles Underlying the Use of the Air Service in the Zone of the Advance, A.E.F." (April 1918), reprinted in Maurer, *The U.S. Air Service*, 2:175.

225. Thomas H. Greer, *The Development of Air Doctrine in the Army Air Arm, 1917–1941* (Washington, D.C.: Office of Air Force History, 1985), 5; Futrell, *Ideas, Concepts, Doctrine*, 12–13.

226. On St. Mihiel, see vol. 3 of Maurer, *The U.S. Air Service*, which is entirely devoted to documentation on the aerial aspects of the battle of St. Mihiel; also, Futrell, *Ideas, Concepts, Doctrine*, 12–13. Morrow, *The Great War in the Air*, 336–38; Greer, *Development of Air Doctrine*, 6; and Hurley, *Billy Mitchell*, 35–37. Mitchell gives his own account in his *Memoirs*, chaps. 30–32.

227. Morrow, *The Great War in the Air*, 338.

228. Elaborate plans to build first, Italian Caproni bombers, and later British Handley-Page bombers were never realized. The United States was unable to produce any long-range bombers in time for use in the war. See Holley, *Ideas and Weapons*, 143–45, 157–58.

229. Gorrell, who graduated from West Point in 1912, had learned to fly in 1915 and served with the 1st Aero Squadron in Mexico the following year. He earned a master's degree in aeronautical engineering from the Massachusetts Institute of Technology, and was in Washington serving as an intelligence officer in the Aeronautical Division when he was selected to join the Bolling Commission. See the introduction to Maurer, *The U.S. Air Service*, 1:4.

230. He also argued that the United States should aim to produce between 3,000 and 6,000 bombers. Gorrell quoted in Holley, *Ideas and Weapons*, 135.

231. Gorrell to Caproni, 31 October 1917, quoted in Atkinson, "Italian Influence," 146. See also Futrell, *Ideas, Concepts, Doctrine*, 13.

232. In November 1917, when General Foulois arrived to take command of the Air Service AEF, he divided the Zone of Advance into "Tactical Aviation" and "Strategical Aviation" branches.

233. Gen. Laurence Kuter, quoted in Maurer, *The U.S. Air Service*, 2:141. The plan itself is reprinted on 141–57.

234. I am indebted to George K. Williams for pointing out this vital connection. In January 1918, Gorrell sent Tiverton a note that read, "I enclose herewith your original notes, which you so kindly sent me, together with two type-

written copies of these notes. Your kindness is sincerely appreciated in sending these to me and your cooperation is very much appreciated." Gorrell to Tiverton, 5 January 1918, Halsbury Papers, AC 73/2, box 2, RAF Museum, Hendon. See also Tiverton's note to Captain Vyvyan, 15 September 1917, in AIR 1/462/15/312/121, in which Tiverton explains that he is offering assistance to the Americans. For a detailed analysis of the Tiverton-Gorrell relationship, see George K. Williams, "'The Shank of the Drill': Americans and Strategical Aviation in the Great War," *The Journal of Strategic Studies* 19, no. 3 (September 1996): 381–431.

235. Gorrell Plan, in Maurer, *The U.S. Air Service*, 2:141–42.

236. Ibid., 2:143.

237. Ibid.

238. Ibid., 2:150.

239. Ibid., 2:142.

240. Maj. E. S. Gorrell, "The Future Role of American Bombardment Aviation," ACTS History, Air Service Field Officer's School, AFHRC, decimal no. 248.222–78. The document, which is undated, was entered into the collections of the Air Service Field Officer's School in 1922. See also Williams, "The Shank of the Drill," 411–23.

241. Gorrell, "The Future Role," 14–15. At the end of the document, Gorrell provided a list of "purposes" aerial bombardment was to serve: "*a*) To cooperate with the ground army on the field of battle; *b*) To attack enemy communications in his rear front; *c*) To carry out strategical bombardment against important targets in his service of the rear; *d*) To keep the enemy's forces fixed in position and to prevent concentration during battle; *e*) To cause dispersion of the enemy's aerial efforts; *f*) To cause dispersion of the enemy's anti-aircraft efforts; *g*) to effect the enemy's morale; *h*) To act as an arm of constant wear upon the enemy; *i*) To act as an arm of intimidation; *j*) If the enemy makes it necessary, to act as an arm of reprisal" (21).

242. Williams, "The Shank of the Drill," 423; see generally 417–23.

243. See extracts from Gorrell's "Early History of the Strategical Section" (written in January 1919 as part of an effort to document the history of the Air Service), reprinted in Maurer, *The U.S. Air Service*, 2:152–53.

244. Williams provided the details of this shift ("Shank of the Drill," 410–11).

245. Memorandum, 18 June 1918, from J. W. McAndrew, Chief of Staff, GHQ, AEF, reprinted in Maurer, *The U.S. Air Service*, 2:192.

246. See Maurer, *The U.S. Air Service*, 2:155.

247. See Maurer's introduction to the "Final Report" in *The U.S. Air Service*, 1:9, and endnote 20. The volume contains a reprinted version of the entire Final Report. See also Williams, "The Shank of the Drill," 410–11.

248. See "Final Report of the Commander-in-Chief, American Expeditionary Forces" (Washington, D.C.: U.S. Government Printing Office, 1919).

249. See Shiner, *Foulois*, 12; Futrell, *Ideas, Concepts, Doctrine*, 15–16.

250. CC 1:16.

251. The team included three intelligence officers and three other ranks under the direction of Major Paul. They worked between December 1918 and Febru-

ary 1919, and their reports can be found in the files of AIR 1. The most thorough examination and analysis of the British bombing survey is in Williams, "Statistics." (The survey is discussed in various places throughout the thesis, but descriptions of the administrative details can be found on pp. 46–48, and 337–38.) A briefer examination of the survey can be found in Wise, *Canadian Airmen*, 321–24.

252. The team was comprised of two officers, three draughtsmen, and a photographer. A leading member was Erskine Childers, author of the thriller, *The Riddle of the Sands*. They were sent to Belgium on 19 November 1918 and returned to Britain on 22 December 1918. The results of this survey can be found in AIR 1/2115/207/56/1.

253. See "Results of Air Raids on Germany Carried out by the 8th Brigade and Independent Force," Air Publication (A.P.) 1225, 3rd ed., Air Ministry, London, January 1920. See also Williams, "Statistics," 340–43.

254. Quoted in Maurer, *The U.S. Air Service*, 4:363–64, introductory section to the "U.S. Bombing Survey." Vol. 4 reprints many of the documents produced in the U.S. Survey, which can be found in original form in "Gorrell's History of the American Expeditionary Forces Air Service 1917–1918," Record Group 120, National Archives and Records Administration (hereafter, NARA), Washington, D.C. The reports on the effects of bombing are in Series R, vol. I and series R, vol. II. See also Williams, "Statistics," 46. The timing of the two surveys did not overlap as the American survey took place from early March to May 1919. Interestingly, the investigators from the two nations did not seem to be aware of each other's efforts.

255. "Chemical and Munitions Factories" report, in AIR 1/1999/204/273/268, p. 1. Later in the same document the authors wrote, "Such damage as was caused was annoying and entailed extra labour, but did not affect the output of the factory in any way" (5).

256. "Blast Furnaces" report, in AIR 1/1999/204/273/269, p. 1. Later in the report the authors made essentially the same point, arguing, "In no case can the material results achieved by any one single raid on a blast furnace be said to have been very striking. Indeed, with one or two exceptions, the amount of material damage wrought had been decidedly disappointing" (p. 15).

257. "Industrial Centres" report in AIR 1/1998/204/273/264; A.P. 1225, 3rd ed., p. 3.

258. They claimed also that "approximately 15 hours of work were lost to the Works" during the month of September ("Blast Furnaces," 12). It is interesting here to note that if the estimate of two to three hours lost per raid was accurate, then one would have expected the hours lost at Völklingen to have been closer to 88 than 15. See AIR 1/1999/204/273/269.

259. AIR 1/1999/204/273/268, p. 1.

260. "Material Effects Resulting From Moral Effects," in AIR 1/1999/204/273/269, pp. 16–17. The foundry at Völklingen was used as an example because "very full statistics" were kept there through the war. Though monetary figures were included in the survey results, they were not provided in a systematic way, and did not give the reader an overall sense of the economic effect of bombing.

261. A.P. 1225, 3rd ed., p. 1.

262. "The General Moral Effect and Its Causes Produced by Day and Night Raids on the B.A.S.F.," in AIR 1/1999/204/273/268.

263. "General Moral Effect," in AIR 1/1999/204/273/269. The report on chemical and munitions factories came to a similar conclusion, pointing out that had the raids been more frequent the results "might have been disastrous." See AIR 1/1999/204/273/268.

264. See "Chemical and Munitions Factories" report, section titled "The General Moral Effect and Its Causes Produced by Day and Night Air Raids on the B.A.S.F." in AIR 1/1999/204/273/268; "Blast Furnaces," report, sections titled "Difficulty of Retaining Employees" and "General Opinion of the Directors as to Our Bombing and the Effect of the Bombing of Blast Furnaces" in AIR 1/1999/204/273/269. See also Williams, "Statistics," 348–50; Wise, *Canadian Airmen*, 322–24.

265. "General Moral Effect," in AIR 1/1999/204/273/269. They pointed out that several factors were crucial if bombing was to achieve a true "moral effect" on the enemy. Attacks, first of all, should be "frequently carried out." Second, they "must be extended over a considerable period, by the end of which the nerves of the male, and more particularly the female, workers begin to feel the strain severely." Finally, they argued that raids must, on at least one occasion, be of a "devastating and terrifying nature," so as to create expectations regarding subsequent raids.

266. See AIR 1/1998/204/273/264.

267. Maj. E. Childers and E.N.G. Morris, 12 March 1919, in AIR 1/2115/207/56/1.

268. See Williams, "Statistics," 340–43. He argues further that A.P. 1225 did "little more than encapsulate and institutionalise the optimistic view of bombing that had been promoted during hostilities" (365). And see generally "Results of Air Raids on Germany," A.P. 1225, 3rd ed.; AIR 1/2104/207/36.

269. Command 100, "Synopsis of British Air Effort During the War," quoted in Williams, "Statistics," 365.

270. See Corum, *The Luftwaffe*, 40–41.

271. H. A. Jones, *The War in the Air*, 6:153.

272. Ibid., 6:154–55. Earlier in the text he argued, "The German people in 1918 were suffering from war weariness, fostered, among other things, by short rations and by Allied propaganda. . . . That is to say, the nerves of the German people, during the time the Independent Force was operating, were at a tension which ensured a maximum moral effect from bombing attacks. The more these were spread, therefore, the greater that effect must be" (138).

273. "Final Report," in Maurer, *The U.S. Air Service*, 1:31; also, 1:17–279. See also, generally, Maurer's introduction (1–14).

274. Information on the U.S. Bombing Survey has been derived from Series R, volumes 1 and 2 of "Gorrell's History of the American Expeditionary Forces, 1917–1919," in "Records of the American Expeditionary Forces (World War I), 1917–1923," record group 120, NARA, Washington, D.C. The reports are also available in reprinted form in Maurer, *The U.S. Air Service*, 4:368–562. Maurer's introduction is quite useful (363–67).

275. See Maurer's introduction, *The U.S. Air Service*, 4:365.

276. See, for instance, the U.S. Survey report on Conflans (in Gorrell's History), which points out that artillery did more damage in the town than aerial bombing (reprinted in Maurer, *The U.S. Air Service*, 4:370).

277. Gorrell's History, U.S. Bombing Survey, Thionville (see ibid., 4:400).

278. Gorrell's History, U.S. Bombing Survey, see, for instance, reports on Metz, Conflans, and Dommary-Baroncourt (ibid., 4:368–73).

279. Gorrell's History, U.S. Bombing Survey, Ludwigshafen (ibid., 4:461–66).

280. Gorrell's History, U.S. Bombing Survey, "Narrative Summary," section titled, "Cost of Protection" (ibid., 4:495–96). Unfortunately, however, the carefully estimated figures offered by the reports were never compared to overall German war expenditures—so the reader did not gain a sense of the comparative significance of these outlays with regard to the German war effort as a whole.

281. See Gorrell's History, U.S. Bombing Survey, Mainz, which stated, "As far as could be gathered from direct questioning the morale of the population was not affected by alarms, but from slips in the conversation and one or two confidential sources it appears that they were quite worried" (ibid., 4:469).

282. Gorrell's History, U.S. Bombing Survey, Coblenz (ibid., 4:481).

283. See for instance, the U.S. Bombing Survey on Burbach, which claimed that "[o]n one occasion . . . when 4 men were killed by a bomb, the women working in an adjacent plant became hysterical and threatened to give up work but were calmed in the course of a day or two." (ibid., 4:440). The report on Völklingen noted, "During the several raids that took place, some of the women employees became hysterical and their lack of control had its effect upon the workmen in the same building" (ibid., 4:444).

284. Gorrell's History, U.S. Bombing Survey, Metz (ibid., 4:369).

285. Gorrell's History, U.S. Bombing Survey, Burbach (ibid., 4:440); U.S. Bombing Survey, Frankfurt (ibid., 4:475). On the issue of worker bonuses generally, see the "Narrative Summary" (ibid., 4:496).

286. U.S. Bombing Survey, Düren (Maurer, *The U.S. Air Service*, 4:486); U.S. Bombing Survey, Thionville (4:402); U.S. Bombing Survey, Ehrang (4:434); U.S. Bombing Survey, Narrative Summary, Moral Effect (4:498).

287. U.S. Bombing Survey, Cologne (ibid., 4:485).

288. U.S. Bombing Survey, Bonn (ibid., 4:482).

289. Gorrell's History, U.S. Bombing Survey, "Narrative Summary" (Maurer, *The U.S. Air Service*, 4:498–99).

290. Gorrell's History, U.S. Bombing Survey, "Narrative Summary," section titled "Criticisms of Bombing in the Present War" (ibid., 4:501–2).

291. Ibid. The statement on British views began, "It might be well to add that in many conversations with officers of the British Independent Air Force there was a growing feeling of dissatisfaction against their bombing policy."

292. Ibid. One might speculate that this officer was Tiverton or Sykes.

293. The "Narrative Summary" makes specific reference to this issue on several occasions, stating at one point, "Too much emphasis cannot be given to the importance of hindering the enemy's military organization" (ibid., 4:501–2).

294. Gorrell's History, U.S. Bombing Survey, "Narrative Summary," section titled "Criticisms of Bombing in the Present War" (ibid., 4:501–2). It is important to point out here that the Americans were not critical of the direct bombing of troops in the field, which they recognized to have an immediate effect on the morale of those troops.

295. U.S. Bombing Survey, "Narrative Summary," section titled "Suggestions for Future Bombing Campaigns." (ibid., 4:502–3).

296. In his "Final Report," the Chief of the Air Service openly acknowledged the debt owed to the British by American aviators. See "Final Report," in Gorrell's History, published in *Air Service Information Circular* 2, no. 180 (15 February 1921) and reprinted in Maurer, *The U.S. Air Service*, 1:17–279.

Chapter 2
Britain in the Interwar Years

1. On the disproportionate weight that is accorded to (1) information that fits in with an actor's prevailing conceptions; (2) information that is derived from firsthand experience; and (3) information that is revealed in the course of a consequential event such as a war, see Robert Jervis, *Perception and Misperception in International Politics* (Princeton: Princeton University Press, 1976), 117–20, 235, 239, 266–68.

2. On the "cult of the offensive," see Jack Snyder, *The Ideology of the Offensive: Military Decision Making and the Disasters of 1914* (Ithaca: Cornell University Press, 1984); Snyder, "Civil-Military Relations and the Cult of the Offensive, 1914 and 1984," and Stephen Van Evera, "The Cult of the Offensive and the Origins of the First World War," both in *International Security* 9, no. 1 (Summer 1984): 58–146; Tim Travers, *The Killing Ground: The British Army, the Western Front and the Emergence of Modern Warfare, 1900–1918* (London: Unwin Hyman, 1987), 37–97; Michael Howard, "Men against Fire: Expectations of War in 1914," *International Security* 9, no. 1 (Summer 1984): 41–57.

3. See also Trenchard's memo for distribution to Corps and Divisional Commanders, with covering note by Lt. Gen. L. E. Kiggell, 9 April 1917, in AIR 1/522/16/12/5, Public Records Office, London; Gen. W. R. Robertson, Chief of the Imperial General Staff (CIGS), "Air Raids and the Bombing of Germany," 6 October 1917, in AIR 9/8. Trenchard's original 1916 memo is reproduced in Maurice Baring, *R.F.C. H.Q., 1914–1918* (London: G. Bell, 1920), 180–84.

4. "Air Superiority," unsigned paper, 1919, in AIR 9/8, p. 4.

5. The literature on cognitive consistency has explanatory power here. See Jervis, *Perception and Misperception*, 193, 203, esp. 221.

6. Trenchard, "Long-Distance Bombing," 26 November 1917, in Trenchard Papers (hereafter TP), MFC 76/1/67, RAF Museum, Hendon, UK; Haig to CIGS (Robertson), 2 October 1917, in AIR 1/522/16/12/5; "Independent Force, Royal Air Force," unsigned and undated document describing the early history of the IF, in AIR 9/6. (The document, the authors note, is based on a GHQ file on bombing policy, 1721/11G, 17 July 1917 to 31 March 1918.)

7. Trenchard to Weir, 1 May 1918, in TP, MFC 76/1/20, c I 17; H. A. Jones, *The War in the Air* (Oxford: Oxford University Press, 1922), 6:170–73; WF (see note 1 of Introduction), 1:43. Jones argued that Trenchard was reluctant to take aircraft away from the other services in part because he could not foresee exactly what type of fighter would be required by the force.

8. Trenchard to Sykes, 4 August 1918, in AIR 1/460/15/312/100.

9. [Tiverton?] memo, F.O.3 section, Air Staff, 8 August 1918, in AIR 1/460/15/312/100.

10. J. M. Spaight, *The Sky's the Limit* (London: Hodder and Stoughton, 1940), 18.

11. "Air Power and National Security," Air Staff, January 1921, copy in TP, MFC 76/1/21; Air Staff Memorandum No. 11A, March 1924, in AIR 9/8, PRO.

12. T. H. O'Brien, *Civil Defence* (London: HMSO, 1955), 11; Raymond Fredette, *The Sky on Fire: The First Battle of Britain, 1917–1918* (New York: Holt, Rinehart & Winston, 1966), 186, 212–13.

13. Wing Commander J.E.A. Baldwin, "Experiences of Bombing with the Independent Force in 1918," in "A Selection of Essays from the Work of Officers attending the First Course at the Royal Air Force Staff College, 1922–1923," pp. 4–5, 7–8, Air Publication 956, Air Ministry, December 1923, at the Library of the RAF Staff College, Bracknell, Berkshire, UK; now part of the Joint Services Command and Staff College, Swindon, Wiltshire, UK.

14. Air Commodore H.R.M. Brooke-Popham, "The Air Force," delivered to the Royal United Services Institution on 3 December 1919, and published in *The Journal of the Royal United Services Institution* 65, no. 457 (February 1920). See p. 55.

15. Commandant's lecture, "Air Warfare," RAF Staff College, 1924, in AIR 1/2385/228/10.

16. Minute by Trenchard (25 July 1923), quoted in John Ferris in "Fighter Defence Before Fighter Command: The Rise of Strategic Air Defence in Great Britain, 1917–1934," *The Journal of Military History* 63, no. 4 (October 1999): 848.

17. See Robert Jervis, "Deterrence and Perception," *International Security* 7, no. 3 (winter 1982–1983): 15–16.

18. See Jervis, *Perception and Misperception*, 186–191; Richard Ned Lebow, *Between Peace and War: The Nature of International Crises* (Baltimore: Johns Hopkins University Press, 1981), 103–7.

19. During the war there were 103 air raids against Britain (51 by zeppelin and 52 by aircraft); they caused 4,820 casualties (including 1,413 deaths). The June and July Gotha attacks on London caused 832 casualties (including 216 deaths). See O'Brien, *Civil Defence*, 11.

20. Fredette, *The Sky on Fire*, 196, 218; James Corum, *The Luftwaffe: Creating the Operational Air War, 1918–1940* (Lawrence: University Press of Kansas, 1997), 36. See also Barry Powers, *Strategy Without Slide Rule* (London: Croom Helm, 1976), 74.

21. For the best and most detailed examination of this topic, see Ferris, "Fighter Defence Before Fighter Command."

22. Richard Titmuss has criticized these estimates on a host of statistical grounds. See his *Problems of Social Policy* (London: HMSO, 1950), 12–13, esp. note 1, for the history of the multiplier and its flaws. See also O' Brien, *Civil Defence*, 13; Fredette, *The Sky on Fire*, 232–33.

23. Trenchard might have used the word "psychological" in his own rhetoric, but, as he explained later in his career, he shied away from the word as he had difficulty spelling it. See Trenchard's comments at the conclusion of a lecture by Dr. E. B. Strauss on "The Psychological Effects of Bombing," reprinted in the *Journal of the Royal United Services Institution* 534 (May 1939): 282.

24. Memo of September 1916 reprinted in Maurice Baring, *R.F.C.H.Q., 1914–1918* (London: G. Bell, 1920), 180–84. See also Trenchard's 26 November 1917 paper called "Strategic and Tactical Considerations Involved in Long Distance Bombing," in AIR 1/725/97/7, in which it was stated that long-distance bombing "is indeed only an expansion of operations which have been going on . . . daily and nightly under the Royal Flying Corps on the Western Front." See also Neville Jones, *The Origins of Strategic Bombing* (London: William Kimber, 1973), 162–163; Michael Paris, *Winged Warfare* (New York: Manchester University Press, 1992), 242–43.

25. See Air Publication 302, "Fighting in the Air," (March) 1917 ed., London, issued by the General Staff. Copy at the RAF Museum, Hendon. For a similar sentiment, see Air Publication 159, "Notes on Observation from Aeroplanes," (April) 1918, London. Copies of both documents are at the RAF Museum, Hendon.

26. Maj. Stewart L. Murray, *The Peace of the Anglo-Saxons* (London: Watts, 1905), 34; Sir Frederick Sykes, "Review of Air Situation and Strategy for the Information of the Imperial War Cabinet," 27 June 1918, in AIR 9/8. It is reprinted as Appendix V in Sykes's memoir, *From Many Angles* (London: Harrap, 1942).

27. Trenchard stated, "It will be remembered that, owing to the great popular outcry, it was considered necessary to start an Air Force." See "Why the Royal Air Force Should be Maintained as separate from the Navy and Army," 11 September 1919, in TP, MFC 76/1/21.

28. See Brock Millman, "British Home Defence Planning and Civil Dissent, 1917–1918," *War in History* 5, no. 2 (April 1998): 220; Lloyd George, *War Memoirs* (London: Ivor Nicholson and Watson, 1934), 4:1925–63; Bernard Waites, *A Class Society at War* (Providence, R.I.: Berg, 1987), 225–30.

29. Winston Churchill, "Memorandum of Protection from Air Raids," 5 October 1917, quoted in Powers, *Strategy Without Slide Rule*, 60, also 61; Waites, *A Class Society at War*, 225–30.

30. Waites, *A Class Society at War*, 59, 191–93, 207, 231; Powers, *Strategy Without Slide Rule*, 58; Titmuss, *Problems of Social Policy*, 12–13, note 1.

31. Powers, *Strategy Without Slide Rule*, 62; Charles Stienon, "The Zeppelin Raids and Their Effect on England," 333–38.

32. Churchill, "Munitions Possibilities of 1918," 21 October 1917, extract printed as Appendix IV in H. A. Jones, *The War in the Air: Appendices* (Oxford: Oxford University Press, 1937), 19; see also 18–21.

33. Brooke-Popham, "The Air Force," 55.

34. "Air Power and National Security," Air Staff, January 1921, in TP, MFC 76/1/21.

35. See, for instance, "The Responsibility of the Royal Air Force of the Future in the Defence of These Islands Against Invasion," Air Staff, May 1921, and "Air as the Primary Medium of War with Particular Reference to the British Isles," Air Staff, May 1921; both in TP, MFC 76/1/21.

36. Air Raid Precautions committee conclusions quoted in Titmuss, *Problems of Social Policy*, 18.

37. See Titmuss, *Problems of Social Policy*, 18.

38. Neville Jones makes a number of similar arguments in his critique of the Air Staff in *The Beginnings of Strategic Air Power, 1923–1939* (London: Frank Cass, 1987), 34.

39. Ferris has made the argument that Trenchard was so fully able to dominate RAF strategy in part because other senior officers were not forceful. See John Ferris, *The Evolution of British Strategic Policy, 1919–1926* (London: Macmillan, 1989), 7. Trenchard himself admitted in 1919 that "many good officers have left [the RAF] owing to the uncertainty as to the future of the Air Force." See "Memorandum on Why the Royal Air Force Should be Maintained as Separate from the Navy and the Army," 11 September 1919, in TP, MFC 76/1/21. Also, N. Jones, *The Beginnings of Strategic Air Power*, 22–28; Powers, *Strategy Without Slide Rule*, 164–67; Malcolm Smith, *British Air Strategy Between the Wars* (Oxford: Clarendon, 1984), 19–28; and, though it is not quite as helpful here as one might hope, Andrew Boyle, *Trenchard* (New York: W. W. Norton, 1962), 324–34. Trenchard's own (albeit after the fact) explanation of events can be found in "A Memorandum by Marshal of the R.A.F the Viscount Lord Trenchard," [1947] in AIR 1/1999/204/273/270. He argues that he accepted Churchill's offer to become CAS because he felt that allowing the RAF to be divided up by the army and navy would be a "retrograde step." He believed that air power would develop better on its own than it would under the aegis of Britain's dominant service, the navy.

40. Malcolm Smith has written that "Trenchard's extraordinary personality was, without doubt, one of the greatest assets of the RAF in the fight for survival, once he had become converted to the idea of a separate Air Ministry" (*British Air Strategy*, 23). See also Powers, *Strategy Without Slide Rule*, 164–67.

41. Ferris, *Strategic Policy*, 67–68, 83.

42. "Memorandum on the Status of the Royal Air Force by the Chief of Air Staff," 20 July 1919, in TP, MFC 76/1/21.

43. See Ferris, *Strategic Policy*, 4, 17–18, 20–21. Ferris argues that though some scholars date the "Ten Year Rule" from 1919, this is incorrect since it was never really enforced for the Navy and the RAF before 1925, and since the phrase itself was not used until 1926 (and was not used regularly until after it was revoked).

44. See Ferris, *Strategic Policy*, 63–68, 73–74, 85–87. Also, Smith, *British Air Strategy*, 28–31; and Powers, *Strategy Without Slide Rule*, 170–74. Book-length accounts of the policy have been produced by Philip Towle, *Pilots and Rebels* (London: Brassey's, 1989) and David Omissi, *Air Power and Colonial Control* (New York: St. Martin's, 1990).

45. For RAF defenses of air control, see "Memorandum by the Air Staff on the Effects Likely to be Produced by Intensive Aerial Bombing of Semi-Civilized People," n.d. [1922], in TP, MFC 76/1/21; "Aircraft in Frontier Warfare," [1922?], AIR 9/6; Squadron Leader John Slessor "Air Control. The Other Point of View," May 1931, in AIR 69/9.

46. During its first year of operation in Iraq for instance, air control reduced British expenditures in the region from 20.1 million pounds to 6.6 million pounds—and by the sixth year in Iraq, expenses were as low as 1.65 million pounds. See Powers, *Strategy Without Slide Rule*, 173.

47. Richard R. Muller, "Close Air Support: The German, British, and American Experiences, 1918–1941" in *Military Innovation in the Interwar Period*, ed. Williamson Murray and Allen Millett (New York: Cambridge University Press, 1996), 171.

48. "Air Staff Memorandum on the Policy Which Should Govern the Distribution of Air Forces and Some Considerations as to How They Should be Employed," April 1920, in AIR 9/8; "Aircraft in Frontier Warfare," n.d. [1922], in AIR 9/6.

49. "Development and Employment of the Heavy Bomber Force," 22 September 1941, Papers of Lord Portal (hereafter PP), folder 2c., Christ Church Library, Oxford.

50. Ferris, *Strategic Policy*, 74–76, 83–86.

51. On these debates, see Ferris, *Strategic Policy*, 84–85, 89–91; Powers, *Strategy Without Slide Rule*, 178–82; Boyle, *Trenchard*, 396–98; Stephen Roskill, *Naval Policy Between the Wars, Vol. I, The Period of Anglo-American Antagonism, 1919–1929* (London: Collins, 1968), 264–68.

52. David Edgerton, *England and the Aeroplane* (London: Macmillan, 1991), 41–43.

53. Ibid., 47; see also 13, 47–49.

54. Lloyd George quoted in Ferris, *Strategic Policy*, 127; see, generally pp. 107–9, 126–32. See also Ferris, "The Theory of a French Air Menace: Anglo-French Relations and the British Home Defence Air Force Programmes, 1921–1925," *The Journal of Strategic Studies* 10 (1987): 62–83; Neil Young, "British Home Defence Planning in the 1920s," *The Journal of Strategic Studies* 11, no. 4 (1988): esp. 494–97.

55. Memo by Air Staff for the Committee on Imperial Defence, 8 November 1921, in TP, MFC 76/1/21.

56. See Ferris, *Strategic Policy*, 129–32; Young, "British Home Defence Planning," 498.

57. See "The RAF in the Bombing Offensive Against Germany, Prewar Evolution of Bomber Command, 1917–1939," in AIR 41/39, pp. 25–27; WF, vol. 4, Appendix 1 (Minutes of a Conference held in the room of the Chief of the Air Staff, Air Ministry, on 19 July 1923), 66, 1:54–56. Also, N. Jones, *The Beginnings of Strategic Air Power*, 28–30.

58. Ferris, "Fighter Defence Before Fighter Command: The Rise of Strategic Air Defence," 848–52; on Bullock, see 851.

59. See Ferris, "Fighter Defence," 852; AIR 41/39, p. 27.

60. Trenchard quoted in Ferris, "Fighter Defence," 851.

61. Ferris, "Fighter Defence," 855.

62. See War Office Staff Exercise, Buxton (9–13 April 1923), 2nd Conference, Address by Chief of the Air Staff, with covering note from Air Commodore Brooke-Popham, 2 May 1923, in AIR 9/8.

63. Air Staff Memorandum No. 11A, March 1924, AIR 9/8, PRO.

64. An eleven-fold increase in the national debt between 1914 and 1918 meant that by the late 1920s, interest payments alone consumed some 40 percent of central government spending. See Paul Kennedy, *The Realities Behind Diplomacy* (Glasgow: Fontana, 1981), 228.

65. Ferris, *Strategic Policy*, 170–72.

66. Ferris, "Fighter Defence," 862.

67. The former, for instance, could carry only four 112-pound or two 230-pound bombs to targets within 250 miles of its base. See AIR 41/39, pp. 35–38, 42.

68. Churchill quoted in AIR 41/39, p. 43.

69. See John Ferris, "'The Greatest Power on Earth': Great Britain in the 1920s," *The International History Review* 13, no. 4 (November 1991): 730.

70. Edgerton, *England and the Aeroplane*, 22, 35.

71. Ibid., 22, 25, 37.

72. See N. Jones, *The Beginnings of Strategic Air Power*, 55.

73. The shortcomings of navigational training in the interwar RAF are discussed in detail in WF, 1:60–61 and 1:110–14; N. Jones, *The Beginnings of Strategic Air Power*, 59–64; Sir John Slessor, *The Central Blue* (London: Cassell, 1956), 205–6; and Flight Lt. Alec Ayliffe, "RAF Navigation Between the Wars," in *A History of Navigation in the Royal Air Force* (Brighton: Royal Air Force Historical Society, 1997), 12–33.

74. AIR 41/39, pp. 41–42; N. Jones, *The Beginnings of Strategic Air Power*, 63–65.

75. Ferris, "Fighter Defence," 876. Other commentaries on these exercises include: Scot Robertson, *The Development of RAF Strategic Bombing Doctrine, 1919–1939*" (Westport, Conn.: Praeger, 1995), 96–108; Smith, *British Air Strategy*, 72; Maj. C. C. Turner, "British and Foreign Air Exercises of 1931," *Journal of the Royal United Services Institution*, 76, no. 504 (November 1931): 731–43; Maj. F. A. de V. Robertson, "Air Exercises, 1932," *Journal of the Royal United Services Institution*, 77, no. 508 (November 1932): 808–814.

76. See S. Robertson, *RAF Strategic Bombing Doctrine*, 98, 108. See also Scot Robertson's, "On a Wing and a Prayer: The Development of RAF Strategic Bombing Doctrine, 1919–1939," (doctoral thesis, University of New Brunswick, Canada, 1989), 193–94.

77. Yool quoted in S. Robertson, *RAF Strategic Bombing Doctrine*, 184. See also Smith, *British Air Strategy*, 72.

78. Turner, "British and Foreign Air Exercises," 731, 733–34.

79. Ferris, "Fighter Defence," 880.

80. Ibid., 879.

81. Slessor, *The Central Blue*, 204.

82. On interwar amateurism see generally Brian Bond, *British Military Policy Between the Two World Wars* (Oxford: Clarendon, 1980), esp. chapter 2. On

the impact of culture on British interwar military thinking, see Elizabeth Kier, *Imagining War* (Princeton: Princeton University Press, 1997) 89–139. Kier, however, tends to overstate cultural distinctions between the Army and the RAF, giving the RAF more credit than it deserved for encouraging "individuality" and "freedom of thought" (130).

83. Shelford Bidwell and Dominick Graham have documented this trend toward amateurism in the interwar Royal Artillery. They argued that *The Journal of the Royal Artillery*, which, right after World War I had been filled with technical articles, disintegrated into "a sort of house magazine rather than a serious professional journal, with articles on pig-sticking, shooting, and even a motoring holiday in Spain." See Shelford Bidwell and Dominick Graham, *Firepower* (Boston: Allen and Unwin, 1985), 157–58.

84. Slessor, *The Central Blue*, 84; see 82–85 generally.

85. "Operations Record Book (RAF Form 540), the former Library of the RAF Staff College Library, now part of the Joint Services Command and Staff College. See also, Maj. F. A. de V. Robertson, "The Royal Air Force Staff College," *Flight*, 20 July 1933.

86. See Allan D. English, "The RAF Staff College and the Evolution of RAF Strategic Bombing Policy, 1922–1929," (master's thesis, Royal Military College, Canada, 1987), 51–58, esp. 57. See also his article of the same title in *The Journal of Strategic Studies* 16, no. 3 (September 1993): 419–23, esp. 421. Subsequent citations will refer to the journal article.

87. See English, "The RAF Staff College," 423, and generally, 411–12, 419–23. See also "Notes for the Use of Officers Attending Courses," RAF Staff College, 1924, in the RAF Museum Library.

88. Slessor, *The Central Blue*, 82. Indeed, the fences for the drag hunt were made deliberately difficult so as to provoke many "traditional forced landings" among many of the participants—evidently much to the delight of gathered onlookers, referred to as "ghouls." See *The Hawk*, 1930 and 1931, articles titled, "Camberly Week." A complete set of *The Hawk* can be found at the RAF Museum.

89. Commandant's lecture, "Air Warfare," RAF Staff College, [1921], in AIR 1/2385/228/10, pp. 1–2.

90. E. Ludlow-Hewitt, "Air Warfare," lecture to the 6th course, RAF Staff College (February 1928), in the papers of Sir Arthur Tedder, Box B270 (2 of 2), the RAF Museum archive, Hendon, U.K.

91. H. A. Jones, *The War in the Air*, 6:431.

92. Ludlow-Hewitt, "Air Warfare," section VII, "Direct Air Action" (1928).

93. Trenchard, "Memorandum by the Chief of the Air Staff for the Chiefs of Staff Sub-Committee on The War Object of An Air Force," 2 May 1928, reproduced in WF, 4:71–76, esp. 72–73.

94. Ibid., 4:73.

95. Ibid., 4:75. The RAF War Manual, published less than two months later, conveyed a similar idea: "A single air raid on such vital centres may bring work to a standstill over a large area during the whole period of the raid and prolonged attack consisting of air raids at short intervals may be expected to result in such dislocation and confusion as a consequence of the continual stoppage of

work and the strain on the workers, that supplies essential to the successful continuance of operations will not be forthcoming." See RAF War Manual, Part I, Operations, chap. 8, para. 15 (Air Publication 1300), July 1928, Air Historical Branch, Ministry of Defence, London.

96. Air Vice-Marshal Sir John Slessor (Commander, No. 5 Group, RAF), memo, 28 October 1941, p. 3, in Papers of Sir John Slessor, file XII D, Bomber Policy 1935/45, Air Historical Branch, Ministry of Defence, London. (The Slessor Papers have since been moved to the Public Record Office.)

97. In the 1928 RAF Staff College entrance exam, one examiner pointed out that, while London was a more exposed target for air attack than Paris, "the English [were] more stubborn and have a less imaginative temperament than the French, and are therefore less susceptible to bombing." See English, "The RAF Staff College," 421.

98. RAF War Manual, Part I, Operations, chap. 1, para. 6.

99. RAF War Manual, Part I, Operations, chap. 8, paras. 24–26.

100. Trenchard, "Memorandum by the CAS to the Chiefs of Staff Subcommittee," May 1928, in WF, 4:75.

101. These critiques of Trenchard's May 1928 Memorandum are reprinted in WF, Appendix 2, 4:76–83.

102. See Trenchard's May 1928 Memorandum in WF, Appendix 2, 4:73–74.

103. Ibid., 4:74.

104. Ibid., 4:81–82.

105. "An Address given by the Chief of the Air Staff to the Imperial Defence College on the War Aim of the Air Force," October 1928, in AIR 2/675.

106. Ibid., 4.

107. In explaining this point, the CAS wrote, "Defence in the air requires an altogether disproportionate strength and as the defence is found to be inadequate, the outcry for better and more defence, growing in strength, forces the high command to hold back still more of its units. Gradually by this process one air force comes to be thrown on to the defensive altogether" (ibid., 6).

108. Ibid., 5.

109. See *The Hawk* (the RAF Staff College journal and yearbook), December 1930, 10–11.

110. P. B. Joubert de la Ferte, "The Employment of Air Forces in War," 28 October 1932, in AIR 69/13.

111. H. A. Jones interview with Lord Trenchard, 11 April 1934, in AIR 8/67. In an address to the newly opened RAF Staff College (1922), Trenchard argued that students must be given opportunities to hone their abilities to state a case "clearly and concisely." He pointed out, "In my early days no such opportunities occurred, or perhaps I failed to see them . . . and at the various meetings I attend now I sometimes feel a difficulty in doing justice to ideas that come to me from my staff that in themselves merit the clearest and most concise exposition" (TP, MFC 76/1/21). See also the "Afterword" by Sir John Slessor in Fredette's *The Sky on Fire*, 253.

112. Sir Maurice Dean quoted in John Terraine, "Theory and Practice of Air War: The Royal Air Force," in *The Conduct of the Air War in the Second World War: An International Comparison*, ed. Horst Boog (Providence, R.I.: Berg,

1992), 469. Terraine himself wrote, "It may be said, without straining verity, that bombing was what the RAF was all about. . . . [B]ombing was what the RAF understood by air warfare, and bombing was what it intended to perform. It is chiefly for that reason . . . that cooperating with the Army and the Navy went right out of fashion between the wars" (470).

113. On the 1939 exercise, see Lee Kennett, "Developments to 1939," in *Case Studies in the Development of Close Air Support* (Washington, D.C.: Office of Air Force History, 1990), 28.

114. Muller, "Close Air Support, 151–52, 164–65.

115. Ibid., 167.

116. Sir John Slessor, *Air Power and Armies* (Oxford: Oxford University Press, 1936).

117. Liddell Hart quoted in S. F. Wise, *Canadian Airmen and the First World War*, vol. 1 of *Official History of the Royal Canadian Air Force* (Toronto: University of Toronto Press, 1980), 575. Wise argues that the ground support role "disappeared quickly and completely from the corpus of doctrine upon which RAF procurement and training was based." Also, Muller, "Close Air Support," 169.

118. Interestingly, J. M. Spaight's 1930 book, *Air Power and the Cities* (London: Longmans, Green), argued that naval bombardments had, in general, been as discriminate as possible. Spaight, who was considered sympathetic to the RAF, made the argument that the air service ought to try to achieve the same standard.

119. Unsigned article, "Bombs Cause Resentment," in *The Hawk*, December 1930, 26–27. See also unsigned article, "Some Aspects of International Law in Air Warfare," in *The Hawk*, December 1930, 37–46. It was standard for contributors to *The Hawk* to remain unidentified.

120. Air Vice-Marshal T. Webb-Bowen, "An Appreciation on the Employment of the Air Defence of Great Britain Bomber Formations Against the Western European Confederation During the First Month of Operations," March 1933, in AIR 2/675, pp. 2, 7.

121. Webb-Bowen explained, "Having examined closely all the available targets, I came to the conclusion that it would be quite impossible to achieve the aim by considering material damage alone. That would imply continuous and sustained attack on one object after another until each was thoroughly destroyed. With scattered objectives and a small force . . . the time which would be taken to break down any particular service essential to the continued existence of the nation, would be altogether excessive. I decided that the aim must be achieved by exerting moral pressure on the enemy." See "Remarks by Air Vice-Marshal Sir Tom Webb-Bowen ('A' Syndicate) at the Final Conference on 15.3.33," in AIR 2/675, p. 1.

122. P. B. Joubert de la Ferte, *The Aim of the Royal Air Force*, May 1933, in AIR 2/675.

123. Ibid., 2.

124. Ibid.

125. Ibid.

126. Ibid., 12.

127. Ibid., 10.

128. Portal to DCAS, Minute, 2 August 1933, in AIR 2/675.

129. He stated at the top of his memo: "This file, which has been dormant for some time, deals with the 'War Aim of the R.A.F.' and contains various complaints and criticisms to the effect that the definition of the Aim which was originally agreed to by the Chiefs of Staff is nowhere clearly and concisely explained, although it is referred to in various places in the War Manual, Part I" (Memo from Group Captain A. T. Harris to D.D.O.I., 1 March 1935, in AIR 2/675).

130. Unsigned draft, *The War Aim of the Royal Air Force*, 15 November 1935, in AIR 2/675, p. 1.

131. Ibid., 9.

132. Slessor, *Air Power and Armies*, 65–66.

133. Of British public opinion in the 1920s, John Ferris made an observation that might apply equally to the 1930s. "British public opinion," he wrote, "remained contradictory and unpredictable: simultaneously able to support the most pacific and aggressive of international actions; and to favour the maintenance of British prestige and Wilsonian internationalism, the strongest navy on earth and reduced spending on the armed forces." See Ferris, " 'The Greatest Power on Earth,' " 735.

134. On air disarmament and British policy see Uri Bialer's important study *The Shadow of the Bomber* (London: Royal Historical Society, 1980). Bialer wrote: "Failure to substantiate Britain's adherence to the cause of disarmament, by securing a binding convention, was considered to be an eventuality pregnant with grave domestic political consequences" (9). See also AIR 41/39, pp. 32–36.

135. Admiralty Memorandum (April 1932) quoted in Bialer, *The Shadow of the Bomber*, 24.

136. The quotation is from a letter from Harris to Portal, 30 October 1932, in AIR 9/34. I thank John Ferris for making the document available to me.

137. On the bomber ban issue, see generally Phillip S. Meilinger, "Clipping the Bomber's Wings: The Geneva Disarmament Conference and the Royal Air Force, 1932–1934, *War in History* 6, no. 3 (1999): 306–30.

138. P.R.C. Groves, *Behind the Smoke Screen* (London: Faber and Faber, 1934), 29.

139. Groves, "The New Warfare" and "England Without a Defence," *The Times* (London), 21 March and 24 April 1922. They were reprinted in *Our Future in the Air: A Survey of the Question of British Air Power* (London: Hutchinson, 1922). Excerpts of the articles were printed in Eugene Emme, ed., *The Impact of Air Power* (Princeton: Van Nostrand, 1959), 176–81.

140. See Groves's *Times* (London) articles are reprinted in Emme, *The Impact of Air Power*, 177–79.

141. Barry Powers has written, "Each year the House of Commons had its seizure of air power bombast when the Air Service budget requirements were presented" (*Strategy Without Slide Rule*, 138).

142. See ibid., 107–57.

143. B. H. Liddell Hart, *Paris, or the Future of War* (New York: E. P. Dutton, 1925; reprint, New York: Garland, 1972), 28–29. He argued further, "The liv-

ing alone retain the power to admit defeat, and since wars, therefore, are ended by surrender and not by extermination, it becomes apparent that defeat is the result not of loss of life . . . but by loss of moral" (31).

144. Ibid., 36–37.

145. Liddell Hart, *Paris*, 39.

146. Ibid., 39–40.

147. Ibid., 41–42. Reading recommendations for RAF officers were listed in Squadron Leader R. Graham, "Some Notes on Preparing for the Staff College," *R.A.F. Quarterly* 1, no. 1 (1930).

148. I. F. Clarke, *Voices Prophesying War, 1763–1984* (New York: Oxford University Press, 1966), 164–65.

149. The Committee was a subcommittee of the CID, working under the direction of the Home Office. For details about its workings, see O'Brien, *Civil Defence*, 14–15.

150. See O'Brien, 15–25; the quotes appear on 16 and 19. See also Powers, who provides a summary, in *Strategy Without Slide Rule*, 120–24.

151. See N. Jones, *The Beginnings of Strategic Air Power*, 37–41.

152. Lawrence quoted in Powers, *Strategy Without Slide Rule*, 150–51.

153. I. F. Clarke, *Voices Prophesying War*, 169–70.

154. For some overviews of Douhet in English from this period, see unsigned article, "The Air Doctrine of General Douhet," *The Royal Air Force Quarterly* 4, no. 2 (April 1933): 164–67; "General Giulio Douhet—An Italian Apostle of Air Power" and "Air Warfare—The Principles of Air Warfare by General Giulio Douhet," *The Royal Air Force Quarterly* 7, no. 2 (April 1936): 148–51, 152–68. For recent authoritative accounts of Douhet's thought, see Azar Gat, "Futurism, Proto-fascist Italian Culture and the Sources of Douhetism," *War and Society* 15, no. 1 (May 1997): 31–51; *Fascist and Liberal Visions of War* (Oxford: Clarendon Press, 1998), 43–79.

155. Gat, "Futurism," 39.

156. See, for instance, Slessor to Liddell Hart, 31 October 1947, and Liddell Hart to Slessor, 12 November 1947, Liddell Hart Papers, folder L.H. 1/644, Centre for Military Archives, King's College, London.

157. Douhet asserted that "when the working personnel of a factory sees one of its machine shops destroyed, even with a minimum loss of life, it quickly breaks up and the plant ceases to function." See Douhet's *Command of the Air*, trans. Dino Ferrari (Coward-McCann, 1942; reprint, Washington, D.C.: Office of Air Force History, 1983), 22–23.

158. Douhet, *Command of the Air*, 10.

159. Michael Sherry, *The Rise of American Air Power* (New Haven: Yale University Press, 1987). In a perceptive critique of the interwar air prophets, he has written, "They could not really imagine a future except one crudely extrapolated from contemporary experience. Dismissing most of the war's record, they simplistically assumed that bomb damage . . . would be a simple multiple of previous experience: a tenfold increase in bomb tonnage yielding ten times the panic and dislocation" (27).

160. Maj. F. A. de V. Robertson, "Air Exercises, 1932," *Journal of the Royal United Services Institution*, 77, no. 508 (November 1932): 808.

161. House of Commons Debates, 10 November 1932, vol. 270, col. 632. See also, Bialer, *The Shadow of the Bomber*, 21.

162. Baldwin quoted in Overy, "Air Power and Deterrence Theory Before 1939," *The Journal of Strategic Studies* 15, no. 1 (March 1992): 79.

163. Bialer, *The Shadow of the Bomber*, 28–31.

164. Ibid., 32–40. The remainder of *The Shadow of the Bomber* (41–160) covers British efforts through 1939. A sense of the sincerity of British efforts in the early 1930s can be discovered in the documents relating to the Conference, in AIR 8/173. For other descriptions of these events, see AIR 41/39, pp. 251–54; Smith, *British Air Strategy*, 112–21; Kennett, *A History of Strategic Bombing*, 58–71.

165. L.E.O. Charlton, *War From the Air* (London: Thomas Nelson, 1935), 166.

166. Ibid., 170–71.

167. Ibid., 173. As urban historian Joseph Konvitz has written, "Predictions of air raids on cities exploited contemporary concerns about the nature and behavior of crowds in the modern city. . . . It seems as if strategists, reacting to contemporary anxieties about class conflict and antisocial behavior in cities, projected fears about cities into a theory of air war." See Joseph Konvitz, "Cities as Targets: Conceptions of Strategic Bombing, 1914–1945," paper no. 85, December 1987, Woodrow Wilson International Center for Scholars, Washington, D.C., p. 5.

168. Frank Morison, *War on Great Cities* (London: Faber and Faber, 1937), 181–83, 194–206.

169. Research on high explosive or incendiary bombs had suffered due to efforts at economy; see Titmuss, *Problems of Social Policy*, 6–7. For further detail, see O'Brien, *Civil Defence*, 52–60.

170. Titmuss, *Problems of Social Policy*, 9.

171. See O'Brien, *Civil Defence*, 53; Titmuss, *Problems of Social Policy*, 14. In raids on Barcelona, the figure cited was 3,000 casualties for forty-two tons of bombs. Of this number, 1,000 were killed and the remainder injured (the latter number was divided arbitrarily by the Air Raid Precautions Dept. into "slightly" and "badly" injured). Thus it was estimated that for every ton of bombs, twenty-four persons would be killed, twenty-four would be badly injured, and another twenty-four slightly injured.

172. See Report by the Advisory Committee on London Casualty Organization, 20 July 1938, in Ministry of Health (MH) 76/128, Public Records Office, London.

173. Titmuss, *Problems of Social Policy*, 19–21. The government had, in general, however, recognized that there would not be enough personnel available for such crowd control duties, and the discipline of civilians would have to hold without the aid of uniformed officers.

174. Ibid., 19–21.

175. See John Rickman, M.D., "Mental Aspects of A.R.P.," and Dr. Maurice B. Wright, "Psychological Emergencies in Wartime," in *War Wounds and Air Raid Casualties* [articles reprinted from the *British Medical Journal*] (London: H. K. Lewis, 1939).

176. Many bomber squadrons were equipped with the same light, single-engined machines given to the two-seater fighter squadrons. See AIR 41/39, pp. 35–36.

177. To understand rearmament one must understand how the British services perceived the German threat. See Wesley K. Wark, *The Ultimate Enemy: British Intelligence and Nazi Germany, 1933–1939* (Ithaca: Cornell University Press, 1985). See generally 35–79.

178. For an authoritative overview of British aircraft production during the interwar and early wartime years, see Sebastian Ritchie, *Industry and Air Power* (London: Frank Cass, 1997).

179. Smith, *British Air Strategy*, 110. See Smith generally on rearmament, as well as Williamson Murray, *The Change in the European Balance of Power, 1938–1939* (Princeton: Princeton University Press, 1984); G. C. Peden, *The Treasury and British Rearmament, 1932–1939* (Edinburgh: Scottish Academic Press, 1979); Robert Paul Shay, Jr., *British Rearmament in the Thirties* (Princeton: Princeton University Press, 1977); N. Gibbs, *Grand Stategy*, vol. 1, *Rearmament Policy* (London: HMSO, 1976); and N. Jones, *The Beginnings of Strategic Air Power*, 71–149.

180. See Slessor, *The Central Blue*, 164; also "Memorandum on the Bomber Strength of Great Britain Relative to Other Powers," [1937], in AIR 9/76. (This document details comparative numbers but does not address the issue of what Britain's enemies—especially Germany—might do with their aircraft.) See also Wark, *The Ultimate Enemy*, 65, 67; and Paul Kennedy, "British Net Assessment and the Coming of the Second World War," *Calculations: Net Assessment and the Coming of World War II*, ed. Williamson Murray and Allan R. Millett (New York: Free Press, 1992), 29–30.

181. Wark, *The Ultimate Enemy*, 35.

182. The body was comprised of Sir Maurice Hankey (Chair); Sir Robert Vansittart, Permanent Head of the Foreign Office; Sir Warren Fisher, Permanent Secretary to the Treasury; and the three Chiefs of Staff (including Sir Edward Ellington for the RAF).

183. Smith, *British Air Strategy*, 130.

184. Ibid., 130–34; Kennedy, "British Net Assessment," 46.

185. Wark, *The Ultimate Enemy*, 38–39; see Wark generally on intelligence in these years.

186. Slessor, *The Central Blue*, 205.

187. At that point, the British were considering whether it might not be a good idea to cancel Part V (German disarmament) of the Versailles Treaty before the Germans repudiated it. They also hoped that it might be possible to negotiate some guarantee for the East European states, and to persuade Germany to rejoin the League. The Foreign Secretary believed that Germany might like to be made an "honest woman." See Smith, *British Air Strategy*, 146–47.

188. See Wark, *The Ultimate Enemy*, 43; see also 43–45. Also, J. A. Cross, *Lord Swinton* (Oxford: Clarendon Press, 1982), 136–37.

189. Smith, *British Air Strategy*, 163–65.

190. On Swinton's early years of service to the nation in this capacity, see Cross, *Lord Swinton*, 134–79. Also, Smith, *British Air Strategy*, 158, 160.

191. This was an advance over the existing system in which "Air Defence"

had included both fighters and bombers. See AIR 41/39, pp. 110A–110E; also, Terraine, "Theory and Practice of Air War," 23; Smith, *British Air Strategy*, 41.

192. In his memoirs, Slessor pointed out that those in Plans, Air Ministry, were "not in close, day-to-day touch with technical developments" (*The Central Blue*, 205); also, Terraine, "Theory and Practice of Air War," 24.

193. "Record of a Discussion which took place Between the Prime Minister and a deputation from both Houses of Parliament on July 28, 1936," in AIR 9/8, esp. pp. 1–9.

194. Wark, *The Ultimate Enemy*, 56–59, 70.

195. On the background to the JPC and the October 1935 draft appreciation it produced, see ibid., 188–94; for a critique of the 1936 paper and the responses to it, see 196–202. The paper is discussed in detail in AIR 41/39, pp. 145–150; WF, vol. 4 contains an extract on 88–95. On the differences between the services regarding strategy at this point, see David Dilks, "The Unnecessary War? Military Advice and Foreign Policy in Great Britain, 1931–1939," in *General Staffs and Diplomacy Before World War II*, ed. Adrian Preston (London: Croom Helm, 1978).

196. JPC Paper 155 quoted in AIR 41/39, p. 146. See also Wark, *The Ultimate Enemy*, 196–202.

197. JPC Paper 155 quoted in AIR 41/39, p. 147.

198. Ibid., pp. 149–150. In their review of the JPC plan, the Chiefs of Staff endorsed an air counteroffensive in response to German attacks on Britain, but observed that German airfields were not a very satisfactory target for the initial phase of war. They pointed out, though, that such targets would at least "have the advantage of reducing the scale of attack upon our own vitals and of directing our offensive against an unmistakably military target, thus leaving to the enemy the odium of the initiative in bombing places where large populations are concentrated" (COS Paper 549, 15 February 1937, quoted in AIR 41/39, p. 151).

199. See WF, 4:90.

200. Wark, *The Ultimate Enemy*, 63–65.

201. See James Corum, "The Spanish Civil War: Lessons Learned and Not Learned by the Great Powers," *The Journal of Military History* 29, no. 2 (April 1998): 315–16.

202. Report by R. V. Goddard, Chairman, Joint Intelligence Sub-Committee (Spain), 21 September 1937, in AIR 2/2190. A similar argument appears in an RAF intelligence assessment of the war in Spain, July 1937, based on the reports of Gen. Alfred Kindelan, Chief of the Nationalist Air Forces, in AIR 8/219.

203. He was aware that there was a growing concern within the army that they might find themselves opposed by troops enjoying considerable air support. He felt that any tendency to sympathize with such concerns must be resisted. See Minute, DDOps to DCAS September 1937 (day not clear in original), in AIR 5/1132.

204. Minute, DD Plans to DCAS, 1 Dec. 1937, in AIR 2/2190.

205. Republican Spain: General Report by Wing Commander R.V. Goddard, 11 March 1938, decimal file no. 512.04F. Office of Air Force History, Bolling AFB, Washington, D.C.

206. Ibid., 10, 18. Also, R. Dan Richardson, "The Development of Airpower

Concepts and Air Combat Techniques in the Spanish Civil War," *Air Power History* 40, no. 1 (Spring 1993): 19.

207. Goddard, General Report [on Spain], 22; also, 17.

208. Ibid., 18–19.

209. Ibid., 20–21.

210. Report of the British Consul in Valencia, quoted in AIR 41/39, p. 337.

211. Goddard, General Report, 22. Generally Goddard found that air attacks, instead of demoralizing the population, had often had the effect of turning them more firmly against Franco (10).

212. Ibid., 21, 27.

213. AIR 41/39, p. 334. See in general, pp. 333–40.

214. See, for example, Minute, DCAS to DSD, 2 February 1937, in AIR 2/2613.

215. Goddard. General Report, 22.

216. See "Extract from W / C Goddard's Report on Visit to Republican Spain, February 1938," in AIR 2/2613.

217. Goddard, General Report, 11 and 22.

218. Minute, DDOps to DCAS, 23 November 1936, in AIR 2/2613.

219. Ibid.

220. Minute, DSD to DCAS, 30 November 1936, in AIR 2/2613.

221. Minute, DCAS to DSD, 1 February 1937, in AIR 2/2613.

222. See "The Question of Fighter Escorts for Bombers," in the Agenda for the 9th Meeting of the Air Fighting Committee, 9 June 1937, in Air 2/2613.

223. The head of Fighter Command, Air Chief Marshal Sir Hugh Dowding, argued that single-seater fighters could only be used as "distant escorts," and thus could be easily drawn off and out of touch with the formation. Therefore he concluded that a single-seater should be ruled out of consideration—and the majority of the Committee agreed with him. See Minutes of the 9th Meeting of the Air Fighting Committee, Air Ministry, 9 June 1937, in AIR 2/2613, esp. pp. 9–11.

224. WF, 1:96.

225. Conference held in DCAS's Room, Air Ministry, Whitehall, on Thursday, 6 April 1939, to discuss Bomber Command War Readiness—Agenda Part I, in AIR 8/270.

226. Letter, ACAS to AOC in C., Bomber Command, 12 August 1939, in AIR 2/2613; also, "The Escort Fighter," FC/s.24744/DO/Ops., 7 March 1942, in AIR 2/2613; "Heavy Bomber Escorts," FC/S.24744 Headquarters, Fighter Command (Tactics), 7 March 1942, in AIR 2/2613.

227. David Dilks has written that Chamberlain may have perceived himself as having a "mission" to prevent the disaster of another world war. See "The Unnecessary War?" 119; also Paul Kennedy, *The Realities Behind Diplomacy*, 240–43.

228. Kennedy (*The Realities Behind Diplomacy*) writes, "The most cruel dilemma facing British decision makers as they contemplated the various external threats of the 1930s was . . . that the defence chiefs and the economic 'watchdogs' at the Treasury and Bank of England were both correct—and both wrong. The country could either have a balanced economy but with inadequate forces

to protect itself and its overseas interests against those threats; or it could have much larger armaments and a bankrupt economy. It could not have both, and the post-Munich decision to abandon Treasury controls on defence spending simply meant that one hazard had been replaced by another" (234–35).

229. WF, 1:75. See also Slessor, *The Central Blue*, 156–85, on plans for Scheme J and his personal role in shaping them.

230. Swinton quoted in Wark, *The Ultimate Enemy*, 61.

231. See Aide-Mémoire by Inskip, 9 December 1937, in AIR 8/226; it is reprinted in WF, 4:96–98. See also Wark, *The Ultimate Enemy*, 61–62.

232. He articulated his view further in an interim report dated 15 December 1937. See Smith, *British Air Strategy*, 182–91.

233. Additional examinations of Inskip's role can be found in Shay, *British Rearmament in the Thirties*, 164–96; Cross, *Lord Swinton*, 181–90; Wark, *The Ultimate Enemy*, 61–63; WF, 1:70–85. See also, generally, Brian Bond, *British Military Policy Between the Two World Wars* (Oxford: Clarendon, 1980).

234. WF, 1:77–78.

235. See Wark, *The Ultimate Enemy*, 62; also WF, 1:77.

236. Smith, *British Air Strategy*, 185, 189. Secretary of State for Air Lord Swinton also put up a struggle against Inskip's designs, claiming that, in war, success would "go to the nation which can most quickly overcome the will of his opponent to continue the fight." See Cross, *Lord Swinton*, 194; Shay, *British Rearmament in the Thirties*, 172–73.

237. WF, 1:91–92.

238. Slessor, *The Central Blue*, 160. Later in the book he argued that, among other things, "our growing awareness of the miserable inadequacy of our counteroffensive resources in the near future" helped to justify "beyond all argument the allocation of first priority to the defensive fighter" (180).

239. Quoted in Terraine, *A Time for Courage*, 82.

240. On this point Terraine comments, "The British generally dislike contemplating uncomfortable truths and look askance at those who announce them" (ibid., 90). See also Slessor, *The Central Blue*, 206.

241. On reconnaissance and photographic interpretation see Sebastian Cox, "Sources and Organisation of RAF Intelligence and its Influence on Operations," in *The Conduct of the Air War*, 555–59. Also, Slessor, *The Central Blue*, 203–7.

242. Terraine, *A Time for Courage*, 83–84. See also AIR 41/39, which concluded, "It is hardly wisdom after the event to suggest that the Air Staff and its subordinate branches showed in this matter a marked lack of imaginative forethought. By a little hard and logical deduction from their often repeated strategical doctrines and from what they knew about the new aircraft already, they might well have anticipated and provided in time for most of the urgent requirements which the Commander-in-Chief of Bomber Command had to demand in November of 1937" (167).

243. On this debate see S. Robertson, *RAF Strategic Bombing Doctrine*, 113–20.

244. See "Air Staff Note on Bombing Policy to be Discussed by the Bombing Policy Sub-Committee," 8 March 1938, in AIR 2/8812. (The Bombing Commit-

tee had begun meeting in 1934. Still, four years later, little was known for sure about bombing methods.)

245. Minutes of the 1st Meeting of the Bombing Policy Sub-Committee of the Bombing Committee, Air Ministry, 22 March 1938, in AIR 2/8812. The subcommittee also recorded the opinion that Bomber Command ought to arrange more frequent exercises "in locating unfamiliar targets in various parts of the country."

246. AIR 41/39, p. 174.

247. AIR 41/39, pp. 51–52, 176. In 1932 the CAS ruled that no bomb greater than 500 lbs. was required by the RAF.

248. AIR 41/39, p. 35.

249. There has been a debate in the political science literature over who deserves credit for insuring that the British paid attention to defensive measures on the eve of World War II. Barry Posen gives credit to civilian intervention, arguing that without it, the "RAF never would have invested sufficient resources in Fighter Command." Stephen Peter Rosen takes issue with this. Though he acknowledges that "civilian intervention in the late 1930s eventually altered the balance of resources in favor of fighter aircraft," he points out that one must look at the activities of the RAF itself in the development of air defense in the years prior to 1935. He believes that the success of the air defense net used in 1940 was the product of "long-standing interest on the part of the RAF leadership in the problems of command, control, communications and intelligence in support of defensive fighter operations." See Barry Posen, *The Sources of Military Doctrine* (Ithaca: Cornell University Press, 1984), 161, and, generally, 159–76; Stephen Peter Rosen, *Winning the Next War* (Ithaca: Cornell University Press, 1991), 15, and, generally, 15–19; also, Rosen, "New Ways of War: Understanding Military Innovation," *International Security*, 13, no. 1 (summer 1988): 148–49. The recent work of John Ferris has supported Rosen.

250. Alan Beyerchen, "From Radio to Radar: Interwar Military Adaptation to Technological Change in Germany, the United Kingdom, and the United States," in *Military Innovation in the Interwar Period*, 269–70, 275–76.

251. David Zimmerman, "Tucker's Acoustical Mirrors: Aircraft Detection Before Radar," *War and Society*, 15, no. 1 (May 1997): 96.

252. It consisted of Tizard (Chairman), Wimperis, A. P. Rowe (Secretary), P.M.S. Blackett, a Nobel Laureate of Manchester University, and A. V. Hill, another Nobel Laureate from University College, London. On these decisions, see Cross, *Lord Swinton*, 172–79.

253. Tizard went to Watson-Watt at first to rule out the possibility of developing a "death ray" weapon. Watson-Watt laid this to rest, but took up the work on target location based on a cue from a Post Office Report of June 1932, which reported that aircraft interfered with radio signals and re-radiated them. Terraine, *A Time for Courage*, 22; Beyerchen, "From Radio to Radar," 279–80.

254. Beyerchen, "From Radio to Radar," 238–87.

255. See "Answers to Questions Raised by D.D. Plans in His Minute Dated 11.3.38" (with covering note by Slessor to ACAS attached), in AIR 2/2948.

256. Ibid., 1–2, 6, 12.

257. "The Composition and Strength of the Royal Air Force—Air Staff Pol-

icy," in AIR 2/2948. See also "Air Staff Note on Bombing Policy," 8 March 1938, in AIR 2/8812.

258. Air Council Letter and Note, 26 November 1938, quoted in WF, 1:80–81.

259. R. J. Overy, *The Air War* (New York: Stein and Day, 1980), 15. See also WF, 1:75.

260. See Cross, *Lord Swinton*, 208–219. See also Smith, *British Air Strategy*, 209–10.

261. See Smith, *British Air Strategy*, 218, and "The Air Threat and British Foreign and Domestic Policy," in *The Conduct of the Air War in the Second World War*, 617; Williamson Murray, "The German Air Force and the Munich Crisis," in *War and Society*, edited by Brian Bond and Ian Roy (New York: Holmes and Meier, 1976); Kennedy, "British Net Assessment," 30–31. For the personal view of one who was inside the RAF during the Czech crisis, see Sir John Slessor, *The Central Blue*, esp. 144–235. For Chamberlain's views see House of Commons Debates, 6 October 1938, vol. 339.

262. Wark, *The Ultimate Enemy*, 66–67.

263. Ibid., 69.

264. Slessor, *The Central Blue*, 153–54.

265. See the *Times* (London), 1–30 September 1938. For the quoted material on shop preparations, see "Effects in the Shops: ARP Precautions," 30 September 1938.

266. Slessor, *The Central Blue*, 153.

267. Edgerton, *England and the Aeroplane*, 47–49.

Chapter 3
The United States in the Interwar Years

1. Memo on "Doctrines of the Army Air Corps" with covering note from the War Plans Division of the War Department General Staff, 21 December 1934, p. 4, in record group (hereafter RG) 18, central decimal files (hereafter CDF) 321.9, box 485, National Archives and Records Administration (hereafter NARA), Washington, D.C.

2. Memo from the Office of the Chief of the Air Corps to the Commandant, Air Corps Tactical School (ACTS), Langley, Virginia, 1 September 1928, p. 4, in RG 18, CDF 321.9, box 485, NARA.

3. As Michael Sherry has observed, "Prophecy, political debate, and cultural imagination shaped a benign image of aviation, thereby making the bomber seem attractive as an instrument of American ideals but remote as a weapon of war" (*The Rise of American Air Power* [New Haven: Yale University Press, 1987], 23).

4. Section titled, "The Routine of a Day Bombardment Group," in "Provisional Manual of Operations," 23 December 1918. Reprinted in Maurer Maurer, ed., *The U.S. Air Service in World War I* (Washington, D.C.: Office of Air Force History, 1978), 2:276.

5. William C. Sherman, "Tentative Manual for the Employment of Air Service," 1919. Reprinted in Maurer, *The U.S. Air Service*, 2:313–408.

6. "Tentative Manual," 316, in Maurer, *The U.S. Air Service*, vol. 2. To support his assertions he cited an incident in which a division of "first class troops" that had received "with equanimity" four thousand shells in its sector per day was nonetheless "greatly disturbed and harassed" by the efforts of one persistent day bomber.

7. Ibid., reprinted in Maurer, *The U.S. Air Service*, 2:314.

8. See *Air Service Information Circular*, 30 June 1920 (Washington, D.C., Government Printing Office); also Maurer, *The U.S. Air Service*, 2:314, 384.

9. Robert Frank Futrell, *Ideas, Concepts, Doctrine: A History of Basic Thinking in the United States Air Force* (Maxwell AFB, Ala.: Air University Press, 1971), 20.

10. Newton Baker, "Report of the Secretary of War," in *War Department Annual Reports, 1919*, vol. 1 (Washington, D.C.: Government Printing Office, 1920), 74–75.

11. Baker said of air power, "The art itself is so new and so fascinating, and the men in it have so taken on the character of supermen, that it is difficult to reason coldly" ("Report of the Secretary of War," 68–70).

12. *History of the Air Corps Tactical School, 1920–1940*, USAF Historical Studies Number 100 (Maxwell AFB, Ala.: USAF Historical Division, Air University, 1950), 4. Also, Robert T. Finney, *History of the Air Corps Tactical School, 1920–1940* (Washington, D.C.: Center for Air Force History, 1992), p. 8.

13. See "Program of Instruction, Air Service Tactical School [Langley Field, Va.]," October 15, 1923 to June 14, 1924, in Air Force Historical Research Center (hereafter AFHRC), decimal no. 248.192.

14. Milling wrote, "In the same broad sense that the Navy assists the infantry, so also does the Air Force." "But," he added, "[the Air Service] . . . must seek out our doctrine, as with the Navy, in the element in which it operates" ("Air Tactics," in Air Service Field Officers School [Langley Field, Va.], Training Regulations No. 440–15 [1922], 8 and 13. See AFHRC, file no. 248.101-4A).

15. Thomas H. Greer, *The Development of Air Doctrine in the Army Air Arm, 1917–1941* (Washington, D.C.: Office of Air Force History, 1985), 36–37.

16. Milling, "Air Tactics," 4–5.

17. Ibid., 3–4, 13.

18. Spaatz to Lt. H. W. Cook, 13 February 1923, Papers of Carl Spaatz (hereafter SP), box 2, diary, Library of Congress Manuscript Room, Washington, D.C.

19. Milling, "Air Tactics," 7–10.

20. Air Service Tactical School, "Bombardment Course" 1924–1925, p. 4. See AFHRC dec. file no. 248.101-9.

21. Ibid., 4.

22. Memo to Maj. Carl Spaatz from W. G. Kilner, A.S. Executive, 15 August 1925, in Papers of Carl Spaatz, box 3, diary.

23. See Craven and Cate (CC) 1:20–25.

24. On the Air Service organizational debates of the immediate postwar period, see Maurer Maurer, *Aviation in the U.S. Army, 1919–1939* (Washington, D.C.: Office of Air Force History, 1987), 39–52; also Futrell, *Ideas, Concepts, Doctrine*, 19–21.

25. See for instance, memo from Gen. Mason Patrick, "The Reorganization of Air Forces for National Defense," 19 December 1924, in SP, box 3.

26. See Alfred F. Hurley, *Billy Mitchell: Crusader for Air Power* (Bloomington: Indiana University Press, 1975); Mark Clodfelter, "Molding Airpower Convictions: The Development and Legacy of William Mitchell's Strategic Thought," in *The Paths of Heaven: The Evolution of Airpower Theory*, ed. Phillip Meilinger (Maxwell AFB, Ala.: Air University Press, 1997), 79–114; Walter Millis, *Arms and Men* (New Brunswick: Rutgers University Press, 1986, 3rd printing), 254–58.

27. Andrew Boyle, *Trenchard* (New York: W. W. Norton, 1962), 299.

28. Mitchell's *Skyways*, quoted in CC, 1:42.

29. William Mitchell, *Our Air Force: The Keystone of National Defense* (New York: E. P. Dutton, 1921), xix.

30. Ibid., xxii. Mitchell argued, "Warfare today between first-class powers includes all of the people of the nations so engaged—men, women and children. This inclusion of women and children is not merely a sentimental and economic one, but during the last war was an actual one from a military standpoint. . . . The entire nations were combatant forces. We must expect, therefore, in case of war, to have the enemy attempt to destroy any or all of our combatant or industrial forces—his attacks being entirely controlled by the dictates of strategy, and the means of bringing the war to a quick conclusion."

31. Ibid., 177.

32. According to Mitchell, "The personnel of entire cities—men, women and children—can be destroyed by gas attacks from the air" (ibid., xxii–xxiii).

33. On this point, see Clodfelter, "Molding Airpower Convictions," 97.

34. The quote is from Millis, *Arms and Men*, 257. See also David E. Johnson, *Fast Tanks and Heavy Bombers: Innovation in the U.S. Army, 1917–1945* (Ithaca: Cornell University Press, 1998), 81–90.

35. Hurley, *Billy Mitchell*, 93.

36. Clodfelter, "Molding Airpower Convictions," 98.

37. Futrell, *Ideas, Concepts, Doctrine*, 26.

38. Maurer, *Aviation*, 74.

39. Ibid., 191–221.

40. On the early years of ACTS, see *History of the Air Corps Tactical School*, 7–11.

41. See Sherry, who points out that "in a typical year, 2.5 per cent of all army aviators died in crashes" (*The Rise of American Air Power*, 51).

42. Quoted in CC, 1:45.

43. See ACTS, *Bombardment* (Washington, D.C.: U.S. Government Printing Office, 1926). Like many of the ACTS texts, the 1926 text lists no specific individual as its author.

44. Ibid., 72. See also, Thomas Greer, *The Development of Air Doctrine in the Army Air Arm, 1917–1941* (1955, reprint, Washington, D.C.: Office of Air Force History, 1985), 41; Johnson, *Fast Tanks and Heavy Bombers*, 208–9.

45. ACTS, *Bombardment* (1926), 63–64.

46. See Greer, *The Development of Air Doctrine*, 40–43; Peter Faber, "Interwar U.S. Army Aviation and the Air Corps Tactical School: Incubators of American Airpower," in *The Paths of Heaven*, 215.

47. Futrell, *Ideas, Concepts, Doctrine*, 28; Greer, *The Development of Air Doctrine*, 19–20.

48. Quoted in Futrell, *Ideas, Concepts, Doctrine*, 32.

49. William C. Sherman, *Air Warfare* (New York: The Ronald Press, 1926), 6.

50. Ibid., 211.

51. Ibid., 197. Sherman also recognized that gas bombs might be a feature of any future air war (203–5).

52. Ibid., 214.

53. Ibid., 217.

54. Ibid., 218.

55. Memo, Office of the Chief of the Air Corps to the Commandant, ACTS, 1 September 1928 (along with "The Doctrine of the Air Force" with covering note by C. C. Culver, Commandant, ACTS, 30 April 1928) in RG 18, CDF 321.9 (Doctrine of the AAC), box 485, NARA.

56. On the manuevers of 1929, see Maurer, *Aviation*, 239–45.

57. Frank quoted in Futrell, *Ideas, Concepts, Doctrine*, 33.

58. On Walker see, Martha Byrd, *Kenneth N. Walker: Air Power's Untempered Crusader* (Maxwell AFB, Ala.: Air University Press, 1997); for quote, see xi. See also, generally, Thomas Fabyanic, "A Critique of United States Air War Planning, 1941–1944" (Ph.D. diss., St. Louis University, 1973).

59. See generally, Terry Gwynn-Jones, *Farther and Faster: Aviation's Adventuring Years, 1909–1939* (Washington, D.C.: Smithsonian Institution Press, 1991). Also, Sherry, *The Rise of American Air Power*, 38–41.

60. Maurer, *Aviation*, 284.

61. On the development of the GHQ, see generally, Maurer, *Aviation*, 283–98; Futrell, *Ideas, Concepts, Doctrine*, 36–43; Greer, *The Development of Air Doctrine*, 67–75. See also "The Army Air Corps for 1934," an information circular produced by the Air Corps in December 1934, in AFHRC, decimal file no. 167.6-11 (1932–1935).

62. See CC, 1:62.

63. Futrell, *Ideas, Concepts, Doctrine*, 34; Maurer, *Aviation*, 285; Faber, "Interwar U.S. Army Aviation," 198–200; John F. Shiner, "Benjamin D. Foulois: In the Beginning," in *Makers of the United States Air Force* (Washington, D.C.: Office of Air Force History, 1987), 26.

64. Maurer, *Aviation*, 289–91.

65. Ibid., 285–89. Also, Shiner, "Benjamin D. Foulois," 26; and Greer, *The Development of Air Doctrine*, 69.

66. Maurer, *Aviation*, 345–50.

67. So-called because each separate plan was designated by a color, for instance the plan for attack by Great Britain was called RED, and the plan for attack by Japan, ORANGE.

68. Futrell, *Ideas, Concepts, Doctrine*, 34–35.

69. Maurer, *Aviation*, 300; Shiner, "Bejamin D. Foulois," 29–33.

70. Historian Robin Higham has written, "Airline men were frequently ex-officers whose ambitions could not be satisfied under peacetime military conditions, and they regarded themselves as professional airmen and the military as amateurs" (*Air Power: A Concise History* [New York: St. Martin's Press, 1972], 75). In a feisty article titled, "An Army Air Mail Flyer Speaks," Capt. Ira Eaker defended Air Corps capabilities and pilots. He pointed out that while the Air

Corps had pioneered many of the technologies that made flying safe and efficient, commercial pilots had easier access to them because the Air Corps budget was so tight. See Eaker, "An Air Mail Flyer Speaks," with covering note (approving release by General Westover) of 14 March 1934 in RG 18, CDF 232, box 1, NARA.

71. Maurer, *Aviation*, 315; Shiner, "Benjamin D. Foulois," 30–31. The Air Corps had a completion rate for scheduled flights of only 65.83 percent.

72. Maurer, *Aviation*, 315–17, 347–50. The Air Corps had asked for $35 million for fiscal year 1935. Congress cut it back to $25 million. The air mail incident, however, prompted President Roosevelt to call for additional appropriations, and congress granted a five-million-dollar increase.

73. Brig. Gen. Frank M. Andrews quoted in "Long-Range Air planes Most Flexible Defense," in *The Air Corps News Letter* 18, no. 9 (15 May 1935), 1 (published by the Information Division, Air Corps; originals at Bolling Air Force Base, Washington, D.C.).

74. Expenditures went up from a total of $30 million in 1935 to $32 million in fiscal year 1936, to $41.1 million in 1937, to $50.9 million in 1938, to $83.1 million in 1939 (Maurer, *Aviation*, 347, 350).

75. Editorial, "Wings Over Europe," *Manchester Guardian*, 12 April 1935; reprinted in the *Air Corps Newsletter* (Washington, D.C.) under the heading "Widespread Air Bombardment Contemplated By European Powers" (15 May 1935): 3. The editorial claimed that bombing would be used not only against military targets, but also against "vital centers" in order to demoralize the civilian population.

76. CC, 1:60–61.

77. The aircraft's rudder and elevator controls had not been unlocked. See Maurer, *Aviation*, 354. On the B-17, see also Futrell, *Ideas, Concepts, Doctrine*, 42–43, and Greer, *Development of Air Doctrine*, 46–47.

78. Quoted in Futrell, *Ideas, Concepts, Doctrine*, 43. On the B-17 see also, Stephen McFarland and Wesley Phillips Newton, *To Command the Sky* (Washington, D.C.: Smithsonian Institution Press, 1991), 33–34.

79. CC, 1:67.

80. Robert Wiebe, *The Search for Order, 1877–1920* (New York: Hill and Wang, 1967), 14, 77–78; also Louis M. Hacker, *American Problems of Today* (New York: F. S. Crofts, 1938).

81. For general information on labor unrest in this period, see Dwight Lowell Dumond, *America in Our Time, 1896–1946* (New York: Henry Holt, 1947), 439–42.

82. Sherry, *The Rise of American Air Power*, 43.

83. Edison quoted in "'Viper' Weapons," *The Literary Digest*, 24 December 1921.

84. See, for instance, "Strafing New York from the Clouds," *The Literary Digest*, 8 June 1929, p. 60.

85. See "Can Enemy Planes Wipe Out America?" *Popular Science*, June 1931; Stuart Chase, "The Two-Hour War," *The New Republic*, 8 May 1929.

86. See Brig. Gen. William Mitchell, "Air Power vs. Sea Power," *The American Review of Reviews*, March 1921, p. 277.

87. In addition, Air Service / Air Corps members engaged in a variety of activities designed to promote the utility and versatility of aircraft, including: fire fighting, border patrolling, crop dusting, and aerial mapping. See Faber, "Interwar U.S. Army Aviation and the Air Corps Tactical School," 188–192.

88. Phillip Meilinger, "Alexander de Seversky and American Airpower," in *The Paths of Heaven*, 239–77.

89. See Arlington B. Conway, "Death from the Sky," *The American Mercury*, February 1932, p. 167; John Edwin Hogg, "The Bogey of War in the Air," *The Forum*, December 1934, p. 347; W. F. Kernan, "Our Reception for Bombers," *The American Mercury*, June 1935, p. 206.

90. Conway, "Death from the Sky," 167–172. He adjusted his casualty figures for the lower population density of New York compared to London.

91. Ibid., 175. Michael Sherry offers some interesting insights on interwar critiques of the air power enthusiasts (*The Rise of American Air Power*, 62–64).

92. Memo by the Secretary of State, 25 May 1932, in *Foreign Relations of the United States* (hereafter FRUS) 1932, vol. 1 (Washington, D.C.: U.S. Government Printing Office (USGPO), 1948), 183.

93. See for instance the preparatory documents for the Geneva Disarmament Conference, containing the views of the War Department, the Navy, and the Commerce Department, in RG 18, CDF 337 (Disarmament Conference), box 559, NARA.

94. FRUS, 1932, 1:186–91.

95. See Bialer, *The Shadow of the Bomber* (London: Royal Historical Society), 33.

96. Memo of a Trans-Atlantic Telephone Conversation between Hoover and Stimson in Washington, and Gibson and Davis in Geneva, 21 June 1932, 12 noon; Memo of a Trans-Atlantic Telephone Conversation between Hoover and Stimson in Washington, and Davis in Geneva, 21 June 1932, 2:10 P.M., FRUS, 1932, 1:197–207, quotation on 198.

97. Memo of a Trans-Atlantic Telephone Conversation between Hoover and Stimson in Washington and Davis in Geneva, 21 June 1932, 2:10 P.M., FRUS, 1:202–7.

98. Bialer, *The Shadow of the Bomber*, 33–40. See also Phillip Meilinger, "Clipping the Bomber's Wings," *War in History* 6, no. 3 (1999): 320–21.

99. These were the adjectives used by Jonathan Mitchell in his essay, "Death Rides the Wind," *The New Republic*, 26 May 1937, p. 63.

100. Sherry, *The Rise of American Air Power*, 69.

101. Matthews quoted in "Barcelona Horrors," *Time* magazine, 28 March 1938.

102. Mitchell, "Death Rides the Wind," 64. On this general topic, see also Sherry, *The Rise of American Air Power*, 73–74.

103. Maj. Ira Eaker, "The Air Corps Tactical School," *Air Corps Newsletter*, 19, no. 8 (15 April 1936): 9.

104. Lt. Col. John F. Curry to the Chief of the Air Corps, 8 April 1932, in AFHRC, decimal file no. 248.192, 1929–1939; Col. A. G. Fisher, "Forward on Maxwell Field," *Air Corps Newsletter* 9, no. 8 (15 April 1936): 1.

105. On the Air Corps Tactical School and its relationship to the army, see Sherry, *The Rise of American Air Power*, 51.

106. ACTS, "Air Warfare" text of "Air Force" course, 1938, in AFHRC, file no. 248.101-1.

107. See "Proposed Training Regulations No. 440-15, Air Corps, Employment of Air Corps Troops" 4 April 1935, from the War Department General Staff," in RG 18, CDF (Doctrines of the AAC) box 485, NARA.

108. Futrell, *Ideas, Concepts, Doctrine*, 47.

109. See ACTS, "Program of Instruction," 1934–35, Command and Staff Regular Course, in AFHRC, decimal file no. 248.192; ACTS, "Comparison of Courses," 1 July 1934, in AFHRC, decimal file no. 248.192. Also, Finney, *History of the Air Corps Tactical School*, 8.

110. Lt. Col. E. L. Hoffmann, memo, 24 October 1935, in AFHRC, file no. 248.126, 1934–1936.

111. Maj. Ira Eaker, "The Air Corps Tactical School," *Air Corps Newsletter* 19, no. 8 (15 April 1936): 10.

112. Lt. Col. Harold George, "Department of Air Tactics and Strategy," *Air Corps Newsletter*, 19, no. 8 (15 April 1936): 2. ACTS graduates had to know about the other services as well, and to that end students were given instruction in field artillery, cavalry, infantry, and chemical warfare.

113. ACTS, "Bombardment Aviation," typescript, December 1930, in AFHRC, decimal file no. 248.101-9, pp. 6, 8–9. See also "Bombardment Aviation," printed text, February 1931, in AFHRC, decimal file no. 248.101-9, which appears to be a slightly revised, printed version of the December 1930 text.

114. The text "Bombardment Aviation," February 1931, reads, "The merits of this policy are apparent" (10).

115. "Bombardment Aviation," December 1930, pp. 13, 16. This argument was put forward again in the February 1931 "Bombardment Aviation" text, p. 13.

116. ACTS, "Bombardment Aviation," December 1930, pp. 17–18.

117. Ibid., 15. This criticism was repeated in the February 1931 "Bombardment Aviation" text, p. 12.

118. And they added, "Bombing since the war has conclusively proved that the bomb is a tremendously powerful agent of destruction. Consequently, there should be no temptation for air commanders of the future to violate the principle of the objective" (ACTS, "Air Force" text, 1930, in AFHRC, decimal file no. 248.101-1, p. 45).

119. Ibid., 5.

120. ACTS, "Air Force Objectives," in "Air Force" text, 1934–35, in AFHRC, decimal file no. 248.101-1, p. 1. And they added, "Air power finds its objectives not only in the hostile land, sea, and air forces, but also in the economic, social, and political life of the enemy. Thus it is able to place strong, direct pressure initially upon those decisive objectives that modern warfare, heretofore, has been able only to influence indirectly" (2).

121. ACTS, "Air Warfare," in "Air Force" text, 1938, in AFHRC, decimal file no. 248.101-1.

122. Maj. General Frank M. Andrews, Address to the National Aeronautic Association, 16 January 1939, in AFHRC, decimal file no. 248.211-20.

123. ACTS, "Air Force" text, 1930, p. 5.

124. ACTS, "Air Force Objectives," in "Air Force" text, 1934–35, p. 1.

125. Maj. Harold Lee George, "An Inquiry into the Subject 'War'" (lecture delivered at ACTS, [1934?]), in AFHRC, decimal file no. 248.11-9.

126. ACTS, "Air Force" text, 1931, in AFHRC, file no. 248.101-1, p. 53. The authors indicated that the decision on raids would be based on such things as an estimate of the likely results as weighed against the suffering of women and children, and the likely effect upon public opinion in neutral countries (53).

127. ACTS, "International Aerial Regulations" text, 1933–34, in AFHRC, decimal file no. 248.101-16, 1933–1934, p. 53. The quotation in the text came directly from M. W. Royse's book, *Aerial Bombardment and the International Regulation of Warfare* (New York: Harold Vinal, 1928), 237.

128. ACTS, "International Aerial Regulations" text, 1933–34, p. 31.

129. Maj. B. Q. Jones, "The G.H.Q. What Will It Do?," *Air Corps Newsletter* 18, no. 11 (15 June 1935): 13.

130. ACTS, "Air Force Objectives," in "Air Force" text, 1934–35, p. 2.

131. Ibid., 2–3.

132. Ibid., 3. The authors' own discussion of an attack on an enemy water supply provided a rather grim scenario in this realm. They wrote, "The water supply system of a city is very vulnerable. Reservoirs can be gassed, aqueducts cut, and dams or pumping facilities destroyed. The effects upon the civil population will be immediate and far reaching; sanitation will fail and the possibility of epidemic disease will become acute" (4).

133. Ibid., 5.

134. Stephen L. McFarland, *America's Pursuit of Precision Bombing, 1910–1945* (Washington, D.C.: Smithsonian Institution Press, 1995), 90–91.

135. In his memoir, Wilson claimed that he was the sole originator of the "key node" targeting theory in the United States (in 1934), and that the idea had come to him in a dream. He also claimed that no air theorist had expounded anything like the "key node" theory before he invented it. See Donald Wilson, *Wooing Peponi* (Monterey, Cal.: Angel Press, 1974), 237. It is certainly possible that Wilson was not aware of the development of the theory in Britain, and perhaps he thought he was "inventing" it. But it actually had a long history, and elements of it had formed a consistent refrain in American air doctrine since the WWI U.S. bombing survey. Wilson did, however, articulate the theory in a detailed form for his classes and helped to write it into ACTS manuals.

136. ACTS, "Air Warfare," in "Air Force" text, 1 February 1938, in AFHRC, decimal file no. 248.101-1, p. 14.

137. For details on the development of the Norden bombsight and its role in precision bombing doctrine, see Stephen McFarland, *America's Pursuit of Precision Bombing*, esp. 68–88. McFarland explains the focus on high-altitude bombing on 84–86.

138. Reflecting on his thoughts and actions much later, Wilson wrote, "The recently-acquired weapon of precision bombing gave us an instrument which could cause collapse of this industrial fabric by depriving the web of certain essential elements—as few as three main systems such as transportation, electric power and steel manufacture would suffice." See Donald Wilson, "Origin of a Theory for Air Strategy," *Aerospace Historian* 18, no. 1 (March 1971): 19. See

also Greer (who interviewed Wilson in 1952), *The Development of Air Doctrine*, 57–58; McFarland, *America's Pursuit of Precision Bombing*, 92–93.

139. Maj. Donald Wilson to 1st Lt. John S. Gullett, 2 October 1933, in AF-HRC, decimal file no. 248.126.

140. Maj. Donald Wilson to Maj. William H. Crom, 14 November 1933, in AFHRC, decimal file no. 248.126. The letters by Donald Wilson can be found at the AFHRC, under decimal file nos. 248.126 and 248.12601.

141. Memo from Col. A. G. Fisher, Commandant of ACTS, to the Chief of the Air Corps, 21 August 1935, and attachment, 26 August 1935, in AFHRC, decimal file no. 248.12606.

142. Notes for "Air Power and the City" (lecture delivered at ACTS), 15 April 1936, AFHRC decimal no. 248.2019A-12.

143. Fairchild said, "In going over the course I find some very large question marks" (Maj. Muir S. Fairchild to Maj. John Y. York, 28 October 1937, in AFHRC, decimal file no. 248.12601).

144. Ibid., 2–3. See also Fabyanic, "A Critique of United States Air War Planning," 43–44.

145. Lt. Laurence Kuter, "Bombing Probabilities" (lecture), in the course "Bombardment Aviation," at ACTS, 18 October 1935, in USAFHRC, decimal no. 248.222, p. 3. Similarly Maj. Harold George argued, "We are concerned . . . in determining how air power should be employed in the next war and what constitutes the principles governing its employment, not by journeying into the hinterlands of wild imaginings but by traveling the highway of common sense and logic." Maj. Harold Lee George, "An Inquiry into the Subject 'War,'" Air Corps Tactical School, Dept. of Air Tactics and Strategy, [1934/5?], in AFHRC, decimal file no. 248.11-9, p. 1.

146. Maj. Harold Lee George, among others at ACTS, spoke frequently of the vulnerabilities and interdependencies "which our present civilization has created" ("An Inquiry into the Subject 'War'").

147. Bruce Barton, "After Roosevelt—What?" *Colliers* magazine, 21 January 1939, pp. 13, 35–36.

148. McFarland, *America's Pursuit of Precision Bombing*, 94–98; quotation on 95.

149. Thomas Greer has written, "By 1933, with the high-speed heavy bombers almost a reality, and with the emerging concept of long range, precision attack becoming dominant at ACTS, ground support aviation fell into neglect" (*The Development of Air Doctrine*, 66–67).

150. See Lee Kennett, "The U.S. Army Air Forces and Tactical Air War in the Second World War," in *The Conduct of the Air War in the Second World War*, ed. Hoorst Boog (Providence, R.I.: Berg, 1992), 459–460; R. Muller, "Close Air Support: The German, British, and American Experiences, 1918–1941," in *Military Innovation in the Interwar Period*, ed. Williamson Murray and Allan Millett (Cambridge: Cambridge University Press, 1996), 173.

151. Kennett, "The U.S. Army Air Forces and Tactical Air War," 460.

152. On the issue of defenses and fighter escorts in American planning generally, see I. B. Holley, "An Enduring Challenge: The Problem of Air Force Doctrine," in *The Harmon Memorial Lectures in Military History, 1959–1987*, ed.

H. Borowski (Washington, D.C.: Office of Air Force History, 1988), 428–30; and Holley's "Of Saber Charges, Escort Fighters, and Spacecraft," *Air University Quarterly Review* 34, no. 6 (1983): 5–11. For an investigation of the problem as it existed in both the United States and in Britain, see Williamson Murray, "The Influence of Pre-War Anglo-American Doctrine on the Air Campaigns of the Second World War," in *The Conduct of the Air War in the Second World War*, 235–53.

153. Spaatz quoted in B. L. Boylan, "The Development of the American Long Range Escort Fighter" (Ph. D. diss., University of Missouri, 1955), 12.

154. Sherman, *Air Warfare*, 227–28.

155. ACTS, *Bombardment* (1926 text), 9.

156. Boylan, "Long Range Escort Fighter," 58.

157. Ibid., 13–14, 58–61.

158. ACTS, "Bombardment Aviation," 1930, p. 12. The historical section was published as a separate monograph in 1938, under the heading the "Genesis of Bombardment Aviation."

159. Ibid., 13–14. This argument utilized an extended quote from H. A. Jones's official history, *The War in the Air*, 2:473–75.

160. ACTS, "Air Force" (1930 text), p. 44.

161. Ibid., 72.

162. Ibid., 53–54.

163. Ibid. Later in the text the authors examined some of the records of Trenchard's IF in order to determine when bomber formations were likely to get through; their examination produced no conclusive results. They argued simply, "These World War examples indicate that sometimes the success of the bombardment mission will be prevented by pursuit, and that at other times it will be successful in spite of hostile pursuit" (88).

164. Ibid., 64, 88.

165. Ibid., 67. The preceding sentences of the quote stated, "An air force gains superiority over its enemy, ground and air, through superior leadership resulting in better plans; by fortitude including physical and moral courage, and the ability to maintain a high morale under adversity; and above all through the realization that a striking force once in the air, cannot be stopped."

166. ACTS, "Air Force" (1930 text), 87.

167. Quoted in Boylan, "Long Range Escort Fighter," 16–17.

168. Westover quoted in CC, 1:65.

169. Quoted in Boylan, "Longe Range Escort Fighter," 17. See also Futrell, *Ideas, Concepts, Doctrine*, 42.

170. Major General Foulois, "Developments in Organization, Armament, and Equipment of the Air Corps," lecture to the Army War College, 22 October 1934, in RG 18, CDF 350.001 (lectures), box 565, NARA.

171. John F. Shiner, "The Heyday of the GHQ Air Force, 1935–1939," in Bernard C. Nalty, ed. *Winged Sword, Winged Shield: A History of the United States Air Force*, vol. 1 (Washington, D.C.: Air Force History and Museums Program, 1997), 142.

172. See Futrell, *Ideas, Concept, Doctrine*, 43.

173. C. L. Chennault, "The Role of Defensive Pursuit," 1933, in AFHRC,

decimal file no. 248-282-4, p. 12. On Chennault's views generally, see Greer, *The Development of Air Doctrine*, 58–67; Johnson, *Fast Tanks and Heavy Bombers*, 156–57.

174. Shiner, "The Heyday," 141. See also Boylan, "Long Range Escort Fighter," 20–21; Greer, *The Development of Air Doctrine*, 58–59.

175. Col. W. C. McChord, Chief, War Plans and Training Division, Air Corps, "Memorandum for the Executive," 3 July 1936, in RG 18, CDF 381 (war plans), box 771, NARA.

176. Shiner, "The Heyday," 141; Byrd, *Kenneth N. Walker*, 33–38.

177. ACTS, "Bombardment," 1935 text, AFHRC dec. no. 248.101-9, p. 140.

178. Boylan, "Long Range Escort Fighter," 26–29.

179. Quoted in ibid., 33.

180. Ibid., 60–61; Stephen McFarland and Wesley Phillips Newton, *To Command the Sky* (Washington, D.C.: Smithsonian Institution Press, 1991), 102–3.

181. Boylan, "Long Range Escort Fighter," 38–45. The ACTS 1939 "Pursuit" manual had reintroduced the idea of a single-seater escort, although it was tentative about when and how the planes might be employed.

182. See Robert Frank Futrell, "Historical Evaluation of the Combined Bomber Offensive: Twenty Years and Two Wars Later" (paper delivered at the Second Annual Military History Symposium, U.S. Air Force Academy, 2–3 May 1968), 3–4; also, CC, 1:604.

183. One historian, writing in 1962, laconically described the impact of the Spanish civil war: "The Allies, uninvolved, developed strategic doctrine unimpeded by the Spanish experience." See John F. Guilmartin, "Aspects of Air Power in the Spanish Civil War," *Air Power Historian* 9, no. 2 (April 1962): 86.

184. James S. Corum, "The Spanish Civil War: Lessons Learned and Not Learned by the Great Powers," *The Journal of Military History* 62 (April 1998): 320–22.

185. CC, 1:84.

186. H. H. Arnold and Ira C. Eaker, draft chapter for *This Flying Game*, update, [1937/38], p. 3. Located in H. H. Arnold Papers, box 228, Library of Congress Manuscript Room, Washington, D.C.; also Corum, "The Spanish Civil War," 318–19.

187. Arnold and Eaker, draft chapter, *This Flying Game*, 8. In support of the same point, Arnold wrote, "The powers, capabilities, and limitations of bombardment aircraft have not been properly tested in Spain. So, let us be careful not to draw lessons about heavy bombardment from the air work in that theatre. . . . [T]here has been no major effort to interrupt the commercial and industrial life in Spain by the use of large forces of heavy bombardment aviation."

188. Ibid., 13. The views expressed in the draft chapter had commonalities with two reports—one on Spain and one on China—written by Col. Ira Eaker in late 1937. See "General Summary and Comment on Air Fighting, Spain" and "General Summary and Comment on Air Fighting, Far East" prepared by Col. Eaker, 1 December 1937, in RG 18, CDF 385, box 775, NARA.

189. Canevari added, "There would be . . . numerous bases and points of supply, powerful national air industries working at top speed, and large reserves

of trained pilots" (Lt. Col. Emilio Carnevari, "Forecasts from the War in Spain," portions translated and reprinted in *Air Corps Newsletter* 21: no. 7 [1 April 1938]: 9).

190. H. H. Arnold and Ira C. Eaker, *Winged Warfare* (New York: Harper Bros., 1941), 168.

191. Ibid., 169.

192. Ibid., 170–71.

193. R. Dan Richardson, "The Development of Airpower Concepts and Air Combat Techniques in the Spanish Civil War," *Air Power History* 40, no. 1 (Spring 1993): 14.

194. Kindelan quoted in Richardson, "The Development of Airpower Concepts," 14.

195. He added, "In no circumstance has one seen bombing machines attacked by the enemy pursuit until this latter has endeavored to get rid of these escorting planes, whether by engaging them in combat or by waiting until the escort single-seaters and bombing planes have separated" ("Air Warfare in Spain," *Air Corps Newsletter*, 20, no. 15 (1 August 1937): 6. The author of the original article was not identified, but it may have been André Langeron, who wrote a similar-sounding article for *Les Ailes* in April 1937.

196. Richardson. "The Development of Airpower Concepts," 16.

197. Boylan, "Long Range Escort Fighter," 29–30.

198. See for instance, "Recollections of a Flyer in Spain," reprint from *L'Air*, August 11–20, 1938, with note of receipt from General Arnold, 16 December 1938, in RG 18, CDF 385, box 775, NARA. "Report of Observations pertaining to Equipment, etc., Japan, China" from Frank D. Sinclair, Sikorsky Aircraft Corp. 17 August 1938, with covering note to Chief of Air Corps from Maj. Cortlandt S. Johnson, 29 August 1938, in RG 18, CDF 385, box 774, NARA.

199. Arnold quoted in Boylan, "Long Range Escort Fighter," 40; see also McFarland and Newton, *To Command the Sky*, 35–36.

200. Arnold and Eaker, *Winged Warfare*, 176.

201. ACTS, "Bombardment," 1935 text, cited in Fabyanic, "A Critique of United States Air Planning," 33.

202. Sherry, *The Rise of American Air Power*, 53.

Chapter 4
Rhetoric and Reality, 1939–1942

1. Terence O'Brien, *Civil Defence* (London: HMSO, 1955), 281.

2. There were exceptions. In 1928, J.F.C. Fuller had speculated that a future air war was unlikely to begin with all-out attacks on cities since "no nation in the near future will be in a position to place all, or the majority of its war eggs in the air basket" (*On Future Warfare* [London: Sifton Praed, 1928], 214).

3. See unsigned document, "The General Policy for the Employment of the Air Striking Force at the Outset of a War," 27 September 1938, in AIR 8/251, Public Record Office, London. For an overview of these issues, see AIR 41/39, pp. 254–64; WF, 1:97–100.

4. WF, 1:91. See generally WF, 1:93–106; Malcolm Smith, *British Air Strategy Between the Wars* (Oxford: Clarendon, 1984), 269–305.

5. The Industrial Intelligence Committee had been set up in 1929 and overhauled in 1936. An air targets subcommittee collected and analyzed data on Germany, trying to base targeting decisions on as comprehensive and informed a foundation as possible. On the outbreak of war, such intelligence operations were brought under the purview of the Intelligence Department of the Ministry of Economic Warfare (MEW). It would take some time, however, for the MEW to rationalize its relationship with the Air Staff, and with the Joint Intelligence Committee (JIC) of the Committee of Imperial Defence (CID)—the latter committee allowing for the intelligence directors of the three services to work with a staff in order to supply agreed-upon appreciations to the Chiefs of Staff and the CID. For a thorough overview of intelligence organization in Britain, see F. H. Hinsley et al., *British Intelligence in the Second World War* vol. 1 (London: HMSO, 1979), 3–43.

6. WF, 1:92–93, 260–62.

7. WF, 1:94.

8. See "Western Plans," 1 September 1939, in AIR 9/96; AIR 9/135, esp. "Memorandum on German Forests," 7 August 1940; and AIR 9/139, esp. "Chemical Board Crop Subcommittee, First Report," 6 March 1941. Other plans drawn up but given lower priority included attacks on the German fleet at sea or in harbor (W.A.12 and W.A.7); attacks on the Kiel canal (W.A.9); attacks on enemy administrative offices (W.A.13). Plans for sowing mines (W.A.15) and dropping propaganda leaflets (W.A.14) were also compiled.

9. See Smith, *British Air Strategy*, 289.

10. Ludlow-Hewitt calculated that if a determined attack were made on Germany, his medium bomber force would be eliminated in three and a half weeks, and the heavy bomber force in seven and a half (WF, 1:95).

11. WF, 1:96–97.

12. See "Appreciation on the Attack of German War Industry" (for the period 1 April to 1 August 1939), January 1939, and "Memorandum on Air Attack Against the Ruhr Area and Navigable Waterways Leading Thereto," 11 April 1940, both in AIR 9/102; "Summary of Plans for Action by the Air Striking Force Against Enemy War Industry" and "Note on the Course of Action to be adopted from the point of view of the 'Air' War as soon as 'Gloves off' Policy is approved by the Government," 10 September 1939, along with "Western Plans," 1 Sept. 1939, in AIR 9/96.

13. "Note on the Course of Action" and "Summary of Plans for Action," 10 September 1939, in AIR 9/96.

14. In light of this, Ludlow-Hewitt suggested that bombing categories be renamed as "Destructive bombing" (subdivided into 'precise targets' and 'target groups') and "Harassing Bombing." See Minutes of the 1st Meeting of the Bombing Policy Sub-Committee, 22 March 1938, in AIR 2/8812.

15. "Notes of a Meeting at General Gamelin's Headquarters at 10:30 A.M. 24 Tuesday October 1939," in AIR 14/194.

16. WF, 1:96.

17. "Minutes of a Meeting to Discuss the Assumptions Required for War Planning," 30 November 1938, in AIR 9/96, pp. 3–4.

18. Ludlow-Hewitt, "Readiness for War Report," 10 March 1939, in AIR 14/298; Ludlow-Hewitt to Under-Secretary of State, Air Ministry, 25 May 1939, in AIR 8/258.

19. Newall, "Covering Memorandum by CAS on Letter from Air Officer Commanding-in-Chief, Bomber Command, BC/S.21588/C.-in-C. dated 25th May 1939," for 176th Progress Meeting, Bomber Command Policy, in AIR 8/258. See also WF, 1:101.

20. AIR 41/39, p. 255.

21. AIR 41/39, p. 256–57.

22. See "Appreciation on the Attack of German War Industry," January 1939.

23. See AIR 41/39, pp. 249–51; Sir John Slessor, *The Central Blue* (London: Cassell, 1956), 213–14.

24. "Air Ministry Instructions and Notes on the Rules to be Observed By the Royal Air Force in War," and covering note, A. H. Self (Air Ministry) to Air Officer Commanding-in-Chief, Bomber Command, 22 August 1939, in AIR 14/249. Since taking the "gloves off" right away was the only means through which Britain might be of help to Poland, it was understood in Britain that any immediate assistance to the Poles would be sacrificed for longer-term imperatives. See also J. M. Spaight, formerly secret annex to *Air Power and War Rights* (1947), in AIR 41/5, Section D, "British Bombing Policy."

25. The text of Roosevelt's appeal can be found in *Foreign Relations of the United States*, 1939, vol. 1 (Washington, D.C.: Government Printing Office, 1956), 541–42; also Eugene Emme, ed., *The Impact of Air Power* (Princeton: Van Nostrand, 1959), 68.

26. AIR 41/39, pp. 264–71.

27. "Air Ministry Instructions governing Naval and Air Bombardment," 5 June 1940 (from Bomber Command to Headquarters, Groups 2 through 6), in AIR 14/249.

28. These were supported by two thousand reserve aircraft of fighter and coastal reconnaissance types. There were also nearly thirty-five squadrons overseas. See J.R.M. Butler, *Grand Strategy*, vol. 2, September 1939–June 1941 (London: HMSO, 1957), 33–35.

29. Brereton Greenhous et al., *The Crucible of War, 1939–1945*, vol. 3 of *The Official History of the Royal Canadian Air Force* (Toronto: University of Toronto Press, 1994), 530. The chapters of the volume on Bomber Command were written by Stephen J. Harris.

30. Anthony Verrier, *The Bomber Offensive* (London: B.T. Batsford, 1968), 82; WF, 138–139.

31. WF, 1:138–39.

32. WF, 1:100, 105–6.

33. See Greenhous et al., *The Crucible of War*, 532–34. Even after the ban was lifted, the RAF continued to prohibit leaflet drops west of Saarbrücken, Frankfurt, Päderborn, and Bremen in order to reduce the chance of incursions into the airspace of France and the Low Countries.

34. Draft of "The Attack of German War Potential by Night," 13 January 1940, Plans (Op.), in AIR 9/102.

35. WF, 1:140, 204–11.

36. Douglas quoted in WF, 1:145. See also, generally, John Terraine, "Theory and Practice of the Air War: The Royal Air Force," in *The Conduct of the Air War in the Second World War: An International Comparison*, ed. Hoorst Boog (Providence, R.I.: Berg, 1992), 467–95.

37. For an overview, see Hinsley, *British Intelligence*, 1:234–35.

38. WF, 1:141, 146, 265–66, 288–89. The importance of oil had been understood before the war and, accordingly, the Cabinet set up a special committee under Lord Hankey to advise on the topic. After the war began, a special intelligence committee—under Geoffrey Lloyd—was set up to advise the Hankey committee and prepare estimates for the Chiefs of Staff. While the MEW also provided information on oil, the Lloyd committee drew information from a variety of sources, including the Allies' great oil companies. For an overview of the Lloyd committee's impact on targeting at this point, see Hinsley, *British Intelligence*, 1:241–44.

39. Churchill quoted in David Reynolds, "Churchill and the British Decision to Fight On in 1940: Right Policy, Wrong Reasons," in *Diplomacy and Intelligence During the Second World War*, ed. Richard Langhorne (Cambridge: Cambridge University Press, 1985), 156–57; see generally 147–67.

40. Ibid., 157.

41. Churchill quoted in ibid., 157–58. See also: WF, 1:280–83; Hinsley, *British Intelligence*, 1:238–39; Harold Nicholson, *The War Years, 1939–1945* (London: Collins, 1967), 62.

42. Basil Collier, *The Defence of the United Kingdom* (London: HMSO, 1957), 225. Of the summer of 1940, Webster and Frankland wrote perceptively that "before Bomber Command had become the master of any skill, it was forced to become the jack-of-all-trades" (WF, 1:144).

43. See Malcolm Smith, "The Air Threat and British Foreign and Domestic Policy: The Background to the Strategic Air Offensive," in *The Conduct of the Air War in the Second World War*, 622–23.

44. Sebastian Cox, "The Sources and Organization of RAF Intelligence" in *The Conduct of the Air War in the Second World War*, 577. In the September 1940 issue of *The Royal Air Force Quarterly*, J. M. Spaight argued optimistically, "Our great and shining hope is in the air. It is there that we shall achieve victory, there that we shall bring home to the Germans the truth that they who take the sword will perish by the sword" ("Victory and the Bombing of Hinterlands," *The Royal Air Force Quarterly*, 11, no. 4 [September 1940]: 335).

45. Portal to Air Ministry, 16 July 1940, and Agenda for Air Staff Conference, sent to Portal 21 July 1940, quoted in WF, 1: 150–51.

46. Churchill quoted in Charles Messenger, *Bomber Harris and the Strategic Bombing Offensive* (New York: St. Martin's, 1984), 39.

47. Vice Chief of Air Staff Sir Richard Peirse wrote directly to Churchill urging a continuation of attacks against aircraft and oil targets. See Peirse to Churchill, 5 September 1940, in AIR 8/41.

48. WF, 1:153.

49. See Hinsley, *British Intelligence*, 1:315.

50. Portal, "Review of Bombing Policy: Note by Air Officer Commanding-in-Chief, Bomber Command," 30 September 1940, in AIR 9/443.

51. See "Notes of a Meeting Held on 23 October 1940 to Discuss Bombing Policy," in AIR 9/443. Portal argued that the maximum use of fire be made in such attacks. When the issue of reprisals was raised, the gathered policymakers agreed that the RAF could no longer be bound by fear of what the enemy might do and argued as well that it would be preferable for the Germans to make reprisal raids than for them systematically to attack British industry.

52. Not until the Luftwaffe attacked Coventry (14 November) was Bomber Command given a city center as its aim point. See WF, 1:215.

53. Ian McLaine, *Ministry of Morale* (London: Allen and Unwin, 1979), 7.

54. Harold Nicholson, recruited by Churchill to serve in the Ministry of Information, was angry about the attacks made on it. He admitted, though, the there was some foundation for the criticism due to the ministry's failures of organization. See Nicholson, *The War Years, 1939–1945*, 104–5.

55. Richard Titmuss, *Problems of Social Policy* (London: HMSO, 1950), 339.

56. Harold Nicholson, *The War Years, 1939–1945*, ed. Nigel Nicholson (New York: Atheneum, 1967), 2:105–6; 114–16.

57. McLaine, *Ministry of Morale*, 94, 97.

58. "War, Drunkenness, and Suicide," *Nature* 146 (20 July 1940): 90. Also McLaine, *Ministry of Morale*, 109–136; Titmuss, *Problems of Social Policy*, 339–42.

59. Dr. Felix Brown, "Civilian Psychiatric Air Raid Casualties," *The Lancet* (31 May 1941): 691. See also, R. J. Bartlett, "The Civilian Population Under Bombardment," *Nature* no. 3736 (7 June 1941): 700–701; P. E. Vernon, "Psychological Effects of Air Raids," *The Journal of Abnormal and Social Psychology* 36, no. 4 (October 1941): 457–76.

60. Vernon, "Psychological Effects of Air Raids," 474.

61. Ibid., 475; Dr. R. D. Gillespie, *Psychological Effects of War on Citizen and Soldier* (New York: W. W. Norton, 1942), 209–11.

62. Cited in Richard Overy, *Why the Allies Won* (London: Jonathan Cape, 1955), 109.

63. The British official historians noted that judgment on the question tended to rest on "speculative reasoning which had strong appeal to certain minds" (see WF, 1:270).

64. Count Stephan Zamoyski to Sir Richard Peirse, 4 January 1941; Sir Richard Peirse to Sir Charles Portal, 8 January 1941; Sir Charles Portal to Sir Richard Peirse, 12 January 1941; and Sir Richard Peirse to Gen. W. Sikorski, 15 January 1941; in the Papers of Lord Portal (hereafter PP), folder 9 B, Correspondence with C-in-C Bomber Command, 1941, Christ Church, Oxford.

65. This was the result of poor weather. Bomber Command devoted three nights to oil, six to industrial cities, six to Channel ports, and nineteen to naval targets. See Peirse to Portal, 28 February 1941, in PP, folder 9B.

66. WF, 1:299.

67. Portal to Peirse, message, [28] February 1941, in PP, folder 9B.

68. Note by Chief of the Air Staff (2nd Draft), 3 March 1941, in PP, folder 9B; Portal to Director of Plans, 28 Febrary 1941, in AIR 8/424; "Information Required for Dominion Prime Ministers," 4 December 1940, in AIR 8/424.

69. Peirse to Portal, 5 March 1941, in PP, folder 9B.

70. Directive to Bomber Command (Freeman to Peirse), 9 March 1941, quoted in WF, 1:165. The official historians write that if Bomber Command had been at this stage "left free to carry out the oil plan it would probably have done a great deal more damage to its prestige than to its targets" (165–66).

71. WF, 1:167.

72. See Bottomley to V.C.A.S., memo 17 May 1941, in AIR 20/3359.

73. WF, 1:169, 280–83.

74. WF, 1:280–81, 296–98.

75. Trenchard to Churchill, memo, 19 May 1941, quoted in WF, 1:169–70.

76. Minutes of a Meeting held by CAS on Monday, 2 June 1941, to Discuss Bombing Policy, in AIR 20/2795. Trenchard elaborated on these views later, in a meeting of the Parliamentary Air Committee on 15 October 1941. He argued that the Germans disliked being kept out of bed at night, and that "the German civilian population were much further apart from their officials than were our people over here." In the end, he argued, "the moral effect would eventually shake them." Notes of a Meeting of Parliamentary Air Committee, 15 October 1941, in AIR 8/424.

77. Minutes, 2 June 1941, pp. 1–2.

78. Minutes, 2nd June 1941, p. 2. During the period between June and December 1941, Bomber Command had available to it for operations only 380 medium and 40 heavy bombers. See J.M.A. Gwyer and J.R.M. Butler, *Grand Strategy*, vol. 3, *June 1941–August 1942*, Part 1, (London: HMSO, 1964), p. 27.

79. Minutes, 2nd June 1941, p. 4.

80. WF, 1:170–71.

81. DCAS (Bottomley) to Peirse, 28 July 1941, in AIR 8/424; WF, 1:171–74.

82. The official wording in the report was as follows: "Of the total sorties, only about one in five get within five miles of the target." Of planes recorded as attacking the target (a percentage of total sorties), the ratio was one in three. The Butt Report is reproduced in WF, 4:205–13. See also, WF, 1:178–80. Mr. Butt, a civil servant and member of the War Cabinet Secretariat, examined over 600 photographs of night bomber sorties that had been flown between the beginning of June and the end of July. Though he could not claim that his figures were perfect, he did feel confident that his general conclusions were correct.

83. For Peirse's reaction, see the introduction to this book.

84. Churchill to CAS (Portal), Personal Minute, 3 September 1941, in PP, folder 2B; Prime Minister's Minutes, July–September 1941; Churchill to CAS, Personal Minute, 15 September 1941, in PP, folder 2B.

85. See "Extract from Conclusions of W.M. (41) 84th meeting held on 19th August 1941," in AIR 8/424.

86. Portal to DCAS, 28 September 1941, in AIR 8/424.

87. VCAS to CAS, 2 October 1941, in AIR 20/2795; CAS to VCAS, 5 October 1941, in AIR 8/424.

88. Prime Minister to Secretary of State for Air, 11 April 1942, in AIR 8/424.

89. Portal to Peirse, 30 November 1940, in AIR 8/407.

90. WF, 1:185, 302.

91. German statistics detailing bombs dropped on dummy installations can be found in Edward B. Westermann, "Sword in the Heavens: German Ground-Based Air Defenses, 1914–1945" (Ph.D. diss., University of North Carolina, at Chapel Hill, 2000), esp. 185–86, 233–34. For statistics on the Berlin raid, see 233.

92. Mark K. Wells, *Courage and Air Warfare* (London: Frank Cass, 1995), 114.

93. Portal to Peirse, 23 November 1941, in PP, folder 9 (correspondence with Commander in Chief of Bomber Command); see also WF, 1:185–86, 254–57. Portal had longstanding concerns about Peirse's attention to weather. See, for instance, Portal to Peirse, 30 November 1940, in AIR 8/407.

94. The directive is reprinted in WF, 4:143–48; see also WF, 1:322–24. British scientist Sir Henry Tizard had earlier proposed an alternative: very fast bombers with improved armament. The technical problems remained to be solved though, and thus city bombing appeared the most feasible near-term alternative. See "Notes on the Bomber Striking Force," 23 July 1941, in AIR 8/424.

95. Air Vice-Marshal Slessor, ACAS (Policy), "Bombardment Policy" memo, 29 October 1942, in AIR 8/424.

96. See, for example, DCAS (Harris) to Portal, 26 April 1941, in AIR 8/424. Harris's early history is detailed in his autobiography, *Bomber Offensive* (London: Collins, 1947). See also Dudley Saward, *Bomber Harris* (Garden City, NY: Doubleday, 1985), and Messenger, *Bomber Harris and the Strategic Bombing Offensive*.

97. Wesley K. Wark, *The Ultimate Enemy: British Intelligence and Nazi Germany, 1933–1939* (Ithaca: Cornell University Press, 1985), 188–202.

98. Harris, *Bomber Offensive*, 277.

99. Harris to Trenchard, 14 April 1943, Harris Papers, (hereafter HP) folder 50, RAF Museum, Hendon, United Kingdom.

100. Harris, *Bomber Offensive*, 83, also 86–89.

101. Ibid., 88.

102. Webster and Frankland (WF) foreshadow the problem in 1:345.

103. See S. Zuckerman, *From Apes to Warlords* (New York: 1978), 140–48; Appendix II reprints "Qualitative Study of Total Effects of Air Raids," Ministry of Home Security, Research and Experiments Dept. 2770, 8 April 1942. Interestingly, Noble Frankland has recently asserted that Zuckerman's critique of Cherwell was ex post facto; in early 1942, Frankland claims, Zuckerman himself was not opposed to area bombing. See Frankland's letter to the *Times Literary Supplement*, 4 September 1998, p. 17.

104. See Zuckerman, *From Apes to Warlords*, 143–44; McLaine, *Ministry of Morale*, 123–124. The quote is from WF, 1:332–33.

105. See WF, 1:331–32. Commenting on the implications of the Cherwell minute, the official historians described it starkly and honestly as a plan of attack designed to "render the German industrial population homeless, spiritless, and, in so far as possible, dead." See WF, 2:22.

106. See WF, 1:329.

107. On Stalin's views, see Overy, *Why the Allies Won*, 101–3.

108. Harris added, "[S]o much so that we are tempted to the somewhat cynical remark that only Admiral King of the United States Navy and the Air Ministry itself still remain to be converted to the bomber idea" (Harris to Trenchard, 1 Dec. 1943, in HP, folder 50).

109. I am indebted to Vincent Orange for stressing this point to me in personal correspondence. See Vincent Orange, "World War II: Allied and National Command," *The Journal of the Royal Air Force Historical Society*, no. 16 (1996): 12–21. See also WF, 3:29.

110. Harris's 17 June minute to Churchill is quoted in WF, 1:341.

111. Harris, Untitled paper of 28 August 1942, sent with covering note to Portal on 3 September 1942, in AIR 8/424; see also HP, folder 77.

112. Churchill to Sinclair, 13 March 1942, in PP folder 2D.

113. In October 1917, Churchill wrote, "It is improbable that any terrorization of the civil population which could be achieved by air attack would compel the Government of a great nation to surrender." See Churchill's "Munitions Possibilities of 1918," reprinted in H. A. Jones, *The War in the Air: Appendices* (Oxford: Oxford University Press, 1937), Appendix IV, 19; Winston Churchill, "Let the Tyrant Criminals Bomb!" *Colliers*, 14 January 1939, pp. 12–13, 36.

114. Those arguments are detailed in this book's introduction.

115. On Churchill's views see Reynolds, "Churchill and the British Decision," 160–162. Harold Nicholson also expected a quick American entry into the war. In a letter of 19 June 1940, he wrote, "I think it practically certain that the Americans will enter the war in November, and if we can last till then, all is well" (*The War Years, 1939–1945*, 96).

116. CC, 1:104, 107–108; Futrell, *Ideas, Concepts, Doctrine*, 48–49. The first of thirty-nine upgraded B-17s, incorporating improvements based on a year's worth of flight testing, was delivered to Wright Field, Ohio, on 3 February. See "Air Corps Ready for Army Expansion Program," 3 April 1939, and "First of Improved Flying Fortresses Delivered to Army," 4 February 1939, War Department Press Releases, in AFHRC dec. no. 167.6-11 (1936–1939).

117. Overy, *Why the Allies Won*, 110. Also, generally, Jeffery S. Underwood, *The Wings of Democracy: The Influence of Air Power on the Roosevelt Administration, 1933–1941*(College Station: Texas A&M University Press, 1991).

118. Forrest C. Pogue, *George Marshall: Education of a General*, vol. 1 (New York: Viking, 1963), 323.

119. I. B. Holley, *Buying Aircraft: Matériel Procurement for the Army Air Forces* (Washington, D.C.: Office of the Chief of Military History, 1964), 200–201.

120. Figures are from Futrell, *Ideas, Concepts, Doctrine*, 50–51.

121. Sherry, *The Rise of American Air Power*, 81; Evan Huelfer, "Sacred Treasures: How the Casualty Issue Shaped the American Military Establishment: 1919–1941" (Ph.D. diss., University of North Carolina, Chapel Hill, 2000), 356–57, 406–7.

122. See "Anglo-American Air Collaboration," an Air Ministry Historical Narrative written by the Air Historical Branch in August 1946, pp. 18–25; copy

in the Papers of Carl. A. Spaatz (SP), box 70, Library of Congress Manuscript Collection, Washington, D.C.

123. See Slessor's personal memo, undated [March 1941?], in the Papers of Sir John Slessor, file XII C (Bomber Policy, 1939–1945), formerly located at the Air Historical Branch, Ministry of Defence, London, and now housed at the Public Record Office, London.

124. Harris continued, "The Yanks resent and ignore our advice. . . . In consequence one watches them, in spite of our protests and offers of help, laboriously plodding round the whole gamut of detailed error through which we ourselves have so painfully laboured during the past twenty years" (Harris to Freeman, 15 September 1941, in HP, folder H98).

125. Ibid., 5.

126. Richard G. Davis, *Carl A. Spaatz and the Air War in Europe* (Washington, D.C.: Smithsonian Institution Press, 1993), 53, 56; and "Carl A. Spaatz and the Development of the Royal Air Force-U.S. Army Air Corps Relationship, 1939–1940," *The Journal of Military History* 54, no. 4 (October 1990): 470.

127. Spaatz quoted in Davis, *Spaatz*, 52

128. See AWPD/1, Munitions Requirements of the AAF, 12 August 1941, in AFHRC, decimal no. 145.82. For analyses of the plan, see Haywood S. Hansell, *The Strategic Air War Against Germany and Japan* (Washington, D.C.: Office of Air Force History, 1986); *The Air Plan That Defeated Hitler* (Atlanta: Higgins-McArthur, 1972); James C. Gaston, *Planning the American Air War* (Washington, D.C.: National Defense University Press, 1982); CC, 1:131–50; Greer, *The Development of Air Doctrine*, 123–27; Fabyanic, "A Critique of United States Air War Planning," 49–78; and Davis, *Spaatz*, 60.

129. See AWPD/1; Fabyanic, "A Critique of United States Air War Planning," 54–56.

130. See Davis, *Spaatz*, 435–36; and Richard G. Davis, "Operation Thunderclap: The US Army Air Forces and the Bombing of Berlin," *The Journal of Strategic Studies* 14, no. 1 (March 1991): 90–111.

131. AWPD/1, tab 3, Escort Fighters, p. 1. See also, generally, I. B. Holley, Jr., "The Development of Defensive Armament for U.S. Army Bombers, 1918–1941: A Study in Doctrinal Failure and Production Success," in *The Conduct of the Air War in the Second World War*, 131–47.

132. AWPD/1, tab 3, Escort Fighters, p. 3.

133. Davis, *Spaatz*, 60–61.

134. Ibid., 64.

135. McFarland, *America's Pursuit of Precision Bombing, 1910–1945*, 98, 102.

136. See Gwyer and Butler, *Grand Strategy*, vol. 3, part 1, pp. 315–74.

137. CC, 1:115; "Anglo-American Air Collaboration," 54, 63.

138. The Americans found the idea of bombing at night incompatible with their orientation toward the destruction of selected industrial targets. And they also felt that the British had sent out smaller forces than were needed to do the job, had sacrificed experienced leaders, and had not given their crews enough rest. At the same time, though, they realized that the British had been operating under less than ideal circumstances, and that much of their air strength had

been devoted to sea and sea-related targets. See "History of the Eighth Air Force," volume 1, Headquarters, Eighth Air Force, February 1945, p. 40, in AFHRC, dec. file no. 520.01-3.

139. The Americans believed that two fighter groups (equipped with P-47s) would be necessary initially while American crews developed their technique. "Anglo-American Air Collaboration," 65.

140. Ibid., 66.

141. Noble Frankland, "The Combined Bomber Offensive" (lecture delivered to the Second Annual Military History Symposium, United States Air Force Academy, 2–3 May 1968), 7–8; copy in the Papers of Sir Robert Saundby, AC 72/12, box 5, RAF Museum, Hendon, United Kingdom.

142. See CC, 2:298.

143. RAF bombers would occasionally be called upon to aid in, or to do diversionary work for U.S. day bombing operations. See "Anglo-American Air Collaboration," 113–15.

144. "History of the Eighth Air Force," 1:76, 77. See also "Target Priorities of the Eighth Air Force," Headquarters, Eighth Air Force, Office of the Director of Intelligence, 15 May 1945, in AFHRC, dec. no. 520.317A; CC, 2:215–16.

145. See Charles W. MacArthur, *Operations Analysis in the US Eighth Air Force in World War II* (Providence, R.I.: The American Mathematical Society, 1990), 8–9; CC, 2:353–56.

146. CC, 2:353–55.

147. CC, 2:221–22.

148. CC, 2:217, 226.

149. On the effect of the North Africa campaign, see Records of Commanders Meeting, 10 November 1942, in SP, box 10, diary; on Arnold's concerns, see Davis, *Spaatz*, 99.

150. Churchill to Roosevelt, 16 September 1942, in AIR 8/711. In order to bolster FDR's enthusiasm, Churchill made an argument he himself did not fully believe: "[W]e know our night bombing offensive is having a devastating effect."

151. Churchill wrote, "Whether the Fortresses and Liberators will be able to bomb far into Germany by day is one of the great tactical questions of the war and one that is at present unanswered. . . . We do not think the claims of fighters shot down by Fortresses are correct though made with complete sincerity, and the dangers of daylight bombing will increase terribly once outside fighter protection and as the range lengthens" (Churchill to Hopkins, 16 October 1942, in AIR 8/711). Churchill was not opposed to daylight bombing per se; he merely felt that it would be impossible without long-range fighter escort.

152. The circle included Marshal of the Royal Air Force Sir Charles Portal, Chief of the Air Staff, RAF; Sir Archibald Sinclair, Secretary of State for Air; and Air Vice-Marshal John Slessor, Assistant Chief of the Air Staff for Policy. The documents on this internal debate can be found in AIR 8/711.

153. Portal, "Note on US Bomber Force," memo, 26 September 1942, in AIR 8/711.

154. Slessor to Portal, minute, 26 September 1942, in AIR 8/711.

155. Slessor to Sinclair, minute, 26 September 1942, AIR 8/711.

156. See Sinclair to Churchill, minute, 28 October 1942, and also "Note by the Secretary of State for Air," [October?] 1942, in AIR 8/711. In the latter, Sinclair wrote, "Americans are much like other people—they prefer to learn from their own experience. In spite of some admitted defects—including lack of experience—their leadership is of a high order, and the quality of their air crews is magnificent. If their policy of day bombing proves to their own satisfaction to be unsuccessful or prohibitively expensive they will abandon it and turn to night action. . . . They will not turn aside from day bombing till they are convinced that it has failed: they will not be convinced except by their own experience." See also WF, 1:360–63.

157. Portal to Churchill, minute, 7 November 1942, in AIR 8/711. On 12 January 1943, Sinclair once again urged Churchill to be diplomatic, and to give the Americans a chance (see Sinclair to Churchill, minute, 12 January 1943, in AIR 8/711).

158. Col. Edgar P. Sorenson to the Chief of the Air Corps, 20 May 1941; copy in AFHRC, decimal file no. 145.82.

159. See Davis, *Spaatz*, 97.

160. CC, 2:298.

161. See "Special Studies of Bombing Results," Headquarters, Army Air Forces, Director of Intelligence Service (19 October 1942), in SP, box 203. The authors wrote, for instance, that the British attack on Rostock "may well be cited by future airmen as a classic example of misdirected bombardment effort" (Special Study No. 1, p. 15). See also CC, 2:298–300.

Chapter 5
The Combined Bomber Offensive, 1943–1945

1. Only 2.5 percent of Bomber Command crews could be expected to survive two tours. See Mark Wells, *Courage and Air Warfare* (London: Frank Cass, 1995), 101, 127; Portal to Air Chief Marshal Sir Christopher Courtney, 24 December 1942, in AIR 8/1942, Public Record Office, London.

2. Text of General Eaker's Presentation to Prime Minister Churchill at the Casablanca conference, January 1943, in AFHRC (Maxwell AFB, Ala.), decimal no. 520.54C, p. 5. See also Gen. Ira Eaker, memo on "Night Bombing," 8 October 1942, in Papers of Carl A. Spaatz (hereafter, SP), box 10, diary, Library of Congress Manuscript Collection, Washington, D.C.

3. The Casablanca directive is reprinted in WF, 4:153–54.

4. "Report of Committee of Operations Analysts (COA) with Respect to Economic Targets Within the Western Axis," 8 March 1943; copy in SP, box 67 ("Air War Plans, Combined Bomber Offensive").

5. See "The Combined Bomber Offensive from the U.K.," 12 April 1943, in SP, box 67. The previously mentioned 8 March 1943 report by the COA had argued that "the principal reason for an early attack on the German aircraft industry is to neutralize German fighter aircraft strength in order to decrease losses and increase effectiveness of later bombardment operations."

6. "The Combined Bomber Offensive from the United Kingdom as approved by the Combined Chiefs of Staff, 14 May 1943, in WF, Annexes and Appen-

dices, 4:273–83. On Casablanca and Pointblank generally, see WF, 2:10–32; CC, 2:274–307, 348–76. See also, William R. Emerson, "Operation POINT-BLANK: A Tale of Bombers and Fighters," in *The Harmon Memorial Lectures in Military History, 1959–1987,* ed. Harry R. Borowski (Washington, D.C.: Office of Air Force History, 1988), 441–72; Davis, *Spaatz,* 161–65. See also Office of the Director of Intelligence, Headquarters, Eighth Air Force, "Target Priorities of the Eighth Air Force," 15 May 1945, in AFHRC, decimal no. 520.317A; "The Combined Bomber Offensive from the U.K." (Eaker Plan), Eighth Air Force 12 April 1943, in SP, box 67. The six systems included submarine construction yards and bases; the German aircraft industry; ball bearings; oil; synthetic rubber and tires; and military transport vehicles. See the Pointblank directive, reprinted in WF, 4:275.

7. "Report of Committee of Operations Analysts with Respect to Economic Targets Within the Western Axis," 8 March 1943; "The Combined Bomber Offensive from the U.K.," 12 April 1943, in SP, box 67.

8. See Pointblank directive in WF, 4:277.

9. See Harris to Eaker, 15 April 1943, copy in SP, box 67; WF, 2:28–30.

10. WF, 2:5. On 10 February 1944, Portal sent Churchill a minute telling him how he might in the future answer a question that had been posed by an American officer, "Why had not the R.A.F. the courage to bomb Germany by day?" He suggested pointing out that the Americans had not yet bombed Berlin, while Bomber Command had dropped 33,000 tons of bombs on the target. He also suggested that Churchill point out that in 1943 Bomber Command had: "*a*) despatched three times as many sorties to Germany [as the USAAF]; *b*) attacked targets in Germany with nearly four times as many aircraft; *c*) dropped nearly six times the weight of bombs on Germany; and *d*) lost nearly three times as many aircraft and more than twice as many airmen in attacking Germany" (Papers of Lord Portal [hereafter PP], folder 5A, Prime Minister's Minutes, January–December 1944; in Christ Church Library, Oxford).

11. Credit for these developments is due in part to Harris for his constant pressure regarding improved navigation. See Harris to Portal, 17 April 1942, and Portal to Harris, 20 April 1942, in PP, folder 9C. On radar aids, navigation aids, and bombsights, see WF, 4:3–24, 31–39.

12. WF, 3:300–330; Brereton Greenhous, *The Crucible of War, 1939–1945,* vol. 3 of *The Official History of the Royal Canadian Air Force* (Toronto: University of Toronto Press, 1994), 689–700.

13. Unsigned article, "Battle of Europe: High Road to Hell," *Time* magazine, 7 June 1943, pp. 27–30.

14. Berlin, for instance, had a key point rating of 545, while Dresden had one of 70. I am grateful to Andrew Lambert for allowing me access to the Blue Books at the RAF Staff College, Bracknell, United Kingdom.

15. Harris to Bottomley, 20 December 1943, Papers of Sir Arthur Harris (hereafter HP), folder 47, RAF Museum, Hendon, United Kingdom. Harris referred to those on the Air Staff who supported the bombing of oil targets as "the oily boys," and those who were interested in ball bearings as the "Schweinfurt fans." See Harris to Portal, 21 October 1942, in PP, folder 9C. See also Harris to Eaker, 15 April 1943, copy in SP, box 67.

16. These attitudes are prevalent throughout Harris' wartime correspondence. One might see, for instance, his letter to Portal of 5 March 1942, or of 24 August 1942, in PP, folder 9C (correspondence with CinC Bomber Command, 1942).

17. "Note on the Role and Work of Bomber Command," 8 July 1942, HP, folder 77, p. 4.

18. On RAF-Royal Navy rivalry, and on RAF Coastal Command's immensely important wartime campaigns, see Christina J. M. Goulter, *A Forgotten Offensive* (London: Frank Cass, 1995).

19. Sinclair to Harris, 28 August 1943, in HP, folder 79.

20. Tedder quoted in Vincent Orange, "World War II: Allied and National Command," *The Journal of the Royal Air Force Historical Society* no. 16 (1996): 19.

21. Harris told Eaker, "There is no difficulty in achieving our object . . . There is difficulty only in convincing those in whose hands lies the power to grasp this opportunity. The whole weight of enemy propaganda against the efficiency of our bomber offensive centres now on the prevention of their enlightenment" (Harris to Eaker, 15 April 1943; copy in SP, Box 67).

22. See Harris to Portal, 5 March 1942, in PP, folder 9C.

23. On the Ministry of Information's unwillingness to tell the unvarnished truth about Bomber Command, see Ian McLaine, *Ministry of Morale* (London: Allen and Unwin, 1979), 160–66.

24. Harris to Sir Arthur Street, Under Secretary of State, Air Ministry, 25 October 1943, in AIR 14/843. This correspondence was brought to my attention by Stephen J. Harris.

25. Harris to Street, 25 October 1943, in AIR 14/843, p. 2. Just over a month later, Lord Salisbury would send a letter of concern to Secretary of State for Air Sir Archibald Sinclair, asking if it was indeed Harris's intention to attack the German civilian population. Sinclair attempted to assuage Salisbury's fears by pointing out that there had been no change in the government's policy. He explained that "Harris is an airman, and he thinks of Germany in terms of War. He thinks of Berlin as the heart of the German war organism." Sinclair then went on to list for Salisbury the many war manufactures represented in the capital city. See Salisbury to Sinclair, 26 November 1943, and Sinclair to Salisbury, 29 November 1943; copies in HP, folder H79.

26. Street to Harris, 15 December 1943, in AIR 14/843.

27. Harris to Street, 23 December 1943, in AIR 14/843. (See also Street to Harris, 15 December 1943.) Street finally answered Harris on 2 March 1944. He explained that while the Air Ministry recognized that "the attack on Germany's war economy must entail heavy casualties to the civil population your directive neither requires nor enjoins direct attack on German civilians as such." But he then added that there had been no attempt "to disguise from the public the fact that your Command's attacks are aimed at the destruction of vast acreages of industrial cities." Harris was prepared to settle on such wording. On 7 March he wrote Street to say that he was "relieved to find . . . explicit recognition of the fact that Bomber Command's attacks aim deliberately at the destruction of vast acreages of German industrial cities." See Street to Harris, 2 March 1944, and Harris to Street, 7 March 1944, in AIR 14/843.

28. McLaine, *Ministry of Morale*, 161–63.

29. Bomber Command Staff, "Bomber Command, 1942" report, in HP, folder H77.

30. "A Result of Recent R.A.F. Attacks," with covering note from Portal to Churchill, 23 September 1942, in PP, folder 3B, Prime Minister's Minutes, July–September 1942; "R.A.F. Attacks and German Morale," 29 March 1943, copy in SP, box 203, file: "Results: Morale"; H. Freeman Matthews to Sir Archibald Sinclair, 11 March 1943, in HP, folder 79.

31. See, for example, Harris to Portal, 24 August 1942, PP, folder 9C. Writing to the prime minister on 3 November 1943, Harris argued that, with regard to devastation in German towns "what actually occurs is much more than can be seen in any photograph." Harris to Churchill, 3 November 1943, in HP, folder 77.

32. See "Report by the Chief of the Air Staff and Commanding General, U. S. Eighth Air Force on Progress Made by the R.A.F. and U.S. Eighth Air Force in the Combined Bomber Offensive," 7 November 1943, in National Archives, RG 243 sec. 3, envelope 194, pp. 3–4; Transcript of remarks by Gen. H. H. Arnold, to a conference of editors, writers, and broadcasters at the Pentagon, 18 October 1943, in SP, box 94.

33. Eaker to Spaatz, 8 October 1942, in SP, box 10, diary.

34. See Eaker to Eisenhower, 13 April 1943, in SP, box 67.

35. See WF, 2:16; CC, 1:667–68, 607–11; CC, 2:214–15.

36. See "Target Priorities of the Eighth Air Force," Headquarters Eighth Air Force, 15 May 1945, Office of Air Force History, Bolling AFB, Ala., dec. no. 520.317A; Stephen McFarland and Wesley Phillips Newton, *To Command the Sky* (Washington, D.C.: Smithsonian Institution Press, 1991), 96; WF, 2:27.

37. Eaker quoted in McFarland and Newton, *To Command the Sky*, 97–98.

38. See unsigned article, "The American Bombing Effort," *The Royal Air Force Quarterly* 14, no. 4 (September 1943): 1, 7, copy in the Papers of Ira C. Eaker, box 21, Library of Congress Manuscript Collection, Washington, D.C.

39. CC, 2:333–35. An intelligence report received by the British Air Staff on 4 November indicated that whereas the Pointblank directive had aimed at reducing Luftwaffe fighter aircraft to less than 700 (available for use in the west), the Germans would have over twice that number available in December, and as many as 1,700 by the time the Allied landings on the continent were scheduled to take place. See Greenhous, *The Crucible of War*, 732

40. WF, 2:33, 36–37.

41. CC, 2:357–58.

42. WF, 2:39; Noble Frankland, *The Bombing Offensive Against Germany* (London: Faber and Faber, 1965), 77; CC, 2:681–83, 704.

43. "Arnold Calls Bomber Blow at Nazi Plant Worth Cost," *New York Times*, 16 October 1943, p. 1.

44. "Arnold Calls . . . ," 16 October 1943.

45. "The first sixteen and a half months of operations of the Eighth Air Force, through the end of 1943, were largely a period of experiment, preparation, and accumulation of strength," said the War Department Bureau of Public Relations on 29 March 1944. See "Strategy of Bomber Offensive Against Germany Explained," in SP, box 84.

46. This correspondence, of October 1943, is detailed in WF, 2:42–45. Portal may have found this exchange ironic, in light of the superior tone Arnold had used in a letter to Portal of 9 March 1942. See Papers of H. H. Arnold (hereafter AP), box 38. Library of Congress Manuscript Collection, Washington, D.C.

47. Eaker pressed Arnold for more H2X-equipped airplanes and told him that it would be necessary to increase operational losses in order to push the bombing offensive in overcast conditions (a tradeoff he deemed "worthwhile.") Finally, Eaker told Arnold that there would be no visual targets available in Germany for the entire month. See Eaker to Arnold, 16 November 1943; copy in SP, box 82.

48. See WF, 2:46–52.

49. For a description of this important shuffling of command, see Richard G. Davis, *Carl A. Spaatz and the Air War in Europe* (Washington, D.C.: Smithsonian Institution Press, 1993), 273–79. Despite the great differences in their approaches to strategic bombing, Harris and Eaker actually had a strong friendship. For example, see letter, Harris to Eaker, 18 June 1945, in HP, folder 28.

50. See Davis, *Spaatz*, 289–90.

51. The British view was summed up well in a letter from Portal to Churchill, of 3 June 1941. The CAS told the prime minister, "Experience has shown . . . that the long range fighter is not able to operate successfully with the radius of action of the enemy's short range fighter force." Churchill responded simply, "This closes many doors of hope and opportunity" (in PP, folder 2 [Correspondence with prime minister, April–June 1941]).

52. AWPD/2, quoted in WF, 2:77.

53. CC, 2:334–35.

54. CC, 2:654–55.

55. WF, 2:78–82. A prototype of the first Mustang was produced in a mere 127 days.

56. For a sense of the strength and scope of American industrial production at this point in the war, see Paul Kennedy, *The Rise and Fall of the Great Powers* (New York: Random House, 1987), 353–55.

57. Bernard Lovell, *Echoes of War: The Story of H2S Radar* (Bristol: Adam Hilger, 1991), 148.

58. Eaker to Portal, 15 March 1943; copy in SP, box 81 ("Bombing Overcast"); Eaker to Arnold, 16 November 1943; copy in SP, box 82 ("Bombing Overcast Operations").

59. See W. Hays Parks, "'Precision and 'Area' Bombing: Who Did Which and When?" *The Journal of Strategic Studies* 18, no. 1 (March 1995):145–74, esp. 148, 153. In a question period following remarks to the press in October 1943, Arnold admitted that the Americans "do pattern bombing sometimes." But he confused the issue and misled those present by implying that pattern bombing, rather than the normal mode of all operations, was a distinct form, "done more for the breaking of morale of the people, confusion, and that sort of stuff in a community, and for destroying a city, more than it is to knock out any objective, which is what we are trying to do" (Gen. Henry H. Arnold, Transcript of remarks made at a conference of editors, writers, and broadcasters, 18 October 1943, in SP, box 94).

60. Memo from the CG, Army Air Forces, "Combined Chiefs of Staff Air Plan for the Defeat of Germany", 1 November 1943 in AP, box 39.

61. See Davis, *Spaatz*, 296–298. See also, Richard G. Davis, "German Railyards and Cities: US Bombing Policy 1944–1945," *Air Power History* 42, no. 2 (Summer 1995), 48–49.

62. Unsigned report to Spaatz, Navigational Errors in Operations, Headquarters, United States Strategic Air Forces in Europe, 4 March 1944, in SP, box 17 (diary).

63. Doolittle to Spaatz and Anderson, 14 February 1944, in SP, box 17 (diary), p. 2. In a meeting held in Maj. Gen. F. L. Anderson's office on 28 October 1944, several of the members present remarked on the continued unwillingness of crews to use offset bombing equipment. "They are prone to gamble on getting a lucky visual at the last minute," one remarked. See Minutes of Conference held in General Anderson's Office, 28 October 1944, in SP, box 19 (diary).

64. Gen. Arnold to Asst. Chief of Air Staff, Materiel, Maintenance & Distribution, memo, 26 April 1943, in AP, box 38. In January 1943 the British had prepared a report arguing that in area attacks, incendiary bombs caused— pound for pound—five times more damage than high explosive bombs. See "Incendiary Attack of German Cities," Air Ministry, January 1943; copy in SP, box 80 (Bombing Methods).

65. Parks, "Precision and 'Area' Bombing," 155–56; Davis, "German Railyards," 48. Some American commanders could not believe statistics indicating that American daylight bombing accuracy was sometimes poorer than RAF night raids. One wrote, "If anyone says that RAF night bombing with PFF is more accurate than Fortress day bombing, I'd instinctively call him a liar" (Comment on carrier sheet, Eighth Air Force, 26 October 1943, in SP, box 76 [Bombing Accuracy]).

66. WF, 2:32, 36.

67. Harris to the prime minister, 3 November 1943, in HP, folder H 77.

68. See WF, 2:31, footnote 2, and 33–36.

69. The letter is reproduced in WF, 2:54–55.

70. For excellent coverage of the battle of Berlin, see Greenhous, *The Crucible of War*, 729–95, esp. 731–35.

71. WF, 190–21; Greenhous, *The Crucible of War*, 730–60, esp. 734–46. For the figure on German fighter strength, see WF, 2:46.

72. Harris to Under Secretary of State, Air Ministry, 25 February 1944, in AIR 14/843.

73. Untitled report by the ACAS (I), 11 March 1944, in AIR 14/843; Air Marshal Sir Douglas C. S. Evill to Harris, 29 March 1944, in AIR 14/843. See also, Directorate of Intelligence (0), "RAF Attacks and German Morale," 29 March 1943; copy in SP, box 203 ("Results, Morale").

74. Extract from Air Ministry Weekly Intelligence Summary, no. 240, 8 April 1944; copy in SP, box 67.

75. The losses at Nuremburg would represent the largest Bomber Command loss of the war. See Martin Middlebrook and Chris Everitt, *The Bomber Command War Diaries*, rev. ed. (Leicester: Midland Publishing, 1996), 487.

76. See Emerson, "Operation POINTBLANK," 446–449; WF, 2:269–300, esp. 280–81; Davis, *Spaatz*, 296–333.

77. See Portal's letter to Harris of 8 January 1945 (in PP, folder 10C, pp. 6–7), in which he felt compelled to make the case for the American contribution.

78. Forward by the Commanding General for "Evaluation of Results of Strategic Bombardment Against the Western Axis (to the Report on the Progress of the CBO by A2, 10 December 1943)," copy in SP, Box 67; "Air Plan for the Defeat of Germany," memo from the Commanding General, Army Air Forces, 1 November 1943, in AP, box 39.

79. Spaatz to Doolittle, 26 January 1944, in SP, box 84 ("Strategic Bombing Concept"); Doolittle to Spaatz, "Tentative Plan for the Completion of the Combined Bomber Offensive," 11 March 1944, in SP, box 17 (diary). See also Davis, *Spaatz*, 298–303.

80. See Davis, *Spaatz*, 319–27; CC, 3:30–66. For a contemporary account of the operation, see Anderson to Arnold, "Script for Teletype," 27 February 1944, in SP, box 67 (Air War Plans, CBO).

81. "'Overlord'—The Employment of Bomber Forces in Relation to the Outline Plan," 12 February 1944, in SP, box 17, (diary).

82. On these command arrangements and the debates they engendered, see Davis, *Spaatz*, 341–44, and "Royal Air Force / United States Air Force Co-operation: Higher Command Structure and Relationships," (lecture to the Royal Air Force Historical Society, 29 October 1990 and published in that Society's "Proceedings," no. 9). On Tedder's views, see his *Air Power in War* (London: Hodder and Stoughton, 1947), 108. On the background to the railway (transportation) plan, see W. W. Rostow, *Pre-Invasion Bombing Strategy* (Austin: University of Texas Press, 1981), 7–14.

83. Harris, "The Employment of the Night Bomber Force in Connection with the Invasion of the Continent from the U.K.," memo, 13 January 1944, in PP, folder 10B.

84. Portal sent Harris the Air Ministry's comments, along with a pointed cover letter, on 30 January. See "Comments on Bomber Command Memorandum for the Employment of Night Bombers in Connection with Overlord," with covering note by Portal, 30 January 1944, in PP, folder 10B.

85. See Harris's letter to Portal of 24 March 1944, in HP, folder 83.

86. WF, 3:27.

87. See "Memorandum, Anderson to Spaatz," 14 February 1944, in SP, box 17 (diary); "Memorandum, Brig. Gen. C. P. Cabell, Col. C. G. Williamson, and Col. R. D. Hughes, to Lt. Gen. Carl Spaatz," with accompanying plan for the operation of the United States Strategic Air Forces for the Completion of the Combined Bomber Offensive, 5 March 1944, in SP, box 67 (Air War Plans, Combined Bomber Offensive), esp. "Prospect for Ending Air Attack Against German Morale," and "Re-examination of Previously Recommended Target Systems, Summary and Conclusions." See also Rostow, *Pre-Invasion Bombing Strategy*, 15–23, 36–43.

88. Tedder stated that the railway plan "should force the enemy to pass all traffic in the 'Overlord' area through a comparatively small number of lines. See

"Final Minutes of a Meeting Held on Saturday March 25th to Discuss the Bombing Policy in the Period Before 'Overlord,'" copy in AIR 37/1125.

89. Spaatz argued that the Germans would use their fighter force to defend against oil targets, whereas they might not use it for the defense of railway attacks. See "Final Minutes," in AIR 37/1125, p. 6. On the debate over targeting in general, and Spaatz's views specifically, see Davis, *Spaatz*, 341–418.

90. Eisenhower said that everything he had read had convinced him that apart from the attack on the German air force, the transportation plan was the only one that offered a reasonable chance of the air forces making an important contribution to the land battle during the first vital weeks of Overlord. See "Final Minutes," in AIR 37/1125, pp. 3–4.

91. Roosevelt quoted in Davis, *Spaatz*, 403. On this issue, see generally 400–403.

92. Davis, "German Railyards," 54.

93. Harris to Under Secretary of State, 7 April 1944, in PP, folder 10B.

94. Harris to Lovett, 3 April 1944, in HP, folder 28.

95. Portal to Harris, 12 April 1944; Harris to Portal, 15 April 1944; and Portal to Harris, 16 April 1944; in PP, folder 10B.

96. Attritional attacks on rail centers are estimated to have reduced rail traffic by 30 percent by 20 May 1944, and another 27 percent by mid-July. Rail cuts may have accounted for some 19 percent of the reduction in the same interval. See William F. Whitmore's "Logistics as a Target System" (1952), cited in Rostow, *Pre-Invasion Bombing Strategy*, 72–73, and notes 39 and 40. See also Greenhous, *The Crucible of War*, 797–98, 808–9.

97. W.W. Rostow, *Pre-Invasion Bombing Strategy*, 52–56.

98. Ibid., 56–65, 72–87.

99. See Davis, *Spaatz*, 414.

100. Ibid., 426–32.

101. CC, 3:172–76.

102. Eisenhower memo to Tedder quoted in Davis, *Spaatz*, 430.

103. On Portal's views, see "Final Minutes," AIR 37/1125, p. 5.

104. Göring quoted in Davis, *Spaatz*, 442. See generally, F. H. Hinsley et al., *British Intelligence in the Second World War*, vol. 3, Part 2 (New York: Cambridge University Press, 1988), 497–532.

105. Davis, *Spaatz*, 395–400, 403–8; Rostow, *Pre-Invasion Bombing Strategy*, 52–53.

106. Davis, *Spaatz*, 440.

107. See CC, 3:228–38; Davis, *Spaatz*, 453–82. On heavy bombers in close support, see Ian Gooderson, *Air Power at the Battlefront* (London: Frank Cass, 1998), 125–64.

108. Davis, *Spaatz*, 503; also "An Evaluation of the Effects of the Bomber Offensive in Landing Operations in France," with covering letter from Maj. Gen. F. L. Anderson to Maj. Gen. Andrei Sharapov, 13 October 1944, in SP, box 19 (diary).

109. On Thunderclap, see Davis, *Spaatz*, 432–39; WF, 3:52–55, 98–103.

110. WF, 3:55–56. A mid-September memo by the British Chiefs of Staff

reiterated the priority of oil attacks, but added, "Rapid developments in the strategic situation are now taking place. It may become desirable in the immediate future, to apply the whole of the strategic bomber effort to the direct attack of German morale." Memorandum by the British Chiefs of Staff, CCS 520/3 (Octagon), 12 September 1944, p. 4; copy in SP, box 18, (diary).

111. Eisenhower concluded by stating, "The policies under which you are now operating will be unchanged unless in my opinion an opportunity arises where a sudden and devastating blow may have an incalculable result." See Spaatz to Eisenhower, 24 August 1944, and Eisenhower message to Spaatz, 28 August 1944, in SP, Box 18 (diary).

112. Spaatz quoted by Davis in "German Railyards," 52. In recent years the topic of morality and American strategic bombing has garnered attention in the literature. See Ronald Schaffer, *Wings of Judgment* (New York: Oxford University Press, 1985); Michael Sherry, *The Rise of American Air Power* (New Haven, Conn.: Yale University Press, 1987); Conrad C. Crane, *Bombs, Cities, and Civilians* (Manhattan: University Press of Kansas, 1993). For an earlier but still useful study, see Gary Shandroff, "The Evolution of Area Bombing in American Doctrine and Practice" (Ph.D. diss., New York University, 1972).

113. AWPD / 1 argued that: "Timeliness of attack is most important in the conduct of air operations directly against civil morale. If the morale of the people is already low because of sustained suffering and deprivation and because the people are losing faith in the ability of the armed forces to win a favorable decision, then heavy and sustained bombing of cities may crash that morale entirely" (AWPD / 1 quoted in Davis, *Spaatz*, 435–36).

114. Davis, *Spaatz*, 435.

115. Ibid., 433, 494–95.

116. Davis, *Spaatz*, 438.

117. For details of the program, see Crane, *Bombs, Cities, and Civilians*, 78–92.

118. Ibid., 83–84.

119. See Col. C. G. Williamson (for Spaatz) to Doolittle, "Double-Azon Controlled Aircraft," 24 June 1944, in SP, box 18 (diary); Cypher Telegram, Joint Staff Mission to AMMSO, 11 November 1944, in AIR 8/838; Annex I to CCS 729, 11 November 1944, in AIR 8/838.

120. Employment of War-Weary U.S. Bombers Against German Industrial Targets, J.S.M. 362, C.O.S. Meeting, 13 November 1944, in AIR 8/838.

121. See related documents in AIR 8/838, especially Extract from Minutes of DO (45) 1st meeting, 26 January 1945.

122. Roosevelt to Churchill, telegram, 29 March 1945; Employment of War-Weary U.S. Bombers, note by the Chief of the Air Staff, COS (45) 246 (O), 10 April 1945; Churchill to Truman, telegram 14 April 1945; and Truman to Churchill, telegram 17 April 1945, all in AIR 8/838. Also, Sherry, *The Rise of American Air Power*, 263.

123. The British Chiefs of Staff argued, "Any relaxation of the tempo of our attacks against his [Germany's] oil installations will provide opportunity for rehabilitation and dispersal." See Memorandum by the British Chiefs of Staff, CCS 520/3 (Octagon), 12 September 1944, pp. 3–4, in SP, box 18 (diary);

Spaatz, "Future Plans for United States Strategic Air Forces in Europe," 24 August 1944, in SP, box 18 (diary). On the oil campaign generally, see CC, 3:280–302, 640–46; WF, 3:225–43; Davis, *Spaatz*, 490–95. Another important source on this point, which highlights the role of Ultra in target planning, is Hinsley, vol. 3, pt. 2, pp. 497–532, 605–24. On the targeting debates, see generally, WF, 3:65–74.

124. Deputy Chief of the Air Staff to Air Officer Commanding-in-Chief, Bomber Command, 25 September 1944, with "Directive for the Control of Strategic Bomber Forces in Europe," (attached); copy in SP, box 18 (diary). For further detail on command arrangements and the debates about it, see Davis, *Spaatz*, 483–90.

125. See Davis, *Spaatz*, 496–97.

126. Of the 12.9 percent of bombs that hit within the factory perimeter, 1.8 percent of the total failed to explode, 7.6 percent landed in empty spaces, and 1.3 percent hit pipelines and other utilities. See United States Strategic Bombing Survey (USSBS), Oil Division Final Report, 2nd ed., January 1947, p. 121.

127. These figures are from Davis, *Spaatz*, 500.

128. Ibid., 433–35.

129. The force bombed through 8/10ths to 10/10ths cloud cover fully 50 percent of the time. In addition, heavy bomber accuracy was dramatically affected by the number of combat boxes attacking a given target. The accuracy achieved by the first three boxes of the formation was over twice as great as that of succeeding groups. See Operational Analysis Section of the Eighth Air Force, "AAF Bombing Accuracy, Report No. 2," in RG 18, box 550, Air Adjutant General Files, 470 (classified, bulky file), National Archives and Records Administration (NARA), Washington, D.C. Report No. 2 also is summarized in Charles W. McArthur, *Operations Analysis in the U.S. Army Eighth Air Force in World War II* (Providence, R.I.: American Mathematical Society, 1990), 287–98.

130. Spaatz to Arnold, "H2X Pathfinders," 14 January 1944, in SP, box 17 (diary); Conference on Bombing Accuracy, 22–23 March 1945, USSTAF Armament memorandum no. 14-3 (1 April 1945), in SP, box 76 (Bombing Accuracy), esp. pp. 10–11.

131. Headquarters Eighth Air Force Operational Research Section, Report on H2X Operations During September Against Targets in Ludwigshafen and Mannheim, 25 October 1944, p. 3, in SP, box 82 (Bombing, Overcast Ops.).

132. See Headquarters Eighth Air Force, "The Oxford Experiment in H2X Bombing," 20 November 1944, in SP, box 81 (Bombing Overcast, Analytical Studies II); Braxton to Spaatz, Memo: Utilization of Improved B.T.O. Equipment by Eighth Air Force, 22 March 1944, in SP, box 17 (diary); unsigned memo to Arnold, Navigational Errors in Operations, 4 March 1944, in SP, box 17 (diary).

133. Davis, *Spaatz*, 508, 564–71; Davis, "German Railyards," 46–63.

134. Davis, *Spaatz*, 570 (and also 565). On the ballistic properties of incendiaries, see Maj. Gen. O. P. Echols (Asst. Chief of Air Staff, Matériel, Maintenance and Distribution), Memo, "Incendiary Bombs," 28 April 1943, in AP, box 38.

135. The memo is reprinted in Davis, *Spaatz*, 508. Davis points out, "This policy made it open season for bombing Germany's major cities in any weather."

136. Ibid., 505; WF, 3:45–51.

137. Max Hastings makes this point, stating, "Harris saw his own role in the ultimate Trenchardian sense, as the independent director of a campaign that he was entitled to wage in his own way for as long as he possessed the confidence of his superiors" (*Bomber Command* [New York: Dial Press, 1979], p. 388).

138. On the origins of the correspondence, see WF, 3:80–81. The correspondence itself can be found in PP, folders 10B and 10C. On 22 December 1944, Portal wrote, "[I]f you allow your obvious doubts in this direction to influence your conduct of operations I very much fear that the prize may yet slip through our fingers. Moreover, it is difficult for me to feel that your staff can be devoting its maximum thoughts and energies to the accomplishment of your first priority task if you yourself are not wholeheartedly in support of it" (Portal to Harris, 22 December 1944, p. 2, in PP, folder 10C). On 8 January 1944, Portal restated the same point, claiming, "I can never feel entirely satisfied that the oil offensive is being conducted with maximum effectiveness by Bomber Command until I feel sure that you and your staff have really come to believe in it" (Portal to Harris, 8 January 1945, in PP, folder 10C).

139. Harris, "The Employment of the Night Bomber Force in 'Connection with the Invasion of the Continent From the U.K.," 13 January 1944, esp. pp. 7–8, in HP, folder 77; Harris to the Undersecretary of State, Air Ministry, 7 April 1944, in PP, folder 10B.

140. If they did in fact have such concerns, their instincts were correct. See, for instance, Michael Walzer, *Just and Unjust Wars* (New York: Basic Books, 1976), 251–63.

141. Harris to Portal, 1 November 1944, in PP, folder 10B.

142. Portal to Harris, 5 November 1944; Harris to Portal, 6 November 1944; Portal to Harris, 12 November 1944; in PP, folder 10B. In his letter to Portal of 18 January 1945, Harris would again raise his resentment over what he perceived to be inordinate interference with his command prerogatives. He argued, "In fact I hold now only the tactical, technical and administrative command of a force whose operations are otherwise dictated virtually ad hoc by the climate, the Air Ministry, SHAEF, and enemy reactions—in that order of impact and import" (in PP, folder 10C).

143. Harris to Portal, 12 December 1944; Harris to Portal, 28 December 1944; in PP, folder 10C.

144. Harris to Portal, 28 December 1944, in PP, folder 10B.

145. In fact, it was difficult to disperse oil production. Some dispersal was achieved by building small distillation plants in sheltered places and increasing the number of benzol plants, but this could only make a small contribution to the total supply. In addition, the plants were too complicated to build quickly. See WF, 3:231.

146. Portal to Harris, 8 January 1945, in PP, folder 10C; Portal to Harris, 12 November 1944; in PP, folder 10B. Also WF, vol. 3:242–43; Hinsley et al., *British Intelligence*, vol. 3, pt. 2 , p. 531, also Appendix 25, pp. 913–24. See

also Greenhous, *The Crucible of War*, 847; Ralph Bennett, "Ten-tenths Cloud Cover: Intelligence and Bomber Command," in *Behind the Battle: Intelligence in the War with Germany, 1939–1945* (London: Sinclair-Stevenson, 1994), 133–67. In 1961, Webster and Frankland strongly implied that Bomber Command did not take full advantage of an opportunity presented to it by the oil offensive. They speculated that attacks that might have been undertaken in October and November were likely to have been as effective as the attacks that were in fact undertaken by Harris (after great pressure from Portal) in December and January (WF, 3:242–43). In 1988, F. H. Hinsley and his coauthors argued that while intelligence information on the increasingly critical German oil situation spurred the USSTAF to greater efforts against the target in mid-September, the intelligence "produced no change . . . in Bomber Command's programme." The authors added that Bomber Command made "only token gestures to the oil offensive, a strategy by which the Air Staff now set great store." In their concluding remarks on the issue, they pointed out that, "it is not possible to doubt that, effected in July or August and maintained into the autumn, comparable marginal diversion of its effort from areas bombing to the oil offensive would have brought forward to an earlier date the reduction of German production to the low level it reached in September and would at least have prevented it from recovering" (Hinsley, vol. 3: part 2, pp. 514, 516, and 531). In Greenhous (*The Crucible of War*), Stephen Harris argued, "It would be an exaggeration to say the the AOC-in-C ever did his utmost to knock out the German oil industry. Operations in November and December featured an eclectic mix of objectives in which the proportion of sorties given over to the destruction of the enemy's synthetic oil plants was less than one in four" (847). Recently, however, Sebastian Cox has argued that instead of mere ex post facto arguments, Harris's assertions that weather and other tactical factors put constraints on him were indeed legitimate claims at the time. See Cox's introduction to Harris's *Despatch on War Operations* (London: Frank Cass, 1995), xxi–xxiii.

147. Portal told Harris, "In view of the doubt which exists as to the point to which area attacks must be carried to be decisive in themselves, it is clearly the sounder policy now to employ the bomber forces so that they can make a calculable contribution to the offensive as a whole." (Portal to Harris, 8 January 1945, in PP, folder 10C).

148. JIC (44) 301 (0) quoted in Hinsley et al., *British Intelligence*, vol. 3, part 2, p. 516.

149. In his letter of 8 January 1945, Portal felt compelled to challenge Harris's assertion that the United States would have made a greater contribution to the war if it had come in on the area offensive. Insisting that enemy countermeasures had gotten ahead of Bomber Command before it was able to bring the area offensive to a decisive point, Portal argued that it was only the American air campaign that had made Overlord possible and had given Bomber Command "a new lease on life" in its own campaign (Portal to Harris, 8 January 1945, in PP, folder 10C).

150. Harris to Portal, 24 January 1945, in PP, folder 10C.

151. Portal to Harris, 20 January 1945, in PP, folder 10C. See also, generally,

Hastings, *Bomber Command*, 385–88; Denis Richards, *Portal of Hungerford* (London: Heinemann, 1977), 317–32; Richards, *The Hardest Victory* (London: Hodder and Stoughton, 1994), 261–75.

152. Portal began his letter of 20 January 1945: "I am sorry to see from your letter of the 18th January in reply to mine of the 8th that I have failed to convince you of the soundness of the oil plan" (Portal to Harris, 20 January 1945, in PP, folder 10C.

153. Harris to Portal, 18 January 1945, in PP, folder 10C.

154. Portal added, "We must wait until after the war before we can know for certain who was right and I sincerely hope that until then you will continue in command of the force which has done so much towards defeating the enemy and has brought such credit and reknown to yourself and to the Air Force" (Portal to Harris, 20 January 1945, in PP, 10C).

155. When Portal read the draft version of the official history, which argued that he had "virtually abdicated" his responsibilities by not removing Harris, he threatened to sue for libel if it was not withdrawn. See Richards, *The Hardest Victory*, 265–67.

156. Harris to Portal, 22 February 1945, in HP, folder 84.

157. See, for instance, Harris's debates with Portal over weather, in Harris to Portal, 1 November 1944; Portal to Harris, 5 November 1944; Harris to Portal, 6 November 1944; in PP, folder 10B.

158. See Sebastian Cox's introduction to *The Strategic Air War Against Germany* (London: Frank Cass, 1998), xxiv. This volume reprints the original BBSU report.

159. WF, 3:84–85. In *The Hardest Victory*, Richards argues that Portal exerted direct leverage over Harris in this debate because Portal's questioning of Harris's decisions resulted in Bomber Command devoting increased attention to oil targets, not only in November but again in January, after the tactical emergency provoked by the Battle of the Bulge (266–67).

160. WF, 3:200.

161. Harris to Portal, 22 February 1945, in HP, folder 84.

162. Harris to Portal, 10 May 1945, quoted in Richards, *Portal of Hungerford*, 327.

163. Julian Allen (Asst. to Director of Intelligence) to Brig. Gen. G. C. McDonald, memo, 21 January 1945, in SP, box 23 (diary).

164. See Davis, "German Railyards," 58.

165. Ibid., 56–57.

166. WF, 3:98–104.

167. Notes of the Allied Commander's Conference held at SHAEF, 1 February 1945, in AFHRC, files K239.046-38.

168. Headquarters, Eighth Air Force, Intops Summary no. 290, 0001 hours 14 February to 2400 hours 14 February 1945, in RG 243, sec. 4 2A (5) f-h, folder G, NARA.

169. WF, 3:107–9, inc. note 5 on 108–9, and 111.

170. One of the objectives of Clarion was to overwhelm the German's normal repair organization. See "General Plan for Maximum Effort Attack Against Transportation Objectives," 17 December 1944, in AIR 14/915.

171. When Spaatz had earlier discussed Clarion with Tedder, the latter noted that tactical air units had been engaged in a modified Clarion for some time. See Notes of the Allied Air Commanders' Conference, 1 February 1945; Notes of the Allied Commanders' Conference, 15 February, 1945; and Notes of the Allied Air Commanders' Conference, 1 March 1945; in AFHRC, K239.046-38. On the day before Clarion commenced, General Spaatz was careful to stress to commanders that press releases must emphasize the military value of the sites on the target list. See Schaffer, *Wings of Judgment*, 86–95; Sherry, *The Rise of American Air Power*, 144, 260–63.

172. "8,000 Planes Batter Nazis Close to Two Fronts," *New York Times*, 15 Feb. 1945, p. 1; "Rail City Blasted," *New York Times*, 16 Feb. 1945, p. 1; "Smashing Blows at Dresden," *Times* (London), 15 Feb. 1945, p. 4.

173. "The Air Assault," *Times* (London), 16 February 1945, p. 5

174. Kurt Vonnegut, who was in Dresden during the raid (as a POW) and managed to survive, described the city as "about as sinister as a wedding cake" (*Fates Worse Than Death*, [New York: Knopf, 1992], 100). See generally, WF, 3:107–9; Davis, *Spaatz*, 556–57.

175. Verrier, *The Bomber Offensive*, 301.

176. On British public opinion generally see: WF, 3:114–17; Greenhous, *The Crucible of War*, 725–26; Stephen Garrett, *Ethics and Air Power in World War II* (New York: St. Martin's, 1993), 89–105.

177. "Smashing Blows at Dresden," *Times* (London), 15 February 1945, p. 4

178. Churchill note of 28 March 1945, reprinted in WF, 3:112.

179. Churchill note of 1 April 1945, reprinted in WF, 3:117.

180. Churchill to Truman (prime minister's personal telegram), 14 April 1945, in AIR 8/838. See also note by the ACAS (P), "Employment of US War Weary Bombers," COS (45) 246 (O), 11 April 1944, in AIR 8/838.

181. Harris argued that "either we continue as in the past or we very largely stand down altogether. The last alternative would certainly be welcome. I take little delight in the work and none whatever in risking my crews avoidably" (Harris to Bottomley, 29 March 1945, in HP, folder 9).

182. Notes of the Allies Air Commanders' Conference, 1 March 1945, in AFHRC, decimal no. K239.046-38. At Pforzheim all but 10 of the 388 bombers dispatched bombed the target from low-level, creating a firestorm that engulfed the city and killed over 17,000 persons.

183. Eisenhower responded, to Harris's satisfaction, on 6 March 1945 (Harris to Eisenhower, 2 March 1945, and Eisenhower to Harris, 6 March 1945 [with covering note of 7 March 1945], in AIR 8/843).

184. See, for instance, Harris's letters to Portal of 26 October 1944 and 22 February 1945, in HP, folders 83, 84.

185. Documents pertaining to this affair can be found in the collections of the AFHRC, dec. file no. K239.046-38, 14–15 February 1945. See also Davis, *Spaatz*, 543–64; Schaffer, *Wings of Judgment*, 95–103; Sherry, *The Rise of American Air Power*, 261–63.

186. See, for instance, the April 1945 issue describing the Americans as the "pin point" specialists, and the RAF as "saturation" bombers (Assistant Chief of Air Staff, Intelligence, *Impact*, April 1945, p. 46).

187. Bruce Bliven, "The B-29," *The New Republic*, 1 January 1945, pp. 19–21; "Bombing Civilians in Europe," *The New Republic*, 19 April 1943, p. 494.

188. See, for instance, the story "Terror Bombing", which appeared in Washington's *Evening Star* on Monday 19 February 1945. It stated, "Since the dispatch was cleared through the strict Allied censorship, its authenticity may be accepted. But it fails to make clear precisely what is meant by 'terror bombing' in this instance."

189. Transcript of USAAF press conference held 21 February 1945. (The speaker was not identified, but it was probably Gen. Barney Giles, who did many similar conferences.) See RG 18, entry 55, box 30, NARA.

190. Ibid., 3, 11.

191. See WF, 3:113.

192. Sherry, *The Rise of American Air Power*, 263.

193. See Davis, *Spaatz*, 568–69.

194. Ibid; see also his "German Railyards," 58.

195. Extract from Minutes of COS (45) 80th Meeting, 29 March 1945: COS (45) 233 (0), Area Bombing, Note by the Air Staff, 4 April 1945, in AIR 8/427.

196. Harris to Portal, 24 January 1945, in PP, folder 10C.

197. See Note by the Chief of the Air Staff, COS (45) 263 (0), Revised Directive for Strategic Air Forces in Europe, 16 April 1945, in AIR 8/427.

198. The argument to the Secretary of State for Air is from Harris's letter to Sinclair, 1 June 1945, in AIR 20/2987. See also Harris to Portal, 15 June 1945, in HP, folder 84; and Harris to Portal, 1 June 1945, in PP, folder 10C.

199. Had Hirohito's surrender not come when it did, the almost unfathomable power of this bomber force would have rained down relentlessly upon Japan, making all the wartime strategic bombing up to that point, even the atomic attacks, seem modest in comparison.

200. Harris to Bottomley, 29 March 1945, in HP, folder 9.

201. On the arrangements for the Twentieth Air Force, see Air Staff Meeting Minutes, 3 April 1944, in RG 18, AAG 42–44, 337 (class bulky), box 357, NARA.

202. Quoted in Crane, *Bombs, Cities, and Civilians*, 126.

203. Sherry, *The Rise of American Air Power*, 101–2.

204. Ibid., 105–8.

205. Ibid., 109–14.

206. Crane, *Bombs, Cities, and Civilians*, 126; Sherry, *The Rise of American Air Power*, 112.

207. Sherry, *The Rise of American Air Power*, 160.

208. Ibid., 124–25.

209. Incendiary tests were repeated in April 1944, at Eglin Base, Florida. See Kenneth P. Werrell, *Blankets of Fire* (Washington, D.C.: Smithsonian Institution Press, 1996), 48–49.

210. Ibid., 50.

211. Quoted in ibid., 51.

212. On Arnold at the Quebec conference, see Crane, *Bombs, Cities, and Civilians*, 127.

213. Werrell, *Blankets of Fire*, 52–53.

214. Ibid., 53.

215. For an excellent summary of these problems, see ibid., 84–85.

216. Werrell, *Blankets of Fire*, 98, 112.

217. Crane, *Bombs, Cities, and Civilians*, 127–28.

218. Haywood Hansell, *The Strategic Air War Against Germany and Japan* (Washington, D.C.: Office of Air Force History, 1986), 141, 164–66.

219. See Office of Information Services, Headquarters, Army Air Forces, "Highlights of the Twentieth Air Force," [1945], in AFHRC, dec. file no. 760.01, Misc. 314.7 (Twentieth Air Force), 1942–1945.

220. For this history, see Headquarters, XXI Bomber Command, "Analysis of Incendiary Phase of Operations, 9–19 March 1945," in AFHRC, dec. file no. 760.01, 1 July–2 September 1945, vol. 7, Narrative History, Headquarters Twentieth Air Force; and Staff Presentation, 10 April 1945, Binder XIII, Operations Div. Reports, Docs. 103–109, in AFHRC, dec. file no. 760.01, 1 July–2 September 1945, vol. 14, Narrative History, Twentieth Air Force.

221. Sherry, *The Rise of American Air Power*, 257–58.

222. Hansell, *The Strategic Air War*, 211, also 167, 177.

223. Sherry, *The Rise of American Air Power*, 257–58.

224. Hansell, *The Strategic Air War*, 212–13; Sherry, *The Rise of American Air Power*, 159.

225. Warren B. Moscow, "Not a Building is Left in 15 Square Miles," *New York Times*, 11 March 1945, p. 13, see also p. 1.

226. See "Highlights of the Twentieth Air Force," and "Analysis of Incendiary Phase of Operations"; both in AFHRC. Also, Crane, *Bombs, Cities, and Civilians*, 127–29.

227. W. H. Lawrence, "World Peak Blow," *New York Times*, 2 August 1945, pp. 1–2.

228. Sherry, *The Rise of American Air Power*, 131.

229. Untitled article, *The Nation*, 24 March 1945, p. 318.

230. "Analysis of Incendiary Phase of Operations," in AFHRC, p. 6

231. "Highlights of the Twentieth Air Force," in AFHRC, p. 2.

232. The very next sentence noted, "Never in the history of aerial warfare has such destruction been achieved at such moderate cost." See "Third Report of the Commanding General of the Army Air Forces to the Secretary of War," 12 November 1945, published as *The War Reports of General of the Army George C. Marshall, General of the Army H. H. Arnold, and Fleet Admiral Ernest J. King*, foreword by Walter Millis (Philadelphia: Lippincott, 1947), 440, graphic on 441. This was kindly brought to my attention by Jacob Vander Meulen.

233. In 1947, James Conant (who would become a staunch defender of the atomic bomb decision) criticized theologian Reinhold Niebuhr for implying that Hiroshima was somehow ethically distinct from the air raids that had preceded it in the Far East. See Barton J. Bernstein, "Seizing the Contested Terrain of Early Nuclear History," in *Hiroshima's Shadow* ed. Kai Bird and Lawrence Lifschultz (Stony Creek, Conn.: Pamphleteer's Press, 1998), 165.

234. Joint Statement on Strategic Bombing by Air Ministry and U.S. Strategic Air Forces in Europe, Air Ministry News Service, Air Ministry Bulletin no.

18598, 30 April 1945, in Slessor Papers, file XII C (Bomber Policy, 1939–1945), formerly at Air Historical Branch, now at Public Records Office, London.

235. The British survey has recently been published, with an analytical introduction by Sebastian Cox, under the title *The Strategic Air War Against Germany, 1939–1945* (London: Frank Cass, 1998).

236. David MacIsaac, *Strategic Bombing in World War II* (New York: Garland, 1976), 38.

237. Formal proposals for a bombing survey were drawn up almost simultaneously in March 1944 at AAF Headquarters in Washington, and at USSTAF Headquarters in London. On the History of the United States Bombing Survey, see generally MacIsaac, *Strategic Bombing*. See also "The British and United States Surveys of the Strategic Bombing Offensive," in WF, 4:40–41; CC, 3:789–92.

238. This study was sometimes known as the "Coffin Report" as it was prepared under the direction of Lt. Col. Caleb Coffin. See MacIsaac, *Strategic Bombing*, 97–98.

239. Mr. H. C. Alexander, president of J. P. Morgan and Co., was second in command. The number of military personnel engaged in the Survey rose to over 1,400 by August 1945. See MacIsaac, *Strategic Bombing*, 68.

240. The Summary Report was a condensed version of the longer Over-all Report.

241. MacIsaac, *Strategic Bombing*, 144.

242. On all of these criticisms, problems, and attempts to correct them, see WF, 4:50–53.

243. Harris urged that British assessment efforts neither "exaggerate the effects of what has been done in the interests of propaganda," nor fall into the temptation of "writing down our own achievement in the interests of 'objectivity' and 'conservative estimates'" (Harris to Undersecretary of State, Air Ministry, 26 October 1944, in AIR 14/902). See WF, 4:40–58, and Sebastian Cox's introduction to *The Strategic Air War Against Germany, 1939–1945*.

244. Of this episode, the official historians write, "It was an unfortunate decision, made against the advice of all those who were able to judge the advantages of such an enquiry. It is the main reason why no authoritative pronouncement has ever been made in Britain, then or since, on the conduct and results of the strategic offensive" (WF, 4:45, also 41–43).

245. Minutes of a Meeting held at Air Ministry, to Discuss the Formation and Function of the British Bombing Survey Unit, 31 May 1945, in AIR 14/902; The Formation of British Bombing Survey Unit, 13 June 1945, in AIR 14/902; WF, 4:45–47.

246. MacIsaac, *Strategic Bombing*, 141–44.

247. Gian Peri Gentile, "Advocacy or Assessment? The United States Strategic Bombing Survey of Germany and Japan," *The Pacific Historical Review*, 66, no. 1 (February 1997): 66–68.

248. See United States Strategic Bombing Survey, "The Effects of Strategic Bombing on the German War Economy," 31 October 1945, esp. pp. 1–14, 146, and 157, where Galbraith argued, "Bombing not only destroyed capacity, but also increased it—in the sense that capacity was utilized which might have been neglected in the absence of bombing. Although bombing caused output losses, it

also stimulated rationalization and expansion." The differences of opinion regarding the survey are summarized nicely in Gentile, "Advocacy or Assessment," 53–79; on this point see 60–62.

249. For a recent critique of Galbraith's methods and conclusions, see James G. Roche and Barry Watts, "Choosing Analytic Measures," *The Journal of Strategic Studies* 14, no. 2 (June 1991): 172–84.

250. See USSBS, "The Effects of Strategic Bombing on the German War Economy," 13.

251. USSBS, "The Impact of the Allied Air Effort on German Logistics," 2nd ed., January 1947 (1st ed., 3 November 1945), esp. 5.

252. CC, 3:794.

253. USSBS, "The Effects of Strategic Bombing on the German War Economy," 159.

254. USSBS, "Oil Division Final Report," 25 August 1945 (1st ed.), see esp. 2, 6, 7–8; USSBS, "The Effects of Strategic Bombing on the German Economy," 82 and 161.

255. CC, 3:800–801.

256. USSBS, Over-all Report, 107.

257. CC, 3:792.

258. Gen. Omar N. Bradley, Military Advisor, USSBS, "Effect of Air Power on Military Operations (Western Europe)," 15 July 1945; copy in AIR 40/1131; see esp. pp. xi, 1–4, 9–17, 64–65.

259. USSBS, "Area Studies Division Report," 29 October 1945, pp. 22–24.

260. USSBS, "The Effects of Strategic Bombing on German Morale," pp. 1–3, and 53–54; "Over-all Report (European War)," 30 September 1945, pp. 97–98.

261. Fred Charles Iklé, *The Social Impact of Bomb Destruction* (Norman: University of Oklahoma Press, 1958), 15.

262. USSBS, "The Effects of Strategic Bombing on German Morale," 2–3.

263. Gentile, "Advocacy or Assessment," 68–70.

264. Nitze added, "Based on a detailed investigation of all the facts, and supported by the testimony of the surviving Japanese leaders involved, it is the Survey's opinion that certainly prior to 31 December 1945, and in all probability prior to 1 November 1945, Japan would have surrendered even if the atomic bombs had not been dropped, even if Russia had not entered the war, and even if no invasion had been planned or contemplated" (USSBS, "Summary Report, Pacific War," 1 July 1946 (Washington, D.C., USGPO) 26). See also Gentile, "Advocacy or Assessment?" 71–72, 55–58.

265. See MacIsaac, *Strategic Bombing*, 119–35; Gentile, "Advocacy or Assessment?" 62–66, 77–79.

266. Ofstie quoted in MacIsaac, *Strategic Bombing*, 132.

267. "Third Report of the Commanding General of the Army Air Forces," 12 November 1945, p. 437; reprinted in *The War Reports of General of the Army George C. Marshall, General of the Army H. H. Arnold, and Fleet Admiral Ernest J. King.*

268. The authors argued that if aid to ground forces rendered the strategic campaign "less effective than it might have been," the "final victory was no less complete" (CC, 3:804, also 797).

269. CC, 3:797, also 792–93; 795–96, 805. The authors made clear however that it had taken an enormous effort to erode the robust German transport net. They also credited the RAF for blocking the main north German canals. They concluded, "The Germans did not give up easily. Their will to operate the railroads was strong to the very last, and they worked furiously and efficiently to keep up their most vital movements. But nothing could save their transportation system" (3:796–97).

270. See especially Alfred C. Mierzejewski, *The Collapse of the German War Economy, 1944–1945* (Chapel Hill: University of North Carolina Press, 1988). Ideas about the transportation campaign were used by Edmund Dews in his study, "NATO Inland Transport as a Potential Rear-area Target System: Lessons from German Experience in World War II, Office of the Assistant Secretary of Defense / Program Analysis and Evaluation, N-1522-PA&E, June 1980.

271. Report of the British Bombing Survey Unit, "The Strategic Air War Against Germany, 1939–1945," p. 130; copy of original document given to the author by Lord Zuckerman.

272. Report of the British Bombing Survey Unit, "The Strategic Air War Against Germany, 1939–1945," pp. 79 and 97; WF, 3:89. The authors explained that in the very final stages of the war, area bombing also had an effect on oil and communications, but they also explained that, by that point, so many different factors were contributing to Germany's final collapse that it is very difficult to separate them out. (WF, 4:54).

273. It was published under the title, *Sir Arthur T. Harris: Despatch on War Operations*, by the Frank Cass Publishing Company, London. It contains a helpful introduction by Sebastian Cox.

274. CC, 3:791.

275. See for example the concerns expressed by Air Chief Marshal R. Saundby to Undersecretary of State, Air Ministry, 11 April 1945, in AIR 14/902.

276. Harris wrote, early in the book, "As a matter of strict calculation it was therefore obvious that the policy of destroying industrial cities, and the factories in them, was not merely the only possible one for Bomber Command at that time; it was also the best way of destroying Germany's capacity to produce war material" (*Bomber Offensive*, 88).

277. Ibid., 265.

278. Ibid., 261–62.

279. See Harris's *Despatch on War Operations*. The reprint contains Harris's full text, as well as the Air Staff statement of March 1948. The original document is, and has been, available in HP, folder 5.

280. Harris, *Despatch*, 33–38.

281. Ibid., 39–40.

282. The arguments of some of the early critics of strategic bombing are noted in David MacIsaac, "What the Bombing Survey Really Says," *Air Force Magazine*, June 1973, pp. 60–63.

283. Lord Tedder, *Air Power in War* (London: Hodder and Stoughton, 1948), 29. Though he set out no specific formula for its achievement, and explained that it could be neither permanent nor absolute, Tedder nonetheless made clear that such superiority was a prerequisite for all else (53, also 34, 39 42).

284. Ibid., 87, 90–91, 97–98.

285. WF, 3:284.

286. Ibid., 3:288–89.

287. Harris concluded that Webster, because of his affiliation with the London School of Economics, had leftist leanings. Harris assessed Frankland, on grounds that are far from obvious, to be a disgruntled former RAF navigator and a "rabid individual." See Noble Frankland, "Some Thoughts about and Experience of Official Military History," *Journal of the Royal Air Force Historical Society*," no. 17 (1997): 7–18.

288. WF, 3:291–93.

289. The authors added, "In the event, the Eighth Air Force was cast by a combination of resolution and rigidity into headlong assault on the German fighter force. It was almost involved in tragic defeat, but the ultimate result was the downfall of the Luftwaffe" (WF, 2:38–39).

290. See Greenhous, *The Crucible of War*, 856–57, 865–66.

291. Ibid., 867.

292. Gerhard Weinberg, *A World at Arms: A Global History of World War II* (Cambridge: Cambridge University Press, 1994), esp. 773–74.

293. Overy, *Why the Allies Won*, 130–33.

294. Anglo-American losses, Overy points out, were far lower than those of the other fighting powers (*Why the Allies Won*, 127–28). In the conclusion to his comprehensive history of General Spaatz and the World War II strategic air war, American historian Richard G. Davis credited strategic bombing for ending the war months earlier than otherwise might have been the case—and thereby saving the lives not only of Allied soldiers but also of those suffering at the hands of the Third Reich (*Spaatz*, 596).

295. R. J. Overy, "Rationalization and the 'Production Miracle' in Germany during the Second World War," in *War and Economy in the Third Reich*, ed. R. J. Overy (New York: Oxford University Press, 1994), 343–75; on these points see esp. p. 373.

296. Following Overy, Cox levels a general critique of the BBSU authors for their heavy reliance on a flawed analysis of the German war economy written by Dr. Rolf Wagenfuehr, a former senior official in the Reich Statistical Office. See Cox's introduction to the BBSU Report, in *The Strategic Air War Against Germany 1939–1945*; for quoted material see p. xxx.

297. WF, 3:4.

Conclusion

1. "Third Report of the Commanding General of the Army Air Forces to the Secretary of War," 12 November 1945; reprinted in *The War Reports of Gen. George C. Marshall, Gen. H. H. Arnold, and Fleet Adm. Ernest J. King*, foreword by Walter Millis (Philadelphia: Lippincott, 1947), 462.

2. Quoted in Futrell, *Ideas, Concepts, Doctrine: A History of Basic Thinking in the United States Air Force, 1907–1964* (Maxwell AFB, Ala.: Air University Press, 1971), 109.

3. O'Donnell quoted in Conrad C. Crane, "Raiding the Beggar's Pantry: The Search for Air Power Strategy in the Korean War," *The Journal of Military History* 63, no. 4 (October 1999): 889.

4. Crane, "Raiding the Beggar's Pantry," 893–903.

5. Mark Clodfelter, *The Limits of Air Power* (New York: Free Press, 1989), 21.

6. LeMay quoted in Thomas Hone, "Strategic Bombardment Constrained: Korea and Vietnam" in *Case Studies in Strategic Bombardment* ed. R. Cargill Hall (Washington, D.C.: Air Force History and Museums Program, 1998), 517.

7. Crane, "Raiding the Beggar's Pantry," 905.

8. Ibid., 912.

9. Ibid., 914.

10. Ibid., 918; Clodfelter, *The Limits of Air Power*, 18–20.

11. Crane, "Raiding the Beggar's Pantry," 918. See also Clodfelter, *The Limits of Air Power*, 23.

12. Zimmerman quoted in Futrell, *Ideas, Concepts, Doctrine*, 177.

13. Ibid., 177, 180–81.

14. See Crane, "Raiding the Beggar's Pantry," 920; John T. Greenwood, "The Emergence of the Postwar Strategic Air Force, 1943–1953," in *Air Power and Warfare*, ed. Alfred Hurley and Robert Ehrhart (Washington, D.C.: U.S. Air Force 1979), 236. Clodfelter, *The Limits of Air Power*, 27; and generally, Dennis M. Drew, "Air Theory, Air Force, and Low Intensity Conflict: A Short Journey to Confusion" in Meilinger, ed., *The Paths of Heaven: The Evolution of Air Power Theory* (Maxwell AFB, Ala.: Air University Press), 321–55.

15. Manual 1–8 (1954), quoted in Clodfelter, *The Limits of Air Power*, 28.

16. Clodfelter, *The Limits of Air Power*, 39–56.

17. Hone, "Strategic Bombardment Constrained," 495–96.

18. Earl Tilford, "Setup: Why and How the U.S. Air Force Lost in Vietnam," *Armed Forces and Society* 17, no. 3 (1991): 327.

19. Robert A. Pape, Jr., "Coercive Air Power in the Vietnam War," *International Security*, 15, no. 2 (Fall 1990): 103–46, esp. 123–24; and Pape, *Bombing to Win: Air Power and Coercion in War* (Ithaca: Cornell University Press, 1996), 174–210.

20. Clodfelter, *The Limits of Air Power*, 205.

21. Pape, *Bombing to Win*, 199–209.

22. Milton quoted in Tilford, "Setup," 335; Clodfelter, *The Limits of Air Power*, 206–8.

23. Clodfelter, *The Limits of Air Power* 201–2; Tilford, "Setup," 334–36, 338.

24. Pape, *Bombing to Win*, 209; Thomas Griffith, "Air Pressure: Strategy for the New World Order?" at www.airpower.maxwell.af.mil/airchronicles/apj/apj94/griffith.html.

25. Clodfelter, *The Limits of Air Power*, 203.

26. Compare, for example, William J. Perry, "Desert Storm and Deterrence," *Foreign Affairs* 70, no. 4 (Fall 1991): 66–82; Lt. Col. John F. Jones, Jr., "Giulio Douhet Vindicated: Desert Storm 1991," *Naval War College Review* 65, no. 4 (Autumn 1992); Thomas Keaney and Eliot Cohen, *Gulf War Air Power Survey Summary Report* (Washington, D.C.: USGPO, 1993), 235–25; Stephen D. Biddle, "Victory Misunderstood: What the Gulf War Tells Us about the Future of Conflict," *International Security* 21, no. 2 (Fall 1997): 139–79; Lt. Col. David

S. Fadok, "John Boyd and John Warden: Airpower's Quest for Strategic Paralysis," in *The Paths of Heaven*, 357–98; Richard G. Davis, "Strategic Bombardment in the Gulf War" in *Case Studies in Strategic Bombardment*, edited by Cargill Hall (Washington, D.C.: Air Force History Program), 527–621.

27. Compare, for example, Ernest Blazer, "Aerial Battle," *Washington Times*, 20 August 1998, p. 8; Richard P. Hallion, "When the World Dials 911, the Air Force Responds," *Washington Times*, 22 August 1998, p. C2; Brig. General Edward H. Simmons, "Can Our National Security Stand on One Leg?" *Washington Times*, 31 August 1998, p. 16; Ivo H. Daalder and Michael E. O'Hanlon, *Winning Ugly: NATO's War to Save Kosovo* (Washington, D.C.: The Brookings Institution, 2000); Daniel A. Byman and Matthew C. Waxman, "Kosovo and the Great Air Power Debate," *International Security* 24, no. 4 (Spring 2000): 5–38; Barry Posen, The War for Kosovo," *International Security*, 24, no. 4 (Spring 2000): 39–84.

28. In recent years, calls have been made for a radical rethinking of U.S. air power doctrine. See, for example, Harold R. Winton, "A Black Hole in the Wild Blue Yonder: The Need for a Comprehensive Theory of Air Power," *Air Power History*, 39, no. 4 (Winter 1992): 32–42; Dennis M. Drew, "Desert Storm as a Symbol: Implications of the Air War in the Desert," *Airpower Journal* 6, no. 3 (Fall 1992): 5–13. See also, I. B. Holley, Jr., "Reflections on the Search for Airpower Theory," in *The Paths of Heaven*, 579–99.

Bibliography of Archival Sources

British Sources

Public Record Office, London:
AIR 1 Air Historical Branch Records, Series I
AIR 2 Air Ministry Correspondence
AIR 8 Chief of Air Staff papers
AIR 9 Directorate of Plans
AIR 14 Bomber Command
AIR 20 Unregistered Papers
AIR 40 Directorate of Intelligence
AIR 41 Air Historical Branch Narrative Histories
CAB 65, 66–68, 79, 84, and 101
Papers of Sir John Slessor

Royal Air Force Museum, Hendon, United Kingdom:
The Hawk (Royal Air Force Staff College Yearbook)
Papers of the Earl of Halsbury
Papers of Sir Arthur Harris
Papers of Sir Robert Saundby
Papers of Lord Tedder
Papers of Sir Hugh Trenchard

Air Historical Branch, Ministry of Defence, London:
Papers of Sir Edgar Ludlow Hewitt
Royal Air Force Manuals

Library of the RAF Staff College (Bracknell, Berkshire), now part of the Joint
    Services Command and Staff College, Swindon, Wiltshire, United Kingdom:
Operations Record Book
Staff College papers, including early records, lectures, and student papers

Christ Church Library, Oxford, United Kingdom:
Papers of Lord Portal
(used by permission of the Head of the Air Historical Branch, RAF)

Centre for Military Archives, King's College, London:
Liddell Hart Papers

Imperial War Museum, London:
Manuscripts and letters on aerial bombing in World War I

Canadian Sources

Copies of AIR 1
National Library of Canada, Ottawa:

Copies of AIR 9 and AIR 14
National Defence Headquarters, Ottawa, Canada:

U.S. Sources

Library of Congress Manuscript Collection, Washington, D.C.:
Papers of Frank Andrews
Papers of H. H. Arnold
Papers of Newton Baker
Papers of Ira C. Eaker
Papers of Curtis LeMay
Papers of Carl A. Spaatz

National Archives and Records Administration, Washington, D.C.:
RG 18 Records of the Army Air Forces
RG 107 Records of the Secretary of War
RG 120 Records of the American Expeditionary Forces (WWI)
RG 218 Records of the Joint Chiefs of Staff
RG 243 Records of the United States Strategic Bombing Survey
RG 339 Records of Headquarters, Army Air Forces

United States Air Force Historical Research Center (AFHRC), Maxwell AFB, Alabama:
Lectures to the Air War College
Records of the Air Corps Tactical School
Records of the Air Service Field Officer's School
Records of Air Service Tactical School
Records of the Eighth Air Force
Records of the Twentieth Air Force

Office of Air Force History, Bolling AFB, Washington, D.C.:
Air Corps Newsletter, original copies (1926–39)
Records of the Air Corps Tactical School (microfilm copies of holdings at the Air Force Historical Research Center)
Records of the Air Service Field Officers' School (microfilm copies of holdings at the Air Force Historical Research Center)
Additional documents including AWPD/1; World War II bombing analyses; internal histories of the Eighth Air Force; analyses of Bomber Command (by American wartime analysts); documents pertaining to Anglo-American cooperation in the Combined Bomber Offensive; notes of Allied Air Commanders Conferences; and aviation rare books collection

United States Army Military History Institute, Carlisle Barracks, Pennsylvania:
Army War College Curricular Archives
Papers of Ira C. Eaker, and Eaker oral history interview

United States Military Academy Library, West Point, New York:
Papers of Gen. George A. Lincoln

Duke University Library, Special Collections Department:
Air Intelligence Bulletin, American Expeditionary Forces, 1917–18
The Hawk (Royal Air Force Staff College Yearbook)